Behavioral Biometrics for Human Identification:
Intelligent Applications

Liang Wang
University of Melbourne, Australia

Xin Geng
Southeast University, China

Medical Information Science
REFERENCE

MEDICAL INFORMATION SCIENCE REFERENCE

Hershey · New York

Director of Editorial Content:	Kristin Klinger
Senior Managing Editor:	Jamie Snavely
Assistant Managing Editor:	Michael Brehm
Publishing Assistant:	Sean Woznicki
Typesetter:	Michael Brehm
Cover Design:	Lisa Tosheff
Printed at:	Yurchak Printing Inc.

Published in the United States of America by
Medical Information Science Reference (an imprint of IGI Global)
701 E. Chocolate Avenue
Hershey PA 17033
Tel: 717-533-8845
Fax: 717-533-8661
E-mail: cust@igi-global.com
Web site: http://www.igi-global.com/reference

Library of Congress Cataloging-in-Publication Data

Behavioral biometrics for human identification : intelligent applications /
Liang Wang and Xin Geng, editors.
        p. cm.
  Includes bibliographical references and index.
  Summary: "This edited book provides researchers and practitioners a
comprehensive understanding of the start-of-the-art of behavioral biometrics
techniques, potential applications, successful practice, snf available
resources"--Provided by publisher.
  ISBN 978-1-60566-725-6 (hbk.) -- ISBN 978-1-60566-726-3 (ebook) 1.
Biometric identification. I. Wang, Liang, 1975- II. Geng, Xin, 1978-
  TK7882.B56B39 2010
  006.4--dc22
                            2009006953

British Cataloguing in Publication Data
A Cataloguing in Publication record for this book is available from the British Library.

All work contributed to this book is new, previously-unpublished material. The views expressed in this book are those of the authors, but not necessarily of the publisher.

Table of Contents

Detailed Table of Contents

This chapter presents a taxonomy of the latest behavioural biometrics including some future oriented approaches. Current research in the field is examined and analyzed, along with the features used to describe different types of behaviour. After comparing accuracy rates for verification of users using different behavioural biometric approaches, researchers address privacy issues which arise or might arise in the future with the use of behavioural biometrics. Finally, generalized properties of behaviour are addressed, as well as the influence of environmental factors on observed behaviour and potential directions for future research in behavioural biometrics.

For establishing trust in the security of IT products, security evaluations by independent third-party testing laboratories are the first choice. In some fields of application of biometric methods (e.g., for protecting private keys for qualified electronic signatures), a security evaluation is even required by legislation. The common criteria for IT security evaluation form the basis for security evaluations for which a wide international recognition is desired. Within the common criteria, predefined security assurance requirements describe actions to be carried out by the developers of the product and by the evaluators. The assurance components that require clarification in the context of biometric systems are related to vulnerability assessment. This chapter reviews the state of the art and gives a gentle introduction to the methodology for evaluating the security of biometric systems, in particular of behavioral biometric verification systems.

Chapter 3

    F. Cherifi, University of Caen, France
    B. Hemery, University of Caen, France
    R. Giot, University of Caen, France
    M. Pasquet, University of Caen, France
    C. Rosenberger, University of Caen, France

We present in this chapter an overview of techniques for the performance evaluation of behavioral biometric systems. The BioAPI standard that defines the architecture of a biometric system is presented in the first part of the chapter. The general methodology for the evaluation of biometric systems is given, including statistical metrics, definition of benchmark databases, and subjective evaluation. These considerations rely with the ISO/IEC19795-1 standard describing the biometric performance testing and reporting. The specificity of behavioral biometric systems is detailed in the second part of the chapter in order to define some additional constraints for their evaluation. This chapter is dedicated to researchers and engineers who need to quantify the performance of such biometric systems.

Chapter 4

    Y. Pratheepan, University of Ulster, UK
    J.V. Condell, University of Ulster, UK
    G. Prasad, University of Ulster, UK

This chapter presents multiple methods for recognizing individuals from their "style of action/actions," that is, "biometric behavioural characteristics." Two forms of human recognition can be useful: the determination that an object is from the class of humans (which is called human detection), and the determination that an object is a particular individual from this class (which is called individual recognition). This chapter focuses on the latter problem. For individual recognition, this chapter considers two different categories. First, individual recognition using "style of single action," for example, hand waving and partial gait, and second, individual recognition using "style of doing similar actions" in video sequences. The "style of single action" and "style of doing similar actions," for example, behavioural biometric characteristics, are proposed as a cue to discriminate between two individuals. Nowadays multibiometric security systems are available to recognise individuals from video sequences. Those multibiometric systems are combined with finger print, face, voice, and iris biometrics. This chapter reports multiple novel behavioural biometric techniques for individual recognition based on "style of single action" and "style of multiple actions" (i.e., analysing the pattern history of behavioural biometric motion), which can be additionally combined with finger print, face, voice, and iris biometrics as a complementary cue to intelligent security systems.

Chapter 5

    Kenneth Revett, University of Westminster, UK

Behavioral biometrics is a relatively new form of authentication mechanism which relies on the way a person interacts with an authentication device. Traditional instances of this approach include voice, signature, and keystroke dynamics. Novel approaches to behavioral biometrics include biosignals such as the electroencephalogram and the electrocardiogram. The biosignal approach to user authentication has been shown to produce equal error rates on par with more traditional behavioral biometric approaches. In addition, through a process similar to biofeedback, users can be trained with minimal effort to produce computer-based input via the manipulations of endogenous biosignal patterns. This chapter discusses the use of biosignal based biometrics, highlighting key studies and how this approach can be integrated into a multi-biometric user authentication system.

The Gabor wavelets are employed regularly in various biometrics applications because of their biological relevance and computational properties. These wavelets have kernels similar to the 2D receptive field profiles of the mammalian cortical simple cells. They exhibit desirable characteristics of spatial locality and orientation selectivity, and are optimally localized in the space and frequency domains. Physiological, biometric systems, such as face, fingerprint, and iris based human identification have shown great improvement in identification accuracies if Gabor wavelets are used for feature extraction. Moreover, some behavioral biometric systems, such as speaker and gait based applications have shown more than 7% increase in identification accuracies. In this study, we provide a brief discussion on the origin of Gabor wavelets, then an illustration of "how to use Gabor wavelets" to extract features for a generic biometric application is discussed. We also provide an implementation pseudocode for the wavelet. It also offers an elaborate discussion on biometric applications with specific emphasis on behavioral biometric systems that have used Gabor wavelets. We also provide guideline for some biometric systems that have not yet applied Gabor wavelets for feature extraction.

With the increasing demands of visual surveillance systems, human identification at a distance is an urgent need. Gait is an attractive biometric feature for human identification at a distance, and recently has gained much interest from computer vision researchers. This chapter provides a survey of recent advances in gait recognition. First, an overview on gait recognition framework, feature extraction, and classifiers is given, and then some gait databases and evaluation metrics are introduced. Finally, research challenges and applications are discussed in detail.

Human identification from gait is a challenging task in realistic surveillance scenarios in which people walking along arbitrary directions are viewed by a single camera. However, viewpoint is only one of the many covariate factors limiting the efficacy of gait recognition as a reliable biometric. In this chapter, we address the problem of robust identity recognition in the framework of multilinear models. Bilinear models, in particular, allow us to classify the "content" of human motions of unknown "style" (covariate factor). We illustrate a three-layer scheme in which image sequences are first mapped to observation vectors of fixed dimension using Markov modeling, to be later classified by an asymmetric bilinear model. We show tests on the CMU Mobo database that prove that bilinear separation outperforms other common approaches, allowing robust view- and action-invariant identity recognition. Finally, we give an overview of the available tensor factorization techniques, and outline their potential applications to gait recognition. The design of algorithms insensitive to multiple covariate factors is in sight.

Jimin Liang, Xidian University, China
Changhong Chen, Xidian University, China
Heng Zhao, Xidian University, China
Haihong Hu, Xidian University, China
Jie Tian, Xidian University, China

Multisource information fusion technology offers a promising solution to the development of a superior classification system. For gait recognition problems, information fusion is necessary to be employed under at least three circumstances: 1) multiple gait feature fusion, 2) multiple view gait sequence fusion, and 3) gait and other biometrics fusion. Feature concatenation is the most popular methodology to integrate multiple features. However, because of the high dimensional gait data size and small available number of training samples, feature concatenation typically leads to the well-known curse of dimensionality and the small sample size problems. In this chapter, we explore the factorial hidden Markov model (FHMM), an extended hidden Markov model (HMM) with a multiple layer structure, as a feature fusion framework for gait recognition. FHMM provides an alternative to combining several gait features without concatenating them into a single augmented feature, thus, to some extent, overcomes the curse of dimensionality and small sample size problem for gait recognition. Three gait features, the frieze feature, wavelet feature, and boundary signature, are adopted in the numerical experiments conducted on CMU MoBo database and CASIA gait database A. Besides the cumulative matching score (CMS) curves, McNemar's test is employed to check on the statistical significance of the performance difference between the recognition algorithms. Experimental results demonstrate that the proposed FHMM feature fusion scheme outperforms the feature concatenation method.

Ahmed Awad E. Ahmed, University of Victoria, Canada
Issa Traore, University of Victoria, Canada

In this chapter, we will introduce the concepts behind the mouse dynamics biometric technology, present a generic architecture of the detector used to collect and process mouse dynamics, and study the various factors used to build the user's signature. We will also provide an updated survey on the researches and industrial implementations related to the technology, and study possible applications in computer security.

In this chapter, we investigate repetitive human activity patterns and individual recognition in thermal infrared imagery, where human motion can be easily detected from the background regardless of the lighting conditions and colors of the human clothing and surfaces and backgrounds. We employ an efficient spatiotemporal representation for human repetitive activity and individual recognition, which represents human motion sequence in a single image while preserving spatiotemporal characteristics. A statistical approach is used to extract features for activity and individual recognition. Experimental results show that the proposed approach achieves good performance for repetitive human activity and individual recognition.

This chapter describes the use of visual attention characteristics as a biometric for authentication or identification of individual viewers. The visual attention characteristics of a person can be easily monitored by tracking the gaze of a viewer during the presentation of a known or unknown visual scene. The positions and sequences of gaze locations during viewing may be determined by overt (conscious) or covert (subconscious) viewing behaviour. Methods to quantify the spatial and temporal patterns established by the viewer for both overt and covert behaviours are proposed. The former behaviour entails a simple PIN-like approach to develop an independent signature while the latter behaviour is captured through three proposed techniques: a principal component analysis technique ('eigenGaze'); a linear discriminant analysis technique; and a fusion of distance measures. Experimental results suggest that both types of gaze behaviours can provide simple and effective biometrics for this application.

A speaker recognition system verifies or identifies a speaker's identity based on his/her voice and is considered as one of the most convenient biometric characteristic for human machine communication. This chapter introduces several speaker recognition systems and examines their performances under various conditions. Speaker recognition can be classified into either speaker verification or speaker identification. Speaker verification aims to verify whether an input speech corresponds to a claimed identity, and speaker identification aims to identify an input speech by selecting one model from a set of enrolled speaker models. Both the speaker verification and identification system consist of three essential elements: feature extraction, speaker modeling, and matching. The feature extraction pertains to extracting essential features from an input speech for speaker recognition. The speaker modeling pertains to probabilistically modeling the feature of the enrolled speakers. The matching pertains to matching the input feature to various speaker models. Speaker modeling techniques including Gaussian mixture model (GMM), hidden Markov model (HMM), and phone n-grams are presented, and in this chapter, their performances are compared under various tasks. Several verification and identification experimental results presented in this chapter indicate that speaker recognition performances are highly dependent on the acoustical environment. A comparative study between human listeners and an automatic speaker verification system is presented, and it indicates that an automatic speaker verification system can outperform human listeners. The applications of speaker recognition are summarized, and finally various obstacles that must be overcome are discussed.

Chapter 14
Concetto Spampinato, University of Catania, Italy

The chapter is so articulated: the next section will tackle the state of art of the attention theory, with the third paragraph related to the computational models that implement the attention theories, with a particular focus on the model that is the basis for the proposed biometric systems. Such an algorithm will be used for describing the first biometric system. The following section will tackle the people recognition algorithms carried out by evaluating the FOAs distribution. In detail, two different systems are proposed: 1) A face recognition system that takes into account both the behavioral and morphological aspects, and 2) a pure behavioral biometric system that recognizes people according to their actions evaluated by a careful analysis of the extracted FOAs.

Chapter 15
Zhenan Sun, NLPR, CAS, China
Bangyu Li, NLPR, CAS, China
Tieniu Tan, NLPR, CAS, China

Automatic writer identification is desirable in many important applications, including banks, forensics, archeology, and so forth. A key and still open issue in writer identification is how to represent the distinctive and robust features of individual handwriting. This chapter presents three statistical feature models of handwritings in paragraph-level, stroke-level, and point-level, respectively, for text-independent writer identification. The three methods evolve from coarse to fine, showing the technology roadmap of handwriting biometrics. The proposed methods are evaluated on CASIA handwriting databases and perform well in both Chinese and English handwriting datasets. The experimental results show that fine scale handwriting primitives are advantageous in text-independent writer identification. The best performing method adopts the probability distribution function and the statistical dynamic features of tripoint primitives for handwriting feature representation, achieving 95% writer identification accuracy on CASIA-HandwritingV2 with 1,500 handwritings from more than 250 subjects. And a demo system of online writer identification is developed to demonstrate the potential of current algorithms for real world applications.

Chapter 16

A novel keystroke biometric system for long-text input was developed and evaluated for user identification and authentication applications. The system consists of a Java applet to collect raw keystroke data over the Internet, a feature extractor, and pattern classifiers to make identification or authentication decisions. Experiments on over 100 subjects investigated two input modes–copy and free-text input–and two keyboard types–desktop and laptop keyboards. The system can accurately identify or authenticate individuals if the same type of keyboard is used to produce the enrollment and questioned input samples. Longitudinal experiments quantified performance degradation over intervals of several weeks and over an interval of two years. Additional experiments investigated the system's hierarchical model, parameter settings, assumptions, and sufficiency of enrollment samples and input-text length. Although evaluated on input texts up to 650 keystrokes, we found that input of 300 keystrokes, roughly four lines of text, is sufficient for the important applications described.

Chapter 17

Biometric-key computation is a process of converting a piece of live biometric data into a key. Among the various biometrics available today, the hand signature has the highest level of social acceptance. The general masses are familiar with the use of handwritten signature by means of verification and acknowledgement. On the other hand, cryptography is used in multitude applications present in technologically advanced society. Examples include the security of ATM cards, computer networks, and e-commerce. The signature crypto-key computation is, hence, of highly interesting as it is a way to integrate behavioral biometrics with the existing cryptographic framework. In this chapter, we report a dynamic hand signatures-key generation scheme which is based on a randomized biometric helper. This scheme consists of a randomized feature discretization process and a code redundancy construction. The former enables one to control the intraclass variations of dynamic hand signatures to the minimal level and the latter will further reduce the errors. Randomized biometric helper ensures that a signature-key is easy to be revoked when the key is compromised. The proposed scheme is evaluated based on the 2004 Signature Verification Competition (SVC) database. We found that the proposed methods are able to produce keys that are stable, distinguishable and secure.

Chapter 18

This chapter expends behavior based intrusion detection approach to a new domain of game networks. Specifically, our research shows that a behavioral biometric signature can be generated based on the strategy used by an individual to play a game. We wrote software capable of automatically extracting behavioral profiles for each player in a game of poker. Once a behavioral signature is generated for a player, it is continuously compared against player's current actions. Any significant deviations in behavior are reported to the game server administrator as potential security breaches. In this chapter, we report our experimental results with user verification and identification as well as our approach to generation of synthetic poker data and potential spoofing approaches of the developed system. We also propose utilizing techniques developed for behavior based recognition of humans to the identification and verification of intelligent game bots. Our experimental results demonstrate feasibility of such methodology.

Chapter 19
    Xiaoli Zhou, University of California - Riverside, USA
    Bir Bhanu, University of California - Riverside, USA

This chapter introduces a new video based recognition system to recognize noncooperating individuals at a distance in video, who expose side views to the camera. Information from two biometric sources, side face and gait, is utilized and integrated for recognition. For side face, an Enhanced Side Face Image (ESFI), a higher resolution image compared with the image directly obtained from a single video frame, is constructed, which integrates face information from multiple video frames. For gait, the Gait Energy Image (GEI), a spatiotemporal compact representation of gait in video, is used to characterize human walking properties. The features of face and gait are extracted from ESFI and GEI, respectively. They are integrated at both of the match score level and the feature level by using different fusion strategies. The system is tested on a database of video sequences, corresponding to 45 people, which are collected over several months. The performance of different fusion methods are compared and analyzed. The experimental results show that (a) the idea of constructing ESFI from multiple frames is promising for human recognition in video and better face features are extracted from ESFI compared to those from the original side face images; (b) the synchronization of face and gait is not necessary for face template ESFI and gait template GEI; and (c) integrated information from side face and gait is effective for human recognition in video. The feature level fusion methods achieve better performance than the match score level methods fusion overall.

Foreword

The science of biometrics has advanced considerably over the past decade. It has now reached a position where there is general acceptance that people are unique by biometrics, and can be identified by them. Issues that remain for general resolution include the more pragmatic aspects, such as implementation issues (not just how the systems can operate, but also how people can interact with them) and analysis of results and performance. Given this acceptance, it is then correct that the research agenda should develop a wider remit.

That this is already happening is reflected in the diversity of new conference agendas on biometrics and of the emergence of new texts, such as this one. That makes this text very timely indeed. It is also very timely for its novelty: this is the first text on behavioural biometrics for human identification.

That a person can be identified by behavioural activities is entirely consistent with the notion of biometrics. The techniques for automated writer identification have a long history; gait is an inherently behavioural biometric wherein identity is reflected by the nature of variation of human body pose. Having been a long-time researcher in biometrics, I have seen the research path from concept to implementation many times. There is an ideas phase, where the notions of identity verification/recognition are first exposed. When this has been achieved, there is an issue of performance evaluation, and later on standardised analysis. Then, there is the need for real-time implementation in a system convenient for use and deployment. Finally, there is the need to convince the general public not just that these systems do indeed ascertain identity, but also that they work and are generally acceptable. This is the first text on behavioural biometrics, and is at the nascent stage of this new technology.

It is not surprising that some of oldest behavioural biometrics are to be found in extended and contemporary form within this volume. There are works here in describing text-independent writer identification, and keystroke input which is of increasing importance given the prevalence of web technologies. Given its importance as a behavioural biometric, it is no surprise that there are works here which survey the recent advances in gait, and which extend identification approaches by using bilinear models, and by gait feature fusion. An extension to these is to recognise people by their style of performing particular actions.

There is of course a wider remit in behaviour than there is in biometrics, for behaviour can concern not only personal variation, but also their interaction with a computer system or another device. In this we are found to be individual by the way we behave, as well as by physical characteristic. That is reflected here in that there are approaches based on using biosignals (electroencephalogram and electrocardiogram data), on a user's mouse dynamics, on a user's gaze when viewing familiar and unfamiliar scenes, and on a user's visual attention. Taking the approaches beyond more conventional biometrics, it is even show how recognition can be achieved based on a user's game-playing strategy.

The advance of recognition technique is usually paralleled by advance in the enabling technologies, and by advance in evaluation and that is to be found here. This new text contains works which define the remit by it taxonomy, which consider security evaluation to increase confidence, and on techniques and standard for performance evaluation. The technology concerns technique, here by Gabor wavelets, and by sensor technology, here by infrared. There is natural concern of security and by deployment of fusion to enhance recognition capability. In these respects, this text approaches major areas of interest in these new approaches.

The editorial team has assembled an impressive set of contributors and an impressive variety of contributions. I believe they encompass the majority of areas consistent with a new technology, covering basis, implementation, and evaluation. I look forward to analysing and discussing the content of this first text on behavioural biometrics, to the research that it contains, and that which it inspires.

Mark S. Nixon
University of Southampton
February 2009

Mark Nixon *is the Professor in Computer Vision at the University of Southampton UK. His research interests are in image processing and computer vision, especially when applied in biometrics. His team has developed new techniques for static and moving shape extraction which have found application in biometrics and in medical image analysis. His team was early workers in face recognition, later came to pioneer gait recognition and more recently joined the pioneers of ear biometrics. Amongst research contracts, he was Principal Investigator with John Carter on the DARPA supported project Automatic Gait Recognition for Human ID at a Distance. He chaired BMVC 98 and with Josef Kittler he co-chaired IEEE FG 2006 and AVBPA 2003, was Publications Chair for ICPR 2004 and is currently program chair for ICB and BTAS. His computer vision book, co-written with Alberto Aguado, Feature Extraction and Image Processing was published in 2002 by Academic Press and the 2nd Edition in 2007. With Tieniu Tan and Rama Chellappa, his book Human ID based on Gait which is part of the Springer Series on Biometrics, was published in 2005. Mark Nixon is a Fellow of the IAPR and of the IET.*

Preface

Automatic biometric recognition techniques are becoming increasingly important in corporate and public security systems. The term "biometric" is derived from the Greek words bio (life) and metric (to measure). There are two types of biometrics that can be used for human identification or verification: physical biometrics and behavioral biometrics. Physical biometrics, such as fingerprint and iris, have already been widely acknowledged and used in many real applications. As a relatively new technology, behavioral biometrics help verify a person's identity through some measurable activity patterns, for example, speaker recognition (i.e., analyzing vocal behavior), signature recognition (i.e., analyzing signature dynamics), gait recognition (i.e., analyzing walking patterns), keystroke dynamics (i.e., analyzing keyboard typing patterns), mouse dynamics (i.e., analyzing mouse moving patterns), and so forth.

Biometrics has been studied for many years. However, up to the present, most work is on physical biometrics, which naturally becomes main contents of the existing publications. Although some of them mentioned behavioral biometrics as an important category in addition to physical biometrics, they did not provide comprehensive survey and profound insight into this emerging technique. Over the past few years, people with both academic and industrial background have begun to realize the importance and advantages of behavioral biometrics, which consequently leads to a rapid development in this exciting area. Therefore, it is now very opportune to summarize what has happened and to indicate what will happen in this exciting area. To the best of our knowledge, this edited book is the first literature mainly focusing on behavioral biometrics, which will be very attractive and useful to those who are interested in these innovative recognition techniques and their promising applications. In particular, this book covers as much as possible about behavioral biometrics including basic knowledge, the state-of-the-art techniques, and realistic application systems, which will be very helpful to both researchers and practitioners.

The objective of this book is to discuss typical behavioral biometrics and to collect the latest advances in behavioral biometric techniques including both theoretical approaches and real applications. This edited book is anticipated to provide researchers and practitioners a comprehensive understanding of the start-of-the-art of behavioral biometrics techniques, potential applications, successful practice, available resources, and so forth. The book can serve as an important reference tool for researchers and practitioners in biometrics recognition, a handbook for research students, and a repository for technologists.

The target audience of this book includes the professionals and researchers working in the field of various disciplines, for example, computer vision, pattern recognition, information technique, psychology, image processing, artificial intelligence, and so forth. In particular, this book provides a comprehensive introduction to the latest techniques in behavioral biometrics for researchers. It is also attractive to the managers of those organizations seeking reliable security solutions.

In this edition, many topics of interest are highlighted. The following gives some brief introductions to each chapter included in this book.

Chapter 1, "Taxonomy of Behavioural Biometrics," presents taxonomy of the state-of-the-art in behavioural biometrics which are based on skills, style, preference, knowledge, motor-skills, or strategy used by people while accomplishing different everyday tasks, such as driving an automobile, talking on the phone, or using a computer. Current research in the field is examined and analyzed along with the features used to describe different types of behaviours. After comparing accuracy rates for verification of users using different behavioural biometric approaches, researchers address privacy issues which arise or might arise in the future with the use of behavioural biometrics. Finally, generalized properties of behaviour are addressed, as well as influence of environmental factors on observed behavior, and potential directions for future research in behavioural biometrics.

Chapter 2, "Security Evaluation of Behavioral Biometric Systems," reviews the state of the art of the methodology for evaluating the security of biometric systems, in particular of behavioral biometric verification systems. For increasing the confidence in the security of IT products, security evaluations by independent third-party testing laboratories are the first choice. In some fields of application of biometric methods (e.g., for protecting private keys for qualified electronic signatures), a security evaluation is even required by legislation. The common criteria for IT security evaluation form the basis for security evaluations for which a wide international recognition is desired. Within the common criteria, predefined security assurance requirements describe actions to be carried out by the developers of the product and by the evaluators. The assurance components that require clarification in the context of biometric systems are related to vulnerability assessment.

Chapter 3, "Performance Evaluation of Behavioral Biometric Systems," presents an overview of techniques for the performance evaluation of behavioral biometric systems. The BioAPI standard that defines the architecture of a biometric system is presented. The general methodology for the evaluation of biometric systems is given including statistical metrics, definition of benchmark databases, and subjective evaluation. These considerations rely with the ISO/IEC19795-1 standard describing the biometric performance testing and reporting. The specificity of behavioral biometric systems is detailed in order to define some additional constraints for their evaluation. This chapter is dedicated to researchers and engineers who need to quantify the performance of such biometric systems.

Chapter 4, "Individual Identification from Video based on 'Behavioural Biometrics'," presents multiple methods for recognizing individuals from their "style of action/actions", that is "biometric behavioural characteristics." Two forms of human recognition can be useful: the determination that an object is from the class of humans (i.e., human detection), and the determination that an object is a particular individual from this class (i.e., individual recognition). For individual recognition, this chapter considers two different categories, first individual recognition using "style of single action" (i.e., hand waving and partial gait) and second individual recognition using "style of doing similar actions" in video sequences. The "style of single action" and "style of doing similar actions," are proposed as a cue to discriminate between two individuals. Nowadays multibiometric security systems are available to recognise individuals from video sequences. This chapter also reports multiple novel behavioural biometric techniques for individual recognition based on "style of single action" and "style of multiple actions," which can be additionally combined with finger print, face, voice, and iris biometrics as a complementary cue to intelligent security systems.

Chapter 5, "Behavioral Biometrics: A Biosignal Based Approach", discusses the use of biosignal based biometrics, highlighting key studies and how this approach can be integrated into a multi-biometric user authentication system. The deployment of behavioral biometrics relies on the way a person interacts with an authentication device. Typical instances of this approach include voice, signature, and keystroke dynamics. Novel approaches to behavioral biometrics include biosignals such as the electroencephalogram and the electrocardiogram. The biosignal approach to user authentication has been shown to produce equal error rates on par with more traditional behavioral biometric approaches. Through a process similar to biofeedback, users can be trained with minimal effort to produce computer-based input via the manipulations of endogenous biosignal patterns.

Chapter 6, "Gabor Wavelets in Behavioral Biometrics," provides a brief discussion on the origin of Gabor wavelets, and then an illustration of "how to use Gabor wavelets" to extract features for a generic biometric application is discussed. Gabor wavelets are employed regularly in various biometrics applications because of their biological relevance and computational properties. These wavelets exhibit desirable characteristics of spatial locality and orientation selectivity, and are optimally localized in the space and frequency domains. Physiological, biometric systems such as face, fingerprint, and iris based human identification have shown great improvement in identification accuracy if Gabor wavelets are used for feature extraction. Moreover, some behavioral biometric systems such as speaker and gait-based applications have shown a more than 7% increase in identification accuracy. This study also provides an implementation pseudocode for the wavelet, as well as presenting an elaborate discussion on biometric applications with specific emphasis on behavioral biometric systems that have used Gabor wavelets and providing guideline for some biometric systems that have not yet applied Gabor for feature extraction.

Chapter 7, "Gait Recognition and Analysis," provides a survey of recent advances in gait recognition. With the increasing demands of visual surveillance systems, human identification at a distance is an urgent need. Gait is an attractive biometric feature for human identification at a distance, and recently has gained much interest from computer vision researchers. First, an overview on gait recognition framework, feature extraction, and classifiers is given in this chapter, and then some gait databases and evaluation metrics are introduced. Finally, research challenges and applications are discussed in detail.

Chapter 8, "Multilinear Modeling for Robust Identity Recognition from Gait," illustrates a three-layer scheme in which image sequences are first mapped to observation vectors of fixed dimension using Markov modeling, to be later classified by an asymmetric bilinear model, for human identification from gait. Gait recognition is a challenging task in realistic surveillance scenarios in which people walking along arbitrary directions are shot by a single camera. However, viewpoint is only one of the many covariate factors limiting the efficacy of gait recognition as a reliable biometrics. In this chapter the problem of robust identity recognition in the framework of multilineal models is addressed. Bilinear models, in particular, allow one to classify the "content" of human motions of unknown "style" (covariate factor). Tests are shown on the CMU Mobo database to prove that bilinear separation outperforms other common approaches, allowing robust view- and action-invariant identity recognition. In addition, an overview of the available tensor factorization techniques is given, and their potential applications to gait recognition are outlined.

Chapter 9, "Gait Feature Fusion using Factorial HMM," explores the factorial hidden Markov model (FHMM), an extended hidden Markov model (HMM) with a multiple layer structure, as a feature fusion framework for gait recognition. FHMM provides an alternative to combining several gait features without concatenating them into a single augmented feature, thus, to some extent, overcomes the curse of dimensionality and small sample size problem for gait recognition. Three gait features, the frieze feature, wavelet feature, and boundary signature, are adopted in the numerical experiments conducted on CMU MoBo database and CASIA gait database A. Besides the cumulative matching score (CMS) curves, McNemar's test is employed to check on the statistical significance of the performance difference between the recognition algorithms. Experimental results demonstrate that the proposed FHMM feature fusion scheme outperforms the feature concatenation method.

Chapter 10, "Mouse Dynamics Biometric Technology," introduces the concepts behind the mouse dynamics biometric technology. Mouse dynamics can be described as the characteristics of the actions received from the mouse input device for a user, while interacting with a graphical user interface. One of its key strengths compared to traditional biometric technologies is that it allows dynamic and passive user monitoring. As such, it can be used to track reliably and continuously legitimate and illegitimate users throughout computing sessions. This chapter presents a generic architecture of the detector used to collect and process mouse dynamics, and studies the various factors used to build the user's signature. This chapter also provides an updated survey on the researches and industrial implementations related to the technology, and studies possible applications in computer security.

Chapter 11, "Activity and Individual Human Recognition in Infrared Imagery," investigates repetitive human activity patterns and individual recognition in thermal infrared imagery, where human motion can be easily detected from the background regardless of the lighting conditions and colors of the human clothing and surfaces, and backgrounds. An efficient spatiotemporal representation for human repetitive activity and individual recognition, which represents human motion sequence in a single image while preserving spatiotemporal characteristics, is employed. A statistical approach is used to extract features for activity and individual recognition. Experimental results show that the approach achieves good performance for repetitive human activity and individual recognition.

Chapter 12, "Gaze Based Personal Identification," describes the use of visual attention characteristics as a biometric for authentication or identification of individual viewers. The visual attention characteristics of a person can be easily monitored by tracking the gaze of a viewer during the presentation of a known or unknown visual scene. The positions and sequences of gaze locations during viewing may be determined by overt (conscious) or covert (subconscious) viewing behaviour. Methods to quantify the spatial and temporal patterns established by the viewer for both overt and covert behaviours are proposed. The former behaviour entails a simple PIN-like approach to develop an independent signature while the latter behaviour is captured through three proposed techniques: a principal component analysis technique ('eigenGaze'); a linear discriminant analysis technique; and a fusion of distance measures. Experimental results suggest that both types of gaze behaviours can provide simple and effective biometrics for this application.

Chapter 13, "Speaker Verification and Identification," introduces several speaker recognition systems and examines their performances under various conditions. Speaker recognition can be classified into either speaker verification or speaker identification. Both the speaker verification and identification system consist of three essential elements: feature extraction, speaker modeling, and matching. The feature extraction pertains to extracting essential features from an input speech for speaker recognition. The speaker modeling pertains to probabilistically modeling the feature of the enrolled speakers. The matching pertains to matching the input feature to various speaker models. Speaker modeling techniques including Gaussian mixture model (GMM), hidden Markov model (HMM), and phone n-grams are presented, and their performances are compared under various tasks. Several verification and identification experimental results presented in this chapter indicates that speaker recognition performances are highly dependent on the acoustical environment. A comparative study between human listeners and an automatic speaker verification system is presented, and it indicates that an automatic speaker verification system can outperform human listeners. The applications of speaker recognition are summarized, and finally various obstacles that must be overcome are discussed.

Chapter 14, "Visual Attention for Behavioral Biometric Systems," proposes novel behavioral biometric applications based on the human visual attention system. More in detail, two biometrics systems based on how humans recognize faces, bodies, postures, and so forth, are discussed, according to the distribution of the focuses of attention (FOAs, that represent the most interesting parts in a visual scene) that are fixations reproducing the ability of humans in the interpretation of visual scenes. Indeed the pattern of these fixations and the choice of where to send the eye next are not random but appear to be guided.

Chapter 15, "Statistical Features for Text-independent Writer Identification," presents three statistical feature models of handwritings in paragraph-level, stroke-level, and point-level, respectively, for text-independent writer identification. Automatic writer identification is desirable in many important applications including banks, forensics, archeology, and so forth. A key and still open issue in writer identification is how to represent the distinctive and robust features of individual handwriting. The proposed three methods evolves from coarse to fine, showing the technology roadmap of handwriting biometrics, and are evaluated on CASIA handwriting databases. Experimental results show that they perform well in both Chinese and English handwriting datasets, and fine scale handwriting primitives are advantageous in text-independent writer identification. The best performing method adopts the probability distribution function and the statistical dynamic features of tri-point primitives for handwriting feature representation, achieving 95% writer identification accuracy on CASIA-HandwritingV2 with 1,500 handwritings from more than 250 subjects. And a demo system of online writer identification is developed to demonstrate the potential of current algorithms for real world applications.

Chapter 16, "Keystroke Biometric Identification and Authentication on Long-Text Input," introduces a novel keystroke biometric system for long-text input for identification and authentication applications. The system consists of a Java applet to collect raw keystroke data over the Internet, a feature extractor, and pattern classifiers to make identification or authentication decisions. Experiments on over 100 subjects investigated two input modes–copy and free-text input–and two keyboard types–desktop and laptop keyboards. The system can accurately identify or authenticate individuals if the same type of keyboard is used to produce the enrollment and questioned input samples. Longitudinal experiments quantified performance degradation over intervals of several weeks and over an interval of two years. Additional experiments investigated the system's hierarchical model, parameter settings, assumptions, and sufficiency of enrollment samples and input-text length.

Chapter 17, "Secure Dynamic Signature-Crypto Key Computation," reports a dynamic hand signatures-key generation scheme which is based on a randomized biometric helper. Biometric-key computation is a process of converting a piece of live biometric data into a key. Among the various biometrics available today, the hand signature has the highest level of social acceptance. On the other hand, cryptography is used in multitude applications present in technologically advanced society. The signature crypto-key computation is hence of highly interesting as it is a way to integrate behavioral biometrics with the existing cryptographic framework. This proposed scheme consists of a randomized feature discretization process and a code redundancy construction. The former enables one to control the intraclass variations of dynamic hand signatures to the minimal level and the latter will further reduce the errors. Randomized biometric helper ensures that a signature-key is easy to be revoked when the key is compromised. The proposed scheme is evaluated based on the 2004 Signature Verification Competition (SVC) database, and results show that the proposed methods are able to produce keys that are stable, distinguishable and secure.

Chapter 18, "Game Playing Tactic as a Behavioral Biometric for Human Identification," expends behavior based intrusion detection approach to a new domain of game networks. Specifically, this research shows that a behavioral biometric signature can be generated based on the strategy used by an individual to play a game. Software capable of automatically extracting behavioral profiles for each player in a game of poker is written. Once a behavioral signature is generated for a player, it is continuously compared against player's current actions. Any significant deviations in behavior are reported to the game server administrator as potential security breaches. In this chapter, experimental results with user verification and identification, as well as our approach to generation of synthetic poker data and potential spoofing approaches of the developed system, are reported. Also, utilizing techniques developed for behavior based recognition of humans to the identification and verification of intelligent game bots is proposed.

Chapter 19, "Multimodal Biometrics Fusion for Human Recognition in Video," introduces a new video based recognition system to recognize noncooperating individuals at a distance in video, who expose side views to the camera. Information from two biometric sources, side face and gait, is utilized and integrated for recognition. For side face, an Enhanced Side Face Image (ESFI), a higher resolution image compared with the image directly obtained from a single video frame, is constructed, which integrates face information from multiple video frames. For gait, the Gait Energy Image (GEI), a spatiotemporal compact representation of gait in video, is used to characterize human walking properties. The features of face and gait are extracted from ESFI and GEI, respectively. They are integrated at both of the match score level and the feature level by using different fusion strategies. The system is tested on a database of video sequences, corresponding to 45 people, which are collected over several months. The performance of different fusion methods are compared and analyzed. The experimental results show that (a) the idea of constructing ESFI from multiple frames is promising for human recognition in video and better face features are extracted from ESFI compared to those from the original side face images; (b) the synchronization of face and gait is not necessary for face template ESFI and gait template GEI; and (c) integrated information from side face and gait is effective for human recognition in video. The feature level fusion methods achieve better performance than the match score level methods fusion overall.

This book is an immediate and timely effort to review the latest progress in behavioral biometrics. Attempts of behavioral biometrics recognition in real world applications bring more realistic challenging problems in addition to the theoretical methodologies. As a reference book on various behavioral biometrics technologies, it contains an excellent collection of technical chapters written by authors who are worldwide recognized researchers and practitioners on the corresponding topics.

The readers of this book can learn about the state of the art of behavioral biometric techniques. They can be inspired of research interest in this exciting and promising area. They can be guided how to follow the right ways for their specific research and applications. They can learn about the potential applications of behavioral biometrics systems, research challenges, and possible solutions.

Liang Wang
University of Melbourne, Australia

Xin Geng
Southeast University, China
January 18, 2009

Acknowledgment

Automatic biometric recognition techniques are becoming increasingly important in corporate and public security systems. However, up to the present, most of the existing publications are on physical biometrics. To the best of our knowledge, this edited book is the first literature focusing on behavioral biometrics, which is very helpful to both researchers and practitioners. Therefore, we would like to express our sincere thanks to IGI Global to offer us the opportunity to edit such a book on this exciting area.

During the edition of this book, we received much help and support. First of all, we would like to thank all of the authors for submitting their wonderful works and apologize that not all chapter submissions could be accepted. We are also grateful to all of the chapter reviewers for their remarkable efforts on providing timely reviews of high quality. It was a great honor to have those worldwide leading experts join the Editorial Advisory Board of this book. They are Prof. Ahmed Awad (University of Victoria, Canada), Prof. Bir Bhanu (University of California, Riverside, USA), Prof. Hubert Cardot (Université François-Rabelais de Tours, France), Prof. Stan Li (Chinese Academy of Sciences, China), Prof. Mark Nixon (University of Southampton, UK), Prof. Tieniu Tan (Chinese Academy of Sciences, China), Prof. Anastasios Venetsanopoulos (Ryerson University, Canada), and Prof. David Zhang (Hong Kong Polytechnic University, China). We appreciate their valuable suggestions to strengthen the overall quality of this book and help to promote this publication. We are especially grateful to Prof. Mark Nixon for his time in writing the foreword for this book.

This book could not be possible without the help of the people involved at IGI Global. As a full-service publishing company, IGI Global staff handles all tasks related to production, registration, marketing and promotion, overseas distribution, and so on. As well as thanking the financial and technical support from IGI Global, special thanks go to Rebecca Beistline (Assistant Development Editor) and Christine Bufton (Administrative Editorial Assistant), for their assistance in guiding us each step of the way.

Liang Wang
University of Melbourne, Australia

Xin Geng
Southeast University, China
January 18, 2009

Chapter 1
Taxonomy of Behavioural Biometrics

Roman V. Yampolskiy
University of Louisville, USA

Venu Govindaraju
University at Buffalo, USA

ABSTRACT

This chapter presents a taxonomy of the latest behavioural biometrics, including some future oriented approaches. Current research in the field is examined and analyzed along with the features used to describe different types of behaviour. After comparing accuracy rates for verification of users using different behavioural biometric approaches, researchers address privacy issues which arise or might arise in the future with the use of behavioural biometrics. Finally, generalized properties of behaviour are addressed as well as influence of environmental factors on observed behaviour and potential directions for future research in behavioural biometrics.

INTRODUCTION TO BEHAVIORAL BIOMETRICS

With the proliferation of computers in our every day lives need for reliable computer security steadily increases. Biometric technologies provide user friendly and reliable control methodology for access to computer systems, networks and workplaces (Angle, Bhagtani, & Chheda, 2005; Dugelay, et al., 2002; Lee & Park, 2003). The majority of research is aimed at studying well established physical biometrics such as fingerprint (Cappelli, Maio, Maltoni,

Wayman, & Jain, 2006) or iris scans (Jain, Ross, & Prabhakar, 2004d). Behavioural biometrics systems are usually less established, and only those which are in large part based on muscle control such as keystrokes, gait or signature are well analyzed (Bolle, Connell, Pankanti, Ratha, & Senior, 2003; Delac & Grgic, 2004; Jain, Pankanti, Prabhakar, Hong, & Ross, 2004c; Ruggles, 2007; Solayappan & Latifi, 2006; Uludag, Pankanti, Prabhakar, & Jain, 2004).

Behavioural biometrics provide a number of advantages over traditional biometric technologies. They can be collected non-obtrusively or even without the knowledge of the user. Collection of

DOI: 10.4018/978-1-60566-725-6.ch001

behavioural data often does not require any special hardware and is so very cost effective. While most behavioural biometrics are not unique enough to provide reliable human identification they have been shown to provide sufficiently high accuracy identity verification. This chapter is based on "Behavioral Biometrics: a Survey and Classification." by R. Yampolskiy and V. Govindaraju, which appeared in the International Journal of Biometrics, 1(1), 81-113. The chapter presents a new comprehensive overview and improvements on research previously published in a number of publications including: (Yampolskiy, 2006, 2007a, 2007b, 2007c, 2007d, 2008a, 2008b; Yampolskiy & Govindaraju, 2006a, 2006b, 2007a, 2007b, 2008)

In accomplishing their everyday tasks human beings employ different strategies, use different styles and apply unique skills and knowledge. One of the defining characteristics of a behavioural biometric is the incorporation of time dimension as a part of the behavioural signature. The measured behaviour has a beginning, duration, and an end (Bioprivacy.org, 2005a). Behavioural biometrics researchers attempt to quantify behavioural traits exhibited by users and use resulting feature profiles to successfully verify identity (Bromme, 2003). In this section authors present an overview of most established behavioural biometrics.

Behavioural biometrics can be classified into five categories based on the type of information about the user being collected. Category one is made up of authorship based biometrics, which are based on examining a piece of text or a drawing produced by a person. Verification is accomplished by observing style peculiarities typical to the author of the work being examined, such as the used vocabulary, punctuation or brush strokes.

Category two consists of Human Computer Interaction (HCI) based biometrics (Yampolskiy, 2007a). In their everyday interaction with computers human beings employ different strategies, use different style and apply unique abilities and knowledge. Researchers attempt to quantify such

traits and use resulting feature profiles to successfully verify identity. HCI-based biometrics can be further subdivided into additional categories, first one consisting of human interaction with input devices such as keyboards, computer mice, and haptics which can register inherent, distinctive and consistent muscle actions (Bioprivacy.org, 2005b). The second group consists of HCI-based behavioural biometrics which measure advanced human behaviour such as strategy, knowledge or skill exhibited by the user during interaction with different software.

Third group is closely related to the second one and is the set of the indirect HCI-based biometrics which are the events that can be obtained by monitoring user's HCI behaviours indirectly via observable low-level actions of computer software (Yampolskiy, 2007b). Those include system call traces (Denning, 1987), audit logs (Ilgun, Kemmerer, & Porras, 1995), program execution traces (Ghosh, Schwartzbard, & Schatz, 1999a), registry access (Apap, Honig, Hershkop, Eskin, & Stolfo, 2002), storage activity (Pennington, et al., 2002), call-stack data analysis (Feng, Kolesnikov, Fogla, Lee, & Gong, 2003b) and system calls (Garg, Rahalkar, Upadhyaya, & Kwiat, 2006 ; Pusara & Brodley, 2004). Such low-level events are produced unintentionally by the user during interaction with different software.

Same HCI-based biometrics are sometimes known to different researchers under different names. IDS based on system calls or audit logs are often classified as utilizing program execution traces and those based on call-stack data as based on system calls. The confusion is probably related to the fact that a lot of interdependency exists between different indirect behavioural biometrics and they are frequently used in combinations to improve accuracy of the system being developed. For example system calls and program counter data may be combined in the same behavioural signature or audit logs may contain information about system calls. Also one can't forget that a human being is indirectly behind each one of those reflections of behaviour and so a large degree of correlation is to be expected.

Fourth and probably the best researched group of behavioural biometrics relies on motor-skills of the users to accomplish verification (Yampolskiy, 2007c). Motor-skill is an ability of a human being to utilize muscles. Muscle movements rely upon the proper functioning of the brain, skeleton, joints, and nervous system and so motor skills indirectly reflect the quality of functioning of such systems, making person verification possible. Most motor skills are learned, not inherited, with disabilities having potential to affect the development of motor skills. Authors adopt definition for motor-skill based behavioural biometrics, a.k.a. *kinetics,* as those biometrics which are based on innate, unique and stable muscle actions of the user while performing a particular task (Caslon. com.au, 2005).

Fifth and final category consists of purely behavioural biometrics. Purely behavioural biometrics are those which measure human behaviour directly not concentrating on measurements of body parts or intrinsic, inimitable and lasting muscle actions such as the way an individual walks, types or even grips a tool (Caslon.com.au, 2005). Human beings utilize different strategies, skills and knowledge during performance of mentally demanding tasks. Purely behavioural biometrics quantify such behavioural traits and make successful identity verification a possibility.

All of the behavioural biometrics reviewed in this chapter share a number of characteristics and so can be analyzed as a group using seven properties of good biometrics presented by Jain et al. (Jain, Bolle, & Pankanti, 1999; Jain, et al., 2004d). It is a good idea to check them before declaring some characteristics suitable for the automated recognition of individuals.

- **Universality:** Behavioural biometrics are dependent on specific abilities possessed by different people to a different degree or not at all and so in a general population

universality of behavioural biometrics is very low. But since behavioural biometrics are only applied in a specific domain, the actual universality of behavioural biometrics is a 100%.

- **Uniqueness:** Since only a small set of different approaches to performing any task exists uniqueness of behavioural biometrics is relatively low. Number of existing writing styles, different game strategies and varying preferences are only sufficient for user verification not identification unless the set of users is extremely small (Adler, Youmaran, & Loyka, 2006).
- **Permanence:** Behavioural biometrics exhibit a low degree of permanence as they measure behaviour which changes with time as person learns advanced techniques and faster ways of accomplishing tasks. However, this problem of concept drift is addressed in the behaviour based intrusion detection research and systems are developed capable of adjusting to the changing behaviour of the users (Koychev & Schwab, 2000; Tsymbal, 2004).
- **Collectability:** Collecting behavioural biometrics is relatively easy and unobtrusive to the user. In some instances the user may not even be aware that data collection is taking place. The process of data collection is fully automated and is very low cost.
- **Performance:** The identification accuracy of most behavioural biometrics is low particularly as the number of users in the database becomes large. However verification accuracy is very good for some behavioural biometrics.
- **Acceptability:** Since behavioural biometric characteristics can be collected without user participation they enjoy a high degree of acceptability, but might be objected to for ethical or privacy reasons.
- **Circumvention:** It is relatively difficult to get around behavioural biometric systems

as it requires intimate knowledge of someone else's behaviour, but once such knowledge is available fabrication might be very straightforward (Schuckers, 2002). This is why it is extremely important to keep the collected behavioural profiles securely encrypted.

BACKGROUND ON BEHAVIORAL RESEARCH

It is often the case in the scientific discovery process that multiple sub-fields of science study the same concept simultaneously but are not aware of the contributions made in the other fields to what essentially is the same problem. Multiple disciplines use different motivation for their research as well as create unique vocabulary to deal with the problem at hand. A lot of progress in finding a solution to such a problem can be made by realizing similarity of research goals and making scientists realize the wealth of available techniques from other fields which may be used with little to no modification for solving a problem at hand. We start by presenting just such a problem addressed by many fields, which are relatively unaware of each other, but all attempt to model human behaviour.

- **User Profiling:** is studied by researchers in the field of Intrusion Detection. It consists of observing someone interacting with a computer, creating a model of such behaviour and using it as a template for what is considered a normal behaviour for that particular user. If the behaviour of supposedly the same user is significantly different we can speculate that perhaps it is a different user masquerading as the user whose profile is stored in our security system as a template.
- **User Modelling:** is studied for marketing and customization purposes. It aims at creating a representation of the user for the purpose of customizing products and service to better suite the user. For example software can be made to only display options which are in the field of interest of this particular user making it easier for him to interact with an otherwise very complicated piece of software.
- **Opponent Modelling:** is related to the field of Game Theory and studies different models for understanding and predicting behaviour of players in different games. While for many games such as chess it is sufficient for victory to play the best possible strategy and ignore the unique behaviour of your opponent in many other games such as poker it is not. Having a well performing prediction model of your opponent's behaviour can give you an edge necessary to defeat him in an otherwise equal game.
- **Criminal Profiling:** as done by police and FBI investigators is the practice of trying to determine personality and identity of an individual who has committed a crime based on the behaviour, which was exhibited during the criminal act.
- **Jury Profiling:** is a technique used by lawyers to attempt to predict how a particular potential juror will vote with respect to the verdict based on juror's current behaviour, answers to a questioner and overall physical and psychological appearance of the juror.

While the researchers faced with the above problems represent relatively unrelated disciplines they are all essentially trying to achieve the same exact goals. They want to be able to do the following: By analyzing past and current actions create an accurate model of individual human's behavior capable of predicting future actions based on a given situation and environmental factors. Given a description of behavior either identify an individual likely to conduct himself in such manner or to verify if a given individual is likely to behave in such a way (Yampolskiy, 2008a).

Basically in its most generalized form the problem boils down to a mapping from the set of behaviors to individuals and vise versa. However we can ask if it is possible to create more complicated mappings between personality and behavior.

Given occurrence of some behavior by an individual can we predict happening of another smilingly unrelated behavior by the same individual? It is obvious that in the case of related behaviors the answer is definitely - yes, for example someone who buys a first and second album by a famous rap artist is likely to also purchase a third one. But in the case of completely unrelated behaviors we don't have any strong evidence supporting or disproving possibility of such correspondence. For example do people who collect stamps are also more likely to enjoy horseback riding?

Some research suggests that there is a connection between one set of behaviors and another. Rentfrow et al. in the Journal of Personality and Social Psychology report that they found a connection between person's musical preferences and other unrelated social behaviors (Rentfrow & Gosling, 2005). The most famous example from the field of data mining tells us that people who buy diapers also tend to buy beer while at the store. Clearly this is a very interesting and beneficial area of research. The possible applications for cross-behavioral prediction are numerous. Perhaps it is possible to make judgments about intelligence or health of an individual from something as benign as routine computer interaction. Maybe we can learn to judge suitability of a potential mate from table manners or find a reliable business partner by watching a person park his car.

Another interesting question to ask is: if two different individuals have similar behavioral profiles and individual A performs a novel behavior is it likely that individual B will also perform the same

behavior in the near future. Intuitively it seems very plausible, for example, if two different people recently got married and left on a honeymoon we can expect that seeing one of them buy baby related items may allow us to predict similar purchases by the other in the nearest future. Obviously in this contrived example we had alternative ways of figuring this out.

It would seem desirable to have a single discipline devoted to solving such an important problem for many fields, but in reality a number of somewhat different fields all attempt to work on it to some degree, not mentioning the fields listed above we have:

- **Behaviormetrics:** which studies human behavior on the basis of statistics and information technology. Methodology in behavioral sciences is studied and mathematical or statistical models for understanding human behavior are developed (Yutaka, 2005).
- **Behavioral Sciences:** "essentially investigates the decision processes and communication strategies within and between organisms in a social system. BS encompasses all the disciplines that explore the behavior and strategies within and between organisms in the natural world. It involves the systematic analysis and investigation of humans and animal behavior, through controlled and naturalistic experimental observations and rigorous formulations" (Wikipedia.org, 2005).

Both of which can be put under a more general umbrella of science of psychology defined as: "scientific study of human behavior, mental processes, and how they are affected and/or affect an individuals or group's physical state, mental state, and external environment. It's goal is to describe, understand, predict, and modify behavior" (Elissetche, 2005).

DESCRIPTION OF BEHAVIOURAL BIOMETRICS

Table 1 shows behavioural biometrics covered in this paper classified according to the five categories outlined above (Yampolskiy & Govindaraju, 2008). Many of the reviewed biometrics are cross listed in multiple categories due to their dependence on multiple behavioural attributes. In addition enrolment time and verification time (D =days, H=hours, M=Minutes, S=Seconds) of the listed biometrics is provided as well as any hardware required for the collection of the biometric characteristic data. Out of all the listed behavioural biometrics only two are believed to be useful not just for person verification but also for reliable large scale person identification, those are: signature/handwriting and speech. Other behavioural biometrics may be used for identification purposes but are not reliable enough to be employed in that capacity in the real world applications.

Presented next are short overviews of the most researched behavioural biometrics listed in alphabetical order (Yampolskiy & Govindaraju, 2008).

Audit Logs

Most modern operating systems keep some records of user activity and program interaction. While such audit trails can be of some interest to behavioural intrusion detection researchers, specialized audit trails specifically designed for security enforcement can be potentially much more powerful. A typical audit log may contain such information as: CPU and I/O usage, number of connections from each location, whether a directory was accessed, a file created, another user ID changed, audit record was modified, amount of activity for the system, network and host (Lunt, 1993). Experimentally it has been shown that collecting audit events is a less intrusive technique than recording system calls (Wespi, Dacier, & Debar, 2000). Because an enormous amount of

auditing data can be generated overwhelming an intrusion detection system it has been suggested that a random sampling might be a reasonable approach to auditing data (Anderson, 1980). Additional data might be helpful in distinguishing suspicious activity from normal behaviour. For example facts about changes in user status, new users being added, terminated users, users on vocations, or changed job assignments might be needed to reduce the number of false positives produced by the IDS (Lunt, 1993). Since so much potentially valuable information can be captured by the audit logs a large number of researchers are attracted to this form of indirect HCI-based biometric (Denning, 1987; Ilgun, et al., 1995; Ko, Fink, & Levitt, 1994; Lee, Stolfo, & Mok, 1999; Li, Wu, Jajodia, & Wang, 2002; Michael, 2003; Michael & Ghosh, 2000; Seleznyov & Puuronen, 1999; Ye, 2000).

Biometric Sketch

Bromme et al. (Al-Zubi, Brömme, & Tönnies, 2003; Brömme & Al-Zubi, 2003) proposed a biometric sketch authentication method based on sketch recognition and a user's personal knowledge about the drawings content. The system directs a user to create a simple sketch for example of three circles and each user is free to do so in any way he pleases. Because a large number of different combinations exist for combing multiple simple structural shapes sketches of different users are sufficiently unique to provide accurate authentication. The approach measures user's knowledge about the sketch, which is only available to the previously authenticated user. Such features as the sketches location and relative position of different primitives are taken as the profile of the sketch. Similar approaches are tried by (Varenhorst, 2004) with a system called Passdoodles and also by (Jermyn, Mayer, Monrose, Reiter, & Rubin, 1999) with a system called Draw-a-Secret. Finally a V-go Password requests a user to perform simulation of simple actions such

Table 1. Classification and properties of behavioural biometrics (©2008. Inderscience Publishers Ltd. Used with permission.)

Classification of the Various Types of Behavioural Biometrics	Authorship	Direct Human Computer Interaction		Indirect Human Computer Interaction	Motor Skill	Purely Behavioural	Properties of Behavioural Biometrics			
		Input Device Interaction Based	Software Interaction Based				Enrolment time	Verification time	Identification	Required Hardware
Audit Logs				•			D	D	N	Computer
Biometric Sketch	•					•	M	S	N	Mouse
Blinking					•		M	S	N	Camera
Call-Stack				•			D	H	N	Computer
Calling Behaviour						•	D	D	N	Phone
Car Driving Style						•	H	M	N	Car Sensors
Command Line Lexicon			•			•	H	H	N	Computer
Credit Card Use						•	D	D	N	Credit Card
Dynamic Facial Features					•		M	S	N	Camera
Email Behaviour	•		•			•	D	M	N	Computer
Gait/Stride					•		M	S	N	Camera
Game Strategy			•			•	H	H	N	Computer
GUI Interaction				•			D	H	N	Computer
Handgrip					•		M	S	N	Gun Sensors
Haptic		•			•		M	M	N	Haptic
Keystroke Dynamics		•			•		M	S	N	Keyboard
Lip Movement					•		M	S	N	Camera
Mouse Dynamics		•			•		M	S	N	Mouse
Network Traffic				•			D	D	N	Computer
Painting Style	•					•	D	D	N	Scanner
Programming Style	•		•			•	H	H	N	Computer
Registry Access				•			D	H	N	Computer
Signature/Handwriting					•		M	S	Y	Stylus
Storage Activity				•			D	D	N	Computer
System Calls				•			D	H	N	Computer
Tapping					•		M	S	N	Sensor
Text Authorship	•					•	H	M	N	Computer
Voice/Speech/Singing					•		M	S	Y	Microphone

as mixing a cocktail using a graphical interface, with the assumption that all users have a personal approach to bartending (Renaud, 2003).

Blinking

(Westeyn, Pesti, Park, & Starner, 2005; Westeyn & Starner, 2004) have developed a system for identifying users by analyzing voluntary song-based blink patterns. During the enrolment phase user looks at the system's camera and blinks to the beat of a song he has previously chosen producing a so-called "blinkprint". During verification phase the user's blinking is compared to the database of the stored blinked patterns to determine which song is being blinked and as a result user identification is possible. In addition to the blink pattern itself supplementary features can also be extracted such as: time between blinks, how long the eye is held closed at each blink, and other physical characteristics the eye undergoes while blinking. Based on those additional features it was shown to be feasible to distinguish users blinking the same exact pattern and not just a secretly selected song.

Call-Stack

Feng et al. (Feng, Kolesnikov, Fogla, Lee, & Gong, 2003a) developed a method for performing anomaly detection using call stack information. The program counter indicates the current execution point of a program; and since each instruction of a program corresponds to a unique program counter this information is useful for intrusion detection. The idea is to extract return addresses from the call stack and generate an abstract execution path between two program execution points. This path is analyzed to decide whether this path is valid based on what has been learned during the normal execution of the program. Return addresses are a particularly good source of information on suspicious behaviour. The approach has been shown capable of detecting some attacks that could not

be detected by other approaches, while retaining a comparable false positive rate (Feng, et al., 2003a). Additional research into call-stack-based intruder detection has been performed by Giffin et al. (Giffin, Jha, & Miller, 2004) and Liu et al. (Liu & Bridges, 2005).

Calling Behavior

With the proliferation of the mobile cellular phone networks, communication companies are faced with the increasing amount of fraudulent calling activity. In order to automatically detect theft of service many companies are turning to behavioural user profiling with the hopes of detecting unusual calling patterns and be able to stop fraud at an earliest possible time. Typical systems work by generating a user calling profile which consist of use indicators such as: date and time of the call, duration, called ID, called number, cost of call, number of calls to a local destination, number of calls to mobile destinations, number of calls to international destinations and the total statistics about the calls for the day (Hilas & Sahalos, 2005). Grosser et al. (Grosser, Britos, & García-Martínez, 2005) have shown that neural networks can be successfully applied to such a feature vector for the purpose of fraud detection. Cahill et al. (Cahill, Lambert, Pinheiro, & Sun, 2000) have addressed ways to improve the selection of the threshold values which are compared with account summaries to see if fraud has taken place. Fawcett et al. (Fawcett & Provost, 1997) developed a rule-learning program to uncover indicators of fraudulent behaviour from a large database of customer transactions.

Car driving style

People tend to operate vehicles in very different ways, some drivers are safe and slow others are much more aggressive and often speed and tailgate. As a result, driving behavior can be successfully treated as a behavioural biometric. Erdogan et al.

(Erdogan, et al., 2005a; Erdogan, et al., 2005b; Erzin, et al., 2006) have shown that by analyzing pressure readings from accelerator pedal and brake pedal in kilogram force per square centimetre, vehicle speed in revolutions per minute, and steering angle within the range of -720 to + 720 degrees it is possible to achieve genuine versus impostor driver authentication. Gaussian mixture modelling was used to process the resulting feature vectors, after some initial smoothing and sub-sampling of the driving signal. Similar results were obtained by Igarashi et al. (Igarashi, et al., 2004) on the same set of multimodal data. Liu et al. (Liu & Salvucci, 2001) in their work on prediction of driver behaviour have demonstrated that inclusion of the driver's visual scanning behaviour can further enhance accuracy of the driver behaviour model. Once fully developed, driver recognition can be used for car personalization, theft prevention, as well as for detection of drunk or sleepy drivers. With so many potential benefits from this technology, research in driver behaviour modelling is not solely limited to the biometrics community (Kuge, Yamamura, & Shimoyama, 1998; Oliver & Pentland, 2000).

Command Line Lexicon

A popular approach to the construction of behaviour based intrusion detection systems, is based on profiling the set of commands utilized by the user in the process of interaction with the operating system. A frequent target of such research is UNIX operating system, probably due to it having mostly command line nature. User's differ greatly in their level of familiarity with the command set and all the possible arguments which can be applied to individual commands. Regardless of how well a user knows the set of available commands; most are fairly consistent in their choice of commands used to accomplish a particular task.

A user profile typically consists of a list of used commands together with corresponding frequency counts, and lists of arguments to the commands. Data collection process is often time consuming since as many as 15,000 individual commands need to be collected for the system to achieve high degree of accuracy (Maxion & Townsend, 2002b; Schonlau, et al., 2001). Additional information about the secession may also be included in the profile such as the login host and login time, which help to improve accuracy of the user profile as it is likely that users perform different actions on different hosts (Dao & Vemuri, 2000). Overall, this line of research is extremely popular (Lane & Brodley, 1997a, 1997b; Marin, Ragsdale, & Surdu, 2001; Yeung & Ding), but recently a shift has been made towards user profiling in a graphical environment such as Windows as most users prefer convenience of a Graphical User Interface (GUI). Typical features extracted from the user's interaction with a windows based machine include: time between windows, time between new windows, number of windows simultaneously open, and number of words in a window title (Goldring, 2003; Kaufman, Cervone, & Michalski, 2003).

Credit Card Use

Data mining techniques are frequently used in detection of credit card fraud. Looking out for statistical outliers such as unusual transactions, payments to far away geographical locations or simultaneous use of a card at multiple locations can all be signs of a stolen account. Outliers are considerably different from the remainder of the data points and can be detected by using discordancy tests. Approaches for fraud related outlier detection are based on distance, density, projection, and distribution analysis methods. A generalized approach to finding outliers is to assume a known statistical distribution for the data and to evaluate the deviation of samples from the distribution. Brause et al. (Brause, Langsdorf, & Hepp, 1999) have used symbolic and analog number data to detect credit card fraud. Such transaction information as account number, transaction type, credit card type, merchant ID, merchant address, etc. were used in their rule based model. They have also shown that analog data alone can't serve as a satisfying source for detection of fraudulent transactions.

Dynamic Facial Features

Pamudurthy et al. (Pamudurthy, Guan, Mueller, & Rafailovich, 2005) proposed a dynamic approach to face recognition based on dynamic instead of static facial features. They track the motion of skin pores on the face during a facial expression and obtain a vector field that characterizes the deformation of the face. In the training process, two high-resolution images of an individual, one with a neutral expression and the other with a facial expression, like a subtle smile, are taken to obtain the deformation field (Mainguet, 2006).

Smile recognition research in particular is a subfield of dynamic facial feature recognition currently gaining in prominence (Ito, Wang, Suzuki, & Makino, 2005). The existing systems rely on probing the characteristic pattern of muscles beneath the skin of the user's face. Two images of a person in quick progression are taken, with subjects smiling for the camera in the second sample. An analysis is later performed of how the skin around the subject's mouth moves between the two images. This movement is controlled by the pattern of muscles under the skin, and is not affected by the presence of make-up or the degree to which the subject smiles (Mainguet, 2006).

Email Behaviour

Email sending behaviour is not the same for all individuals. Some people work at night and send dozens of emails to many different addresses; others only check mail in the morning and only correspond with one or two people. All this peculiarities can be used to create a behavioural profile which can serve as a behavioural biometric characteristic for an individual. Length of the emails, time of the day the mail is sent, how frequently inbox is emptied and of course the recipients' addresses among other variables can all be combined to create a baseline feature vector for the person's email behaviour. Some work in using email behaviour modelling was done by Stolfo et al. (Stolfo, Hershkop, Wang, Nimeskern, & Hu, 2003a; Stolfo, et al., 2003b). They have investigated possibility of detecting virus propagation via email by observing abnormalities in the email sending behaviour, such as unusual clique of recipients for the same email. For example sending the same email to your girlfriend and your boss is not an everyday occurrence.

De Vel et al. (Vel, Anderson, Corney, & Mohay, 2001) have applied authorship identification techniques to determine the likely author of an email message. Alongside the typical features used in text authorship identification authors also used some email specific structural features such as: use of a greeting, farewell acknowledgment, signature, number of attachments, position of re-quoted text within the message body, HTML tag frequency distribution and total number of HTML tags. Overall, almost 200 features are used in the experiment, but some frequently cited features used in text authorship determination are not appropriate in the domain of email messages due to the shorter average size of such communications.

Gait/Stride

Gait is one of the best researched muscle control based biometrics (BenAbdelkader, Cutler, & Davis, 2002; Kale, et al., 2004; Nixon & Carter, 2004), it is a complex spatio-temporal motor-control behaviour which allows biometric recognition of individuals at a distance usually from captured video. Gait is subject to significant variations based on changes in person's body weight, waddling during pregnancy, injuries of extremities or of the brain, or due to intoxication (Jain, et al., 1999). Typical features include: amount of arm swing, rhythm of the walker, bounce, length of steps, vertical distance between head and foot, distance between head and pelvis, maximum distance between the left and right foot (Kalyanaraman, 2006).

Game Strategy

Yampolskiy et al. (Yampolskiy, 2006; Yampolskiy & Govindaraju, 2006b, 2007b) proposed a system for verification of online poker players based on a behavioural profile which represents a statistical model of player's strategy. The profile consists of frequency measures indicating range of cards considered by the player at all stages of the game. It also measures how aggressive the player is via such variables as percentages of re-raised hands. The profile is actually human readable meaning that a poker expert can analyze and understand strategy employed by the player from observing his or her behavioural profile (poker-edge.com, 2006). For example just by knowing the percentage of hands a particular player chooses to play pre-flop it is possible to determine which cards are being played with high degree of accuracy.

Ramon et al. (Ramon & Jacobs, 2002) have demonstrated possibility of identifying Go players based on their style of game play. They analyzed a number of Go specific features such as type of opening moves, how early such moves are made and total number of liberties in the formed groups. They also speculate that the decision tree approach they have developed can be applied to other games such as Chess or Checkers.

Jansen et al. (Jansen, Dowe, & E., 2000) report on their research in chess strategy inference from game records. In particular they were able to surmise good estimates of the weights used in the evaluation function of computer chess players and later applied same techniques to human grandmasters. Their approach is aimed at predicting future moves made by the players, but the opponent model created with some additional processing can be utilized for opponent identification or at least verification. This can be achieved by comparing new moves made by the player with predicted once from models for different players and using the achieved accuracy scores as an indication of which profile models which player.

GUI Interaction

Expanding on the idea of monitoring user's keyboard and mouse activity Garg et al. (Garg, et al., 2006) developed a system for collecting Graphical User Interface (GUI) interaction-based data. Collected data allows for generation of advanced behavioural profiles of the system's users. Such comprehensive data may provide additional information not available form typically analyzed command line data. With proliferation of GUI based systems a shift towards security systems based on GUI interaction data, as opposed to command line data, is a natural progression. Ideally the collected data would include high-level detailed information about the GUI related actions of the user such as: left click on the Start menu, double click on explorer.exe, close Notepad.exe window, etc. Software generated by Garg et al. records all possible low-level user activities on the system in real time, including: system background processes, user run commands, keyboard activity and mouse clicks. All collected information is time stamped and pre-processed to reduce the amount of data actually used for intrusion detection purposes (Garg, et al., 2006).

Handgrip

Developed mostly for gun control applications grip-pattern recognition approach assumes that users hold the gun in a sufficiently unique way to permit user verification to take place. By incorporating a hardware sensor array in the gun's butt Kauffman et al. (Kauffman, Bazen, Gerez, & Veldhuis, 2003; Veldhuis, Bazen, Kauffman, & Hartel, 2004) were able to get resistance measurements in as many as 44 x 44 points which are used in creation of a feature vector. Obtained pressure points are taken as pixels in the pressure pattern image used as input for verification algorithm based on a likelihood-ratio classifier for Gaussian probability densities (Kauffman, et al., 2003). Experiments showed that more experienced gun users tended to be more accurately verified as compared to first time subjects.

Haptic

Haptic systems are computer input/output devices which can provide us with information about direction, pressure, force, angle, speed, and position of user's interactions (Orozco, Asfaw, Adler, Shirmohammadi, & Saddik, 2005; Orozco, Asfaw, Shirmohammadi, Adler, & Saddik, 2006). Because so much information is available about the user's performance a high degree of accuracy can be expected from a haptic based biometrics system. Orozco et al. (Orozco, et al., 2005; Orozco, et al., 2006) have created a simple haptic application built on an elastic membrane surface in which the user is required to navigate a stylus through the maze. The maze has gummy walls and a stretchy floor. The application collects data about the ability of the user to navigate the maze, such as reaction time to release from sticky wall, the route, the velocity, and the pressure applied to the floor. The individual user profiles are made up of such information as 3D world location of the pen, average speed, mean velocity, mean standard deviation, navigation style, angular turns and rounded turns.

In a separate experiment Orozco et al. (Trujillo, Shakra, & Saddik, 2005) implement a virtual mobile phone application where the user interacts through a haptic pen to simulate making a phone call via a touch pad. The keystroke duration, pen's position, and exerted force are used as the raw features collected for user profiling.

Keystroke Dynamics

Typing patterns are characteristic to each person, some people are experienced typists utilizing the touch-typing method, and others utilize the hunt-and-peck approach which uses only two fingers. Those differences make verification of people based on their typing patterns a proven possibility, some reports suggest identification is also possible (Ilonen, 2006). For verification a small typing sample such as the input of user's password is sufficient, but for recognition a large amount of keystroke data is needed and identification is based on comparisons with the profiles of all other existing users already in the system.

Keystroke features are based on time durations between the keystrokes, inter-key strokes and dwell times, which is the time a key is pressed down, overall typing speed, frequency of errors (use of backspace), use of numpad, order in which user presses shift key to get capital letters and possibly the force with which keys are hit for specially equipped keyboards (Ilonen, 2006; Jain, et al., 1999). Keystroke dynamics is probably the most researched type of HCI-based biometric characteristic (Bergadano, Gunetti, & Picardi, 2002 ; Monrose & Rubin, March 2000), with novel research taking place in different languages (Gunetti, Picardi, & Ruffo, 2005), for long text samples, (Bartolacci, et al., 2005; Curtin, et al., 2006) and for email authorship identification (Gupta, Mazumdar, & Rao, 2004).

In a similar fashion Bella et al. (Bella & Palmer, 2006) have studied finger movements of skilled piano players. They have recorded finger motion from skilled pianists while playing a musical keyboard. Pianists' finger motion and speed with which keys are struck was analyzed using functional data analysis methods. Movement velocity and acceleration were consistent for the participants and in multiple musical contexts. Accurate pianists' classification was achieved by training a neural network classifier using velocity/acceleration trajectories preceding key presses.

Lip Movement

This approach originally based on the visual speech reading technology attempts to generate a model representing lip dynamics produced by a person during speech. User verification is based on how close the generated model fits observed lip movement. Such models are typically constructed around spatio-temporal lip features. First the lip region needs to be isolated from the video feed, and then significant features of lip contours are extracted typically from edges and gradients. Lip features include: the mouth opening or closing, skin around the lips, mouth width, upper/lower lip width, lip opening height/width, distance between horizontal lip line and upper lip (Broun, Zhang, Mersereau, & Clements, 2002; Shipilova, 2006). Typically lip dynamics are utilized as a part of a multimodal biometric system, usually combined with speaker recognition based authentication (Jourlin, Luettin, Genoud, & Wassner, 1997; Luettin, Thacker, & Beet, 1996; Mason, Brand, Auckenthaler, Deravi, & Chibelushi, 1999; Wark, Thambiratnam, & Sridharan, 1997), but standalone usage is also possible (Mok, Lau, Leung, Wang, & Yan, 2004).

Mouse Dynamics

By monitoring all mouse actions produced by the user during interaction with the Graphical User Interface (GUI), a unique profile can be generated which can be used for user re-authentication (Pusara & Brodley, 2004). Mouse actions of interest include general movement, drag and drop, point and click, and stillness. From those a set of features can be extracted for example average speed against the distance travelled, and average speed against the movement direction (Ahmed & Traore, 2005a, 2005b). Pusara et al. (Pusara & Brodley, 2004) describe a feature extraction approach in which they split the mouse event data into mouse wheel movements, clicks, menu and toolbar clicks. Click data is further subdivided

into single and double click data.

Gamboa et al. (Gamboa & Fred, 2003, 2004) have tried to improve accuracy of mouse-dynamics-based biometrics by restricting the domain of data collection to an online game instead of a more general GUI environment. As a result applicability of their results is somewhat restricted and the methodology is more intrusive to the user. The system requires around 10-15 minutes of devoted game play instead of seamless data collection during the normal to the user human computer interaction. As far as the extracted features, x and y coordinates of the mouse, horizontal velocity, vertical velocity, tangential velocity, tangential acceleration, tangential jerk and angular velocity are utilized with respect to the mouse strokes to create a unique user profile.

Network Traffic

Network level intrusion detection is somewhat different from other types of intrusion detection as the monitored activity originates outside the system being protected. With the increase in popularity of Internet and other networks an intruder no longer has to have physical access to the system he is trying to penetrate. This means that the network dataflow arriving on different system ports and encoded using different protocols needs to be processed and reviewed. IDS based on network traffic analyze various packet attributes such as: IP protocol-type values, packet size, server port numbers, source and destination IP prefixes, Time-To-Live values, IP/TCP header length, incorrect IP/TCP/UDP checksums, and TCP flag patterns. During the baseline profiling period the number of packets with each attribute value is counted and taken as normal behaviour (Kim, Jo, & Suh, 2006). Any deviation from the normal baseline profile may set an alert flag informing network administrator that an attack is taking place. Many behaviour based security systems have been developed based on the concept of network level attack detection (Novikov, 2005;

Novikov, Yampolskiy, & Reznik, 2006a, 2006b; Silva, Santos, Silva, & Montes, 2004; Sommer & Paxson, 2003; Zhang & Manikopoulos, 2003) and the general area of network traffic analysis is highly applicable for improved network and network application design (Liu & Huebner, 2002; Thompson, Miller, & Wilder, 1997).

Painting Style

Just like authorship of literary works can be attributed based on the writers style, so can the works of art be accredited based on the style of the drawing. In particular the subtle pen and brush strokes characteristic of a particular painter can be profiled. Lyu et al. (Lyu, Rockmore, & Farid, 2004) developed a technique for performing a multi-scale, multi-orientation painting scan decomposition. This decomposition changes the basis from functions maximally localized in space to one in which the basis functions are also localized in orientation and scale. By constructing a compact model of the statistics from such a function it is possible to detect consistencies or inconsistencies between paintings and drawings supposedly produced by the same author.

Programming Style

With the increasing number of viruses, worms, and Trojan horses it is often useful in a forensic investigation to be able to identify an author of such malware programs based on the analysis of the source code. It is also valuable for the purposes of software debugging and maintenance to know who the original author of a certain code fragment was. Spafford et al. (Spafford & Weeber., 1992) have analyzed a number of features potentially useful for the identification of software authorship. In case only the executable code is available for analysis, data structures and applied algorithms can be profiled as well as any remaining compiler and system information, observed programming skill level, knowledge of the operating system and choice of the system calls. Additionally use of predefined functions and provisions for error handling are not the same for different programmers.

In case the original source files are available a large number of additional identifying features become accessible such as: chosen programming language, code formatting style, type of code editor, special macros, style of comments, variable names, spelling and grammar, use of language features such as choice of loop structures, the ratio of global to local variables, temporary coding structures, and finally types of mistakes observable in the code. Software metrics such as number of lines of code per function, comment-to-code ratio and function complexity may also be introduced (Spafford & Weeber., 1992). Similar code features are discussed by Gray et al. (Gray, Sallis, & MacDonell, 1997) and in Grantzeskou et al. (Frantzeskou, Gritzalis, & MacDonell, 2004).

Registry Access

Apap et al. (Apap, et al., 2002) proposed a new type of host-based security approach they call Registry Anomaly Detection (RAD) that monitors access to the Windows registry in real time and detects the actions of malicious software. Windows registry stores information about hardware installed on the system, which ports are used, user profiles, policies, user names, passwords and configuration settings for programs. Most programs access a certain set of registry keys during normal operation. Similarly most users use only a certain subset of programs available on the machine. This results in a high degree of regularity in registry interaction during the normal operation of the system. However, malicious software may substantially deviate from this regular activity and can be detected. Many attacks involve starting programs which have rarely been used in the past or changing keys that have never been changed before. If a RAD system is trained on clean data, then these kinds of registry operations will appear abnormal to the system and result in issue of an alert (Apap, et al., 2002).

Signature/Handwriting

Signature verification is a widely accepted methodology for confirming identity (Herbst & Coetzer, 1998; Jain, Griess, & Connell, 2002; Lei, Palla, & Govindaraju, 2004; Nalwa, 1997). Two distinct approaches to signature verification are traditionally recognized based on the data collection approach, they are: on-line and off-line signature verification also known as static and dynamic approaches (Riha & Matyas, 2000). In the off-line signature verification the image of the signature is obtained using a scanning device, possibly some time after the signing took place. With on-line signature verification special hardware is used to capture dynamics of the signature, typically pressure sensitive pens in combination with digitizing tablets are utilized. Because on-line data acquisition methodology obtains features not available in the off-line mode, dynamic signature verification is more reliable (Muralidharan & Wunnava, 2004).

With on-line signature verification in addition to the trajectory coordinates of the signature, other features like pressure at pen tip, acceleration and pen-tilt can be collected. In general signature related features can be classified into two groups: global and local. Global features include: signing speed, signature bounding box, Fourier descriptors of the signature's trajectory, number of strokes, and signing flow. Local features describe specific sample point in the signature and relationship between such points, for example distance and curvature change between two successive points may be analyzed as well as x and y offsets relative to the first point on the signature trajectory, and critical points of the signature trajectory (Muralidharan & Wunnava, 2004; Plamondon & Lorette, 1989).

Signature-based user verification is a particular type of general handwriting based biometric authentication. Unlike with signatures, handwriting-based user verification/recognition is content independent, which makes the process somewhat more complicated (Ballard, Lopresti, & Monrose, 2006; Ballard, Monrose, & Lopresti, 2006; Ramann, Vielhauer, & Steinmetz, 2002). Each person's handwriting is seen as having a specific texture. The spatial frequency and orientation contents represent the features of each texture (Zhu, Tan, & Wang, 2000). Since handwriting provides a much more substantial biometric characteristic sample in comparison to signatures respective verification accuracy can be much greater.

Soft Behavioural Biometrics

Jain et al. (Jain, Dass, & Nandakumar, 2004a, 2004b) define soft biometrics as: "…traits as characteristics that provide some information about the individual, but lack the distinctiveness and permanence to sufficiently differentiate any two individuals". They further state that soft biometric traits can either be continuous such as height or weight or discrete such as gender or ethnicity. Authors propose expending the definition to include soft behavioural biometrics, which also can be grouped into continuous and discrete types. Continuous soft behavioural biometric traits include measurements produced by various standardized tests, some of the most popular such tests are IQ test for intelligence, and verbal sections of SAT, GRE, GMAT for language abilities. Discrete soft behavioural biometrics are skills which a particular person either has or does not have. Examples of such include ability to speak a particular foreign language, knowledge of how to fly a plane, ride a motorcycle, etc.

While such soft behavioural biometrics are not sufficient for identification or verification of individuals they can be combined with other biometric approaches to increase system accuracy. They can also be used in certain situations to reject individual's verification claim. For example in a case of academic cheating a significantly fluctuating score on a repeatedly taken standardized test can be used to suspect that not the same person answered all the questions on a given test (Jacob & Levitt, 2004).

Storage Activity

Many actions of intruders became visible at the storage level interface. Manipulation of system utilities (to add backdoors), tampering with audit logs (to destroy evidence), resetting of attributes (to hide changes) and addition of suspicious content (known virus) all show up as the changes in the storage layer of the system. A storage-based security system analyzes all requests received by the storage server and can issue alerts about suspicious activity to the system administrator. Additionally it can slow down the suspected intruder's storage access or isolate intruder via a forking of version trees to a sandbox. Storage-based security approach has the advantage of being independent from the client's operating system and so can continue working after the initial compromise, unlike host-based security systems which can be disabled by the intruder (Pennington, et al., 2002). Research using storage activity is fast gaining in popularity with intrusions being detected at the block storage level (Stanton, Yurcik, & Brumbaugh, 2005), in Storage Area Network (SAN) environments (Banikazemi, Poff, & Abali, 2005), object-based storage devices (Zhang & Wang, 2006), workstation disk drives (Griffin, et al., 2003) and in the context of the overall intrusion detection (Stanton, et al., 2005).

System Calls

A system call is the method used by a program to request service from the operating system, or more particularly, the operating system kernel. System calls use a special instruction which causes the processor to transfer control to a more privileged code segment. Intruder detection can be achieved by comparing an application's run-time system calls with a pre-defined normal system call behaviour model. The assumption is that as long as the intruder can't make arbitrary system calls, it is unlikely that he can achieve his desired malicious goals (Lam, Li, & Chiueh, 2006). Following the original work of Forest et al. (Hofmeyr, Forrest, & Somayaji, 1998; Warrender, Forrest, & Pearlmutter, 1999) a number of researchers have pursuit development of security systems based on analyzing system call sequences (Ghosh, Schwatzbard, & Shatz, 1999b; Giffin, et al., 2004; Lam, et al., 2006 ; Marceau, 2000; Nguyen, Reiher, & Kuenning, 2003; Wagner & Dean, 2001). Typically a model of normal system call behavior is learned during the training phase which is a baseline-state assumed to be free of attacks (Bhatkar, Chaturvedi, & Sekar, May 2006), alternative approaches use static analysis of the source code or binary code (Giffin, et al., 2004). A number of representation schemas for the behavioral model have been proposed, including strings (Warrender, et al., 1999; Wespi, et al., 2000), finite state automata and push down automata (Feng, et al., 2003a; Giffin, et al., 2004).

Tapping

Henderson et al. (Henderson, White, Veldhuis, Hartel, & Slump, 2002; Henderson, Papakostas, White, & Hartel, 2001) have studied the idea of tapping recognition, based on the idea that you are able to recognize who is knocking on your door. They concentrated on the waveform properties of the pulses which result from tapping the polymer thick-film sensor on a smart card. Produced pressure pulses are further processed to extract useful features such as: pulse height, pulse duration, and the duration of the first inter-pulse interval. The recognition algorithm utilized in this research has been initially developed for processing of keyboard dynamics, which is a somewhat similar technology of recognizing tapping with respect to keyboard keys.

Text Authorship

Email and source code authorship identification represent application and improvement of techniques developed in a broader field of text authorship determination. Written text and spoken word once transcribed can be analyzed in terms of vocabulary and style to determine its authorship. In order to do so a linguistic profile needs to be established. Many linguistic features can be profiled such as: lexical patterns, syntax, semantics, pragmatics, information content or item distribution through a text (Halteren, 2004). Stematatos et al. (Stamatatos, Fakotakis, & Kokkinakis, 1999) in their analysis of modern Greek texts proposed using such text descriptors as: sentence count, word count, punctuation mark count, noun phrase count, word included in noun phrase count prepositional phrase count, word included in prepositional phrase count and keyword count. Overall area of authorship attribution is very promising with a lot of ongoing research (Juola & Sofko, 2004; Koppel & Schler, 2004; Koppel, Schler, & Mughaz, 2004).

Voice/Speech/Singing

Speaker identification is one of the best researched biometric technologies (Campbell, 1997; Ciota, 2004; Sanderson & Paliwal, 2001). Verification is based on information about the speaker's anatomical structure conveyed in amplitude spectrum, with the location and size of spectral peaks related to the vocal tract shape and the pitch striations related to the glottal source of the user (Kalyanaraman, 2006). Speaker identification systems can be classified based on the freedom of what is spoken (Ratha, Senior, & Bolle, 2001):

- **Fixed text:** The speaker says a particular word selected at enrolment.
- **Text dependent:** The speaker is prompted by the system to say a particular phrase.

- **Text independent:** The speaker is free to say anything he wants, verification accuracy typically improves with larger amount of spoken text.

Feature extraction is applied to the normalized amplitude of the input signal which is further decomposed into several band-pass frequency channels. A frequently extracted feature is a logarithm of the Fourier Transform of the voice signal in each band along with pitch, tone, cadence, and shape of the larynx (Jain, et al., 1999). Accuracy of voice based biometrics systems can be increased by inclusion of visual speech (lip dynamics) (Jourlin, et al., 1997; Luettin, et al., 1996; Mason, et al., 1999; Wark, et al., 1997) and incorporation of soft behavioural biometrics such as accent (Deshpande, Chikkerur, & Govindaraju, 2005; Lin & Simske, 2004). Recently some research has been aimed at expanding the developed technology to singer recognition for the purposes of music database management (Tsai & Wang, Jan. 2006a) and to laughter recognition. Currently, the laughter-recognition software is rather crude and cannot accurately distinguish between different people (Ito, et al., 2005; Mainguet, 2006).

Some of the presented approaches are not sufficiently unique, permanent, easily collectable or difficult to circumvent but they can be seen as behavioural counterparts of "soft" physical biometrics well recognized in the field. Soft biometrics are also not strong enough to be a backbone of a standalone biometric security system, but are nonetheless valuable in improving accuracy of multimodal systems. Likewise, we believe that multimodal behaviour-based biometric systems will be able to take advantage of many of technologies presented in our survey and therefore it is important to include them in order to make our survey as comprehensive and as useful as possible to the largest number of researchers and developers. For example game strategy alone may not be sufficient for person identification but combined

Figure 1. Examples of Behavioural Biometrics: a) Biometric Sketch, b) Blinking, c) Calling, d) Car Driving, e) Command Line Lexicon, f) Credit Card Use, g) Dynamic Facial Features, h) Email, i) Gait, j) Game Strategy, k) GUI Interaction, l) Handgrip, m) Haptic, n) Keystrokes, o) Lip Movement, p) Mouse Dynamics, q) Painting Style, r) Programming Style, s) Signature, t) Tapping, u) Text Authorship, v) Voice. Adopted from (Yampolskiy & Govindaraju, 2008)

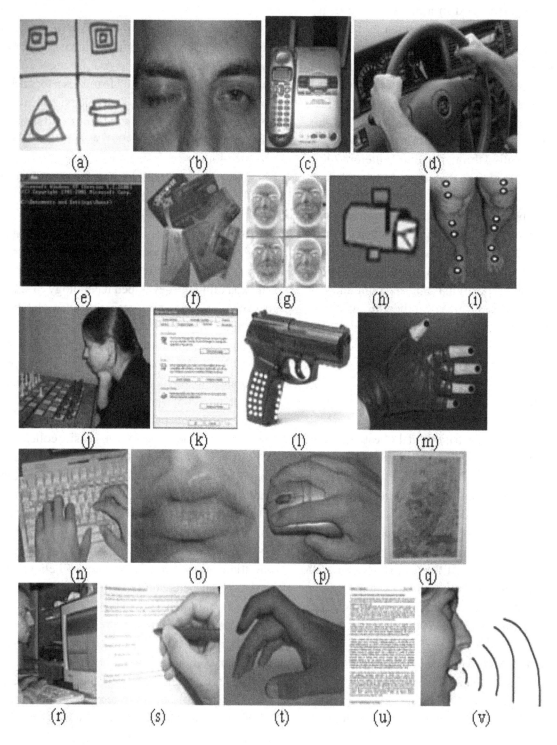

with keyboard dynamics and mouse movements it might be sufficiently discriminative. Also as breakthroughs are made in the field of behavioural biometrics it is likely that some of the described technologies will become easier to collect and harder to circumvent.

Practically all behavioural biometrics are not strong enough for person identification only for verification purposes and so the assumption is always made that we are dealing with a cooperating subject who wishes to positively verify his identity. For all behaviours even for low level ones an un-cooperating subject can completely change his behaviour in order to avoid being successfully profiled by the security system. This is an inherent limitation of most behavioural biometric systems. (see Figure 1)

NEW BEHAVIOURAL BIOMETRIC MODALITIES

Because behavioural biometrics are a new and still developing field even such basic concept as what qualifies as a behavioural biometric is still not universally excepted. In our detailed survey we have chosen to only cover approaches in which behaviour in question is under full or at least partial control of the individual exhibiting it. In this section we presented a number of approaches which have been classified as behavioural biometrics by other researchers in the field (Revett, 2008) and which as a rule are not under the full control of the subject. Despite our personal belief that such methods do not fall under the definition of behavioural biometrics we feel it is necessary to include such approaches for the sake of completeness of presentation of the state-of-the-art in the field at least until any ambiguity about them is resolved by the scientific community.

Odor as a Biometric

Animals, for example dogs, are perfectly capable of recognizing people based on odor. Idea behind this type of authentication is to create an Electronic Nose (ENose) capable of sniffing out person's identity. The ENose consists of a collection of sensors each one serving as a receptor for a particular odor. Once a significant number of odors can be profiled by the system it becomes an interesting pattern recognition problem to match odor-print to people. This is a promising line of research and is still in the early stages of development with no functional systems available on the market (Korotkaya, 2003).

Heart Beat Sound

Recently some research effort was put towards investigation of the possibility of using heart sound as a biometric for human identification. The main advantage of using heart sound as a biometric is that it cannot be easily spoofed as compared to other, particularly non-physical biometric modalities. Preliminary results show that with optimally selected parameters, an identification rate of up to 96% is achievable for a small database of seven persons (Phua, Dat, Chen, & Shue, 2006). The heart beat is known as the Inherent Liveness Biometrics because "The way the human heart beats" biometric characteristic is only valid for a living person (Preez & Soms, 2005).

BIOLOGICAL SIGNALS AS A BEHAVIORAL BIOMETRICS

A number of biological signals have been classified as behavioural biometrics in recent literature (Marcel & Millan, 2007; Revett, 2008; Thorpe, Oorschot, & Somayaji, 2005). Numerous examples include the electrocardiogram (ECG), the electroencephalogram (EEG), and the electrooculogram (EOG) as well as some emerging technologies, like Brain-Computer Interface (BCI), Human-Computer Interface (HCI), and Electrocenphlogram Interface (EEGI), NHCI (Neural Human-Computer Interface) and NI (Neural Interface) (Lawson, 2002). In addition to electrical activity, neural activity also generates other types of signals, for example magnetic and metabolic, that could be utilized in a BCI. Magnetic activity is recordable with magnetoencephalography (MEG), brain metabolic activity as mirrored by changes in blood flow can be measured with positron emission tomography (PET), and functional magnetic resonance imaging (fMRI) (Marcel & Millan, 2007). There are also invasive BCI signal recording methods such as implanted electrodes (Thorpe, et al., 2005).

ECG as a Behavioural Biometric

The ECG is a recording of the electrical activity produced by the beating of the heart. A series of sensors are positioned over the heart and pick up the electrical signals produced by various regions of the heart during the pumping cycle. The recording of the heartbeat generates a unique and reliable profile for any particular individual. Recent experiments provide sufficient evidence to suggest that it is a highly discriminative biometric modality in some cases near 100% accurate (Revett, 2008).

Brainwaves: EEG as a Behavioural Biometric

The electroencephalogram (EEG) is a recording of the electrical activity of the brain. Numerous studies demonstrate that the brainwave pattern of every individual is unique and that the EEG can be used for biometric identification (Marcel & Millan, 2007). EEG signal changes with variation in types of cognitive activities. The signal itself can be isolated from the background noise through a series of filters. The idea behind this approach is to associate a particular EEG signature with a

particular set of thoughts, such as recorded during type or human computer interaction (Revett, 2008). Correct classification of individual in the accuracy range of 80% to 100% has been achieved in recent experiments (Mohammadi, Shoushtari, Ardekani, & Shamsollahi, 2006).

PassThoughts

Thorpe et al. proposed using Brain Computer Interface (BCI) technology to have a user directly transmit his thoughts to a computer (PassThoughts). The system extracts entropy from a user's brain signal upon reading a thought. The brain signals are processed in an accurate and repeatable way providing a changeable, authentication method resilient to shoulder-surfing. The potential size of the space of a pass-thought system is not clear at this point but likely to be very large, due to the lack of bounds on what composes a thought (Thorpe, et al., 2005). (see Table 2)

SOFTWARE INTERACTION BIOMETRIC TECHNOLOGIES

Up to this point a lot of research in behavioural biometrics concentrated on a very low level be-

Table 2. Accuracy rates for novel behavioural biometric modalities

Behavioral Biometric	Publication	Accuracy Rate
Musicians' Finger Movements	(Bella & Palmer, 2006)	84%
Odor	(Korotkaya, 2003)	-
Heart Beat	(Phua, et al., 2006)	96%
electrocardiogram (ECG)	(Revett, 2008)	100%
electroencephalogram (EEG)	(Mohammadi, et al., 2006)	80-100%
PassThoughts	(Thorpe, et al., 2005)	90%

haviour of the users such as keystroke dynamics and mouse movements which are used to interact with a computer. While relatively accurate, those behavioural biometrics only concentrate on manifestations of behaviour dependent on physical abilities of an individual and completely ignore higher level intentional behaviours, which may provide superior descriptors for successfully verifying identity of human beings.

User interaction with almost every type of software can be used to generate a personalized behavioural signature capable of verifying user's identity. While some research in that area has been done, particularly with command line interfaces (Maxion & Townsend, 2002a; Schonlau, et al., 2001) and more recently with spoint and click interfaces (Goldring, 2003) much more can be accomplished. Usually low-level side effects of user activity are all that is taken to generate a user profile (Yampolskiy, 2007b). For example one study concentrated on things like number of open windows, time between new windows and number of words in a window title(Goldring, 2003). As the technology advances it may become possible to use higher-level behaviours to generate more accurate user profiles:

- **Operating system interaction behaviour:** A profile consists of OS specific behaviours of the user. Almost every task in a modern OS can be accomplished with multiple equally well performing approaches. So a user's choice of doing some task may constitute a single data point in the behavioural signature. For example using a desktop icon to start an application as apposed to going through the Start button in the MS Windows environment. Dozens if not hundreds of similar choices provide a wealth of behavioural information sufficient to verify if the same user is interacting with the OS.
- **Web browsing behaviour:** Just as unique as the OS manipulation behaviour can be

the set of actions user takes to work with a network such as Internet. The choice of web browser, search engine, collection of often-visited sites and other similar web related choices could be a great personal identifier. Online searching behaviour can be a particularly telling descriptor since the choice of keywords used, topics of searching and skill necessary to construct complicated logical predicates say a lot about who the person is.

- **Email checking/sending behaviour:** In addition to the different people we all chose to communicate with via email, we all have unique ways of composing emails. Even a simple task of replying to an email can be done very differently. Some people choose to include the original message in the response there is others insist on deleting it (Vel, et al., 2001). Some add a complicated personalized signature to the end of the message while others simply send "regards". The number of emails sent and received also greatly varies. Many other personal choices can also be considered such as how a person reads his new messages. Some people tend to read them all first and choose to reply to some at a later time, while others always immediately reply to a new message not wishing to keep the sender waiting for a response.
- **Word processing behaviour:** There is a million different ways to format a document (Yampolskiy, 2007d). Choices of fonts, styles, paragraph structure and so on can be as unique as the users who compose those documents. In addition a great amount of additional information can be collected about the actual writing of the individual such as common topic, vocabulary size, common spelling and grammatical errors.
- **Media interaction behaviour:** Modern computers serve as DVD players, stereo

systems, photo albums and art galleries to name just some media related applications. How a user organizes a play list of songs, speed with which he looks through a photo album and which news feeds he likes to listen too can be used to tell different users a part.

- **Photo editing behaviour:** An operation of complicated photo processing software such as Photoshop requires a significant level of skill. Just like with OS or word processors no two users will perform many complicated tasks exactly the same way. Since many different images require similar processing we can quickly collect enough data to start verifying user identities in the creative environments such as provided by image processing software.

- **Any other software:** An attentive reader can clearly notice a pattern in the above behavioural biometrics related to software use. All software provides many ways and options for accomplishing similar tasks. The more complicated a piece of software is the more unique will be a behavioural signature generated by the user of the said piece of software. This might be particularly true in security sensitive domains of power management companies and intelligence agency's databases where verifying user's identity is a task second in importance only to the primary function of the software.

VIDEO SURVEILLANCE BIOMETRICS

Big brother is watching you. The surveillance cameras are no longer limited to convenience stores. Banks, libraries, airports, factories and even street corners are under constant observation not to mention prisons, police stations, and government buildings. For example in London there are at least 500,000 cameras in the city, and one

study showed that in a single day a person could expect to be filmed 300 times (Stecklow, Singer, & Patrick, 2005). With such a wealth of data it is only logical that we will try to use this information to find, recognize, identify and verify people.

Obviously the best approach to doing so is via face recognition but since it is not always possible, as in the cases there no clear face shot is available, alternative biometric solutions can be exploited. Gait has been one such alternative being researched at multiple centres around the world. We propose a number of behaviour-based biometrics, which can be extracted from surveillance videos and analyzed without inconveniencing even a single person with document checks, body searches and similar extreme measures.

Today the processing necessary to obtain desired behavioural information may be well beyond capabilities of our technology, but the capabilities of biometric science are quickly growing and it is entirely possible to have prototypes of such technologies available in a few years and working systems in a decade or so. In any case, the first step is to identify what technology is desirable to have before any such technology begins its way from research lab to the deployment in the field, and this is precisely this first step this paper aims at taking:

- **Eating and drinking behaviour:** Since many restaurants and café houses with outside sitting enjoy the security provided by surveillance cameras it is possible to consider person's eating habits as a behavioural biometric. The type of a diet a person follows such as vegetarian, vegan, kosher, or Atkins is a good personal descriptor. How a person eats, how they hold a fork, use a napkin, cut their stake all that can be useful for identification purposes. What sides they choose with their meal, do they use a lot of salt, paper or hot sauce all such information can add uniqueness to their behavioural signature. Additionally we can consider interaction with the restaurant staff such as ordering and tipping habits.

- **Interaction with electronics:** In our everyday life we are constantly using different electronic devices. We get money from ATMs, talk on our cell phones, watch TV or listen to radio, in all such situations we are very particular about just how we interact with the above-mentioned devices. If we take cell phones as an example some people prefer to use speakerphone while others go with a hands free ear set. We all use different dialling fingers, hold phone at a different angle, and keep the phone in various locations in or on our wardrobe. Similar observations can be made about all other interactions with electronics, from TV channel flipping habits to notebook carrying style.

- **Driving Style**: Be it an automobile or a plane the way we control such a contraption is very unique. Take driving for example, how fast one accelerates, applies breaks, makes turns all can be taken to uniquely identify a particular driver (Erdogan, et al., 2005a; Erdogan, et al., 2005b; Erzin, et al., 2006). An in car computer can provide lots of such information to supplement outside monitoring by traffic cameras. This intimate knowledge of the driver's behaviour can be used to identify an incident of auto theft or to customize the car's handling to a particular driver.

- **Shopping habits**: Shopping habits of people have long been subject to intense Data Mining scrutiny in hopes of finding ways to improve sales and increase success of special promotions. For a behavioural profile we can look at what form of payment a person uses. Do they go with a shopping cart or a basket, which order do the take scanning shelves of different products, not to mention which products they select and

how those products can be used to better characterize them.

- **Exercise routine**: Lots of people try to stay lean and healthy by going to the gym. Gyms provide an enormous amount of personal choices for the individual. Hundreds of different machines each one with unique settings options, swimming pools, saunas, and locker rooms. A security system can keep track of the times of attendance, duration of exercise, machines and weights used, and type of exercises performed.

- **Dress and appearance choices**: Many people have a very unique dress style, often with a particular piece of attire so unique it is sufficient to immediately identify them. Even though the daily choice of wardrobe changes the style frequently remains the same. Some people like loose hanging T-shirts, some prefer cloths so tight they have hard time putting it on. Hats, high heels, scarves, jewellery, hairstyles all allow us to show our personality and at the same time to successfully profile us.

- **Vocabulary**: while voice has long been used to identify people we can add a lot of additional variables to the successful behavioural equation. What languages does a person speak, what words he likes to use a lot, even overuse? How big is his vocabulary and what words he never uses? Is he very talkative? How many words per unit of time? The above descriptors can easily be used not just with spoken word but with emails, writings, reports basically any documents.

- **Other Behaviours**: Any skill behaviour, any preference or anything else which makes us who we are can be used as a behavioural descriptor. The list below is not all-inclusive and is only meant to spark ideas for novel research directions and groundbreaking projects. Can a behavioural biometric system be developed around:

Working habits, Social behaviour (social contacts, hand shaking), Knowledge (what types of information this person knows about), Sense of humour (how a person laughs), Temper (aggressive, passive), Intelligence (capacity to learn and remember, behaviour in a classroom environment), Interests (books, hobbies), Athletic ability (fighting style, dancing style, swimming style), Talents (drawing, singing, playing musical instruments), Likes / dislikes (rap music, tanning), Sexual preferences and physical preference for others, Strategy for using tools, Grooming and hygiene habits, Picture taking(picture posing and acting), Public speaking(presenting mannerisms), Psychological disorders (paranoia, schizophrenia), Credit cards(use and payment pattern), Seat choice(on a plain or movie theatre), Investing(stocks, bank account preferences), Interaction with animals(pets).

GENERAL PROPERTIES OF BEHAVIOR

While the set of possible behaviours is truly infinite it might be possible to find some measurable properties of behaviour, which can be found in all behaviours and correspond well between different behaviours in the same individual. This would be extremely useful in Multi-modal Behavioural Biometrics (MBB) in which multiple different behaviours are used together to create a single profile. Examples of MBB include combining mouse movement data with keyboard dynamics or voice with lip motion and typically significantly increase accuracy of the system. Ideally at the same time those cross-behavioural property measurements will be somewhat different between different individuals making it easier to tell different people apart. Some possible cross-behavioural properties are presented below:

- **Speed:** how fast a behaviour is performed. Examples may include typing speed and number of words spoken per minute.
- **Correctness:** number of mistakes as compared to the desired behaviour in a given situation. For example number of mistyped characters or slips of the tongue.
- **Redundancy:** useless repetitiveness of the same behaviour per time period. For example saying same thing twice.
- **Consistency:** a statistical measurement of how similar this person's behaviour is from one data taking section to the other. Some people are more predictable than others and tend to follow the same routine more precisely.
- **Rule obedience:** some people believe that rules are made to be broken. They park next to fire hydrants, cheat on exams, take 10 items to a 7 or less items cash register and abuse the proper rules of spoken language. The opposite of that behaviour is strict following of the rules to the point of absurdity, such as putting a seatbelt on to sit in a parked car. In any case people of those two types are relatively consistent in their rule obedience across different behaviours.

INFLUENCE OF ENVIRONMENT ON BEHAVIOR

One of the problems with behavioral biometrics is that human behavior itself is not perfectly repetitive. People act differently based on their current mood, illness, sleep deprivation, drugs, stress, conflict, hunger, previous events and surrounding environment. For example, a person who did not get enough sleep may act irritated, shout a lot and be sloppy at performing his work duties. While fully understanding human emotions may be well beyond capability of modern computers it might be possible to incorporate the effects of the environment into the behavioral model.

The main component of the environment is the geo-spatial location of the individual. The same person will act very differently if they are in privacy of their home or at a public event. In terms of computer networks we can observe that a person who is connecting to the network from his home computer may perform different actions as compared to the times he was accessing the network from his work computer (Kim, et al., 2006). This leads us to the following thesis: location influences behavior. We are not claiming that knowing individual's location is sufficient condition for predicting his or her behavior, but we propose that it is one of the factors knowing which may increase the accuracy of behavior prediction.

As more and more computers and mobile devices such as cell phones come equipped with GPS (Global Positioning System) chips identifying location of an individual will become trivial. For now individual's location can be obtained by looking up IP address information for the computer from which individual is accessing the network.

Continuing with our previous example of a person accessing a network from different locations and assuming that the network in question is Internet we can predict that if an individual is accessing Internet from his home computer he will be more likely to check the schedule of movies at a local theatre playing within the next hour then to perform a search for suppliers of aluminium tubing (assuming he works in the acquisitions department). So knowing the geo-spatial location of an individual our behaviour prediction model can be fine-tuned to produce much better results. While the above example is trivial, it might be possible to anticipate some changes in behaviour caused by any number of factors and include such changes in our dynamic personal behaviour model.

However good our algorithms are it is still very possible for a behaviour based biometric to generate a number of false alarms. This can be seen as a significant shortcoming, but can also be viewed as beneficial. Suppose the system triggers an alarm for an abnormal behaviour pattern, but quick investigation positively verifies individual's identity. So now we can conclude that for some reason the individual is not acting like himself. This information can be beneficial for example in the domain of games, more specifically Poker. Knowing that a very strong player is not using his usual superior strategy may be very valuable. It is possible the player in question is on *tilt* (temporary psychological instability) and so will likely make some bad decisions which a good player can take advantage of. A similar example in workplace may indicate that an individual is out of it, and is likely to be performing a substandard level work and so it might benefit the company to temporarily remove that employee from his position, maybe sending him on a well-needed vocation.

GENERALIZED ALGORITHM FOR PURELY BEHAVIORAL BIOMETRICS

In this section we describe a generalized algorithm for purely behavioural biometrics, which can be applied to any type of high level decision based human activity. The first step is to break up the behaviour in question into a number of atomic operations each one corresponding to a single decision, idea or a choice. Ideally all possible operations should be considered, but in a case of behaviour with a very large repertoire of possible operations a large subset of most frequent operations might be sufficient.

User's behaviour should be observed and a frequency count for the occurrence of the atomic operations should be produced. The resulting frequency counts form a feature vector which is used to verify or reject the user based on the similarity score produced by a similarity function. An experimentally determined threshold serves as a decision boundary for separating legitimate users from intruders. In case user identification is attempted a neural network or a decision tree approach might be used to select the best matching user from the database of existing templates. Below outline of the proposed generalized algorithm is presented:

1. Pick behaviour
2. Break up behaviour into component actions
3. Determine frequencies of component actions for each user
4. Combine results into a feature vector profile
5. Apply similarity measure function to the stored template and current behaviour
6. Experimentally determine a threshold value
7. Verify or reject user based on the similarity score comparison to the threshold value

Step 5 in the above algorithm is not trivial and over the years a lot of research has gone into understanding what makes a good similarity measure function for different biometric systems. A good similarity measure takes into account statistical characteristics of the data distribution assuming enough data is available to determine such properties (Lee & Park, 2003). Alternatively expert knowledge about the data can be used to optimize a similarity measure function, for example a weighted Euclidian distance function can be developed if it is known that certain features are more valuable then others. The distance score has to be very small for two feature vectors belonging to the same individual and therefore representing a similar strategy. At the same time it needs to be as large as possible for feature vectors coming from different individuals, as it should represent two distinct playing strategies (Yampolskiy & Govindaraju, 2006b).

Lee et al. (Lee & Park, 2003) describe the following method for making a similarity measure based on the statistical properties of the data: data is represented as a random variable $x=(x1,...,xD)$ with dimensionality D. The data set $X=[xn|n=1,...$,$N]$ can be decomposed into sub-sets $Xk = [xnk|nk = 1,..., Nk]$ $(k=1,...,K)$, where each sub-set Xk is made up of data from the class Ck corresponding to an individual k. For identification the statistical properties of data Xnk are usually considered, which can be represented by a probability density function $pk(x)$. If $pk(x)$ for each k, for given data x, it is possible to calculate $f(pk(x))$, where f is a monotonic function and find a class Ck maximizing $pk(x)$. The similarity measure between a new data item and the centre of mean μk of class Ck is given by the Euclidean distance. If covariance matrix Σk for $pk(x)$ is estimated, then the similarity measure defined as $-\log pk(x)$ is the Mahalanobis distance (Lee & Park, 2003).

In the context of behavioural biometrics Euclidean distance (Sturn, 2000), Mahalanobis distance (Yampolskiy & Govindaraju, 2007b) and Manhattan distance (Sturn, 2000; Yampolskiy & Govindaraju, 2007b) are among the most popular similarity measure functions.

COMPARISON AND ANALYSIS

All behavioural biometrics essentially measure human actions which result from specific to every human skills, style, preference, knowledge, motor-skills or strategy. Table 3 summarizes what precisely is being measured by different behavioural biometrics as well as lists some of the most frequently used features for each type of behaviour. Indirect HCI-based biometrics are not included as they have no meaning independent of the direct human computer interaction which causes them.

Motor-skill based biometrics measure innate, unique and stable muscle actions of users performing a particular task. Table 4 outlines which muscle groups are responsible for a particular motor-skill as well as lists some of the most frequently used features for each muscle control based biometric approach.

While many behavioural biometrics are still in

Table 3. Behavioural biometrics with traits and features (©2008. Inderscience Publishers Ltd. Used with permission.)

Behavioural Biometric	Measures	Features
Biometric Sketch	Knowledge	location and relative position of different primitives
Calling Behaviour	Preferences	date and time of the call, duration, called ID, called number, cost of call, number of calls to a local destination, number of calls to mobile destinations, number of calls to international destinations
Car driving style	Skill	Pressure from accelerator pedal and brake pedal, vehicle speed, steering angle
Command Line Lexicon	Technical Vocabulary	used commands together with corresponding frequency counts, and lists of arguments to the commands
Credit Card Use	Preferences	account number, transaction type, credit card type, merchant ID, merchant address
Email Behaviour	Style	Length of the emails, time of the day the mail is sent, how frequently inbox is emptied, the recipients' addresses
Game Strategy	Strategy/Skill	Count of hands folded, checked, called, raised, check-raised, re-raised, and times player went all-in
Haptic	Style	3D world location of the pen, average speed, mean velocity, mean standard deviation, navigation style, angular turns and rounded turns
Keystroke Dynamics	Skill	time durations between the keystrokes, inter-key strokes and dwell times, which is the time a key is pressed down, overall typing speed, frequency of errors (use of backspace), use of numpad, order in which user presses shift key to get capital letters
Mouse Dynamics	Style	x and y coordinates of the mouse, horizontal velocity, vertical velocity, tangential velocity, tangential acceleration, tangential jerk and angular velocity
Painting Style	Style	subtle pen and brush strokes characteristic
Programming Style	Skill, Style, Preferences	chosen programming language, code formatting style, type of code editor, special macros, comment style, variable names, spelling and grammar, language features, the ratio of global to local variables, temporary coding structures, errors
Soft Behavioural Biometrics	Intelligence, Vocabulary, Skills	word knowledge, generalization ability, mathematical skill
Text Authorship	Vocabulary	sentence count, word count, punctuation mark count, noun phrase count, word included in noun phrase count prepositional phrase count, word included in prepositional phrase count and keyword count

their infancy some very promising research has already been done. The results obtained justify feasibility of using behaviour for verification of individuals and further research in this direction is likely to improve accuracy of such systems. Table 5 summarizes obtained accuracy ranges for the set of direct behavioural biometrics for which such data is available. Table 6 reports detection rates and error rates for indirect human computer interaction based behavioural biometrics.

An unintended property of behavioural profiles is that they might contain information which may be of interest to third parties which have potential to discriminate against individuals based on such information. As a consequence intentionally revealing or obtaining somebody else's behavioural profile for the purposes other than verification is highly unethical. Examples of private information which might be revealed by some behavioural profiles follow:

- **Calling Behaviour:** Calling data is a particularly sensitive subject since it might reveal signs of infidelity or interest in non-traditional adult entertainment.
- **Car driving style:** Car insurance

Table 4. Motor-skill biometrics with respective muscles and features (Standring, 2004)

Motor Skill Based Biometric	Muscles Involved	Extracted Features
Blinking	orbicularis oculi, corrugator supercilii, depressor supercilii	time between blinks, how long the eye is held closed at each blink, physical characteristics the eye undergoes while blinking
Dynamic Facial Features	levator labii superioris, levator anguli oris zygomaticus major, zygomaticus minor, depressor labii inferioris, depressor anguli oris, buccinator, orbicularis oris	motion of skin pores on the face
Gait/Stride	tibialis anterior, extensor hallucis longus, extensor digitorum longus, peroneus tertius, extensor digitorum brevis, extensor hallucis brevis, gastrocnemius, soleus, plantaris, popliteus, flexor hallucis longus flexor digitorum longus	amount of arm swing, rhythm of the walker, bounce, length of steps, vertical distance between head and foot, distance between head and pelvis, maximum distance between the left and right foot
Handgrip	abductor pollicis brevis, opponens pollicis, flexor pollicis brevis, adductor pollicis, palmaris brevis, abductor minimi digiti, flexor brevis minimi digiti	resistance measurements in multiple points
Haptic	abductor pollicis brevis, opponens pollicis,| flexor pollicis brevis, adductor pollicis, palmaris brevis, abductor minimi digiti,| flexor brevis minimi digiti, opponens digiti minimi, lumbrical, dorsal interossei, palmar interossei	3D world location of the pen, average speed, mean velocity, mean standard deviation, navigation style, angular turns and rounded turns
Keystroke Dynamics	abductor pollicis brevis, opponens pollicis, flexor pollicis brevis, adductor pollicis, palmaris brevis, abductor minimi digiti, flexor brevis minimi digiti, opponens digiti minimi, lumbrical, dorsal interossei, palmar interossei	time durations between the keystrokes, inter-key strokes and dwell times, which is the time a key is pressed down, overall typing speed, frequency of errors (use of backspace), use of numpad, order in which user presses shift key to get capital letters
Lip Movement	levator palpebrae superiorisj, levator anguli oris, mentalis, depressor labii inferioris, depressor anguli oris, buccinator, orbicularis oris, risorius	Mouth width, upper/lower lip width, lip opening height/width, distance between horizontal lip line and upper lip
Mouse Dynamics	abductor pollicis brevis, opponens pollicis, flexor pollicis brevis, adductor pollicis, palmaris brevis, abductor minimi digiti, flexor brevis minimi digiti, opponens digiti minimi, lumbrical, dorsal interossei	x and y coordinates of the mouse, horizontal velocity, vertical velocity, tangential velocity, tangential acceleration, tangential jerk and angular velocity
Signature/ Handwriting	abductor pollicis brevis, opponens pollicis, flexor pollicis brevis, adductor pollicis, palmaris brevis, abductor minimi digiti, flexor brevis minimi digiti, opponens digiti minimi, lumbrical, dorsal interossei, palmar interossei	coordinates of the signature, pressure at pen tip, acceleration and pen-tilt, signing speed, signature bounding box, Fourier descriptors of the signature's trajectory, number of strokes, and signing flow
Tapping	abductor pollicis brevis, opponens pollicis, flexor pollicis brevis, adductor pollicis, palmaris brevis, abductor minimi digiti, flexor brevis minimi digiti	Pulse height, pulse duration, and the duration of the first inter-pulse interval
Voice/ Speech	cricothyroid, posterior ricoarytenoid, lateral cricoarytenoid, arytenoid, thyroarytenoid	logarithm of the Fourier transform of the voice signal in each band along with pitch and tone

companies may be interested to know if a driver frequently speeds and is an overall aggressive driver in order to charge an increased coverage rate or to deny coverage all together.

- **Command Line Lexicon:** Information about proficiency with the commands might be used by an employer to decide if you are sufficiently qualified for a job involving computer interaction.

- **Credit Card Use:** Credit card data reveals information about what items you frequently purchase and in what locations you can be found violating your expectation of privacy. For example an employer might be interested to know if an employee buys a case of beer every day indicating a problem with alcoholism.

Table 5. Recognition and error rates of behavioural biometrics (©2008. Inderscience Publishers Ltd. Used with permission)

Behavioural Biometric	Publication	Detection Rate	FAR	FRR	EER
Biometric Sketch	Bromme 2003 (Brömme & Al-Zubi, 2003)				7.2%
Blinking	Westeyn 2004 (Westeyn & Starner, 2004)	82.02%			
Calling Behaviour	Fawcett 1997 (Fawcett & Provost, 1997)	92.5%			
Car driving style	Erdogan 2005 (Erdogan, et al., 2005a)	88.25%			4.0%
Command Line Lexicon	Marin 2001 (Marin, et al., 2001)	74.4%		33.5%	
Credit Card Use	Brause 1999 (Brause, et al., 1999)	99.995%		20%	
Email Behaviour	de Vel 2001 (Vel, et al., 2001)	90.5%			
Gait/Stride	Kale 2004 (Kale, et al., 2004)	90%			
Game Strategy	Yampolskiy 2007 (Yampolskiy & Govindaraju, 2007b)				7.0%
Handgrip	Veldhuis 2004 (Veldhuis, et al., 2004)				1.8%
Haptic	Orozco 2006 (Orozco, et al., 2006)		25%		22.3%
Keystroke Dynamics	Bergadano 2002 (Bergadano, et al., 2002)		0.01%	4%	
Lip Movement	Mok 2004 (Mok, et al., 2004)				2.17%
Mouse Dynamics	Pusara 2004 (Pusara & Brodley, 2004)		0.43%	1.75%	
Programming Style	Frantzeskou 2004 (Frantzeskou, et al., 2004)	73%			
Signature Handwriting	Jain 2002 (Jain, et al., 2002) Zhu 2000 (Zhu, et al., 2000)	95.7%	1.6%	2.8%	
Tapping	Henderson 2001 (Henderson, et al., 2001)				2.3%
Text Authorship	Halteren 2004 (Halteren, 2004)		0.2%	0.0%	
Voice/Speech Singing	Colombi 1996 (Colombi, Ruck, Rogers, Oxley, & Anderson, 1996) Tsai 2006 (Tsai & Wang, Jan. 2006b)				0.28% 29.6%

Table 6. Detection and false positive rates for indirect biometrics (©2008. Inderscience Publishers Ltd. Used with permission)

Type of Indirect Biometric	Publication	Detection Rate	False Positive Rate
Audit Logs	Lee (Lee, et al., 1999)	93%	8%
Call-Stack	Feng (Feng, et al., 2003b)	-	1%
GUI Interaction	Garg (Garg, et al., 2006)	96.15%	3.85%
Network Traffic	Zhang (Zhang & Manikopoulos, 2003)	96.2%	.0393%
Registry Access	Apap (Apap, et al., 2002)	86.9%	3.8%
Storage Activity	Stanton (Stanton, et al., 2005)	97%	4%
System Calls	Ghosh (Ghosh, et al., 1999b)	86.4%	4.3%

- **Email Behaviour:** An employer would be interested to know if employees send out personal emails during office hours.
- **Game Strategy:** If information about game strategy is obtained by the player's opponents it might be analyzed to find weaknesses in player's game and as a result give an unfair advantage to the opponents.
- **Programming Style:** Software metric obtained from analysis of code may indicate a poorly performing coder and as a result jeopardize the person's employment.

Additionally, any of the motor-skill based biometrics may reveal a physical handicap of a person and so result in potential discrimination. Such biometrics as voice can reveal emotions, and the face images may reveal information about emotions and health (Crompton, 2003). Because behavioural biometric indirectly measures our thoughts and personal traits any data collected in the process of generation of a behavioural profile needs to be safely stored in an encrypted form.

CONCLUSION

In this chapter authors have presented only the most popular behavioural biometrics but any human behaviour can be used as a basis for personal profiling and for subsequent verification. Some behavioural biometrics which are quickly gaining ground but are not a part of this survey include profiling of shopping behaviour based on market basked analysis (Prassas, Pramataris, & Papaemmanouil, 2001), web browsing and click-stream profiling (Fu & Shih, 2002; Goecks & Shavlik, 2000; Liang & Lai, 2002), and even TV preferences (Democraticmedia.org, 2001). To make it easier to recognize newly proposed approaches as behavioural biometrics we propose a definition of what properties constitute a behavioural biometric characteristic. We define behavioural biometric as any quantifiable actions of a person. Such ac-

tions may not be unique to the person and may take a different amount of time to be exhibited by different individuals.

Behavioural biometrics are particularly well suited for verification of users which interact with computers, cell phones, smart cars, or points of sale terminals. As the number of electronic appliances used in homes and offices increases so does the potential for utilization of this novel and promising technology. Future research should be directed at increasing overall accuracy of such systems, for example by looking into possibility of developing multimodal behavioural biometrics, as people often engage in multiple behaviours at the same time., for example, talking on a cell phone while driving or using keyboard and mouse at the same time (Dahel & Xiao, 2003; Humm, Hennebert, & Ingold, 2006; Jain, Nandakumar, & Ross, 2005).

Fields as diverse as marketing, game theory, security and law enforcement all can greatly benefit from accurate modeling of human behavior. One of the aims of this chapter was to show that the problem at hand is not unique to any given field and that a solution found once might benefit many industries without a need for rediscovering it for each sub-field.

General introduction to the field of biometrics and more particularly behavioral biometrics is given alongside the benefits of this non-intrusive approach. An overview of possible software based behavioral biometrics was given followed by a large exploratory section on potential future lines of research in video surveillance based behavioral biometrics. We proposed and explored some novel behavioral biometrics and research paths as well as some universal descriptors of behavior in general. It was followed with an analysis of how behavior can be influenced by the environment in particular location of the individual engaging in the behavior.

There are a number of conclusions we can draw from the above discussion. Fruitful lines of research will investigate relationship between behavior and identity, different behaviors and correlations in future actions between people who share same personality traits. It may prove extremely valuable for multi-modal behavioral biometrics to study universal behavioral descriptors such as speed and correctness. Much more could to be done to better understand precisely how outside factors such as location influence human behavior and is it possible to predict the changes in behavior if changes in the environment are known.

Because many of the presented technologies represent behavioural biometrics which are not strong enough to serve as a backbone of a complete security system on their own, we suggest that a lot of research in behavioural biometrics be geared towards multimodal behavioural biometrics. Successful research in this area would allow for development of systems with accuracy levels sufficient not just for identity verification, but also for person identification obtained as a result of combining different behaviours. Breakthroughs in purely behavioural biometrics research will also undoubtedly lead to improvements in associated applications such as product customization, development of tailored opponents in games as well as multitude of competency assessment tools.

Future of behavioral research looks very bright. The next decade will bring us technologies providing unprecedented level of security, product customization, social compatibility and work efficiency. Ideas presented in the section on novel behavioral biometrics provide a wealth of opportunities for interesting research and development. A great side effect of such research would be general greater understanding of human behavior, personality and perhaps human mind itself.

REFERENCES

Adler, A., Youmaran, R., & Loyka, S. (2006). *Towards a measure of biometric information.* Retrieved on August 2, 2006, from http://www. sce.carleton.ca/faculty/adler/publications/2006/ youmaran-ccece2006-biometric-entropy.pdf

Ahmed, A. A. E., & Traore, I. (2005a, June). *Anomaly intrusion detection based on biometrics.* Paper presented at the Workshop on Information Assurance, United States Military Academy, West Point, NY.

Ahmed, A. A. E., & Traore, I. (2005b, October). *Detecting computer intrusions using behavioral biometrics.* Paper presented at the Third Annual Conference on Privacy, Security, and Trust, St. Andrews, New Brunswick, Canada.

Al-Zubi, S., Brömme, A., & Tönnies, K. (2003, September 10-12). *Using an active shape structural model for biometric sketch recognition.* Paper presented at the DAGM, Magdeburg, Germany (pp. 187-195).

Anderson, J. P. (1980). *Computer security threat monitoring and surveillance.* Fort Washington, PA: James P. Anderson Company.

Angle, S., Bhagtani, R., & Chheda, H. (2005, March 27-30). *Biometrics: A further echelon of security.* Paper presented at the First UAE International Conference on Biological and Medical Physics.

Apap, F., Honig, A., Hershkop, S., Eskin, E., & Stolfo, S. (2002). *Detecting malicious software by monitoring anomalous windows registry accesses.* Paper presented at the Fifth International Symposium on Recent Advances in Intrusion Detection (pp. 16-18).

Ballard, L., Lopresti, D., & Monrose, F. (2006, October). *Evaluating the security of handwriting biometrics.* Paper presented at the 10th International Workshop on Frontiers in Handwriting Recognition (IWFHR06), La Baule, France (pp. 461-466).

Ballard, L., Monrose, F., & Lopresti, D. P. (2006, July-August). *Biometric authentication revisited: Understanding the impact of wolves in sheep's clothing.* Paper presented at the Fifteenth USENIX Security Symposium, Vancouver, BC, Canada.

Banikazemi, M., Poff, D., & Abali, B. (2005, April 11-14). *Storage-based intrusion detection for storage area networks (SANs)*. Paper presented at the 22ⁿᵈ IEEE/13ᵗʰ NASA Goddard Conference on Mass Storage Systems and Technologies (pp. 118- 127).

Bartolacci, G., Curtin, M., Katzenberg, M., Nwana, N., Cha, S.-H., & Tappert, C. C. (2005). *Long-text keystroke biometric applications over the Internet.* Paper presented at the MLMTA (pp. 119-126).

Bella, S. D., & Palmer, C. (2006). Personal identifiers in musicians' finger movement dynamics. *Journal of Cognitive Neuroscience*, ▪▪▪, 18.

BenAbdelkader, C., Cutler, R., & Davis, L. (2002). *Person identification using automatic height and stride estimation.* Paper presented at the IEEE International Conference on Pattern Recognition.

Bergadano, F., Gunetti, D., & Picardi, C. (2002). User authentication through keystroke dynamics. [TISSEC]. *ACM Transactions on Information and System Security*, 5(4), 367–397. doi:10.1145/581271.581272

Bhatkar, S., Chaturvedi, A., & Sekar, R. (2006, May). *Dataflow anomaly detection.* Paper presented at the IEEE Symposium on Security and Privacy.

Bioprivacy.org. (2005a). *FAQ. BioPrivacy Initiative.* Retrieved on July 22, 2005, from http://www.bioprivacy.org/faqmain.htm

Bioprivacy.org. (2005b). *FAQ's and definitions.* International Biometric Group, LLC. Retrieved on October 2, 2005, from http://www.bioprivacy.org/bioprivacy_text.htm

Bolle, R., Connell, J., Pankanti, S., Ratha, N., & Senior, A. (2003). *Guide to biometrics.* New York: Springer.

Brause, R., Langsdorf, T., & Hepp, M. (1999). *Neural data mining for credit card fraud detection.* Paper presented at the 11ᵗʰ IEEE International Conference on Tools with Artificial Intelligence (pp. 103-106).

Bromme, A. (2003, July 6-9). *A classification of biometric signatures.* Paper presented at the International Conference on Multimedia and Expo (ICME '03) (pp. 17-20).

Brömme, A., & Al-Zubi, S. (2003, July 24). *Multifactor biometric sketch authentication.* Paper presented at the BIOSIG, Darmstadt, Germany (pp. 81-90).

Broun, C. C., Zhang, X., Mersereau, R. M., & Clements, M. A. (2002). Automatic speechreading with applications to speaker verification. *Eurasip Journal on Applied Signal Processing, Special Issue on Joint Audio-Visual Speech Processing*.

Cahill, M., Lambert, D., Pinheiro, J., & Sun, D. (2000). *Detecting fraud in the real world.* (Tech. Rep.). Bell Labs, Lucent Technologies.

Campbell, J. P. (1997). Speaker recognition: A tutorial. *Proceedings of the IEEE*, 85(9), 1437–1462. doi:10.1109/5.628714

Cappelli, R., Maio, D., Maltoni, D., Wayman, J. L., & Jain, A. K. (2006). Performance evaluation of fingerprint verification systems. *IEEE Transactions on Pattern Analysis and Machine Intelligence*, 28(1), 3–18. doi:10.1109/TPAMI.2006.20

Caslon.com.au. (2005). *Caslon-analytics.* Retrieved on October 2, 2005, from http://www.caslon.com.au/biometricsnote8.htm

Ciota, Z. (2004, October 10-13). *Speaker verification for multimedia application.* Paper presented at the IEEE International Conference on Systems, Man and Cybernetics (pp. 2752- 2756).

Colombi, J., Ruck, D., Rogers, S., Oxley, M., & Anderson, T. (1996). *Cohort selection and word grammar effects for speaker recognition.* Paper presented at the IEEE International Conference on Acoustics, Speech, and Signal Processing, Atlanta, GA (pp. 85-88).

Crompton, M. (2003). *Biometrics and privacy: The end of the world as we know it or the white knight of privacy?* Paper presented at the 1st Biometrics Institute Conference.

Curtin, M., Tappert, C. C., Villani, M., Ngo, G., Simone, J., Fort, H. S., et al. (2006, June). *Keystroke biometric recognition on long-text input: A feasibility study.* Paper presented at the Workshop Sci Comp/Comp Stat (IWSCCS 2006), Hong Kong.

Dahel, S. K., & Xiao, Q. (2003, June 18-20). *Accuracy performance analysis of multimodal biometrics.* Paper presented at the IEEE Information Assurance Workshop on Systems, Man, and Cybernetics Society (pp. 170- 173).

Dao, V., & Vemuri, V. (2000, December 11-15). *Profiling users in the UNIX OS environment.* Paper presented at the International ICSC Conference on Intelligent Systems and Applications, University of Wollongong Australia.

Delac, K., & Grgic, M. (2004, June 16-18). *A survey of biometric recognition methods.* Paper presented at the 46th International Symposium Electronics in Marine, ELMAR-2004, Zadar, Croatia (pp. 184-193).

Democraticmedia.org. (2001). *TV that watches you: The prying eyes of interactive television. A report by the Center for Digital Democracy.* Retrieved June 11, 2001, from www.democraticmedia.org/privacyreport.pdf

Denning, D. E. (1987). An intrusion-detection model. *IEEE Transactions on Software Engineering, 13*(2), 222–232. doi:10.1109/TSE.1987.232894

Deshpande, S., Chikkerur, S., & Govindaraju, V. (2005, October 17-18). *Accent classification in speech.* Paper presented at the Fourth IEEE Workshop on Automatic Identification Advanced Technologies (pp. 139-143).

Dugelay, J.-L., Junqua, J.-C., Kotropoulos, C., Kuhn, R., Perronnin, F., & Pitas, I. (2002, May). *Recent advances in biometric person authentication.* Paper presented at the IEEE Int. Conf. on Acoustics Speech and Signal Processing (ICASSP), Special Session on Biometrics, Orlando, FL.

Elissetche, M. M. (2005). *Social science dictionary.* Retrieved on October 6, 2005, from http://www.elissetche.org/dico/p.htm

Erdogan, H., Ercil, A., Ekenel, H., Bilgin, S., Eden, I., & Kirisci, M. (2005a). Multimodal person recognition for vehicular applications. *LNCS, 3541*, 366–375.

Erdogan, H., Ozyagci, A. N., Eskil, T., Rodoper, M., Ercil, A., & Abut, H. (2005b, September). *Experiments on decision fusion for driver recognition.* Paper presented at the Biennial on DSP for in-vehicle and mobile systems, Sesimbra, Portugal.

Erzin, E., Yemez, Y., Tekalp, A. M., Erçil, A., Erdogan, H., & Abut, H. (2006). Multimodal person recognition for human-vehicle interaction. *IEEE MultiMedia, 13*, 18–31. doi:10.1109/MMUL.2006.37

Fawcett, T., & Provost, F. (1997). Adaptive fraud detection. *Data Mining and Knowledge Discovery, 1*(3), 291–316. doi:10.1023/A:1009700419189

Feng, H., Kolesnikov, O., Fogla, P., Lee, W., & Gong, W. (2003a, May 11-14). *Anomaly detection using call stack information.* Paper presented at the IEEE Security and Privacy, Oakland, CA.

Feng, H. H., Kolesnikov, O. M., Fogla, P., Lee, W., & Gong, W. (2003b). *Anomaly detection using call stack information.* Paper presented at the IEEE Symposium on Security and Privacy (pp. 62-78).

Frantzeskou, G., Gritzalis, S., & MacDonell, S. (2004, August). *Source code authorship analysis for supporting the cybercrime investigation process.* Paper presented at the 1st International Conference on E-Business and Telecommunication Networks-Security and Reliability in Information Systems and Networks Track, Setubal, Portugal (pp. 85-92).

Fu, Y., & Shih, M. (2002, June). *A framework for personal Web usage mining.* Paper presented at the International Conference on Internet Computing (IC'2002), Las Vegas, NV (pp. 595-600).

Gamboa, H., & Fred, A. (2003). *An identity authentication system based on human computer interaction behaviour.* Paper presented at the 3rd Intl. Workshop on Pattern Recognition in Information Systems (pp. 46-55).

Gamboa, H., & Fred, A. (2004). *A behavioral biometric system based on human computer interaction.* Paper presented at the SPIE (pp. 5404-5436).

Garg, A., Rahalkar, R., Upadhyaya, S., & Kwiat, K. (2006, June 21-23). *Profiling users in GUI based systems for masquerade detection.* Paper presented at The 7th IEEE Information Assurance Workshop (IAWorkshop 2006), West Point, NY.

Ghosh, A. K., Schwatzbard, A., & Shatz, M. (1999b, April). *Learning program behavior profiles for intrusion detection.* Paper presented at the 1st USENIX Workshop on Intrusion Detection and Network Monitoring, Santa Clara, CA (pp. 51-62).

Giffin, J., Jha, S., & Miller, B. (2004, February). *Efficient context-sensitive intrusion detection.* Paper presented at the 11th Annual Network and Distributed Systems Security Symposium (NDSS), San Diego, CA.

Goecks, J., & Shavlik, J. (2000). *Learning users' interests by unobtrusively observing their normal behavior.* Paper presented at the International Conference on Intelligent User Interfaces, New Orleans, LA (pp. 129-132).

Goldring, T. (2003). User profiling for intrusion detection in windows NT. *Computing Science and Statistics, 35.*

Gray, A., Sallis, P., & MacDonell, S. (1997). *Software forensics: Extending authorship analysis techniques to computer programs.* Paper presented at the In Proc. 3rd Biannual Conf. Int. Assoc. of Forensic Linguists (IAFL'97).

Griffin, J. L., Pennington, A. G., Bucy, J. S., Choundappan, D., Muralidharan, N., & Ganger, G. R. (2003). *On the feasibility of intrusion detection inside workstation disks.* (Tech. Rep. CMU-PDL-03-106). Carnegie Mellon University.

Grosser, H., Britos, H., & García-Martínez, R. (2005). *Detecting fraud in mobile telephony using neural networks.* (LNAI, pp. 613-615).

Gunetti, D., Picardi, C., & Ruffo, G. (2005). *Keystroke analysis of different languages: A case study.* Paper presented at the Proc. of the Sixth Symposium on Intelligent Data Analysis (IDA 2005), Madrid, Spain (pp. 133-144).

Gupta, G., Mazumdar, C., & Rao, M. S. (2004). Digital forensic analysis of e-mails: A trusted e-mail protocol. *International Journal of Digital Evidence, 2*(4).

Halteren, H. v. (2004). *Linguistic profiling for author recognition and verification.* Paper presented at the ACL-2004.

Henderson, N. J., White, N. M., Veldhuis, R. N. J., Hartel, P. H., & Slump, C. H. (2002). *Sensing pressure for authentication*. Paper presented at the 3rd IEEE Benelux Signal Processing Symp. (SPS), Leuven, Belgium (pp. 241-244).

Henderson, N. Y., Papakostas, T. V., White, N. M., & Hartel, P. H. (2001). *Polymer thick-film sensors: Possibilities for smartcard biometrics*. Paper presented at the Sensors and Their Applications XI (pp. 83-88).

Herbst, B., & Coetzer, H. (1998). *On an offline signature verification system*. Paper presented at the 9th Annual South African Workshop on Pattern Recognition (pp. 39-43).

Hilas, C., & Sahalos, J. (2005, October 15-16). *User profiling for fraud detection in telecommunication networks*. Paper presented at the 5th International Conference on Technology and Automation (ICTA 2005), Thessaloniki, Greece (pp. 382-387).

Hofmeyr, S. A., Forrest, S., & Somayaji, A. (1998). Intrusion detection using sequences of system calls. *Journal of Computer Security, 6*, 151–180.

Humm, A., Hennebert, J., & Ingold, R. (2006, July 10-12). *Scenario and survey of combined handwriting and speech modalities for user authentication*. Paper presented at the 6th International Conference on Recent Advances in Soft Computing (RASC'06), Canterbury, UK (pp. 496-501).

Igarashi, K., Miyajima, C., Itou, K., Takeda, K., Itakura, F., & Abut, H. (2004). *Biometric identification using driving behavioral signals*. Paper presented at the Proc. 2004 IEEE International Conference on Multimedia and Expo (pp. 65-68).

Ilgun, K., Kemmerer, R. A., & Porras, P. A. (1995). State transition analysis: A rule-based intrusion detection approach. *Software Engineering, 21*(3), 181–199.

Ilonen, J. (2006). *Keystroke dynamics*. Retrieved on July 12, 2006, from www.it.lut.fi/kurssit/03-04/010970000/seminars/ilonen.pdf

Ito, A., Wang, X., Suzuki, M., & Makino, S. (2005). *Smile and laughter recognition using speech processing and face recognition from conversation video*. Paper presented at the International Conference on Cyberworlds (pp. 437-444).

Jacob, B. A., & Levitt, S. D. (2004). *To catch a cheat*. Paper presented at the Education Next Retrieved from www.educationnext.org

Jain, A., Griess, F., & Connell, S. (2002). Online signature verification. *Pattern Recognition, 35*, 2963–2972. doi:10.1016/S0031-3203(01)00240-0

Jain, A. K., Bolle, R., & Pankanti, S. (1999). *BIOMETRICS: Personal identification in networked society*. Norwell, MA: Kluwer Academic Publishers.

Jain, A. K., Dass, S. C., & Nandakumar, K. (2004a). *Can soft biometric traits assist user recognition?* Paper presented at the SPIE Defense and Security Symposium, Orlando, FL, April 2004.

Jain, A. K., Dass, S. C., & Nandakumar, K. (2004b, July). *Soft biometric traits for personal recognition systems*. Paper presented at the International Conference on Biometric Authentication (ICBA), Hong Kong (pp. 731-738).

Jain, A. K., Pankanti, S., Prabhakar, S., Hong, L., & Ross, A. (2004c, August). *Biometrics: A grand challenge*. Paper presented at the International Conference on Pattern Recognition, Cambridge, UK.

Jain, A. K., Ross, A., & Prabhakar, S. (2004d). An introduction to biometric recognition. *IEEE Trans. Circuits Syst. Video Technol, 14*, 4–20. doi:10.1109/TCSVT.2003.818349

Jain, K., Nandakumar, K., & Ross, A. (2005). Score normalization in multimodal biometric systems. *Pattern Recognition, 38*(12), 2270–2285. doi:10.1016/j.patcog.2005.01.012

Jansen, A. R., Dowe, D. L., & E., G. (2000). *Farr inductive inference of chess player strategy.* Paper presented at the 6th Pacific Rim International Conference on Artificial Intelligence (PRICAI'2000) (pp. 61-71).

Jermyn, I., Mayer, A., Monrose, F., Reiter, M. K., & Rubin, A. D. (1999, August 23-26). *The design and analysis of graphical passwords.* Paper presented at the 8th USENIX Security Symposium, Washington, D.C.

Jourlin, P., Luettin, J., Genoud, D., & Wassner, H. (1997). Acoustic-labial speaker verification. *Pattern Recognition Letters, 18*(9), 853–858. doi:10.1016/S0167-8655(97)00070-6

Juola, P., & Sofko, J. (2004). *Proving and improving authorship attribution.* Paper presented at the CaSTA-04 The Face of Text.

Kale, A., Sundaresan, A., Rajagopalan, A. N., & Cuntoor, N., RoyChowdhury, A., Kruger, V., et al. (2004). Identification of humans using gait. *IEEE Transactions on Image Processing, 13*(9). doi:10.1109/TIP.2004.832865

Kalyanaraman, S. (2006). *Biometric authentication systems a report.* Retrieved from http://netlab.cs.iitm.ernet.in/cs650/2006/termpapers/sriramk.pdf

Kauffman, J. A., Bazen, A. M., Gerez, S. H., & Veldhuis, R. N. J. (2003). *Grip-pattern recognition for smart guns.* Paper presented at the 14th Annual Workshop on Circuits, Systems, and Signal Processing (ProRISC), Veldhoven, The Netherlands (pp. 379-384).

Kaufman, K., Cervone, G., & Michalski, R. S. (2003). *An application of symbolic learning to intrusion detection: Preliminary results from the LUS methodology* (No. MLI 03-2). Fairfax, VA: George Mason University.

Kim, Y., Jo, J.-Y., & Suh, K. (2006, April). *Baseline profile stability for network anomaly detection.* Paper presented at the IEEE ITNG 2006, Internet and Wireless Network Security Track, Las Vegas, NV.

Ko, C., Fink, G., & Levitt, K. (1994, December). *Automated detection of vulnerabilities in privileged programs by execution monitoring.* Paper presented at the 10th Annual Computer Security Applications Conference (pp. 134-144).

Koppel, M., & Schler, J. (2004, July). *Authorship verification as a one-class classification problem.* Paper presented at the 21st International Conference on Machine Learning, Banff, Canada (pp. 489-495).

Koppel, M., Schler, J., & Mughaz, D. (2004, January). *Text categorization for authorship verification.* Paper presented at the Eighth International Symposium on Artificial Intelligence and Mathematics, Fort Lauderdale, FL.

Korotkaya, Z. (2003). Biometrics person authentication: Odor. Retrieved on October 12, 2008, from http://www.it.lut.fi/kurssit/03-04/010970000/seminars/korotkaya.pdf

Koychev, I., & Schwab, I. (2000). *Adaptation to drifting user's interests.* Paper presented at the Workshop: Machine Learning in New Information Age, Barcelona, Spain.

Kuge, N., Yamamura, T., & Shimoyama, O. (1998). *A driver behavior recognition method based on driver model framework.* Paper presented at the Society of Automotive Engineers.

Lam, L.-c., Li, W., & Chiueh, T.-c. (2006, June). *Accurate and automated system call policy-based intrusion prevention.* Paper presented at the International Conference on Dependable Systems and Networks (DSN 2006).

Lane, T., & Brodley, C. E. (1997a). *An application of machine learning to anomaly detection.* Paper presented at the 20th Annual National Information Systems Security Conference (pp. 366-380).

Lane, T., & Brodley, C. E. (1997b). *Detecting the abnormal: Machine learning in computer security* (No. ECE-97-1). West Lafayette: Purdue University

Lawson, W. (2002). *The new wave ("Biometric access & neural control").* Retrieved on November 24, 2008, from http://www.icdri.org/biometrics/new_wave.htm

Lee, K., & Park, H. (2003). A new similarity measure based on intraclass statistics for biometric systems. *ETRI Journal, 25*(5), 401–406. doi:10.4218/etrij.03.0102.0017

Lee, W., Stolfo, S. J., & Mok, K. W. (1999). *A data mining framework for building intrusion detection models.* Paper presented at the IEEE Symposium on Security and Privacy, Oakland, CA.

Lei, H., Palla, S., & Govindaraju, V. (2004). *ER2: An intuitive similarity measure for online signature verification.* Paper presented at the Ninth International Workshop on Frontiers in Handwriting Recognition (IWFHR'04) (pp. 191-195).

Li, Y., Wu, N., Jajodia, S., & Wang, X. S. (2002). *Enhancing profiles for anomaly detection using time granularities.* Paper presented at the Journal of Computer Security (pp. 137-157).

Liang, T. P., & Lai, H.-J. (2002). *Discovering user interests from Web browsing behavior.* Paper presented at the Hawaii International Conference on Systems Sciences, HI.

Lin, X., & Simske, S. (2004, November 7-10). *Phoneme-less hierarchical accent classification.* Paper presented at the Thirty-Eighth Asilomar Conference on Signals, Systems, and Computers (pp. 1801- 1804).

Liu, A., & Salvucci, D. (2001, August 5-10). *Modeling and prediction of human driver behavior.* Paper presented at the 9th HCI International Conference, New Orleans, LA (pp. 1479-1483).

Liu, D., & Huebner, F. (2002, November 6-8). *Application profiling of IP traffic.* Paper presented at the 27th Annual IEEE Conference on Local Computer Networks (pp. 220-229).

Liu, Z., & Bridges, S. M. (2005, April 4-6). *Dynamic learning of automata from the call stack log for anomaly detection.* Paper presented at the International Conference on Information Technology: Coding and Computing (ITCC 2005) (pp. 774-779).

Luettin, J., Thacker, N. A., & Beet, S. W. (1996). *Speaker identification by lipreading.* Paper presented at the 4th International Conference on Spoken Language Processing (ICSLP'96).

Lunt, T. (1993). *Detecting intruders in computer systems.* Paper presented at the Conference on Auditing and Computer Technology.

Lyu, S., Rockmore, D., & Farid, H. (2004). A digital technique for art authentication. *National Academy of Sciences, 101*(49), 17006-17010.

Mainguet, J.-F. (2006). *Biometrics,* Retrieved on July 28, 2006, from http://perso.orange.fr/fingerchip/biometrics/biometrics.htm

Marceau, C. (2000, September 19-21). *Characterizing the behavior of a program using multiple-length n-grams.* Paper presented at the New Security Paradigms Workshop, Cork, Ireland.

Marcel, S., & Millan, J. (2007). Person authentication using brainwaves (EEG) and maximum a posteriori model adaptation. *IEEE Transactions on Pattern Analysis and Machine Intelligence, 29*(4), 743–752. doi:10.1109/TPAMI.2007.1012

Marin, J., Ragsdale, D., & Surdu, J. (2001). *A hybrid approach to the profile creation and intrusion detection.* Paper presented at the DARPA Information Survivability Conference and Exposition (DISCEX II'01).

Mason, J. S. D., Brand, J., Auckenthaler, R., Deravi, F., & Chibelushi, C. (1999). *Lip signatures for automatic person recognition.* Paper presented at the In IEEE Workshop, MMSP (pp. 457-462).

Maxion, R. A., & Townsend, T. N. (2002a, June 23-26). *Masquerade detection using truncated command lines.* Paper presented at the International Conference of Dependable Systems and Networks, Washington, D.C.

Maxion, R. A., & Townsend, T. N. (2002b). *Masquerade detection using truncated command lines.* Paper presented at the International Conference on Dependable Systems and Networks (DNS-02).

Michael, C. C. (2003, April 22-24). *Finding the vocabulary of program behavior data for anomaly detection.* Paper presented at the DARPA Information Survivability Conference and Exposition (pp. 152-163).

Michael, C. C., & Ghosh, A. (2000, October). *Using finite automata to mine execution data for intrusion detection: A preliminary report.* Paper presented at the Third International Workshop in Recent Advances in Intrusion Detection, Toulouse, France.

Mohammadi, G., Shoushtari, P., Ardekani, B. M., & Shamsollahi, M. B. (2006). *Person identification by using AR model for EEG signals.* Paper presented at the World Academy of Science, Engineering and Technology.

Mok, L., Lau, W. H., Leung, S. H., Wang, S. L., & Yan, H. (2004, October 24-27). *Person authentication using ASM based lip shape and intensity information.* Paper presented at the International Conference on Image Processing (pp. 561-564).

Monrose, F., & Rubin, A. D. (2000, March). Keystroke dynamics as a biometric for authentication. *Future Generation Computing Systems (FGCS) Journal: Security on the Web (special issue).*

Muralidharan, N., & Wunnava, S. (2004, June 2-4). *Signature verification: A popular biometric technology.* Paper presented at the Second LACCEI International Latin American and Caribbean Conference for Engineering and Technology (LACCEI'2004), Miami, FL.

Nalwa, V. S. (1997). Automatic online signature verification. *Proceedings of the IEEE, 85,* 215–239. doi:10.1109/5.554220

Nguyen, N., Reiher, P., & Kuenning, G. H. (2003, June 18-20). *Detecting insider threats by monitoring system call activity.* Paper presented at the IEEE Systems, Man, and Cybernetics Society Information Assurance Workshop (pp. 45-52).

Nixon, M. S., & Carter, J. N. (2004). *On gait as a biometric: Progress and prospects.* Paper presented at the EUSIPCO, Vienna.

Novikov, D. (2005). *Neural networks to intrusion detection.* Unpublished MS thesis, Rochester Institute of Technology, Rochester, NY.

Novikov, D., Yampolskiy, R. V., & Reznik, L. (2006a, April 10-12). *Anomaly detection based intrusion detection*. Paper presented at the Third International Conference on Information Technology: New Generations (ITNG 2006), Las Vegas, NV (pp. 420-425).

Novikov, D., Yampolskiy, R. V., & Reznik, L. (2006b, May 5). *Artificial intelligence approaches for intrusion detection*. Paper presented at the Long Island Systems Applications and Technology Conference (LISAT2006), Long Island, NY (pp. 1-8).

Oliver, N., & Pentland, A. P. (2000). *Graphical models for driver behavior recognition in a SmartCar*. Paper presented at the IEEE Intelligent Vehicles Symposium.

Orozco, M., Asfaw, Y., Adler, A., Shirmohammadi, S., & Saddik, A. E. (2005, May 17-19). *Automatic identification of participants in haptic systems*. Paper presented at the IEEE Instrumentation and Measurement Technology Conference, Ottawa, Canada.

Orozco, M., Asfaw, Y., Shirmohammadi, S., Adler, A., & Saddik, A. E. (2006, March 25-29). *Haptic-based biometrics: A feasibility study*. Paper presented at the IEEE Virtual Reality Conference, Alexandria, VA.

Pamudurthy, S., Guan, E., Mueller, K., & Rafailovich, M. (2005, July). *Dynamic approach for face recognition using digital image skin correlation*. Paper presented at the Audio- and Video-based Biometric Person Authentication (AVBPA), New York.

Paper presented at the IEEE International Conference on Multimedia and Expo (ICME '02) (pp. 573-576).

Pennington, A. G., Strunk, J. D., Griffin, J. L., Soules, C. A. N., Goodson, G. R., & Ganger, G. R. (2002). *Storage-based intrusion detection: Watching storage activity for suspicious behavior*. (No. CMU--CS-02-179). Carnegie Mellon University.

Phua, K., Dat, T. H., Chen, J., & Shue, L. (2006). *Human identification using heart sound*. Paper presented at the Second International Workshop on Multimodal User Authentication, Toulouse, France.

Plamondon, R., & Lorette, G. (1989). Automatic signature verification and writer identification: The state of the art. *Pattern Recognition, 22*(2), 107–131. doi:10.1016/0031-3203(89)90059-9

poker-edge.com. (2006). *Stats and analysis. Poker-edge.com* Retrieved on June 7, 2006, from http://www.poker-edge.com/stats.php

Prassas, G., Pramataris, K. C., & Papaemmanouil, O. (2001, June). *Dynamic recommendations in Internet retailing*. Paper presented at the 9th European Conference on Information Systems (ECIS 2001).

Preez, J., & Soms, S. H. (2005). *Person identification and authentication by using "the way the heart beats."* Paper presented at the ISSA 2005 New Knowledge Today Conference, Sandton, South Africa.

Pusara, M., & Brodley, C. E. (2004). *User reauthentication via mouse movements*. Paper presented at the ACM Workshop on Visualization and Data Mining for Computer Security, Washington, D.C. (pp. 1-8).

Ramann, F., Vielhauer, C., & Steinmetz, R. (2002). *Biometric applications based on handwriting*.

Ramon, J., & Jacobs, N. (2002). *Opponent modeling by analysing play*. Paper presented at the Computers and Games workshop on Agents in Computer Games, Edmonton, Albera, Canada.

Ratha, N. K., Senior, A., & Bolle, R. M. (2001, March). *Automated biometrics.* Paper presented at the International Conference on Advances in Pattern Recognition, Rio de Janeiro, Brazil.

Renaud, K. (2003). Quantifying the quality of Web authentication mechanisms. A usability perspective. *Journal of Web Engineering, 0*(0). Retrieved from http://www.dcs.gla.ac.uk/~karen/papers/j.pdf

Rentfrow, P. J., & Gosling, S. D. (2003). The do-re-mi's of everyday life: The structure and personality correlates of music preferences. *Journal of Personality and Social Psychology, 84,* 1236–1256. doi:10.1037/0022-3514.84.6.1236

Revett, K. (2008). *Behavioral biometrics: A remote access approach.* Chichester, UK: Wiley.

Riha, Z., & Matyas, V. (2000). *Biometric authentication systems.* Paper presented at the FI MU Report Series.

Ruggles, T. (2007). *Comparison of biometric techniques.* Retrieved on May 27, 2007, from http://www.bio-tech-inc.com/bio.htm

Sanderson, C., & Paliwal, K. K. (2001). *Information fusion for robust speaker verification.* Paper presented at the 7th European Conference on Speech Communication and Technology (EUROSPEECH'01), Aalborg.

Schonlau, M., DuMouchel, W., Ju, W.-H., Karr, A. F., Theus, M., & Vardi, Y. (2001). Computer intrusion: Detecting maquerades. *Statistical Science, 16*(1), 1–17.

Schuckers, S. A. C. (2002). Spoofing and anti-spoofing measures. *Information Security, 7*(4), 56–62.

Seleznyov, A., & Puuronen, S. (1999). *Anomaly intrusion detection systems: Handling temporal relations between events.* Paper presented at the 2nd International Workshop on Recent Advances in Intrusion Detection (RAID'99).

Shipilova, O. (2006). *Person recognition based on lip movements.* Retrieved on July 15, 2006, from http://www.it.lut.fi/kurssit/03-04/010970000/seminars/shipilova.pdf

Silva, L. S., Santos, A. F. d., Silva, J. D. d., & Montes, A. (2004). A neural network application for attack detection in computer networks. *Instituto Nacional de Pesquisas Espanciais.*

Solayappan, N., & Latifi, S. (2006). *A survey of unimodal biometric methods.* Paper presented at the Security and Management, Las Vegas, NV (pp. 57-63).

Sommer, R., & Paxson, V. (2003). *Enhancing byte-level network intrusion detection signatures with context.* Paper presented at the 10th ACM Conference on Computer and Communications Security.

Spafford, E. H., & Weeber, S. A. (1992, October). *Software forensics: Can we track code to its authors?* Paper presented at the 15th National Computer Security Conference (pp. 641-650).

Stamatatos, E., Fakotakis, N., & Kokkinakis, G. (1999, June). *Automatic authorship attribution.* Paper presented at the Ninth Conf. European Chap. Assoc. Computational Linguistics, Bergen, Norway (pp. 158-164).

Standring, S. (2004). *Gray's anatomy: The anatomical basis of medicine and surgery.*

Stanton, P. T., Yurcik, W., & Brumbaugh, L. (2005, June 15-17). *FABS: File and block surveillance system for determining anomalous disk accesses.* Paper presented at the Sixth Annual IEEE Information Assurance Workshop (pp. 207-214).

Stecklow, S., Singer, J., & Patrick, A. (2005). Watch on the Thames. *The Wall Street Journal.* Retrieved on October 4, 2005, from http://online.wsj.com/public/article/sb112077340647880052-ckyzgab0t3asu4udfvnpwroaqcy_20060708.html

Stolfo, S. J., Hershkop, S., Wang, K., Nimeskern, O., & Hu, C.-W. (2003a, September). *A behavior-based approach to securing e-mail systems.* Paper presented at the Mathematical Methods, Models, and Architectures for Computer Networks Security.

Stolfo, S. J., Hu, C.-W., Li, W.-J., Hershkop, S., Wang, K., & Nimeskern, O. (2003b). *Combining behavior models to secure e-mail systems* (No. CU Tech. Rep.). Retrieved from www1.cs.columbia. edu/ids/publications/EMT-weijen.pdf

Sturn, A. (2000). *Cluster analysis for large scale gene expression studies.* Unpublished Masters thesis, The Institute for Genomic Research, Rockville, MD.

Thompson, K., Miller, G., & Wilder, R. (1997). Wide area Internet traffic patterns and characteristics. *IEEE Network, 11,* 10–23. doi:10.1109/65.642356

Thorpe, J., Oorschot, P. C. v., & Somayaji, A. (2005, October 23). *Pass-thoughts: Authenticating with our minds.* Paper presented at the Workshop on New Security Paradigms, Lake Arrowhead, CA (pp. 45-56).

Trujillo, M. O., Shakra, I., & Saddik, A. E. (2005). *Haptic: The new biometrics-embedded media to recognizing and quantifying human patterns.* Paper presented at the 13th Annual ACM International Conference on Multimedia, Hilton, Singapore (pp. 387-390).

Tsai, W.-H., & Wang, H.-M. (2006a, January). Automatic singer recognition of popular music recordings via estimation and modeling of solo vocal signals. *IEEE Transactions on Audio, Speech, and Language Processing, 14*(1), 330–341. doi:10.1109/TSA.2005.854091

Tsai, W.-H., & Wang, H.-M. (2006b, January). Automatic singer recognition of popular music recordings via estimation and modeling of solo vocal signals. *IEEE Transactions on Audio, Speech, and Language Processing, 14*(1), 330–341. doi:10.1109/TSA.2005.854091

Tsymbal, A. (2004). *The problem of concept drift: Definitions and related work* (No. TCD-CS-2004-15). Dublin, Ireland: Trinity College.

Uludag, U., Pankanti, S., Prabhakar, S., & Jain, A. K. (2004). Biometric cryptosystems: Issues and challenges. *Proceedings of the IEEE, 92*(6). doi:10.1109/JPROC.2004.827372

Varenhorst, C. (2004). *Passdoodles: A lightweight authentication method.* Retrieved on July 27, 2004, from http://people.csail.mit.edu/emax/papers/varenhorst.pdf

Vel, O. D., Anderson, A., Corney, M., & Mohay, G. (2001). *Mining e-mail content for author identification forensics.* Paper presented at the SIGMOD: Special Section on Data Mining for Intrusion Detection and Threat Analysis.

Veldhuis, R. N. J., Bazen, A. M., Kauffman, J. A., & Hartel, P. H. (2004). *Biometric verification based on grip-pattern recognition.* Paper presented at the Security, Steganography, and Watermarking of Multimedia Contents (pp. 634-641).

Wagner, D., & Dean, D. (2001). *Intrusion detection via static analysis.* Paper presented at the IEEE Symposium on Security and Privacy.

Wark, T., Thambiratnam, D., & Sridharan, S. (1997). *Person authentication using lip information.* Paper presented at the IEEE 10th Annual Conference, Speech and Image Technologies for Computing and Telecommunications (pp. 153-156).

Warrender, C., Forrest, S., & Pearlmutter, B. (1999, May 9-12). *Detecting intrusions using system calls: Alternative data models.* Paper presented at the IEEE Symposium on Security and Privacy Oakland, CA (pp. 133-145).

Wespi, A., Dacier, M., & Debar, H. (2000). *Intrusion detection using variable-length audit trail patterns.* Paper presented at the Recent Advances in Intrusion Detection (RAID).

Westeyn, T., Pesti, P., Park, K., & Starner, T. (2005, July). *Biometric identification using song-based eye blink patterns.* Paper presented at the Human Computer Interaction International (HCII), Las Vegas, NV.

Westeyn, T., & Starner, T. (2004). *Recognizing song-based blink patterns: Applications for restricted and universal access.* Paper presented at the Sixth IEEE International Conference on Automatic Face and Gesture Recognition (p. 717).

Wikipedia.org. (2005). *Behavioural sciences.* Retrieved on October 6, 2005, from http://en.wikipedia.org/wiki/behavioral_sciences

Yampolskiy, R. V. (2006, February 24). *Behavior based identification of network intruders.* Paper presented at the 19th Annual CSE Graduate Conference (Grad-Conf2006), Buffalo, NY.

Yampolskiy, R. V. (2007a, April 2-4). *Human computer interaction based intrusion detection.* Paper presented at the 4th International Conference on Information Technology: New Generations (ITNG 2007), Las Vegas, NA (pp. 837-842).

Yampolskiy, R. V. (2007b, October 9-11). *Indirect human computer interaction-based biometrics for intrusion detection systems.* Paper presented at the 41st Annual IEEE International Carnahan Conference on Security Technology (ICCST2007), Ottawa, Canada (pp. 138-145).

Yampolskiy, R. V. (2007c, April 11-12). *Motor-skill based biometrics.* Paper presented at the 6th Annual Security Conference, Las Vegas, NV.

Yampolskiy, R. V. (2007d, April 2-4). *Secure network authentication with passtext.* Paper presented at the 4th International Conference on Information Technology: New Generations (ITNG 2007), Las Vegas, NA (pp. 831-836).

Yampolskiy, R. V. (2008a). Behavioral modeling: An overview. *American Journal of Applied Sciences, 5*(5), 496–503.

Yampolskiy, R. V. (2008b). *Computer security: From passwords to behavioral biometrics.* London: New Academic Publishing.

Yampolskiy, R. V., & Govindaraju, V. (2006a, December 16-18). *Similarity measure functions for strategy-based biometrics.* Paper presented at the International Conference on Signal Processing (ICSP 2006), Vienna, Austria.

Yampolskiy, R. V., & Govindaraju, V. (2006b, April 17-22). *Use of behavioral biometrics in intrusion detection and online gaming.* Paper presented at the Biometric Technology for Human Identification III. SPIE Defense and Security Symposium, Orlando, FL.

Yampolskiy, R. V., & Govindaraju, V. (2007a). Direct and indirect human computer interaction based biometrics. *Journal of Computers, 2*(8), 76–88.

Yampolskiy, R. V., & Govindaraju, V. (2007b, April 9-13). *Dissimilarity functions for behavior-based biometrics.* Paper presented at the Biometric Technology for Human Identification IV. SPIE Defense and Security Symposium, Orlando, FL.

Yampolskiy, R. V., & Govindaraju, V. (2008). Behavioral biometrics: A survey and classification. [IJBM]. *International Journal of Biometric, 1*(1), 81–113. doi:10.1504/IJBM.2008.018665

Ye, N. (2000). *A Markov chain model of temporal behavior for anomaly detection.* Paper presented at the IEEE Systems, Man, and Cybernetics Information Assurance and Security Workshop.

Yeung, D. Y., & Ding, Y. (2001). (n.d.) Host-based intrusion detection using dynamic and static behavioral models. *Pattern Recognition, 36,* 229–243. doi:10.1016/S0031-3203(02)00026-2

Yutaka, K. (2005). *Behaviormetrics.* Retrieved on October 6, 2005, from http://koko15.hus.osaka-u.ac.jp/

Zhang, Y., & Wang, D. (2006, July 12-15). *Research on object-storage-based intrusion detection.* Paper presented at the 12th International Conference on Parallel and Distributed Systems (ICPADS) (pp. 68- 78).

Zhang, Z., & Manikopoulos, C. (2003, August 11-13). *Investigation of neural network classification of computer network attacks.* Paper presented at the International Conference on Information Technology: Research and Education (pp. 590- 594).

Zhu, Y., Tan, T., & Wang, Y. (2000). *Biometric personal identification based on handwriting.* Paper presented at the 15th International Conference on Pattern Recognition (ICPR'00) (p. 2797).

Chapter 2
Security Evaluation of Behavioral Biometric Systems

Olaf Henniger
Fraunhofer Institute for Secure Information Technology, Germany

ABSTRACT

For establishing trust in the security of IT products, security evaluations by independent third-party testing laboratories are the first choice. In some fields of application of biometric methods (e.g., for protecting private keys for qualified electronic signatures), a security evaluation is even required by legislation. The common criteria for IT security evaluation form the basis for security evaluations for which wide international recognition is desired. Within the common criteria, predefined security assurance requirements describe actions to be carried out by the developers of the product and by the evaluators. The assurance components that require clarification in the context of biometric systems are related to vulnerability assessment. This chapter reviews the state of the art and gives a gentle introduction to the methodology for evaluating the security of biometric systems, in particular of behavioral biometric verification systems.

INTRODUCTION

Behavioral biometric characteristics, like the voice or handwritten signatures, are generally used for verification, i.e. for confirming a claimed identity through comparisons of biometric features, but rarely for identification, i.e. for finding identifiers attributable to a person through search among biometric features in a database, (see, e.g., ISO 19092, 2008). Therefore, we concentrate in this chapter on biometric verification systems.

Biometric verification systems are often embedded in larger systems as security mechanisms for user authentication purposes. Since the biometric characteristics of a person are bound to that person and cannot easily be presented by others, biometric methods can increase the binding of authentication processes to persons. It is, of course, a precondition that the biometric security mechanisms themselves are sufficiently secure (Prabhakar, Pankanti, & Jain, 2003).

DOI: 10.4018/978-1-60566-725-6.ch002

There are long-established standards and best practices for ensuring IT security, including such for preventing and mitigating such threats as the unwarranted or unwanted dissemination, alteration, or loss of information. These apply also to biometric systems. The means to achieve security are largely cryptographic, but there are also other security mechanisms, like tamper-proof enclosures, log files, locked doors, guardians, or the separation of responsibilities. In addition to the general IT security issues, there are security issues specific to biometric systems: their recognition accuracy and fraud resistance. These are the subject of this chapter.

As most users lack the resources and expertise to evaluate the security of IT products on their own and are unwilling to rely solely on claims put forth by the developers, security evaluations by independent third-party testing laboratories are the first choice for building confidence in the security of IT products. In some fields of application of biometric technologies, a security evaluation based on officially recognized criteria like the Common Criteria for IT security evaluation (ISO/IEC 15408), also known simply as the Common Criteria, is even required by legislation (see section "Specific requirements" below).

This chapter is structured as follows: The next section provides a general introduction to the Common Criteria security assurance requirements. Section "Vulnerability analysis" clarifies the evaluation methodology that is specific to biometric systems. The final section briefly summarizes the main conclusions.

SECURITY ASSURANCE REQUIREMENTS

General

To achieve comparability of the results of security evaluations, evaluation criteria have been standardized by several national and international standardization bodies. The Common Criteria for IT security evaluation (ISO/IEC 15408) arose as a basis for a wide international recognition of evaluation results. They comprise two large catalogues:

- Security functional requirements for describing the security functionality of an IT product (ISO/IEC 15408-2), and
- Security assurance requirements for describing the level of assurance provided by a security evaluation (ISO/IEC 15408-3).

The security assurance requirements define actions required from developers and evaluators. General guidance on how to perform these actions is provided in the Common Evaluation Methodology (ISO/IEC 18045). In addition to this, there are more specific guidance documents for specific purposes. A Biometric Evaluation Methodology was developed to supplement the Common Evaluation Methodology with respect to the evaluation of biometric systems (Common Criteria Biometric Evaluation Methodology Working Group, 2002). ISO/IEC 19792 (2008) specifies basic guidance on security evaluations of biometric systems independently of the Common Criteria or any other specific evaluation and certification schemes.

The security requirements are grouped into components, families and classes. A component is the smallest unit selectable for an evaluation. A family is a grouping of components that share security objectives, but differ in emphasis or rigor. A class is a grouping of families with a common focus.

The security assurance components are furthermore grouped into seven predefined Evaluation Assurance Levels (EALs). These levels, EAL1–EAL7, correspond to increasing degrees of confidence in the security of the Target of Evaluation (TOE) to be gained by increasing efforts for testing and design verification. Table 1 lists for each EAL the required security assurance com-

Table 1. Evaluation assurance level summary (ISO/IEC 15408-3)

Assurance class	Assurance family	Assurance components						
		EAL1	EAL2	EAL3	EAL4	EAL5	EAL6	EAL7
Development	Security architecture (ADV_ARC)	–	1	1	1	1	1	1
	Functional specification (ADV_FSP)	1	2	3	4	5	5	6
	Implementation representation (ADV_IMP)	–	–	–	1	1	2	2
	Security function internals (ADV_INT)	–	–	–	–	2	3	3
	Security policy modeling (ADV_SPM)	–	–	–	–	–	1	1
	TOE design (ADV_TDS)	–	1	2	3	4	5	6
Guidance documents	Operational user guidance (AGD_OPE)	1	1	1	1	1	1	1
	Preparative procedures (AGD_PRE)	1	1	1	1	1	1	1
Life-cycle support	Configuration management capabilities (ALC_CMC)	1	2	3	4	4	5	5
	Configuration management scope (ALC_CMS)	1	2	3	4	5	5	5
	Delivery (ALC_DEL)	–	1	1	1	1	1	1
	Development security (ALC_DVS)	–	–	1	1	1	2	2
	Flaw remediation (ALC_FLR)	–	–	–	–	–	–	–
	Life-cycle definition (ALC_LCD)	–	–	1	1	1	1	2
	Tools and techniques (ALC_TAT)	–	–	–	1	2	3	3
Security Target (ST) evaluation	Conformance claims (ASE_CCL)	1	1	1	1	1	1	1
	Extended components definition (ASE_ECD)	1	1	1	1	1	1	1
	ST introduction (ASE_INT)	1	1	1	1	1	1	1
	Security objectives (ASE_OBJ)	1	2	2	2	2	2	2
	Security requirements (ASE_REQ)	1	2	2	2	2	2	2
	Security problem definition (ASE_SPD)	–	1	1	1	1	1	1
	TOE summary specification (ASE_TSS)	1	1	1	1	1	1	1
Tests	Coverage (ATE_COV)	–	1	2	2	2	3	3
	Depth (ATE_DPT)	–	–	1	2	3	3	4
	Functional tests (ATE_FUN)	–	1	1	1	1	2	2
	Independent testing (ATE_IND)	1	2	2	2	2	2	3
Vulnerability assessment	Vulnerability analysis (AVA_VAN)	1	2	2	3	4	5	5

ponents. For details of the assurance components see ISO/IEC 15408-3.

Specific Requirements

For products for qualified electronic signatures (which are deemed legally equivalent to handwritten signatures), national legislation may require a security evaluation based on internationally acknowledged criteria such as the Common Criteria. For instance, the German ordinance on electronic signatures (2001) requires that the evaluation must cover

- at least the evaluation assurance level EAL4, augmented with an advanced methodical vulnerability analysis showing resistance to attacks with a high attack potential (assurance component AVA_VAN.5), for
  - secure signature creation devices,
  - technical components for key generation, and
  - technical components for certification services used outside a specially secured trust center,
- at least the evaluation assurance level EAL3, augmented with an advanced methodical vulnerability analysis showing resistance to attacks with a high attack potential (assurance component AVA_VAN.5), for
  - other components of signature creation applications and
  - signature verification applications,
- at least the evaluation assurance level EAL3 for
  - technical components for certification services used within a specially secured trust center.

If biometric user authentication methods are to be used in products for qualified electronic signatures instead of a knowledge-based user authentication method, they have to show a level of security equivalent to that of the knowledge-based user authentication method, i.e. resistance to attacks with a high attack potential. If a biometric method is used in addition to a knowledge-based user authentication method, then a methodical vulnerability analysis showing resistance to attacks with a moderate attack potential (assurance component AVA_VAN.4) is sufficient by way of exception. In other fields of application than that of the creation of qualified electronic signatures, similar evaluation requirements may apply.

The assurance components that require clarification in the context of biometric systems are those in the family AVA_VAN (vulnerability analysis) within the class AVA (vulnerability assessment). These assurance components are discussed in section "Vulnerability analysis".

Protection Profiles for Biometric Systems

The evaluation of the security of an IT product is based on a set of security requirements (both, security functional requirements and security assurance requirements) within a Security Target (ST) document. A TOE is to be evaluated against the corresponding ST.

An implementation-specific ST may be compliant to a reusable, implementation-independent Protection Profile (PP). A PP document defines a set of security requirements for a class of TOEs. A PP should include the set of security assurance requirements predefined for an EAL, possibly augmented with additional assurance requirements. A PP expresses common security requirements useful for many users and to be met by diverse manufacturers. A PP can be developed by user associations, governmental authorities, or other parties interested in defining a common set of security requirements. Several PPs related to biometrics have been developed (UK CESG,

2001; U.S. Information Assurance Directorate, 2007; German Federal Office for Information Security, 2008).

PPs and STs themselves have to be evaluated to demonstrate their completeness, consistency, technical soundness, and suitability for practical use. If different PPs are to be used in a composite evaluation, e.g. a biometric PP together with smart card PPs, they have to fit together. This should be checked separately by an evaluation.

VULNERABILITY ANALYSIS

Introduction

The assurance components AVA_VAN.4 ("Methodical vulnerability analysis") and AVA_VAN.5 ("Advanced methodical vulnerability analysis") require that the evaluator

- identifies, based on the documentation provided by the developer, a list of (preferably all) potential vulnerabilities in the TOE, the source of which is largely general experience,
- conducts penetration tests based on the identified potential vulnerabilities to determine whether the TOE is resistant to attacks with
  - a moderate attack potential, in case of AVA_VAN.4, or
  - a high attack potential, in case of AVA_VAN.5.

The attack potential is well defined in ISO/IEC 18045. The attack potential is a measure of the minimum effort to be expended in an attack to be successful. Essentially, it depends on the required expertise (general and target-specific knowledge) and resources (time, access to the target, equipment). The higher the attackers' motivation (value of the asset), the higher efforts they may exert. The Australian Biometrics Institute's

White Paper (2008) outlines guidelines how to calculate the attack potential for attacks specific to biometric systems.

In older versions of the Common Criteria, the resistance of a TOE security function to direct attacks (i.e. not to bypassing, deactivating, corrupting, etc.) was referred to as Strength of Function (SOF) and was to be evaluated in a separate assurance component. Now, the SOF is regarded as the resistance to just a particular type of attacks and is to be evaluated within the assurance components of the AVA_VAN family. The three SOF levels correspond to resistance to direct attacks as follows:

- **SOF-basic:** resistance to attacks with a low attack potential, i.e. to a casual breach of the security;
- **SOF-medium:** resistance to attacks with a moderate attack potential, i.e. to a straightforward or intentional breach of the security;
- **SOF-high:** resistance to attacks with a high attack potential, i.e. to a deliberately planned or organized breach of the security.

Vulnerabilities in Biometric Systems

Overview

Given their variety, it is difficult to generalize about biometric systems and their vulnerabilities. Each type of biometric system has its own potential vulnerabilities that need to be taken into consideration during the vulnerability analysis. However, different biometric systems have many elements in common. Figure 1 illustrates the general flow of information within a biometric system and identifies potential points of attack.

Figure 1. Examples of points of attack in a biometric system

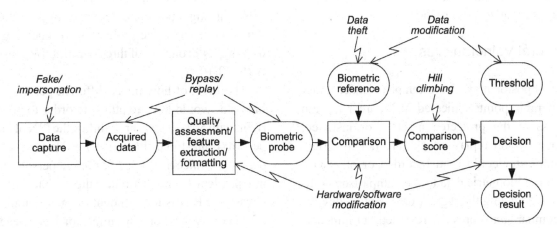

Vulnerabilities Specific to Biometric Systems

Unlike PINs (Personal Identification Numbers) and passwords, not all biometric characteristics are secrets. For instance, anyone can take photographs of someone else's face. Other biometric characteristics such as vein patterns or the handwritten-signature dynamics are harder to spy out. A main threat to assets under protection by a biometric system is that of impersonation, i.e. of an impostor masquerading as another person who is enrolled and gaining access to the protected assets.

Forgeries of behavioral biometric characteristics may take several forms requiring different impostor skill levels (ISO/IEC TR 19795-3):

- **Random forgery (zero-effort impostor attempt):** attempt in which an impostor presents their own biometric characteristics as if attempting successful verification against their own biometric reference;
- **Accidental forgery:** attempt in which an impostor without knowledge of the original biometric characteristics presents any behavior;
- **Simple forgery:** attempt in which an impostor with knowledge of the original biometric characteristics mimics them from memory without practice;

- **Simulated forgery:** attempt in which an impostor mimics an example of the original biometric characteristics without prior practice;
- **Skilled forgery:** attempt in which an impostor mimics the original biometric characteristics after practicing.

If unwatched, an impostor may also attempt to impersonate another person by use of

- a dummy (in case of physiological biometric characteristics), e.g. a silicone or gummy finger, or
- a reproducing device (in case of behavioral biometric characteristics), e.g. an autopen machine for automatic signing or a voice recorder.

A challenging problem is that the same person possesses only a limited number of fall-back characteristics that could replace compromised biometric characteristics in case of successful attacks (Ratha, Connell, & Bolle, 2001). In contrast to this, if a PIN or password is compromised, they can easily be replaced by new ones. Replacing sniffed biometric characteristics would not help much if the same type of attack succeeds also against the fall-back characteristics. Hence, the resistance of biometric systems to fake, impersonation, bypass and replay attacks is crucial.

General Vulnerabilities

The impostor may also attempt to attack other vulnerable points indicated in Figure 1 to gain access to the protected assets. For instance, if bypass and replay attacks are not thwarted, an impostor could send recorded or otherwise acquired biometric data to the comparison component, evading the regular data capture device. If comparison scores are revealed, an impostor could systematically modify biometric probes in a hill climbing attack to obtain comparison scores closer and closer to the decision threshold until this threshold is met.

Excursus: Attack Resistance of Knowledge-Based Authentication

For comparison: The strength of a 6–8-digit numeric PIN with three permitted attempts is considered high (prEN 14890-1, 2007). The strength of knowledge-based user authentication by means of a PIN or password is related to the probability of guessing the PIN or password. The more digits the PIN has, the more different characters, and the fewer retries are permitted, the lower is the probability of guessing the PIN, and the higher is the strength of the knowledge-based user authentication method.

For instance, the probability of guessing, in a single attempt, a 6-digit PIN containing numerals from 0 through 9 is $P_1 = 10^{-6}$ (assuming that all 6-digit permutations of the 10 numerals represent equally probable valid PINs). If all possible PIN values could be tried one after the other (brute-force attack on the PIN of a single person), then the probability of guessing the PIN in the next attempt would increase from failed attempt to failed attempt since the number of values left to try decreases. After 10^6 attempts the impostor would with 100% certainty have determined the right PIN. In order to prevent brute-force attacks on the PIN of a single person, the number of permitted retries is limited. The probability of guessing a 6-digit PIN in one out of three permitted attempts is $P_3 = 3 \cdot 10^{-6}$.

The PINs of how many different persons an impostor would have to attack in order to guess right, with 50% or 95% probability, the PIN of one person (brute-force attack on the PINs of several persons)? Since the PINs of different persons are independent from each other, the probability of guessing a PIN is independent from the number of persons for whom the impostor has already failed to guess the PIN. An impostor would have to try the PINs of $\log_{(1-P3)} 0.5 = 231,049$ different persons in order to have a 50% chance to guess the PIN of one person. In order to have even 95% confidence, an impostor would have to try the PINs of $\log_{(1-P3)} (1 - 0.95) = 998,576$ different persons. Organizational measures can protect well against this residual risk.

However, the security of PINs and passwords is not only related to the probability of guessing them, but also to their memorability and the risks of PIN or password sniffing. The longer a PIN or password is, the lower is the probability of guessing, yet the higher is the probability that its owner makes a written note of it (contrary to the usual security recommendations). This must be taken into account when evaluating the security of knowledge-based user authentication methods and when comparing their security with that of biometric methods.

Attack Resistance of Biometric Verification Systems

Biometric Performance Metrics

The strength of a biometric system lies in its ability to tell different persons apart and is related to its false accept rate (FAR), but also to other factors such as the binding of the biometric characteristics to persons. The FAR of a biometric verification system (where the user explicitly claims an identity) is the proportion of impostor attempts falsely declared to match the biometric reference within a permitted number of attempts (ISO/IEC 19795-1). For biometric identification systems (where users make no explicit claims to identity), the false-positive identification-error rate (FPIR) is not an invariant of the system, but depends on the number of enrolled persons.

The FAR of a behavioral biometric system depends on the nature of impostor attempts under consideration. It has to be distinguished between

- zero-effort FAR, i.e. the FAR regarding zero-effort impostor attempts, and
- active-impostor FAR, i.e. FAR regarding active impostor attempts.

The zero-effort FAR is meaningful for biometric systems based on physiological characteristics like fingerprints or irides, where impostors can hardly influence the outcome in their favor, but is not relevant for predicting the practical performance of systems based on behavioral characteristics like handwritten signatures, where the impostors can easily take action to influence the outcome in their favor. For instance, it is unlikely in practice that impostors claiming to be someone else present their own handwritten signatures (that would be zero-effort impostor attempts). They would rather take efforts to forge the signature of the persons they claim to be.

For determining whether a behavioral biometric system is sufficiently resistant to attacks with a high attack potential, the FAR is to be measured using skilled forgeries. For determining resistance to attacks with a moderate attack potential, measuring the FAR with respect to attacks requiring a lower skill level may be sufficient.

Statistical Performance Testing

The FAR of a biometric system can be measured experimentally with a certain statistical confidence

- off-line using pre-existing or specially collected test databases (technology evaluation) or
- on-line in a prototype or simulated application using a test population representative of the intended target population (scenario evaluation).

The FAR measured in the test population is an estimate for the "honest" FAR in the target population. General guidance on the test subject selection and test data acquisition is given in Mansfield & Wayman (2002) and ISO/IEC 19795-1.

The statistical confidence interval of the FAR estimate depends on the size of the test population. If you want to show, with a small probability of error, very low error rates, then an unwieldily large number of independent observations are necessary. Based on the assumption that the two possible outcomes of all verification attempts (acceptance or rejection) were independent from each other and that the error probability is the same in each attempt, i.e. that the sequence of attempts forms a Bernoulli process, the Rule of 3 and the Rule of 30 (ISO/IEC 19795-1) provide lower bounds to the number of attempts needed for showing a certain recognition accuracy:

- **Rule of 3:** If no error is observed in N independent attempts, then the honest error rate is with 95% confidence lower or equal $3/N$.
- **Rule of 30:** If at least $M \geq 30$ errors are observed in N independent attempts, then the honest error rate lies with 90% confidence within $\pm 30\%$ of the observed error rate M/N.

Independent attempts mean that the outcome of any attempt does not depend on the outcomes of the previous ones. In general, the attempts are independent from each other if each impostor and each enrollee is involved in only one impostor attempt. In case of behavioral biometric characteristics, the attempts are also considered independent from each other if impostors are allowed to mimic several enrollees, but each enrollee is subject to only one impostor attempt (possibly after an impostor has practiced the enrollee's behavior). If a biometric verification system has falsely accepted an impostor as an enrollee once, it is likely that it would falsely accept him as this enrollee again and again. Repeated dependent trials would bias the FAR estimate for a biometric verification system. That's why it is preferable to have few attempts by many different persons rather than many repeated attempts by only few persons.

If you wanted to show an error rate of 10^{-6} (which corresponds to the probability of guessing a 6-digit numeric PIN right in a single attempt), then as per Rule of 30 around $30 \cdot 10^6$ impostor attempts were necessary to observe 30 errors. In order that the impostor attempts are independent from each other, each biometric reference has to come from a different person. Thus, biometric references were needed from $30 \cdot 10^6$ different persons. If you relax the independence of the observations and collect, e.g., 25 genuine samples and 25 forgeries for each test subject, as Ortega-Garcia et al. (2003) did in the signature subcorpus of the MCYT database, and compare all genuine samples with all associated forgeries, then at least $n = 48,000$ different test subjects were needed in order to implement the impostor attempts ($25^2 n > 30 \cdot 10^6$). While making better use of available test subjects, this approach leads to a degradation of the statistical confidence.

As per Rule of 3, at least $3 \cdot 10^6$ impostor attempts were necessary to show an error rate of 10^{-6}. In order that the impostor attempts are independent from each other, biometric references were needed from $3 \cdot 10^6$ different persons. If you

again relax the independence of observations and collect and compare 25 references and 25 forgeries for each test subject, then biometric samples were still needed from at least $n = 4,800$ different persons in order to implement the attacks ($25^2 n > 3 \cdot 10^6$).

Due to the difficulties to attain the theoretically recommendable test sizes in practice, the Common Criteria Biometric Evaluation Methodology Working Group (2002) recommends using the largest test population that can be reasonably managed.

Correspondence Between Accuracy and Attack Resistance

Apparently, validating very low error rates with high confidence is not practicable due to the size of test population required. However, if all strengths and weaknesses of biometric systems and of PINs and passwords are duly taken into account in their entirety, then a biometric system need not necessarily achieve a FAR of 10^{-6} in order that its strength can be assessed as as high as that of a 6-digit numeric PIN (which may be guessed right in a single attempt with a probability of 10^{-6}). A higher FAR may be sufficient. The FAR of a biometric method and the probability of guessing a PIN should not be equated. Systematically trying different PINs in a brute-force attack is much simpler than systematically presenting different biometric characteristics. The stronger binding of biometric characteristics to the person, as compared to that of a PIN, needs to be taken into account in the evaluation (Statham, 2005).

Assume the FAR of a biometric method is $FAR_1 = 10^{-4}$ in case of a single permitted attempt. Unlike the probability of guessing a PIN, which increases from failed attempt to failed attempt because the number of permutations left to try decreases, the probability of a biometric false acceptance in the next attempt does not increase from failed attempt to failed attempt. Also after 10^4 attempts a brute-force attack against the biometric reference of a single person would succeed only with a probability of $FAR_{10}4 = 1 - (1 - FAR_1)^{104}$ = 0.632 (63.2%). In order to prevent brute-force attacks on the biometric reference of a single person, the number of permitted retries is limited also for biometric methods. For instance, in case of five permitted attempts, the FAR is still FAR_5 = $1 - (1 - FAR_1)^5 = 4,999 \cdot 10^{-4}$.

How many different persons would the impostors have to try to impersonate in order to be falsely accepted with 50% or 95% probability as one of the persons? Since the biometric characteristics of different persons are independent from each other, the probability of being falsely accepted is independent from the number of persons whom the impostors have already failed to impersonate. The impostors would have to try to impersonate $\log_{(1-FAR5)} 0.5 = 1,386$ different persons in order to have a 50% chance to be falsely accepted once at the latest in the fifth attempt. In order to have 95% confidence to be falsely accepted once in at most five attempts, the impostors would have to try to impersonate $\log_{(1-FAR5)}(1 - 0.95) = 5,991$ different persons.

Also this residual risk appears acceptable for a TOE resistant to attacks with a high attack potential if the inherently increased resistance of biometric systems to brute-force attacks, compared to that of a PIN or password, is taken into account. Organizational measures preventing impostors from accessing that many targets may protect well against this residual risk.

Specifying error rate requirements to meet security needs in applications using biometrics is not a purely technical, but also political issue. Specifying error rate requirements for biometric systems is in some way similar to setting road speed limits. The lower a speed limit is enforced, the lower may be the road fatality rate, but the more impeded is the traffic flow. If the traffic is not to come to a standstill, a residual risk of fatal traffic accidents, which should be reduced by all conceivable safety measures, must still be accepted. Similarly, the lower the FAR of a biometric system, the lower may be the fraud rate, but the system may be less usable.

Several attempts to define a fixed mapping between error rates of a biometric system and its strength of function have already been made (e.g. in the Common Criteria Biometric Evaluation Methodology Working Group's Biometric Evaluation Methodology (2002) and in working drafts of ISO/IEC 19792), but did not find universal approval because these mappings did not reflect all strengths and weaknesses of biometric systems. All strengths and weaknesses of biometric systems vs. PINs and passwords need to be taken into account in their entirety when comparing their attack resistance.

Usability of Biometric Verification Systems

While the FAR is a measure for the security of a biometric verification system, the false reject rate (FRR) is a measure for the usability of the system. The FRR of a biometric verification system is the proportion of genuine attempts falsely declared not to match the biometric reference after the permitted number of retries.

Both, a low FAR and a low FRR are desirable. However, these two requirements run contrary to each other. The lower the FAR at a certain threshold value, i.e. the fewer impostor attempts get through, the higher is the FRR, i.e. the more genuine enrollee attempts are rejected, and vice versa. It must be tested whether an acceptable FRR is maintained while an acceptable FAR is achieved. Therefore, FAR values should always be accompanied with the associated FRR value.

The FRR is the lower, the more retries are permitted in case of rejections. The outcomes of retries by the same person, however, are not independent from each other. Therefore, the FRR in case of m permitted attempts cannot be deduced without further assumptions or experiments from the FRR in case of a single permitted attempt.

User-Dependent Variability

Significant differences in the attack resistance and perceived usability may show up among the users of a biometric verification system (Doddington et al., 1998). These differences may be due to differences in the stability and the forgeability of the biometric characteristics of the individual users, but also to differences in the skills applied when attempting to forge them. Per-user error rates, measured over multiple genuine and forgery attempts, help to find out the worst-case performance of a biometric system.

SUMMARY

Biometric methods may replace knowledge-based user authentication methods in many application fields, provided that their recognition accuracy and attack resistance are sufficiently high. Their strengths lie in freeing users from the burden of recalling PINs or passwords from memory and in increasing the binding of authentication processes to persons. Moreover, the presentation of behavioral biometric characteristics such as handwritten signatures, which are in general not presented coincidentally or unintentionally, is regarded as evidence of a deliberate decision on the part of a user.

Biometric systems, however, are not immune to attacks: Their security may be broken, expending a certain amount of efforts, by faking or imitating biometric characteristics using e.g. gummy fingers or handwritten signature forgeries. Even during normal use, occasional recognition errors (false acceptances and false rejections) cannot be completely avoided as the biometric characteristics of a person may vary from presentation to presentation. In particular, the capability of behavioral biometric characteristics as an exclusive means of authentication appears limited because some aspects of behavior may be rather easily imitated by other people and there are many people whose behav-

ioral characteristics are quite variable. However, behavioral biometric characteristics may still be used in addition to other authentication methods to enhance security and usability.

Quantifying the security of a biometric system is difficult and requires taking all its strengths and weaknesses into account. The details of how to do this are not all resolved yet and, anyway, go beyond the scope of this chapter. The error rates (FAR and FRR) of a biometric verification system can be determined only experimentally. In order to provide, with high confidence, evidence of low error rates, a great number of verification attempts are necessary. In case of behavioral biometric characteristics the objective evaluation of security is made more difficult by the fact that the observed error rates depend largely on the skill level used in forgery attempts. The attack potential of direct and indirect attacks that the biometric system is able to withstand is to be classified as basic, moderate, or high based on the efforts necessary for effecting these attacks.

A lack of evidence and trust in the security of biometric systems is an obstacle to their application. In high-security application areas like the banking sector or for the protection of private keys for qualified electronic signatures, so far, biometric technologies, in particular behavioral biometric technologies, are rarely used. As yet, no biometric products have been evaluated and awarded a Common Criteria certificate at an evaluation assurance level sufficiently high for security applications. Only few biometric products have attained a certificate, and if so, only on the evaluation assurance level EAL2 (Canadian Communications Security Establishment, 2001; Australian Defence Signals Directorate, 2003; TÜViT, 2005). This is not only because the security of biometric products may still need to be improved, but also because the IT security evaluation methodology is quite complex and not easily applicable to biometric products.

REFERENCES

Australian Biometrics Institute. (2008). *Biometric vulnerability: A principled assessment methodology*. White paper.

Australian Defence Signals Directorate. (2003). *EAL2 certification report for Iridian technologies KnoWho authentication server and private ID*. Certification Report 2003/31.

Canadian Communications Security Establishment. (2001). *EAL2 certification report for Bioscrypt™ Enterprise for NT logon version 2.1.3*. Certification Report 383-4-8.

Common Criteria Biometric Evaluation Methodology Working Group. (2002). *Biometric evaluation methodology*. Version 1.0.

Doddington, G., Liggett, W., Martin, A., Przybocki, M., & Reynolds, D. (1998). Sheep, goats, lambs, and wolves: A statistical analysis of speaker performance in the NIST 1998 speaker recognition evaluation. In *International Conference on Spoken Language Processing*, Sydney, Australia.

Draft European Standard prEN 14890-1. (2007). *Application interface for smart cards used as secure signature creation devices–part 1: Basic services*.

Final Committee Draft ISO/IEC 19792. (2008). *Information technology–security techniques–security evaluation of biometrics*.

German Federal Office for Information Security. (2008). *Biometric verification mechanisms protection profile (BVMPP)*. Common Criteria Protection Profile BSI-CC-PP-0043.

German Government. (2001). *Ordinance on electronic signatures*.

International Standard ISO 19092. (2008). *Financial services–biometrics–security framework*.

International Standard ISO/IEC 15408-1. (2005). *Information technology–security techniques–evaluation criteria for IT security–part 1: Introduction and general model*.

International Standard ISO/IEC 15408-2. (2008). *Information technology–security techniques–evaluation criteria for IT security–part 2: Security functional components*.

International Standard ISO/IEC 15408-3. (2008). *Information technology–security techniques–evaluation criteria for IT security–part 3: Security assurance components*.

International Standard ISO/IEC 18045. (2008). *Information technology–security techniques–methodology for IT security evaluation*.

International Standard ISO/IEC 19795-1. (2006). *Information technology–biometric performance testing and reporting–part 1: Principles and framework*.

Mansfield, A. J., & Wayman, J. L. (2002). *Best practices in testing and reporting performance of biometric devices*. NPL Report CMSC 14/02.

Ortega-Garcia, J., Fiérrez-Aguilar, J., Simon, D., Gonzalez, J., Faundez-Zanuy, M., & Espinosa, V. (2003). MCYT baseline corpus: A bimodal biometric database. *IEEE Proceedings Visual Image Processing*, *150*(6), 395–401. doi:10.1049/ip-vis:20031078

Prabhakar, S., Pankanti, S., & Jain, A. K. (2003). Biometric recognition: Security and privacy concerns. *IEEE Security & Privacy*, March/April, 33–42

Ratha, N. K., Connell, J. H., & Bolle, R. M. (2001). Enhancing security and privacy in biometrics-based authentication systems. *IBM Systems Journal*, *40*(3).

Statham, P. (2005). Threat ananlysis–how can we compare different authentication methods? In *Biometric Consortium Conference*, Arlington, VA.

Technical Report ISO/IEC 19795-3. (2007). *Information technology–biometric performance testing and reporting–part 3: Modality-specific testing.*

TÜViT. (2005). *EAL2 certification report for authentication engine of VOICE.TRUST server version 4.1.2.0.* Certification Report TUVIT-DSZ-CC-9224.

UK CESG. (2001). *Biometric device protection profile (BDPP).* Draft issue 0.82.

U.S. Information Assurance Directorate. (2007). *U.S. government biometric verification mode protection profile for basic robustness environments.* Version 1.1.

U.S. Information Assurance Directorate. (2007). *U.S. government biometric verification mode protection profile for medium robustness environments.* Version 1.1.

Chapter 3
Performance Evaluation of Behavioral Biometric Systems

F. Cherifi
University of Caen, France

B. Hemery
University of Caen, France

R. Giot
University of Caen, France

M. Pasquet
University of Caen, France

C. Rosenberger
University of Caen, France

ABSTRACT

We present, in this chapter, an overview of techniques for the performance evaluation of behavioral biometric systems. The BioAPI standard that defines the architecture of a biometric system is presented in the first part of the chapter. The general methodology for the evaluation of biometric systems is given including statistical metrics, definition of benchmark databases, and subjective evaluation. These considerations rely with the ISO/IEC19795-1 standard describing the biometric performance testing and reporting. The specificity of behavioral biometric systems is detailed in the second part of the chapter in order to define some additional constraints for their evaluation. This chapter is dedicated to researchers and engineers who need to quantify the performance of such biometric systems.

INTRODUCTION

Biometrics is now a technology that is present in our daily life. It is used as for example in airports (passport verification), offices (access control, biometric USB key...) and even in some places in the world for banking operations... Different biometric modalities can be used for the identification / verification of an individual (face recognition, keystroke dynamics recognition, DNA analysis...) (Mahier et al., 2008).

DOI: 10.4018/978-1-60566-725-6.ch003

The characterization of an human by considering its behavior in its daily life operations (gait, signature dynamics, voice...) (Han et al. 2006; Muramatsu & Matsumoto, 2007; Petrovska-Delacretaz et al., 2007) or through its interactions with a computer (mouse dynamics, keystroke dynamics...) represents an interesting and open area in research (Hwang et al., 2006; Orozco et al., 2006).

The performance evaluation of such biometric systems is very important for many reasons:

- To be used in a real (that is to say in an industrial) context, the quality of a biometric system must be precisely quantified. The context of use, the efficiency, the robustness of the algorithm must be defined to determine if it fulfills the requirements of a particular industrial application (logical access, physical access, e-commerce...) ;
- The comparison of different biometric modalities is essential to qualify their relative advantages and drawbacks ;
- The performance evaluation is also necessary in order to facilitate the research in this field (Hemery et al., 2006). We need a reliable evaluation method in order to put into obviousness the benefit of a new biometric system.

The objective of this chapter is to make an overview on evaluation techniques that are used in the state of the art to quantify the performance of behavioral biometric systems. An engineer or a researcher will find in the proposed chapter, the different criteria or methods he can use to validate a biometric system he intends to use in a real context. A behavioral biometric system can be evaluated by considering the general approach to evaluate a biometric system while taking into account the specificity of this type of modality.

The plan of the chapter is given below. In the section 1, we present the general approaches for the evaluation of a biometric system. It necessitates generally to use a benchmark database (Hemery

et al., 2007) and a set of criteria (computation time, FAR...). The benchmark database can be composed of real biometric templates or synthetic ones. We present different solutions from the state of the art. Section 3 focuses on specificities of behavioral biometric systems. We present their specificities that must be taken into account for their evaluation. Section 4 concerns the future trends that must be achieved in order to facilitate research progress in this domain. We conclude this chapter in section 5.

GENERAL EVALUATION METHODOLOGIES

Introduction

A biometric system is composed of different steps (see Figure 1). There are mainly two processes in the use of a biometric system. The enrollment phase has for objective to determine a model of an individual given the characteristics acquired by the selected biometric sensor. The identification / verification phase uses this model to make a decision an individual.

The international standards committee for biometrics within ISO (ISO/IEC JTC1 SC37) developed a complete specification and reference implementation for a standardized API (BioAPI Consortium, 2005). The purpose of the BioAPI Specification is to define an open system standard application program interface (API) which allows software applications to communicate with a broad range of biometric technologies in a common way.

Figure 2 shows the interaction between the three BioAPI 2.0 components: applications, BioAPI Framework, and BSPs (Biometric Service Providers). The BioAPI 2.0 specification implements two APIs. The first one is the API which is the interface between the BioAPI Framework which supports the functions in the API specification and application. The second is

Figure 1. Diagram summarizing the various phases of a biometric system (Adapted from: ISO/IEC JTC 1/SC 37 Part 1 Overview Standards Harmonization Document)

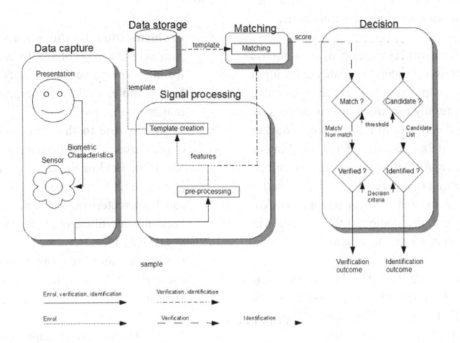

the Service Provider Interface (SPI) that is the interface between the BioAPI Framework which invokes the functions in the SPI specification and to support the functions of the SPI specification and BSPs. The BioAPI Framework is responsible for the management of BSPs and for the mapping of function calls from an API function to an SPI function within the appropriate BSP.

The performance evaluation of biometric systems is a crucial problem. It is generally realized within three contexts (ISO, 2006):

- **Technology evaluation:** It consists in testing an algorithm on a standardized corpus. The objective is to determine if the developed biometric system *a priori* meets the requirements. Testing is carried out using offline processing of the data and the results of technology tests are repeatable ;
- **Scenario evaluation:** The testing is carried out on a complete system in an environment that models a real-world target

Figure 2. BioAPI components (Adapted from BioApi, 2005)

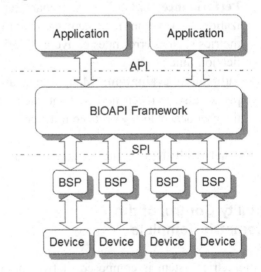

application of interest. Test results will be repeatable only to the extent that the modeled scenario can be carefully controlled ;

- **Operational evaluation:** It is an online test in real conditions. In general, operational test results will not be repeatable because of unknown and undocumented differences between operational environments.

The performance evaluation of a biometric system generally considers the quality of the input data and the output result. In order to evaluate them, we generally use an empirical process by considering the system as a black box (Thacker et al., 2008). In this case, the internal working of the associated algorithms is not studied. The black box generates an output result given a biometric template as input and a set of parameters. We identified within this context different issues in the evaluation of biometric systems:

- **Quality control of the biometric template:** This quality is necessary to be quantified before the enrollment or verification/identification step ;
- **Definition of benchmark databases:** It is a challenge as it is used in the two first evaluation contexts ;
- **Performance evaluation:** The characterization of a biometric system uses many metrics such as error rates or average verification time ;
- **Subjective evaluation:** Many other aspects must be taken into account such as the user acceptability or its confidence.

We detail all these issues in the next sections.

Quality Control of the Biometric Template

A biometric system is composed of two main components: a sensor that permits to acquire the biometric template and some algorithms for the enrollment and the verification/ identification steps. The quality of the biometric template is essential to guarantee a correct behavior of the biometric system. Many problems can alter this

quality mainly because of three reasons (ISO, 2006):

- **Problems due to the sensor:** incorrect parameterization (volume for audio, focus for image based sensor...), dirty sensor (as for example, optical fingerprint sensor), transmission error...
- **Problems due to the user:** incorrect use of the sensor (too far from the microphone, not in the field of the camera...), behavior (stress, tension, mood or distractions), personal characteristic (accent, handicap...), personal modifications (haircut change, keystroke...)...
- **Problems due to the environment:** conditions of acquisition (noise, light, humidity...)...

In the BioAPI standard, the quality of the biometric template can be evaluated by the BSP. If the quality (a score between 0 and 100) is considered as insufficient, the user is asked to acquire again the template.

Many specifications by the ISO organization defined some evaluation criteria for the quality of few biometric templates such as face, fingerprint or Iris. Other biometric modalities are currently studied such as the signature, voice or hand shape. If we consider as for example the face modality, the evaluation of the template takes into account the resolution of the image, the size of the face in terms of pixels in the image or the compression rate used to store the face image.

Definition of Benchmark Databases

In order to compare different biometric systems, we need generally to compute their performance following the same protocol (acquisition conditions, test database, metrics...). The testing database contains many samples specific to a biometric modality and each sample is associated to an individual. By comparing the performance of different systems on the same database and with the same experimental conditions (number of samples used in the enrollment step, thresholds), we can decide which system performs better. In this case, it provides us a relative evaluation of biometric systems.

These benchmark databases aim to be as close as possible as real use cases. By the way, a database must contain enough samples from an individual for the enrollment step. Moreover, a database is generally composed of two parts. The first one is used for the enrollment and the second one for the identification/verification task. A database must also contain a large number of individuals because the performance of biometric systems generally decreases as the number of user increases. Finally, the samples must represent most of different possible alterations that could be seen in a real use, as for example noisy or incomplete biometric data.

A benchmark database can contain real samples from individuals, which reflect the best the real use cases. Nevertheless, it is difficult to create such a database for several reasons. First of all, it can be difficult and costly to collect samples from a high number of individuals. Moreover, all samples must be acquired in the same conditions. This constraint can be very difficult to fulfill (as for example the guarantee to have the same lighting conditions for the face capture). Samples must then be acquired with some alterations to represent difficulties during the identification/verification task. Finally, each sample must be annotated by an human. A database can be specific to a modality, like the USF HumanID gait database (Sarkar et al., 2005), but can also be multimodal like the MCYT-100 database (Ortega-Garcia et al, 2003) which contains samples of fingerprint and signature for the same individual.

A benchmark can also contain synthetic samples. The creation of such a database is easier but is less significant. The main advantage of synthetic database is that alterations on samples are fully controlled. This enables to verify the robustness

of a biometric system face to a specific alteration. Such a database has been realized for fingerprints (Cappelli et al., 2002) as for example and used in the Fingerprint Verification competition in 2006 (FVC 2006). Figure 3 shows some examples of synthetic fingerprints. Alterations are simulated to make the fingerprint more realistic.

Performance Evaluation

The performance evaluation has for objective to provide some quantitative measures on the efficiency of biometric systems. The classical statistical metrics used to quantify the performance of a biometric system are:

- **Computation time:** the necessary time for the acquirement, enrollment, verification / identification ;
- **True positive (TP):** number of users that have been correctly authenticated ;
- **False positive (FP):** number of impostors that have been authenticated ;
- **False reject rate (FRR):** Proportion of authentic users that are incorrectly denied. It is calculated as:

FRR = 1-TP/(number of genuine users)

- **False accept rate (FAR):** proportion of impostors that are accepted by the biometric system. It is calculated as:

FAR = FP/(number of impostor users)

- **Failure-to-enroll rate (FTE):** proportion of the user population for whom the biometric system fails to capture or extract usable information from biometric sample. This failure may be caused due to behavioral or physical conditions pertaining to the subject which hinder its ability to present correctly the required biometric information ;

Figure 3. Some examples of synthetic fingerprints generated by SfinGe (Maltoni, 2004)

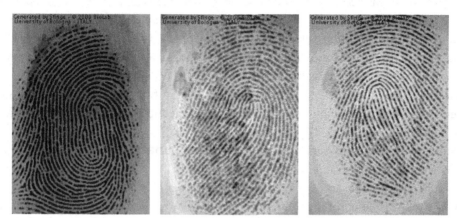

- **Failure-to-acquire rate (FTA):** proportion of verification or identification attempts for which a biometric system is unable to capture a sample or locate an image or signal of sufficient quality ;

- **False match rate (FMR):** The rate for incorrect positive matches by the matching algorithm for single template comparison attempts. FMR equals FAR when the biometric system uses one attempt by a user to match its own stored template ;

- **False non-match rate (FNMR):** The rate for incorrect negative matches by the matching algorithm for single template comparison attempts. FNMR equals FRR when the biometric system uses one attempt by a user to match its own stored template ;

- **Identification rank:** It is the smallest value k for which a user's correct identifier is in the top k identifiers returned by an identification system ;

- **Receiver operating characteristic curve (ROC curve):** The method most commonly used to assess the performance of a biometric system is the ROC curve. The aim is to plot a curve representing FAR according to the FRR. In order to plot this type of curve, we have to changes the value of the decision threshold. For each value of

the threshold, we calculate the associated FRR and FAR that we plot on the curve. The advantage of this method is that it gives a compact representation of the performance of a biometric system through a single curve allowing the comparison of different biometric systems. In order to compare easily several biometric systems, we can then compute the area under the curve AUC and the equal error rate ERR where FAR = FRR. The optimal result is obtained if the AUC equals 1 and the ERR equals 0 ;

- **Detection error trade-off curve (DET curve):** DET curve (Adler et al., 2007) is a ROC curve which has its linear scale replaced by a scale based on a normal distribution, to make it more readable and usable. In this case, the curve flattens and tends towards the right. The benefits of the DET curves are the same as those of ROC curves, but they allow in addition to compare biometric systems that have similar performance. An example of a DET curve can be seen on Figure 4 ;

- **Cumulative match characteristic curve (CMC curve):** This curve plots the identification rank values on the x-axis and the probability of correct identification at or below that rank on the y-axis.

Figure 4. Example of DET curves used for the performance comparison of face recognition systems (Adapted from Adler et al., 2007)

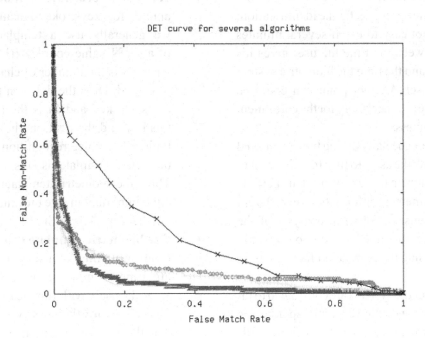

- **Precision/recall curve (PR curve):** This curve (Muller et al, 2001) has a similar behavior to ROC curves. In order to draw the PR curve, we plot the positive predictive value (PPR = TP /(TP+FP)), also known as the precision versus the recall. We can then compute AUC and ERR in a similar way as in ROC curves. One advantage is that we do not need the number of true negative in this method.

The most used methods are the DET curves, ROC curves and the PR curves.

Subjective Evaluation

The performance evaluation is not the only thing to take into account when we have to consider a biometric system. To be accepted by users in real conditions (physical or logical access as for example), a biometric system must fulfill some other properties such as the acceptability, the easiness of use or the confidence in the system.

The acceptability denotes the way how users perceive the biometric system and interact with it. The acceptability is highly dependent of the culture of users. As for example, Asian users hardly accept to have a contact with a biometric sensor. This implies that biometric systems with contact less sensors, such as iris recognition, are better accepted by Asian users that biometric systems that need a contact, such as the fingerprint recognition. Another example, European users prefer fingerprint recognition to iris recognition.

The confidence in a biometric system is very close to its acceptability, as it is also highly dependent of the culture of users. It denotes how the reliability of a biometric system is perceived by users. Generally, users have a better confidence in biological biometric system than in behavioral biometric system. Fingerprint recognition or a DNA analysis is often considered, quite rightly, to be better than voice recognition. In the same time, the more the modality is efficient, such as the DNA analysis, the more it invades privacy and the less the acceptability is high.

The easiness of use depends on the quality of the sensor and the interface with users. It also depends on the time necessary for the identification: the system is not easy to use if several minutes are needed between the time the user gives his biometric data and the time the biometric system identifies the user. Another point that could be considered is the time necessary for the enrollment step and its easiness.

It is possible, especially during the operational evaluation, to ask the users to fill a form in order to have their opinion on these aspects. This permits to have complementary information on different biometric systems. A statistical analysis of the answers must be performed in order to keep only reliable users using the correlation factors or Chi square tests.

Finally, biometric systems are confronted to juridical problems concerning data corresponding to template of biometric system users. This depends mainly of the country where the biometric system is used. Each country has its own lawn concerning the protection of private data. As for example, in France, the use of computer devices to treat and save private data is regulated by the CNIL (French data protection authority). By the way, to use a biometric system, a French company must warn the CNIL and asks for their authorization before being able to collect samples and names used in biometric systems.

We detailed in this section the general scheme for the evaluation of any biometric system. We focus in the next section on behavioral ones and we put into obviousness their specificity.

THE SPECIFICITY OF BEHAVIORAL BIOMETRICS

Behavioral biometric systems are specific. Many characteristics make them difficult to define and to quantify their performance:

- **The biometric template contains generally temporal information.** As for example, for keystroke dynamics analysis, we generally use a template composed of a set N value couples $\{(D_i, F_i)\ i=1..N\}$ where N is the number of characters in the password, D_i is the duration time the user presses a key and F_i is the time between this key and the next one in the password typing. For voice recognition systems, the biometric template is a sampled signal. Thus, the biometric template is generally quite important in size meaning that the parameters space is high ;

- **The biometric template can change with time according to users.** If we keep in mind the example of keystroke dynamics analysis, users with time learn how to type more efficiently their password. That means that the biometric template can be quite different compared to the one obtained after the enrollment step (Hocquet et al., 2007). Another example, the dynamics of signature can also change a lot with time as it becomes a reflex for the user. This variability has multiple consequences. The first one concerns the number of templates for the enrollment step that is generally higher than other types of biometric systems. The second consequence is that the verification / identification algorithm should take into account this variability in order to make a correct decision. Another point concerns the testing of such biometric systems with biometric data that must embed this difficulty ;

- **The behavior as biometric characteristic can be very different for an individual given its age, culture and experience.** The evaluation of a behavioral biometric system is often realized considering a large diversity of users.

We focus in the next sections on impacts of these remarks on the evaluation of behavioral biometric systems.

Benchmark Definition

Benchmark definition is really important for the performance evaluation of biometric systems.

As mentioned previously in the chapter, a benchmark database can be composed of real biometric templates (from test users) or synthetic ones. The definition of synthetic templates is easier for behavioral biometric data. Indeed, many behavioral modalities can be synthesized rather easily such as keystroke dynamics, voice, lip movements, mouse dynamics, signature dynamics... For morphological biometric modalities, it is much more difficult to do. The ability to generate more easily synthetic biometric templates is an advantage for the evaluation of such systems.

Generally, a biometric model (generated after the enrollment phase) is computed for the same person given 2 or 3 capture sessions. As for example, the AR face database has been created considering two sessions with an interval between them of 15 days (Phillips & al., 2000). The difficulty of behavioral biometric systems is that the biometric template naturally changes with time. Indeed, a human is a nice machine who wants to do things quicker. As a consequence, a benchmark database for behavioral modalities needs more capture sessions in order to take into account this variation. As for example, Awad & Traore in the approach they proposed in 2005 for computer intrusion detection with behavioral biometrics has been validated with biometric data acquired during 9 sessions (Awad & Traore, 2005). The number of capture sessions is important but also the period of time between them. This shows the difficulty and the cost of such benchmark definition for this type of biometric modality.

The variability of behavioral biometric templates is really important if we compare morphological ones. Indeed, the fingerprint of individuals from different cultures or age is not so different. If we consider now the behavioral biometric modalities such as the keystroke dynamics, voice or gait, the associated template can be very different from individuals at different ages. As a consequence, the benchmark database must embed all the variability of biometric templates to be representative of real applications. As for example, Janakiraman & Sim (Janakiraman & Sim, 2007) tested their keystroke authentication method on users that were Chinese, Indian or European origin. This is so an additional constraint for the definition of benchmark databases.

Robustness Analysis

The behavior of an individual is very dependent on many factors like his mood, emotion, tiredness or health... As for example, voice recognition systems are very sensitive to all these factors. In order to be used in a real context, one has to test the robustness of a biometric system face to all these modifications.

Behavioral biometric systems can be very sensitive according to the sensor (keystroke dynamics, mouse dynamics...). The behavior of an individual can be different for multiple sensors. As for example, the template generated during the enrollment based on keystroke dynamics for an individual and a given keyboard cannot easily be used for the verification on another keyboard (Clarke & Furnell, 2007). Indeed, the performance in term of EER can be quite high (>10%) in this case.

Another point concerns the robustness of behavioral biometric systems face to attacks. The main difficulty for these systems is that anybody can try to duplicate a biometric template. As for example, it is not very hard to launch the verification given its keystroke dynamics, voice or gait. That does not mean that the chance to be authenticated is necessary higher but it is very easy to make a try. For morphological biometric systems, it is much more difficult even if as for example, fingerprints can be duplicated with some effort to launch one verification.

Discussion

In order to evaluate a behavioral biometric system, one could use the general methodology described in the previous section by using benchmark databases and classical performance metrics. Nevertheless, several aspects must be taken into account to consider the specificity of such systems:

- The number of sessions for the definition of biometric templates for testing such a biometric system must be high (≥ 3) ;
- The sessions must be relatively spaced in order to take into account the natural change of behaviors of individuals ;
- Behavioral biometric templates can be in general easily synthesized. This approach for the definition of a benchmark database is interesting. It allows to test a large number of biometric templates and to control their alterations to quantify the robustness of the system ;
- The benchmark database must contain some fake biometric templates to also test the robustness of the system ;

- A benchmark database must embed a large diversity of users (culture, age...);
- The performance evaluation of behavioral biometric systems must be realized using the same sensor during the enrollment and verification / identification steps.

EXPERIMENTAL RESULTS

We present the evaluation of a keystroke dynamics verification system (Hocquet et al., 2007) as illustration of the proposed methodology. We first detail the protocol of the experiment we realized.

Protocol

We asked 15 individuals to participate for this experiment. Figure 5 shows some information on these individuals considering their age. Three females and twelve males participated to this experiment. All the involved individuals use a computer in their daily life. We explained them before starting the objectives of the experiment and the acquisition process. Each user tried two times in the first session before we record the biometric data.

Figure 6 presents the dates where sessions have been realized.

Figure 5. Repartition of users' ages for the experiment

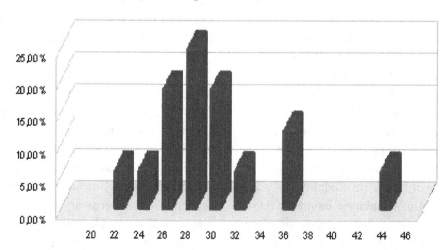

The biometric template contains: time between two keys pressure, time between two keys release, time between one pressure and one release and time between one release and one pressure. We asked each individual for each session to type 5 times the same password "GREYC Laboratory". We measured many data such as the time necessary for each user to type all of them, the number of mistyping and of course, the data that will be used as biometric template. To quantify the objective evaluation performance of this biometric system, we used for each individual, 5 biometric templates for the enrollment step and the 10 last for the verification one. To complete this objective evaluation experiment, we also realized a subjective evaluation test by asking the users to answer the questions shown in Box 1.

Results

Figure 7 presents some statistics on the capture process. The FTA value is quite important for some individuals (the user wants to type the sentence too fast, users not enough concentrated…). The average FTA value equals 16% which is important.

Figure 8 shows as illustration the biometric template acquired for an individual in a session. We can remark that the biometric template is quite stable.

The resulting ROC curve is given in Figure 9 and Figure 10. The computed EER value equals 20.5%. The performance of this biometric system is not really important for this study as the main objective is to illustrate in this part, the different elements to take into account for its evaluation. If we want to obtain a FAR value equals to 0,

Figure 6. Session dates for the experiment

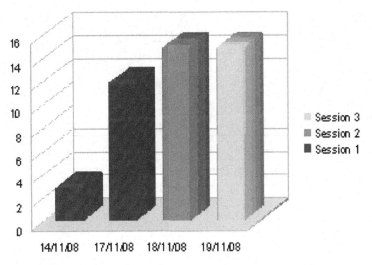

Box 1.

Q1: Is the verification fast? **Yes, no**
Q2: Is the system easy to use? **Yes, no**
Q3: Are you ready to use this system in the future? **Yes, no, do not know**
Q4: Do you feel confident in this system? **Yes, no**
Q5: Do you feel embarrassed when using this system? **Yes, no, do not know**
Q6: What is your general appreciation of the system? **Very good, good, average, bad**

Figure 7. FTA value for each individual for all sessions

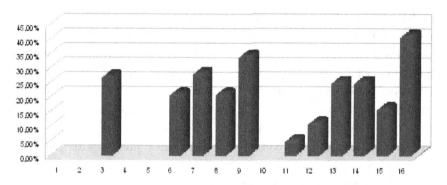

Figure 8. Plot of the biometric data for an individual for one session (5 acquisitions)

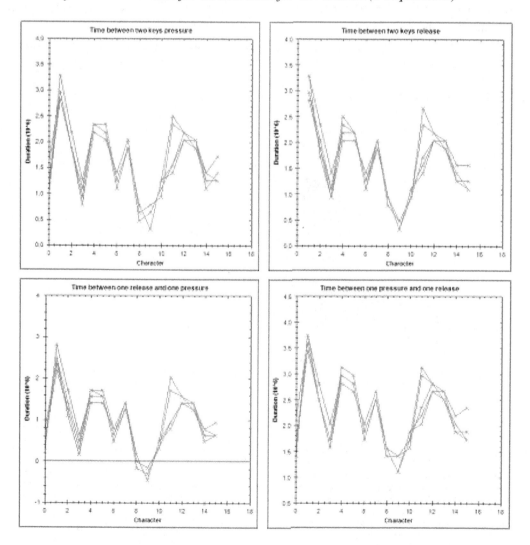

the FRR value equals 50.16%. That means if we want none impostor, we have to set the value of the threshold having as consequence to reject genuine in 50.16% cases.

In order to quantify the robustness of the selected biometric system, we made an experiment consisting in generating random synthetic keystroke dynamics. Given the 5 biometric templates used in the enrollment step, we compute an average biometric template denoted $E[T]$. We generated different biometric templates $T_i i=1:15$ given $E[T]$ and adding a random alteration by controlling its standard deviation. Figure 11 shows some examples of altered biometric templates given $E[T]$ for an order value equals to 2.

Figure 12 shows the evolution of the EER value considering the standard deviation of the alteration of $E[T]$. We can notice that a small alteration has a great impact on the EER value; this means that this biometric system is not very robust.

We give now the results of the subjective evaluation experiment. We obtained for some questions similar answers for all users. As for example, all users found that the verification is fast. 93% of them considered the system is easy to use and is non intrusive for their privacy.

Figure 13 shows the results of the subjective evaluation. Even if the biometric system is not very efficient (EER = 20.7%), nearly 50% of users are ready to use it in the future. The general appreciation is good for 60% of users.

For a logical control access, this biometric system even with a very bad value of the EER, could be an interesting solution as it necessitates none additional sensor (all computer has a keyboard), it is very simple to use. This subjective study (even if realized with a low number of individuals) shows that the perception of users is interesting to take into account.

FUTURE TRENDS

How can we make progress for the evaluation of behavioral biometric systems?

The constraints and the cost for the evaluation of behavioral biometric systems are extremely prohibitive. High quality benchmark databases must be available for the research community taking into account the previous constraints. These databases would facilitate the testing and the development of new behavioral biometric systems. They also would able to compare different enrollment and identification / verification algorithms to increase the knowledge in the domain. Actually, a researcher in the domain

Figure 9. Scores distribution

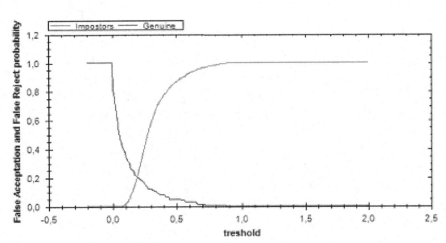

Figure 10. Roc curve

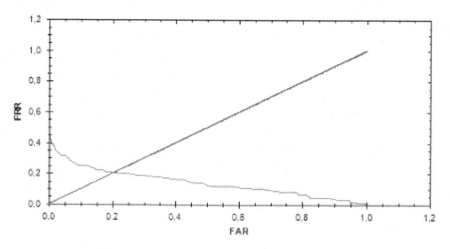

generally creates its own database to validate the proposed system. It is generally difficult to say if the database is representative of real use cases and if the system achieves better than others in the state of the art.

The European BioSecure network of excellence (http://biosecure.it-sudparis.eu/) had for objective as for example to realize benchmark databases for different biometric modalities. If we

consider behavioral modalities, only the speech was concerned. An organization should deliver for free to researchers some benchmark databases. It could be also a good thing to ask researchers to implement their biometric system following the BioAPI requirements. The cost of implementation is not so important and the benefit is high as a BSP is only a DLL file that can be transferred without giving the source code.

Figure 11. Three examples of random alteration (order 2) of the average biometric of an individual

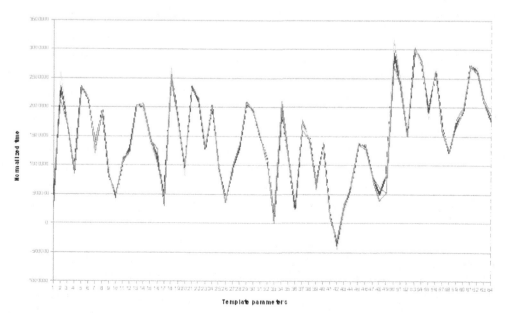

Figure 12. Evolution of the EER value given the amount of alterations

Figure 13.

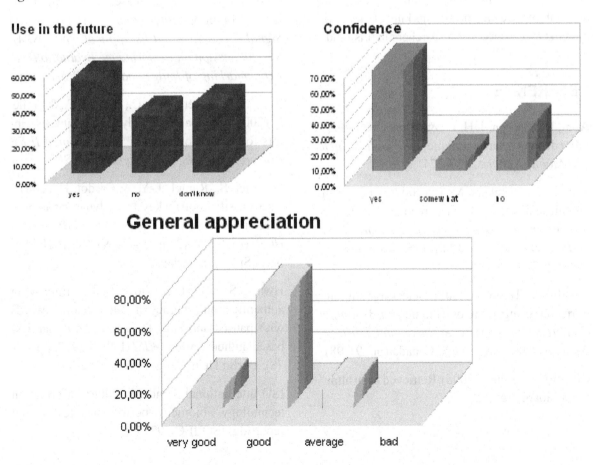

The statistical evaluation of biometric systems is important but is not sufficient. A biometric system to be used in real conditions must be easy to use, not reluctant to use... Subjective evaluation is a domain that needs a lot of research to take into account the user as the central element in the biometric system.

CONCLUSION

We presented in this chapter several issues for the evaluation of behavioral biometric systems. We detailed the BioAPI standard that defines the architecture and the evaluation of biometric systems in a general context. Behavioral biometric modalities are currently under standardization.

Much specificity of behavioral biometric systems had been detailed in the second part of this chapter. These considerations must be taken into account for the evaluation of this kind of biometric systems by engineers or researchers in this field.

REFERENCES

Abut, H., Hansen, J. H. L., & Takeda, K. (2005). Is our driving behavior unique? *DSP for In-Vehicle and Mobile Systems*, 257-274.

Adler, A., & Suckers, M. E. (2007). Comparing human and automatic face recognition performance. *IEEE Transactions on Systems, Man, and Cybernetics*, *37*, 1248–1255. doi:10.1109/TSMCB.2007.907036

Awad, A., & Traore, I. (2005). Detecting computer intrusions using behavioral biometrics. *3rd Annual Conference on Privacy, Security, and Trust*, St. Andrews, New Brunswick, Canada (pp. 91-98).

BioApi Consortium. (2005). Retrieved from http://www.bioapi.org/

Cappelli, R., Maio, D., & Maltoni, D. (2002). Synthetic fingerprint-database generation. *16th International Conference on Pattern Recognition (ICPR), 3.*

Clarke, N. L., & Furnell, S. M. (2007). Advanced user authentication for mobile devices. *Computers & Security*, *26*, 109–119. doi:10.1016/j.cose.2006.08.008

Han, J., & Bhanu, B. (2006). Individual recognition using gait energy image. *IEEE Transactions on Pattern Analysis and Machine Intelligence*, *28*(2), 316–322. doi:10.1109/TPAMI.2006.38

Hanley, J. A., & McNeil, B. J. (1982). The meaning and use of the area under a receiver operating characteristic (ROC) curve. *Radiology*, *143*, 29–36.

Hemery, B., Rosenberger, C., & Laurent, H. (2007). The ENSIB database: A benchmark for face recognition. *International Symposium on Signal Processing and Its Applications (ISSPA), Special Session on Performance Evaluation and Benchmarking of Image and Video Processing*.

Hemery, B., Rosenberger, C., Toinard, C., & Emile, B. (2006). Comparative study of invariant descriptors for face recognition. *8th International IEEE Conference on Signal Processing (ICSP)*.

Hocquet, S., Ramel, J.-Y., & Cardot, H. (2007). User classification for keystroke dynamics authentication. *International Conference on Biometrics (ICB)* (LNCS 4642, pp. 531-239). Berlin Heidelberg: Springer-Verlag.

Hwang, S., Lee, H., & Cho, S. (2006). Improving authentication accuracy of unfamiliar passwords with pauses and cues for keystroke dynamics-based authentication. *WISI* (LNCS 3917, pp. 73-78). Berlin Heidelberg: Springer-Verlag.

ISO International Standard. (2006). Information technology—biometric performance testing and reporting. ISO/IEC 19795-1.

Janakiraman, R., & Sim, T. (2007). Keystroke dynamics in a general setting. *International Conference on Biometrics (ICB)* (LNCS 4642, pp. 584-593). Berlin Heidelberg: Springer-Verlag.

Mahier, J., Pasquet, M., Rosenberger, C., & Cuozzo, F. (2008). Biometric authentication. In *IGI encyclopedia of information science and technology, 2nd edition*

Maltoni, M. (2004). Generation of synthetic fingerprint image databases. In N. Ratha & R. Bolle (Eds.), *Automatic fingerprint recognition systems*. Springer.

Muller, H., Muller, W., Squire, D. M., Marchand-Maillet, S., & Pun, T. (2001). Performance evaluation in content-based image retrieval: Overview and proposals. *Pattern Recognition Letters, 22,* 593–601. doi:10.1016/S0167-8655(00)00118-5

Muramatsu, D., & Matsumoto, T. (2007). Effectiveness of pen pressure, azimuth, and altitude features for online signature verification. *Proceedings of the International Conference on Advances in Biometrics (ICB)* (LNCS 4642, pp. 503-512). Springer.

Orozco, M., Asfaw, Y., Shirmohammadi, S., Adler, A., & El Saddik, A. (2006). Haptic-based biometrics: A feasibility study. *Symposium on Haptic Interfaces for Virtual Environment and Teleoperator Systems (HAPTICS)* (pp. 265-271).

Ortega-Garcia, J., Fierrez-Aguilar, J., Simon, D., Gonzalez, J., Faundez-Zanuy, M., & Espinosa, V. (2003). MCYT baseline corpus: A bimodal biometric database. *IEEE Procedings of Image and Signal Processing, 150,* 395–401. doi:10.1049/ip-vis:20031078

Petrovska-Delacretaz, D., El Hannani, A., & Chollet, G. (2007). Text-independent speaker verification: State of the art and challenges. ([]. *Progress in nonlinear speech processing*.]. *LNCS, 4391,* 135–169.

Phillips, P. J., Moon, H., Rizvi, S. A., & Rauss, P. J. (2000). The FERET evaluation methodology for face-recognition algorithms. *IEEE Transactions on Pattern Analysis and Machine Intelligence Archive, 22*(10), 1090–1104. doi:10.1109/34.879790

Sarkar, S., Phillips, P. J., Liu, Z., Vega, I. R., Grother, P., & Bowyer, K. W. (2005). The humanID gait challenge problem: Data sets, performance, and analysis. *IEEE Transactions on Pattern Analysis and Machine Intelligence, 27,* 162–177. doi:10.1109/TPAMI.2005.39

Thacker, N. A., Clark, A. F., Barron, J. L., Ross Beveridge, J., Courtney, P., & Crum, W. R. (2008). Performance characterization in computer vision: A guide to best practices. *Computer Vision and Image Understanding, 109,* 305–334. doi:10.1016/j.cviu.2007.04.006

KEY TERMS AND DEFINITIONS

Behavioral biometric: A Behavioral Biometric is a measurable behavior trait that is acquired over time for the identification or identity verification of an individual.

Benchmark: A database composed of biometric templates supposed to represent real cases for the performance evaluation of biometric systems.

Biometric Application Programming Interface (BioAPI): The BioAPI specification enables different biometric systems to be developed by the integration of modules from multiple independent companies.

Enrollment: The process of collecting biometric samples from a person and the subsequent preparation and storage of biometric reference templates representing that person's identity.

False Acceptance Rate (FAR): Rate at which an impostor is accepted by an identification system.

False Rejection Rate (FRR): Rate at which the authorized user is rejected from the system.

Equal Error Rate (EER): This error rate corresponds to the point at which the FAR and FRR cross (compromise between FAR and FRR).

Chapter 4
Individual Identification from Video Based on "Behavioural Biometrics"

Y. Pratheepan
University of Ulster, UK

J.V. Condell
University of Ulster, UK

G. Prasad
University of Ulster, UK

ABSTRACT

This chapter presents multiple methods for recognizing individuals from their "style of action/actions," that is, "biometric behavioural characteristics." Two forms of human recognition can be useful: the determination that an object is from the class of humans (which is called human detection), and the determination that an object is a particular individual from this class (which is called individual recognition). This chapter focuses on the latter problem. For individual recognition, this chapter considers two different categories. First, individual recognition using "style of single action," that is, hand waving and partial gait, and second, individual recognition using "style of doing similar actions" in video sequences. The "style of single action" and "style of doing similar actions," that is, behavioural biometric characteristics, are proposed as a cue to discriminate between two individuals. Nowadays, multibiometric security systems are available to recognise individuals from video sequences. Those multibiometric systems are combined with finger print, face, voice, and iris biometrics. This chapter reports multiple novel behavioural biometric techniques for individual recognition based on "style of single action" and "style of multiple actions" (i.e., analysing the pattern history of behavioural biometric motion), which can be additionally combined with finger print, face, voice, and iris biometrics as a complementary cue to intelligent security systems.

DOI: 10.4018/978-1-60566-725-6.ch004

INTRODUCTION

A biometric is a unique, measurable characteristic or trait of a human being for automatically recognizing or verifying their identity. There are two types of biometrics that can be used for the purposes of human identification or verification: physical biometrics and behavioural biometrics. Physical biometrics, such as fingerprint and iris, have already been widely acknowledged and used in many real applications. Behavioural biometric is based on an action taken by a person (source: http://www.authentec.com/technology-biometrics-overview.html - retrieved on 29/08/2008.) and is generally very hard to copy from one person to another. It is well known that humans intuitively use some behavioural characteristics such as "gait" or "style of action" to recognize each other.

A biometric system is essentially a pattern recognition system which recognizes a user by determining the authenticity of a specific physiological or behavioural characteristic possessed by the user. Several important issues must be considered in designing a practical biometric system. They have the principles of acquisition, feature extraction, matching and decision in common (see Figure 1).

Depending on the context, a biometric system can operate either in a verification (authentication) or an identification mode. Verification (*Am I who I claim I am?*) involves confirming or denying a person's *claimed identity*. On the other hand, in identification, the system has to recognize a person (*Who am I?*) from a list of N users in the template database. Identification is a more challenging problem because it involves 1:N matching compared to 1:1 matching for verification. This chapter considers individual identification problem rather than individual verification problem.

In intelligent security systems, identification of humans and their activities is generally one of the most important tasks. Examples of such systems are intelligent security systems that detect unknown or suspicious people entering restricted door entrances or an interface robot that acts as an interface for taking known users' commands and presenting results. Consider a scenario that if a person needs to go through a security enabled door then he/she may needs to prove his/her identity. An intelligent security system should offer a natural and reliable solution to the problem of identifying a person based on "who is he/she" rather than "what he/she knows" (i.e. password) or "what he/she carries" (i.e. key or ID cards) (Jain, Bolle & Pankanti, 1999).

As a relatively new technology, behavioural biometrics help to identify a person's identity through some measurable activity patterns, e.g., speaker recognition (i.e., analyzing vocal behaviour), signature recognition (i.e., analyzing signature dynamics), gait recognition (i.e., analyzing walking patterns), keystroke dynamics (i.e., analyzing keyboard typing patterns), mouse dynamics (i.e., analyzing mouse moving patterns), etc. Recently security systems operate using multibiometric techniques, combined with anatomical

Figure 1. Basic structure of behavioural biometrics systems

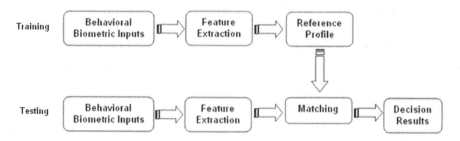

and behavioural characteristics. A commercial multi-biometric system called BioID (Frischholz & Dieckmann, 2000) (www.bioid.com) integrates the face, voice and lip movement of an individual. BioID solutions represent an advanced, people-oriented solution: with BioID, instead of typing in a password or using a PIN, the user simply looks into a standard video camera and says his or her name to get authenticated. Sharath Pankanti and Anil K. Jain (Pankanti & Jain, 2008) implement a multi-behavioural system using face, voice and finger print for person identification, see Figure 2.

Security systems can be made to determine or verify a person's identity based on his/her anatomical (i.e. finger print, face, iris or voice) and behavioural characteristics or body language (i.e. gait and hand waving). Gait includes the dynamics of the human walking motion. In order to properly interact with people an intelligent security system has to detect people and identify them using their "style of action" (the way of doing actions, say individual body language or their behavioural characteristics).

GreenDot (http://movement.nyu.edu/Green-DotProject/ - retrieved on 26/12/2008) is a research project that investigates motion capture, pattern recognition, and "Intrinsic Biometrics" techniques to detect human body language in video. Through techniques similar to those used in speech recognition, this project applies machine learning to train a computer system to compare the detected body language of an individual in a video, to that of a database of other subjects. The goal of the project is to train a computer to recognize a person based on his/her motions. The human body language covers a variety of different sub-languages such as small-scale body language, e.g., hand-gesture or facial expression, and large-scale body language, e.g., a complete human action such as walking, running, hand waving, etc. The large-scale body language (i.e. walking and sequence of similar actions) and small-scale body language (i.e. hand waving) are considered in this chapter.

Figure 2. Beyond fingerprinting: Sharath Pankanti and Anil K. Jain (Pankanti, & Jain, 2008)

Further, two different humans doing the same action may be similar but cannot be identical as the way of doing the same action (i.e. the style of action) between individuals is known to be different. That is, each individual has his/her own "behavioural" characteristics. It is important to find a behavioural characteristic features to discriminate two individuals. Then it is possible to recognize each individual using similarity measure methods or classification techniques.

Find the discrimination between individuals based on actions is to find how they "act" in particular events. Therefore there is a need to extract and find this information from video sequences using a "style of action" similarity measure. The question that pose here is, if it is not possible to obtain the lower body part of walking sequences then how do recognise individuals using upper body parts? Therefore this chapter is interested in this behavioural characteristic called style of "hand waving" action. Hence for individual identification based on "style of single action" first "hand waving" action sequences are considered for the experiments. The whole motion information in

Figure 3. The motion history image (MHI) (b) for two individuals: I1 (top) and I2 (bottom)

a　　　　　　　　　　　　　　　　b

the particular action needs to be considered for the similarity measure. The Motion History Image (MHI) (Bobick & Davis, 2001) technique is used to obtain a single image template from the whole motion information of a particular event (see Figure 3).

Here the MHI is used as our motion feature extractor. Due to the speed variant, the numbers of frames are not going to be the same for different individuals with similar action sequences. A simple periodic detection method is applied to find the number of frames involved in an individual's action sequence.

Two different approaches are applied for the similarity measure based on the hand waving style of action. In the first approach the Hausdroff distance based similarity measure is applied. In the second approach Hu moments (Hu, 1962) is applied to the calculated MHI image to get the seven dimensional (7D) transformation invariant feature vector. Based on these feature vectors the Support Vector Machines (SVM) is then applied for individual classification. A shorter version appears in the literature (Pratheepan, Prasad & Condell, 2008).

Next, gait sequence is considered for "style

of single action" based individual identification. There has been an explosion of research on individual recognition in recent years based on gait (Little & Boyd, 1998; Nixon, Carter, Nash, Huang, Cunado & Stevenage, 1999; Bobick & Johnson, 2001). The most recognized and earliest psychophysical study of human perception of gait was carried out by Johansson (Johansson, 1975) using moving light displays (MLD). The initial experiments showed that human observers are remarkably good at perceiving the human motion that generated the MLD stimuli. Cutting et al. (Cutting, Prott & Kozlowski, 1978) studied human perception of gait and their ability to identify individuals using MLD.

The above psychological evidence and computational approaches justify that individual recognition can be done using people's walking sequences, i.e. human gait has enough information to discriminate individuals. Most of the research has been done using full-cyclic period gait sequences rather than partial gait sequences. Motion information is one of the best cues which can be used to recognize individuals.

The first question is, if it is not possible to obtain full-cyclic walking sequences then how do we recognise individuals? The number of frames in individuals walk sequences, even from a particular individual's sequence, may vary because of the speed. Therefore the second question is, how do calculate a similarity measure between the different numbers of frames based on the "behavioural characteristics" information. This chapter attempts to answer these questions. Therefore in this chapter partial gait sequences is considered for individual identification. As a solution, the Longest Common Subsequence (LCS) approach is applied on partial gait sequences to identify individuals in image sequences.

Next, individual identification based on "style of multiple actions" is considered instead of the single action. For the experiment the individuals' image sequences with multiple actions are selected. In particular the actions observed are that individuals enter the room, pick up the pen, sit down, write their name, get up and leave the room etc (see Figure 4). All observations are taken for individual identification. The feature vector for each image in the sequence is calculated based on motion information. The feature vectors are clustered into groups to represent the actions using the K-means algorithm. Similar actions are represented after clustering the feature vectors in each cluster. The mean of the vectors are calculated from each cluster and this mean vector is the "code-word". Each code-word represents a different action.

For the purpose of individual identification a similarity measure is needed to match a new image sequence against those sequences already available in the database, and find whether or not the same individual appears in those database sequences. If two image sequences are captured from a particular person in a different time then the length of these two sequences need not be with the equal number of frames depending on both the speed and movement performance. Therefore image sequence alignment is important for the similarity measure. Here the DTW (Dynamic Time Warping) (Andrea, 2001) alignment algorithm is

used for sequence alignment with an assumption that start and end frames are correctly aligned. A short version appears in the literature (Pratheepan, Torr, Condell & Prasad, 2008).

This chapter is organized as follows: Section 2 explains individual identification based on "style of single action" work. This section gives technical details of the individual identification based on "hand waving" and "partial gait" systems including periodicity detection, Motion History Image (MHI), the Hausdorff Distance, Hu moments, SVM classification, Dimensional Reduction and Longest Common Sequence (LCS). Section 3 explains individual identification based on "style of multiple actions" and technical detail of the Dynamic Time Warping (DTW) algorithm. The experiments results are explained in section 4. Finally, a discussion and conclusion are presented in Section 5.

INDIVIDUAL IDENTIFICATION BASED ON "STYLE OF SINGLE ACTION"

The question that address in this section is how can discriminate individuals in video sequences using their "Style of Action". To find the discrimination between individuals based on actions is to find how they "act" in particular event. A method is implemented to extract and find this information from video sequences using a "style of action" (i.e., Time-invariant action parameters that characterize the motion appearance (shape).) similarity measure.

Individual Identification Using "Hand Waving" Action Sequences

The whole motion information in the particular action needs to be considered for the similarity measure. Using the Motion History Image (MHI) technique the whole motion information from a particular event can convert as a single image template. Here MHI is used as a motion feature

Figure 4: Enter, sit down, write name, stand up and leave image sequences

extractor. Due to the speed variant, the numbers of frames are not going to be the same for different individuals with similar action sequences. Therefore a periodic action detection method is applied to find the number of frames involved in an individual's action sequence. The novelty of the method is that it is simpler and more reliable than the Fourier transformation methods (Liu & Picard, 1998; Polana & Nelson, 1993) as it was tested against those published previously.

Finding the Periodicity of Action

Periodicity detection is based on the similarity for motion detected binary consecutive image frames. Here, $S_i = R \cdot B_i$ is used as the similarity measure function. Here there is a need to convert the 2D vectors to 1D vectors for the dot product. In this equation S_i are the similarity measure values, R_i is the reference image (shown at the left side of Figures 5 and 6) and B_i is the motion detected binary test image. B_i is calculated as:

$$B_i(x,y) = \begin{cases} 1 & if \quad |f_{i+1}(x,y) - f_i(x,y)| > \alpha \\ 0 & otherwise \end{cases}$$

$$(1)$$

where $f_i(x,y)$ and $f_{i+1}(x,y)$ are the intensity values of each pixel at location *(x,y)* at frames i and $i+1$ respectively, $B_i(x,y)$ is the binary image representing regions of motion, α is a threshold value and $i \in (f_s, f_e - 1)$ (i.e. the last calculation should be with f_e

and f_{e-1}). Also f_s and f_e are the start and end frames respectively from the selected test sequence.

Figures 5 and 6 show similarity measure graphs. The x-axis and y-axis represent frame numbers and similarity measure values respectively. The peak values in these graphs represent a higher similarity measure with the reference frame and the test sequence. The first higher value in the graph shows that the first similarity occurs when the individuals hands go down, the second higher values shows that the second similarity occurs when the individuals hands go up and the third higher value shows that the third similarity occurs when the individuals hand go down etc. Therefore the periodicity is calculated as the number of frames between two higher similarity measure values (represented as horizontal lines at the bottom of Figures 5 and 6). The number of frames is now used to generate MHI images.

Motion History Image (MHI)

A motion history image (MHI) is a kind of temporal template. Let $I(u,v,k)$ be the kth frame of pixels intensities of an image sequence and let $D(u,v,k)$ be the binary image that results from pixel intensity change detection. That is by thresholding $|I(u,v,k)-I(u,v,k-1)>th|$, where *th* is the minimal intensity difference between two images for change detection. A MHI, say H_θ, contains the temporal history of motion at that point represented by θ which is the period of time to be considered. The implementation of the MHI is then as follows (Davis & Bobick, 1997):

Figure 5. Periodicity measure graph for individual 1

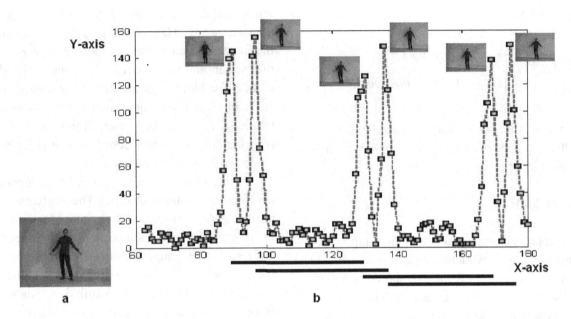

Figure 6. Periodicity measure graph for individual 2

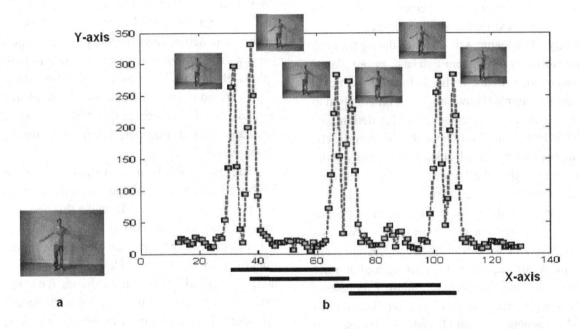

$$H_\theta(u,v,k) = \begin{cases} \theta & if \quad D(u,v,k) = 1 \\ \max[0, H_\theta(u,v,k-1)] & otherwise \end{cases}$$

(2)

Moreover, in Davis's problem (Davis & Bobick, 1997) definition, it is not known when the movement of interest begins or ends. Therefore they needed to vary the observed period θ. As with assumption that the beginning and the end of a hand waving are known, there is no need to vary θ. Therefore the modified MHI operator is modified as:

$$H(u,v,k) = \begin{cases} k & if \quad D(u,v,k)=1 \\ H(u,v,k-1) & otherwise \end{cases}$$

(3)

where $H(u,v,k) = 0$ for $k = 0$ and $0 \leq k \leq K$. k is the sequence of frames during which the motion is stored.

Approach-1

This approach consists of three main components, namely, feature extractor, matcher and decision modules. Ideally, the feature set should be unique for each person (i.e. extremely small inter-person similarity) and also invariant with respect to changes in the different samples of the same behavioural characteristic collected from the same person (i.e. extremely small intra-person variability). The feature sets obtained during training are stored in the system database as templates. During identification, the feature set extracted from the sample (known as query) is compared to the templates by the matcher, which determines the degree of similarity between the feature sets. The decision module decides on the identity of the person based on the degree of similarity between the templates and the query.

For the feature extraction first MHI images are generated from image sequences. Two different sets of hand waving sequences are used - one set of sequences for training and another set of sequences for testing. Figure 7 represents the sample image frames from two individual's video sequences (I1 and I2) which were used for training. Figure 8(a) shows the image sequences corresponding to the MHI for the two different individuals I1 and I2.

Canny edge detection (Canny, 1986) is applied to the MHI images. Figure 8(b) shows the results of canny edge detection (Canny, 1986). This edge detected shape of the motion information template is manually cropped to only contain the rectangular area where any "Hand Waving" action occurs in the image sequence. Due to the variant size of the human and the camera zoom, the cropped rectangular block regions are further resized to HxW block regions using bilinear interpolation (Rafael & Richard, 2003). Here H=60 and W=80 (number of pixels) represent height and width respectively of each block region.

An ideal shape **A** is calculated which is a model or reference for the target object. These references are calculated for each and every individual using the mean of the set of their sequences of cropped and resized MHI templates. Figure 9(a) represents the rectangular block region of reference template for a particular individual, I1. Similarly a "Shape" **B** for a new object is calculated by its cropped and resized MHI template and further "Dilate" it to allow slight variation on "Shape", see Figure 9(b). In the experiments, MHI images corresponding to the same action carried out by the same person can have a significant variation due to their "physical mood". Dilation is applied to allow slight variation on transformations on individual's template, i.e. it is expected this "dilated" image can handle slight intra-person variations on the "hand waving" action.

Here, the problem of individual recognition is how to decide if a "Shape" B is an instance of a particular "Shape" A. To make this decision the similarity measure between "Shapes" A and B is calculated. Therefore, an efficient template matching method - the Hausdorff Distance method – is used for comparing shapes. It can say that B is an instance of the object A if the partial Hausdorff distance from A (the reference object) to B (the new object) is at most some threshold *d*. The threshold values are defined for each and every individual as *d1* for individual 1 and *d2* for individual 2, etc. Based on these threshold values individual discrimination is carried out based on their "style of action" or behavioural characteristics information.

Figure 7. Image sequences used for training

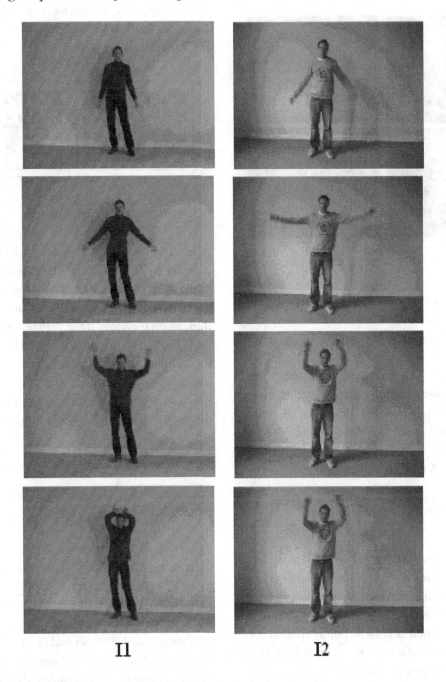

I1   I2

Hausdorff Distance

Consider the directed Hausdorff Distance. It is defined as follows: Let A and B be two finite point sets. The distance from A to B is given by

$$h(A,B) = \max_{a \in A} \min_{b \in B} \|a - b\|$$

(4)

This measures the maximum distance from a point in A to its nearest point in B. The main strength of the Hausdorff distance is that it does

Figure 8. The MHI (a) and detected edges (b)

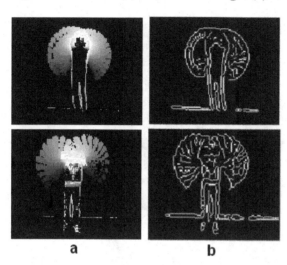

a   b

Figure 9. (a) Rectangular block for edges detected for the cropped MHI from individual I1 (b) Dilated image from the edge detected and cropped MHI for individual I1

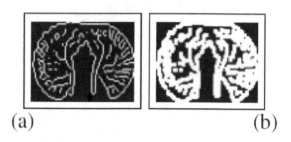

(a)   (b)

not require that points in A and B exactly match (Huttenlocher, Klanderman & Rucklidge, 1993). In particular, moving the points by a small amount only changes the Hausdorff distance by a small amount. This is extremely important for recognizing objects based on their shapes. Here the modified version of the Hausdorff distance method is used based on Felzenszwalb's work (Felzenszwalb, 2001). The partial Hausdorff distance from A to B is defined as

$$h_K\left(A,B\right) = K^{th}_{a \in A} \min_{b \in B} \|a - b\|$$

(5)

where K^{th} denotes the Kth largest value. For example, by taking K = |A|/2, the partial distance reflects the median distance from points in A to their closet points in B. Note that $h_K(A,B) \le d$ holds exactly when at least K points from A are at a distance at most d from some point in B. It is common to interpret this decision function using the notation of dilation. The dilation of B by r is denoted B^r and it consists of the set of points that are at a distance at most r from some point in B. Using the concept of dilation, $h_K(A,B) \le d$ holds when at least K points from A are contained in B^d. Now remember that A and B correspond to

points from images. These sets can be represented as n dimensional vectors, where n is the number of pixels in the images. Let A be the vector representation of A. A is a binary vector, where the ith dimension indicates if the ith pixel in the image is in A. Using the vector representation of the sets, the number of points from **A** contained in **B^d** is exactly the dot product **A.B^d**. So the decision function is represented based on the Hausdorff distance as a linear threshold function:

$$h_K(A,B) \le d \ \hat{U} \ A \cdot B^d \ge K$$

(6)

Approach-2

The method that described in approach-1 is invariant with translation, scale and rotation. But to make invariant on transformations, the edge detected MHI images are manually cropped and resized in approach-1. In approach-2 the manual operations, such as crop and resize, are ignored. Instead in this approach-2 the Hu moments are directly applied to the calculated MHI image to get the seven dimensional (7D) transformation invariant feature vector. Based on these feature vectors a Support Vector Machines (SVM) classification is applied for individual identification.

Hu Moments

Invariants based on moments of the coefficients are used up to third order. Traditionally, these features have been widely used in pattern recognition applications to recognize the geometrical shapes of different objects. A density distribution function f (Hu, 1962) is taken for calculation. The $(p+q)^{th}$ order central moment $\mu_{pq}(f)$ of f is given by

$$\mu_{pq}(f) = \int_R \int_R (x - x_c)^p (y - y_c)^q f(x, y)(x - x_c)(y - y_c)$$

(7)

where (x_c, y_c) is the center of mass and $(p, q) \in N$. Here R represents the set of real numbers and N represents the set of all natural numbers.

The Homogeneity Condition

The following orthogonal (and translational) invariants have been derived by Hu (1962).

$$I_1 = \mu_{20} + \mu_{02}$$

(8)

$$I_2 = (\mu_{20} - \mu_{02})^2 + 4\mu_{11}^2$$

(9)

$$I_3 = (\mu_{30} - 3\mu_{12})^2 + (3\mu_{21} - \mu_{03})^2$$

(10)

$$I_4 = (\mu_{30} + \mu_{12})^2 + (\mu_{21} + \mu_{03})^2$$

(11)

$$I_5 = (\mu_{30} - 3\mu_{12})(\mu_{30} + \mu_{12})((\mu_{30} + \mu_{12})^2 - 3(\mu_{21} + \mu_{03})^2) + (3\mu_{21} - \mu_{03})(\mu_{21} + \mu_{03})(3(\mu_{03} + \mu_{12})^2 - (\mu_{21} + \mu_{03})^2)$$

(12)

$$I_6 = (\mu_{20} - \mu_{02})((\mu_{30} + \mu_{12})^2 - (\mu_{21} + \mu_{03})^2) + 4\mu_{11}(\mu_{30} + \mu_{12})(\mu_{21} + \mu_{03})$$

(13)

$$I_7 = (3\mu_{21} - \mu_{03})(\mu_{30} + \mu_{12})((\mu_{30} + \mu_{12})^2 - 3(\mu_{21} + \mu_{03})^2) - (\mu_{30} - 3\mu_{12})(\mu_{21} + \mu_{03})(3(\mu_{30} + \mu_{12})^2 - (\mu_{21} + \mu_{03})^2)$$

(14)

Naively, it might composes the following feature vector $I \in R^7$:

$$I = [I_1 I_2 I_3 I_4 I_5 I_6 I_7]$$

(15)

Without scaling of the elements the computation of the Euclidean norm of the difference between such feature vectors leads to arbitrary results. Therefore it proceeds as follows. Firstly, it is observed that

$$\mu_{pq}(\lambda f) = \lambda \mu_{pq}(f), \text{ for all } \lambda^1 0$$

(16)

The homogeneity condition means that we demand a homogeneous change in the elements of a feature vector if the density distribution f is multiplied by the said scalar λ. Obviously, this condition is not satisfied by equations (8-15) (Zeeuw, 2002). The following operator is applied based on (Zeeuw, 2002):

$$R_p(u) = sign(u)|u|^{1/p} \text{ for } p \in N \text{ and } u \in R$$

(17)

When applied to an invariant I_k it produces again an invariant. It can easily be verified that the feature vector,

$$\hat{I} = [I_1 R_2(I_2) R_3(I_3) R_4(I_4) R_5(I_5) R_6(I_6) R_7(I_7)]$$

(18)

does satisfy the homogeneity condition (Zeeuw, 2002). This vector is used as the feature vector for this approach.

Support Vector Machine (SVM)

The problem of learning a binary classifier can be expressed as that of learning the function f: $R^n \rightarrow \pm1$ that maps patterns x onto their correct classification y as $y = f(x)$. In the case of an SVM, the function f takes the form

$$f_{svm}(x) = \sum_{i=1}^{N} y_i \alpha_i k(x, x_i) + b$$

(19)

where N is the number of training patterns, (x_i, y_i) is training pattern i with its classification, α_i and b are learned weights, and k(., .) is a kernel function. Here, a linear function is used as the kernel for which $\alpha_i > 0$ are denoted support vectors. The surface *f(x) = 0* defines a hyperplane through the feature space as defined by the kernel k (.,.). The weights α_i and b are selected so that the number of incorrect classifications in the training set is minimized, while the distances from this hyperplane to the support vectors are maximized. This is achieved by solving the optimization problem (Gunn, 1998).

Minimize

$$\alpha^* = \arg\min_{\alpha} \frac{1}{2} \sum_{i=1}^{N} \sum_{j=1}^{N} \alpha_i \alpha_j y_i y_j k(x_i, x_j) - \sum_{k=1}^{N} \alpha_i$$

with constraints, (20)

$$0 \leq \alpha_i \leq C, \sum_{i=1}^{N} y_i \alpha_i = 0$$

The constant C affects the tolerance to incorrect classifications. Using optimal parameters α_i, Equation (19) with any support vector (x_i, y_i) as in data can be used to find b. In each binary SVM, only one class is labelled as "1" and the other is labelled as "-1". The one-versus-all method uses a winner-takes-all strategy. Multi-class SVMs are usually implemented by combining several two-class SVMs. If there are M classes, SVM will construct M binary classifiers by learning. The multi-class SVMs are used in the experiments.

Individual Identification Using "Partial Gait" Sequences

The aim of this work is to recognize individuals using the "style of walk" information alone. That is, the same person can act in walking sequences with different types and colour of clothing, even though the algorithm needs to recognize that individual properly.

This work considers the fronto-parallel view of a walking person to be that which is perpendicular to the direction of walk. The image sequences of

four individuals (A, B, C and D) are collected using a stationery camera i.e. walk image sequences with static background.

Silhouette Feature Extraction

To remove the effect of changing clothing colour, only the silhouettes of the walking subjects are used in the representation. In addition, the silhouettes are scaled to remove the effect of changing depth of the walking subject in the view of the camera. For the foreground segmentation the background subtraction is applied and then binarized using a suitable threshold. Morphological operators such as erosion and dilation (Rafael & Richard, 2003) are first used to further filter spurious pixels. Small holes inside the extracted silhouettes are then filled. A connected component extraction is finally applied to extract a connected region with the largest size motion area of the walking human. The motion area included by the bounding box (Figure 10) is cropped, then re-scaled using a bilinear method (Rafael & Richard, 2003) into a fixed size SxS image (S = 64, number of pixels). Figure 11 shows normalized silhouettes of two individual's walking sequences.

The size of these cropped images is considerable. Therefore a dimensionality reduction needs to be applied before applying the classification algorithm. This is done using Principal Components Analysis (PCA) on those images.

Dimensionality Reduction

Dimensionality Reduction using PCA is applied successfully in many applications. Sirovich et al (Sirovich & Kirby, 1987) has applied this technique for face recognition. In this work also the PCA technique is used for individual recognition.

The image set is defined as $\{y(i)| \; i = 1, 2, \ldots, M\}$, where M is the number of images in the set. Next the average image $\hat{y}$ is calculated, which is the mean image of all images in the set. An image matrix P is constructed by subtracting $\hat{y}$ from each image and stacking the resulting vectors column-wise. Let, P be NxM, where N is the number of pixels in each image.

In this experiment 114 images are used for training, i.e. M = 114. Each image size is 64x64, i.e. N = 4096 and N > M. If we consider the covariance matrix Q, where Q=PP^T, then Q is NxN and N>M. Calculation of the eigenvectors of a matrix as large as Q is computationally intensive. For improvement the implicit covariance matrix $\hat{Q}$ is used, where: $\hat{Q} = P^TP$. Note that $\hat{Q}$ is an MxM matrix and therefore much smaller than Q. Here M eigenvectors of $\hat{Q}$ can be computed. These can be computed much faster than the first M eigenvectors of Q due to the disparity in the size of the two matrices. It can be shown that the M largest eigenvalues and corresponding eigenvectors of Q can be determined from the M eigenvalues and eigenvectors of $\hat{Q}$ as: $\lambda_i = \hat{\lambda}_i$, and $e_i = \hat{\lambda}^{-1/2}P\hat{e}_i$ (Nayar, Murase & Nene, 1986). Here, λ_i and e_i are the ith eigenvalue and eigenvector of Q, while $\hat{\lambda}_i$ and $\hat{e}_i$ are the ith eigenvalue and eigenvector of $\hat{Q}$. Previous research has proved that only a few eigenvectors are necessary for visual recognition. Therefore, we use the first k eigenvectors calculated corresponding to the largest k eigenvalues. The k-dimensional subspace spanned by these eigenvectors is called the eigenspace. Singular Value Decomposition (SVD) is applied to the data set as N is much larger than M (Nayar, Murase & Nene, 1986). It is not viable, however, when more than M eigenvectors are needed.

Figure 12 shows the eigenvalues calculated

Figure 10. Silhouette extraction method

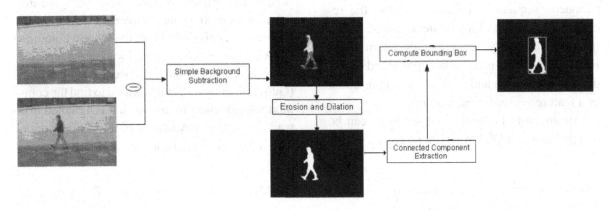

Figure 11. The silhouettes of individuals A and B's walking sequences

Figure 12. Eigenvalues obtained from applying SVD algorithm on the entire training sequence

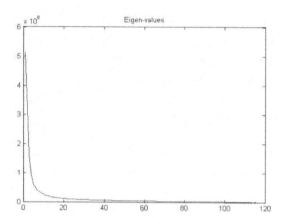

by the SVD algorithm for the training image sequence. The first 40 eigenvalues are greater than zero and then the eigenvalues tend to zero. Therefore, the first 40 eigenvectors corresponding to these 40 eigenvalues are used to reconstruct silhouette sequences. Figure 13 shows the reconstruction result of a silhouette image. Using this dimensionality reduction algorithm, each image in the sequence can be represented by a k dimensional vector and this vector is represented as a feature vector for each image.

An image in the individual sequence can be mapped to a point $f(i)$, where $f(i) = [e_1, e_2, ..., e_k]$ $^{T}y(i)$, in the eigenspace. Here, $f(i)$ is the kth dimensional feature vector for image $y(i)$. Therefore, a sequential movement can be represented as a trajectory in the eigenspace. An example of walking patterns for four different individuals is shown in Figure 14. This is the eigenspace representation of the individual trajectory manifolds.

Recognition Stage

Walking sequences are periodic and cyclic. In the walking sequence all the phases which match the known poses are called a walk-cycle. An example of a human walk-cycle is shown in Figure 15. If an image sequence contains a walk-cycle then that sequence can be called a full walking sequence.

Murase et al (Murase & Sakai, 1996) and He et al (He & Debrunner, 2000) assumed their database had the full cyclic walking sequence data. If any sequence does not have a walk-cycle then it can say those sequences are partial sequences. For the partial case the above two methods did not give any solution for partial data comparison. To solve this problem, it is needed to find the longest common subsequence from both partial walking sequences. The Longest Common Sequence (LCS) algorithm (Guo & Siegelmann, 2004) is used to find the common subsequence. In this work it is assumed that walk sequences may consist of full cyclic motion data or partial motion data.

Figure 13. Left: Silhouette obtained from test sequence. Middle: Mean image. Right: Reconstructed image using first 40 eigenvectors

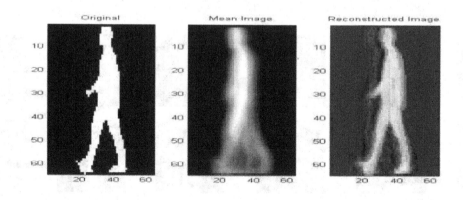

Figure 14. Trajectory of 4 individuals in 3D space made of first 3 eigenvectors

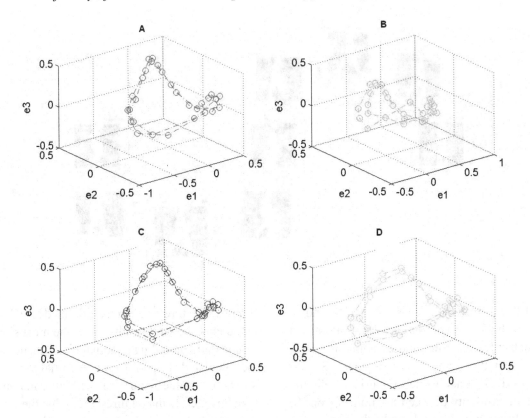

Longest Common Subsequence

The Longest Common Sequence (LCS) Algorithm finds the longest subsequence that two sequences have in common, regardless of the length and number of intermittent non-matching symbols. For example, the sequences "abcdefg" and "axbydezzz" have a sequenced length of four ("abde") as their longest common subsequence. Figure 16 given below shows further information.

Formally, the LCS problem is defined as follows: Given a sequence $X=(x_1, x_2,...,x_m)$, and a sequence $Y=(y_1,y_2,...,y_n)$, find a longest common sequence $Z=(z_1,z_2,...,z_k)$. The solution to the LCS problem involves solving the following recurrence equation, where the cost for the edit operations stored in C is:

$$C(i,j) = \begin{cases} 0 & if(i=0)or(j=0) \\ C(i-1,j-1)+1 & if(i,j>0)and(x_i=y_j) \\ \max[C(i,j-1),C(i-1,j)] & if(i,j>0)and(x_i \ne y_j) \end{cases}$$

(21)

Using LCS as a similarity measure between two sequences has the advantage that the two sequences can have different lengths and have intermittent non-matches. In the context of individual recognition, this allows for the use of partial walking sequences with noisy inputs.

Given two image sequences (S1 and S2) the 40-dimensional feature vector is calculated, as described before, for each frame in those sequences. Further those vectors are normalized to unit length to then apply the correlation measure between two frames: c = xᵀy, where c is the correlation value between 0 and 1, x and y are the normalized vec-

Figure 15. The silhouettes from a walk-cycle

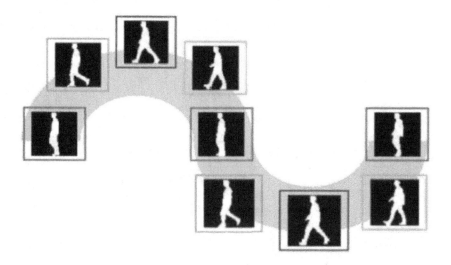

tors of the corresponding frames from S_1 and S_2 respectively. These correlation values are stored in a matrix C. The rows and columns in matrix C represent the frames from sequence S_1 and S_2 respectively. Each value in matrix C tells the degree of similarity between the frames from S_1 and S_2. From experimental results the correlation value greater then or equal to 0.7 gives similar

frames. The threshold value is defined as 0.7 from good experimental results. Now the most similar frames corresponding to both these sequences can be calculated. To do this, it is essential to find the maximum value for each row. If that maximum value is greater than a threshold value then it can be say that the frames represented by the rows and columns are similar (or equal).

Figure 16. The longest common sequence "abde" found from the two strings "abcdefg" and "axbydezzz" using LCS algorithm

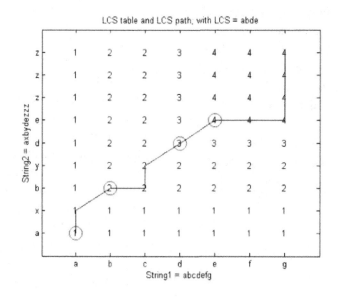

It is important to find the similar frames before applying the LCS algorithm as there is a calculation in LCS algorithm that, if $(x_i = y_j)$ then $c(i, j) = c(i-1, j-1) + 1$. A set of pair of frames can be found using the Longest Common Sequence algorithm, which are similar frames from two walk sequences S1 and S2. The values from the matrix C corresponding to each pair of frames from the set are summed and finally we find the mean value. This mean value gives the final measure of the two sequences.

INDIVIDUAL IDENTIFICATION USING "STYLE OF MULTIPLE ACTIONS"

The image sequences of three individuals (A, B, and C) are taken. The local space-time intensity gradient (Sx, Sy, St) is calculated at each space-time point (x, y, t) for each frame in the sequence. The absolute values of the temporal derivatives are found in all pixels of the image frame and ignore all space-time points (x, y, t) for which the temporal derivative is below some threshold, thus performing the calculation mostly on the points which participate in the event. Let the thresholded image with the detected object be divided into 10 x 10 bins.

Each bin has a numeric value of the total number of pixels which have non-zero values. The values in each bin are stacked into a 100-dimensional vector. This 100-dimensional vector is used as a feature to represent each frame (Figure 17).

There are many actions available from the individuals image sequences: enter, pick up the pen, sit down, write their name, get up and leave etc. The frames are clustered into groups to represent the actions (here it is assumed that the number of groups = 9). Consider the whole image frames from these three image sequences and apply the K-means algorithm. After clustering, the 100-D vectors in each cluster represent similar actions. The mean of the vectors from each cluster is calculated and this mean vector is the "code-word". Each code-word represents a different action.

For the purpose of individual re-identification a similarity measure is needed to match a new image sequence against the image sequences those already stored in a database and find whether or not the same individual appears in those sequences.

Figure 17. 100D feature vector generation for image frame in sequence

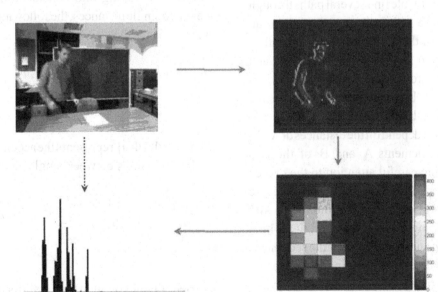

If two image sequences are captured from a particular person in a different time then the length of these two sequences need not be with the equal number of frames depending on both the speed and movement performance. Therefore image sequence alignment is important for the similarity measure. Here the DTW (Dynamic Time Warping) (Andrea, 2001) alignment algorithm is used for sequence alignment with an assumption that start and end frames are correctly aligned.

Dynamic Time Warping (DTW) Algorithm

The DTW algorithm is successfully applied in the previous research such as speech recognition and DNA sequence analysis, etc. This algorithm performs time alignment and normalization by computing a temporal transformation allowing two sequences to be matched. The DTW algorithm is discussed based on (Andrea, 2001).

When compare two distinct sequences A_n and B_m of length n and m, respectively, the variation in duration must not play a significant part of the determination of their similarity score. To find the best alignment between A and B one needs to find the minimum distance path through the grid (see Figure 18). It is possible find several paths through the grid, and one path will give the minimum distance between them. In Figure 18, the path $P = \{p_1, ..., p_s, ..., p_k\}$, where $p_s = \{i_s, j_s\}$ and i_s and j_s are the indices from A and B, which minimizes the total distances between them, i.e. P gives the best alignment path between A and B.

This path must depend on the distances $d(A_i, B_j)$ between single elements A_i and B_j of the two sequences paying careful attention to the choice of the indices i and j. Hence, such a measure can define only after finding two monotonically increasing warping functions Φ_a and Φ_b, which both preserve the temporal order of the sequences and relate the indices of their individual elements to the common time index t. Mathematically, this is expressed as:

Figure 18. The warping function

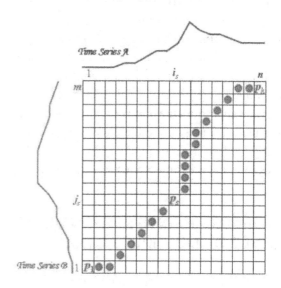

$$\begin{cases} \Phi_a(t-1) \leq \Phi_a(t) \, \Phi_b(t-1) \leq \Phi_b(t) \\ \Phi_a(t) = i \qquad\qquad \Phi_b(t) = j \end{cases} \tag{22}$$

Since there are a lot of possible functions, the similarity measure between a pair of patterns A_n and B_m can be consistently defined by taking the warping functions which minimize the accumulated sum of weighted single element similarities. Taking into consideration all these weighted single distances, the following similarity function is used.

$$d_{(\Phi_a, \Phi_b)}(A_n, B_m) = \min_{(\Phi_a, \Phi_b)} \left\{ s(\Phi_a, \Phi_b) \right\} \tag{23}$$

where $s\{(\Phi_a, \Phi_b)\}$ represents the accumulated sum of the distortions between single elements, i.e.

$$s(\Phi_a, \Phi_b) = \frac{1}{W(\Phi_a, \Phi_b)} \sum_{t=1}^{T} d\left(A_{\Phi_a(t)}, B_{\Phi_b(t)}\right) w(t) \tag{24}$$

Here T is the common time scale for the warping function Φ_a and Φ_b. Also $w(t)$ is a non-negative weighting function in terms of the common axis index which takes into account the temporal variability of the movement by controlling the contributions of each short-term distortion $d\left(A_{\Phi_a(t)}, B_{\Phi_b(t)}\right)$. The term $W(\Phi_a, \Phi_b)$ is a global normalization factor which is usually set to,

$$W\left(\Phi_a, \Phi_b\right) = \sum_{t=1}^{T} w(t) \quad (25)$$

A time alignment between two sequences can be seen as a path through a 2-dimensional lattice structure in which the single sequence components of the first sequence are reported along the x-axis and the second along the y-axis. Equation (22) is then evaluated exactly at the points the path traverses.

Finding the best alignment between two sequences amounts to determining the path which leads to a global minimum distance value among all allowable routes through the grid. Each path represents a mapping of the other sequence according to the chosen warping functions. Since start and end points of both sequences fix a temporal limit for the movement, besides the monotonicity constraint, the warping functions must satisfy the additional conditions:

$$\begin{cases} \Phi_a\left(1\right) = \Phi_b\left(1\right) = 1 \\ \Phi_a\left(T\right) = n \quad \Phi_b\left(T\right) = m \end{cases} \quad (26)$$

Next local continuity constraints are defined to express the allowable individual moves to reach a given point within the grid structure. It is easy to verify that these constraints cause some points of the grid to be excluded from the region which can be crossed be the optimal path. There are many local continuity constraints applicable to the DTW algorithm. As a local continuity constraint a particular type of DTW algorithm called the Quasi-symmetric DTW Algorithm (Andrea, 2001) is used for application. Locally, the values

of the weighting function w(t) are associated with the path constraints to express a preference for allowable pathways. The function w(t) is called a slope weighting function since it is related to the slope of the local path constraints. Larger function values indicate less preferable paths as a higher local difference represents a less likely match.

An efficient method for minimizing the distance function in equation (23) with embedded time alignment and normalization results from the application of the dynamic programming technique. The fundamental idea is a recursive decomposition of the optimization problem into sub-problems assuming the Bellman's principle of optimality stating that all sub-problem solutions are already optimal solutions. Define a path from node (s, t) to (u, v), $\{(s, t), (i_1, j_1), (i_2, j_2), ..., (u, v)\}$. Bellman's principle of optimality: $(s, t) \rightarrow (u, v) = (s, t) \rightarrow (w, x) * (w, x) \rightarrow (u, v)$ where $*$ denotes concatenation of the path segments. In the case paths of the optimal one are already paths with minimal distance. That is, we do not need to exhaustively search for the best path. Instead we can build the best path by considering a sequence of partial paths and retaining the best local path. The same slope weighting function is used as described in (Andrea, 2001):

$$w(t) = \Phi_a(t) - \Phi_a(t-1) + \Phi_b(t) - \Phi_b(t-1) \quad (27)$$

which locally attempts to maintain a strong bias toward non diagonal path movements. Due to this selection the global normalization factor $W(\Phi_a, \Phi_b)$ in equation (22) results to assume the expression

Method

a) Take an image sequence that needs to be matched to another sequence.

b) For each frame in the image sequence, find the most suitable code-word. This operation converts an image frame sequence into a code-word sequence.

c) Apply the DTW algorithm for code-word sequences to do alignment and find the distance. Actually this alignment is based on actions.

EXPERIMENTAL RESULTS

First the individual identification experiment is considered using "hand waving" action sequences. A challenging database (http://www.nada.kth.se/cvap/actions/ - retrieved on 29/08/08) of action sequences is used for the evaluation,. Actually the outdoor sequences are very challenging. Figure 19, the out door action sequences, shows the variation of light, scale of the individual's appearance and texture of clothing are different from the training sequences (indoor action sequences).

Results from Periodicity Detection

Table 1 shows periodicity detection results for 6 different individuals using our periodicity detection method. As is common in periodicity estimation we use the average value of the periodicities computed over several cycles. However, the pe-

riodicity is used as half the computed periodicity as it only considers motion from the bottom to the top. Compared with the manual periodicity detection results, the periodicity method's experimental results show that it is very accurate and reliable for periodicity detection.

Results from approach-1

Here two experiments are discussed. In experiment 1, the indoor sequences are divided into two equal parts and used the first half of the sequence for training and the second half for testing. In experiment 2, indoor sequences are used for training and outdoor sequences for testing. In total 25 individuals were used for these two experiments. The reference template that is used for the similarity measure for the sample of 6 individuals is shown in Figure 20.

Similarity measure matrices between individual's indoor-indoor and indoor-outdoor sequences are shown in Tables 2 and 3 respectively. Here, the already known individuals are represented by the reference templates R1, R2..., R25. The row templates are taken from unknown individuals (T1, T2,..., T25) and the system needs to find which individual appears in each sequence. The values

Figure 19. Challenging test sequences that were used for individual recognition. Each image represents a different individual

Table 1. Periodicity detection (number of frames) using the automated method

Individuals	InSeq		OutSeq	
	auto.	manual	auto.	manual
I1	20	20	20	20
I2	16	17	18	18
I3	21	22	22	22
I4	17	17	17	17
I5	19	19	18	19
I6	18	18	18	18

of Tables 2 and 3 show the similarity measures between two sequences calculated using the partial hausdorff distance method. The maximum value in each row indicates a high similarity between that particular reference (known) and unknown individuals.

The values corresponding to (T3, R3) from Tables 2 and 3 are 307 and 296. It is already known that R3 represents individual 3. Therefore 290 is technically defined as threshold value to recognise T3 as individual 3. Based on this concept using Tables 2 and 3 threshold values (340, 350, 290,

Figure 20. MHI template images for 6 individuals

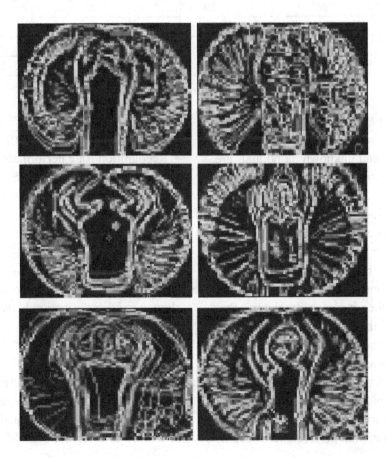

Table 2. Similarity measure matrix for indoor - indoor (InIn) sequences

Individuals	R1	R2	R3	R4	R5	-	R24	R25
T1	*370*	313	212	262	264	-	256	216
T2	314	*397*	244	281	278	-	281	272
T3	225	246	*307*	202	200	-	204	280
T4	268	264	207	*284*	219	-	236	296
T5	251	268	206	234	*296*	-	314	251
-	-	-	-	-	-	-	-	-
T24	234	292	250	212	288	-	*348*	280
T25	238	299	262	270	254	-	304	*314*

Table 3. Similarity measure matrix for indoor - outdoor (InOut) sequences

Individuals	R1	R2	R3	R4	R5	-	R24	R25
T1	*358*	273	282	274	280	-	269	271
T2	306	*364*	161	290	268	-	286	286
T3	213	208	*296*	221	224	-	240	251
T4	268	242	247	*286*	246	-	287	268
T5	256	260	226	231	*282*	-	268	264
-	-	-	-	-	-	-	-	-
T24	207	298	249	296	272	-	*306*	264
T25	256	285	264	268	257	-	256	*298*

280, 280,..., 300,290) are defined for individuals (I1, I2, ..., I25) respectively. It is accepted that reference (known) and unknown individuals are similar if the similarity measure value is greater than or equal to the predefined threshold value. Based on these threshold values, a recognition rate performance is computed for the individual recognition system. The 1250 samples are used for the performance rate recognition, i.e. 625 samples from each Table. Considering columns R4 and R5 in Tables 2 and 3 then it can easily identify that five values greater than or equal to 280 as well as the diagonal values. It is then assumed that the diagonal values assure recognition of similar individuals. Therefore these five values are giving a "false recognition". A total of 122 "false recognitions" were indentified from experiments 1 and 2. The experimental performance recogni-

tion rate is given by: $RR = \frac{PN}{TS} * 100$, where RR = Recognition Rate performance, PN = Positive or Negative samples and TS = Total Samples. The experimental results gave Positive and False Recognition rates of 90.24% (i.e. 1128/1250) and 9.76% (i.e. 122/1250) respectively. To the best of our knowledge, currently any other research or experimental results do not available to compare these experimental research results with. Results show good discrimination between individuals.

Results from Approach-2

Here 7D Hu moments are used as a feature vector for the SVM training and testing. A total of 25 individuals are taken from the database. Twenty five different SVM classifiers (i.e. SVM01, SVM02,...,

Table 4. SVM classification results for InOut sequences

Classifiers	I1	I2	I3	I4	-	I24	I25
SVM01	*-0.38*	-1.00	-0.64	-1.00	-	-1.00	-0.43
SVM02	-1.00	*0.58*	-1.00	-1.00	-	-0.65	0.02
SVM03	-0.96	-1.00	*0.53*	-1.00	-	-0.93	-0.82
SVM04	-1.00	-1.00	-1.00	*1.00*	-	-1.00	-0.91
-	-	-	-	-	-	-	-
SVM24	-1.00	-0.75	-1.00	-1.00	-	*0.46*	-0.87
SVM25	-0.40	-1.00	-1.00	-0.89	-	-1.00	*1.00*

SVM25) are generated for 25 individuals. These classifiers are used to classify the new individuals whether they are already known or not. In training, +1 and -1 are assigned for positive and negative samples respectively. Therefore individuals are recognised based on the table values greater than 0. Table 4 shows the classification results against individuals (I1, I2,..., I25). If the row SVM01 is considered against column I1 (i.e.−0.38) and SVM02 against I25 (i.e.0.02) then these values represent misclassification. In addition 19 further misclassifications are identified in the experiments. Otherwise each of the SVM classifiers recognised individuals correctly. For example, say SVMC3 recognised I3 as positive and the remainder of the individuals as negative. A 96.64% (i.e. 604/625) positive recognition rate and a 3.36% (i.e. 21/625) negative recognition rate are calculated from this experiment. This is a better result than our previous approach.

Results for "Partial Gait" Sequences

In Table 5, the already known individual's data is represented in rows. Frames 1 to 8 are taken from this data as a partial sequence. The column data are taken from the unknown individuals and there is a need to find which individuals appear in those sequences. Frames 4 to 13 are taken from this data as partial data. It can be expect that the common subsequence should contain frames 4 to 8. Due to noise it varies slightly.

For the maximum value in each column it can find the corresponding row (i.e, column represents the unknown person). This maximum value indicates the high similarity between the row and column. Therefore individuals appearing in corresponding rows and columns are the same person. Here also the threshold value is defined as 0.9 for good experimental results. Therefore if the highest value is greater than this threshold value then we accept that the same person is available in both sequences.

Table 5. Similarity matrix for known - unknown sequences

Individuals	1-Seq	2-Seq	3-Seq	4-Seq
S1	*0.9458*	0.8305	0.8908	0.8542
S2	0.7586	*0.9877*	0.8036	0.8006
S3	0.8979	0.8748	*0.9571*	0.8867
S4	0.8735	0.7285	0.8783	*0.9031*

Table 6. Similarity matrix for known - unknown sequences

Individuals	A1	A2	A3
A2	*0.0608*	0.2213	0.2976
B2	0.2543	*0.0698*	0.2588
C2	0.2514	0.1179	*0:0917*

Significant progress has been made in individual identification using their "style of walk" over the past few years. Compared with Gait i.e. "style of walk", not much progress has been made in individuals recognition using their "style of actions".

Results for Multiple Action Sequences

Three individuals have chosen for this experiment: individuals A, B and C with similar height and width. Table 6 shows the time normalized accumulated distance between individual's sequences (see Figure 21). The diagonal elements represent the smallest value in each row. The smallest value shows that individuals appearing in the two sequences are similar based on their "style of doing actions" i.e. "behavioural biometric characteristics".

CONCLUSION

In this chapter, several new systems are proposed for individual recognition using their "style of single action" and "style of multiple actions". They can be applied individually to identify individuals in video sequences. For the "style of action" based individual identification the hand waving action is considered for approach-1 and approach-2. Firstly a periodicity detection method calculates the number of frames involved in the action of each individual. Secondly, a Motion History Image (MHI) is extracted directly from the images using the detected number of frames.

In the approach-1, the canny edge detector is applied to the motion history image to generate the feature vector. Feature reference templates are generated for each individual and stored in the database. The partial Hausdorff Distance

Figure 21. The path with the minimum distance between two individuals sequences. Path towards the diagonal gives the minimum distance

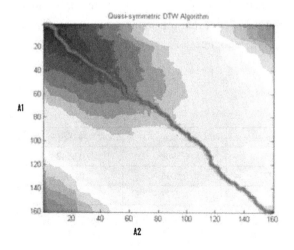
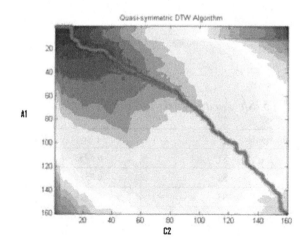

measure is applied for the similarity measure between reference templates and new individuals feature template to find out whether the new individuals are already known. This approach is invariant to transformation variations as dilation and partial Hausdorff distance are used. However it is partially dependent on manual operations such as cropping and resizing.

To overcome the manual operations in the second approach, Hu moments are applied directly to the MHI images for feature generation. Then SVM classification is applied on these feature vectors and the results show a good recognition rate. This approach does not include any manual operations. Edge detection is dependency by light conditions. Therefore approach-1's accuracy may be affected by light conditions. MHI may not prove to be a good solution if the actions which overlap occur. In that case instead of MHI the Motion History Volume (MHV) can be used. Also tree theory could be investigated in future work for matching the detected edges in approach-1.

Further "style of action" based individual identification, the partial gait sequences are also used for individual identification. Here the LCS (Longest Common Sequences) algorithm is used for the similarity measure calculation. Reasonable results are obtained from this experiment. The "Style of multiple actions" based individual identification approach considered the sequence of particular actions (i.e., sit down, write name, stand up etc.). It gave good similarity measures between two different individuals' actions sequences based on DTW similarity measure. The main constraint in the DTW method is that the first and last frames in the video sequence should be aligned properly. Ongoing work applies N-Cut clustering to individual's video sequences.

All the above approaches could be applied as behavioural characteristics for multi-biometric individual recognition systems.

REFERENCES

Andrea, C. (2001). Dynamic time warping for offline recognition of a small gesture vocabulary. *International Conference on Recognition, Analysis and Tracking of Faces and Gestures in Real-Time Systems* (pp. 82-89).

Bobick, A., & Davis, J. (2001). The recognition of human movement using temporal templates. [PAMI]. *IEEE Transactions on Pattern Analysis and Machine Intelligence, 23*(3), 257–266. doi:10.1109/34.910878

Bobick, A. F., & Johnson, A. Y. (2001). Gait recognition using static, activity specific parameters. *Proceedings of the IEEE Conference on Computer Vision and Pattern Recognition, CVPR* (pp. 423-430).

Canny, J. (1986). A computational approach to edge detection. *IEEE Trans. Pattern Analysis and. Machine Intelligence (PAM)I, 8*(6), 679-698.

Cutting, J., Prott, D., & Kozlowski, L. (1978). A biomechanical invariant for gait perception. *Journal of Experimental Psychology. Human Perception and Performance, 4*(3), 357–372. doi:10.1037/0096-1523.4.3.357

Davis, J. W., & Bobick, A. F. (1997). The representation and recognition of action using temporal templates. In *Proceedings of the IEEE Computer Society Conference on Computer Vision and Pattern Recognition* (pp. 928-934).

Felzenszwalb, P. F. (2001). Learning models for object recognition. *Proceedings of the IEEE Conference on Computer Vision and Pattern Recognition* (pp. 1056-1062).

Frischholz, R., & Dieckmann, U. (2000). BioID: A multimodal biometric identification system. *IEEE Computer, 33*(2), 64–68.

Gunn, S. R. (1998). *Support vector machines for classification and regression.* (Tech. Rep. No. 6459). Image, Speech, and Intelligent Systems Research Group, University of Southampton.

Guo, A., & Siegelmann, H. (2004). Time-warped longest common subsequence algorithm for music retrieval. *Proc of the Fifth International Conference on Music Information Retrieval (IS-MIR)* (pp. 10-14).

He, Q., & Debrunner, C. H. (2000). Individual recognition from periodic activity using hidden markov models. *Proceedings IEEE Workshop on Human Motion,* (pp. 47-52).

Hu, M. (1962). Visual pattern recognition by moment invariants. *I.R.E. Transactions on Information Theory, IT-8,* 179–187.

Huttenlocher, D. P., Klanderman, G. A., & Rucklidge, W. J. (1993). Comparing images using the Hausdorff distance. [PAMI]. *IEEE Transactions on Pattern Analysis and Machine Intelligence, 15*(9), 850–863. doi:10.1109/34.232073

Jain, A. K., Bolle, R., & Pankanti, S. (Eds.). (1999). *Biometrics: Personal identification in networked society.* Kluwer Academic Publishers.

Johansson, G. (1975). Visual motion perception. *Scientific American, 232*(6), 76–88.

Little, J. J., & Boyd, J. E. (1998). Recognizing people by their gait: The shape of motion. [The MIT Press.]. *Videre: Journal of Computer Vision Research, 1*(2), 1–32.

Liu, F., & Picard, R. W. (1998). Finding periodicity in space and time. *Proceedings of the IEEE Sixth International Conference on Computer Vision* (pp. 376-382).

Murase, H., & Sakai, R. (1996). Moving object recognition in eigenspace representation: Gait analysis and lip reading. *Pattern Recognition Letters, Elsevier Science, 17*(2), 155–162. doi:10.1016/0167-8655(95)00109-3

Nayar, S. K., Murase, M., & Nene, S. A. (1986). Parametric appearance representation. In *Early visual learning.* Oxford: Oxford University Press.

Nixon, M., Carter, J., Nash, J., Huang, P., Cunado, D., & Stevenage, S. (1999). Automatic gait recognition. *Proceedings of the IEE Colloquium on Motion Analysis and Tracking* (pp. 31-36).

Pankanti, S., & Jain, A. K. (2008). Beyond fingerprinting. *Scientific American,* 79–81.

Polana, R., & Nelson, R. (1993). Detecting activities. In *Proceedings of the IEEE Computer Society Conference on Computer Vision and Pattern Recognition* (pp. 2-7).

Pratheepan, Y., Prasad, G., & Condell, J. V. (2008). Style of action based individual recognition in video sequences. *Proceeding of the IEEE International Conference on Systems, Man, and Cybernetics (SMC)* (pp. 1237-1242).

Pratheepan, Y., Torr, P. H. S., Condell, J. V., & Prasad, G. (2008). Body language based individual identification in video using gait and actions. *The Third International Conference on Image and Signal Processing (ICISP)* (pp. 368-377).

Rafael, C. G., & Richard, E. W. (2003). *Digital image processing.* Pearson Education, second edition.

Sirovich, L., & Kirby, M. (1987). Low dimensional procedure for the characterization of human faces. *Journal of the Optical Society of America. A, Optics, Image Science, and Vision, 4*(3), 519–524. doi:10.1364/JOSAA.4.000519

Zeeuw, P. M. (2002). *A toolbox for the lifting scheme on quincunx grids (LISQ).* (Tech. Rep. PNA-R0224). Centrum voor Wiskunde en Informatica.

Chapter 5
Behavioral Biometrics:
A Biosignal Based Approach

Kenneth Revett
University of Westminster, UK

ABSTRACT

Behavioral biometrics is a relatively new form of authentication mechanism which relies on the way a person interacts with an authentication device. Traditional instances of this approach include voice, signature, and keystroke dynamics. Novel approaches to behavioral biometrics include biosignals, such as the electroencephalogram and the electrocardiogram. The biosignal approach to user authentication has been shown to produce equal error rates on par with more traditional behavioral biometric approaches. In addition, through a process similar to biofeedback, users can be trained with minimal effort to produce computer-based input via the manipulations of endogenous biosignal patterns. This chapter discusses the use of biosignal based biometrics, highlighting key studies and how this approach can be integrated into a multibiometric user authentication system.

INTRODUCTION

Behavioral biometrics is an approach to user verification and/or identification based on the *way* a person interacts with the biometrics device. Some of the most prominent instantiations include keystroke dynamics, mouse dynamics, signature, voice, gait, and odor (Revett, 2008). In order to serve as a biometric, the input must not only be unique, but must be convenient, reliable, and difficult to replicate.

The uniqueness of behavioral biometrics refers to individual differences in the way people interact with the verification device. With respect to signature verification as an example – how unique are our signatures? In part, this depends on how closely one looks at a signature. A clerk in a shop may provide a quick glance when comparing a signature to that written on the back of a credit card. At the other extreme, an off-line signature verification system may extract several features including pen pressure or wavelet transform of a digitized version when comparing a signature to a reference exemplar

DOI: 10.4018/978-1-60566-725-6.ch005

(Coetzer et al., 2004). The question remains - are signatures sufficiently unique to provide unequivocal person authentication? The data suggests that error rates on the order of 5% or less - depending on the verification methodology employed (see Kholmatov, 2001 for a comprehensive discussion on this topic) are obtainable. Other behavioral biometrics produce similar error rates – though large variations have been published, depending on the exemplar matching approach employed, the quality of the data, and the features extracted (see Revett, 2008 for details).

Convenience in the context of biometrics is intimately related to familiarity in many respects – if we are used to entering a password/PIN, then this form of user verification in the stricter context of biometrics is not prohibitive. Typically, most behavioral based biometrics utilize familiar functions and hence convenience is not an issue. For instance, gait analysis can be performed in real-time – for example, while users are approaching a gate at an airport. In addition, convenience refers to the level of invasiveness of the biometric. One may consider a retinal scan as invasive – simply because we are not used to engaging in such activities – even though there is no inherent risk to the user. This sense of user acceptability/convenience is one of the key factors in the rapid deployment of behavioral based biometrics.

The reproducibility factor refers to the trial-to-trial variation produced by a user when entering their biometric verification details. Are signatures constant over time, do we type exactly the same way, does our voice change with our state of health? The obvious answer is that there are variations in these behaviors as they are influenced by our emotional and/or physical state – which in turn influences our physiology/behavior in non-linear and potentially complex ways. To date, there has been no systematic study within the field of behavioral or physiological based biometrics that has investigated the issue of inherent variability on the resulting accuracy of the biometric. On the contrary, most research focuses on trying to

enhance accuracy by reducing data variability via filtering and deploying multiple machine learning techniques. Typically, the reproducibility is quantified by measuring the false acceptance rate (FAR) and the false rejection rate (FRR) has yet to be solved. Users wish to be authenticate without being rejected too frequently (thus minimizing FRR), while the possibility of a successful intruder is minimized (FAR). The cross-over error rate (CER) is defined as the intersection of the FAR/FRR, as a function of some authentication threshold. One can then equate reproducibility with the value of the CER – all other factors being held equal. The last factor to consider is the difficulty in replicating a user's authentication details – which is intimately related to uniqueness and reliability. For instance, a password that is drawn from a dictionary can easily be cracked using a dictionary based off-line attack. The information content of the biometric is critical in terms of discriminating the authentic owner from an impostor. The critical issue is the depth of the feature space of the biometric: how many features can be extracted from the authentication approach? In a noisy environment such as voice or signature – the cardinality of the feature space can compensate for the inherent noise levels. Clearly, enhancing the feature space of a biometric reduces the success rate of impostors (lowers FAR). One approach to augmenting the depth of the feature space is combining different authentication approaches – the multi-biometric approach. For instance, voice and signature, or password and voice can be employed together to enhance the degrees of freedom for classification purposes (see Ross & Jain, 2003). Again, there is a trade-off here – the richer the feature space – the more one has to remember – or at least the more one must practice their biometric details if they are behavioral.

In addition to the multi-biometric approach, one must consider whether we have exhausted the full spectrum of authentication approaches. In this chapter, the author proposes that there are additional biometric approaches that have not yet been fully explored: these are based on biosignals such as the use of the electrocardiogram (ECG) and electroencephalogram (EEG). The claim is that the deployment of biosignals provides at the very least a novel approach to user authentication that contains all the essential features of more traditional behavioral biometrics. The rest of this chapter is organized as follows. First, a general introduction to the respective biosignals is presented, followed by a series of case studies demonstrating the utility of these approaches. The issue of where biosignals actually fit into the physiological or behavioral biometric ontology is discussed as well. It is argued that they fit into the later framework – in which case the definitions and/or distinctions between physiological and behavioral biometrics needs addressing. The benefits of a fusion based approach (at the sensor level) is discussed, via a description of the ENOBIO sensor system. Lastly, the integration of the ENOBIO system into the HUMABIO virtual reality environment is discussed as a model of a potential future of behavioral biometrics.

BACKGROUND

The current frontier in behavioral biometrics is the deployment of biological based signals such as the electrocardiogram (ECG) and the electroencephalogram (EEG). These signals are generated by the heart and brain respectively – and are recorded using standard equipment in a generally non-invasive fashion. In one approach, the recorded signals are used directly as a biometric signature (which may be pre-processed). This approach relies on the inherent individuality of the biosignal. Several studies have examined the heritability – and thus the genetic basis for ECG and EEG signals (see van Beijsterveldt et al., 1995, Pilia et al., 2006, Tang et al., 2006, Dalageorgou et al., 2007 for more details). If there is a genetic basis for biosignals, then one can expect that there will be a significant level of individuality.

The data suggests that for ECG, there is genetics accounts for approximately 60% of the variability (Pilia et al., 2006). The authors claim that further variability can be accounted for by environmental factors such as diet and emotional state. These results imply that there may be distinct differences in features within ECGs that allow one to map an ECG to an individual. With respect to EEG, studies of sib-pair populations indicate that even subjects related genetically demonstrate inherent variability in their EEGs – especially when considering low and high alpha bands – upwards of 65% (see Tang et al., 2006, Chorlian et al., 2007). These results could be interpreted as defining an upper bound on the discriminative capacity of approaches relying solely on raw biosignal data. There is strangely not a lot of data that examines the general population with respect to inherent variability of biosignals. The data reported above is for genetically related individuals – which on the one hand might imply that those that are not genetically related would yield larger variability and hence more individuality. One the other hand – the populations are closed so to speak – and hence a larger more open population may yield more possibilities of duplicates arising. This clearly should be an area of active research – and we must wait for the data to draw any conclusions.

In addition to utilizing raw biosignal data, one can examine the effect of training- biofeedback – as a means of individualizing our biosignals. The interesting field of brain-computer interfacing (BCI) provides a wealth of data regarding the ability to modulate EEG rhythms through simple training procedures (applicable to the ECG?). The BCI industry developed as a tool for assisting people with disabilities (Birbaumer et al., 1999). The concepts developed were then applied to the human-computer interface more generally (Wolpaw et al., 2002). Currently, research efforts are underway to utilize this technology for biometric purposes (Thorpe et al., 2005). If through training – one can modify – or tailor our biosignals(both EEG and ECG) – then one can build upon the inherent variability due to genetics alone – and raise the expected ceiling of uniqueness to acceptable values. As many of the case studies presented later in this chapter indicate – the results in terms of classification accuracy are already quite significant without incorporating these issues. It would be very interesting to incorporate the biological aspects with the machine learning aspects (the current focus) to see just how far this envelope can be pushed in terms of classification accuracy.

There are several issues that must be addressed when deploying the biosignal approach to biometric based authentication. For one, what sort of equipment is required? The goal of behavioral biometrics is to minimize (if not eliminate) the amount of specialized equipment required for the authentication process. The second issue is how individual are these signals – are they sufficiently unique to allow them to be deployed for user verification purposes? This issue is critical – in terms of the likelihood of impostor success – and also, with respect to EEG as a tool for the brain-computer interface – how adaptable are these signals? In the next section, we explore the use of the ECG as a biometric, looking at the inherent variability of this technology with respect to signal production.

ECG Based Biometrics

The electrocardiogram (ECG) has a long and venerable history, beginning officially in 1887 with the first publication of a human electrocardiogram (Waller, 1887). The ECG is a record of the electrical activity of the heart, which generally follows an extremely rhythmic pattern. The basis of the ECG lies in the nervous innervation of the heart muscle, which consists of two separate pumps (left and right). In brief, the heart receives venous blood from the vena cava (inferior and superior), replenishes it with oxygen (via the pulmonary system), and then delivers oxygenated blood through the circulatory system (via the aorta). In order to control the activity of the heart, which consists

of millions of cardiac muscle fibers and related nervous tissue, the pumps must act in a coordinated fashion. The muscle fibers are connected together to form a large syncytium – a collection of cells that are electrically connected to one another, and therefore allow current to pass across the heart muscle very quickly. In addition to the left and right pumps, there is a further division, top (atria) and bottom (ventricles). These divisions are separated from one another through a non-conducting fibrous tissue that serves to electrically insulate them. Therefore, the atria and ventricles can function separately – the atria (contracting first) followed by ventricular contraction. In a typical cardiac cycle (the events that occur from one heartbeat to the next), the atria contract first (via the cardiac pacemaker, the sino-atrial node), and the current flows throughout the right and left atria. There is an electrical connection between the atria and the ventricles (the A-V bundle), which allows propagation of current from the atria to the ventricles, which react about 160 ms after the atria contract. This arrangement allows the ventricles to fill with blood before they contract. These electrical events form the basis of the electrocardiograph, and the resulting trace is what we typically term the ECG (axes are electrical potential (mV) over time (s)).

The ECG displays several characteristic inflection points, which impart the clinical utility of this biometric. These inflection points are labeled as: P wave, QRS complex, and the T wave (see Figure 1 for details). Typically, the QRS complex consists of the separate waves (Q, R, & S), but this is not always the case across subjects. The P wave is the result of depolarization of the atria (from the activity of the heart's pace maker, the sino-atrial node (SA node)), which is immediately followed by atrial contraction. After approximately 160 ms, the QRS complex occurs as the result of depolarization of the ventricles. Lastly, the T wave represents ventricular repolarization, that is the start of relaxation of the ventricles in preparation for the next cardiac cycle.

Figure 1. A typical ECG pattern for a single heart beat, with indications of the principle fiduciary marks and corresponding intervals which are typically used for feature construction for machine learning approaches to automated ECG classification (source: http://www.jonbarron.org/images/ecg2.jpg)

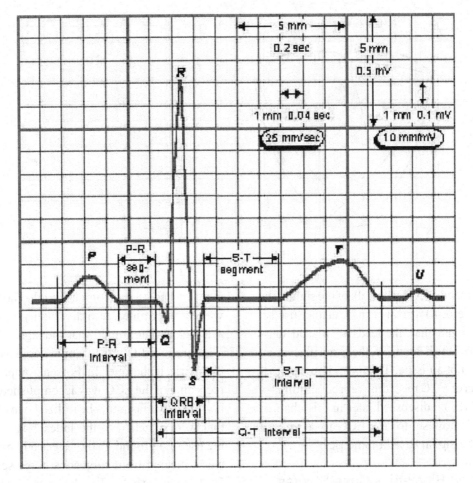

Note that there are other minor waves that occur – principally as a result in slight changes in pressure in the left and right atria (termed a, c and v waves). These will not be discussed further in this chapter, and the interested reader can consult textbooks on anatomy and physiology for more details (see Guyton and Hall, 2000, chapters 9-13). Given that the cardiac cycle is fairly consistent, what is required is a reliable means of recording the electrical impulses that generate the 5 inflection points.

There are several recording techniques that have been employed to generate an ECG. As with all electrical signal recordings from human tissue, specialized conductive leads are used to record the small electrical changes (on the order of 10 mV) associated with nervous tissue activity. Typically, what is termed a 12-lead ECG monitoring system is employed (see Figure 2 for details). These monitoring systems employ bipolar limb leads – the term bipolar indicates that the signal is recorded from different sides of the heart – such as the left and right limbs. Typically, 3 limb leads are used in producing a clinically useful ECG – labeled lead I (connected to left and right arms), lead II (connecting the right arm and left leg), and lead III (connecting the left arm and left leg). In addition, there are other leads – but the three

Figure 2. (A) The 10 ECG leads of Waller. (B) Einthoven limb leads and Einthoven triangle. The Einthoven triangle is an approximate description of the lead vectors associated with the limb leads (Source: http://butler.cc.tut.fi/~malmivuo/bem/bembook/15/15.htm)

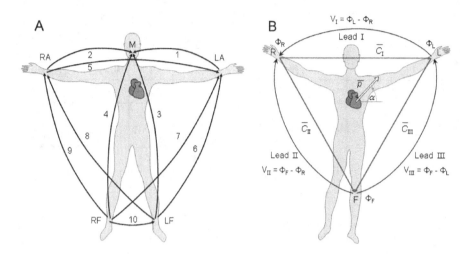

leads mentioned provide the bulk of the signal (the general waveform) typical of an ECG trace used in clinical settings. Since the leads are placed some distance from the heart itself, the exact placement is typically not an issue. This is an important issue in terms of ECG recording reproducibility – a topic that will be discussed later in this chapter. The stage is now set for the ECG to serve as a candidate biosignal based biometric.

ECG Based Biometrics Case Studies

The heartbeat can be used as a liveliness test – a test to see if the input signals presented are from a living person or a clever reproduction attempting to spoof the biometric sensor. In addition, it can be used as a legitimate biometric modality as first described by Forsen (Forsen et al., 1977). Since this idea was first proposed, several successful case studies deploying ECG have been published. In this section, a sample of published studies will be presented, focusing on the methodology and the resulting error rates.

The use of the ECG as a biometric was examined in detail by Forsen (Forsen et al., 1977), in a prescient paper that also discussed the deploy-

ment of EEG as a biometric tool. The first task was to determine the individuality of the ECG – if it was determined that the signal is unique – he proposed that this would serve as a useful biometric technique. In Forsen's approach, the recording of the ECG was accomplished in a very non-invasive fashion – he utilized two electrodes that were attached to the index fingers without the use of a ground lead or electrode paste. Data was collected from subjects at three sessions of 30-40 seconds each. The data was filtered with a 3 KHz cutoff frequency and the data was digitized for subsequent analysis (for more details consult Forsen et al., 1977). A total of 10 features were utilized for classification purposes: five time intervals and five amplitude differences. The time points correspond to the 5 major deflection points in the signal (labeled P,Q,R,S, & T). These features are utilized to produce a reference vector for the individual. When the same user requests authentication, several heartbeats are recorded (takes a few seconds only), and the average of the authentication request trials is compared with the reference vector. The results of this approach, based on type I and type II errors were extremely encouraging, yielding values of 1.2% and 1.1%

respectively. This is a phenomenal result – considering the small number of features utilized.

Biel and colleagues proposed the use of ECG as a new approach to human identification in 2001 (Biel et al., 2001). In their approach they utilized the standard 12-lead ECG to record from a subject cohort consisting of 20 healthy volunteers (aged 2- - 55 years). From the digitized signal, they extracted a total of 30 features for each of the ECG recordings, yielding a data matrix containing 360 features (30 feature/lead). Their first pre-processing step was to reduce the number of features to a more manageable size. The first stage in dimensionality reduction was to use either limb or chest leads (there were six in their study). The authors opted to use the limb leads, as they tend to be less sensitive to placement variations which may occur when different experimenters apply the leads (the same applies to repeated placement across subjects for a single experimenter). This process reduced the number of features in half. Further analysis of the correlation matrix resulted in reducing the feature space to 12 features, based on whether a feature was highly correlated to other features – redundancy in the data (for a fuller discussion on reduction of attribute features in ECG analysis (Mitra et al., 2006). With a reduced feature set, the authors employed the SIMCA (soft independent modeling of class analogy) to generate a principle component analysis (PCA) model for each class (i.e. each individual in the study). Using PCA score plots for each of the features, a clustering of the data according to the selected attributes was generated, which ultimately was used for classification purposes. The data was partitioned into training and test examples, and supervised learning techniques such as neural networks can be utilized for automated classification purposes. Generally, speaking, the classification results were very high – on the order of 99% or better, depending on the attributes set used. Note that the authors explore the classification accuracy of a range of feature vectors – please consult the paper for

relevant details. The classification accuracy was on par with that of Forsen's work – and further provides information regarding the information content of the attribute feature subspace – which is an important result from this work.

Silva and colleagues published results indicating a successful classification rate of over 99% from a collection of 26 subjects, using a contingency matrix analysis approach similar to that of Biel and colleagues (Silva et al., 2007). The principal addition to the literature from this study is the use of a small sample of cardiac cycles – utilizing only 63 seconds worth of ECG recording. The study reported an accuracy rate of 92% when utilizing a single heart beat for the 26 subjects, and 100% accuracy when the full 63 seconds worth of recording was utilized. The feature space used in this study was significantly larger (53 features) than the number utilized by Biel – which may be the reason why the classification accuracy was high with a short data sample. There is always a trade off between the size of the feature space and the coverage derived from taking repeated measures.

Shen and colleagues published a paper discussing how a one-lead ECG electrode system could provide satisfactory identity verification of 100%, depending on which classification algorithm was utilised (Shen et al., 2002). This work is useful in that it demonstrates that a reduced lead system can acquire sufficient data for highly accurate person identification from ECG data. The authors analyzed data from the MIT/BIH database, which consists of ECG recordings from healthy volunteers for use in machine learning development and medical analysis.

A study by Israel and colleagues examined the stability of the ECG as a biometric modality (Israel et al., 2005). Their results indicate that the features extracted for classification purposes were independent of sensor location, invariant to the individual's state of anxiety, and unique to an individual. The authors reported that the ECG trace properties were determined by the magnitude of the signal alone – any timing differences between ECG inflexion points were independent of position. Thus, psychological state changes such as anxiety could be corrected for by appropriate normalization techniques. This process scales the heartbeat to a unit length – and hence removes any temporal variations that may occur between heartbeats. This implies that variations in heart rate yield fixed changes within the fiduciary marks – and the analysis provided by the authors support this hypothesis. This paper therefore addressed one potential criticism of the ECG based approach to biometrics: sample variability. The results from this study indicate that variability based on the affective state of the subject can be neutralized through normalization techniques, with classification accuracies of 97% or higher for normal and anxiety provoked subjects. Variations in cardiac physiology however remain to be examined by this approach – which is (or at least should be) an area of future study.

A study by Mehta & Lingayat yielded over 99% classification accuracy (both in terms of sensitivity and positive predictive value) when using either a single lead or a 12-lead ECG database (Mehta & Lingayat, 2007). In this study, the authors deployed the use of support vector machines (SVM) to perform data extraction, based principally on the QRS wave component of the ECG. The authors claim that once the QRS complex was located, the other wave components could easily be identified relative to the QRS complex. This approach is significant in that there may be less room for signal variation if one focuses on a sub-sample of the data. These results held whether they used the full 12-lead or single-lead system, yielding classification accuracy of over 99%, depending on the classifier used.

In a study published by Wang and colleagues, the use of the ECG as a biometric was examined using autocorrelation (AC) in conjunction with discrete cosine transform (DCT) (Wang et al., 2008). The authors also employed the use of the MIT-BIH heartbeat database in order to examine the classification accuracy of this novel approach to person identification. Typically, features of ECGs are extracted using fiducial marks such as QRS complexes (see Biel, et al., 2001, Israel, et al., 2005). In this study, features were extracted without the prior identification of fiducial marks, using a combination of AC and DCT. The method entails four stages: i) windowing the ECG traced (pre-processed) into non-overlapping windows, where each window is longer than the average heartbeat, ii) estimation of the normalized autocorrelation of each window, iii) discrete cosine transform over the lags of the autocorrelation signal, and iv) classification based on significant coefficients of the DCT. These results from this approach yielded a subject recognition rate of 100%, depending on the dataset that was used. An advantage of this approach over all others so far discussed is the elimination of the fiduciary marks from the data – only local data is required for the feature extraction process. This means the classification stage is largely independent of errors associated with fiduciary discovery – which might imply that the system is more stable to subtle changes in the ECG. This again remains an active area of on-going research.

Lastly, Rainville and colleagues published an article that discussed the relationship between basic emotions and cardiorespiratory activity (Rainville et al., 2005). The purpose of this study was to determine if there was a correlation between four basic emotional states (fear, anger, sadness, and happiness) and a variety of cardiorespiratory attributes associated with the statistical properties of the respiratory period and heart rate variability. The authors in this study extracted a set of features that characterise the R-R interval – that is the peak-to-peak interval between successive heart beats (5 features). In addition, data was collected on standard respiratory features such as the mean respiratory period (6 features). Lastly, R-R features occurring within respiratory cycles were recorded (5 features), along with spectral features for both the RR interval and respiration, yielding a total of 18 features. A statistical analysis approach was taken, in order to determine the effect emotion had on each of these features. More specifically, an exploratory principal component analysis (PCA) was performed to remove any redundant features. A log transformation of the data was performed and any datum that lied outside the mean +/- 3SD was removed. Smoothing was performed on the respiratory data using the mean of a 1-s window and transformed into instantaneous measurements of period and amplitude. For the spectral data, exact Fast Fourier Transform (FFT) analysis was performed on 2^{14} data samples (81.92 s) of the RR tachogram and the smoothed respiratory data. The exploratory PCA reduced the set of 5 factors that accounted for more than 91% of the variance in the data. In the final analysis, the authors were able to produce a heuristic decision tree with significant predictive power – that is the task was to predict the emotion (into one of the 4 mentioned categories) based on the data. The nodes of the tree were clearly dependent on heart rate and spectral features (i.e. existence of high frequency components), modulated by respiratory features (i.e. whether or not there were changes in respiration).

The case studies presented so far are but a small sample of the literature on the use of ECG as a biometric. Space does not permit a full-scale survey of this exciting literature – but it is hoped that what has been presented provides some insight into the line of approach taken by researchers in this field. There are several issues that must be considered when investigating whether a feature will be suitable for a biometric. For one, reproducibility is a critical issue – especially in the context of behavioral biometrics. As a behavioral biometric, one envisions the use of signatures, speech, and keystroke/mouse dynamics. The possibility for the lack of reproducibility has led many researchers to believe these approaches are not stable enough for high security installations. On the other hand, physiological biometrics such as retinal and iris scans, and fingerprints yield a perception of superior accuracy and hence have been employed in high security installations. The principal reason for this demarcation, in terms of perceived (and real in many instances) security of physiological biometrics is their stability over time. The question is where does an ECG fit into this demarcation – should it be behavioral or physiological? We probably are not able to control our heartbeat to any significant degree of precision – but it does vary over time based on our emotional state, not withstanding any changes in general health. This is true of various behavioral biometrics – our signatures can vary with time as does our typing style. Physiological biometrics prides itself on the stereotypical nature of anatomy – the retina doesn't change based on any controllable/ willed emotional state – any more than we can change the minutiae on our fingertips. So in this authors perspective, biosignals such as ECG (and as discussed further in this chapter, the electro-encephalogram) serve as intermediaries between behavioral and physiological biometrics, leaning more towards the former. As with the EEG, there is the possibility of changing some features of our heart rate within limits through training, just as we can learn to modify our brain wave patterns (brain computer interface). This possibility then places constraints on the feature extraction process – which must be robust enough to include those features that are behaviorally modifiable. This is potentially a philosophical issue that warrants further investigation from the community.

EEG Based Biometrics

The electroencephalogram (EEG) is a recording of the electrical activity of the brain recorded on the scalp. The first EEG recordings were published by the German psychiatrist Hans Berger in 1929 (Berger, 1929). As with the ECG, voltage sensitive electrodes are typically employed, which in this case are placed on the scalp, recording the electrical activity occurring in the brain of all organisms with central nervous systems. The EEG reflects the on-going activity of large collections of neurons, the functional unit of nervous tissue. The currents generated by nervous tissue activity is very small, on the order of 10-50 μV – which reflects the simultaneous activity of millions of neurons (the brain has on the order of 10^{11} neurons – so this is really a small fraction of the total). The neurons must have a particular orientation – they must all be aligned in the same direction – and must be firing synchronously in order for a signal to be recordable from the scalp. If these conditions are met, a bewildering array of data can be generated which reflects the current activity of the brain.

The brain may be considered to be a collection of modules that serve particular functions (see Fodor for an excellent discussion on the modularity of mind, Fodor, 2001). These modules serve physiological functions such as emotion, memory, vision, and related sensory, motor, and higher order cognitive functions to put it very briefly. These modules act independently – but also in collaboration with other modules. Thus the behavior of the brain – the brain state at a particular point in time - is dependent on the states of all the individual modules plus their interactions. The brain therefore is a dynamical system, whose next state is determined by the current state and some finite number of previous states. Hence during the performance of a particular task – even if performed repeatedly by the same individual – different brain states activation patterns will be generated and hence the EEG will vary accordingly.. So how does one go about extracting useful information from such a dynamical system? One must first start by looking at the data – a sample of which is presented in Figure 3.

EEG generates a tremendous amount of data – where a single recording deploying anywhere from 18-256 electrodes are positioned on the scalp, each providing a time series sampled at 0.5-1.0 KHz. A typical EEG recording can be generated in two different modalities: passive and active (see Figure 3 for an example from EEGLAB). In the passive scenario, the EEG data is acquired from a random brain state – that is the individual may simply be seated in a chair and asked to relax when the recording takes place. In the active method, the subject is asked to perform a particular cognitive task, such as identifying a picture of their mother from a collection of portraits. Data recorded passively has traditionally been used as a diagnostic tool – such as identifying sleep patterns, epilepsy, and brain disorders such as schizophrenia and Alzheimer's disease (Luck, 2005). From an analysis point of view, the gross features of the recording, such as the amplitude and frequency components are useful as diagnostic features. There is a large literature on the automated classification of disease states based on passive EEG recordings (WHO, 2006). On the other hand, active EEG recordings are more subtle in that the recordings are generally produced in a within-participant design – in that a background control recording is made, and superimposed on this background, the subject is asked to perform a specific task, usually repeatedly. The challenge is to be able to detect changes in the EEG recording when the subject performs a cognitive task – relative to background activity. Part of the difficulty is identifying specific responses that are reliably correlated with the engagement of a specific cognitive task. In addition to detecting a change associated with the performance of a particular task, one would like to know which part(s) of the brain was/were responsible for performing the task. If one assumes a modular processing mode for human nervous systems (at least in part), then one would like to be able to associate particular regions of the brain with particular activities. In the EEG literature, this is termed the *inverse problem* – based on a map of cortical activity (recorded by the montage of electrodes covering the scalp), one would like to know which region(s) of the brain (in 3D space) was responsible for that pattern of recorded activity at that particular electrode (over all electrodes). Unfortunately, this is still an unsolved problem, as the system is under-determined for such an analysis – and

Figure 3. A snapshot of an EEG recording taken from the EEGLAB site (Data originated from the EE-GLAB home page: http://sccn.ucsd.edu/eeglab/)

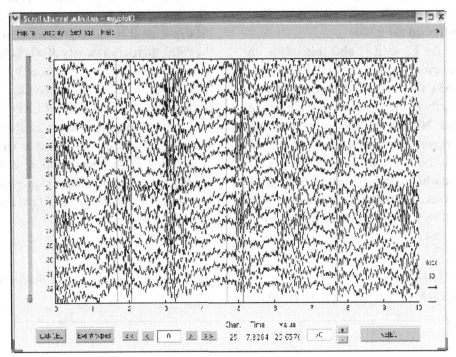

remains a very active area of research. But such analyses have yielded considerable insights into hidden features contained within EEG data under active conditions, termed event-related potentials (ERPs). ERPs therefore may provide the basis for a "signature" that is associated with a cognitive task that may contain enough individuality to serve as a useful biometric.

An ERP is a change in the EEG signal that arises when the brain performs a given cognitive (or motor/sensory) task. They are manifest as subtle changes in the on-going electrical signals, which yield characteristic changes in three principal features: polarity, amplitude, and latency. The polarity is either positive (usually a downward deflection) or negative (upward deflection), forming a collection of peaks and troughs in the recording. The amplitude of the peaks and troughs is a reflection of the synchronicity of the neural activity structures responsible for generating the signal. The latency refers to when the ERP oc-

curs relative to the stimulus presentation – the ERP is typically time-locked to the presentation of the stimulus. Since the power of the EEG signal is very low – one typically enhances the signal-to-noise ratio by averaging a collection of data samples, usually by asking the subject to perform a given task repeatedly – possibly 20 or more repetitions are required. These repetitions are termed 'epochs' – and the software bundled with the EEG equipment is able to mark on the recording (and digitally) when these epochs occur. By combining the epochs (averaging), and subtracting the background from them – one can enhance the signal to noise ratio of the data occurring during the epochs – which are pooled together. The subtraction process then will remove the background noise, enhancing the real changes that occurred during the performance of the cognitive task. Researchers then study the EEG signals that have been epoched – correlating them with the cognitive task – and attempt to correlate them

111

with particular regions of the brain (the inverse problem). Short of solving the inverse problem, a number of ERPs have been discovered, the first of them was termed the P300.

The P300 (or P3 as it is also termed) is an example of an event related potential (ERP) (Sutton et al., 1965). The terminology is derived both from the polarity of the signal ('P' for a positive deflection and 'N' for a negative deflection) and the latency (reported in milliseconds) or ordinal position ('3' is the 3rd wave). So a P300 is a positive deflection which occurs 300 ms after stimulus presentation (see Figure 4 for an example of a P300 ERP). The P300 is typically produced in

what is termed an "odd-ball" paradigm. This is a scenario in which a subject is presented with a stimulus to identify and a stimulus not related to the expected stimulus is presented. In addition to the P300, there are a variety of other characteristic signals (ERPs) that are produced by the brain in response to typical stimuli (see Luck, 2005 for a comprehensive exposition of ERPs). The question relevant to us is whether ERPs can be used as a brain signature – analogous to a hand written signature, for user identification. In the following section, a series of case studies is presented which explore the utility of EEG as a tool for user identification.

Figure 4. A P300 displayed at 3 different recording locations (along the mid-line of the brain) (source: mantas.dtiltas.lt/Mantas_Puociauskas_P300.html)

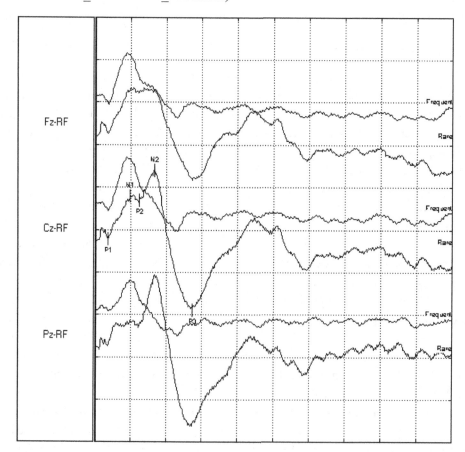

EEG Based Biometrics Case Studies

As previously mentioned, Forsen was the first to propose that EEG signals could be deployed for user verification (Forsen et al., 1977). This study examined the use of EEG as a possible biometric on a theoretical basis – setting the stage for all subsequent EEG based biometrics. Since this publication, a number of studies have investigated the utility of EEG as a biometric – and the results have born out his original intuition – that it does serve as a useful tool. In the following, case studies employing active EEG signal acquisition schemes will be examined in order to illustrate the typical data processing approaches and the associated classification accuracies.

A study published in 2007 by Marcel and Millan illustrated the use of brainwaves (EEG) for person authentication using maximum a posteriori model adaptation (Marcel & Millan, 2007). In this study, a quasi-active EEG data was acquired from nine subjects using a cap with 32 electrodes positioned according to the standard international 10-20 system. The samples were collected over several days, with 4 sessions recorded each day while the subjects were sitting relaxed in a normal chair. For each session (lasting 4 minutes with 5-10 minute breaks between them), the subjects were asked to perform various tasks such as imagining a repetitive self-paced left/right hand movements and as a 3rd task, the subjects were asked to generate words that began with the same randomly selected letter. The resulting EEG was epoched according to the particular task, which was used for subsequent model development. The authors cleansed the data by filtering to enhance the SNR, derived the power spectral density over a small window, which was used for building a Gaussian mixture world model. From this generic model, a subject specific model was generated and the likelihood that the data corresponds to a particular subject can be compared with the likelihood that the data corresponds to the world model. If the ratio is greater then a data derived threshold, then

the particular subject in question is identified. The authors report the classification accuracy based on the HTER (half total error rate), which is the mean of the FAR and FRR. The authors report the HTER for each of the three tasks groups (all performed by the same individuals), which were varied from 4.8 – 50%. These error rates were extremely variable, and the range could not be accounted for based on the number of Gaussians employed. The authors did note a trend that the error rates were task dependent, with the left arm movement providing the lowest error rates. Though this study did not provide useful error rates, the study was one of the first to examine the use of EEG for person identification in a practical scenario. Probably the major difficulty was the use of the MAP model – which requires a significant amount of data to generate an accurate model. No such follow study has been published as far as this author is aware of.

Using an autoregression (AR) model, Mohammadi and colleagues were able to produce a classification system with a classification accuracy score between 80-100% (Mohammadi et al., 2006). The AR model is used to model the EEG time series as a linear difference equation in the time domain. The model includes some number of previous time points plus an error term that incorporates white noise input that is considered to be identical and independently distributed. To estimate the AR parameters, the Yull-Walker approach was utilised. The classification task employed a competitive neural network approach, trained with a reinforcement learning approach. The data was acquired from ten healthy volunteers, using a 100-lead montage sampled at 170 Hz (24 second sample duration). For each subject there were 4,080 samples which were divided into 8 epochs of 3 seconds duration for each. For classification purposes, a portion of the data vectors were deployed for training and the remaining was used to test the classification accuracy of the trained network. The resulting classification accuracy varied from 80-100%, depending in part on how many channels were used for each subject data vector. The authors indicate that using the AR parameters from different channels improved the classification accuracy considerably.

An intriguing idea employing the notion of thought based authentication, Palaniappan published a report indicating that EEG associated with a particular cognitive task could be used to classify individuals (Palaniappan, 2005). In this study, a collection of BCI derived EEG datasets from four subjects was employed. The subjects were placed in a sound controlled booth and a six-electrode montage (10-20 system compliant, with dual mastoid references) and asked to perform a series of mental tasks such as figure rotation, mental arithmetic, visual counting, and mental letter composition. The data was sampled at 250 Hz and band-pass filtered between 0.1 and 100 Hz., recorded for 10s during each of the four mental tasks. Each task was repeated for 10 sessions, which were held on different weeks. In addition to the four mental tasks, a baseline task was also produced where the subjects were asked to sit calmly under the same circumstances as the performance of the mental tasks. The data was reduced into a set of features based on AR modeling, and the AR coefficients were extracted (of order six). This process yielded a set of 36 features for each EEG segment/mental thought. The author then employed linear discriminant analysis as the classification tool in this study. The author reports classification in terms of error, which varied between 0 – 3.5%, depending on the number of features employed and the type of cross-validation technique employed. The author noted that by combining the AR coefficients for two or more mental tasks, the resulting classification error was reduced to 0.33% on average when all four mental tasks were combined into a single feature vector.

In an interesting paper entitled "Pass-thoughts, authenticating with our minds," the notion that we may be able to authenticate – for instance entering a password simply by *thinking* of the password (Thorpe et al., 2005). The basis of this work is that through the deployment of a BCI (brain computer interface) based mechanism, which relies on the use of EEG acquired signals from a subject. A key issue with BCI is the notion of feedback – a form of operant conditioning, where a subject can control to certain degrees the likelihood of generating an event, such as a P300. As a result of training, where the subject is asked to consciously focus on a particular task, and with appropriate feedback (closed-loop BCI), the subject generates the required response (P300 at the correct time) more reliably. What is required is that the response is mapped onto a particular command – such as moving a cursor or depressing a key on a virtual keyboard presented on the computer screen. Though much of this work has focused on assisting patients in locked in states (i.e. patients suffering from a stroke, unable to move their limbs but are cognitively normal), there has been some research investigating the suitability of this technology as a novel approach to user identification.

Though this strategy is still in the development stage, it should be possible in the near future to create an authentication method based on EEG and/or ECG that is both convenient (no passwords to remember), secure – it is difficult to replicate someone's thought patterns, and accurate. The HUMABIO (www.humabio-eu.org) project, funded by the EU FP6, has implemented a system exploring the use of this technology – fusing several behavioral biometrics (EEG, gait, ECG) into an integrated automated authentication scheme within a virtual reality framework (Figure 5 presents an example of this technology). In line with this scheme, a HUMABIO collaborator, STARFAST, has developed a wireless wearable EEG/ECG biometric system (based on the ENOBIO sensor). Riera and colleagues have published data indicating accuracy levels approaching 100%, depending on the fusion approach taken (Riera et al., 2007a). It is believed that the advances in biosignal analysis, modified for use as a biometric

Figure 5. The traffic simulator: The heart of the HUMABIO authentication system (www.humabio-eu. org). This system employs both EEG and EOG that records user's responses and builds a user profile used for subsequent user authentication

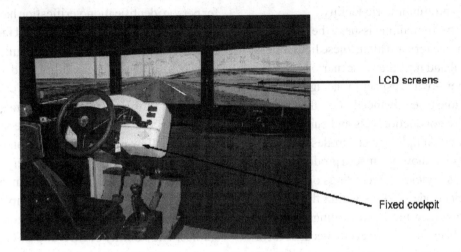

will provide a new venue for secure authentication without compromising user acceptance.

FUTURE WORKS

The studies presented in this chapter provide a range of examples in the deployment of *biosignals* as a viable approach to behavioral bioemtrics. Biosignals, such as the ECG and EEG reflect on-going dynamical biological processes. In a sense, they lie at the interface between behavioral and physiological biometrics. The issue is how much control do we have over them? Can we control our brain patterns sufficiently? Can we exercise biofeedback-based control to regulate our heart rates to a sufficient degree? Through the use of BCI based technology - users can be trained with a minimal amount of effort to control the production of event-related potentials (ERPs) as an example. What is required is a method of authentication that relies on the production of ERPs – one that involves a significant cognitive component. Current methodologies do not entail a significant amount of cognitive processing. For instance, the P300 speller could be used as an alternative to textual passwords – and could be employed in a cancelable fashion. A variety of game-based approaches – or scenario-based approaches could be used as the authentication interface. Through an enrollment process – which includes a training process - an individual's brain wave patterns can be honed and thus serve as the biometric signature. In addition, other factors, such as the emotional state of a user can be incorporated into the signature – fusion at the sensor level. For instance, Picard and colleagues have demonstrated that affective psychological states can be discriminated with a variety of machine learning modeling strategies (Picard et al., 1977). The relevant question to be addressed is: "How well can a computer recognize human emotional states?" Picard and colleagues have addressed this important question in the context of Clyne's set of basic emotions: anger, hate, grief, platonic love, romantic love, joy, and reverence – with a control of no emotion (see Clynes, 1977). The authentication protocol could then consist of a cognitive task that also elicits affective states – recorded with minimalist ECG and EEG equipment. This combination of features – strictly at the biosignal level – augment the feature space considerably – and of course can be employed in combination with more traditional behavioral biometric interfaces. Thus, a critical future trend must be the production of a user-friendly multibiometric facility.

There are two remaining issues to be addressed if we are to move forward along these lines: one is technological and the other is scenario based. As for the former – with respect to biosignals – the technology must be advanced such that we no longer require conduction gels and cumbersome EEG skullcaps. Simple dry electrodes are being developed which show promise in producing high quality results – yielding recordings on par with traditional electrode systems within the next 12 months. With respect to ECG recordings, portable halters have been in use for several decades now. Current research indicates that even less invasive devices such as photoplethysmyographs (which measure blood pressure volume) that fit onto a fingertip provide a significant level of information directly related to ECG activity (see McCraty et al., 1995, Cacioppo et al., 2000, Picard et al., 2000 for details). It is simply a matter of demand that is driving the technology – so this barrier can be effectively removed from the equation.

As far as scenarios are concerned – virtual reality based systems provide an environment that is not only useful – but exciting to many users. Virtual reality environments provide a wealth of input modalities – visual, auditory, and tactile inputs are typical of high-end systems such as that developed on the ENOBIO system. These are obviously high-end systems not suitable for common usage. Instead, a VRML or X3D based VR application can be easily developed and deployed over the internet which provides audio-visual inputs – which should be sufficient for developing a cognitive based approach. With this approach – the array of scenarios is virtually unlimited – the constraints really are imposed on the required hardware – the technological issues mentioned previously.

CONCLUSION

The use of biosignals, specifically ECG and EEG, for person identification/verification has considerable promise. As a biometric, several factors must be addressed: individuality of the signal, stability, ease of use, user acceptability, and robustness to attack. The brief selection of case studies presented in this chapter demonstrate, via low error rates, that these biosignals are sufficiently unique to allow person identification – based on the use of imposter data. To date, very few if any studies have deployed intruder data in this context (see Riera et al., 2007b for an example) – so the verdict must await the results of corroborating studies. The stability of ECG and EEG biosignals is an important issue that has not been properly addressed in the literature. One would assume based on physiological principals that barring drastic changes in the cardiovasculature system, that the ECG will be stable over time. As with any useful behavioral biometric, one does not assume that once collected, it will remain in use for a sustained period of time (this is in contrast to physiological biometrics). Typically, a behavioral biometric such as keystroke dynamics will be adaptive, in that the BIR will be updated over time to reflect any changes in the behavior of the owner (Revett, 2006). The same principal could be applied to and ECG BIR as well, without compromising the underlying assumptions of a behavioral based biometric. One would assume however, that the ECG trace would be more stable than a person's typing style or signature. With respect to EEG biosignals, it will in part depend on whether the data is acquired in a passive or active format. Generally speaking, the EEG is a dynamical time series. To date, the vast majority of biometric applications utilizing EEG employ the passive approach (though see Palaniappan & Mandic, 2007 for an exception). The principal reason for using the passive data is that there is less pre-processing that needs to be performed – and fewer electrodes are required to unambiguously generate ERPs. These issues are being addressed by researchers in the brain-computer interface community, which relies heavily on the use of ERPs for mental/thought control

Ease of use is a very significant issue in the context of biosignal acquisition. With respect to ECG acquisition, portable holters are routinely deployed to allow real-time 24 hr (or more) monitoring of a patient suspected of having cardiac abnormalities. These holters are very unobtrusive and can be connected to a receiving station using standard wireless technology. New dry electrodes are being developed for use as EEG recording electrodes. This is in contrast to the traditional conductivity gel and skullcap that most experimental psychology laboratories deploy – which are unacceptable for biometric security deployment. Dry electrodes obviate the need for conducting gel – so the last issue is the number of electrodes. For electrophysiological studies – most montages contain at least 20 electrodes, with many high-resolution setups deploying 256. In the STARFAST system, 2 dry electrodes were deployed (plus a reference lead), which were placed on the forehead. This montage can be implemented in a cap that the user can simply place on their head during the authentication phase. The technological advances will continue in this area – especially if there is promise for use in alternative and ubiquitous scenarios such as use authentication.

User acceptability is always an issue with the widespread deployment of biometrics. Fingerprint scanners for instance are very easy to use – they are quick – a simple 2-second press of the thumb and you will be authenticated (hopefully!). Within the behavioral biometrics domain, signature and keystroke/mousestroke dynamics are also very acceptable means of authentication. The question remains whether the mode of data acquisition within the biosignal realm will be accepted by the user community? Clearly with ECG, the use of very lightweight portable holter based ECG devices with wireless connections to the authenticating device (typically a PC), the lack of conducting gels

will make this technology suitable for most users. As for EEG signal acquisition, the deployment of montages that consists of 2 forehead electrodes plus the ground lead reduces the wiring closet so to speak, making the device appear less ominous. In addition, technological advances in the use of dry electrodes – obviating the need for conductive gel – will make this approach much more user friendly. The apparatus can be fitted into a cap-like structure. The ENOBIO sensor integrates ECG and EEG into a single cap-like apparatus that is easily fitted onto the head, without compromising classification accuracy. It is believed that as the demand for such devices increases, there will be concomitant technological advances to satisfy market demand.

Lastly, the issue of robustness to attack is a critical facet of any biometric. Notwithstanding the inherent error rates of the methodology, one must consider the vulnerability of the approach to attacks. Typically, approaches such as fingerprints are subject to spoofing – fingers can be removed and placed on the scanner – so a liveliness test has been incorporated into higher-end fingerprint based biometric installations. Liveliness is not an issue with ECG/EEG based biometrics – as by definition death can be defined as a brain-state without any EEG activity or ECG! Whether someone could develop a structure (e.g. human like brain/robot) that could produce the required signals is a possibility that must be considered. In order to counteract these possibilities, a more dynamic test might be utilized. For instance, Rainville and colleagues have reported correlations between cardiorespiratory activity and emotional state (Rainville et al., 2006). The authentication protocol might require inducing a change in the emotional state of the person to be authenticated – possibly via a virtual reality environment (such as that offered by HUMABIO) – and the appropriate change to the cardiorespiratory system (measured via the ECG) would need to be produced. Again, an intelligent spoofer could then produce a series of appropriate changes in the ECG response, mapped to the possible categories of emotional states. This possibility will depend on the dimensionality of the set of states and the exemplars within each state. Similarly, the use of ERPs for EEG recordings provides a much richer set of testing scenarios than using passive EEG data. There is a rich literature on the deployment of visual and auditory stimuli and the resulting characteristic changes induced in the human brain. A very large repertoire of stimuli can be generated, each resulting in a unique global pattern of brain activity that would require producing a brain on par with that of a human (non-human primates do not exhibit the full range of variations). Fusion of ECG and EEG would present a virtually insurmountable task for spoofing – probably much more difficult than the highest end physiological biometric in existence today.

In the final analysis, the future of behavioral biometrics is at the very least much more exciting than that of physiological based biometrics (in this author's opinion of course!). For one, the data is acquired in a more dynamic fashion – allowing the individual's personality and mental processes to become part of their authentication process. One of the consequences of this approach is an augmented sense of personal responsibility in protecting our personal information – our identity in an electronic age. Increasing our awareness of computer security is a major step towards enhancing the productivity of living in an electronic world – allowing greater utilization of current and future technologies. Augmenting the repertoire of biometric security capacities provides enhanced levels of protection that will engender a freer utilization of the resources available in the electronic world.

REFERENCES:

Berger, H. (1929). Über das Elektroenkephalogram des Menschen . *Arch. f. Psychiat.*, *87*, 527–570.

Biel, L., Pettersson, O., Philipson, L., & Wide, P. (2001). ECG analysis: A new approach in human identification. *IEEE Transactions on Instrumentation and Measurement*, *50*(3), 808–812. doi:10.1109/19.930458

Birbaumer, N., Ghanayim, N., Hinterberger, T., Iversen, I., Kotchoubey, B., & Kubler, A. (1999). A spelling device for the paralysed. *Nature*, *398*, 297–298. doi:10.1038/18581

Cacioppo, J. T., Berntson, G. G., Larsen, J. T., & Poehlmann, K. M. (2000). The psychophysiology of emotion. In M. Lewis & J. M. Haviland-Jones (Eds.), *The handbook of emotion*, 2nd edition (pp. 173-191). New York: Guilford Press.

Chang, C. K. (2005). *Human identification using one lead ECG*. M.S. thesis, Department of Computer Science and Information Engineering, Chaoyang University of Technology, Taiwan.

Clynes, D. M. (1977). *Sentics: The touch of the emotions*. Anchor Press/Doubleday.

Coetzer, J., Herbst, B. M., & du Preez, J. A. (2004). Offline signature verification using the discrete radon transform and a hidden Markov model. *EURASIP Journal on Applied Signal Processing*, *4*, 559–571. doi:10.1155/S1110865704309042

Electroencephalography. (n.d.). Retrieved on August 1, 2008, from http://butler.cc.tut.fi/~malmivuo/bembook/13/13.html

Fodor, J. (2001). The modularity of mind. Cambridge, MA: MIT Press. (12th ed.).

Forsen, G., Nelson, M., & Staron. (1977). *Personal attributes authentication techniques*. Rome Air Development Center, Report RADC-TR-77-1033, ed. A.F.B. Griffis, RADC, New York.

Guyton, A. C., & Hall, J. E. (2000). *Textbook of medical physiology*. Saunders Company, 10th edition.

Israel, S., Irvine, J., Cheng, A., Wiederhold, M., & Wiederhold, B. (2005). ECG to identify individuals. *Pattern Recognition, 38*(1), 133–142. doi:10.1016/j.patcog.2004.05.014

Kholmatov, A. (2003). *A biometric identity verification using online and offline signature verification*. MSc Thesis, Sabanci University, Turkey.

Luck, S. J. (2005). An introduction to the event related potential technique. Cambridge, MA: MIT Press.

Marcel, S., & Millan, J. del R. (2007). Person authentication using brainwaves (EEG) and maximum A posteriori model adaptation. *IEEE Transactions on Pattern Analysis and Machine Intelligence . Special Issue on Biometrics, 29*(4), 743–752.

McCraty, R., Atkinson, M., Tiller, W. A., Rein, G., & Watkins, A. D. (1995). The effects of emotions on short-term power spectrum analysis of heart rate variability. *The American Journal of Cardiology, 76*(14), 1089–1093. doi:10.1016/S0002-9149(99)80309-9

Mehta, S. S., & Lingayat, N. S. (2004). Comparative study of QRS detection in single lead and 12-lead ECG based on entropy and combined entropy criteria using support vector machine. *Journal of Theoretical and Applied Information Technology, 3*(2), 8–18.

Mitra, S., Mitra, M., & Chaudhuri, B. B. (2006). A rough-set-based inference engine for ECG classification. *IEEE Transactions on Instrumentation and Measurement, 55*(6), 2198–2206. doi:10.1109/TIM.2006.884279

Mohammadi, G., Shoushtari, P., Ardekani, B. M., & Shamsollahi, B. (2006, February 11). Person identification by using AR model for EEG signals. *Proceedings of the World Academy of Science, Engineering, and Technology* (pp. 281-285).

Palaniappan, R. (2005). Multiple mental thought parametric classification: A new approach for individual identification. *International Journal of Signal Processing, 2*(1), 222–225.

Palaniappan, R., & Mandic, D. P. (2007). Biometrics from brain electrical activity: A machine learning approach. *The Journal of VLSI Signal Processing, 29*(4), 738–742.

Picard, R. W., Vyzas, E., & Healey, J. (2001). Toward machine emotional intelligence: Analysis of affective physiological state. *IEEE Transactions on Pattern Analysis and Machine Intelligence, 23*(10), 1175–1191. doi:10.1109/34.954607

Rainville, R., Bechara, A., Naqvi, N., & Damasio, A. R. (n.d.). Basic emotions are associated with distinct patterns of cardiorespiratory activity. *International Journal of Psychophysiology.*

Revett, K. (2008). Behavioral biometrics: A remote access approach. West Sussex, UK: John Wiley & Sons.

Revett, K., Gorunescu, F., Gorunescu, G., Ene, M., Sérgio Tenreiro de Magalhães, S., & Santos, H. M. D. (2006, April 20-22). Authenticating computer access based on keystroke dynamics using a probabilistic neural network. *International Conference on Global E-Security*, London, UK (pp. 65- 71).

Riera, A., Dunne, S., Cester, I., & Ruffini, G. (2007a). *STAFAST: A wireless wearable EEG/ECG biometric system based on the ENOBIO sensor.*

Riera, A., Soria-Frisch, A., Caparrini, M., Grau, C., & Ruffini, G. (2007b). Unobtrusive biometric system based on electroencephalogram analysis. *EURASIP Journal on Advances in Signal Processing.*

Ross, A., & Jain, A. (2003). Information fusion in biometrics. *Pattern Recognition Letters, 24*(13), 2115–2125. doi:10.1016/S0167-8655(03)00079-5

Shen, T. W., Tompkins, W. J., & Hu, Y. J. (2002, October 23-26). One-lead ECG for identity verification. *Proceedings of the Second Joint EMBS/BMES Conference*, Houston, TX (pp. 62-63).

Silva, H. H. P., Gamboa, H. F. S., & Fred, A. L. N. (2007, April). Applicability of lead V$_2$ ECG measurements in biometrics. *Proc International Educational and Networking Forum for eHealth, Telemedicine, and Health ICT-Med-e-Tel*, Luxembourg.

Sutton, S., Braren, M., Zubin, J., & John, E. R. (1965). Evoked-potential correlates of stimulus uncertainty. *Science, 150*(3700), 1187–1188. doi:10.1126/science.150.3700.1187

Thorpe, J., Oorschot, P. C., & Somayaji, A. (2005). Passthoughts: Authenticating with our minds. In *Proceedings of New Security Paradigms Workshop*, Lake Arrowhead (pp. 45-56).

Waller, A. D. (1887). A demonstration on man of electromotive changes accompanying the heart's beat. [London.]. *The Journal of Physiology, 8,* 29–234.

Wang, Y., Agrafioti, F., Hatzinakos, D., & Plataniotis, K. N. (2008, January). Analysis of human electrocardiogram for biometric recognition. *EURASIP Journal on Advances in Signal Processing*.

WHO. (2006). *Neurological disorders: Public health challenges*. report published by the World Health Organization. ISBN: 92 4 156336 2.

Wolpaw, J. R., Birbaumer, N., Mcfarland, D. J., Pfurtscheller, G., & Vaughan, T. M. (2002). Brain-computer interfaces for communication and control. *Clinical Neurophysiology, 113,* 767–791. doi:10.1016/S1388-2457(02)00057-3

Chapter 6
Gabor Wavelets in Behavioral Biometrics

M. Ashraful Amin
City University of Hong Kong, Hong Kong

Hong Yan
City University of Hong Kong, Hong Kong

ABSTRACT

The Gabor wavelets are employed regularly in various biometrics applications because of their biological relevance and computational properties. These wavelets have kernels similar to the 2D receptive field profiles of the mammalian cortical simple cells. They exhibit desirable characteristics of spatial locality and orientation selectivity, and are optimally localized in the space and frequency domains. Physiological, biometric systems such as face, fingerprint, and iris based human identification have shown great improvement in identification accuracies if Gabor wavelets are used for feature extraction. Moreover, some behavioral biometric systems such as speaker and gait based applications have shown more than 7% increase in identification accuracies. In this study, we provide a brief discussion on the origin of Gabor wavelets, then an illustration of "how to use Gabor wavelets" to extract features for a generic biometric application is discussed. We also provide an implementation pseudocode for the wavelet. It also offers an elaborate discussion on biometric applications with specific emphasis on behavioral biometric systems that have used Gabor wavelets. We also provide guideline for some biometric systems that have not yet applied Gabor wavelets for feature extraction.

INTRODUCTION

Biometrics involves the development of statistical and mathematical methods applicable to data analysis problems in the biological sciences. More specifically, the term "biometrics" is derived from

DOI: 10.4018/978-1-60566-725-6.ch006

the Greek words bio (life) and metric (to measure). The sole purpose of biometrics is either identification or verification. This is performed based on two unique characteristics of human; the physiological uniqueness and the behavioral uniqueness. Physiological uniqueness is the characteristics that people are born with, which include fingerprint, face, and iris, etc. Behavioral uniqueness is the characteristics that people adapt to as they grow-up, which include gait, speech, etc. These are called behavioral, because uniqueness of these acts is expressed through behavior of an individual, for example, the way one walks (gait), and talks (speech).

Possibly the first known example of biometrics in practice was in India and China around the 15th century, where children's palm prints and footprints was marked on paper with ink to distinguish the young children from one another and also to analyze their future. In the 1960's, scientists started to use computer for automated face and speech recognition. Many applications have been developed and different approaches have been taken into account to further modify the existing systems. Among all approaches, biologically inspired computational methods such as Gabor Wavelets are more powerful in terms of optimality, as they seem to be in coherence with the physics of the natural world.

In 1946 using Schwarz inequality arguments, Dennis Gabor proved the "indeterminacy relations of quantum mechanics" (Gabor, 1946). He proved that a signal's specificity, simultaneously in time and frequency is fundamentally limited by a lower bound on the product of its bandwidth and duration. Gabor referred to Heisenberg & Weyl's uncertainty-related-proofs for the natural world and derived the uncertainty relation for information. Based on this understanding he found the general family of signals that optimize this trade-off and thus achieve the theoretical lower limit of joint uncertainty in time and frequency. The so-called Gabor signals take the general form:

$$s(t) = e^{\left[-\frac{(t-t_0)^2}{\sigma^2} \right]} e^{i\omega t} \tag{1}$$

Here the complex notation describes the modulation product of a sine wave with arbitrary frequency ω and a Gaussian envelope of arbitrary duration σ occurring at epoch t_0. Gabor also proposed representing arbitrary signals by a pseudo

expansion set of these elementary signals, which he termed "logons" in the information plane, indexed by all different frequencies of modulation and all different epochs of time.

The research on suitability of Gabor's theory in computer vision fund its motivation in the discovery of a group of neuroscientists and psychologists who claimed by showing experimental results that in visual perception natural images are decomposed into Fourier-like spatial-frequency components (Campbell & Robson, 1968; Kulikowski & Bishop, 1981; Maffei & Fiorentini, 1973; Pollen et al., 1971). In 1980 Marcelja published a paper where Dennis Gabor's "Theory of communications" was pointed out to all vision scientists by interpretations of cortical simple cell receptive-field profiles. Then subsequent research (Daugman, 1980; DeValois et al., 1982; Poleen & Ronner, 1981; Tootell et al., 1981) confirmed that usually two to five interleaved regions of simulative-restrictive influences weighted by a tapering envelope constitute the receptive-field profile of a simple cell, and Gabor signals with suitably chosen parameters invariably give a good fit to such spatial profiles.

In a series of works Daugman (Daugman, 1980; Daugman, 1985; Daugman, 1988; Daugman, 1993b) resolved some of the theoretical problems related to the Gabor representations of image. He introduced the two dimensional (2D) Gabor representations because they comport with the basic fact that a visual neuron's receptive field is localized in a 2D spatial visual manifold. Moreover he contributed to the research of the orientation selectivity of simple cells by explicitly analyzing in the uncertainty framework and relating the functionality of the cells to other tuning variables which specifically include spatial frequency and 2D spatial resolution. In order to model the receptive fields of the orientation-selective simple cells, Daugman (Daugman, 1980; Daugman, 1985) generalized the Gabor function (equation 1) to the following 2D form:

$$G(x,y) = \frac{1}{2\pi\sigma\beta} e^{-\pi\left[\frac{(x-x_0)^2}{\sigma^2} + \frac{(y-y_0)^2}{\beta^2}\right]} e^{i[\xi_0 x + \nu_0 y]}$$
(2)

$$\left(T^{wav}I\right)(a,\theta,x_0,y_0) = \frac{1}{\|a\|} \iint dxdy I(x,y)\psi_\theta\left(\frac{x-x_0}{a}, \frac{y-y_0}{a}\right)$$
(3)

where (x_0, y_0) is the center of the receptive field in the spatial domain and (ξ_0, ν_0) is the optimal spatial frequency of the filter in the frequency domain. σ and β are the standard deviations of the elliptical Gaussian along x and y. The 2D Gabor function is thus a product of an elliptical Gaussian and a complex plane wave. The careful mapping of the receptive fields of the simple cells by Jones & Palmer (1987) confirmed the validity of this model.

Pollen and Ronner's (Pollen & Ronner, 1981) discovery of numerous pairs of adjacent simple cells matched in preferred orientation and spatial frequency having a quadrature (90°) phase relationship within their common receptive-field area farther strengthened the basis of Gabor functions in visual cortex because a complex valued 2D Gabor function contains in quadrature projection: an even-symmetric cosine component and an odd symmetric sine component. This important discovery showed that the design of the cells might indeed be optimal mathematically and from natures view the visual cortical cell has evolved to an optimal design for information encoding.

Vision-based neurophysiological evidence (DeValois & DeValois, 1988) suggests that the spatial structure of the receptive fields of simple cells have different sizes. Daugman (1988) and others (DeValois & DeValois, 1988; Porat & Zeevi, 1988) have proposed that an ensemble of simple cells is best modeled as a family of 2D Gabor wavelets sampling the frequency domain in a log-polar manner. This class is equivalent to a family of affine coherent states generated by the affine group. Lee (1996) represents the decomposition of an image $I(x, y)$ into these states called the wavelet transform of the image as:

where a is the dilation parameter, related to σ and β (of equation 2), x_0, and y_0 the spatial translation parameters, θ the orientation parameter of the wavelet. The 2D wavelet elementary function, rotated by θ is:

$$\psi_\theta\left(a,x,y,x_0,y_0\right) = \frac{1}{\|a\|}\psi_\theta\left(\frac{x-x_0}{a}, \frac{y-y_0}{a}\right)$$
(4)

Lee (1996) extended Daugman's (Daugman, 1988) work by deriving a class of 2D Gabor wavelets, with their parameters properly constrained by both, neurophysiological data on simple cells and wavelet theory. Then he illustrated that Daubechie's completeness criteria (Daubechies, 1992) on 1D wavelet extends to 2D. By numerically computing the frame bounds for the physiologically relevant family of 2D Gabor wavelets in different phase space sampling schemes, he explained the conditions under which they form a tight frame. He discovered that the phase space sampling density provided by the simple cells in the primary visual cortex is sufficient to form an almost tight frame that allows stable reconstruction of the image by linear superposition of the Gabor wavelets with their own projection coefficients. He found that this provides representation of high resolution images using coarse neuronal responses.

GABOR FEATURE EXTRACTION FROM SIGNAL PROCESSING VIEW POINT

In signal processing a very common method of extracting features is to acquire the frequency, magnitude and phases information of the signal. Conversely, it could be said that a compound signal is decomposed into preliminary forms to capture the characteristics. The Fourier transform (Stein & Weiss, 1971) is a very common way to analyze signals.

The Fourier Transform

The Fourier transform is a representation of a function as a sum of complex exponentials of varying magnitude, frequency and phases. If $f(x, y)$ is a continuous function (signal) of a real variable (x, y) in the special domain, then the Fourier transform of $f(x, y)$, denoted by $F(\xi, v)$ in the frequency domain at the frequencies (ξ, v), is defined as:

$$F(\xi, v) = \int_{-\infty}^{\infty} \int_{-\infty}^{\infty} f(x, y) e^{-i(2\pi \xi x + i2\pi vy)} dx dy \tag{5}$$

From the equation above it is clear that the Fourier transform is a global representation of the signal. It cannot analyze the signal's local frequency contents or its local regularity. It ignores local regular behaviors. However, the local infor-

mation is important for highly globally irregular signals such as a facial image. So, the windowed Fourier transform is often used to acquire the local characteristics of signals and to overcome the problem of overlooking local characteristics of signals.

The Windowed Fourier Transform

The windowed Fourier transform has a constant time frequency resolution. It extracts the frequency components of a signal at the neighborhood g at a given time (or space for 2D signals such as images). The Windowed Fourier transform can be defined as:

$$WF(\xi, v, x_0, y_0) =$$
$$\int_{-\infty}^{\infty} \int_{-\infty}^{\infty} f(x, y) * g(x - x_0, y - y_0) e^{-i(2\pi \xi x + 2\pi vy)} dx dy \tag{6}$$

In the above formula notice that unlike the Fourier transform for a given signal a family of Fourier transform is recorded. An 1D example of the family generated by time and frequency translations of one atom is shown in Figure 1. Notice that for the windowed Fourier-transform

Figure 1. An illustration of fixed sized windowed Fourier transform

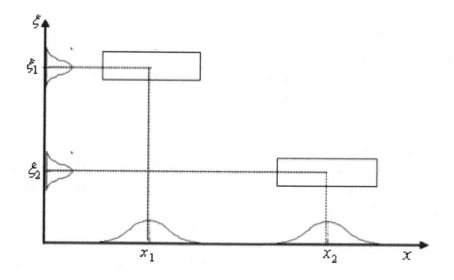

the time and frequency spreads of these functions are constant.

Wavelets

Although the windowed Fourier transform can measure the local variation of time-frequency, it does however apply constant time-window to observe all frequency components. To overcome the problem of fixed size window, wavelet transforms are applied. The wavelet transform replaces the Fourier transform's sinusoidal waves by a family generated by translations and dilations of a window called mother wavelet. For example in figure 2 notice that at location x_1 (time) first the original mother wavelet is applied (left sub-plot) and the frequency response $^1\xi_1$ is recorded. Then a dilated version of the same wavelet is applied (right sub-plot) and the frequency response $^2\xi_1$ is recorded. Now unlike window-Fourier transform the characteristic of the signal at location x_1 (time) is represented combining $^1\xi_1$ and $^1\xi_1$, this is to extract multi-resolution characteristic of local features.

The Gabor Wavelets

When modeling 1D wavelets it is important to carefully consider two key parameters, namely the scale and the 1D location (or time) of the wavelet. However, when modeling 2D wavelets, the additional key variable, orientation, must be considered along with scale and 2D location (or position in an image).

As presented in the equation 3, Gabor's theory can be related with the 2D-wavelet-transform. Consequently a mother wavelet adapted from Daugman's model (*See* equation 2 above) was utilized by (Daubechies, 1992; Daugman, 1988; Laeds et al, 1993; Liu, 2002) as illustrated in the equation below:

$$\psi_{\mu,\nu}(z) = \frac{\|k_{\mu,\nu}\|^2}{\sigma^2} \times e^{-\frac{\|k_{\mu,\nu}\|^2 \|z\|^2}{2\sigma^2}} \times \left[e^{ik_{\mu,\nu}z} - e^{-\frac{\sigma^2}{2}} \right]$$

(7)

where μ and ν define the orientation and scale of the Gabor kernel, $z = (x, y)$, $\|\bullet\|$ denotes the Euclidean norm operator, σ is the standard deviation

Figure 2. Illustration is wavelet transform, different sized window is simultaneously applied at a given time or location

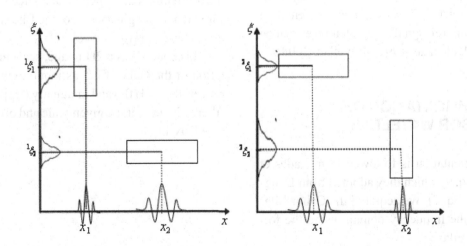

Figure 3. Real part of Gabor kernels at eight orientations and five scales

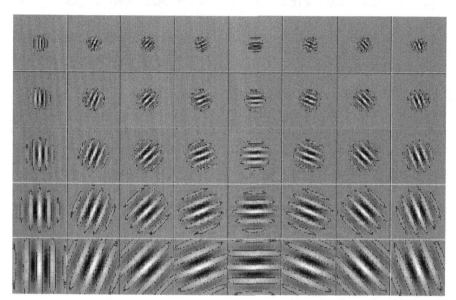

of the Gaussian window and wave vector $k_{\mu,\nu}$ is defined as follows:

$$k_{\mu,\nu} = k_\nu e^{i\phi_\mu}$$

(8)

with the values, $\phi_\mu = \mu\pi/N$ here N is the total number of orientations and $k_\nu = k_{max}/f$ here k_{max} is the maximum frequency, and f is the spacing factor between kernels in the frequency domain. In figure 3 Gabor kernels for the values $\sigma = 2\pi$, $k_{max} = \pi/2$, $f = \sqrt{2}$, $\mu = \{0, 1, ..., 7\}$ (8 different orientations) and $\nu = \{0, 1, ..., 4\}$ (5 different scales) are depicted. More on Gabor representation of spatiotemporal signals such as images can be found at (Maclennan, 1991; Movellan, 2008).

AN IMPLEMENTATION OF THE GABOR WAVELETS

Our implementation is followed from Lades et al., 1993 (Eq. 9) which they adopted from Daugman, 1988 (Eq. 7). We acquired the Gabor filter directly in the frequency domain using the following formula:

$$G(kvec, xvec) =$$
$$\left[\frac{kvec \bullet kvec}{\sigma^2}\right] \times \left[e^{-\frac{[kvec \bullet kvec] \times [xvec \bullet xvec]}{2 \times \sigma^2}}\right] \times \left[e^{i \times [kvec \bullet xvec]} - e^{-\frac{\sigma^2}{2}}\right]$$

(9)

Here *xvec* is the location (x, y) in the 2D filter, $\sigma = 2 \times \pi$ specifies how many oscillations fit inside the Gaussian envelope. The measure of *kvec* is given in the following pseudocode. Note here that there are three major fractions in the above equation, first is the normalization factor, the second is Gaussian factor and the third handles the oscillatory part which is calculated separately for real and imaginary part of the filter from sine and cosine of [*kvec* • *xvec*].

This code takes a 2D image, scale and orientation of the Gabor filter as input argument and returns the real (fR) and imaginary (fI) part of the filtered image for the given scale and orientation. (see Box 1)

Box 1.

```
[fR , fI ] = Gabor_Response (image, scale, orientation)
{ wd = width(image);          //width of the image
ht = hight(image);           //hight of the image
```

$$\varphi = \frac{\pi}{2} - \frac{\text{orientation} \times \pi}{8}; \quad // \text{ angle of the filter}$$

```
σ = 2×π;                     //sigma-the standard deviation of the Gaussian
```

$$\text{kvec} = \left(2^{-(\text{scale}+1)/2}\right) \times \pi; \quad // \text{ length of kvec}$$

$$\text{normfact} = \frac{\text{kvec}^2}{\sigma^2} \quad // \text{ normalization factor;}$$

```
cs = kvec × cos(φ);          // the real part
sn = kvec × sin(φ);          // the imaginary part
```

$$\text{cent} = \frac{\text{wd}}{2} - 1; \quad // \text{ center of the filter}$$

```
// calculate the value for each (x,y) in the filter
    for (j = 0;j < ht;j++)
      for (i = 0;i < wd;i++) {
        if   (j <= cent)
            fac2 = (cent-j);
        else
            fac2 = (ht-(j-cent));
        if(i <= cent)
            fac1 = (cent-i);
        else
            fac1 = (wd-(i-cent));
```

AN EXAMPLE IN FACE RECOGNITION

Usually Gabor wavelets are applied on signals to extract features. For example if we intend to apply Gabor wavelets to extract features from a facial image for face recognition, at first the facial images need to be pre-processed or normalized. As a rule of thumb, for facial images, the eyes and the mouth will always be aligned roughly at the same position in same sized images. Then, Gabor filters for different scales at different orientations are applied on each facial image.

Gabor Feature Representation

Usually Gabor filter/kernel representation of a facial image is obtained by convolving the Gabor filters/kernels at five scales, $v = \{0, 1, …, 4\}$, and eight orientations, $\mu = \{o, 1, 2, …, 7\}$, with the facial image. So, from a single facial image 40 Gabor responses are recorded for this case. Figure

Figure 4. Eight pixel sub-sampling of the image to acquire Gabor filter responses

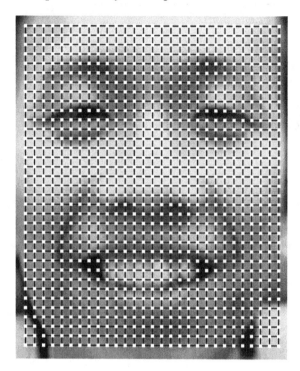

5 presents 40 Gabor magnitude followed by the phase representation of a normalized facial image for the values $\sigma = 2\pi$, $k_{max} = \pi/2$, and $f = \sqrt{2}$. Note here that we show intensity and phase for each filter at each pixel in Figure 5, in reality an 8 pixel sampling is applied as shown in Figure 4.

The result of a Gabor transformation for feature extraction can be seen as a 4th order tensor $TG(u, v, l, m)$ containing filter responses of a facial image (Figure 5). This is a $8 \times 5 \times 29 \times 35$ tensor, where $l = \{1, 2, ..., 29\}$ and $m = \{1, 2, ..., 35\}$ are the indexes along the sub-sample points of the width and height of the image of size 240×292.

If we intend to build a classifier to identify $s = \{1, 2, ..., 30\}$ subjects/individuals/persons, images for each of these individuals is recorded in four poses ($p = \{1, 2, ..., 4\}$) and each pose has e $= \{1, 2, ..., 100\}$ facial images. Applying Gabor filters on each image, a data tensor $D(s, p, e, u, v, l, m)$ is created as shown in Figure 6.

Note that for better illustration, the Gabor filter

responses are presented here in image form. In reality the output of a Gabor function using the convolution $|I(x, y) * \Psi_{\mu,\nu}(x, y)|$ will return a basic Gabor feature vector (refer to implementation section) for the μth orientation at ν^{th} scale, in this case which is a vector of size $n = l \times m = 1015$. So, the practical representation of the whole data set is in fact a 6th order tensor $D(s, p, e, u, v, n)$ which is a $30 \times 4 \times 100 \times 8 \times 5 \times 1015$ tensor. Thus, if in the implementation we want to refer to the response of the kernel $\Psi_{\mu,\nu}(x, y)$ for the ith person's j^{th} pose's k^{th} image in the tensor, we can write $D(i, j, k, \mu + 1, \nu + 1, :)$. Note here that the response for a kernel is considered as a single component even though it is a 1015 element vector and for each of the facial image 40 different components exist in the tensor.

In practice these 40 Gabor feature vectors at 8 orientations and 5 scales are concatenated into a single feature vector (Dailey et al. 2002; Lades et al., 1993; Liu, 2002) as:

$$g = \overset{4}{\underset{\nu=0}{C}}\,\overset{7}{\underset{\mu=0}{C}}\left|I(x, y) * \psi_{\mu,\nu}(x, y)\right| \tag{10}$$

Here, g is the Gabor feature vector. In the right hand side of the equation C denotes the concatenation operation, $*$ denotes the convolution operation and $|\cdot|$ denotes the absolute value operation, $I(x, y)$ is the intensity normalized gray scale image and $\Psi_{\mu,\nu}(x, y)$ is the kernel acquired using equation 7 with μ orientation and ν scale. Here notice that, the data tensor D already contains 40 filter responses for each of the images, so the concatenations are performed on the D by following this formula:

$$\overset{30}{\underset{i=1}{L}}\,\overset{4}{\underset{j=1}{L}}\,\overset{100}{\underset{k=1}{L}}\left(G(i, j, k, :) = \overset{5}{\underset{\nu=1}{C}}\,\overset{8}{\underset{u=1}{C}}D(i, j, k, u, v, :)\right) \tag{11}$$

where L is the looping operation, and G is a 4th order tensor $G(s, p, e, u, v, N)$ is a tensor of

Figure 5. Top: Gabor magnitude representation. Bottom: Gabor phase representation of a facial image

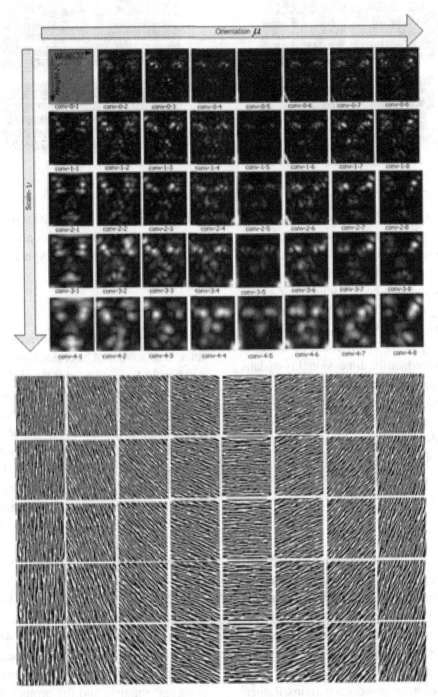

size $30 \times 4 \times 100 \times (1015 \times 40) = 30 \times 4 \times 100 \times 400600$. Finally, this tensor G contains the Gabor representations for the facial images of the whole data set.

Principle Component Analysis (PCA)

It is clear that due to the high dimensionality (40600) of the Gabor feature vectors, any clas-

Figure 6. The 7th order Data tensor's pictorial view

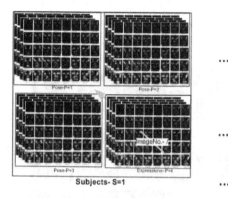

Subjects- S=1

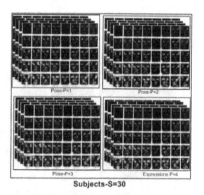

Subjects-S=30

sification technique can hardly be applied to learn the underlying classification rules. So, Principle Component Analysis (PCA) almost always comes with Gabor feature extraction (Dailey et al. 2002; Liu, 2004). Other methods (Belhumeur et al., 1997; Jng et al., 2006; Liu & Wechsler, 2003; Lu et al, 2006; Swets & Weng, 1996; Wang et al., 2005; Wang et al., 2006) could be found in the literature to reduce the dimensionality of data. PCA is a simple statistical method to reduce the dimensionality while minimizing mean squared reconstruction error (Turk & Pentland, 1991). In PCA, the basis vectors are obtained by solving the algebraic eigenvalue problem:

$$\Im^T (XX^T)\Im = \Lambda \tag{12}$$

where $\Im$ and Λ are respectively the matrix of eigenvectors (covariance matrix) and the corresponding diagonal matrix of eigenvalues of the normalized data matrix X. Here notice that, if each column of the X represents a feature vectors then the matrix $XX^T = 40600 \times 40600$ need to be constructed to calculate the covariance matrix $\Im$. But it is virtually impossible for the memory constrains. Rather, the method described in (Turk & Pentland, 1991) is usually employed to construct the covariance matrix $\Im$. The projection of data Y_ε from the original a dimensional space to a subspace spanned by ε

principal eigenvectors (for the top ε eigenvalues) of the covariance matrix $\Im$ is optimal in the mean squared error sense and is expressed as:

$$Y_\varepsilon = \Im_\varepsilon^T X \tag{13}$$

Note that for two important reasons the covariance matrix will not be created for the whole data set. Firstly, because even if the method described in (Turk & Pentland, 1991) is followed, a matrix of size $X^T X = 12000 \times 12000 =$ (as the total number of feature vectors used in this experiment is 30 $\times 4 \times 100$) is needed to be constructed, which is still too large to accommodate. So, 10 subjects as representative feature vectors to create the covariance matrix are chosen. Important point to be noted is that the covariance matrix is not created for all the feature vectors of those 10 subjects. Rather, from the tensor G 400 feature vectors as $G(i, j, k, :)$ are selected, where $i = \{1, 2, ..., 10\}$, $j = \{1, 2, ..., 4\}$ and $k = \{1, 11, ..., 91\}$. Now it is rational to create the covariance matrix following (Turk & Pentland, 1991) as $X^T X = 400 \times 400$ is a manageable number. Finally, all the data of G are projected on the top r principle components of the covariance matrix and the projected tensor $P(s, p, e, r)$ is acquired, here P is a $30 \times 4 \times 100 \times r$ tensor. In practice, the value of r is chosen based on the ratio of "the sum of top r eigenvalues" and "the sum of all N eigenvalues." If the ratio is larger than a certain threshold, for example more than 0.95 then that value of *r* could be chosen. Regarding reconstruction of the original patterns this is significant from mean square error perspective (Turk & Pentland, 1991).

BIOMETRIC APPLICATIONS AND GABOR WAVELETS: NOW AND FUTURE

The primary purpose of biometrics is the identification or verification of either behavioral or physiological human biometric data. Behavioral biometrics is generally used for verification (Yampolskiy & Govindaraju, 2008). Gabor wavelets are alternatively suited best for use in computer aided applications that involve images. However, other signal-processing-based biometrics such as voice based authentication systems, may also utilize Gabor wavelets as a feature extractor. A brief description of various biometric systems (behavioral and physiological) which already apply or have the potential to apply Gabor wavelets follows below.

Behavioral Biometric

Signature and Handwriting-Based Biometrics

Signature recognition has a high level of resistance to imposters as it is quite difficult to copy the behavioral patterns associated with a signature (Jain & Prabhakar, 2004). However, signature recognition biometric systems are vulnerable to error as individuals can easily forget their own signature if the writing of it is not practiced on a regular basis. Despite the problems associated with signature verification, it is a widely accepted methodology for confirming identity (Herbst & Coetzer, 1998; Jain et al, 2002; Leclerc & Plamondon, 1994; Ramann et al., 2002).

Signature-based user verification is a special type of the handwriting-based biometric. However, handwriting-based user verification being content independent, makes the process more complicated and challenging (Ballard et al., 2006; Ramann et al., 2002). Zhu et al. (2000) view each person's handwriting having a specific texture, with the spatial frequency and orientation contents of the handwriting representing the features of each texture. They applied the 2D Gabor filtering technique to extract features of such textures. Finally, a weighted Euclidean distance classifier is applied to perform the identification task. Note here that the strength of Gabor wavelets in texture segmentation and feature extraction is well established method (Clark et al., 1987, Jain & Farrokhnia, 1991).

Not many applications apply wavelets or wavelet type transformations for signature recognition (Leclerc & Plamondon, 1994). A wavelet-based off-line handwritten signature verification system is proposed by Deng et al. (1999). Their system can automatically identify useful and common features which consistently exist within different signatures of the same person. Based on these features, their signature verification system can effectively confirm whether a signature has been made by the same person or not. The system starts with a closed-contour tracing algorithm (Deng et al., 1999), after the curvature signature data is traced it is decomposed into multiresolutional signals using wavelet transforms. In Figure 7 Gabor wavelets responses for a normalized signature data at eight orientations and five scales using the equation 7 is depicted. Note however that the signature data first needs to be detected automatically in an image (Zhu et al., 2007). Thus a certain amount of application dependent preprocessing is required, especially given that signatures in some cases can be different in scale and orientation. Post processing includes PCA, ICA, or LDA based dimensionality reduction techniques (Jain et al., 2000). Moreover, state

Figure 7. Gabor magnitude representation of signature data

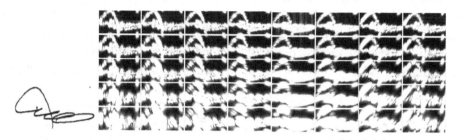

of the art classification tools such as SVM can be applied on the lower dimensional feature to identify writers (Jain et al., 2000).

Dynamic Facial Feature and Facial Biometrics

The facial feature tracking for face recognition or person identification is the dynamic or behavioral approach of face processing based biometrics. In this approach different methods are applied to track facial features assuming that the movement of facial features is unique for an individual. Pamudurthy et al. (2005) track the motion of the skin pores on the face during a facial expression and obtain a vector field that characterizes the deformation of the face. In the training process, two images of an individual are captured with a high-resolution camera, one image with natural expression and the other with a facial expression which could for example include a subtle smile. A similar approach is taken by Ito et al. (2005) while processing facial images for smile and laughter recognition. However, because facial features change with the aging process, both the static and dynamic facial feature based identification represent an important area of research (Geng et al., 2007).

Gabor and other wavelets are also applied in facial feature tracking and identification (Li & Chellappa, 2001). Application of Gabor wavelets in face tracking is a common event in facial recognition (Ferisa et al, 2004). Li and Chellappa (2001) proposed a method for facial features defined on

a grid to be tracked with Gabor attributes. The motion of facial feature points is modeled using global and local processing. A global 2D affine transformation to model the head motion was applied. A local deformation to model the residual motion that was due to inaccuracies in 2D affine modeling and other factors such as facial expression was applied. The basic idea was to track the person dependent change of facial feature points from the Gabor responses recorded at the grid points, and from these characteristics of change verifies the individuals.

Gabor wavelets are very commonly used in static face (Zhao et al., 2003) and facial expression recognition (Dailey et al. 2002). Lades et al. (1993) applied Gabor wavelets for face recognition, using the Dynamic Link Architecture (DLA) framework. At first the DLA computes the Gabor jets and then it performs a flexible template comparison between the resulting image decompositions applying graph-matching methods. In a later work Wiskott et al. (1997) expanded the DLA and developed a Gabor wavelets-based elastic bunch graph matching method which was used to recognize human faces. Lyons et al. (Lyons et al., 1999; Lyons et al., 2000) proposed a two-class categorization of gender, race, and facial expression from facial image based on the 2D Gabor wavelets representation and the labeled elastic graph matching. Donato et al. (1999) have compared a method based on Gabor representation with other techniques, finding that the Gabor provided better performance. In a series of works, Liu combined Gabor features with enhanced fisher linear discriminant methods (Liu, 2002) and kernel PCA with fractional power polynomial models on the Gabor features (Liu, 2004), Liu & Wechsler (2003) applied Gabor+PCA+ICA method for face recognition. Some researches involve identification by near infrared facial image and object that extracts features using Gabor (Braithwaite, 1994; Li, et al., 2007). In section "Gabor Feature Representation" an example is illustrated in detail to explain the application of Gabor wavelets in face recognition.

Gait, Body-Shape and Body-Motion Biometrics

The usual meaning of 'gait' is 'manner of walking' Nixon & Carter (2006). "A given person will perform his or her walking pattern in a fairly repeatable and characteristic way, sufficiently unique that it is possible to recognize a person at a distance by their gait" (Sarkar et al., 2005; Hu, et al. 2004). The performance of gait recognition is effected by many factors, such as the silhouette quality, walking speed, dynamic/static component, elapsed time, shoes, carrying condition (Ben et al., 2002; Haritaoglu et al., 2001), physical and medical condition, disguise, indoor or outdoor location, etc (Boyd, 2004; Nixon & Carter, 2004; Winter, 1991).

Among different representations (Boyd, 2004; Nixon & Carter, 2006; Nixon et al., 2005; Wang et al., 2003.a ; Wang et al., 2003.b; Wang et al., 2004), the averaged gait image is a robust representation for gait recognition task (Han & Bhanu, 2004; Liu & Sharker, 2004; Tao et al., 2007). The averaged gait image is the mean image (pixel by pixel) of silhouettes over a gait cycle within a sequence (Han & Bhanu, 2004; Tao et al., 2007). A gait cycle is a series of stances: from full-stride-stance and heels-together-stance, to full-stride-stance (please see Nixon et al. (2005) for definitions). As suggested in (Liu & Sharker, 2004) usually for averaged gait representation the whole gait sequence is partitioned into a series

of sub–sequences according to the gait period length. Then the binary images (because it is just the silhouette) within one cycle (a sub–sequence) are averaged to acquire a set of mean silhouette images for that whole gait sequence. An example is illustrated in Figure 8. Finally, the Gabor filters (equation 7) are applied on the averaged gait image to acquire the features following the similar method discussed in section "Gabor Future Representation". In Figure 9 an averaged gait image and the Gabor response at 8 orientations and 5 scales for this is presented.

Even though body-shape-based biometrics is not common as a stand alone system, it is useful for development of so-called multimodal biometric systems (Jain et al., 1999). In their work Godil et al. (2003) investigated the utility of static anthropometric distances as a biometric for human identification. The experiment is performed using the 3D landmark data from the CAESAR database (http://www.hec afrl.af.mil/cardlab/CAESAR/index.html). In the database each individual is represented with a simple biometric consisting of distances between fixed rigidly connected body locations. This biometric is clear, and invariant to view and body posture. For implementation they used gross body proportions information to model a computer vision recognition system based on this Euclidian distance measurement. In another body shape based approach Collins et al. (2002) implicitly captured biometric shape cues such as body height, width, and body-part proportions, as well as gait cues such as stride length and amount of arm swing. Relying on a template-matching based feature extraction and nearest-neighbor classifier, they tested their method on "the CMU motion of body (MoBo) database" (Gross & Shi, 2001).

Speaker Identification and Sound-Based Biometrics

Speaker identification is one of the most researched biometric technologies (Campbell, 1997; Ciota,

Figure 8. Averaged gait representation for a gait sequence

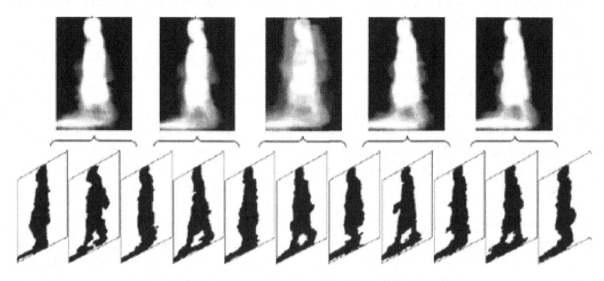

Figure 9. Gabor Wavelet's magnitude response for a single averaged gait representation

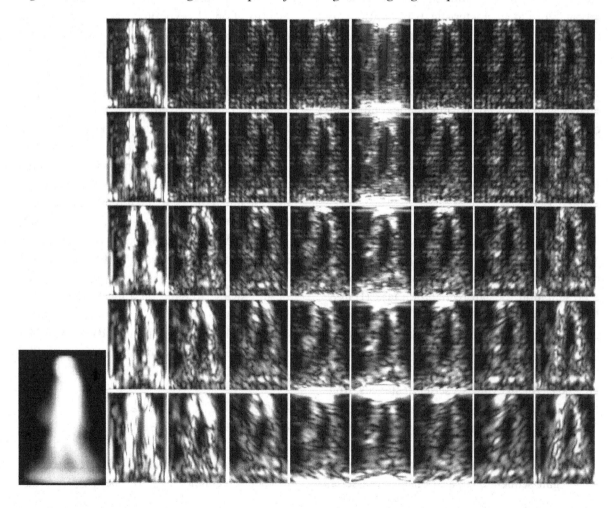

2004). Every speaker has a unique anatomical structure – the most prominent component of which is the vocal cord. Vocal cords invariably produce unique speech which is encoded in the amplitude spectrum and characterized by differences in the location and size of spectral peaks among speakers. This is related to the vocal tract shape and the pitch associated to the glottal (The airstream on the exhalation phase moves unimpeded through the larynx (voice box), pharynx (throat), and oral cavities (mouth)) source of the user.

The basic idea of a voice based recognition system is to record samples of a fixed text spoken by different users. It is also possible to collect the voice data form standard databases (Godfrey & Graff, 1994). Feature extraction is applied to the normalized amplitude of the input signal (recorded speech) which is further decomposed into several band-pass frequency channels. A frequently extracted feature is a logarithm of the Fourier transform of the voice signal in each band along with pitch, tone, cadence, and shape of the larynx (voice box) (Jain et al. 1999).

Application of Gabor filters in speaker identification is not so common. Mildner et al. (2007) proposed a method that not only applies Gabor functions for feature extraction but also optimizes the number of Gabor features required for robust text-independent speaker recognition. They applied the common Gaussian Mixture Model (GMM) (Reynold & Rose, 1995) for classification of three different feature extraction methods and also tested the classification accuracies of different combination of these three methods. These three feature extraction methods are, Mel-Frequency Cepstral Cofficient (MFCC) (Reynold & Rose, 1995), Delta- Mel-Frequency Cepstral Coefficient (DMFCC) (Mildner et al. 2007; Reynold & Rose, 1995) and Gabor filters by filtering a log-compressed Mel-Spectrum representation of a speech (Kleinschmidt, 2002).

Kleinschmidt (2002) applied Gabor as spectro-temporal filters to generate features for speaker recognition. He viewed the time-frequency relation as continuous two dimensional Gabor functions $g(f, t)$, with f frequency and t time as the product of a complex-Euler and a Gaussian as shown in equation 14.

$$g(f,t) = \frac{1}{2\pi\sigma_f\sigma_t} \cdot e^{\left[\frac{-(f-f_0)^2}{2\sigma_f} \frac{-(t-t_0)^2}{2\sigma_t}\right]} \cdot e^{(i\omega_f(f-f_0)+i\omega_t(t-t_0))}$$

(14)

where, t_0 and f_0 are the central time and central frequency, σ_t and σ_f are the standard deviation to define the Gaussian envelop dimensions, ω_t and ω_f are the radian frequencies to define the periodicity. The filtering is performed by calculating the correlation function at all time delays of each input frequency channel with the corresponding part of the Gabor function and a subsequent summation over frequency (Kleinschmidt, 2002). Following this process for each Gabor filter applied on a frame yields one output value. The output at a given center frequency $f_0 = 2284Hz$ for a voice signal is illustrated in Figure 10.

Even though voice based identification research is limited to the speaker recognition methods, recently some research has been extended to the development of technology for singer recognition to manage music databases (Tsai & Wang, 2006). Other applications include identification of individuals from their signature laughter (Ito et al., 2005).

Lip-Movement-Based User Identification

Lip reading is a common techniques for the hearing impaired to infer the speakers words. Interestingly, we all have noticed that while speaking or reading the identical lines of a text, different people will pronounce it different way, and also with substantially different lip movements. Like other biometric authentication systems, user verifica-

Figure 10. a) Mel-scale log magnitude spectrogram of an audio signal. b) The real parts of a 2D-Gabor function with $\omega_t/2\pi = -7Hz$ and $\omega_f/2\pi = -0.2 cycle/channel$. c) Real part of the Gabor filter's response. d) The feature value at $f_0 = 2284Hz$ for the real part. e) Imaginary part of the Gabor filter's response. f) The feature value at $f_0 = 2284Hz$ for imaginary part

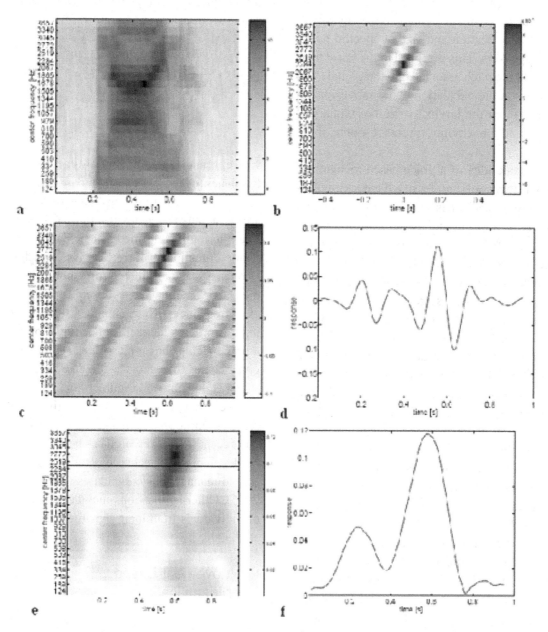

tion can be performed based on the similarity of the generated model (acquired previously from training lip movement sequences) and observed lip movement. These models are usually acquired based on the spatio-temporal lip features. Which includes, edges and gradients of lip contours, mouth opening-closing, texture and color of skin around the lips, mouth width, upper-lower lip width, height-width of lip opening, distance between horizontal lip line and upper lip (Broun,

2002; Shipilova, 2008). Lip-dynamics-based user authentication systems can use Gabor as pre processor as well as feature extractors, specially, for detecting a lip in the facial image, segmenting the lip, acquiring the texture (Clark et al., 1987; Jain & Farrokhnia, 1991). It might also be possible to represent the lip movement image as an averaged lip image (like the average gait representation) and apply Gabor wavelets to extract features. However, overall lip dynamics based identification may not be suitable as a stand alone authentication system rather it is more suitable for a multimodal biometric system (Jain et al. 1999), usually combined with speaker recognition-based authentication where the speaker reads a fixed text (Jourlin et al., 1997; Luettin et al., 1996; Mason et al., 1999; Wark et al., 1997).

Painting-Style Based Biometrics

A Van-Gogh can easily be recognized because of its unique "pen and brush" stroke characteristic. Each painter has his/her own painting style which is expressed in the "pen and brush" stroke and use of colors which can be formally profiled. Lyu et al. (2004) developed a technique for performing multi-scale, multi-orientation painting decomposition from high-resolution scanned images of paintings. In their proposed method an idealized multi-scale and multi-orientation decomposition of frequency space is performed. This decomposition will then change the basis from functions maximally localized in space (pixels), to one in which the basis functions are localized not only in space but also in orientation and scale. They show that by constructing a compact model of the statistics from such representations, it is possible to detect any inconsistencies between paintings and drawings claimed to be produced by the same painter. Even though they did not apply Gabor wavelets for decomposition, it is very possible to utilize the strength of Gabor filters for multi-scale and multi-orientation feature extraction -- both in special and frequency domain given its success in face, gait and speaker identification.

Mouse-Dynamics and Keyboard-Dynamic Based Biometrics

A unique profile can be generated based on the GUI uses and that can be compared later for authentication (Ahmed & Traore, 2005a, Ahmed & Traore, 2005b; Ahmed & Traore, 2007; Pusara, & Brodley, 2004). Ahmed & Traore (2007) extracted discriminating features from general mouse movement, drag and drop, point and click, and stillness. Based on these features they calculated the average speed against the distance traveled and average speed against the movement direction. Pusara & Brodley (2004) adopted different method for feature extraction in which they split the mouse event data into mouse wheel movements, clicks, menu and toolbar clicks. Some mouse-dynamics based recognition systems are unrestricted in which the user is free to use the mouse (Ahmed & Traore, 2007; Pusara, & Brodley, 2004) and some are restricted in which the user is given a specific task with a list of actions they can perform (Gamboa & Fred, 2003; Gamboa & Fred, 2004). Gamboa and Fred (Gamboa & Fred, 2003; Gamboa & Fred, 2004) have tried to improve accuracy of mouse-dynamics-based biometrics by restricting the time and domain of data collection. They use the activities of the mouse while the user plays an online game. This may have shortened the flexibility of this application but it increased the accuracies of authentication. The features they extracted are, x and y coordinates of the mouse, horizontal velocity, vertical velocity, tangential velocity, tangential acceleration, tangential jerk and angular velocity.

Like mouse usage, Keystroke dynamics is also applied for user authentication (Bartolacci et al., 2005; Bella & Palmer, 2006; Hocquet et al., 2007; Ilonen, 2008). For verification, a small typing sample such as the input of user's password is sufficient, but for recognition, a large amount of keystroke data is needed. Identification is performed based upon the comparisons with the pre-registered profiles of all users. Keystroke features can vary from the time durations between the keystrokes to inter-key strokes and dwell times; duration of a key pressed down; overall typing speed; frequency of errors measured from the use of backspace or delete; use of num-pad; order in which user presses shift key to get capital letters; and the force with which keys are hit (this will require special touch and pressure sensitive keyboards) (Ilonen, 2008). The main problem with GUI uses biometric authentication is that, if the system is not considering the characteristics change of a user's GUI dynamics with time, then the false negative error of authentication may increase. This is because the user gets expert using the GUI with time, such as increase in typing speed and becoming comfortable with the mouse uses. It might be possible to apply Gabor as feature extractor in the temporal characteristics of GUI usage.

Physiological Biometrics

Ear Biometrics

Ear biometrics has certain advantages over the more established biometrics. The most prominent advantage is that they have a rich and stable structure that changes very little as a result of the aging process (Hurley et al., 2007). The ear does not suffer from the change in facial expression, and is firmly fixed in the middle of the sides of the head so that the immediate background is predictable. This is very unlike face recognition in which the performance is dependent on the identification of faces in a complex background. In ear recognition PCA is the most popular method (Chang et al., 2003; Hurley et al., 2005). Hurley et al. (2005) proposed an invertible linear transform which transforms an ear image into a force field by pretending that pixels have a mutual attraction proportional to their intensities and inverse to the square of the distance between them, thereby following the principle of Newton's Universal Law of Gravitation. However, it is well-established that if the feature is extracted with Gabor wavelets and then this dimensionality reduction and classification techniques are applied the recognition rate increases (Turk & Pentland, 1991; Nixon et al., 2005; Tao et al., 2007). In Figure 11 an ear image and Gabor magnitude representation of it is illustrated. At this point we should also not forget that the Gabor wavelets can be applied as texture analyzer for ear location identification via segmentation (Clark et al., 1987; Jain & Farrokhnia, 1991).

Fingerprint and Palmprint Based Authentication

Fingerprint biometrics (Lee & Gaensslen, 1991) is a long researched biometric authentication system which is quite similar to the biometric Palmprint recognition application (Zhang, 2004) which has been introduced recently. Fingerprints are the ridge and furrow patterns on the tip of the finger (Tan & Bhanu, 2005) which have been used extensively for person identification (Jain et al., 1997). Fingerprints are fully formed at about seven months of fetal development. Finger ridge configurations do not change throughout the life of an individual (Richards, 2008).

According to Jie et al. (2006) a minutia point can be viewed as an anomaly in locally parallel ridges and it can be captured using the Gabor filters. Before filtering the fingerprint image, Jie et al. (2006) normalize the grey level intensities in the region of interest in each sector (Figure 13.a) separately to a constant mean and variance. Normalization is performed to remove the effects of sensor noise and gray level background due to finger pressure differences. Then they apply a two-stage classifier composed of a K-nearest neighbor classifier in its first stage and a set of neural network classifiers in its second stage. This

Figure 11. Gabor magnitude representation of an ear image

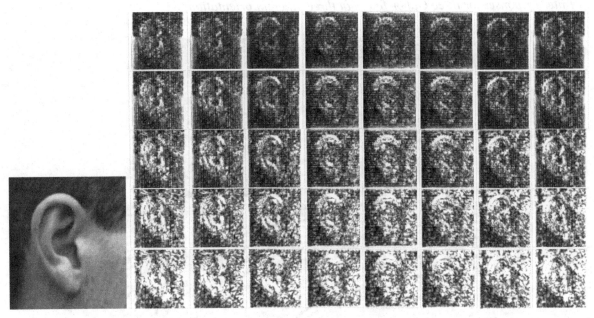

allows them to classify a feature vector extracted applying Gabor wavelets. In Figure 12 a fingerprint image marked with the region of interest (a), normalized and cropped region of interest fingerprint image (b), and Gabor filter response for a given scale at three different orientations (c) is depicted.

Iris and Retina Based Human Identification

The iris begins to form during the third month of gestation (Kronfeld, 1962). Daugman (Daugman, 1993a; Daugman, 2003; Daugman, 2006) investigated the randomness and uniqueness of the human iris. Gabor wavelets was applied on the iris images to extract the phase structure of each iris pattern. The phase structure was extracted by demodulation with quadrature wavelet sampling at several scales. Usually the iris in each image is automatically localized and isolated by algorithms to find its inner (pupil) and outer (limbus) boundaries using circular and arcuate edge detection (Daugman, 1993a). Then each of

the isolated iris patterns is encoded by demodulation (Daugman & Downing, 1995) to extract its detailed phase information using 2D Gabor wavelets. Performing the Exclusive-OR (XOR) operation on the extracted binary representation across the patterns in the database, Daugman and Downing (2001) measured the discriminating ability of the iris patterns. There are other methods (Ahmadi et al., 2007; Boles & Boashash, 1998; Chen et al., 2006; Gan & Liang, 2006; Sanchez-Avila et al., 2002) that apply different types of wavelet based transforms for iris recognition. In Figure 13 you will see an eye image taken with a near infrared camera (a) and the normalized iris representation (b) followed by the magnitude (c) and phase (d) Gabor response for a given scale and orientation.

In 1935 two ophthalmologists Carleton Simon and Isodore Goldstein, while studying eye disease, made a startling discovery: every eye has its own totally unique pattern of blood vessels, which lead to today's retina scanners and retina based biometrics (Simon & Goldstein, 1935). It is very difficult to counterfeit an internal body image

Figure 12. a) A fingerprint image marked with the region of interest. b) Normalized fingerprint image. c) Filter responses for three Gabor filters at three different orientations

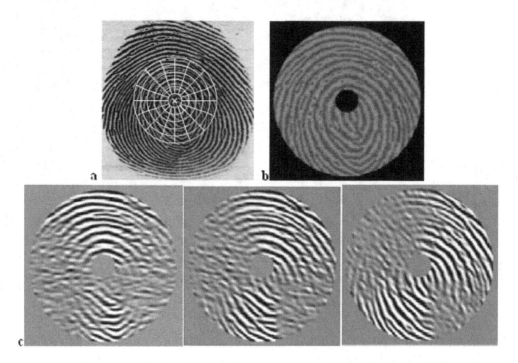

Figure 13. a) An near infrared iris image. b) The normalized iris representation following Daugman (1993). c) The magnitude representation for a scale and orientation of the Gabor filter. d) The phase representation for a scale and orientation of the Gabor filter

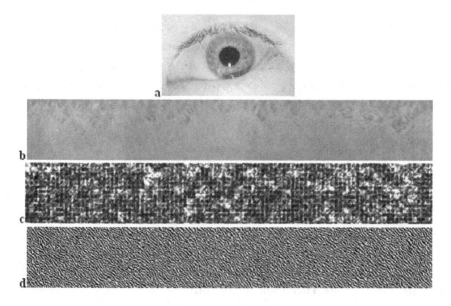

such as the retina/choroids based Identification system, as the person must cooperate so that the data can be collected (Hill, 1999). An attempt to obtain live images of the retina suitable for personal identification is made by (Yokouchi et al., 1974; Ortega et al., 2006). Xu et al. (2005) used the green grayscale retinal image and obtained the vector curve of blood vessel skeleton. Then they defined a set of feature vectors for each image including feature points, directions, and scaling factor. In their method, feature matching consists of finding affine transformation parameters which relate the query and its best corresponding enrolled image.

Farzin, et al. (2008) introduced an algorithm to detect retinal blood vessels, which are applied for feature extracted from a multi-scale code representation of the blood vessel distribution pattern around the optical disk (In the center of the retina is the optical nerve or optical disk (OD), a circular to oval white area measuring about 2×1.5mm across (about 1/30 of retina diameter) (Goh, 2000).). Finally, a similarity measure technique called "modified correlation" is implemented for human identification based on multi-scale blood vessel features. Figure 14 depicts the anatomy of the retina (a) and a retinal fundus image (b) followed by the Gabor based energy estimation (c) combining the 40 Gabor magnitude representations at 8 orientations and 5 scales (d). The retinal vessel structure is unique for each individual hence, the person identification in retina based biometrics systems is performed matching the vessel structure against the stored vessel.

ADVANTAGES OF GABOR WAVELETS

The most successful use of Gabor wavelets is in facial recognition, especially facial expression (Dailey, 2002) and face recognition (Liu, 2004). Liu (2004) showed that Gabor base feature extraction methods can identify individuals with

about 100% accuracy compared to PCA based feature extraction methods that had bellow 90% recognition rate. It is also successfully applied in other physiological Biometrics. In fingerprint based person identification Jie et al. (2006) proposed an application that uses Gabor wavelets as feature extractor which outperforms other feature extraction methods. Like wise for retinal vessel segmentation Farzin, et al. (2008) and iris based perform identification Daugman (2006) showed that Gabor wavelets acquire more relevant features than other feature extraction methods.

In behavioral biometrics the most successful use of Gabor wavelets is in gait based person identification, in a detailed comparison with other feature extraction methods, Tao et al., 2007 have shown that summation based Gabor representation have the highest recognition accuracy of 77% on average with respect to other feature extraction methods which have no more than 70%. Li and Chellappa (2001) have shown that Gabor estimates the facial features in such a way that it is very suitable even for dynamic facial change based person identification. Even if the behavioral biometrics application is not vision based, like speaker recognition, then also Gabor wavelets based feature extraction out performs other feature extraction methods. For example Mildner et al. (2007) have shown that very effective feature extraction method Mel-Frequency Cepstral Coefficients (MFCC) can recognize individuals with about 93% accuracy, however MFCC+ Gabor can recognize with about 99% accuracy for voice data.

Gabor wavelets can be implemented very efficiently since the filters of the wavelet can be pre-calculated and stored in the memory. This makes the applications using Gabor wavelets very fast. From the code provided in this work it is clear that the implementation is not complicated.

The scientific base of the Gabor wavelets is significantly strong. This is because i) Gabor's proposed wavelet is derived in harmony with the physical world as its optimality is mathematically

Figure 14. a) Anatomy of the retina. b) Normalized retinal image. c) Phase congruency acquired from the Gabor based energy calculation. d) Gabor magnitude representation at 40 different scales and orientations of the normalized retinal image

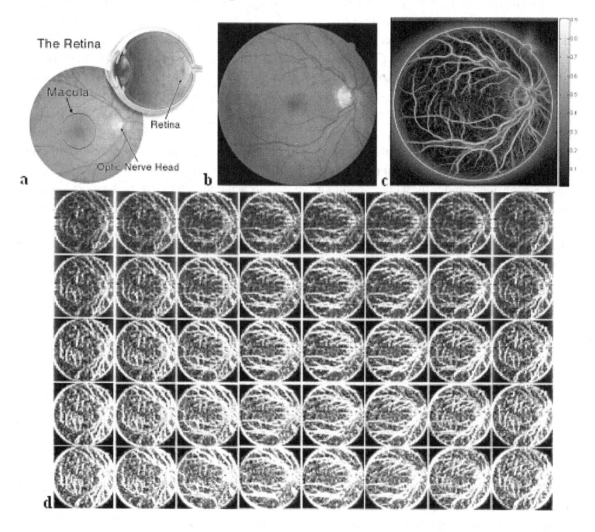

proven (Gabor, 1946), ii) the mammalian visual system which evolved to a state of optimality and completeness by tuning the spatial structure of the receptive fields of simple cells similar to Gabor wavelets (Daugman, 1980; DeValois, 1988; Lee, 1996) makes this method biologically significant iii) different human identification systems specially vision based ones developed using Gabor wavelets based feature extraction methods outperforms other feature extraction methods.

CONCLUSION

Given the success of Gabor wavelets representation in 2D (Soares et al., 2006) and 3D (Wu & Bhanu, 1997) object recognition, most of the time, only the image based biometric systems are thought suitable for application of Gabor wavelets. However, there are other biometric systems such as voice based identification systems (Mildner et al., 2007) that have proven the applicability of Gabor wavelets (Kleinschmidt, 2002). One may think these wavelets are only suitable for physiological biometric (systems that uses static data as input) applications, however, we found that they are also successfully applied in dynamic systems such as behavioral characteristics-based human identification, which includes gait recognition (Tao et al., 2007), and speaker identification (Mildner et al., 2007).

The applicability of Gabor wavelets in many behavioral and physiological biometric systems is yet to be explored. In this chapter we have provided some examples how this wavelets can be applied. For some applications such as iris, fingerprint, the Gabor wavelets are applied as a local feature enhancement operation. However, given the holistic feature extraction ability of this wavelets in face (Liu, 2004) and gait recognition (Tao et al, 2007), other applications such as iris, fingerprint and retina recognition systems are yet to be built with holistically extracted Gabor features.

Applications using Gabor wavelets shows increase in the recognition accuracies for behavioral biometrics. For example, recognition accuracies from gait (Tao et al., 2007) increased 70% to 77%, and speaker identification (Mildner et al., 2007) increased to 99% from 93%. Gabor wavelets is simple to implement as the filters are directly acquired in the frequency domain and a pixel by pixel multiplication with the Fourier transformed image produces the filter response in the frequency domain. For most applications it is possible to pre-compute the filters of the wavelets in the frequency domain and store them in the memory, which makes applications with Gabor wavelets tremendously fast.

Our research show that for three reasons this wavelet should be chosen over other feature extraction methods which are i) different human identification systems developed using Gabor wavelets based feature extraction methods outperforms other feature extraction methods (Liu, 2004, Mildner et al., 2007, Tao et al., 2007), ii) Gabor's proposed wavelet is derived in harmony with the physical world and its optimality is mathemati-

cally proven (Gabor, 1946) which ensures that the features extracted using Gabor wavelet best represents the subject, iii) the mammalian visual system which evolved to a state of optimality and completeness by tuning the spatial structure of the receptive fields of simple cells similar to Gabor wavelets (Daugman, 1980; DeValois, 1988; Lee, 1996) and use of this wavelet is the best candidate to build human-like recognition systems because of its biological significance.

ACKNOWLEDGMENT

This work is supported by a grant from City University of Hong Kong (Project 9610034).

REFERENCE

Ahmadi1, H., Pousaberi, A., Azizzadeh, A., & Kamarei, M. (2007). *An efficient iris coding based on Gauss-Laguerre wavelets.* (LNCS 4642, pp. 917–926).

Ahmed, A. A. E., & Traore, I. (2005a). Anomaly intrusion detection based on biometrics. *IAW, 05,* 452–453.

Ahmed, A. A. E., & Traore, I. (2005b). Detecting computer intrusions using behavioral biometrics. *Conference on Privacy, Security and Trust* (pp. 91-98).

Ahmed, A. A. E., & Traore, I. (2007). A new biometric technology based on mouse dynamics. *IEEE Transactions on Dependable and Secure Computing, 4*(3), 165–179. doi:10.1109/TDSC.2007.70207

Ballard, L., Lopresti, D., & Monrose, F. (2006a). Evaluating the security of handwriting biometrics. *IWFHR '06.* Retrieved from http://hal.inria.fr/docs/00/10/48/11/PDF/cr1108232462618.pdf

Bartolacci, G., Curtin, M., Katzenberg, M., Nwana, N., Cha, S.-H., & Tappert, C. C. (2005). Long-text keystroke biometric applications over the Internet. Retrieved from http://www.csis.pace.edu/~ctappert/srd2005/d3.pdf

Belhumeur, P. N., Hespanha, J. P., & Kriegman, D. J. (1997). Eigenfaces vs. Fisherfaces: Recognition using class specific linear projection. *IEEE Trans. PAMI.*, *19*(7), 711–720.

Bella, S. D., & Palmer, C. (2006). Personal identifiers in musicians' finger movement dynamics. *Journal of Cognitive Neuroscience*, ▪▪▪, 18.

Ben, C., Kader, A. & Davis, L. S. (2002). Detection of people carrying objects: A motion-based recognition approach. *FG'02*, 378-383.

Boles, W. W., & Boashash, B. (1998). A human identification technique using images of the iris and wavelet transform. *IEEE Trans. SP*, *46*(4), 1185–1188. doi:10.1109/78.668573

Boyd, J. E. (2004). Synchronization of oscillations for machine perception of gaits. *J. CVIU*, *96*(1), 35–59.

Braithwaite, R., & Bhanu, B. (1994). Hierarchical Gabor filters for object detection in infrared images. *IEEE Conf. Com. Vision Pattern Recognition*, 628–631.

Broun, C. C., Zhang, X., Mersereau, R. M., & Clements, M. A. (2002). Automatic speechreading with applications to speaker verification. *ICASSP '02*, 1, 685-688.

Campbell, F. W., & Robson, J. G. (1968). Application of Fourier analysis to the visibility of gratings. *The Journal of Physiology*, *197*, 551–566.

Campbell, J. P. (1997). Speaker recognition: A tutorial. *Proceedings of the IEEE*, *85*(9), 1437–1462. doi:10.1109/5.628714

Chang, K., Bowyer, K. W., Sarkar, S., & Victor, B. (2003). Comparison and combination of ear and face images in appearance-based biometrics. *IEEE Trans. PAMI*, *25*(9), 1160–1165.

Chen, Y., Dass, S. C., & Jain, A. K. (2006). Localized iris image quality using 2-D wavelets. (. *LNCS*, *3832*, 373–381.

Ciota, Z. (2004). Speaker verification for multimedia application. *IEEE Int. Conf. SMC*, *3*, 2752–2756.

Clark, M., Bovik, A. C., & Geisler, W. S. (1987). Texture segmentation using Gabor modulation/demodulation. *Pattern Recognition Letters*, *6*, 261–267. doi:10.1016/0167-8655(87)90086-9

Collins, R. T., Gross, R., & Shi, J. (2002). Silhouette-based human identification from body shape and gait. *FG'02*, 366-371.

Dailey, M. N., Cottrell, G. W., Padgett, C., & Adolphs, R. (2002). EMPATH: A neural network that categorizes facial expressions. *Journal of Cognitive Neuroscience*, *14*(8), 1158–1173. doi:10.1162/089892902760807177

Darwin, C. (1859). *On the origin of species by means of natural selection, or the preservation of favoured races in the struggle for life*. London: John Murray, 1st edition.

Daubechies, I. (1992). Ten lectures on wavelets. *61 of CBMS-NSF Regional Conference Series in Applied Mathematics*.

Daugman, J. G. (1980). Two-dimensional spectral analysis of cortical receptive field profiles. *Vision Research*, *20*, 847–856. doi:10.1016/0042-6989(80)90065-6

Daugman, J. G. (1985). Uncertainty relation for resolution in space, spatial frequency, and orientation optimized by two-dimensional visual cortical filters. *Journal of the Optical Society of America*, *2*(7), 1160–1169. doi:10.1364/JOSAA.2.001160

Daugman, J. G. (1988). Complete discrete 2-D Gabor transforms by neural networks for image analysis and compression. *IEEE Trans. ASSP, 36*(7), 1169–1179. doi:10.1109/29.1644

Daugman, J. G. (1993a). High confidence visual recognition of persons by a test of statistical independence. *IEEE Trans. PAMI, 15*, 1148–1161.

Daugman, J. G. (1993b). Quadrature-phase simple-cell pairs are appropriately described in complex analytic form. *Journal of the Optical Society of America, 10*(7), 375–377.

Daugman, J. G. (2003). Demodulation by complex-valued wavelets for stochastic pattern recognition. *International Journal of Wavelets, Multresolution, and Information Processing, 1*(1), 1–17. doi:10.1142/S0219691303000025

Daugman, J. G. (2006). Probing the uniqueness and randomness of iris codes: Results from 200 billion iris pair comparisons. *Proceedings of the IEEE, 94*(11), 1927–1935. doi:10.1109/JPROC.2006.884092

Daugman, J. G., & Downing, C. J. (1995). Demodulation, predictive coding, and spatial vision. *Journal of the Optical Society of America, 12*, 641–660. doi:10.1364/JOSAA.12.000641

Daugman, J. G., & Downing, C. J. (2001). Epigenetic randomness, complexity, and singularity of human iris patterns. *Proceedings of the Royal Society of London, 268*, 1737–1740. doi:10.1098/rspb.2001.1696

Deng, P. S. H., Liao, H. Y. M., Ho, C. W., & Tyan, H. R. (1999). Wavelet-based offline handwritten signature verification. *J. CVIU., 76*(3), 173–190.

DeValois, R. L., & DeValois, K. K. (1988). *Spatial vision*. New York: Oxford Univ. Press.

DeValois, R. L., Yund, E. W., & Hepler, N. (1982). The orientation and direction selectivity of cells in macaque visual cortex. *Vision Research, 22*, 531–544. doi:10.1016/0042-6989(82)90112-2

Donato, G., Bartlett, M. S., Hager, J. C., Ekman, P., & Sejnowski, T. J. (1999). Classifying facial actions. *IEEE Trans. PAMI, 21*(10), 974–989.

Farzin, H., Abrishami-Moghaddam, H., & Moin, M.-S. (2008). A novel retinal identification system. *J. Advances in Signal Processing*, 1-10.

Ferisa, R. S., Kruegerb, V., & Cesar, R. M. Jr. (2004). A wavelet subspace method for real-time face tracking. *Real-Time Imaging, 10*, 339–350. doi:10.1016/j.rti.2004.06.002

Gabor, D. (1946). Theory of communication. *J. Institute of Electronic Engineers, 93*, 429–457.

Gamboa, H., & Fred, A. (2003). An identity authentication system based on human computer interaction behavior. *Intl. Workshop on Pattern Recognition in Information Systems.*, 46-55.

Gamboa, H., & Fred, A. (2004). *A behavioral biometric system based on human computer interaction*. Retrieved from http://www.lx.it.pt/~afred/anawebit/articles/AFredSPIE2004.pdf

Gan, J., & Liang, Y. (2006). Applications of wavelet packets decomposition in iris recognition. (. *LNCS, 3832*, 443–449.

Geng, X., Zhou, Z., & Smith-Miles, K. (2007). Automatic age estimation based on facial aging patterns. *IEEE Trans. PAMI, 29*(12), 2234–2240.

Godfrey, J., & Graff, D. (1994). Public databases for speaker recognition and verification. *ECSA Workshop Automat. Speaker Recognition, 10*, 39–42.

Godil, A., Grother, P., & Ressler, S. (2003). Human identification from body shape. *3DIM'03*, 386-391.

Goh, K. G., Hsu, W., & Lee, M. L. (2000). An automatic diabetic retinal image screening system. *Medical Data Mining and Knowledge Discovery*, 181–210.

Gross, R., & Shi, J. (2001). The CMU motion of body (MoBo) database. (Tech. Rep. CMU-RI-TR-01- 18). Robotics Institute, Carnegie Mellon University.

Han, J., & Bhanu, B. (2004). Statistical feature fusion for gait-based human recognition. *IEEE Int'l Conf. Computer Vision and Pattern Recognition*, 2, 842–847.

Haritaoglu, I., Cutler, R., Harwood, D., & Davis, L. (2001). Backpack: Detection of people carrying objects using silhouettes. *J. CVIU*, 6(3), 385–397.

Herbst, B., & Coetzer, H. (1998). On an offline signature verification system. *South African Workshop on Pattern Recognition*, 39-43.

Hill, R. B. (1999). Retinal identification. In A. Jain, R. Bolle & S. Pankati (Eds.), *Biometrics: Personal identification in networked society*. Berlin: Springer.

Hocquet, S., Ramel, J., & Cardot, H. (2007). User classification for keystroke dynamics authentication. (. *LNCS*, 4642, 531–539.

Hu, W. M., Tan, T. N., Wang, L., & Maybank, S. (2004). A survey of visual surveillance of object motion and behaviors. *IEEE Trans. SMC-C*, 34(3), 334–352.

Hurley, D. J., Arbab-Zavar, B., & Nixon, M. S. (2007). *The ear as a biometric*. Retrieved from http://www.eurasip.org/Proceedings/Eusipco/Eusipco2007/Papers/A1L-B02.pdf

Hurley, D. J., Nixon, M. S., & Carter, J. N. (2005). Force field feature extraction for ear biometrics. *J. CVIU*, 98, 491–512.

Ilonen, J. (2008). *Keystroke dynamics*. Retrieved from www.it.lut.fi/kurssit/03-04/010970000/seminars/Ilonen.pdf

Ito, A., Wang, X., Suzuki, M., & Makini, S. (2005). Smile and laughter recognition using speech processing and face recognition from conversation video. *CW'05*, 437-444.

Jain, A. K., Bolle, R., & Pankanti, S. (1999). *Biometrics: Personal identification in networked society*. Kluwer Academic Publishing.

Jain, A. K., Duin, R. P. W., & Mao, J. (2000). Statistical pattern recognition: A review. *IEEE Trans. PAMI*, 22(1), 4–37.

Jain, A. K., & Farrokhnia, F. (1991). Unsupervised texture segmentation using Gabor filters. *Pattern Recognition*, 24(12), 1167–1186. doi:10.1016/0031-3203(91)90143-S

Jain, A. K., Griess, F., & Connell, S. (2002). Online signature verification. *Pattern Recognition*, 35, 2963–2972. doi:10.1016/S0031-3203(01)00240-0

Jain, A. K., Hong, L., Pankanti, S., & Bolle, R. (1997). An identity authentication system using fingerprints. *Proceedings of the IEEE*, 85(9), 1365–1388. doi:10.1109/5.628674

Jain, A. K., Ross, A., & Prabhakar, S. (2004). An introduction to biometric recognition. IEEE *Trans. CSVT*, 14(1), 4–20.

Jie, Y., Yi fang, Y., Renjie, Z., & Qifa, S. (2006). Fingerprint minutiae matching algorithm for real time system. *Pattern Recognition*, 39(1), 143–146. doi:10.1016/j.patcog.2005.08.005

Jng, X., Wong, H., & Zhang, D. (2006). Face recognition based on 2D fisherface approach. *Pattern Recognition*, 39(4), 707–710. doi:10.1016/j.patcog.2005.10.020

Jones, J. P., & Palmer, L. A. (1987). An evaluation of the two-dimensional Gabor filter model of simple receptive fields in the cat striate cortex. *Journal of Neurophysiology, 58,* 1233–1258.

Jourlin, P., Luettin, J., Genoud, D., & Wassner, H. (1997). Acoustic-labial speaker verification. *Pattern Recognition Letters, 18*(9), 853–858. doi:10.1016/S0167-8655(97)00070-6

Kleinschmidt, M. (2002). *Robust speech recognition based on spectrotemporal processing.* Unpublished doctoral dissertation, University of Oldenburg. Retrieved from http://docserver. bis.uni-oldenburg.de/publikationen/dissertation/2002/klerob02/pdf/klerob02.pdf

Kronfeld, P. C. (1962). Gross anatomy and embryology of the eye. In *The eye.*

Kulikowski, J. J., & Bishop, P. O. (1981). Fourier analysis and spatial representation in the visual cortex. *Experientia, 37,* 160–163. doi:10.1007/BF01963207

Lades, M., Vorbruggen, J. C., Buhmann, J., Lange, J., Von Der Malsburg, C., Wurtz, R. P., & Konen, W. (1993). Distortion invariant object recognition in the dynamic link architecture. *IEEE Transactions on Computers, 42,* 300–311. doi:10.1109/12.210173

Leclerc, F., & Plamondon, R. (1994). Automatic signature verification: The state of the art. *J. PRAI, 8*(3), 643–660.

Lee, H. C., & Gaensslen, R. E. (Eds.). (1991). *Advances in fingerprint technology.* New York: Elsevier.

Lee, T. S. (1996). Image representation using 2D Gabor wavelets. *IEEE Trans. PAMI, 18*(10), 1–13.

Li, B., & Chellappa, R. (2001). Face verification through tracking facial features. *Journal of the Optical Society of America, 18*(12), 2969–2981. doi:10.1364/JOSAA.18.002969

Li, S. Z., Chu, R. F., Liao, S. C., & Zhang, L. (2007). Illumination invariant face recognition using near-infrared images. *IEEE Trans. PAMI, 29*(4), 1–13.

Liu, C. (2002). Gabor feature based classification using the enhanced fisher linear discriminant model for face recognition. *IEEE Trans. IP., 11*(4), 467–476.

Liu, C. (2004). Gabor-based kernel PCA with fractional power polynomial models for face recognition. *IEEE Trans. PAMI, 26*(5), 572–581.

Liu, C., & Wechsler, H. (2003). Independent component analysis of Gabor features for face recognition. *IEEE Trans. NN., 14*(4), 919–928.

Liu, Z., & Sarkar, S. (2004). Simplest representation yet for gait recognition: Averaged silhouette. *IEEE Int'l Conf. Pattern Recognition, 4,* 211–214.

Lu, J., Plataniotis, K. N., Venetsnopulos, A. N., & Li, S. Z. (2006). Ensemble-based discriminant learning with bosting for face recognition. *IEEE Trans. NN., 17*(1), 1–13.

Luettin, J., Thacker, N. A., & Beet, S. W. (1996). Speaker identification by lipreading. *ICSLP '96, 1,* 62-65.

Lyons, M. J., Budynek, J., & Akamatsu, S. (1999). Automatic classification of single facial images. *IEEE Trans. PAMI, 21*(12), 1357–1362.

Lyons, M. J., Budynek, J., Plante, A., & Akamatsu, S. (2000). Classifying facial attributes using a 2-D Gabor wavelet representation and discriminant analysis. *FG '02,* 202-207.

Lyu, S., Rockmore, D., & Farid, H. (2004). A digital technique for art authentication. *Proceedings of the National Academy of Sciences of the United States of America, 101*(49), 17006–17010. doi:10.1073/pnas.0406398101

Maclennan, B. (1991). *Gabor representations of spatiotemporal visual images*. Retrieved from www.cs.utk.edu/~mclennan/papers/GRSTVI.ps

Maffei, L., & Fiorentini, A. (1973). The visual cortex as a spatial frequency analyzer. *Vision Research, 13*, 1255–1267. doi:10.1016/0042-6989(73)90201-0

Marcelja, S. (1980). Mathematical description of the responses of simple cortical cells. *Journal of the Optical Society of America, 70*, 1297–1300. doi:10.1364/JOSA.70.001297

Mason, J. S. D., Brand, J., Auckenthaler, R., Deravi, F., & Chibelushi, C. (1999). Lip signatures for automatic person recognition. *IEEE Workshop, MMSP*, 457-462.

Mildner, V., Goetze, S., Kammeyer, K. D., & Mertins, A. (2007). Optimization of Gabor features for text-independent speaker identification. *ISCAS, 07*, 3932–3935.

Movellan, J. R. (2008). *Tutorial on Gabor filters*. Retrieved from http://mplab.ucsd.edu/wordpress/tutorials/gabor.pdf

Nalwa, V. S. (1997). Automatic online signature verification. *Proceedings of the IEEE*, 215-239.

Nixon, M. S., & Carter, J. N. (2004). On gait as a biometric: Progress and prospects. *EUSIPCO, 04*, 1401–1404.

Nixon, M. S., & Carter, J. N. (2006). Automatic recognition by gait. *Proceedings of the IEEE, 94*(11), 2013–2024. doi:10.1109/JPROC.2006.886018

Nixon, M. S., Tan, T. N., & Chellappa, R. (2005). *Human identification based on gait*. New York: Springer.

Ortega, M., Marino, C., Penedo, M. G., Blanco, M., & Gonzalez, F. (2006). Biometric authentication using digital retinal images. *ACOS, 06*, 422–427.

Pamudurthy, S., Guan, E., Mueller, K., & Rafailovich, M. (2005). Dynamic approach for face recognition using digital image skin correlation. In *Audio and video-based biometrics person authentication*. New York.

Pollen, D. A., Lee, J. R., & Taylor, J. H. (1971). How does the striate cortex begin the reconstruction of the visual world? *Science, 173*, 74–77. doi:10.1126/science.173.3991.74

Pollen, D. A., & Ronner, S. F. (1981). Phase relationships between adjacent simple cells in the visual cortex. *Science, 212*, 1409–1411. doi:10.1126/science.7233231

Porat, M., & Zeevi, Y. (1988). The generalized Gabor scheme of image representation in biological and machine vision. *IEEE Trans. PAMI, 10*(4), 452–468.

Pusara, M., & Brodley, C. E. (2004). User re-authentication via mouse movements. *VizSEC/DMSEC '04*, 1-8.

Ramann, F., Vielhauer, C., & Steinmetz, R. (2002). Biometric applications based on handwriting. *IEEE ICME '02, 2*, 573–576.

Reynold, D. A., & Rose, R. C. (1995). Robust text-independent speaker identification using Gaussian mixture speaker models. *IEEE Trans. SAP, 3*(1), 72–83.

Richards, E. P. (2008). *Phenotype vs. genotype: Why identical twins have different fingerprints?* Retrieved from http://www.forensic-evidence.com/site/ID Twins.html

Sanchez-Avila, C., Sanchez-Reil, R., & Martin-Roche, D. (2002). Iris-based biometric recognition using dyadic wavelet transform. *IEEE AESS Systems Magazine*, 3-6.

Sarkar, S., Phillips, P., Liu, Z., Vega, I., Grother, P., & Bowyer, K. (2005). The humanID gait challenge problem: Data sets, performance, and analysis. *IEEE Trans. PAMI, 27*(2), 162–177.

Shipilova, O. (2008). *Person recognition based on lip movements*. Retrieved from http://www.it.lut.fi/kurssit/03-04/010970000/seminars/Shipilova.pdf

Simon, C., & Goldstein, I. (1935). A new scientific method of identification. *New York State Journal of Medicine, 35*(18), 901–906.

Soares, J. V. B., Leandro, J. J. G., Cesar, R. M. Jr, Jelinek, H. F., & Cree, M. J. (2006). Retinal vessel segmentation using the 2-D Gabor wavelet and supervised classification. *IEEE Trans. MI., 25*(9), 1214–1222.

Stein, E. M., & Weiss, G. (1971). *Introduction to Fourier analysis on Euclidean spaces*. Princeton University Press.

Swets, D. L., & Weng, J. (1996). Using discriminant eigenfeatures for image retrieval. *IEEE Trans. PAMI, 18*(8), 831–836.

Tan, X., & Bhanu, B. (2005). Fingerprint classification based on learned features. *IEEE Trans. SMC-C., 35*(3), 287–300.

Tao, D., Li, X., Wu, X., & Maybank, S. J. (2007). General tensor discriminant analysis and Gabor features for gait recognition. *IEEE Trans. PAMI, 29*(10), 1700–1715.

Tootell, R., Silverman, M., & DeValois, R. L. (1981). Spatial frequency columns in primary visual cortex. *Science, 214*, 813–815. doi:10.1126/science.7292014

Tsai, W.-H., & Wang, H.-M. (2006). Automatic singer recognition of popular music recordings via estimation and modeling of solo vocal signals. *IEEE Trans. ASLP, 14*(1), 330–341.

Turk, M., & Pentland, A. (1991). Eigenfaces for recognition. *Journal of Cognitive Neuroscience, 3*(1), 71–86. doi:10.1162/jocn.1991.3.1.71

Wang, J., Plataniotis, K. N., Lu, J., & Venetsanopoulos, A. N. (2006). On solving the face recognition problem with one training sample per subject. *Pattern Recognition, 39*, 1746–1762. doi:10.1016/j.patcog.2006.03.010

Wang, J., Plataniotis, K. N., & Venetsanopoulos, A. N. (2005). Selecting discriminant eigenfaces for face recognition. *Pattern Recognition Letters, 26*(10), 1470–1482. doi:10.1016/j.patrec.2004.11.029

Wang, L., Tan, T. N., Hu, W. M., & Ning, H. Z. (2003a). Automatic gait recognition based on statistical shape analysis. *IEEE Trans. IP, 12*(9), 1120–1131.

Wang, L., Tan, T. N., Ning, H. Z., & Hu, W. M. (2003b). Silhouette analysis-based gait recognition for human identification. *IEEE Trans. PAMI, 25*(12), 1505–1518.

Wang, L., Tan, T. N., Ning, H. Z., & Hu, W. M. (2004). Fusion of static and dynamic body biometrics for gait recognition. *IEEE Trans. CSVT., 14*(2), 149–158.

Wark, T., Thambiratnam, D., & Sridharan, S. (1997). Person authentication using lip information. *IEEE Conf. Speech and Image Technologies for Computing and Telecommunications, 1*, 153–156.

Winter, D. (1991). *The biometrics and motor control of human gait*. Ontario: Waterloo Biometrics.

Wiskott, L., Fellous, J.-M., & Von Der Malsburg, C. (1997). Face recognition by elastic bunch graph matching. *IEEE Trans. PAMI, 19*, 775–779.

Wu, X., & Bhanu, B. (1997). Gabor wavelet representation for 3-D object recognition. *IEEE Trans. IP, 6*(1), 47–63.

Xu, Z.-W., Guo, X.-X., Hu, X.-Y., & Cheng, X. (2005). The blood vessel recognition of ocular fundus. *ICMLC, 05*, 4493–4498.

Yampolskiy, R. V., & Govindaraju, V. (2008). Behavioral biometrics: A survey and classification. *Int. J. Biometrics*, *1*(1), 81–113. doi:10.1504/IJBM.2008.018665

Yokouchi, H., Yamamoto, S., Suzuki, T., Matsui, M., & Kato, K. (1974). Fundus pattern recognition. *Japanese J. Med. Electronics and Biological Engineering*, *12*(3), 123–130.

Zhang, D. (2004). Palmprint authentication system. In P. Wang (Ed.), *Handbook of pattern recognition and computer vision* (pp. 431-444).

Zhao, W., Chellappa, R., Phillips, P. J., & Rosenfeld, A. (2003). Face recognition: A literature survey. *ACM Computing Surveys*, *35*(4), 399–458. doi:10.1145/954339.954342

Zhu, G. Y., Zheng, Y. F., Doermann, D., & Jaeger, S. (2007). Multiscale structural saliency for signature detection. *IEEE Int'l Conf. Computer Vision and Pattern Recognition*, 1-8.

Zhu, Y., Tan, T., & Wang, Y. (2000). Biometric personal identification based on handwriting. *ICPR '00*, 2, 797-800.

Chapter 7
Gait Recognition and Analysis

Shiqi Yu
Chinese Academy of Sciences/The Chinese University of Hong Kong, China

Liang Wang
The University of Melbourne, Australia

ABSTRACT

With the increasing demands of visual surveillance systems, human identification at a distance is an urgent need. Gait is an attractive biometric feature for human identification at a distance, and recently has gained much interest from computer vision researchers. This chapter provides a survey of recent advances in gait recognition. First, an overview on gait recognition framework, feature extraction, and classifiers is given, and then some gait databases and evaluation metrics are introduced. Finally, research challenges and applications are discussed in detail.

INTRODUCTION

In many countries, CCTV cameras are set up almost everywhere. Cameras are used to monitor streets, building entrances, railway stations, airports, malls, national borders, etc. CCTV is helpful to police investigating the crimes and the video data can be used as evidence in courts. But the video data can suffer from bad quality due to low image resolution. Besides, the cameras are running 24 hours each day, and there are so much video data, it is impossible to view all video data by security staffs. Much of the time, even a suspect walks through a CCTV

camera, no one will recognize him. Because of the far distance most biometric features such as face, iris, palm print and finger print can not be acquired and used for identification. Gait maybe is the best candidate among biometric features for human identification at a distance.

Gait, the manner of walking, is a newly emergent biometric which offers the possibility to recognize people at a distance. Gait recognition, also called gait-based human identification, is receiving more interest from computer vision researchers because of the increasing demands of visual surveillance. Gait recognition aims to recognize people by the way they walk. Compared with those traditional biometric features gait has many unique advantages

DOI: 10.4018/978-1-60566-725-6.ch007

such as non-contact, non-invasive and perceivable at a distance.

Gait seems to be unique: From a biomechanics viewpoint, each person seems to have a distinctive way of walking because gait pattern is mainly determined by the individual's weight, limb lengths, physical dimensions, habitual posture and so on. Walking is a complex action involving synchronized integrated movements of each body segment, joints and the interaction among them (Winter, 1991). Although these movements follow the same basic pattern for all humans, they seem to vary from one individual to another in certain details such as their relative timing and magnitudes. It is the distinguishable variations in the physical properties of human body structures and the behavioral characteristics of walking actions among different subjects that may provide a unique cue to personal recognition. Many earlier studies (Murray, Drought et al., 1964; Murray, 1967) show that gait can be used to identify different persons.

Gait is non-contact and non-invasive: Most biometric features such as finger print, palm print and iris require physical touch or proximal sensing. Although some biometric systems have shown good reliability today, they still lack the users' acceptance to some extent, e.g., the users are unwilling to touch a finger print scanner and dislike closely watching an iris capture device since they think that doing so may be unclean to their hands or harmful to eyes. However, using gait feature would avoid such problems since it does not need the user's interaction other than walking. Gait can be extracted secretly at a distance which naturally advances the acceptance of the users (Cattin, Zlatnik et al., 2001).

Gait is perceivable at a distance: The gait of an individual can be easily captured at a distance. However, the established biometric features such as face, iris and finger print are limited in such capability. To operate successfully, they usually require sensing the cooperative users at close ranges, e.g., finger prints are obtained by the

user's contacting a finger print scanner and faces are taken from near distance in order to produce a resolution high enough for recognition. However at a distance, these biometric features are hardly applicable. Fortunately, gait is still visible in this case. So, from a surveillance perspective, gait is a most attractive modality for recognition at a distance.

Gait is hard to conceal: In applications of biometric recognition, many biometrics can be obscured, altered or hidden. For instance, face may be made up, at low resolution or be hidden with a mask, hands may be even cut off or be obscured, ears are probably invisible due to the occlusion by hair, etc. However, people need to walk. Hence, human gait is usually visible (i.e., the users generally do not disguise or hide their gaits purposely).

Besides human identification, gait can be used in many applications, such as in surveillance video retrieval systems, pedestrian information collection systems and others.

Human identification: For it unique advantages, gait can be used for human identification especially in visual surveillance systems. However, gait can not gain as high recognition rate as iris and finger print. So gait can only be used in a small population. In a large population, gait can be used to find some suspected persons and the security staffs confirm whether they are the persons wanted. Recognition performance can be improved by fusing gait with other biometrics such as face. As gait, face is also perceptible at a distance.

Video retrieval: After a criminal event happens, policemen and security staffs will review a lot of videos to find where the suspects have gone and what the suspects have done. Because there are a lot of cameras mounted everywhere nowadays, there are a lot of videos need to be reviewed. Gait recognition technology can compare each person in videos with suspects and search suspects automatically (Xu and Yan et al., 2007).

Pedestrian information collection: Besides

Figure 1. Gait recognition procedure

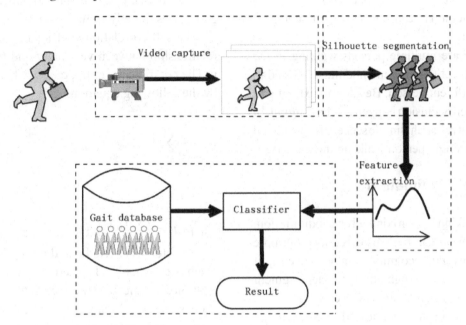

for human identification, gait feature can also be used for gender and age estimation (Davis, & Gao 2004; Yoo, Hwang et al., 2005). In stores, gait analysis technology can help to give statistical results on which gender (or which age group) is more interested with a product. Gait recognition can also identify and tracking customers with no-overlapping cameras. Some valuable information can be picked out by data mining methods.

Like all other biometric features, gait has its shortcomings. For example, it can be affected by some physical factors such as drunkenness, fatigue, pregnancy and injured joints. A person's gait depends on the psychological states (e.g., pleasure and sorrow). Walking surfaces and carrying condition can also affect gait. Compared with most physiological features, gait as a behavioral feature have relatively weaker discriminative power.

GAIT RECOGNITION ALGORITHMS

A typical gait recognition system is shown in Figure 1. Video data is captured by a camera. If

there are walking persons in the video, they are detected and segmented from the background by some motion detection and segmentation methods. Gait features can be extracted from human silhouettes those are segmented from the background. Human identification can be achieved by measuring the similarity between the extracted gait feature and those in a gait database. To extract robust and discriminative feature is an important step in gait recognition.

Silhouette Segmentation

In most applications videos are captured by fixed cameras. Human silhouettes can be extracted by background subtraction and thresholding. The method described in (Wang and Tan et al., 2003) is a simple one to segment human silhouettes. When the background is complex, some sophisticated methods, such as a Gaussian mixture model (Stauffer, & Grimson, 1999), can be used to segment silhouettes. The size of the silhouettes is normally not the same. The silhouette is small when the person is far from the camera, and large when near to the camera. Many current gait recognition methods need normalize silhouettes to the same size.

If there are multiple persons walking in the scenery, object tracking method must be used to identify different person. Besides, to extract gait feature when occlusion happens is challenging. In most current research, simple scenery is considered and only a single person walks in the scenery.

Gait Cycle Estimation

Human walking is approximately periodic motion. So gait motion can be considered as a periodic signal. Many gait recognition methods need split gait videos to some segments, and each segment contains one gait cycle. The gait cycle begins when one foot contacts the ground and ends when that foot contacts the ground again. The width of the silhouette varies periodically when human man walks (Figure 2). Suppose the silhouette width in a video is expressed as $v=[v_1, v_2, ...,v_n]$. An instance extracted from a video in the CASIA Gait Database (Dataset B) is shown in Figure 2. Because of the silhouette segmentation error, the curve in Figure

is not smooth enough. It is a little difficult to get gait cycles directly from the width vector.

The self correlation coefficients indicate the relationship between variable v and the shift of v. The coefficients, $c=[c_1, c_2, ..., c_m]$, are defined by the following equation.

$$c_j = \frac{1}{n}\sum_{k=1}^{n-j}(v_k - u)(v_{j+k} - u)$$

(1)

where $u = \frac{1}{n}\sum_{k=1}^{n}v_k$ and j=1,2,…, m.

If vector v is periodic and period is T, c_j will reach peak when $j=sT$, where $s=1,2,...$. The correlation coefficients of the vector shown in Figure 2 are is shown in Figure 3. It can be found that the curve is smoother than that in Figure 2. The curve reaches local peaks at 12, 24 and 36. Because the silhouette width changing in the first half cycle is similar to that in the next half cycle, the gait period should be 24. Then we can split gait videos to several gait cycles.

Figure 2. Silhouette width vector

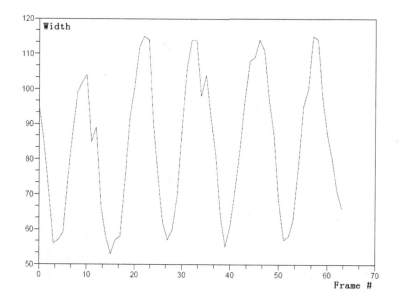

Gait Feature Extraction

According to feature extraction, the methods developed for gait recognition can be roughly divided into two categories: model-based methods and appearance-based ones. Model-based approaches (Johnson, & Bobick, 2001; Yam, Nixon et al., 2002; Wang, Ning et al., 2004)generally aim to recover gait features, such as stride dimensions, limb lengths and kinematics of joint angles, by model matching in each frame of a walking sequence. Appearance-based approaches (Mowbray, & Nixon, 2003; Wang, Tan et al., 2003) usually use the silhouettes as a whole to analyze dynamic features of motion bodies, so these methods are efficient and simple, and most of existing gait recognition approaches belong to this category.

Model-Based Features

The advantages of model-based approaches are those models can handle occlusion and noise better to some extent, and especially, offer the ability to derive gait signatures directly from model parameters. The human body is highly articulated and each part is capable of a variety of motions. Occlusion of different parts of the body happens in most body movements. So choosing a good body model is important to efficiently recover body posture parameters. Three commonly used models are the blob model (Lee, & Grimson, 2002), the stick model (Cunado, Nixon, et al. 2003) and the cylinder model (Kurakake, & Nevatia 1994).

One typical model-based feature extraction method is introduced in (Wang, Ning et al., 2004). The human body model in this work is composed of 14 rigid body parts, including upper and lower torso, neck, two upper arms, two lower arms, two thighs, two lower legs, two feet, and a head, each of which is represented by a truncated cone except for the head, which is represented by a sphere. The feature extracted from a silhouette can be represented by a twelve-dimensional vector $[x, y, \theta_1, \theta_2, ..., \theta_{10}]$, where $[x, y]$ is the global position of human body and $\theta_i, (i=1,2,...,10)$ is the joint angles of shoulders, elbows, hips, knees, and

Figure 3. Self correlation coefficients from a width vector

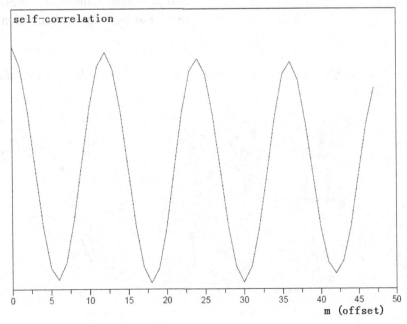

Figure 4. Human body models (Nixon, Tan et al., 2005)

ankles. The human body components are tracked under the Condensation framework. The tracking result and the thigh angle are shown in Figure 4. Similar work can also be found in (Johnson, & Bobick, 2001; Tanawongsuwan, & Bobick, 2001; Zhang, Vogler et al., 2007).

The disadvantage is that the computational costs are high due to the complex matching. In addition, tracking and localizing humans accurately in 3D space in computer vision involving many challenging issues, e.g., camera calibration, modeling human body or motion, self-occlusions, body part labeling, low-resolution images, skeleton fitting, etc.

Appearance-Based Features

The use of silhouette is widely motivated because silhouettes are easier to be acquired than joints and their region-based nature makes them more robust to noise than local information. Furthermore, silhouettes might be extracted from relatively low-resolution images taken at far distances. In (Sarkar, Phillips et al., 2005), a baseline algorithm which uses raw human silhouette as feature is proposed. Each silhouette is expressed by a 0-1 matrix and scaled to the same size. The feature extracted from a video is a 3D hyper-matrix with x, y and t (time) dimensions. The similarity between two silhouettes is the ratio of the number of pixels in their intersection to their union. The similarity

Figure 5. Human body tracking results (the left three) and the thigh angle from four different subjects (Wang, Ning et al., 2004)

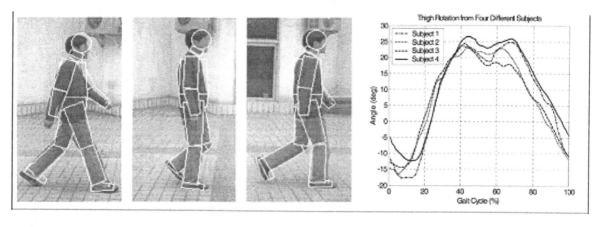

measure between two sequences is chosen to be the median value of the maximum correlation of the gallery sequence with each of these probe gait cycles. The shortcoming of this kind feature is obvious. That is the computational cost is very heavy and much storage is needed.

Silhouette projection is a simple but efficient method which projects a silhouette vertically or horizontally to a vector (Tan, Huang et al., 2007; Tan, Yu et al., 2007). The method is easy to implement and has low computational cost. The projection can reduce the feature dimension greatly. A silhouette and its projection vectors are shown in Figure 6.

Another feature, the gait energy image (GEI), is reported as a good feature which is robust to silhouette errors and image noise (Han, & Bhanu, 2004). GEI is similar with motion-energy image (MEI) and motion-history image (MHI)(Bobick, & Davis, 2001). MEI and MHI are designed for human movement type representation and recognition, but GEI is the gait template for individual recognition. GEI is defined in (Han, & Bhanu, 2004) by:

$$G(x,y) = \frac{1}{N}\sum_{t=1}^{N} I(x,y,t)$$

where N is the number of frames in the sequence I(x,y,t), t is the frame number, x and y are the image coordinate. Figure 7 illustrates how to calculate GEI. To remove the effect of shadows, synthetic gait templates are also used in recognition. The synthetic gait templates are computed from the GEI template by removing the bottom part of the GEI. The authors used real and synthetic gait features and achieved better performance than individual real or synthetic feature classification approaches. The correct classification rates using fusion approach are significantly better than that achieved by the baseline frame matching approach in (Phillips, Sarkar et al., 2002).

Figure 6. A silhouette and its projection vectors

Besides silhouette, another appearance-based feature is contour-based feature. A contour is the outer border of a silhouette. The contour can be easily obtained using a border following algorithm based on connectivity. A contour can express the same information as its corresponding silhouette, but is more compact because only the points on the shape outline are considered. A contour can be further viewed as being in the complex plane (Figure 8). The origin of the complex plane is set as the center of the contour. Each point on the contour can be represented by a complex number $s_i = x_i + j \cdot y_i$, $(i = 1, 2, \cdots, N)$, where N is the number of contour points. Contour-based features are used in many algorithms (Wang, Tan et al., 2003; Wang, Tan et al., 2003; Yu, Wang et al., 2004; Kaziska, & Srivastava, 2006).

Dimension Reduction

The gait feature dimension normally is high, so some feature extraction method are involved to reduce the dimensionality. A common used dimension reduction method is principal components

Figure 7. The silhouettes in a gait cycle and the GEI

analysis (PCA) which performs a linear mapping of the data to a lower dimensional space. After PCA projection, the variance of the data in the low-dimensional representation is maximized. PCA is used in (Wang, Tan et al., 2003) to reduce the dimension of contour-based features. Fourier transform (Mowbray, & Nixon, 2003; Yu, Wang et al., 2004) is also can be used for dimension reduction. PCA and Fourier transform are all unsupervised methods. Linear discriminant analysis (LDA) (Boulgouris, & Chi, 2007; Tao, Li et al., 2007) is a kind of supervised method which best separate different classes.

PCA and LDA are all linear dimension reduction methods. Some researchers using non-linear dimension reduction methods, such as a manifold-based method (Cheng, Ho et al., 2007). In (Cheng, Ho et al., 2007) the gait silhouettes are nonlinearly transformed into low dimensional embedding using Gaussian Process Latent Variable Model (GP-LVM) (Lawrence, 2004), and this method achieved encouraging experimental results.

Classifiers

Most classifiers used in other biometrics can also be used in gait recognition. Simple classifiers such as nearest neighbor (NN) and k-nearest neighbor (kNN) are widely used (Boulgouris, & Chi, 2007; Yu, Wang et al., 2004; Sarkar, Phillips et al., 2005). Because gait data is a kind of time sequence, HMM is also used in some gait recognition methods (Kale, Rajagopalan et al., 2002; Zhang, Vogler et al., 2007).

DATABASES AND PERFORMANCE EVALUATION

In recent years, many gait databases have been created to evaluate gait recognition algorithms. The research on gait recognition has benefited from these gait databases. A good gait database should be large and contains many variations which can affect gait recognition. The earlier databases normally are relative small but many large databases have been created recently, such as the CASIA Gait Database (Yu, Tan et al., 2006), the Gait Challenge Database (Sarkar, Phillips et al., 2005) and the Soton Gait Database (Shutler, Grant et al., 2002).

Figure 8. A contour in the complex plane

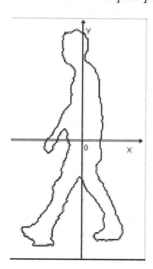

CASIA Gait Database

The CASIA Gait Database (Yu, Tan et al., 2006) is a large multi-sensor (visible camera and thermal camera) database. In it there are three datasets: Dataset A (small size dataset), Dataset B (multi-view dataset) and Dataset C (infrared dataset).

Dataset A (former NLPR Gait Database) was collected on Dec. 10, 2001, including 20 persons. Each person has 12 image sequences, 4 sequences for each of the three directions, i.e. parallel, 45 degrees and 90 degrees to the image plane. The length of each sequence is not identical for the variation of the walker's speed, but it must ranges from 37 to 127. The size of Dataset A is about 2.2GB and the database includes 19139 images.

Dataset B is a large multi-view gait database, which was collected in January 2005. There are 124 subjects, and the gait data was captured from 11 views. The angles between view directions and the walking direction are 0, 18, 36, …, 180 degrees. When a subject was walking, 11 cameras captured videos at the same time, but the videos were not synchronized. Three variations, namely view angle, clothing and carrying condition changes, are separately considered. For each subject, there are 6 normal walking videos, 2 walking in coat videos and 2 walking with bag videos at each view. Altogether there are $(6 + 2 + 2) \times 11 \times 124 = 13,640$ videos.

Dataset C was collected by an infrared (thermal) camera in Jul.-Aug. 2005. It contains 153 subjects and takes into account four walking conditions: normal walking, slow walking, fast walking, and normal walking with a bag. The videos were all captured at night.

The HumanID Gait Challenge Database

The HumanID Gait Challenge Database (Sarkar, Phillips et al., 2005) was created in May, 2001 and November, 2001 at University of South Florida, Tampa. It is an outdoor database. There are 122 subjects in the database and about 33 subjects common between the May and Nov collections. The database consists of subjects walking in elliptical paths in front of the camera(s). Each subject walked circuits around an ellipse. For each subject, there are 5 variations

- 2 different shoe types (A, and B),
- 2 different carrying conditions (with or without a briefcase),
- on 2 different surface types (grass and concrete),
- from 2 different viewpoints (Left or Right) and
- some at 2 different time instants

Compared with other databases, the HumanID Gait Challenge Database contains most variations and is a very challenging database.

Figure 9. Human walking videos from the CASIA Gait Database (Dataset A)

Figure 10. Human walking videos from the CASIA Gait Database (Dataset B)

Figure 11. Human walking videos from the CASIA Gait Database (Dataset C)

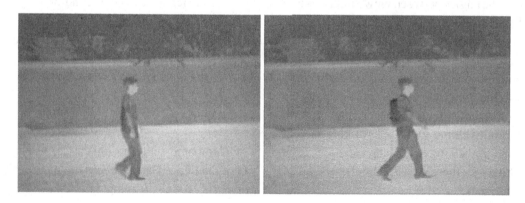

Soton Database

The Soton Database (Shutler, Grant et al., 2002) consists of two dataset, a large one and a small one. The large dataset contains over 100 subjects and is intended to two questions: whether gait is individual across a significant number of people in normal conditions, and to what extent research effort needs to be directed towards biometric algorithms or towards computer vision algorithms for accurate extraction of subjects. The small dataset is intended to investigate the robustness of biometric techniques to imagery of the same subject in various common conditions (carrying items, wearing different clothing or footwear).

Other Databases

Besides the three recent large databases introduced previously, there still some other gait databases which own some unique features. The gait databases used for identification in literature are listed in Table 1.

Figure 12. Human walking videos from the HumanID Gait Challenge Database

Figure 13. Human walking videos from the Soton Database (the larger dataset)

Evaluation Metrics

Even though many gait recognition algorithms have been proposed, comparison of different algorithms and evaluation of an algorithm's robustness to some variations such as the variations of view angle, clothing, shoe types, surface types, carrying condition, illumination, and time are still hard and open problems. Evaluation systems, like FERET for face recognition, should be proposed for gait recognition.

The HumanID Gait Challenge Problem tries to handle this problem. Besides the database described in previous subsection, there are 12 experiments designed to investigate the effect of five variations on performance. The 12 experiments have common gallery set, but the probe sets are different. Each experiment evaluates different variation or different combination of variations. The 12 experiments and the variations that they evaluate are listed in Table 2.

The 12 experiments can evaluate an algorithm's robustness to the 5 variations, and they are challenging experiments. The image quality in the database is relatively low. Besides, the subjects walk in elliptical paths, and the angle between walking direction and the camera is kept changing. So the effect of a variation is relatively hard to be study because of low image quality and view angle changing.

In (Yu, Tan et al., 2006), another evaluation framework is proposed. The framework contains three sets of experiments (Experiment Set A, B and C) is designed to evaluate the effect of three variations: view direction, clothing and carrying condition changing. The gallery sets of these

Table 1. Gait databases used in literature

Database Name	Num. of Subjects	Num. of Sequences	Environment	Time	Variations
UCSD Database	6	42	Outdoor	1998	-
MIT AI Database	24	194	Indoor	2001	View, time
Georgia Tech Database	20	188	Outdoor, indoor, magnetic tracker	2001	View, time, distance
CMU Mobo Database	25	600	Indoor, treadmill	Mar. 2001	6 viewpoints, speed, carrying condition, incline surface
HID-UMD Database (Dataset 1)	25	100	Outdoor	Feb.-May 2001	4 viewpoints
HID-UMD Database (Dataset 2)	55	220	Outdoor	June-July 2001	2 viewpoints
Soton Small Database	12	-	Indoor, green chroma-key backdrop	-	Carrying condition, clothing, shoe, view
Soton Large Database	115	2,128	Indoor, outdoor, treadmill	Summer, 2001	View
Gait Challenge Database	122	1,870	Outdoor	May and Nov. 2001	2 viewpoints, surface, shoe, carrying condition, time
CASIA Database (Dataset A)	20	240	Outdoor	Dec. 2001	3 viewpoints
CASIA Database (Dataset B)	124	13,640	Indoor	Jan. 2005	11 viewpoints, clothing, carrying condition
CASIA Database (Dataset C)	153	1,530	Outdoor, at night, thermal camera	Jul.-Aug. 2005	Speed, carrying condition

three experiment set are the same and contain 124 subjects' normal walking videos. For each view of a subject, there are 6 normal walking sequences. In Experiment Set A the first 4 normal walking sequences are taken as gallery set, and the other 2 sequences are taken as probe set. Considering all combinations between 11 views, there are 11×11 = 121 experiments in Experiment Set A. Experiment Set A is for investigating how view angle affects the gait recognition performance and an algorithm's robustness to view variation. The experimental results using GEI feature are listed in Figure 14. If an algorithm is robust to view variation, its correct classification rates will not decrease greatly when the probe angle and the gallery angle are different.

Experiment Set B is for investigating clothing change, and Experiment Set C is for carrying condition change. There are also 121 experiments

Table 2. The experiments in the HumanID Gait Challenge Problem

Exp.	Num. of subjects	Variations
A	122	View
B	54	Shoe
C	54	Shoe, view
D	121	Surface
E	60	Surface, shoe
F	121	Surface, view
G	60	Surface, shoe, view
H	120	Briefcase
I	60	Shoe, briefcase
J	120	View, briefcase
K	33	Time, shoe, clothing
L	33	Surface, time, shoe, clothing

Figure 14. The correct classification rate (%) in Experiment Set A (using GEI feature)

		Probe angle θ_p (normal walking #5-6)									
		0°	18°	36°	54°	72°	90°	108°	126°	144°	162°	180°
Gallery angle θ_g (normal #1-4)	0°	99.2	31.9	9.3	4.0	3.2	3.2	2.0	2.0	4.8	12.9	37.9
	18°	23.8	99.6	39.9	8.9	4.4	3.6	3.6	5.2	13.7	33.5	10.9
	36°	4.4	37.9	97.6	29.8	11.7	6.9	8.1	13.3	23.4	13.3	2.0
	54°	2.4	3.6	29.0	97.2	23.0	16.5	21.4	29.0	21.4	4.8	1.2
	72°	0.8	4.4	7.3	21.8	97.2	81.5	68.1	21.0	5.6	3.6	1.6
	90°	0.4	2.4	4.8	17.7	82.3	97.6	82.3	15.3	5.2	3.6	1.2
	108°	1.6	1.6	2.0	16.9	71.4	87.9	95.6	37.1	6.0	2.0	2.0
	126°	1.2	2.8	6.0	37.5	33.5	22.2	48.0	96.8	26.6	4.4	2.0
	144°	3.6	5.2	28.2	18.5	4.4	1.6	3.2	43.1	96.4	5.6	2.8
	162°	12.1	39.1	15.7	2.4	1.6	0.8	0.8	2.4	5.2	98.4	28.6
	180°	41.1	19.8	8.1	3.2	2.0	0.8	1.6	3.6	12.5	51.2	99.6

in Set B and Set C, and the experimental results in Experiment Set B and Experiment Set C are listed in Figure 15 and Figure 16. Different from the HumanID Gait Challenge Problem, the CASIA framework can be used to investigate the effect of different variations separately, nor combine the variations together.

VIEW INVARIANT GAIT ANALYSIS

View angle change is a common variation in gait recognition and analysis. One unique advantage of gait is that it can be perceivable at a distance. The subjects do not know they are observed. It can not be expected that all subjects walk along a direction and a subject does not change his/her walking direction. The human silhouettes from different views are different. How to extract discriminative gait features is a really challenging problem.

An early attempt can be found in (Shakhn-arovich, Lee, et al., 2001). An image-based visual hull is computed from a set of monocular views and used to render virtual views for tracking and recognition. The images can be mapped onto the virtual 3D model as texture, and a virtual camera is placed to capture a side-view of the subject. So even no camera is place at the side view of the subject, the side image can also be taken by a virtual camera.

Another attempts use static body parameters recovered from walking videos, such as body height, trunk height and stride for identification. The static body parameters are less sensitive to view variant because they are related to 3D shape of the human body. In (Johnson, & Bobick, 2001) a 4D-walk vector $< d_1, d_2, d_3, d_4 >$ is extracted for human identification. The four elements are defined as follows:

- **d1:** The height of the bounding box around the silhouette.
- **d2:** The distance (L2 norm) between the head and pelvis locations.
- **d3:** The maximum value of the distance between the pelvis and left foot location, and the distance between the pelvis and right foot location.
- **d4:** The distance between the left and right foot.

To reduce the effect of view variation, scale factors are trained to convert the feature vector to a common frame (such as side view frame).

$$f_{new} = s < d_1 \cdot f_1, d_2 \cdot f_2, d_3 \cdot f_3, d_4 \cdot f_4 >$$

Figure 15. The correct classification rate (%) in Experiment Set B (using GEI feature)

Gallery angle θ_g (normal #1-4)	Probe angle θ_p (walking with a coat #1-2)										
		0°	18°	36°	54°	72°	90°	108°	126°	144°	162°	180°
	0°	24.6	6.9	3.2	1.6	0.8	0.8	0.8	0.8	1.6	5.6	8.1
	18°	4.4	27.0	18.5	6.9	0.8	0.8	0.8	2.4	5.6	11.7	2.8
	36°	1.6	8.5	30.2	16.5	1.2	1.2	1.6	6.9	9.3	3.6	0.8
	54°	0.8	2.4	10.1	30.6	5.6	4.4	7.7	14.1	5.6	2.4	0.8
	72°	0.0	2.4	5.6	7.7	31.0	21.8	14.9	8.9	2.8	2.4	0.4
	90°	1.2	2.4	4.0	6.0	20.6	32.7	16.5	6.0	3.6	3.2	0.8
	108°	1.6	2.0	2.4	4.8	17.7	27.8	30.2	9.3	4.8	2.0	1.6
	126°	1.6	1.6	1.6	4.4	10.1	10.1	18.5	26.2	8.9	1.6	1.6
	144°	2.4	2.8	4.0	12.5	4.4	2.4	4.4	18.1	30.6	1.2	2.0
	162°	2.8	7.7	9.7	2.0	0.4	0.8	0.8	1.6	4.0	27.0	6.5
	180°	9.3	6.0	3.2	0.8	1.2	0.0	0.0	1.6	5.6	12.5	27.4

Figure 16. The correct classification rate (%) in Experiment Set C (using GEI feature)

Gallery angle θ_g (normal #1-4)	Probe angle θ_p (walking with a bag #1-2)										
		0°	18°	36°	54°	72°	90°	108°	126°	144°	162°	180°
	0°	80.2	20.2	5.2	2.4	2.4	2.0	2.0	2.0	4.4	14.5	25.8
	18°	16.9	76.2	36.7	7.3	3.6	2.8	2.8	4.8	10.9	18.1	8.1
	36°	3.6	23.0	74.6	24.2	9.3	8.1	7.3	10.5	15.3	6.5	1.6
	54°	0.8	2.8	19.4	66.5	19.0	13.3	14.5	18.5	7.3	4.0	1.6
	72°	0.4	4.8	6.5	8.9	60.5	31.0	22.2	11.7	4.0	3.6	1.2
	90°	0.4	2.8	5.2	8.5	42.3	52.0	31.9	9.7	6.0	3.2	2.0
	108°	1.6	1.2	3.6	7.3	39.9	44.0	57.3	23.4	6.5	3.6	1.6
	126°	0.8	2.8	4.0	17.3	25.4	14.9	27.8	65.7	14.5	2.0	1.6
	144°	2.0	4.8	15.3	11.7	6.9	2.0	4.4	31.9	64.1	2.4	1.2
	162°	7.7	23.8	13.7	3.6	2.4	2.0	2.4	4.4	6.0	68.1	19.0
	180°	30.2	12.9	6.5	2.0	2.0	2.0	1.2	2.8	7.7	31.5	80.2

where s is a global scale factor and d_1-d_4 are scale factors for different feature dimensions. Similar method which also uses walking parameters can be found in (Abdelkader, Cutler et al., 2002). This kind of method has its disadvantage. The possibility of two subjects with similar body parameters will be high when the population is large.

To extract discriminative model-based gait feature is relatively challenging, so some researchers (Kale, Roy et al., 2003; Han, Bhanu, et al. 2005) use appearance-based gait feature synthesis for view invariant gait recognition. Such as a side view (canonical view) is synthesized from any other arbitrary view using a single camera. In (Kale, Roy et al., 2003) the first step is to estimate the azimuth angle under the assumption that the person is walking along a straight line. Two approaches, perspective projection approach and optical flow based SfM one, are proposed for azimuth angle estimation. Experimental results show that the two approaches can achieve numerically close results. After getting the azimuth angle, the next step is to synthesize the gait feature. Here a planar is used to approximate the human body, and then to rotate the planar to the side view. The experiments on a database consists of 12 people proved that the proposed method can improve gait recognition rate.

View variation is a very complex problem because the human body is not a rigid object. Though much work has been done, the problems caused by view variation are far from being solved. To combine human 3D model with appearance-based gait feature is a direction for this problem as indicated in (Lien, Tien, et al. 2007)

CHALLENGES IN GAIT RECOGNITION

In summary, results from early attempts suggest that developing highly reliable gait-based human identification systems in real world are and will continue to be very challenging. The challenges involved in vision-based gait recognition include imperfect foreground segmentation, variations in viewing angle and clothing, changes in gait as a result of mood, walking speed or carrying objects, etc. Because gait is a kind of behavioral biometric, not physical biometric as iris, finger print, etc, there are many factors can affect gait recognition performance. The view variation has been addressed in the previous section, and the other factors are listed as follows.

Clothing: Clothing change is a variation which can greatly affect gait recognition performance. The dependence of gait feature on the appearance of a subject is difficult to remove, unless the joint movements of a walker can be detected or appearance-insensitive features are obtained. However, the appearance of a walking subject contains information about the identity has actually been demonstrated in much previous work. To allow accurate recognition of a person with the change of clothing style, multiple appearance representations of a person with respect to different clothes are probably required.

Carrying conditions: When a subject is carrying an object, whatever a knapsack, handbag or other objects, it will give some effect on gait feature extraction. The carried objects will change the subject's walking style. When a person carries a box using his/her hands, his/her arms will not swim when walking. And some objects will hide some key body components, such as a large handbag will hide the knees movements. It is relatively hard to separate the objects from the human body using computer vision methods. However we can try to detect whether the subject is carrying some objects, and then to call security staffs' attention to the subject.

Distance: Intuitively, the decreases of image resolution related to distances have a great adverse effect on recognition performance. Gait recognition aims to develop such recognition systems that can function at a great distance. It thus needs to translate the resulting performance regarding with different low-resolution images into the associated recognition performance as a function of the viewed distances.

Weather: An all-day biometrics recognition system at a distance must contend with bad weather such as fog, snow and rain. How to reliably extract information of moving human from dynamic scenes under such bad weather is very critical. Currently, some researchers are trying to improve the abilities of human detection and recognition in bad weather to enhance the robustness of gait recognition technique. Other advanced sensors such as infrared, hyper-spectral imaging and radar are also being observed because over video they can be used at night and other low-visibility conditions.

Occlusion: Previous work was mainly implemented under some simplified and controlled conditions, e.g., no occlusion during human walking, relatively simple background. But in real application, occlusions are very common. Human segmentation and tracking algorithms should be developed for identification.

CONCLUSION

During the research on the past decade, it is shown that gait has great potential for human identification at a distance. Although gait recognition is just getting started, it is growing in significance. This chapter has provided an overview on new advances in automatic gait recognition, includes popular gait features, large databases, evaluation metrics and challenges. The existing algorithms have further demonstrated the feasibility of recognizing people by gait. Much work remains to be done, e.g., automatic extraction of view invariant features, removing the effect of clothing and carrying conditions, etc. It is expected that gait recognition will be applied to practical security surveillance systems in the near future.

REFERENCES

Abdelkader, C. B., Cutler, R., et al. (2002). View-invariant estimation of height and stride for gait recognition. *Proceedings of the ECCV 2002 Workshop Copenhagen on Biometric Authentication* (pp. 155-167).

Bobick, A. F., & Davis, J. W. (2001). The recognition of human movement using temporal templates. *IEEE Transactions on Pattern Analysis and Machine Intelligence, 23*(3), 257–267. doi:10.1109/34.910878

Boulgouris, N. V., & Chi, Z. X. (2007). Gait recognition using radon transform and linear discriminant analysis. *IEEE Transactions on Image Processing, 16*, 731–740. doi:10.1109/TIP.2007.891157

Cattin, P. C., Zlatnik, D., et al. (2001). Biometric system using human gait. *Proc. of Mechatronics and Machine Vision in Practice (M2VIP),* Hong Kong.

Cheng, M., Ho, M., et al. (2007). Gait analysis for human identification through manifold learning and HMM. *Proc. of IEEE Workshop on Motion and Video Computing (WMVC'07).*

Cunado, D., & Nixon, M. S. (2003). Automatic extraction and description of human gait models for recognition purposes. *Computer Vision and Image Understanding, 90*(1), 1–41. doi:10.1016/S1077-3142(03)00008-0

Davis, J. W., & Gao, H. (2004). *Gender recognition from walking movements using adaptive three-mode PCA*. Washington, D.C.: IEEE Computer Society.

Han, J., & Bhanu, B. (2004). Statistical feature fusion for gait-based human recognition. *Proc. of the 2004 IEEE Computer Society Conference on Computer Vision and Pattern Recognition,* II842-II847.

Han, J., Bhanu, B., et al. (2005). A study on view-insensitive gait recognition. *Proc. of IEEE International Conference on Image Processing (ICIP 2005),* III (pp. 297-300).

Johnson, A. Y., & Bobick, A. F. (2001). A multiview method for gait recognition using static body parameters. *Proc. of 3rd International Conference on Audio and Video Based Biometric Person Authentication* (pp. 301-311).

Johnson, A. Y., & Bobick, A. F. (2001). A multiview method for gait recognition using static body parameters. *Proc. of 3rd International Conference on Audio and Video Based Biometric Person Authentication* (pp. 301-311).

Kale, A., Rajagopalan, A., et al. (2002). Gait-based recognition of humans using continuous HMMs. *Proc. of 5th IEEE International Conference on Automatic Face and Gesture Recognition* (pp. 336-341).

Kale, A., Roy, A. K., et al. (2003). Towards a view invariant gait recognition algorithm. *Proc. of IEEE Conference on Advanced Video and Signal Based Surveillance* (pp. 143-150).

Kaziska, D., & Srivastava, A. (2006). Cyclostationary processes on shape spaces for gait-based recognition. *Proc. of the 9th European Conference on Computer Vision*, Graz, Austria (pp. 442-453).

Kurakake, S., & Nevatia, R. (1994). Description and tracking of moving articulated objects. *Systems and Computers in Japan, 25*(8), 16–26. doi:10.1002/scj.4690250802

Lawrence, N. (2004). *Probabilistic nonlinear principal component analysis with Gaussian process latent variable models*. (Tech. Rep. CS-04-8). Dept. of Computer Science, Univ. of Sheffield.

Lee, L., & Grimson, W. E. L. (2002). Gait analysis for recognition and classification. *Proc. of 5th IEEE International Conference on Automatic Face and Gesture Recognition* (pp. 155-162).

Lien, C. C., Tien, C. C., et al. (2007). Human gait recognition for arbitrary view angles. *Proc. on the Second International Conference on Innovative Computing, Information and Control, (ICICIC 2007)* (pp. 303-303).

Mowbray, S. D., & Nixon, M. S. (2003). Automatic gait recognition via Fourier descriptors of deformable objects. *Proc. of 4th International Conference on Audio- and Video-based Biometric Person Authentication* (pp. 566-573).

Murray, M. P. (1967). Gait as a total pattern of movement. *American Journal of Physical Medicine, 46*(1), 290–332.

Murray, M. P., & Drought, A. B. (1964). Walking patterns of normal men. *Journal of Bone and Joint Surgery, 46-A*(2), 335–360.

Nixon, M. S., Tan, T., et al. (2005). *Human identification based on gait*. Springer.

Phillips, P. J., Sarkar, S., et al. (2002). The gait identification challenge problem: Data sets and baseline algorithm. *Proc. of International Conference on Pattern Recognition* (pp. 385-388).

Sarkar, S., & Phillips, P. J. (2005). The humanID gait challenge problem: Data sets, performance, and analysis. *IEEE Transactions on Pattern Analysis and Machine Intelligence, 27*(2), 162–177. doi:10.1109/TPAMI.2005.39

Sarkar, S., & Phillips, P. J. (2005). The humanID gait challenge problem: Data sets, performance, and analysis. *IEEE Transactions on Pattern Analysis and Machine Intelligence, 27*(2), 162–177. doi:10.1109/TPAMI.2005.39

Shakhnarovich, G., Lee, L., et al. (2001, December). Integrated face and gait recognition from multiple views. In *Proc. of the 2001 IEEE Computer Society Conference on Computer Vision and Pattern Recognition*, I439–I446, HI.

Shutler, J. D., Grant, M. G., et al. (2002). On a large sequence-based human gait database. *Proc. of 4th International Conference on Recent Advances in Soft Computing* (pp. 66-71).

Stauffer, C., & Grimson, W. E. L. (1999). Adaptive background mixture models for real-time tracking. In *Proc. of IEEE Computer Society Conference on Computer Vision and Pattern Recognition*, 252.

Tan, D., Huang, K., et al. (2007). Uniprojective feature for gait recognition. *Proc. of The 2nd International Conference on Biometrics*, Seoul, Korea (pp. 673-682).

Tan, D., Yu, S., et al. (2007). Walker recognition without gait cycle estimation. *Proc. of The 2nd International Conference on Biometrics*, Seoul, Korea (pp. 222-231).

Tanawongsuwan, R., & Bobick, A. (2001). Gait recognition from time-normalized joint-angle trajectories in the walking plane. *Proc. of the 2001 IEEE Computer Society Conference on Computer Vision and Pattern Recognition* (Vol. 2, pp. 726-731).

Tao, D., & Li, X. (2007). General tensor discriminant analysis and Gabor features for gait recognition. *IEEE Transactions on Pattern Analysis and Machine Intelligence, 29*(10), 1700-1715. doi:10.1109/TPAMI.2007.1096

Wang, L., & Ning, H. (2004). Fusion of static and dynamic body biometrics for gait recognition. *IEEE Transactions on Circuits and Systems for Video Technology, 14*(2), 149–158. doi:10.1109/TCSVT.2003.821972

Wang, L., & Tan, T. (2003). Automatic gait recognition based on statistical shape analysis. *IEEE Transactions on Image Processing, 12*(9), 1120–1131. doi:10.1109/TIP.2003.815251

Wang, L., & Tan, T. (2003). Silhouette analysis-based gait recognition for human identification. *IEEE Transactions on Pattern Analysis and Machine Intelligence, 25*(12), 1505–1518. doi:10.1109/TPAMI.2003.1251144

Winter, D. (1991). *The biomechanics and motor control of human gait: normal, elderly, and pathological*. Waterloo Biomechanics.

Xu, D., & Yan, S. (2007). Marginal Fisher analysis and its variants for human gait recognition and content-based image retrieval. *IEEE Transactions on Image Processing, 16*(11), 2811–2821. doi:10.1109/TIP.2007.906769

Yam, C. Y., Nixon, M. S., et al. (2002). On the relationship of human walking and running: Automatic person identification by gait. *Proc. of International Conference on Pattern Recognition* (pp. 287-290).

Yoo, J. H., Hwang, D., et al. (2005). Gender classification in human gait using support vector machine. *Proceedings of Advanced Concepts for Intelligent Vision Systems 2005*, Antwerp, Belgium (pp. 138-145).

Yu, S., Tan, D., et al. (2006). A framework for evaluating the effect of view angle, clothing, and carrying condition on gait recognition. *Proc. of the 18th International Conference on Pattern Recognition (ICPR06)* (pp. 441-444).

Yu, S., Wang, L., et al. (2004). Gait analysis for human identification in frequency domain. *Proc. of the 3rd International Conference on Image and Graphics* (pp. 282-285).

Zhang, R., & Vogler, C. (2007). Human gait recognition at sagittal plane. *Image and Vision Computing, 25*(3), 321–330. doi:10.1016/j.imavis.2005.10.007

Chapter 8
Multilinear Modeling for Robust Identity Recognition from Gait

Fabio Cuzzolin
Oxford Brookes University, UK

ABSTRACT

Human identification from gait is a challenging task in realistic surveillance scenarios in which people walking along arbitrary directions are viewed by a single camera. However, viewpoint is only one of the many covariate factors limiting the efficacy of gait recognition as a reliable biometric. In this chapter, we address the problem of robust identity recognition in the framework of multilinear models. Bilinear models, in particular, allow us to classify the "content" of human motions of unknown "style" (covariate factor). We illustrate a three-layer scheme in which image sequences are first mapped to observation vectors of fixed dimension using Markov modeling, to be later classified by an asymmetric bilinear model. We show tests on the CMU Mobo database that prove that bilinear separation outperforms other common approaches, allowing robust view- and action-invariant identity recognition. Finally, we give an overview of the available tensor factorization techniques, and outline their potential applications to gait recognition. The design of algorithms insensitive to multiple covariate factors is in sight.

INTRODUCTION

Biometrics has received growing attention in the last decade, as automatic identification systems for surveillance and security have started to enjoy widespread diffusion. Biometrics such as face, iris, or fingerprint recognition, in particular, have been employed. They suffer, however, from two major

DOI: 10.4018/978-1-60566-725-6.ch008

limitations: they cannot be used at a distance, and require user cooperation. Such assumptions are not practical in real-world scenarios, e.g. surveillance of public areas.

Interestingly, psychological studies show that people are capable of recognizing their friends just from the way they walk, even when their "gait" is poorly represented by point light display (Cutting & Kozlowski, 1977). Gait has several advantages over other biometrics, as it can be measured at a distance, is difficult to disguise or occlude, and can be identified even in low-resolution images. Most importantly gait recognition is *non-cooperative* in nature. The person to identify can move freely in the surveyed environment, and is possibly unaware of his/her identity being checked.

The problem of recognizing people from natural gait has been studied by several researchers (Gafurov, 2007; Nixon & Carter, 2006), starting from a seminal work of Niyogi and Adelson (1994). Gait analysis can also be applied to gender recognition (Li et al., 2008), as different pieces of information like gender or emotion are contained in a walking gait and can be recognized. Abnormalities of gait patterns for the diagnosis of certain diseases can also be automatically detected (Wang, 2006). Furthermore, gait and face biometrics can be easily integrated for human identity recognition (Zhou & Bhanu, 2007; Jafri & Arabnia, 2008).

Influence of Covariates

Despite its attractive features, though, gait identification is still far from being ready to be deployed in practice.

What limits the adoption of gait recognition systems in real-world scenarios is the influence of a large number of so-called covariate factors which affect appearance and dynamics of the gait. These include walking surface, lightning, camera setup (viewpoint), but also footwear and clothing, carrying conditions, time of execution, walking speed.

The correlation between those factors can be indeed very significant as pointed out in (Li et al., 2008), making gait difficult to measure and classify.

In the last few years a number of public databases have been made available and can be used as a common ground to validate the variety of algorithms that have been proposed. The USF database (Sarkar et al., 2005), for instance, was specifically designed to study the effect of covariate factors on identity classification in a realistic, outdoor context with cameras located at a distance.

View-Invariance

The most important of those covariate factors is probably viewpoint variation. In the USF database, however, experiments contemplate only two cameras at fairly close viewpoints (with a separation of some 30 degrees). Also people are viewed while walking along the opposite side of an ellipse: the resulting views are almost fronto-parallel. As a result appearance-based algorithms work well in the reported experiments concerning viewpoint variability, while one would expect them to perform poorly for widely separated views.

In a realistic setup, the person to identify steps into the surveyed area from an arbitrary direction. View-invariance (Urtasun & Fua, 2004; Yam et al., 2004; Bhanu & Han, 2002; Kale et al., 2003; Shakhnarovich et al., 2001; Johnson & Bobick, 2001) is then a crucial issue to make identification from gait suitable for real-world applications.

This problem has actually been studied in the gait ID context by many groups (Han et al., 2005). If a 3D articulated model of the moving person is available, tracking can be used as a pre-processing stage to drive recognition. Cunado et al. (1999), for instance, have used their evidence gathering technique to analyze the leg motion in both walking and running gait. Yam et al. (2004) have also worked on a similar model-based approach. Urtasun and Fua (2004) have proposed an approach to gait analysis that relies on fitting 3D temporal motion models to synchronized video sequences. Bhanu and Han (2002) have matched a 3D kinematic model to 2D silhouettes. Viewpoint invariance is achieved in (Spencer & Carter, 2002) by means of a hip/leg model, including camera elevation angle as an additional parameter.

Model-based 3D tracking, however, is a difficult task. Manual initialization of the model is often required, while optimization in a higher-dimensional parameter space suffers from convergence issues. Kale et al. (2003) have proposed as an alternative a method for generating a synthetic side-view of the moving person using a single camera, if the person is far enough. Shakhnarovich et al. (2001) have suggested a view-normalization technique in a multiple camera framework, using the volumetric intersection of the visual hulls of all camera silhouettes. A 3D model is also set up in (Zhao et al., 2006) using sequences acquired by multiple cameras, so that the length of key limbs and their motion trajectories can be extracted and recognized. Johnson and Bobick (2001) have presented a multi-view gait recognition method using static body parameters recovered during the walking motion across multiple views. More recently, Rogez et al. (2006) have used the structure of man-made environments to transform the available image(s) to frontal views, while Makihara et al. (2006) have proposed a view transformation model in the frequency domain, acting on features obtained by Fourier analysis of a spatiotemporal volume.

An approach to multiple view fusion based on the "product of sum" rule has been proposed in (Lu and Zhang, 2007). Different features and classification methods are there compared. The discriminating power of different views has been analyzed in (Huang & Boulgouris, 2008). Several evidence combination methods have been tested on the CMU Mobo database (Gross & Shi, 2001).

More in general, the effects of all the different covariates have not yet been thoroughly investigated, even though some effort has been recently done is this direction. Bouchrika and Nixon (2008) have conducted a comparative study of their influence in gait analysis. Veres et al. (2005) have proposed a remarkable predictive model of the "time of execution" covariate to improve recognition performance. The issue has however been approached so far on an empirical basis, i.e., by trying to measure the influence of individual covariate factors. A principled strategy for their treatment has not yet been brought forward.

Chapter's Objectives

A general framework for addressing the issue of covariate factors in gait recognition is provided by *multilinear* or *tensorial models*. These are mathematical descriptions of the way different factors *linearly* interacts in a mixed training set, yielding the walking gaits we actually observe.

The problem of recovering those factors is often referred to in the literature as *nonnegative tensor factorization* or *NTF* (Tao, 2006). The PARAFAC model for multi-way analysis (Kiers, 2000) has first been introduced for continuous electroencephalogram (EEG) classification in the context of brain-computer interfaces (Morup et al., 2006). A different multi-layer method for 3D NTF has been proposed by Cichocki et al. (2007). Porteus et al. (2008) have introduced a generative Bayesian probabilistic model for unsupervised tensor factorization. It consists of several interacting LDA models, one for each modality (factor), coupled with a Gibbs sampler for inference. Other approaches to NTF can be found in recent papers such as (Lee et al., 2007; Shashua & Hazan, 2005; Boutsidis et al., 2006).

Bilinear models, in particular (Tenenbaum & Freeman, 2000), are the best studied among multilinear models. They can be seen as tools for separating two properties, usually called "style" and "content" of the objects to classify. They allow (for instance) to build a classifier which, given a new sequence in which a *known* person is seen from a view *not* in the training set, can iteratively estimate both identity and view parameters, significantly improving recognition performances.

In this chapter we propose a *three-layer model* in which each motion sequence is considered as an observation depending on three factors (*identity*, *action* type, and *view*). A bilinear model can be trained from those observations by considering two such factors at a time. While in the first layer features are extracted from individual images, in the second stage each feature sequence is given as input to a hidden Markov model (HMM). Assuming fixed dynamics, this HMM clusters the sequence into a fixed number of poses. The stacked vector of such poses eventually represents the input motion as a whole. After learning a bilinear model for such set of observation vectors we can then classify (determine the content of) new sequences characterized by a different style label.

We illustrate experiments on the CMU Mobo database on view-invariant and action invariant identity recognition. They clearly demonstrate that this approach performs significantly better than other standard gait recognition algorithms.

To conclude we outline several possible natural extensions of this methodology to multilinear modeling, in the perspective of providing a comprehensive framework for dealing in a consistent way with an arbitrary number of covariates.

BILINEAR MODELS

Bilinear models were introduced by Tenenbaum & Freeman (2000) as a tool for separating what they called "style" and "content" of a set of objects to classify, i.e., two distinct class labels $s \in [1,...,S]$ and $c \in [1,...,C]$ attributed to each such object. Common but useful examples are font and alphabet letter in writing, or word and accent in speaking.

Consider a training set of K-dimensional observations y_k^{sc}, $k = 1,...,K$ characterized by a style s and a content c, both represented as parameter vectors a^s and b^c of dimension I and J respectively. In the *symmetric* model we assume that these observations can be written as

$$y_k^{sc} = \sum_{i=1}^{I} \sum_{j=1}^{J} w_{ijk} a_i^s b_j^c \tag{1}$$

where a_i^s and b_j^c are the scalar components of the vectors a^s and b^c respectively.

Let W_k denote the k-th matrix of dimension $I \times J$ with entries w_{ijk}. The symmetric model (1) can then be rewritten as

$$y_k^{sc} = (a^s)^T W_k b^c \tag{2}$$

where ^{T} denotes the transpose of a matrix or vector. The K matrices W_k, $k = 1,...,K$ define a *bilinear map* from the style and content spaces to the K-dimensional observation space.

When the interaction factors can vary with style (i.e. w_{ijk}^s depends on s) we get an *asymmetric* model:

$$y^{sc} = A^s b^c. \tag{3}$$

Here A^s denotes the $K \times J$ matrix with entries $\{a_{jk}^s = \sum_i w_{ijk}^s a_i^s\}$, a *style-specific linear map* from the content space to the observation space (see Figure 1-right).

Training an Asymmetric Model

A bilinear model can be fit to a training set of observations endowed with two labels by means of simple linear algebraic techniques. When the training set has (roughly) the same number of measurements y^{sc} for each style and each content class we can use classical singular value decomposition (SVD). If we stack the training data into the $(SK) \times C$ matrix

$$Y = \begin{bmatrix} y^{11} & \cdots & y^{1C} \\ \vdots & \ddots & \vdots \\ y^{S1} & \cdots & y^{SC} \end{bmatrix} \tag{4}$$

the asymmetric model can be written as $Y = AB$ where A and B are the stacked style and content parameter matrices, $A = [A^1 ... A^S]^T$, $B = [b^1 ... b^C]$.

The least-squares optimal style and content parameters are then easily found by computing the SVD of (4), $Y = USV^T$, and assigning

Figure 1. Left: Feature extraction. First a number of lines passing through the center of mass of the silhouette are selected. Then for each such line the distance of the points on the contour of the silhouette from it is computed (here the segment is sub-divided into 10 intervals). The collection of all such distance values for all the lines eventually forms the feature vector representing the image. Right: bilinear modeling. Each observation $\mathbf{y}^{sc}$ is the result of applying a style-specific linear map $\mathbf{A}^s$ to a vector $\mathbf{b}^c$ of some abstract "content space"

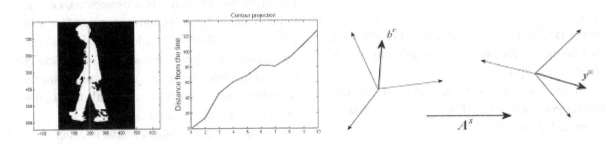

$$A = [US]_{col=1..J}, \quad B = [V^T]_{row=1..J.} \tag{5}$$

If the training data are not equally distributed among all the classes, a least-squares optimum has to be found (Tenenbaum & Freeman, 2000).

Content Classification of Unknown Style

Suppose that we have learnt a bilinear model from a training set of data. Suppose also that a new set of observations becomes available *in a new style*, different from all those already present in the training set, but with *content* labels *among those learned in advance*. In this case an iterative procedure can be set up to factor out the effect of style and classify the content labels of the new observations.

Notice that if we know the content class assignments of the new data we can find the parameters for the new style s' by solving for $A^{s'}$ in the asymmetric model (3). Analogously, having a map $A^{s'}$ for the new style we can easily classify the new "test" vectors y by measuring their distance $\|y - A^{s'}b^c\|$ from $A^{s'}b^c$ for each (known) content vector b^c.

The issue can be solved by fitting a mixture

model to the learnt bilinear model by means of the EM algorithm (Dempster et al., 1977). The EM algorithm alternates between computing the probabilities $p(c|s')$ of the current content label given an estimate s' of the style (E step), and estimating a linear map $A^{s'}$ for the unknown style s' given the current content class probabilities $p(c|s')$ (M step).

We assume that the probability of observing a measurement y given the new style s' and a content label c is given by a Gaussian distribution of the form:

$$p\left(\mathbf{y}|s',c\right) = \exp\left(\frac{-\left\|\mathbf{y} - \mathbf{A}^{s'}b^c\right\|^2}{2\sigma^2}\right). \tag{6}$$

The total probability of such an observation y (notice that the general formulation allows for the presence of more than one unknown style, (Tenenbaum & Freeman, 2000)) is then

$$p(y) = \sum_c p(y|s',c)\,p(s',c) \tag{7}$$

where in absence of prior information $p(s',c)$ is supposed to be equally distributed.

In the E step the EM algorithm computes the joint probability of the labels given the data

$$p\left(s',c|\mathbf{y}\right)=\frac{p\left(\mathbf{y}|s',c\right)p\left(s',c\right)}{p\left(\mathbf{y}\right)} \tag{8}$$

(using Bayes' rule), and classifies the test data by finding the content class c which maximizes $p(c|y) = p(s',c|y)$.

In the M step the style matrix $A^{s'}$ which maximizes the log-likelihood of the test data is estimated. This yields

$$\mathbf{A}^{s'}=\frac{\sum_{c}\mathbf{m}^{s'c}\left(\mathbf{b}^{c}\right)^{T}}{\sum_{c}n^{s'c}\mathbf{b}^{c}\left(\mathbf{b}^{c}\right)^{T}} \tag{9}$$

where $\mathbf{m}^{s'c}=\sum_{y}p(s',c|y)y$ is the mean observation weighted by the probability of having style s' and content c, and $n^{s'c}=\sum_{y}p(s',c|y)$ is a normalization factor.

The effectiveness of the method critically depends on whether the observation vectors actually meet the assumption of bilinearity. However, it was originally presented as a way of finding *approximate* solutions to problems in which two factors are involved, without precise context-based knowledge, and that is the way it is used here.

A Three-Layer Model

In human motion analysis movements, and walking gaits in particular, can be characterized by a number of different labels. They can indeed be classified according to the identity of the moving person, their emotional state, the category of action performed (i.e. walking, reaching out, pointing, etc.), or (if the number of cameras is finite) the viewpoint from which the sequence is acquired.

As a matter of fact, each covariate factor can be seen as an additional label assigned to each walking gait sequence. Covariate-free gait recognition can then be naturally formulated in terms of multilinear modeling (Elgammal and Lee, 2004).

In this chapter we illustrate the use of bilinear models to represent and classify gaits regardless the "style" with which they are executed, i.e., the value of the (in this case single) covariate factor. In practice, this allows us to address problems such as *view-invariant identity recognition* and identity recognition from *unknown* gaits, while ensuring robustness with respect to emotional state, clothing, elapsed time, etcetera.

We propose a *three-layer model* in which each motion sequence is considered as an observation which depends on all covariate factors. A bilinear model can be trained by considering two of those factors at a time. We can subsequently apply bilinear classification to recognize gaits regardless their style.

First Layer: Feature Representation

In gait ID images are usually preprocessed in order to extract the silhouettes of the walking person. We choose here a simple but effective way of computing feature measurements from each such silhouette. More precisely, we detect its center of mass, rescale it to the corresponding bounding box, and project its contours on to one or more lines passing through its barycenter (see Figure 1-left). We favored this approach after testing a number of competing representations: the principal axes of the body-parts as they appear in the image (Lee & Grimson, 2002), size functions (Frosini, 1991), and a PCA-based representation of silhouette contours. All turned out to be rather unstable.

Second Layer: HMMs as Sequence Descriptors

If the contour of the silhouette is projected onto 2 orthogonal lines passing through its barycenter, and we divide each line segment into 10 equally spaced intervals, each image ends up being represented by a 40-dimensional feature vector. Image sequences are then encoded as sequences of feature vectors, in general of different length (duration). To adapt them to their role of inputs for a bilinear model learning stage we need to transform those feature sequences into observation vectors *of the same size*.

Hidden Markov models or HMMs (Elliot et al., 1995) provide us with such a tool.

Even though they have been widely applied to gesture and action recognition, HMMs have rarely been considered as a tool in the gait ID context (He & Debrunner, 2000; Sundaresan et al., 2003), mainly to describe (Kale et al., 2002, He & Debrunner, 2000) or normalize (Liu & Sarkar, 2006) gait dynamics (Kale et al., 2004).

A *hidden Markov model* (HMM) is a finite-state statistical model whose states $\{x_k, k \in N\}$ form a *Markov* chain, i.e., they are such that $P(x_{k+1} | x_0, ..., x_k) = P(x_{k+1} | x_k)$. The only observable quantity in an HMM is a corrupted version y_k of the state called *observation process*.

Using the notation of (Elliot et al., 1995) we can associate the elements of the finite state space $X = \{1, ..., N\}$ with coordinate versors $e_i = [0, ..., 0, 1, 0, ..., 0]^T \in R^N$ and write the model as

$$x_{k+1} = Ax_k + v_{k+1}$$

$$y_{k+1} = Cx_k + diag(w_{k+1})\Sigma x_k. \tag{10}$$

Here $\{v_{k+1}\}$ is a sequence of martingale increments and $\{w_{k+1}\}$ a sequence of i.i.d. Gaussian noises with mean 0 and variance 1. Given a state $x_k = e_j$ the observations y_{k+1} are then assumed to have Gaussian distribution $p(y_{k+1} | x_k = e_j)$ centered around a vector c_j which corresponds to the j-th column of the matrix C.

The parameters of the hidden Markov model (10) are then the "transition matrix" $A = (a_{ij}) = P(x_{k+1} = e_i | x_k = e_j)$, the matrix C collecting the means of the state-output Gaussian distributions $p(y_{k+1} | x_k$

$= e_j)$ and the matrix Σ of the associated variances. The matrices A, C and Σ can be estimated, given a sequence of observations $\{y_1, ..., y_T\}$, using (again) the Expectation-Maximization (EM) algorithm (see (Elliot et al., 1995) for the details).

Let us now go back to the gait ID problem. Given a sequence of feature vectors extracted from all the silhouettes of a sequence, EM yields as output a finite-state representation (an HMM) of the motion. The latter is represented as a series of possible transitions (each associated with a certain probability) between key "poses" mathematically described by the states of the model (see Figure 2). The transition matrix A encodes the sequence's dynamics, while the columns of the C matrix represent the key poses in the observation space.

In the case of cyclic motions, such as the walking gait, the dynamics is rather trivial. It reduces to a circular series of transitions through the states of the HMM (see Figure 2 again). There is no need to estimate the period of the cycle, as the poses are automatically associated with the states of the Markov model by the EM algorithm. For the same reason sequences with variable speed cause no trouble, in opposition to methods based on the estimation of the fundamental frequency of the motion (Little & Boyd, 1998).

Third Layer: Bilinear Model of HMMs

Given the HMM which best fits the input feature sequence, its pose matrix C can be stacked into a single observation vector by simply concatenating its columns.

If we select a fixed number N of states/poses for each sequence, our training set of walking gaits can be encoded as a dataset of such observation vectors. They have homogeneous size, even in the case in which the original sequences had different durations. Such vectors can later be used to build a bilinear model for the input training set of gait motions.

The procedure can then be summarized as follows:

Figure 2. An example of hidden Markov model generated by a gait sequence. The HMM can be seen as a graph where each node represents a state (in this case N=4). Each state is associated with a key "pose" of the walking gait. Transitions between states are governed by the matrix A and are drawn as directed edges with attached a transition probability

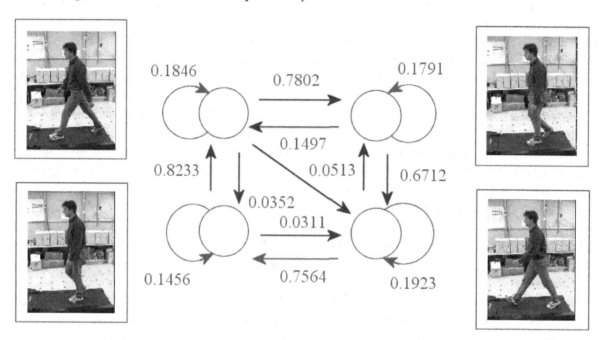

- each training image sequence is mapped to a sequence of feature vectors;
- those feature sequences are fed to the EM algorithm, which in turn delivers an N-state HMM for each training motion;
- the (pose) C matrix of each HMM is stacked to form a single observation vector;
- an asymmetric bilinear model is built as above for the resulting dataset.

The three-layer model we propose is depicted in Figure 3. Given a dataset of walking gaits, we can use this algorithm to built an asymmetric bilinear model from the sequences related to all style labels (covariate factors) but one. This will be our training set. We can then use the bilinear classifier to label the sequences associated with the remaining style (testing set).

EXPERIMENTS

We use here the CMU Mobo database (Gross & Shi, 2001) to extensively test our bilinear approach to gait ID. As its six cameras are widely separated, Mobo gives us the chance of testing the algorithm in a rather realistic setup. In the database 25 different people perform four different walking-related actions: slow walk, fast walk, walking along an inclined slope, and walking while carrying a ball. All the sequences are acquired indoor, with the subjects walking on a treadmill at constant speed. The cameras are more or less equally spaced around the treadmill, roughly positioned around the origin of the world coordinate system (Gross & Shi, 2001). Each sequence is composed by some 340 frames, encompassing 9-10 full walking cycles. We denote the six cameras originally called 3,5,7,13,16,17 by 1,2,3,4,5,6.

Figure 3. The proposed three-layer model. Features (bottom layer) are first extracted from each image of the sequence. The resulting feature sequences are fed to a HMM with a fixed number of states, yielding a dataset of Markov models, one for each sequence (second layer). The stacked versions of the (pose) C matrices of these models are finally used as observation vectors to train an asymmetric bilinear model (top layer)

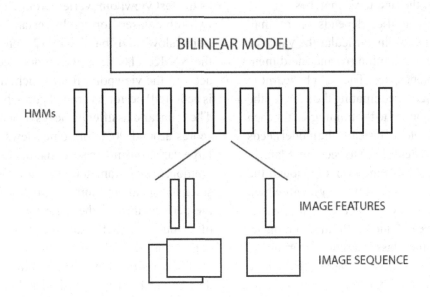

From View-Invariant Gait ID to ID-Invariant Action Recognition

The video sequences of the Mobo database possess three different labels: identity, action, and viewpoint. Therefore we have set up two series of tests in which asymmetric bilinear models are built by selecting identity as content label, and choosing a style label among the two remaining covariates. The two options are: content=ID, style=view (*view-invariant gait ID*); content=ID, style=action (*action-invariant gait ID*).

The remaining factor can be considered as a nuisance. Note that "action" here can be assimilated to classical covariates like walking surface (as the treadmill can be inclined or not) or carrying conditions (as the subject may or not carry a ball).

In each experiment we have formed a different training set by considering the sequences related to all the style labels but one. We have then built

an asymmetric bilinear model as explained above, using the sequences associated with the remaining style label as test data, and measuring the performance of the bilinear classifier.

To gather a large enough dataset we have adopted the period estimation technique of (Sarkar et al., 2005) to sub-divide the original long sequences into a larger number of subsequences, each spanning three walking cycles. In this way we have obtained a collection of 2080 sequences, almost equally distributed among the six views, the 25 IDs, and the four actions. After computing a feature matrix for each subsequence we have applied the HMM-EM algorithm with $N = 2$ states to generate a dataset of pose matrices C, each containing two pose vectors as columns. We have finally stacked those columns into a single observation vector for each subsequence. These observation vectors would finally form our training set. We have used for feature extraction the set of silhouettes provided with the database, after some preprocessing to remove small artifacts from the original images. In the following we report the performances of the algorithm, using both the percentage of correct best matches and the percentage of test sequences for which the correct identity is one of the first three matches.

The bilinear classifier depends on a small number of parameters, in particular the variance σ of the mixture distribution (6) and the dimension J of the content space. They can be learnt in a preliminary stage by computing the score of the algorithm when applied to the training set for each value of the parameters. Basically the model needs a large enough content space to accommodate all the content labels. Most important is though the initial value of the probability $p(c|y)$ with which each test vector y belongs to a content class c. Again, this can be obtained from the training set by maximizing the classification performance, using some sort of *simulated annealing* technique to overcome local maxima.

View-Invariant Identity Recognition

In the first series of tests we have set "identity" as the content label and "viewpoint" as the style label (covariate). This way we could test the view-invariance of the gait ID bilinear classifier. We report here the results of different kinds of tests. To generate Figure 4 the subset of the Mobo database associated with a single action (the nuisance, in this case) has been selected. We have then measured the performance of our bilinear classifier using view 1 as test view, for an increasing number of subjects (from 7 to 25). To get a flavor of the relative performance of our algorithm, we have also implemented a simple nearest neighbor classifier which assigns to each test sequence the identity of the closest Markov model. Distances between HMMs are measured using the standard Kullback-Leibler divergence (Kullback & Leibler, 1951). Figure 4 clearly illustrates how the bilinear classifier greatly outperforms a naive nearest-neighbor (NN) classification of the Markov models built from gait sequences.

The depressing results of the KL-NN approach attest the difficulty of the task. You cannot just neglect the fact that image sequences come from widely separated viewpoints.

Figure 5 compares instead the two algorithms as the test viewpoint varies (from 1 to 6), for the two sub-datasets formed by instances of the actions "slow" and "ball", with 12 identities. Again the NN-KL classifier (which does *not* take into account the viewpoint from which the sequence is acquired) performs around pure-chance levels. The bilinear classifier achieves instead excellent scores around 90% for some views. Relatively large variations in the second plot are due, in our opinion, to the parameter learning algorithm being stuck to a local optimum. Figure 6-left illustrates the performance of the algorithm as a function of the nuisance factor, i.e., the performed action: ball=1, fast=2, incline=3, slow=4.

The classification rate of the bilinear classifier does not exhibit any particular dependence on the nuisance action. We have also implemented for sake of comparison the *baseline algorithm* described in (Sarkar et al., 2005). The latter basically computes similarity scores between a test sequence *SP* and each training sequence *SG* by pairwise frame correlation. The baseline algorithm is used on the USF database (Sarkar et al., 2005) to provide a performance reference.

Figure 6-right compares the results of bilinear classification with those of both the baseline algorithm and the KL-based approach for all the six possible test views, in the complete dataset comprising all 25 identities. The structure introduced by the bilinear model greatly improves the identification performance, rather homogeneously over all the views. The baseline algorithm instead seems to work better for sequences coming from cameras 2 and 3, which have rather close viewpoints, while it delivers the worst results for camera 1, the most isolated from the others (Gross & Shi, 2001). The performance of the KL-based nearest neighbor approach is not distinguishable from pure chance.

Figure 4. View-invariant gait ID for gait sequences related to the same action: "slow" (left) and "ball" (right). View 1 is used as the test view, while all the others are included in the training set. The classification rate is plotted versus an increasing number of subjects (from 7 to 25). The percentage of correct best matches is shown by dashed lines, while the rate of a correct match in the first 3 is plotted by dot-dashed lines. For comparison, the performance of a KL-nearest neighbor classifier on the training set of HMMs is shown in solid black. As a reference pure chance is plotted using little vertical bars

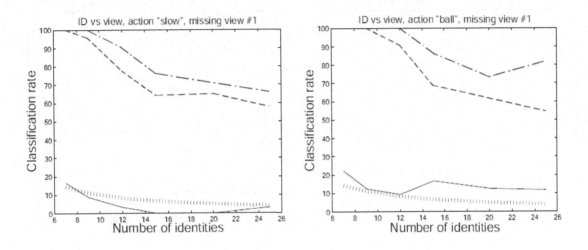

Figure 5. View-invariant gait ID for instances of the actions "slow" (left) and "ball" (right). The classification rate achieved for different test views (from 1 to 6) is plotted. Only the first 12 identities are here considered. Plot styles as above

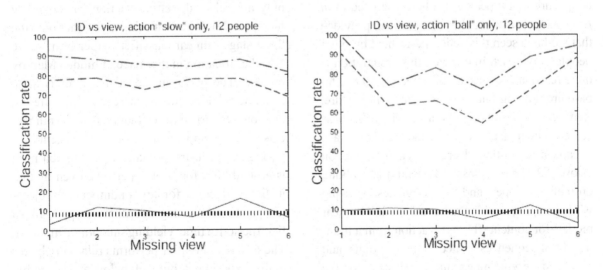

Figure 6. Performance of the bilinear classifier in the view-invariant gait ID experiment. Left: Classification rate as a function of the nuisance (action), test view 1. Right: score for the dataset of sequences related to the action "slow", and different selection of the test view (from 1 to 6). All 25 identities are here considered. The classification rate of the baseline algorithm is the widely spaced dashed line in the right diagram: other line styles as above

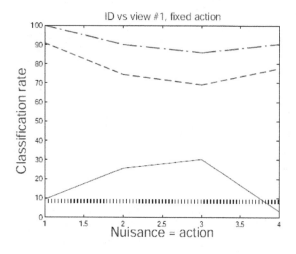 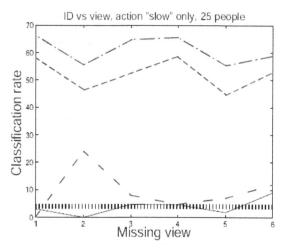

Action-Invariant Identity Recognition

In a different experiment we have validated the conjecture that a person can be recognized *even from an action he/she never performed,* provided that we have seen this action performed by other people in the past. In our case this assumption is quite reasonable, since all the actions in the database are nothing but variants of the gait gesture. Remember that some actions in the Mobo database correspond in fact to covariate factors like surface or carrying conditions. Here "1" denotes the action "slow", "2" denotes "fast", "3" stands for "walking on inclined slope", and "4" designates "walking while carrying a ball". We have then built bilinear models for content=ID, style=action from a training set of sequences related to three actions, and classified the remaining sequences (instances of the fourth action) using our bilinear approach. Figures 7 and 8 support the ability of bilinear classification to allow identity recognition even from unknown gestures (or, equivalently, under different surface or carrying conditions, actions 3 and 4).

Figure 7 shows two diagrams in which identity recognition performances for sequences acquired from viewpoints 1 (left) and 5 (right) only are selected, setting "action" as covariate factor (style). For all missing styles (actions) the three-stage bilinear classifier outperforms naive NN classification in the space of hidden Markov models. The performance of the latter is quite unstable, yielding different results for different unknown covariate values (actions), while bilinear classification appears to be quite consistent.

Figure 8 illustrates that the best-match ratio is around 90% for twelve persons, even though it slightly declines for larger numbers of subjects (the parameter learning algorithm is stopped after a fixed period of time, yielding suboptimal models). The NN-KL classifier performs relatively better in this experiment, but well below an acceptable level.

Figure 7. Action-invariant gait ID for sequences related to viewpoints 1 (left) and 5 (right). The classification rate is plotted versus different possible test actions (from 1 to 4). Only the first 12 identities are here considered. Plot styles as in Figure 4

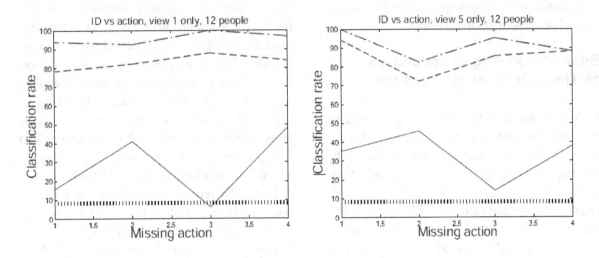

Figure 8. Action-invariant gait ID. In the left diagram sequences related to viewpoint (nuisance) #5 are considered, and "ball" is used as missing action (test style). In the right diagram sequences related to the same viewpoint are considered, and "fast" is used as test action. The classification rate is plotted versus an increasing number of subjects. Styles as above

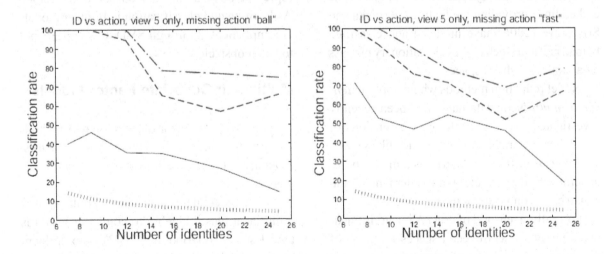

FUTURE DEVELOPMENTS: EXTENSIONS TO MULTILINEAR MODELING

The above experiments seem to prove that bilinear models are indeed capable of handling the influence of one covariate factor in gait recognition. In particular, we have focused above on what is maybe the most important such factor, viewpoint. To provide a comprehensive framework for covariate factor analysis, however, we need to extend our framework to *multilinear* models capable of handling many if not all the involved factors.

We can envisage two possible developments along this line. The first one concerns the compact representation of image sequences *as 3D tensors* instead of stacked column vectors.

Bilinear Modeling of Sequences as Three-Dimensional Tensors

Reduction methods have been largely used to approach the gait recognition problem. Linear techniques in particular are very popular (Abdelkader et al., 2001; Murase & Sakai, 1996; Tolliver & Collins, 2003; Han & Bhanu, 2004). Ekinci et al., for instance (2007), have applied to the problem Kernel PCA. An interesting biologically inspired work (Das et al., 2006) has instead proposed a two-stage PCA to kinematic data to describe gait cycles.

Nonlinear dimensionality reduction has also been recently employed. Locally Linear Embedding has been used in (Honggui & Xingguo, 2004) to detect gait cycles, with the shape of the embeddings providing the features. Kaziska and Srivastava (2006) have modeled and classified human gait as a stochastic cyclostationary process on a nonlinear shape space.

Novel reduction methods which apply to *tensor* or *multilinear* data have also been recently investigated, yielding multilinear extensions of dimensionality reduction techniques like PCA.

A *tensor* or *n*-mode matrix, is a higher order generalization of a vector (first order tensor) and a matrix (second order tensor).

Formally, a tensor A of order N is a multilinear mapping over a set of vector spaces $V_1, ..., V_N$ of dimensions $I_1, ..., I_N$. An element of A is denoted by $a_{i_1,...,i_n,...,i_N}$ where $1 \leq i_n \leq I_n$.

In image analysis and computer vision inputs come naturally in the form of matrices (the images themselves) or third-order tensors (image sequences).

General tensor discriminant analysis has been indeed applied in (Tao et al., 2007) to three different image representations based on Gabor filters. Matrix-based dimensionality reduction has also been applied in (Xu et al., 2006) to averaged silhouettes. A sophisticated application of marginal Fisher analysis on the result of tensor-based dimensionality reduction directly applied to grey-level images can instead be found in (Xu et al., 2007). Lu et al. (2006), on their side, have proposed a multilinear PCA algorithm and applied it to gait analysis. In their novel representation called EigenTensorGait each half cycle, seen as a third-order tensor, is considered as one data sample. He et al. (2005) have proposed a Tensor Subspace Analysis for second-order tensors (images) and compared their results with those produced by PCA and LDA.

A natural extension of the proposed three-layer framework would be the formulation of a model capable of handling observation sequences directly in the form of 3D tensors, instead of having to represent them as packed observation vectors. As learning and classification in bilinear models are implemented through SVD, this appears not to be an obstacle.

Multilinear Covariate Factor Models

A significative extension of the presented methodology to an arbitrary number of covariate factors, though, requires the definition of true *multilinear models*.

A fundamental reference on the application of multilinear/tensor algebra to computer vision is (Vasilescu & Terzopoulos, 2002). The problem of disentangling the different (covariate) factors in image ensembles is there solved through the tensor extension of conventional singular value decomposition, or N-mode SVD (De Lathauwer et al., 2000).

Let us recall the basic notions of tensor algebra and multilinear SVD.

A generalization of the product of two matrices is the product of a tensor and a matrix. The *mode-n product* of a tensor $A \in \mathbb{R}^{I_1 \times \cdots I_n \cdots \times I_N}$ by a matrix $M \in \mathbb{R}^{J_n \times I_n}$, denoted by $A \times_n M$, is a tensor $B \in \mathbb{R}^{I_1 \times \cdots \times I_{n-1} \times J_n \times I_{n+1} \times \cdots I_N}$ whose entries are

$$\left(A \times_n M\right)_{i_1 \cdots i_{n-1} j_n i_{n+1} \cdots i_N} = \sum_{i_n} a_{i_1 \cdots i_{n-1} i_n i_{n+1} \cdots i_N} m_{j_n i_n} \quad (11)$$

The mode-*n* product can be expressed in tensor notation as $B = A \times_n M$.

A matrix is a special case of tensor with two associated vector spaces, a row space and a column space. SVD orthogonalizes these two spaces and decomposes the matrix as $D = U_1 \Sigma U_2^T$, the product of an orthogonal column space associated with the left matrix $U_1 \in \mathbb{R}^{I_1 \times J_1}$ a diagonal singular value matrix $\Sigma \in \mathbb{R}^{J_1 \times J_2}$, and an orthogonal row space represented by the right matrix $U_2 \in \mathbb{R}^{I_2 \times J_2}$.

In terms of the *n*-mode product, the SVD decomposition can be written as $D = \Sigma \times_1 U_1 \times_2 U_2$.

"*N*-mode SVD" (De Lathauwer et al., 2000) is an extension of SVD that orthogonalizes the *N* spaces associated with an order *N* tensor, and expresses the tensor as the *n*-mode product of *N*-orthogonal spaces

$$D = Z \times_1 U_1 \times_2 U_2 \cdots \times_n U_n \cdots \times_N U_N. \quad (12)$$

Tensor *Z*, known as the *core tensor*, is analogous to the diagonal singular value matrix in conventional matrix SVD, but is in general a full tensor (Kolda, 2001). The core tensor governs the interaction between the *mode matrices* U_n, for $n = 1, \ldots, N$. Mode matrix U_n contains the orthonormal vectors spanning the column space of the matrix $D(n)$ resulting from the mode-*n* flattening of *D* (Vasilescu & Terzopoulos, 2002).

The *N*-mode SVD algorithm for decomposing *D* reads then as follows:

1. For $n = 1, \ldots, N$, compute the matrix U_n in (5) by calculating the SVD of the flattened matrix $D(n)$ and setting U_n to be the left

matrix of this SVD.

2. Solve for the core tensor as

$$Z = D \times_1 U_1^T \times_2 U_2^T \cdots \times_n U_n^T \cdots \times_N U_N^T \quad (13)$$

The method has been applied by Vasilescu and Terzopoulos to separate expression, pose, and identity in sets of facial images (*Tensorfaces*). They used a portion of the Weizmann face database of 28 male subjects photographed in 5 different poses under 3 illuminations performing 3 different expressions. Using a global rigid optical flow algorithm they aligned the original 512×352 pixel images to one reference image. The images were then decimated and cropped, yielding a total of 7943 pixels per image. The resulting facial image data tensor *D* was a $28 \times 5 \times 3 \times 3 \times 7943$ tensor, with $N = 5$ modes.

This approach has been later extended to Independent Component Analysis in (Vasilescu & Terzopoulos, 2005), where the statistically independent components of multiple linear factors were learnt.

Wang & Ahuja (2003) have also made use of this technique (often called Higher-Order Singular Value Decomposition or HOSVD) for facial expression decomposition, considering only three factors. A crucial difference with (Vasilescu & Terzopoulos, 2002) is their suggestion to alleviate the computational load by first applying PCA to image pixel to reduce the dimensionality of the problem, leaving HOSVD to deal with the resulting principal dimensions. Recognition is implemented by measuring the cosine distance between new and learnt person or expression vectors in the respective subspaces.

Park and Savvides (2006), on their side, have claimed that the use of higher-order tensors to describe multiple factors is problematic. On one side, it is difficult to decompose the multiple factors of a test image. On the other, it is hard to construct reliable multilinear models with more than two factors as in (12). They have then proposed a novel tensor factorization method based on a least square problem, and solved it using numerical optimization techniques without any knowledge or assumption on the test images. Their results appear fairly good for trilinear models.

A third alternative to multilinear modeling is a novel algorithm for positive tensor factorization proposed in (Welling & Weber, 2001). Starting from the observation that eigenvectors produced by PCA can be interpreted as modes to be linearly combined to get the data, they propose to drop the orthogonality constraint in the associated linear factorization, and simply minimize the reconstruction error under positivity constraint.

The algorithm then factorizes a tensor D of order N into F (not necessarily equal to N) *positive* components as follows

$$D_{i_1,\cdots,i_N} = \sum_{a=1}^{F} A_{i_1,a}^{(1)} \cdots A_{i_N,a}^{(N)} \tag{14}$$

so that the reconstruction error

$$\sum_{i_1,\cdots,i_N} \left(D_{i_1,\cdots,i_N} - \sum_{a=1}^{F} A_{i_1,a}^{(1)} \cdots A_{i_N,a}^{(N)} \right)^2 \tag{15}$$

is minimized. Experiments seem to show that factors produced by PTF are easier to interpret than those produced by algorithms based on singular value decomposition.

An interesting application of multilinear modeling of 3D meshes for face animation transfer can be found in (Vlasic et al., 2005). The application of multilinear algebra to the gait ID problem has been pioneered by Lee and Elgammal (2005) but has not received wide attention later on. Given walking sequences captured from multiple views for multiple people, they fit a multilinear generative model using Higher-Order Singular Value Decomposition which would decompose view

factors, body configuration factors, and gait-style factors.

In the near future the application of positive tensor factorization or multi-linear SVD to tensorial observations like walking gaits will help the field of gait recognition to progress towards a reduction of the influence of covariate factors. This will likely open the way for a wider application of gait biometrics in real-world scenarios.

CONCLUSION

Gait recognition is an interesting biometric which does not undergo the limitations of other standard methods such as iris or face recognition, as it can be applied at a distance to non-cooperative users. However, its practical use is heavily limited by the presence of multiple covariate factors which make identification problematic in real-world scenarios.

In this chapter, motivated by the view-invariance issue in the gait ID problem, we addressed the problem of classifying walking gaits affected by different covariates (or, equivalently, possessing different labels). We illustrated a three-layer model in which hidden Markov models with a fixed number of states are used to cluster each sequence into a fixed number of poses in order to generate the observation data for an asymmetric bilinear model. We used the CMU Mobo database (Gross & Shi, 2001) to set up an experimental comparison between our bilinear approach and other standard algorithms in view-invariant and action-invariant gait ID. We demonstrated that bilinear modelling can improve recognition performances when the test motion is performed in an unknown style.

Natural extensions of the proposed methodology are, firstly, the representation of gait sequences or cycles as 3D tensors instead of stacked vectors. In second order the application of nonnegative tensor factorization or multidimensional SVD to gait data, in order to make identity recognition robust to the many covariate factors present. This will encourage a more extensive adoption of gait identification side by side with other classical biometrics.

REFERENCES

Abdelkader, C. B., Cutler, R., Nanda, H., & Davis, L. (2001). Eigengait: Motion-based recognition using image self-similarity. (LNCS 2091, pp. 284–294). Berlin: Springer.

Bhanu, B., & Han, J. (2002). Individual recognition by kinematic-based gait analysis. In *Proceedings of ICPR02, 3*, 343–346.

Bouchrika, I., & Nixon, M. (2008). Exploratory factor analysis of gait recognition. In *Proc. of the 8th IEEE International Conference on Automatic Face and Gesture Recognition.*

Boutsidis, C., Gallopoulos, E., Zhang, P., & Plemmons, R. J. (2006). PALSIR: A new approach to nonnegative tensor factorization. In *Proc. of the 2nd Workshop on Algorithms for Modern Massive Datasets (MMDS).*

Cichocki, A., Zdunek, R., Plemmons, R., & Amari, S. (2007). Novel multilayer nonnegative tensor factorization with sparsity constraints. (*. LNCS, 4432,* 271–280.

Cunado, D., Nash, J. M., Nixon, M. S., & Carter, J. N. (1999). Gait extraction and description by evidence-gathering. In *. Proceedings of, AVBPA99,* 43–48.

Cutting, J., & Kozlowski, L. (1977). Recognizing friends by their walk: Gait perception without familiarity cues. *Bulletin of the Psychonomic Society, 9,* 353–356.

Das, S. R., Wilson, R. C., Lazarewicz, M. T., & Finkel, L. H. (2006). Two-stage PCA extracts spatiotemporal features for gait recognition. *Journal of Multimedia, 1*(5), 9–17.

De Lathauwer, L., De Moor, B., & Vandewalle, J. (2000). A multilinear singular value decomposition. *SIAM Journal on Matrix Analysis and Applications, 21*(4).

Dempster, A. P., Laird, N. M., & Rubin, D. B. (1977). Maximum likelihood from incomplete data via the EM algorithm. *Journal of the Royal Statistical Society. Series B. Methodological, 39*(1), 1–38.

Ekinci, M., Aykut, M., & Gedikli, E. (2007). Gait recognition by applying multiple projections and kernel PCA. In *Proceedings of MLDM 2007* (LNAI 4571, pp. 727–741.

Elgammal, A., & Lee, C. S. (2004). Separating style and content on a nonlinear manifold. In . *Proceedings of of IEEE Conference on Computer Vision and Pattern Recognition, 1,* 478–485.

Elliot, R., Aggoun, L., & Moore, J. (1995). *Hidden Markov models: Estimation and control.* Springer Verlag.

Frosini, P. (1991). Measuring shape by size functions. In . *Proceedings of SPIE on Intelligent Robotic Systems, 1607,* 122–133.

Gafurov, D. (2007). A survey of biometric gait recognition: Approaches, security, and challeges. In *Proceedings of NIK-2007.*

Gross, R., & Shi, J. (2001). *The CMU motion of body (Mobo) database.* (Tech. Rep.). Pittsburgh, PA: Carnegie Mellon University.

Han, J., & Bhanu, B. (2004). Statistical feature fusion for gait-based human recognition. In *Proceedings of CVPR'04* (Vol. 2, pp. 842–847).

Han, J., & Bhanu, B. (2005). Performance prediction for individual recognition by gait. *Pattern Recognition Letters, 26*(5), 615–624. doi:10.1016/j.patrec.2004.09.011

Han, J., Bhanu, B., & Roy-Chowdhury, A. K. (2005). Study on view-insensitive gait recognition. In *Proceedings of ICIP'05* (Vol. 3, pp. 297–300).

He, Q., & Debrunner, C. (2000). Individual recognition from periodic activity using hidden Markov models. In *IEEE Workshop on Human Motion* (pp. 47–52).

He, X., Cai, D., & Niyogi, P. (2005). Tensor subspace analysis. In *Advances in Neural Information Processing Systems 18 (NIPS)*.

Honggui, L., & Xingguo, L. (2004). Gait analysis using LLE. *Proceedings of ICSP'04*.

Huang, X., & Boulgouris, N. V. (2008). Human gait recognition based on multiview gait sequences. *EURASIP Journal on Advances in Signal Processing*.

Jafri, R., & Arabnia, H. R. (2008). Fusion of face and gait for automatic human recognition. In *Proc. of the Fifth International Conference on Information Technology*.

Johnson, A. Y., & Bobick, A. F. (2001). A multiview method for gait recognition using static body parameters. In . *Proceedings of AVBPA, 01*, 301–311.

Kale, A., Rajagopalan, A. N., Cuntoor, N., & Kruger, V. (2002). Gait-based recognition of humans using continuous HMMs. In . *Proceedings of AFGR, 02*, 321–326.

Kale, A., Roy-Chowdhury, A. K., & Chellappa, R. (2003). Towards a view invariant gait recognition algorithm. In . *Proceedings of, AVSBS03*, 143–150.

Kale, A., Sunsaresan, A., Rajagopalan, A. N., Cuntoor, N. P., Roy-Chowdhury, A. K., Kruger, V., & Chellappa, R. (2004). Identification of humans using gait. *IEEE Trans. PAMI, 13*(9), 1163–1173.

Kaziska, D., & Srivastava, A. (2006). Cyclostationary processes on shape spaces for gait-based recognition. In *Proceedings of ECCV'06* (Vol. 2, pp. 442–453).

Kiers, H. A. L. (2000). Towards a standardized notation and terminology in multiway analysis. *Journal of Chemometrics, 14*(3), 105–122. doi:10.1002/1099-128X(200005/06)14:3<105::AID-CEM582>3.0.CO;2-I

Kolda, T. G. (2001). Orthogonal tensor decompositions. *SIAM Journal on Matrix Analysis and Applications, 23*(1), 243–255. doi:10.1137/S0895479800368354

Kullback, S., & Leibler, R. A. (1951). On information and sufficiency. *Annals of Mathematical Statistics, 22*, 79–86. doi:10.1214/aoms/1177729694

Lee, C.-S., & Elgammal, A. (2004). Gait style and gait content: bilinear models for gait recognition using gait resampling. In . *Proceedings of AFGR, 04*, 147–152.

Lee, C.-S., & Elgammal, A. (2005). Towards scalable view-invariant gait recognition: Multilinear analysis for gait. (. *LNCS, 3546*, 395–405.

Lee, H., Kim, Y.-D., Cichocki, A., & Choi, S. (2007). Nonnegative tensor factorization for continuous EEG classifcation. *International Journal of Neural Systems, 17*(4), 305–317. doi:10.1142/S0129065707001159

Lee, L., & Grimson, W. (2002). Gait analysis for recognition and classification. In . *Proceedings of AFGR, 02*, 155–162.

Li, X. L., Maybank, S. J., Yan, S. J., Tao, D. C., & Xu, D. J. (2008). Gait components and their application to gender recognition. *IEEE Trans. SMC-C, 38*(2), 145–155.

Little, J., & Boyd, J. (1998). Recognising people by their gait: The shape of motion. *IJCV, 14*(6), 83–105.

Liu, Z. Y., & Sarkar, S. (2006). Improved gait recognition by gait dynamics normalization. *IEEE Trans. PAMI, 28*(6), 863–876.

Lu, H., Plataniotis, K. N., & Venetsanopoulos, A. N. (2006). Multilinear principal component analysis of tensor objects for recognition. In *Proc. of the 18th International Conference on Pattern Recognition (ICPR'06)* (Vol. 2, pp. 776–779).

Lu, J. W., & Zhang, E. (2007). Gait recognition for human identification based on ICA and fuzzy SVM through multiple views fusion. *Pattern Recognition Letters, 28*(16), 2401–2411. doi:10.1016/j.patrec.2007.08.004

Makihara, Y., Sagawa, R., Mukaigawa, Y., Echigo, T., & Yagi, Y. (2006). Gait recognition using a view transformation model in the frequency domain. In *Proceedings of ECCV* (Vol. 3, pp. 151–163).

Morup, M., Hansen, L. K., Herrmann, C. S., Parnas, J., & Arnfred, S. M. (2006). Parallel factor analysis as an exploratory tool for wavelet transformed event-related EEG. *NeuroImage, 29*(3), 938–947. doi:10.1016/j.neuroimage.2005.08.005

Murase, H., & Sakai, R. (1996). Moving object recognition in eigenspace representation: Gait analysis and lip reading. *Pattern Recognition Letters, 17*(2), 155–162. doi:10.1016/0167-8655(95)00109-3

Nixon, M. S., & Carter, J. N. (2006). Automatic recognition by gait. *Proceedings of the IEEE, 94*(11), 2013–2024. doi:10.1109/JPROC.2006.886018

Niyogi, S., & Adelson, E. (1994). Analyzing and recognizing walking figures in XYT. In . *Proceedings of CVPR, 94*, 469–474.

Park, S. W., & Savvides, M. (2006). Estimating mixing factors simultaneously in multilinear tensor decomposition for robust face recognition and synthesis. In *Proceedings of the 2006 Conference on Computer Vision and Pattern Recognition Workshop (CVPRW'06)*.

Porteus, I., Bart, E., & Welling, M. (2008). Multi-HDP: A nonparametric Bayesian model for tensor factorization. In *Proc. of AAAI 2008* (pp. 1487–1490).

Rogez, G., Guerrero, J. J., Martinez del Rincon, J., & Orrite-Uranela, C. (2006). Viewpoint independent human motion analysis in man-made environments. In *Proceedings of BMVC'06*.

Sarkar, S., Phillips, P. J., Liu, Z., Vega, I. R., Grother, P., & Bowyer, K. W. (2005). The humanID gait challenge problem: Datasets, performance, and analysis. *IEEE Trans. PAMI, 27*(2), 162–177.

Shakhnarovich, G., Lee, L., & Darrell, T. (2001). Integrated face and gait recognition from multiple views. In . *Proceedings of CVPR, 01*, 439–446.

Shashua, A., & Hazan, T. (2005). Non-negative tensor factorization with applications to statistics and computer vision. In *Proceedings of the 22nd International Conference on Machine Learning* (pp. 792–799).

Spencer, N. M., & Carter, J. N. (2002). Viewpoint invariance in automatic gait recognition. *Proc. of AutoID* (pp. 1–6).

Sundaresan, A., Roy-Chowdhury, A. K., & Chellappa, R. (2003). A hidden Markov model based framework for recognition of humans from gait sequences. In *Proceedings of ICIP'03* (Vol. 2, pp. 93–96).

Tan, D. L., Huang, K. Q., Yu, S. Q., & Tan, T. N. (2007). Orthogonal diagonal projections for gait recognition. In *Proceedings of ICIP'07* (Vol. 1, pp. 337–340).

Tao, D. (2006). Discriminative linear and multilinear subspace methods. Unpublished doctoral dissertation, University of London Birkbeck.

Tao, D., Li, X., Wu, X., & Maybank, S. J. (2007). General tensor discriminant analysis and Gabor features for gait recognition. *IEEE Transactions on Pattern Analysis and Machine Intelligence, 29*(10), 1700–1715. doi:10.1109/TPAMI.2007.1096

Tenenbaum, J. B., & Freeman, W. T. (2000). Separating style and content with bilinear models. *Neural Computation, 12*(6), 1247–1283. doi:10.1162/089976600300015349

Tolliver, D., & Collins, R. (2003). Gait shape estimation for identification. In *Proc. of AVBPA '03* (pp. 734–742).

Urtasun, R., & Fua, P. (2004). *3D tracking for gait characterization and recognition.* (Tech. Rep. No. IC/2004/04). Lausanne, Switzerland: Swiss Federal Institute of Technology.

Vasilescu, M. A. O., & Terzopoulos, D. (2002). Multilinear analysis of image ensembles: Tensor-Faces. In *Proc. of the European Conf. on Computer Vision ECCV '02* (pp. 447–460).

Vasilescu, M. A. O., & Terzopoulos, D. (2005). Multilinear independent component analysis. In *Proceedings of the 2005 IEEE Computer Society Conference on Computer Vision and Pattern Recognition (CVPR'05)* (Vol. 1, pp. 547–553).

Veres, G., Nixon, M., & Carter, J. (2005). Modelling the time-variant covariates for gait recognition. In *Proceedings of AVBPA 2005. Lecture Notes in Computer Science, 3546*, 597–606.

Vlasic, D., Brand, M., Pfister, H., & Popovic, J. (2005). Face transfer with multilinear models. (Tech. Rep. No. TR2005-048). Cambridge, MA: Mitsubishi Electric Research Laboratory.

Wang, H., & Ahuja, N. (2003). Facial expression decomposition. *Proceedings of, ICCV,* 958–965.

Wang, L. (2006). Abnormal walking gait analysis using silhouette-masked flow histograms. In *Proceedings of ICPR '06* (Vol. 3, pp. 473–476).

Welling, M., & Weber, M. (2001). Positive tensor factorization. *Pattern Recognition Letters, 22*(12), 1255–1261. doi:10.1016/S0167-8655(01)00070-8

Xu, D., Yan, S., Tao, D., Lin, S., & Zhang, H.-J. (2007). Marginal Fisher analysis and its variants for human gait recognition and content-based image retrieval. *IEEE Transactions on Image Processing, 16*(11), 2811–2821. doi:10.1109/TIP.2007.906769

Xu, D., Yan, S., Tao, D., Zhang, L., Li, X., & Zhang, H.-J. (2006). Human gait recognition with matrix representation. *IEEE Transactions on Circuits and Systems for Video Technology, 16*(7), 896–903. doi:10.1109/TCSVT.2006.877418

Yam, C., Nixon, M., & Carter, J. (2004). Automated person recognition by walking and running via model-based approaches. *Pattern Recognition, 37*(5), 1057–1072. doi:10.1016/j.patcog.2003.09.012

Zhao, G., Liu, G., Li, H., & Pietikäinen, M. (2006). 3D gait recognition using multiple cameras. In *Proceedings of the 7th IEEE International Conference on Automatic Face and Gesture Recognition* (pp. 529–534).

Zhou, X. L., & Bhanu, B. (2007). Integrating face and gait for human recognition at a distance in video. *IEEE Trans. SMC-B, 37*(5), 1119–1137.

Chapter 9
Gait Feature Fusion using Factorial HMM

Jimin Liang
Xidian University, China

Changhong Chen
Xidian University, China

Heng Zhao
Xidian University, China

Haihong Hu
Xidian University, China

Jie Tian
Xidian University, China

ABSTRACT

Multisource information fusion technology offers a promising solution to the development of a superior classification system. For gait recognition problem, information fusion is necessary to be employed under at least three circumstances: 1) multiple gait feature fusion, 2) multiple view gait sequence fusion, and 3) gait and other biometrics fusion. Feature concatenation is the most popular methodology to integrate multiple features. However, because of the high dimensional gait data size and small available number of training samples, feature concatenation typically leads to the well-known curse of dimensionality and the small sample size problems. In this chapter, we explore the factorial hidden Markov model (FHMM), an extended hidden Markov model (HMM) with a multiple layer structure, as a feature fusion framework for gait recognition. FHMM provides an alternative to combining several gait features without concatenating them into a single augmented feature, thus, to some extent, overcomes the curse of dimensionality and small sample size problem for gait recognition. Three gait features, the frieze feature, wavelet feature, and boundary signature, are adopted in the numerical experiments conducted on CMU MoBo database and CASIA gait database A. Besides the cumulative matching score (CMS) curves, McNemar's test is employed to check on the statistical significance of the performance difference between the recognition algorithms. Experimental results demonstrate that the proposed FHMM feature fusion scheme outperforms the feature concatenation method.

DOI: 10.4018/978-1-60566-725-6.ch009

INTRODUCTION

Biometrics refer to the automatic identification of a person by measuring and analyzing its physiological or behavioral characteristics, such as fingerprints, eye retinas and irises, facial patterns and gait patterns. Gait recognition is the process of identifying an individual by its walking style. In comparison with other biometric characteristics, gait patterns have the advantages of unobtrusive, difficult to conceal, non-invasive and effective at a distance. Therefore, gait recognition has attracted a lot of research interests in recent years.

Feature extraction is a crucial step for gait recognition. It usually comprises the tasks of feature construction, space dimensionality reduction, sparse representations and feature selection. The basic gait feature extraction methods are based on the parameters of human body, such as structural stride parameters (BenAbdelkader et al., 2002), joint angle trajectories (Tanawongsuwan & Bobick, 2001) and five-link biped model (Zhang et al., 2004). Some latterly proposed methods take the gait silhouette as a whole and extract low dimensional feature from it, such as unwrapping the contour into a set of boundary pixel points sampled along its outer-contour (Wang et al. 2003) and self- similarity plot (BenAbdelkader et al., 2004). Robust gait representation tends to be a new research field in gait recognition. The robust gait representation can be applied directly to gait recognition or used for further feature extraction. Han & Bhanu (2006) proposed gait energy image (GEI) to characterize human walking properties, which is an average image of a gait cycle. Gait history image (GHI) (Liu & Zheng, 2007) and gait moment image (GMI) (Ma et al., 2007) were developed based on GEI. GHI preserves the temporal information alongside width the spatial information. GMI is the gait probability image at each key moment of all gait cycles. Lee et al. (2007) introduced a novel spatiotemporal Shape Variation-Based Frieze Pattern (SVB frieze pattern) representation for gait. Lam et al. (2007)

fused two templates, the motion silhouette contour templates (MSCTs) and static silhouette templates (SSTs) for gait recognition.

The foregoing gait feature or representation performs well under some circumstances. However, as for any pattern recognition problem, a single feature can not solve the gait recognition problem thoroughly. Information fusion technology offers a promising solution to the development of a superior classification system. It has been applied to numerous fields and new applications are being explored constantly. For gait recognition problem, information fusion is necessary to be employed under at least three circumstances.

Multiple **gait feature fusion**: Wang et al. (2004) employed both static and dynamic features for recognition using the nearest exemplar classifier. The features were fused on decision level using different combination rules. Lam et al. (2007) presented two gait feature representation methods, the motion silhouette contour templates (MSCTs) and static silhouette templates (SSTs), and performed decision-level fusion by summarizing the similarity scores. Bazin et al. (2005) examined the fusion of a dynamic feature and two static features in a probabilistic framework. They proposed a process for determining the probabilistic match scores using intra and inter-class variance models together with Bayes rule. Han & Bhanu (2004) proposed a method to learn statistical gait features from real templates and synthetic templates to address the problem of lacking gallery gait data. A matching score fusion strategy was therefore applied to improve the recognition performance. Veres et al. (2005) tried to fuse static and dynamic features to overcome the problem when the gallery and probe databases were recorded with a time interval. Generally speaking, superior gait recognition performance was reported when multiple features were employed.

Multiple view gait sequences fusion: While some research attempted the multiview gait recognition problem by warping the original views to the canonical view (Tyagi et al., 2006; Kale et al., 2003), others seek for the information fusion approaches. Wang et al. (2006) presented a multiview gait recognition method based on fusing the similarity scores of two viewpoints by the sum rule, weighted sum rule, product rule and Dempster-Shafer rule. Lu & Zhang (2007) proposed a multiview fusion recognition approach on the decision level, which combined the results of independent component analysis (ICA) and genetic fuzzy support vector machine (GFSVM) using the product of sum (POS) rule.

Gait and other biometrics fusion: Although research conducted in the area of gait recognition has shown the potential of gait-assisted identification, at present, gait is not generally expected to be used as a sole means of identification of individuals in large database; instead, it is seen as a potentially valuable component in a multimodal biometric system (Boulgouris et al., 2005). Liu & Sarkar (2007) explored the possibility of using both face and gait in enhancing human recognition at a distance performance in outdoor conditions. In the prior fusion systems, the side view of gait and the frontal view of face are used (Kale et al., 2004; Shakhnarovich & Darrell, 2002; Shakhnarovich et al., 2001). Zhou & Bhanu (2006; 2007; 2008) combined cues of face profile and gait silhouette from the single camera video sequences.

In the aforementioned literatures, the approaches of information fusion can be roughly classified into two categories: the decision-level fusion and the feature-level fusion. In the decision-level fusion system, multiple classifiers work in hierarchical or in parallel. The outputs of the parallel individual classifiers (subject labels, rank values, or match scores) are combined by some specific fusion rules to produce the final recognition result. Commonly applied fusion rules include majority voting, sum rule, product rule and so on.

While fusion at the decision level has been extensively studied, feature-level fusion is relatively understudied. Zhou & Bhanu (2008) presented a summary of the recent work for the feature-level fusion and pointed out that feature concatenation was the most popular feature-level fusion methodology. Whereas, for most gait recognition applications, the number of available training samples is small, feature concatenation typically results the well-known curse of dimensionality and the small sample size problem (Xu et al., 2006).

In this chapter, we explore an extended hidden Markov models (HMM) framework, factorial HMM (FHMM), for gait recognition as a feature-level fusion structure. HMM-based gait recognition methodology is preferable to other techniques since it explicitly takes into consideration not only the similarity between shapes in the test and reference sequences, but also the probabilities with which shapes appear and succeed each other in a walking cycle of a specific subject (Boulgouris et al. 2005). The FHMM framework provides an interesting alternative to combining several features without the need to combine them into a single augmented feature vector (Logan & Moreno, 1997). It has a multiple layer structure and combines the information from the layers to obtain the model parameters. We treat FHMM as a feature-level fusion structure because feature fusion happens at the training process to obtain the model parameters. It does not produce the recognition result of each individual feature.

In order to testify the FHMM-based feature fusion scheme, three gait features, the frieze feature, wavelet feature, and boundary signature, are adopted in the numerical experiments conducted on the CMU MoBo gait database (Gross & Shi, 2001) and CASIA gait database A (CASIA, 2004). Each two feature pairs are fused by FHMM respectively and their performances are compared with that of feature concatenation and single feature. The performance is evaluated by cumulative matching score (CMS) curves and McNemar's Test.

Figure 1. (A) Hidden Markov model; (B) FHMM with 3 layers

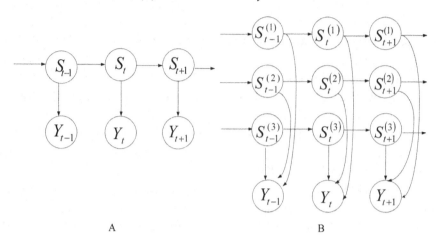

A   B

FHMM-BASED FEATURE FUSION

Model Description

HMM is a probabilistic model which describes a sequence of observation vectors. The structure of HMM is shown in Figure 1 (a). HMM gets its name from two defining properties: First, it assumes that the observation Y_t at time t was generated by some process whose state S_t is hidden from the observer. Second, it hypothesizes that the state of this hidden process satisfies the Markov property. Given the value of S_{t-1}, the current state S_t is independent from all the states prior to $t-1$. HMM-based gait recognition was presented in the book of Kale et al. (2005).

FHMM is an extension of HMM. It was first introduced by Ghahramani & Jordan (1997), who attempted to extend HMM by allowing the modeling of several stochastic random processes loosely coupled. FHMM has a multiple layer structure and provides an interesting alternative to combining several features without merging them into a single augmented feature. It uses a more complex state structure to improve the representational capacity of the HMM. FHMM was firstly applied to speech recognition (Logan & Moreno, 1997, 1998; Betkowska et al., 2006). Betkowska et al.

(2006) used FHMM for speech recognition with the second layers modeling sudden noise. They confirmed that FHMM can improve the clean speech HMM in noisy conditions.

FHMM arises by forming a dynamic belief network composed of several HMM "layers". This is illustrated in Figure 1 (b). Each layer has independent dynamics but that the observation vector depends upon the current state in each of the layers. This is achieved by allowing the state variable in FHMM as a collection of states. A "meta-state" variable as the combination of M states is employed as follows:

$$S_t = S_t^{(1)}, S_t^{(2)}, ..., S_t^{(M)} \qquad (1)$$

where S_t is the "meta-state" at time t, $S_t^{(m)}$ indicates the state of the mth layer at time t and M denotes the number of layers.

For simplicity it is assumed that each layer has the same number of possible states. Let K be the number of states in each layer. A system with M layers requires $M K \times K$ transition matrices with zeros representing illegal transitions. This system could also be represented as a regular HMM with a $K^M \times K^M$ transition matrix. It is preferable to use the $M K \times K$ transition matrices over the K^M

$\times K^M$ equivalent representation for computational simplicity.

It is also assumed that each meta-state variable is a priori uncoupled from other state variables, such that:

$$P(S_t \mid S_{t-1}) = \prod_{m=1}^{M} P(S_t^{(m)} \mid S_{t-1}^{(m)}). \qquad (2)$$

There are two ways of combining the information from the layers to calculate the probability of observation. The first method assumes that the observation is distributed according to a Gaussian distribution with a common covariance and the mean from a linear combination of the state means, named as "linear" FHMM. The second combination method, the "streamed" method, assumes that $P(Y_t|S_t)$ is the product of the distributions of each layer (Y_t is the observation at time t). Refer to Logan & Moreno (1998) for more details.

FHMM for Gait Feature Fusion

The parameters of FHMM are initialized and iteratively estimated as follows. The recognition results are obtained by sorting the log likelihoods that the probe sequence is generated from the training FHMMs.

Parameter Initialization

Number of states K and layers M: The number of states is determined using the method proposed in Kale et al. (2002). The average distortion is used to examine the marginal reduction in the distortion as the change of state numbers. When the average distortion doesn't decrease rapidly, the corresponding state number is chosen. In the following numerical experiments, five state numbers are chosen for CMU MoBo gait database and seven state numbers for CASIA gait database A. The number of layers depends on the number of features to fuse. In the experiments we fuse two kinds of features, hence the number of layers is two.

The transition matrices: The transition matrices are $M K \times K$ matrices. Each of the initial $K \times K$ matrices is initialized as a left-to-right HMM, which allows only transitions from one state to itself and its next state.

Output probability distribution: A gait sequence is always large in size. The large dimension makes it impossible to calculate a common covariance of the observation. So we use an exemplar-based model to calculate the distribution, which achieves the recognition task based on the distance measure between the observed feature vectors and the exemplars. The distance metric and the exemplars are key factors to the algorithm performance. The "streamed" method aforementioned is employed to combine different layers.

Let $Y = \{Y_1, Y_2, ..., Y_T\}$ be the observation vectors of a training cycle, $F^m = \{f_1^m, f_2^m, ..., f_T^m\}$ be the feature vectors of the observation vectors in layer m, and T be the length of the sequence. We divide the observation vectors into K clusters equally and initialize the exemplar element $S_t^{(m)}$ in the mth layer by averaging the feature vectors of the cluster to which the tth feature vector belongs.

In order to avoid calculating high-dimensional probability density functions, we estimate the output probability distribution by an alternative approach based on the distance between the exemplars and the feature vectors (Sundaresan et al. 2003). The output probability distribution of the mth layer is defined as:

$$P(f_t^m \mid S_t^{(m)}) = \alpha \delta_n^m e^{-\delta_n^m \times D(f_t^m, S_t^{(m)})}, \qquad (3)$$

where α is a parameter less than 1, $D(f_t^m, S_t^{(m)})$ is the inner product distance between the tth feature vector f_t^m and the tth state $S_t^{(m)}$ in the mth layer. δ_n^m is defined as:

$$\delta_n^m = \frac{N_n}{\sum_{t \in C_n} D(f_t^m, S_t^{(m)})}, \qquad (4)$$

where N_n is the number of frames in n^{th} cluster. C_n contains the sequence numbers of observation vectors belonging to the nth cluster.

The output probability distribution is represented by:

$$P(Y_t \mid S_t) \propto \prod_{m=1}^{M} P(f_t^m \mid S_t^{(m)}). \qquad (5)$$

Parameter Estimation

The FHMM model parameters are denoted as λ, which include the exemplars, the transition matrices, the output probability distribution and the prior probabilities. The exemplars are initialized and remain unchanged when estimating other parameters. The transition matrices and the prior probabilities are estimated using the Expectation Maximization (EM) algorithm. The exact forward-backward algorithm (Ghahramani & Jordan 1996) is used in the E-step. The naive exact algorithm has the time complexity of $O(TK^{2M})$ if it applies the transformation of the FHMM into an equivalent HMM with K^m states and using the forward-backward algorithm. The exact forward-backward algorithm has time complexity $O(TMK^{(M+1)})$ because it makes use of the independence of the underlying Markov chains to sum over $M K \times K$ transition matrices. Viterbi algorithm is applied to find the most probable path and the likelihood. New exemplars can be obtained through the most probable path and further yields the new output probability distribution. The estimation process is iterated until the likelihood converges to a small specified threshold.

Recognition

First, a probe cycle y is preprocessed and its features are extracted.

Then the output probability distribution of the probe sequence is calculated by the exemplars of the train sequence. The likelihood P_j that the probe sequence is generated by the FHMM parameters λ_j of the jth subject in the training database is calculated as:

$$P_j = P(y \mid \lambda_j) . \qquad (6)$$

If P_m is the largest one among all, we assign the probe sequence to be subject m.

A key problem during calculating the likelihood P_j is how to get the clusters of the probe sequence in case of the given parameters of the training sequence. Two methods can be considered. First, the distances between the features of probe sequence and the exemplars of a training sequence are calculated to form the clusters. The clusters of the same probe sequence may be varied with different training sequences. Second, the probe sequence is equally divided into K clusters, which remain the same for different train sequences. Our experiments adopt the second method.

FEATURE SELECTION

In order to take the advantages of multiple feature fusion, the features are expected to be uncorrelated and supply complementary information for the recognition task. However there is not theoretical guidance about how to select complementary features. In this chapter we intuitively select three kinds of gait features and investigate the feature fusion performance by numerical experiments. In section 4, we further explore the correlation analysis of the selected features.

Figure 2. (A) Sample image of the original silhouette of CMU MoBo gait database; (B) Processed silhouette of (A); (C) Sample image of the original silhouette of CASIA gait database; (D) Processed silhouette of (C)

Figure 3. (A) Preprocessed silhouette image; (B) Frieze feature F_c of (A); (C) Frieze feature F_R of (A); (D) F_R after noise filtering

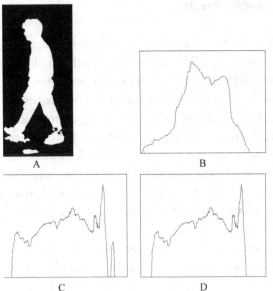

Silhouette Preprocessing

Both the CMU MoBo gait database and the CASIA gait database A offer human silhouettes segmented from the background images. The silhouettes are noisy and need further processing to improve the quality.

Firstly, mathematical morphological operations are used for holes remedy and noise elimination.

Secondly, some big noise blocks, such as the shadow under the feet or other redundant parts of the silhouettes, are removed by eliminating the connected regions whose areas are less than a given threshold. This step is useful to get rid of the separated noise regions, but may fail when the noise is connected with the main body.

Thirdly, all the silhouettes are center aligned to its centroid and scaled to the same height.

Finally, the silhouettes are cropped into the same size. We choose the size of 640×300 for CMU MoBo gait database and 120×96 for CASIA gait database A, which contains most useful information and less noise for most people. Sample silhouette images are shown in Figure 2.

Feature Extraction

Three gait features, the frieze feature, wavelet feature, and boundary signature, are extracted from the preprocessed silhouettes. They are described as follows.

Frieze Feature

The first gait feature representation is the **frieze pattern** (Liu et al., 2002). A two-dimensional pattern that repeats along one dimension is called as a frieze pattern in the mathematics and geometry literature. Consider a binary silhouette image $b(x, y)$ indexed spatially by pixel location (x, y). The first frieze pattern is calculated as $F_C(x) = \Sigma_y b(x, y)$, which is the vertical projection (column sum) of silhouette image. The second frieze pattern $F_R(y) = \Sigma_y b(x, y)$ can be constructed by stacking the row projections. It is considered that F_R contains more information than F_c and some obvious noise can be removed from F_R, as shown in Figure 3. We choose F_R as the first gait feature pattern hereafter in this chapter.

Wavelet Feature

Wavelet transform is regarded as a temporal-frequency localized analysis method, which has both high time resolution in high frequency part and high frequency resolution in low frequency part. It has the property of holding entropy and changing the energy distribution of the image without losing information. Wavelet transform acts on the whole image, which can eliminate the global relativity of the image as well as separate the quantization error to the whole image, thus avoiding artifacts.

We apply two-dimensional wavelet transform to the silhouettes using Harr wavelet base. The wavelet coefficients of approximation sub-image hold most of the useful information and therefore are chosen as the **wavelet feature**.

Boundary Signature

The **silhouette boundary signature** is selected as the third gait feature. A signature is a 1-D functional representation of a boundary and may be generated in various ways. We employ a simple method, which plots the distance from the centroid to the boundary as a function of the corresponding directional angle. Because the gait contours do not contain the same number of points, we partition the gait contour into 36 sectors and calculate the average distance from the centroid to all the points in each sector. The boundary signature is formed by concatenating the average distances, as illustrated in Figure4(c).

NUMERICAL EXPERIMENTS

The CMU MoBo gait database and CASIA gait database A are used to evaluate the proposed FHMM-based feature fusion scheme. The CMU MoBo gait database consists of indoor sequences of 25 subjects walking on a treadmill at two different speeds and captured from 3 different views. The CASIA gait database A includes outdoor sequences of 20 subjects walking in 3 view angles. We conduct experiments on a portion of the databases.

We design experiments to address the following questions:

- **Compare single feature performance.** HMM based recognition using individual feature of wavelet, frieze, and boundary are conducted, respectively. The methods are denoted as HMM(w), HMM(f), and HMM(b) hereafter in figures and tables.
- **Compare the performance of feature concatenation and FHMM-based fusion**

Figure 4. (A) Preprocessed silhouette image; (B) Boundary of (A); (C) Boundary signature

  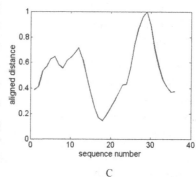

A   B   C

scheme. For simplicity, we only conduct experiments of fusing two features. The methods are denoted in the similar abbreviation. The symbol CON(xy) stands for recognition experiment using HMM and the concatenation of feature x and y. FHMM(xy) stands for experiment of FHMM fusing feature x and y.

The performance of different features and fusion scheme are first shown as cumulative matching scores (CMS) curves. To evaluate the algorithms more comprehensively, we employ McNemar's test to further check on the statistical significance of observed difference in recognition performance.

Evaluation Using CMS Curves

The **CMS curve** is widely used for recognition algorithms comparison, which indicates the probability that the correct identification is included in the top n matches. The CMS curves of the two gait databases are presented separately.

CMS curves of CMU MoBo Gait Database

The lateral sequences of CMU MoBo gait database are adopted and the silhouettes are cropped to the size of 640×300. Four cycles are used for training and two cycles for testing. Two experiments are set up as follows:

(a) S vs. F: Training on slow walk and testing on fast walk.
(b) F vs. S: Training on fast walk and testing on slow walk.

The CMS curves of two experiments are displayed in Figure 5. Some segments of the curves are overlapping with each other, but it is still easy to get the following observations.

For the single feature experiments, the wavelet feature performs best on CMU MoBo database. The boundary feature produces the lowest recognition rates for all rank values. The recognition rates are extremely low for the F vs. S experiment. This suggests that the boundary feature may not be a good gait representation.

For the feature fusion experiments, both feature concatenation and FHMM-based fusion methods obtain higher recognition rates than using single feature alone. Fusion of wavelet and frieze features gives the best results. The FHMM-based fusion scheme outperforms feature concatenation at the first 3 rank values and then the curves merge into one curve, as shown by curves of FHHM(wf) and COM(wf) in Figure 5.

CMS curves of CASIA Gait Database A

The lateral and oblique sequences of CASIA gait database A are adopted and the image sizes are normalized to 120×95. Four cycles are used for training and two cycles for testing. Two experiments are performed as follows:

(a) Lateral test: Training on sequences walking in one direction and testing on sequences walking in the opposite direction.
(b) Oblique test: Same as experiment (a) except for using the oblique sequences.

The experimental results of CMS curves are shown in Figure 6. The recognition rates are not exciting. Recognition using the wavelet feature alone, i.e. HMM(w), gives the best performance. The results of feature fusion using FHMM do not show much advantage. By visually inspecting the silhouette quality of CASIA database, we find that, as an outdoor database, a number of silhouettes are incomplete (body portion lost and broken). The silhouettes are obtained by subtracting background image from the original video frames. Many factors may lead to inaccurate silhouette segmentation, such as similarity of colors of the subject clothes and the background, illumination

Figure 5. CMS curves of CMU MoBo gait database. (A) S vs. F. (B) F vs. S

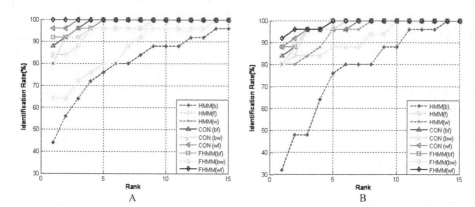

change, the distance between the camera and the subject, and so on. These factors lead to spurious pixels, shadows, holes inside moving subject, noisy contours and, more severely, body portion lost and broken. Silhouette preprocessing can remove spurious pixels and fill small holes. However, for CASIA database, the silhouette height is normalized to eliminate the size difference caused by the changing distance between the subject and the camera. If body portion lost happens, the height normalization operation causes great shape distortion, thus deteriorates the recognition performance.

In order to overcome the low silhouette qual-

ity problem, especially to deal with the body portion lost and broken problem, we propose a new robust gait representation method named as **frame difference energy image (FDEI)**. FDEI is defined as the sum of gait energy image (GEI) and the difference image between the current frame and the next frame. We follow the steps below to construct the FDEI representation of a gait sequence.

Step 1: Clustering and calculating the GEI. The silhouettes of a gait cycle are clustered. We simply divide the sequence into clusters of approximately equal length. The GEI of the cth cluster, denoted as $G_c(x, y)$, is computed as (Han

Figure 6. CMS curves of CASIA gait database A using the origianl silhouettes. (A) The lateral test. (B) The oblique test

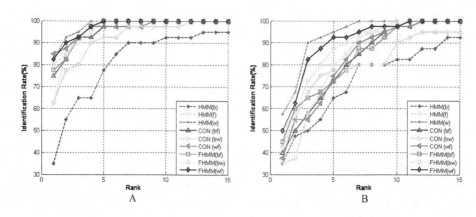

& Bhanu, 2006):

$$G_c(x,y) = \frac{1}{N_c} \sum_{t \in A_c} B(x,y,t), \qquad (7)$$

Where $B(x, y, t)$ is the silhouette image at time t, N_c is the number of frames of the cth cluster, A_c represents the time set of silhouettes in the cth cluster, x and y are the 2D coordinate values.

Step 2: Denoising. $G_c(x, y)$ is denoised by:

$$D_c(x,y) = \begin{cases} G_c(x,y), & if\ G_c(x,y) \geq \varepsilon, \\ 0, & otherwise, \end{cases} \qquad (8)$$

where $D_c(x, y)$ is the denoised image of $G_c(x, y)$. The threshold ε varies with the quality of the silhouettes. $D_c(x, y)$ is named as dominant energy image (DEI).

Step 3: Calculating the positive portion of frame difference. The frame difference is computed as the subtraction of silhouettes $B(x, y, t-1)$ and $B(x, y, t)$. The positive portion $F(x, y, t)$ is obtained by setting the negative values of the frame difference to zero, such that:

$$F(x,y,t) = \begin{cases} B(x,y,t-1) - B(x,y,t), & if\ B(x,y,t-1) > B(x,y,t), \\ 0, & otherwise. \end{cases}$$
$$(9)$$

When $t = 1$, $B(x, y, t - 1)$ is set to the last frame of the cycle.

Step 4: Constructing FDEI. We define FDEI as the summation of $F(x, y, t)$ and its corresponding cluster's DEI, denoted as:

$$FD(x, y, t) = F(x, y, t) + D_C(x, y). \qquad (10)$$

The summation $FD(x, y, t)$ is regarded as the FDEI representation of $B(x, y, t)$.

When silhouette $B(x, y, t)$ is incomplete while $B(x, y, t - 1)$ is complete, the lost portions are compensated and kept in $F(x, y, t)$. When both $B(x, y, t)$ and $B(x, y, t - 1)$ are incomplete, $D_C(x,$

$y)$ can partially compensate the missing portions. In this way, the FDEI representation helps to depress the effect of the lost portions. It also has the advantages of keeping most of the shape details and the gait temporal variation. Figure 7 demonstrates sample images during constructing FDEI, where both $B(x, y, t)$ and $B(x, y, t - 1)$ are incomplete.

After constructing the FDEI for gait sequences in CASIA database A, we repeat the experiments on it. The CMS curves of experiments using FDEI are shown in Figure 8. The recognition rates are much better than that of Figure 6. The performance of frieze feature (HMM(f)) is improved significantly to become the best one among three features for most rank values. However the FDEI does not boost the boundary feature's performance much, especially for the oblique test. This again suggests that boundary feature may not be suitable for gait recognition.

Figure 7. (A) Incomplete silhouette at time t. (B) Silhouette at time t − 1. (C) Frame difference image of (A) and (B). (D) GEI. (E) Denoised GEI. (F) FDEI of (A)

199

Figure 8. CMS curves for CASIA gait database A using FDEI representation. (A) Results of the lateral test. (B) Results of the oblique test

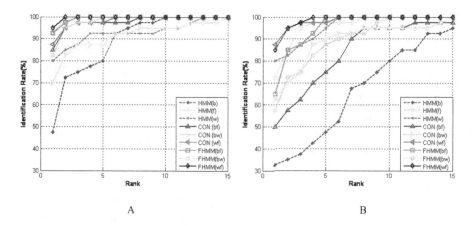

A   B

Based on Figure 8, we get similar conclusion about the feature fusion experiments, i.e., the FHMM-based fusion scheme is superior to feature concatenation method. Also the wavelet and frieze feature are the best feature combination.

Because the CMS curves are sensitive to sampling method and sample size, we further employ McNemar's test to evaluate the algorithms statistically in next section.

Evaluation Using McNemar's Test

Although the CMS curves are widely used for gait recognition performance evaluation, it has some drawbacks. The recognition rates are extremely sensitive to context, including sampling method and sample size (Boyd, 2004). Sometimes the CMS curves are crossed with each other, so it is difficult to make judgement on which algorithm performs better.

In this chapter, we use McNemar's test to address the problem of small sample size. **McNemar's test** is a paired success/failure trials using the binomial model (Beveridge et al., 2001). It is a first order check on the statistical significance of an observed difference of two algorithms. The times of success/failure trials of the compared algorithms are used to calculate the confidence

limits and produce the evaluation results.

After two algorithms, algorithm A and B, are tested on the same data set, four numbers can be obtained: the times that both algorithms fail, algorithm A succeeds but B fails, algorithm A fails but B succeeds, and both algorithms succeed. The trial numbers of succeed/fail are denoted as N_{ff}, N_{sf}, N_{fs}, and N_{ss}, respectively. McNemar's test is defined as:

$$\chi^2 = \frac{\left(N_{sf} - N_{fs}\right)^2}{\left(N_{sf} + N_{fs}\right)}. \tag{11}$$

When $N_{sf} + N_{fs} < 40$, correction for continuity is needed. McNemar's test is re-defined as:

$$\chi^2 = \frac{\left(\left| N_{sf} - N_{fs} \right| - 1\right)^2}{\left(N_{sf} + N_{fs}\right)}. \tag{12}$$

If the number of test is greater than about 30, the central limit theorem applies. In such case, the Z score (standard score) is obtained from equation (12) as:

$$Z = \frac{\left(\left| N_{sf} - N_{fs} \right| - 1\right)}{\sqrt{N_{sf} + N_{fs}}}. \tag{13}$$

If algorithm A and B give very similar results, then Z value will tend to zero. As their difference becomes larger, Z value increases. The confidence limits can be associated with the Z value. More details about McNemar's test refer to Clark & Clark (online).

McNemar's Test on CMU MoBo Gait Database

McNemar's test is carried on CMU MoBo gait database. The experiment setup is the same as above except for only three cycles are used for training and two cycles for testing. We conduct 91 training/testing trials for each subject, hence there are 2275 trials for each pair of algorithms. The results are shown in Table 1.

The first two rows in Table 1 suggest that the wavelet feature is the best choice if only one gait feature is adopted for recognition using the CMU MoBo database. The wavelet feature is obviously superior to the frieze and boundary features.

The third row verifies the advantage of multiple feature fusion. It shows that fusion of two features together achieves better recognition performance than the best individual feature. This is the lowermost requirement for multiple feature fusion.

Comparison results between FHMM and feature concatenation, row 4 to 6 in Table 1, show that our proposed FHMM-based fusion scheme outperforms feature concatenation method. The

conclusion holds no matter which two features are combined.

The last two rows in Table 1 give suggestions on how to choose features when applying FHMM. Among the three features investigated in this chapter, the boundary feature performs worst individually. Therefore it is intuitive to combine the other two better features, frieze and wavelet feature, to achieve the best recognition result. The intuition is proved to be correct by the last two rows in Table 1.

McNemar's test on CASIA gait database A

McNemar's test is carried on the lateral and oblique sequences of CASIA gait database A. Two cycles in one walking direction are used for training and two cycles in the opposite direction for testing. 16 training/testing trials are performed for each subject. There are 320 trails for each pair of algorithms. The results are shown in Table 2.

Based on Table 2, we come to the following conclusions.

For individual feature, the frieze feature performs best, as shown by the first two rows in Table 2. The result is different with that on CMU MoBo database. This may attribute to the illumination and resolution difference between the two databases. Same as the result on CMU database, the boundary feature gives the worst performance.

Table 1. McNemar's test on CMU MoBo database

	N_{ss}	N_{sf}	N_{fs}	N_{ff}	Z value	Confidence (%)
HMM(f) vs. HMM(b)	627	991	117	540	26.227	100
HMM(w) vs. HMM(f)	1529	273	157	316	5.546	100
FHMM(bw) vs. HMM(w)	1675	307	68	225	12.290	100
FHMM(bw) vs. CON(bw)	1853	157	99	166	3.563	100
FHMM(bf) vs. CON(bf)	1952	117	67	139	3.612	100
FHMM(wf) vs. CON(wf)	2013	95	38	129	4.856	100
FHMM(bf) vs. FHMM(bw)	1910	151	74	140	5.067	100
FHMM(wf) vs. FHMM(bf)	1998	98	62	117	2.609	99.5

Table 2. McNemar's test on CASIA database

	N_{ss}	N_{sf}	N_{fs}	N_{ff}	Z value	Confidence (%)
HMM(w) vs. HMM(b)	61	128	24	107	8.436	100
HMM(f) vs. HMM(w)	165	47	33	75	1.565	94.1
FHMM(bf) vs. HMM(f)	183	25	19	93	0.905	81.7
HMM(w) vs. FHMM(bw)	143	53	39	85	1.459	92.6
FHMM(bw) vs. CON(bw)	147	73	36	64	3.448	100
FHMM(bf) vs. CON(bf)	168	42	31	78	1.170	87.9
FHMM(wf) vs. CON(wf)	198	40	24	68	1.875	96.9
FHMM(bf) vs. FHMM(bw)	161	42	23	94	2.357	99.1
FHMM(wf) vs. FHMM(bf)	179	36	15	90	2.941	99.8

In Figure 8 (b), the recognition rate at rank 1 of boundary feature on the oblique sequence is only 32.5%. The low performance of boundary feature makes it infeasible for feature fusion. It is demonstrated by the third and fourth rows in Table 2, where fusing boundary and frieze feature performs better than boundary feature alone, but fusing boundary with the wavelet feature does not bring performance improvement.

Other results in Table 2 produce the same conclusions as Table 1, but the confidence limits are lower. The results verify again the validity of FHMM as a feature fusion scheme.

FEATURE CORRELATION ANALYSIS

Logan & Moreno (1997) pointed out that "there is only an advantage in using the FHMM if the layers model processes with different dynamics" (p. 11); "if the features are indeed highly correlated, FHMM does not seem to offer compelling advantages" (p. 12). However, to the best of our knowledge, it has not been testified by any experiments. From the experimental results in section 4, we may suppose that the wavelet and frieze feature are less correlated, while the frieze and boundary feature are more correlated. Because the features are of different length, it is not possible to directly calculate the correlation

coefficient of them. In this chapter, we attempt **canonical correlation analysis (CCA)** to analyze the relationship between gait features.

CCA is an exploratory statistical method to high-light correlations between two data sets acquired on the same experimental units. Let us denote the two data sets as $X \in R^{n \times p}$ and $X \in R^{n \times q}$, respectively. The columns of X and Y correspond to variables and the rows correspond to experimental units. CCA seeks vector a and b such that the random variables $a^T X$ and $b^T Y$ maximize the correlation $\rho = cor(a^T X, b^T Y)$. $a^T X$ and $b^T Y$ are the first pair of canonical variables. The second pair of canonical variables can be found by seeking vectors maximizing the same correlation subject to the constraint that they are uncorrelated with the first pair of canonical variables. This procedure repeats to find other pairs of canonical variables.

When applying CCA to gait feature correlation analysis, the matrices X and Y represent two different feature sets extracted from the same gait cycle respectively. The columns of them correspond to feature variables and the rows correspond to frames in the gait cycle. Generally speaking, gait feature lengths are much larger than the number of frames in one gait cycle, hence we have $p, q \gg n$. Classical CCA cannot be performed when the number of frames is less than the feature length. One way to solve this problem consists in including a regularization step in the calculation, thus

Table 3. Canonical correlation between features

database	wavelet vs. frieze	boundary vs. frieze	boundary vs. wavelet
CMU	0.9998	0.6168	0.6489
CASIA	0.9569	0.8413	0.4531

named **regularized CCA**. González *et al. (2008)* implemented an R package of regularized CCA, which are used to compute the canonical correlation of feature pairs in this chapter.

Given a gait cycle, the wavelet, frieze and boundary features are extracted, respectively. For each two features combination, the correlation coefficient of the first pair of canonical variables is used to represent the feature correlation. The mean correlation values over all the available sequences in the gait databases are shown in Table 3.

The results in Table 3 do not verify the hypothesis we obtained from the numerical recognition experiments. On the contrary, the correlation between frieze and wavelet feature is the biggest, while boundary and wavelet feature are less correlated. The conclusions hold on both CMU MoBo database and CASIA database A.

We attribute the conflict mainly to the fact that CCA compute the linear correlation between feature sets. However, the HMM and FHMM based recognition algorithms are nonlinear in nature and discern the nonlinear relationship between features. The correlation analysis between features is still an open question and need further investigation.

CONCLUSION

Feature selection and fusion scheme design are two critical problems for successful multiple feature fusion applications. In this chapter we address the second problem by employing FHMM as a feature fusion scheme. The proposed approach is compared with the widely applied feature concatenation method on two public gait databases, CMU MoBo database and CASIA gait database A. Experimental results verify the validity and superiority of the FHMM-based feature fusion scheme.

We deal with the feature selection problem in two ways: (1) conduct experiments on different feature combinations and select the best feature pair by evaluating the recognition performance; (2) analyze the feature correlation using regularized CCA. The methods give conflicting results. We choose to believe the result of recognition experiments and leave the feature correlation analysis problem open for future investigation.

Another contribution of this chapter lies in the performance evaluation. Besides CMS curves, we introduce McNemar's test to evaluate the methods statistically, which gives the confidence limit of one algorithm over another. It must be pointed out that McNemar's test only check the success/failure trial at rank 1. It is better to examine both the CMS curves and McNemar's test result to comprehensively evaluate the algorithms.

ACKNOWLEDGMENT

The research is partially supported by the NSFC (60402038, 60872154), NBRPC (2006CB705700), the Chair Professors of the Cheung Kong Scholars, the Program for Cheung Kong Scholars and Innovative Research Team in University (PCSIRT, Grant No. IRT0645), and the Natural Science Basic Research Plan in Shaanxi Province of China under Program No. SJ08F18.

REFERENCES

Bazin, A. I., Middleton, L., & Nixon, M. S. (2005). Probabilistic fusion of gait features for biometric verification. In . *Proceedings of International Conference on Information Fusion, 2,* 1211–1217.

BenAbdelkader, C., Cutler, R. G., & Davis, L. S. (2004). Gait recognition using image self-similarity. *EURASIP Journal on Applied Signal Processing, 4,* 1–14.

BenAbdelkader, C., Davis, L. S., & Cutler, R. (2002). Stride and cadence as a biometric in automatic person identification and verification. In *Proceedings of the Fifth IEEE International Conference on Automatic Face and Gesture Recognition* (pp. 372-377).

Betkowska, A., Shinoda, K., & Furui, S. (2006). FHMM for robust speech recognition in home environment. In *Proceedings of Symposium on Large-Scale Knowledge Resources* (pp. 129-132).

Beveridge, J. R., She, K., Draper, B. A., & Givens, G. H. (2001). Parametric and nonparametric methods for the statistical evaluation of human ID algorithms. In *Proceedings of the Third Workshop on Empirical Evaluation Methods in Computer Vision* (pp. 535-542).

Boulgouris, N. V., Hatzinakos, D., & Plataniotis, K. N. (2005). Gait recognition: A challenging signal processing technology for biometric identification. *IEEE Signal Processing Magazine, 22,* 78–90. doi:10.1109/MSP.2005.1550191

Boyd, J. E. (2004). Synchronization of oscillations for machine perception of gaits. *Computer Vision and Image Understanding, 96,* 35–59. doi:10.1016/j.cviu.2004.04.004

Clark, A. F., & Clark, C. (n.d.). *Performance characterization in computer vision: A tutorial.* Retrieved from http://peipa.essex.ac.uk/benchmark/tutorials/essex/tutorial.pdf

Gait Database, C. A. S. I. A. (2004). Retrieved from http://www.cbsr.ia.ac.cn/english/Database.asp

Ghahramani, Z., & Jordan, M. I. (1997). Factorial hidden Markov models. *Machine Learning, 29,* 245–273. doi:10.1023/A:1007425814087

González, I., Déjean, S., Martin, P. G. P., & Baccini, A. (2008). CCA: An R package to extend canonical correlation analysis. *Journal of Statistical Software, 23*(12).

Gross, R., & Shi, J. (2001). *The CMU motion of body (MoBo) database.* (Tech. Rep. 01-18). Robotics Institute, Carnegie Mellon University.

Han, J., & Bhanu, B. (2004). Statistical feature fusion for gait-based human recognition. In . *Proceedings of IEEE Computer Society Conference on Computer Vision and Pattern Recognition, 2,* 842–847.

Han, J., & Bhanu, B. (2006). Individual recognition using gait energy image. *IEEE Transactions on Pattern Analysis and Machine Intelligence, 28*(2), 316–322. doi:10.1109/TPAMI.2006.38

Kale, A., Cuntoor, N., & Chellappa, R. (2002). A framework for activity-specific human identification. In *Proc. the Int. Conf. on Acoustics, Speech and Signal Processing* (Vol. 4, pp. 3660-3663).

Kale, A., Roychowdhury, A., & Chellappa, R. (2004). Fusion of gait and face for human identification. In . *Proceedings of Acoustics, Speech, and Signal Processing, 5,* 901–904.

Kale, A., & Sundaresan, A. RoyChowdhury, A., & Chellappa, R. (2005). Gait-based human identification from a monocular video sequence. In *Handbook on pattern recognition and computer vision.* World Scientific Publishing Company.

Lam, T., Lee, R., & Zhang, D. (2007). Human gait recognition by the fusion of motion and static spatiotemporal templates. *Pattern Recognition, 40*(9), 2563–2573. doi:10.1016/j.patcog.2006.11.014

Lee, S., Liu, Y., & Collins, R. (2007). Shape variation-based frieze pattern for robust gait recognition. In *Proceedings of IEEE International Conference on Computer Vision and Pattern Recognition* (pp.1-8).

Lee, T. K. M., Ranganath, S., & Sanei, S. (2006). Fusion of chaotic measure into a new hybrid face-gait system for human recognition. In *. Proceedings of International Conference on Pattern Recognition, 4*, 541–544.

Liu, J., & Zheng, N. (2007). Gait history image: A novel temporal template for gait recognition. In *Proceedings of IEEE International Conference on Multimedia and Expo* (pp. 663-666).

Liu, Y. X., Collins, R. T., & Tsin, Y. H. (2002). Gait sequence analysis using frieze patterns. In *Proceedings of European Conference on Computer Vision* (pp. 659-671).

Liu, Z., & Sarkar, S. (2007). Outdoor recognition at a distance by fusing gait and face. *Image and Vision Computing, 25*, 817–832. doi:10.1016/j.imavis.2006.05.022

Logan, B., & Moreno, P. J. (1997). *Factorial hidden Markov models for speech recognition: Preliminary experiments.* (Tech. Rep. CRL-97-7). Cambrige Research Laboratory.

Logan, B., & Moreno, P. J. (1998). Factorial HMMs for acoustic modeling. In *Proceedings of IEEE International Conference on Acoustics, Speech and Signal Processing* (Vol. 2, pp. 813-816).

Lu, J., & Zhang, E. (2007). Gait recognition for human identification based on ICA and fuzzy SVM through multiple views fusion. *Pattern Recognition Letters, 28*, 2401–2411. doi:10.1016/j.patrec.2007.08.004

Ma, Q., Wang, S., Nie, D., & Qiu, J. (2007). Recognizing humans based on gait moment image. In *Proceedings of Eighth ACIS International Conference on Software Engineering, Artificial Intelligence, Networking and Parallel . Distributed Computing, 2*, 606–610.

Shakhnarovich, G., & Darrell, T. (2002). On probabilistic combination of face and gait cues for identification. In *. Proceedings of Automatic Face and Gesture Recognition, 5*, 169–174.

Shakhnarovich, G., Lee, L., & Darrel, T. l. (2001). Integrated face and gait recognition from multiple views. In *Proceeding of Computer Vision and Pattern Recognition* (Vol. 1, pp. 439–446).

Sundaresan, A., Chowdhury, A. R., & Chellappa, R. (2003). A hidden Markov model based framework for recognition of humans from gait sequences. In *. Proceedings of IEEE International Conference on Image Processing, 2*, 85–88.

Tanawongsuwan, R., & Bobick, A. (2001). Gait recognition from time-normalized joint-angle trajectories in the walking plane. In *Proceeding of IEEE Computer Vision and Pattern Recognition* (Vol. 2, pp. 726–731).

Tyagi, A., Davis, J., & Keck, M. (2006). Multiview fusion for canonical view generation based on homography constraints. *ACM-MM Work. on Video Surveillance and Sensor Networks*, 61-69.

Veres, G. V., Nixon, M. S., Middleton, L., & Carter, J. N. (2005). Fusion of dynamic and static features for gait recognition over time. In *Proceedings of the Eighth International Conference on Information Fusion* (Vol. 2, pp. 1211-1217).

Wang, L., Ning, H., Tan, T., & Hu, W. (2004). Fusion of static and dynamic body biometrics for gait recognition. *IEEE Transactions on Circuits and Systems for Video Technology, 14*(2), 149–158. doi:10.1109/TCSVT.2003.821972

Wang, L., Tan, T. N., Hu, W. M., & Ning, H. Z. (2003). Automatic gait recognition based on statistical shape analysis. *IEEE Transactions on Image Processing, 12*(9), 1120–1131. doi:10.1109/ TIP.2003.815251

Wang, Y., Yu, S., Wang, Y., & Tan, T. (2006). Gait recognition based on fusion of multiview gait sequences. In *Proceedings of the International Conference on Biometrics* (pp. 605-611).

Xu, D., Yan, S., Tao, D., Zhang, L., Li, X., & Zhang, H. (2006). Human gait recognition with matrix representation. *IEEE Transactions on Circuits and Systems for Video Technology, 16*(7), 896–903. doi:10.1109/TCSVT.2006.877418

Zhang, R., Vogler, C., & Metaxas, D. (2004). Human gait recognition. In . *Proceedings of IEEE Computer Vision and Pattern Recognition, 2,* 342–349.

Zhou, X., & Bhanu, B. (2006). Feature fusion of face and gait for human recognition at a distance in video. In . *Proceedings of International Conference on Pattern Recognition, 4,* 529–532.

Zhou, X., & Bhanu, B. (2007). Integrating face and gait for human recognition at a distance in video. *IEEE Transactions on Systems, Man, and Cybernetics. Part B, Cybernetics, 37*(5), 1119–1137. doi:10.1109/TSMCB.2006.889612

Zhou, X., & Bhanu, B. (2008). Feature fusion of side face and gait for video-based human identification. *Pattern Recognition, 41,* 778–795. doi:10.1016/j.patcog.2007.06.019

Chapter 10
Mouse Dynamics Biometric Technology

Ahmed Awad E. Ahmed
University of Victoria, Canada

Issa Traore
University of Victoria, Canada

ABSTRACT

In this chapter the Authors introduce the concepts behind the mouse dynamics biometric technology, present a generic architecture of the detector used to collect and process mouse dynamics, and study the various factors used to build the user's signature. The Authors will also provide an updated survey on the researches and industrial implementations related to the technology, and study possible applications in computer security.

INTRODUCTION

Different types of biometrics are currently available in the market, and are widely used in various security applications. Biometrics can be classified into two categories, "physiological biometrics" and "behavioral biometrics". Physiological biometrics identify the user based on physiological characteristics, such as fingerprints and eye retina/iris scanning, whereas behavioral biometrics depend on detecting the behavioral features of the user, such as signature, voice, and keystroke dynamics.

The utilization of biometrics, however, has so far been limited to identity verification in authentica-

tion and access control systems. Hence important security applications such as intrusion detection systems have been left out of this technology. We have identified two primary reasons for that. First, most biometric systems require special hardware device for biometrics data collection, which restricts their use to only networks segments that provide them, making the systems irrelevant for a significant number of remote users, who operate out of these network segments. Second, most biometric systems require an active involvement of the user who is asked to provide some data sample that can be used to verify his identity. This excludes the possibility of passive monitoring, which is essential for intrusion detection. There is also number of secondary obstacles to the use of biometrics for intrusion

DOI: 10.4018/978-1-60566-725-6.ch010

detection such as whether the technology allows dynamic monitoring, or real-time detection.

A popular biometric system, which escapes some of these limitations, is keystroke dynamics biometrics. Keystroke dynamics does not require special hardware device for data collection (a regular keyboard is enough), and under certain circumstances can be used for dynamic monitoring. The same applies for a newly introduced biometric based on mouse dynamics.

Mouse dynamics is a behavioral biometric which was introduced at the Information Security and Object Technology (ISOT) research lab, University of Victoria in 2003 (Ahmed & Traore, 2003). Mouse Dynamics can be described as the characteristics of the actions received from the mouse input device for a user, while interacting with a graphical user interface. Mouse actions include general mouse movement, drag and drop, point and click, and silence (i.e. no movement). The raw data collected for each mouse movement consists of the distance, time, and angle. The behavioral analysis process utilizes statistical approaches to generate a number of factors from the captured set of actions; these factors are used to construct what is called a Mouse Dynamics Signature (MDS), a unique set of values characterizing the user's behavior measured over a period of time.

Some of the factors consist of calculating the average speed against the traveled distance, or calculating the average speed against the movement direction. Another set of factors can be calculated as a result of studying the histogram of collected measurements (individually or combined) such as the histogram of the types of actions or the durations of the silence periods.

Mouse and keystroke dynamics biometrics are two related technologies, which complement each other. While a mouse is very important for graphical user interface (GUI) –based applications, a keyboard is essential for command –line based applications.

One of its key strengths compared to traditional biometric technologies is that it allows dynamic and passive user monitoring. As such it can be used to track reliably and continuously legitimate and illegitimate users throughout computing sessions.

Mouse Dynamics biometric is appropriate for user authentication (with some limitations). It can be effectively used for dynamic authentication or identity confirmation in cases where the actions of an active user raise some suspicions. The technology is also suitable for continuous monitoring applications such as detecting masqueraders in intrusion detection, or establishing the identity of perpetrators in digital forensics analysis.

In this chapter we will introduce the concepts behind the mouse dynamics biometric technology, present a generic architecture of the detector used to collect and process mouse dynamics, and study the various factors used to build the user's signature. We will also provide an updated survey on the researches and industrial implementations related to the technology, and study possible applications in computer security.

BACKGROUND

In contrast to other behavioral biometrics which were widely studied in computer security, previous works on mouse dynamics have, so far, been limited to user interface design improvement (Chan et al., 2001; Oel et al., 2001; Whisenand & Emurian, 1996). In particular, mouse movement analysis has been the purpose of extensive research works. Studies have been conducted to establish the applicability of Fitts' law in predicting the duration of a movement to a target based on the size of the target and the distance from the starting point to the target (Whisenand & Emurian, 1996). According to Fitts' law, the mean movement time for a movement with distance A to a target with width W is defined as $MT = a$

$+ b(\log_2(2A/W))$, where a and b are empirically determined parameters (Whisenand & Emurian, 1996). In experiments on mouse cursor movements conducted by Whisenand, a special user interface was used to force the user to do specific movements (Whisenand & Emurian, 1999). The user was asked to move the mouse from a specific point approaching a specific object located at a certain distance; the study took into consideration the effect of movement direction and the object size. The study allowed the understanding of several user interface properties related to the shape, size, location, and preferred angle of approach of the target object.

Oel conducted experiments to show that Fitts' law is not suitable to calculate the transfer time of cursor movements, especially if small targets are used (Oel et al., 2001). Since this is the case in most existing GUI interfaces, he introduced, as alternative to Fitts' law, the power model defined as $MT = A.h^k$, where the parameters h and k depend on the width W. The power model gives better results in predicting the movement time of a mouse-based graphical user interface.

From the above we can note that researches conducted on mouse dynamics have focused mainly on the formalization of the measured data after fixing the environment variables. In our research, we target the biometric identification problem by focusing on extracting the behavioral features related to the user and formalizing a way to detect his identity.

To our knowledge the first use of mouse dynamics for biometric analysis was performed in our lab (ISOT) for which we have a pending patent, with priority date in May 2003 (Ahmed & Traore, 2003). We established then through a series of controlled and uncontrolled experiments that mouse dynamics can be considered as a biometric technology. We describe some of these experiments in this chapter, and refer interested to (Ahmed & Traore, 2007) for more details.

Closely related to our work are two more recent papers by Hocquet et al., and Pusara and Brodley,

respectively. Hocquet et al. report the results of an exploratory study, involving ten participants, on the use of mouse dynamics for user authentication (Hocquet et al., 2004). Participants in their study are asked to play a game in which they have to click as quickly as possible on a moving square during a fixed length of time. They collect the mouse coordinates and compute several features such as speed, acceleration, angular velocity, curvature, and the derivative of the curvature curve. Next, they extract from these data the maximum, the minimum, the average, the standard deviation, and the difference between the maximum and minimum. Authentication of an individual is made by comparing such information against some threshold. The performance achieved consists of an equal error rate of 37.5%. In our work, we use a different experimental approach, and furthermore we use a more powerful data analysis technique allowing us to achieve far better performance.

Pusara and Brodley propose a user re-authentication scheme based on mouse movements (Pusara & Brodley, 2004). They collect the raw cursor movement data and extract features such as distance, angle and speed between data points. Using decision tree classifiers, a separate model of normal behavior is built for each application, based on a set of adjustable parameters, which are user specific. The parameters are adjusted by searching through the parameter space to lower false positives and false negatives for each user. The experimental evaluation of their work yields a False Acceptance Rate (FAR) of 1.75% and a False Rejection Rate (FRR) of 0.43%.

Their work is significantly different, however, because their detection model is application dependent. In their approach, they propose to generate a different model for each user per application. Such a scheme cannot realistically be applied for passive monitoring because developing separate models for all possible applications running on a host can quickly become daunting and unmanageable. In contrast, in our work, participants have total freedom to choose which applications

Figure 1. Types of mouse activities

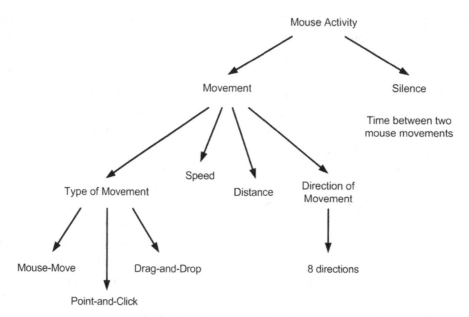

they use and how they use them, more accurately reflecting real-life scenarios.

MOUSE DYNAMICS

Mouse dynamics can be described as the characteristics of the actions received from the mouse input device for a specific user while interacting with a specific graphical user interface (Ahmed & Traore, 2007). Figure 1 illustrates the different categories of mouse activities. Mouse movements can be described by a number of parameters:

- **Type of movement:** Three different types are considered: *Mouse-Move* which is a regular mouse movement from a point to another point; *Point-and-Click* which is a mouse movement followed by a click or a double click; and *Drag-and-Drop* which consists of a movement while maintaining the mouse button down then releasing the mouse button at the end of the action
- **Movement Speed** expressed in pixels per

seconds
- **Traveled Distance** measured in pixels
- **Direction of movement:** eight directions are considered numbered from 1 to 8. Each of the eight directions covers a set of mouse movements performed within a 45-degree area. For instance, direction number 1 represents all actions performed with angles between 0° and 45°, while direction number 2 is responsible for all actions performed between 45° and 90°. Note that we can simply use the angle instead of the direction of movement.

Studying such parameters and categories can help understanding and describing user behavioral characteristics which is a necessary step towards building his signature.

Another category of mouse activities that cannot be ignored is the silence. The silence periods between mouse movements can have a direct link to the main user behavioral characteristics describing the time needed for the user to prepare for the next action. Silence can be dependent on

Figure 2. Raw mouse data. Graph showing a relationship between distance, time, and the type of action based on a sample of intercepted data. Like many behavioral biometrics, the raw mouse data shows strong variability over time

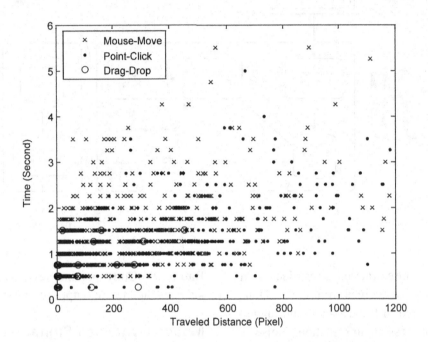

the characteristics of the previously performed action or the action to be performed after, or it can be an independent user behavioral characteristic. Later we will describe an example of feature which belongs to this category.

Figure 2 illustrates sample raw data captured in a user's session. Each point on the figure represents a movement of the mouse with a specific distance, which was completed in a specific time. The type of action is also shown in the figure. As it can be noticed, the raw mouse data shows strong variability over time. So we need to process the data in order to extract distinctive patterns characterizing users' behaviors.

Detection System

Figure 3 shows the architecture of the mouse dynamics detection system proposed in our work. The detector is implemented as client/server software.

The client module, which runs on the monitored machine (i.e. machine that needs to be protected), is responsible for mouse data collection. This data is sent to the server software, which runs on a separate machine. The server software is in charge of analyzing the data and computing a biometric profile. The computed profile is then compared against stored profiles to verify user identity.

Like all other biometric systems, the mouse dynamics detector operates in two modes: enrollment mode and behavior comparison (i.e., verification and identification) mode. The operation of each mode consists of three consecutive stages. In the first stage of the enrollment mode, a data capturing process is conducted by a lightweight software module, which captures all mouse and keyboard actions, and converts them into a set of more organized and meaningful statements.

These statements are directly passed to the next stage of data processing where behavioral

Figure 3. Architecture of the detection system

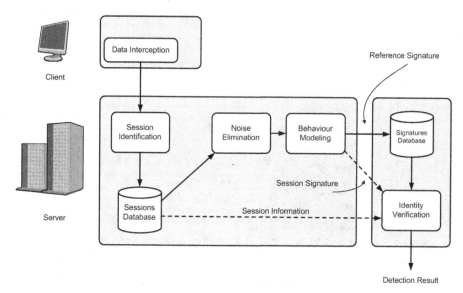

modeling and feature extraction are conducted. At this stage all actions received from the previous stage will be stored in the database and tagged with the current session information. Noise is eliminated from the collected data prior to the behavior modeling process. The behavior modeling component will process the data and extract a set of features representing the Mouse Dynamics Signature (MDS) for the user being monitored. Finally, in the third stage, the generated signature is stored in the signatures database as a reference signature for the enrolled user.

The detection mode shares the first two stages with the enrollment mode. The third stage in this mode is the verification process where the mouse dynamics signature calculated during the data processing stage is compared against the reference signature of the legitimate user. User identification can also be performed at this stage by comparing the signature received from the behavior modeling component to the signatures of all of the enrolled users. The result of this stage consists of a ratio (computed as a percentage) describing how confident the system is about identity matching; we refer to this as Confidence

Ratio (CR). Corresponding session information is also attached to the output of this stage.

Mouse Dynamics Signature

Mouse dynamics Signature consists of a set of features that can describe the user behavior in performing tasks using the mouse. The features can be categorized in two groups:

1. Features which are based on movement characteristics such as movement speed, traveled distance, and type of action. We call them non-histogrammic features.
2. Features which are related to the percentage occurrence of a specific characteristic over the duration of user session. We call them histogrammic features.

In this section we present the mouse dynamics biometrics features and study the characteristics of each feature individually. For each feature we demonstrate how it can be used to differentiate between users. We also show real data captured for different users to illustrate the difference.

Movement Characteristics-Based Features (Non-Histogrammic)

Three different features come under this category as follows:

1. Movement Speed Compared to Traveled Distance.
2. Average Movement Speed per Movement Direction.
3. Average Movement Speed per Type of Action.

Movement Speed Compared to Traveled Distance

This feature captures the relation between the distance traveled on the screen while the user is performing an action (of any type) and the speed of the movement. Figure 4 plots this relation between the two parameters (distance and speed). The figure shows the different ranges of speed a user will cover for distances varying from 25 to 1200 pixels. An increasing pattern of the speed is detected for all users as the traveled distance increases. Curves can follow different shapes, however, as per the figure; the reproducibility of this feature is high. The shape of the curve and the ranges of the speed are the parameters describing this feature. Each of these curves is actually an approximation of the raw data shown in Figure 2 which was calculated using neural networks. The approximation network is an MLP consisting of a single hidden layer containing five nodes. The input to the network is the traveled distance and the output is the speed. The back propagation technique was used to train the network. A split-sample validation technique was used to evaluate different neural network configurations.

Average Movement Speed per Movement Direction

This feature captures the relation between the movement speed and the direction of the performed actions. It involves the calculation of the average speed in each of the eight directions of movement. Figure 5 shows the distribution of the average movement speed against the direction of movement for two different users, User 1 and User 2. The eight points describing this relation not only represent the range of speed expected for each user in a specific direction, but also describe the ratios between these readings.

From the figure we can note that directions 3 and 7 are the highest in speed for User 1 while for User 2 the highest speed occurs for movements in direction 2. The lowest speed for User 1 occurs at direction 5, while for User 2 it occurs at directions 1 and 8. We can also note the high reproducibility of this feature for User 1, while for User 2 a noticeable variation occurs; however, the readings stay in the same range for all of his sessions.

Average Movement Speed per Type of Action

This feature captures the relation between the type of action with respect to the movement speed. Three types of actions are considered: point-and-click (PC), drag-and-drop (DD), and regular mouse movement (MM).

Figure 6 illustrates the relation between the movement speed and the type of performed action for the three recognized types of actions for two different users; ten sessions are shown for each user. Two pieces of information can be extracted from each curve: the range of each entry, and the ratios between the entries.

From the figure we can note that User 2 performs more mouse-move and drag-and-drop actions than User 1, and less point-and-click compared to the same user. We can also note that for User 1 the number of mouse-move actions is almost the same as the number of point-and-click actions, which is not the case for User 2.

Histogrammic Features

Five different features are included in this category:

Figure 4. Movement Speeds for the traveled distance spectrum for two different users. Each curve is computed based on a user session consisting of 2000 actions. Ten sessions are shown for each user

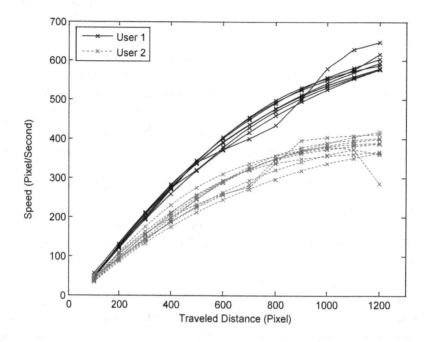

Figure 5. Average Speeds for the different directions of movement for two different users. Each curve is computed for a user session consisting of 2000 actions. Ten sessions are shown for each user

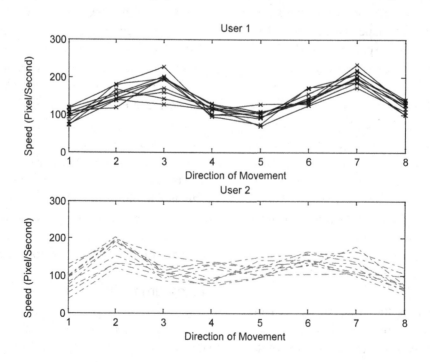

Figure 6. Movement Speeds for the three types of actions. Each curve is computed for a user session consisting of 2000 actions. Ten sessions are shown for each user

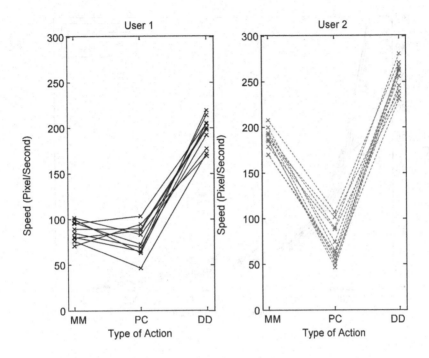

1. Traveled Distance Histogram.
2. Movement Elapsed Time.
3. Silence Time Histogram.
4. Direction of Movement Histogram.
5. Type of Action Histogram.

Traveled Distance Histogram

This feature is based on the distribution of the number of actions performed by the user within different distance ranges. Figure 7 illustrates this feature computed for two different users. Ten histograms are shown for each user representing ten different sessions each consisting of 2000 mouse actions. The figure indicates a noticeable difference between the histograms of the two users.

We can note that the number of actions performed by User 1 with shorter distances (< 100 pixels) is higher than the number of actions performed by User 2. If we take a look at the higher values for the distances, we find the opposite. The number of actions performed by User 1 (for

longer distances) is lower than those performed by User 2 in the same distance range.

We can also notice the high reproducibility of this feature, as shown in Figure 7; the histograms of the ten sessions are very close to each other for each of the users.

Movement Elapsed Time Histogram

This feature describes the distribution of the number of actions performed by a user in different ranges of the elapsed time. The elapsed time is the duration of a performed action. This feature aims to demonstrate the user's behavior based on how often he performs actions with a specific duration.

Figure 8 shows this feature computed for two different users. Ten histograms are shown for each user representing ten different sessions each consisting of 2000 mouse actions. The figure indicates a noticeable difference between the histograms for the two different users. The value and loca-

Figure 7. Traveled Distance Histograms for two different users based on ten sessions for each user

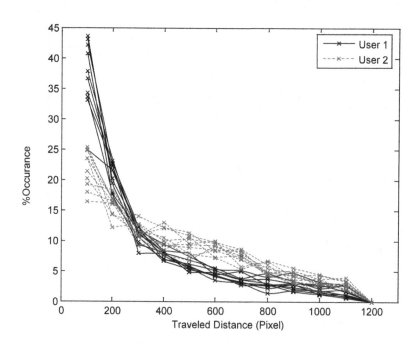

tion of the peak can be used as a distinguishing characteristic. As per the figure 50% of User 1's actions fall in the range of 0.5 to 1 second while for User 2 only 30% of his actions are performed in this range.

We can also notice the closeness of the histograms of the sessions belonging to the same user; this indicates a high reproducibility of this feature.

Silence Time Histogram

Silence time is the time spent by the user performing no mouse actions. This is usually detected by counting the time spent while the mouse position is fixed. This definition covers two categories of silence times. The first category refers to the silence time spent between mouse actions, like the time the user takes to think before performing the action, or if the user is searching for an object on the screen, and so on. The other category is the silence time resulted when the user leaves the computer.

The first category is what concerns us the most, since it reflects a behavioral characteristic of the user. The second category cannot be used for the sake of identity detection; however, it is more suitable for detecting the end of user session or activity period.

Figure 9 shows the histogram of the silence time for two different users; ten sessions are shown for each user. For this feature, the peak of the histogram can be used to differentiate between users. The range the peak occurs in and the percentage value are the most distinguishing parameters. In other words the detection system, analyzing this histogram, should be able to specify the range of the silence period durations that will include most of the silence periods in a session. This range and the number of silence periods in it can be used to differentiate between users.

In figure 9 we can note that about 47% of User 1's silence periods are in the 0.5 to 1 second range, while for user 2 only 30% of his silence periods fall in this range.

Figure 8. Movement Elapsed Time Histogram for two different users showing ten sessions for each of them

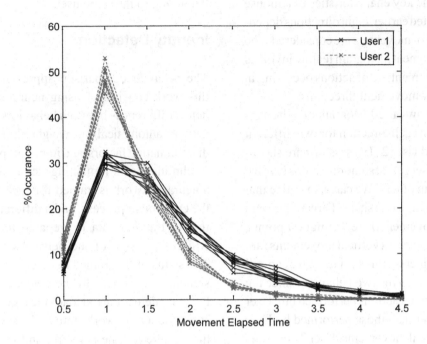

Figure 9. Silence time Histogram for two different users showing ten sessions for each of them

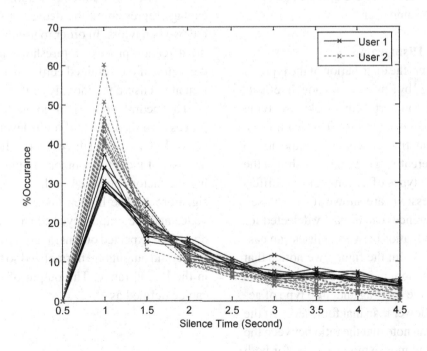

Direction of Movement Histogram

As mentioned previously the direction of movement is one of the key characteristics of a mouse action. As indicated earlier, eight directions dependent on the angle of movement are considered. The direction of movement histogram feature involves calculating the percentage of actions occurring in each of the eight movement directions.

Figure 10 shows the histograms of the performed actions in each direction for two different users, User 1 and User 2. Ten sessions are shown for each user. Observe that some directions involve more actions than others. We can also notice that all curves follow the same shape. Directions 3 and 4 (horizontal movements) are the highest points, while directions 1 and 5 (vertical movements) are the lowest. Considering this similarity, we can still differentiate between the two behaviors since the number of horizontal actions performed buy User 1 is always higher than those performed by User 2, while for vertical movements, User 2 performs more actions than User 1. The reproducibility of this feature is very high; we can notice the closeness of the curves for the different sessions belonging to the same user.

Type of Action Histogram

This feature covers the distribution of the types of actions performed by a user in a session. It reflects the user behavior in performing tasks involving different types of mouse actions. This feature can be very discriminative as people are expected to do tasks in different ways. Figure 11 shows the histogram of the types of actions for two different users; ten sessions are shown for each user. Behavioral differences can be easily detected for the two users and ratios between entries can easily be identified. From the figure, we notice that User 1 performs more mouse movement actions than Users 2, while for drag and drop type of action his count is lower than that for User 2. At the same time, we can note that the ratio between the drag and drop and mouse move actions for both users are totally different. The reproducibility of

this feature is also very high; we can notice the closeness of the curves for the different sessions belonging to the same user.

Identity Detection

The behavior comparison approach adopted in this work consists of using neural networks to detect differences between behaviors. The neural network automatically up weights the most reliable discriminating factors, and improves performance by eliminating the remaining factors. Specifically, a neural network is trained for each user during the enrollment process, and a different combination of training data is prepared for each user, while the design of the networks is the same. The status of the trained network is stored in the signatures database. In the detection mode, the behavior detection unit loads the legitimate user's stored neural network status. The saved status is then applied to the network, and the monitored behavior resulting from session analysis is applied to the neural network. We refer to the output of the network as the confidence ratio (CR), a percentage representing the degree of similarity of the two behaviors. In order to use this number in the detection process, a threshold limit is set to determine if the obtained confidence ratio is sufficient to ensure the identity of the user.

The neural network used in the detection process is a feed-forward multi-layer perceptron network consisting of three layers. The input layer consists of the total number of inputs representing the factors involved in the mouse dynamics signature N. The hidden layer consists of $N+1$ nodes and the output layer consists of only one node. The expected output range is from 0 to 100. Inputs and outputs are normalized so that they fall in the [-1, 1] range. The output of the network can be defined as

Figure 10. Directions of Movement Histograms for two different users showing ten sessions per user. Notice that some directions involve more actions than others. Each of the histograms was created using 2000 actions (of all types) collected over one user session

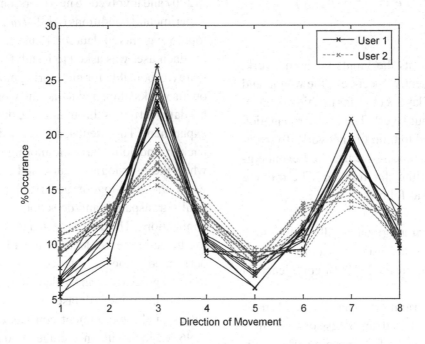

Figure 11. Types of Actions Histograms for two different users showing ten sessions per user; each of the histograms was created using 2000 actions collected over one user session

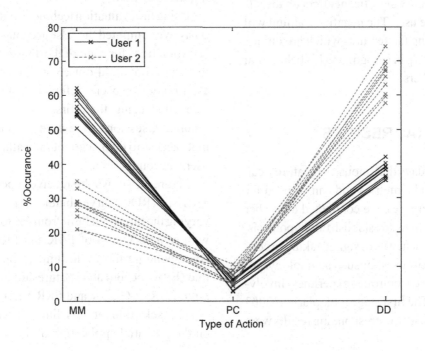

$$CR = \left(\left(\sum_{j=1}^{N+1} w_{2j} \cdot \frac{1}{1 + e^{-\left(\sum_{i=1}^{N} w_{ij} s_i\right) - b_{1j}}} \right) + b_{21} \right) \times 100$$

Where S_i represents the inputs to the network, w_{kl} and b_{kl} represent, respectively, the weight and bias of node l of layer k (k=1 for the hidden layer, k=2 for the output layer). The back propagation algorithm is used to train the network. To expedite the learning process we use the Levenberg-Marquardt algorithm for training. The training data is designed as follows:

- **Positive training:** data collected from 5 sessions for the user trained for an output of 100, meaning 100% confidence in identity.
- **Negative training:** data collected from other users based on 5 sessions per user with an output of 0, meaning 0% confidence in identity.

The trained network will be able to distinguish the features that have significant effect on the CR for the legitimate user. The negative training will also help detecting the features which are unique for the user and help in recognizing his behavioral identity from others.

EXPERIMENTAL RESULTS

In order to validate that mouse signatures can be considered as biometrics and can be used for identification purposes, we conducted a number of experiments aiming to establish this hypothesis. Our main experiment was designed taking in consideration potential uses for such technology. We conducted a large uncontrolled experiment involving two stages. The first stage took place in 2003 and involved 22 users; corresponding results were

reported in see (Ahmed & Traore, 2003; Ahmed & Traore, 2007). The second stage, which was simply an extension of the first stage, took place in 2007 and involved 26 new users, under the same experimental conditions (Akif *et al.*, 2008). So in total, we gathered data for 48 users.

Each user was asked to install the client software (responsible for monitoring mouse actions) on his workstation and to use the workstation for his daily activities throughout the duration of the experiment. The client software, which runs as a background job, starts monitoring user actions when the user-login occurs, and stops running when the user-logout occurs; the software is totally transparent and does not affect any other applications. The data collected was sent directly to a detection server located in our lab. The tasks performed by the users varied from web browsing to word processing and video game playing.

The combined dataset collected for both stages of the experiment consists of a total of 1896 sessions with an average of 40 sessions per user, covering a period of 19 weeks (in total). Overall, 477 hours of raw mouse data was collected, with an average input of 9 hours and 58 minutes per user.

Using the evaluation technique outlined previously, we computed the false acceptance and false rejection rates for each of the 48 users separately through a one-hold-out cross validation test. In each round the users' reference signatures were calculated using their first five sessions, their remaining sessions were used to simulate legitimate access to their accounts and attacks on other users' accounts.

Figure 12 shows the receiver operating characteristic (ROC) curve obtained for this test when varying the threshold limit from 5% to 95%, along with sample values of FAR and FRR and their corresponding threshold limits. The equal error rate (ERR) occurs at 45% threshold limit, at this point FAR=2.6052% and FRR= 2.506%.

The selection of this limit depends mainly on the potential application of the system either

Figure 12. ROC curve for the main experiment showing the relation between FAR, FRR and the selected CR. Sample performance results obtained for different value of the threshold are also shown; the EER is obtained for CR=45%

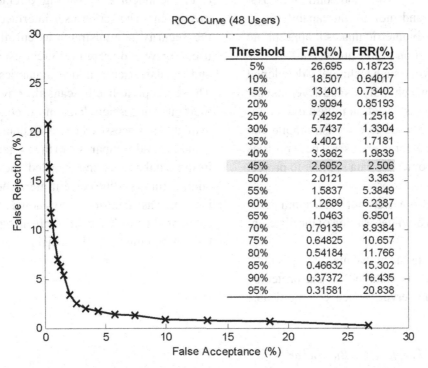

ROC Curve (48 Users)

Threshold	FAR(%)	FRR(%)
5%	26.695	0.18723
10%	18.507	0.64017
15%	13.401	0.73402
20%	9.9094	0.85193
25%	7.4292	1.2518
30%	5.7437	1.3304
35%	4.4021	1.7181
40%	3.3862	1.9839
45%	2.6052	2.506
50%	2.0121	3.363
55%	1.5837	5.3849
60%	1.2689	6.2387
65%	1.0463	6.9501
70%	0.79135	8.9384
75%	0.64825	10.657
80%	0.54184	11.766
85%	0.46632	15.302
90%	0.37372	16.435
95%	0.31581	20.838

aiming to decrease FAR, or FRR, or to maintain an EER for both. For real life implementations we suggest selecting a threshold limit within the 40% to 50% range and the threshold should be progressively tuned according to the evaluation of the collected data and the aimed goal.

In addition to the above experiment, we also conducted in 2003, a controlled experiment to study the impact of having the same hardware, the same application and on top of that, the same set of actions. Seven users were asked to interact with a customized application running on a PC using Windows XP, and to perform exactly the same set of actions. The interaction basically involved a user performing specific actions between two rectangles displayed on the screen. For instance, a user would be asked to drag one rectangle to another or simply click on one of the rectangles. The test was conducted for each of the three types of actions: Mouse-Movement, Point-and-Click,

and Drag-and-Drop. Data was collected over 63 sessions, 9 sessions per participants, and each session consisting of 100 mouse actions. In this stage, a FAR of 2.245% and a FRR of 0.898% was achieved, when the threshold was set to CR=50%. Using a ROC curve, the equal error rate was estimated at about 2.24%. This allows concluding that even by fixing the actions performed by users, mouse dynamics can still be used to discriminate effectively among a small group of users.

More details on this experiment can be found in (Ahmed & Traore, 2003; Ahmed & Traore, 2007).

APPLICATION

Mouse dynamics biometric may be used for dynamic authentication or identity confirmation in cases where the actions of an active user raise some suspicions. However, intrusion detection is the most suitable of the possible applications of this biometric. The passive and continuous user data acquisition and monitoring capabilities of mouse dynamics biometric makes it appropriate for efficient detection of masqueraders.

Biotracker[1] is one such technology developed in the ISOT Lab, which analyzes and develops user interactions patterns based on mouse dynamics. These patterns are used to establish unique and distinctive profiles for every user. These profiles can be used as biometrics data in order to protect individual computer users.

Figure 13 shows a snapshot of the main interface along with a brief description of the different GUI items.

The system consists of two main components. The client, which is installed on the protected machine, and the server, which communicates and receives data from all active clients. The client can be installed on the user's local machine or on the machine he is using to remote login to the system. The server user interface is used by the security administrator to enroll legitimate users, view and search different users sessions, and display user's mouse dynamics signature. The server periodically scans all active users, test their current session data, and if enough data is available it processes the session data to build the signature and compares it to the signatures stored in the database for the enrolled users. Security administrators will receive an alert when a session is flagged as an intrusion. Session details and the calculated confidence ratios are also provided to help in making the right decision.

Figure 13. Main Interface for Biotracker

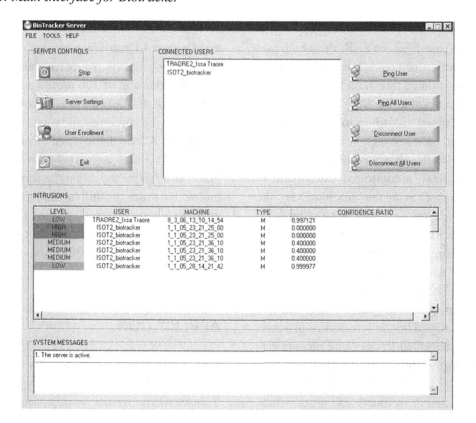

SUMMARY

We have presented, in this chapter, a new system for mouse dynamics recognition. Specifically, we have described the underlying features and presented a neural network model for biometric analysis. We have also described the experiments conducted to evaluate the proposed system and discussed corresponding results. The performance obtained consisting of FAR = 2.4649% and FRR = 2.4614%, although encouraging, does not yet meet the European standard for access control, which requires commercial biometric system to achieve a FAR less than 0.001% and a FRR less than 1% (Polemi, 1997).

More work must be done toward designing better algorithms in order to improve these performance results; we think that is where the future lies for further research work in the field of mouse dynamics biometric.

REFERENCES

Ahmed A. A. E., & Traore I. (2003). System and method for determining a computer user profile from a motion-based input device. Priority Date 2 May 2003, PCT Filling Date 3 May 2004, PCT/CA2004/000669. USPTO Application No. 10/555408, 1 Nov 2005. CIPO Application No. 2535542, 1 Nov 2005.

Ahmed, A. A. E., & Traore, I. (2005). Detecting computer intrusions using behavioral biometrics. *Proc. of 3rd Ann. Conf. on Privacy, Security, and Trust*, Canada (pp. 91-98).

Ahmed, A. A. E., & Traore, I. (2007). A new biometrics technology based on mouse dynamics. *IEEE Transactions on Dependable and Secure Computing, 4*(3), 165–179. doi:10.1109/TDSC.2007.70207

Chan, A., Lau, R. W. H., & Si, A. (2001). A motion prediction method for mouse-based navigation. *Proc. IEEE Computer Graphics International 2001 (CGI'01)* (pp. 139-146).

Hocquet, S., Ramel, J. Y., & Cardot, H. (2004). Users authentication by a study of human computer interactions. *8th Annual (Doctoral) Meeting on Health, Science, and Technology.*

Nazar, A., Traore, I., & Ahmed, A. A. E. (2008). Inverse biometrics for mouse dynamics. [IJPRAI]. *International Journal of Pattern Recognition and Artificial Intelligence, 22*(3), 461–495. doi:10.1142/S0218001408006363

Oel, P., Schmidt, P., & Shmitt, A. (2001). Time prediction of mouse-based cursor movements. *Proc. of Joint AFIHM-BCS Conf. on Human-Computer Interaction IHM-HCI, 2,* 37–40.

Polemi, D. (1997). *Biometric techniques: Review and evaluation of biometric techniques for identification and authentication, including an appraisal of the areas where they are most applicable.* (Tech. Rep.). Retrieved from ftp://ftp.cordis.lu/pub/infosec/docs/biomet.doc

Pusara, M., & Brodley, C. E. (2004). User reauthentication via mouse movements. *Proceedings ACM VizSec/DMSEC'04*, Washington, D.C.

Whisenand, T. G., & Emurian, H. (1996). Effects of angle of approach on cursor movement with a mouse: Consideration of Fitts' law. *Computers in Human Behavior, 12*(3), 481–495. doi:10.1016/0747-5632(96)00020-9

Whisenand, T. G., & Emurian, H. H. (1999). Analysis of cursor movements with a mouse. *Computers in Human Behavior, 15*(1), 85–103. doi:10.1016/S0747-5632(98)00036-3

ENDNOTE

[1] See http://www.isot.ece.uvic.ca/projects/biotracker for more about Biotracker.

Chapter 11
Activity and Individual Human Recognition in Infrared Imagery

Bir Bhanu
University of California - Riverside, USA

Ju Han
University of California - Riverside, USA

ABSTRACT

In this chapter, we investigate repetitive human activity patterns and individual recognition in thermal infrared imagery, where human motion can be easily detected from the background regardless of the lighting conditions and colors of the human clothing and surfaces, and backgrounds. We employ an efficient spatiotemporal representation for human repetitive activity and individual recognition, which represents human motion sequence in a single image while preserving spatiotemporal characteristics. A statistical approach is used to extract features for activity and individual recognition. Experimental results show that the proposed approach achieves good performance for repetitive human activity and individual recognition.

INTRODUCTION

Repetitive human activity involves a regularly repeating sequence of motion events such as walking, running and jogging. Most existing human activity recognition approaches detect human motion in visible spectrum. However, it is very likely that some part of human body or clothing has similar colors as the background colors. In this case, human motion detection using currently available approaches usually fails on these parts of the human body. Moreover,

the existence of shadows is a significant problem in the visible spectrum. In addition, sensors in the visible spectrum do not work under low lighting conditions such as night or indoor environments without any light.

To avoid the disadvantages of using sensors in the visible spectrum, we investigate the possibility of using the thermal infrared (long wave infrared) sensor for human activity analysis and individual recognition. Unlike a regular camera which records reflected visible light, a long wave (8~12μm) infrared camera records electromagnetic radiation emitted by objects in a scene as a thermal image

DOI: 10.4018/978-1-60566-725-6.ch011

Figure 1. An example of human walking, at different times of a day, recorded using a thermal infrared sensor: noon (first row), late afternoon (second row) and night (third row)

whose pixel values represent temperature. In a thermal image that consists of humans in a scene, human silhouettes can be easily extracted from the background regardless of lighting conditions and colors of the human surfaces and backgrounds, because the temperatures of the human body and background are different in most situations (Arlowe, 1992). Figure 1 shows an example of a walking human at different time of a day recorded using a thermal infrared sensor: noon (first row), late afternoon (second row) and night (third row). There are no obvious thermal shadows introduced in the thermal infrared images recorded at noon and late afternoon. Thermal images also have high contrast between the human and the background at night.

In this chapter, we investigate repetitive human activities and individual recognition in thermal infrared imagery. First, human motion is detected and human silhouettes are extracted from the background. Then, we employ an efficient spatio-temporal representation, called Gait Energy Image (GEI), for repetitive human activity and individual recognition. Unlike other representations which consider motion as a sequence of templates (poses), GEI represents human motion sequence in a single image while preserving essential spatio-

temporal information. Finally, we use a statistical approach based on principal component analysis and multi-discriminant to extract features from GEI for activity and individual recognition.

In section 2, related work on object detection, activity and individual recognition is presented. Gait energy image based representation of human motion is discussed in detail in Section 3. Statistical approach for recognition of activities and individuals is presented in Section 4. Experimental results are presented in Section 5. Finally, conclusions of the chapter are provided in Section 6.

RELATED WORK

Object Detection

Over the years many different approaches have been proposed to detect moving objects in color imagery, including running Gaussian average (Wren et al., 1996), mixture of Gaussians (Stauffer & Grimson, 1999), kernel density estimation (Elgammal, Harwood & Davis, 2000), and Eigen-background (Oliver Rosario & Pentland, 2000), etc. These approaches vary in computational complexity and their performance depends on the complexity of background variations. However, images from different kind of sensors generally have different pixel characteristics due to the phenomenological differences between the image formation processes of the sensors. Object detection in thermal infrared imagery has been widely used in automated object recognition in surveillance environments, especially for human detection. Andreone et. al (Andreone et. al, 2002) propose an approach for detecting vehicles in thermal infrared imagery. Initially the attention is focused on portions of the image that contain hot objects only. The result is further investigated exploiting specific vehicle thermal characteristics. Arlowe (Arlowe, 1992) develop an automatic detection systems based on the thermal contrast and motion of human intruders. The conditions and energy transfer mechanisms that lead to difficult thermal detection are discussed in his work. The heat flux balance equation can be used in an iterative computer program to predict the surface temperatures of both the background and the target for human intruder detection. Ginesu et. al (Ginesu et. al, 2004) propose a novel method to detect foreign bodies, which are not detectable using conventional methods, by inspecting food samples using thermographic images. Pavlidis et. Al (Pavlidis, Levine & Baukol, 2000) propose a method for detecting suspects engaged in illegal and potentially harmful activities in or around critical military or civilian installations. Thermal image analysis is performed to detect facial patterns of anxiety, alertness, and/or fearfulness at a distance. Bhanu and Han (Bhanu & Han, 2002) investigated the use of kinematic models for analyzing human motion in infrared video. Nadimi and Bhanu (Nadimi & Bhanu, 2004) investigate phenomenology based models for object detection by fusing color and infrared video. Han and Bhanu (Han & Bhanu, 2007) develop registration techniques for human detection in color and infrared videos. Yoshitomi et. al (Yoshitomi et al., 1997) develop a face identification approach based on thermal image analysis. The front-view face

is first normalized in terms of location and size, the temperature distribution is then measured as well as the locally averaged temperature and the shape factors of face. These features are used for supervised classification by neural network.

Human Activity Recognition

In recent years, various approaches have been proposed for human activity recognition. These approaches generally fall under two major categories: model-based approaches and model-free approaches.

When people observe human motion patterns, they not only observe the global motion properties, but also interpret the structure of the human body and detect the motion patterns of local body parts. The structure of the human body is generally interpreted based on their prior knowledge. Model-based activity recognition approaches focus on recovering a structural model of human motion, and the motion patterns are then generated from the model parameters for activity recognition. Guo & Tsuji (Guo & Tsuji, 1994) represent the human body structure in the silhouette by a stick figure model. The human motion characterized by a sequence of the stick figure parameters are used as input of a neural network for classification. Fujiyoshi and Lipton (Fujiyoshi & Lipson, 1998) analyze the human motion by producing a star skeleton determined by extreme point estimation from the silhouette boundaries extracted. These cues are used to recognize human activities such as walking or running. Sappa et. al (Sappa et al., 2000) develop a technique for human motion recognition based on the study of feature points' trajectories. Peaks and valleys of points' trajectories are first detected to classify human activity using prior knowledge of human body kinematics structure together with the corresponding motion model. In model-based approaches, the accuracy of human model reconstruction strongly depends on the quality of the extracted human silhouette. In the presence of noise or low-resolution data, the estimated parameters may not be reliable.

Model-free approaches make no attempt to recover a structural model of human motion. Polana and Nelson (Polana & Nelson, 1994) analyze human repetitive motion activity based on bottom up processing, which does not require the prior identification of specific parts. Motion activity is recognized by matching against a spatiotemporal template of motion features. Rajagopalan and Chellappa (Rajagopalan & Chellappa, 2000) develop a higher order spectral analysis-based approach for detecting people by recognizing repetitive motion activity. The stride length is determined in every frame, and the bi-spectrum which is the Fourier transform of the triple correlation is used for recognition. Sarkar and Vega (Sarkar & Vega, 2001) discriminate between motion types based on the change in the relational statistics among the detected image features. They use the distribution of the statistics of the relations among the features for recognition. Davis (Davis, 2004) proposes a probabilistic reliable-inference framework to address the issue of rapid and-reliable detection of human activities using posterior class ratios to verify the saliency of an input before committing to any activity classification.

Individual Human Recognition

Various techniques have been proposed for human recognition by gait. Like the classification of human activities these techniques can be divided as model-based and model-free approaches. Little and Boyd (Little & Boyd, 1998) describe the shape of the human motion with scale-independent features from moments of the dense optical flow, and recognize individuals by phase vectors estimated from the feature sequences. Sundaresan et al. (Sundaresan, RoyChowdhury & Chellappa, 2003) proposed a hidden Markov models (HMMs) based framework for individual recognition by gait. Huang et al. (Huang, Harris & Nixon, 1999) extend the template matching method to gait recognition by combining transformation based on canonical

analysis and eigenspace transformation for feature selection. Sarkar et al. (Sarkar et al., 2005) directly measure the similarity between the gallery sequence and the probe sequence by computing the correlation of corresponding time-normalized frame pairs. Collins et al. (Collins, Gross & Shi, 2002) first extract key frames from a sequence and then the similarity between two sequences is computed using the normalized correlation.

REPRESENTATION OF HUMAN MOTION

Repetitive human activity is a cyclic motion where human motion repeats at a stable frequency (Cutler & Davis, 2000). Assuming that the order of poses in a specific repetitive activity is the same among different people, it is possible to compose a spatio-temporal template in a single image instead of an ordered image sequence as usual. The fundamental assumptions made here are: (a) the order of poses in different cycles is the same, i.e., limbs move forward and backward in a similar way among normal people; (b) differences exist in the phase of poses in a motion cycle, the extend of limbs, and the shape of the torso, etc. In this chapter, we propose to use a silhouette based human motion representation, Gait Energy Image (GEI), for both activity recognition and individual recognition. Silhouette-based representation may be dependent on certain environmental conditions, such as camera views and walking surfaces. Model-based human motion representation may partially overcome this limitation with increased computational complexity. An alternative way to solve this problem is to synthesize normalized silhouette (e.g., synthesize side-view silhouette from other views (Kale, Chowdhury & Chellappa, 2003)), or generate synthetic silhouettes that simulate different environmental conditions and summarize invariant gait features from them (Han & Bhanu, 2006).

Human Silhouette Extraction

In this chapter, we suppose that the data have been divided into short image sequences each of which only contains one individual and one activity. It is reasonable to assume the background variation is very small in such a short period (typically less than one minute). Here, we use a simple running Gaussian average (Wren et al., 1996) method for silhouette extraction.

The raw silhouettes are further processed by size normalization (proportionally resizing each silhouette image so that all silhouettes have the same height) and horizontal alignment (centering the upper half silhouette part with respect to its horizontal centroid). In a so-obtained silhouette sequence, the time series signal of lower half silhouette part size from each frame indicates the motion frequency and phase information. The obtained time series signal consists of few cycles and lots of noise, which lead to sidelobe effect in the Fourier spectrum. To avoid this problem, we estimate the motion frequency and phase by maximum entropy spectrum estimation (Little & Boyd, 1998) from the obtained time series signal as shown in Figure 2.

Gait Energy Image

Given the preprocessed binary human silhouette images $B_t(x, y)$ at time t in a sequence, the grey-level gait energy image (GEI) is defined as follows:

$$G(x, y) = \frac{1}{N} \sum_{t=1}^{N} B_t(x, y)$$

$$(1)$$

where N is the number of frames in the complete cycle(s) of a silhouette sequence, t is the frame number in the sequence (moment of time), x and y are values in the 2D image coordinate. As expected, GEI reflects major shapes of silhouettes and their changes over the motion cycle. We refer to it as gait energy image because: (a) each silhouette image is the space-normalized energy image of human walking at this moment; (b) GEI is the time-normalized accumulative energy image of human walking in the complete cycle(s); (c) a pixel with higher intensity value in GEI means that human walking occurs more frequently at this position (i.e., with higher energy).

GEI Properties

In comparison with the activity representation by binary silhouette sequence, GEI representation saves both storage space and computation time for recognition and is less sensitive to silhouette noise in individual frames. Consider a noisy silhouette image $B_t(x, y)$ that is formed by the addition of noise $\eta_t(x, y)$ to an original silhouette image $f_t(x, y)$, that is, $B_t(x, y) = f_t(x, y) + \eta_t(x, y)$, where we assume that at every pair of coordinates (x, y) the noise at different moments t is uncorrelated and identically distributed. Under these constraints, we further assume that $\eta_t(x, y)$ satisfies the following distribution:

$$\eta_t(x, y) = \begin{cases} \eta_{1t}(x, y), & \text{if } f_t(x, y) = 1 \\ \eta_{2t}(x, y), & \text{if } f_t(x, y) = 0 \end{cases}$$

$$(2)$$

Where:

$$\eta_{1t}(x, y): \quad P\{\eta_t(x, y) = -1\} = p, P\{\eta_t(x, y) = 0\} = 1 - p$$
$$\eta_{2t}(x, y): \quad P\{\eta_t(x, y) = 1\} = p, P\{\eta_t(x, y) = 0\} = 1 - p$$

we have:

$$E\{\eta_t(x, y)\} = \begin{cases} -p, & \text{if } f_t(x, y) = 1 \\ p, & \text{if } f_t(x, y) = 0 \end{cases}$$

$$(3)$$

and

Figure 2. The time series signal of lower half silhouette size for different frames of walking humans

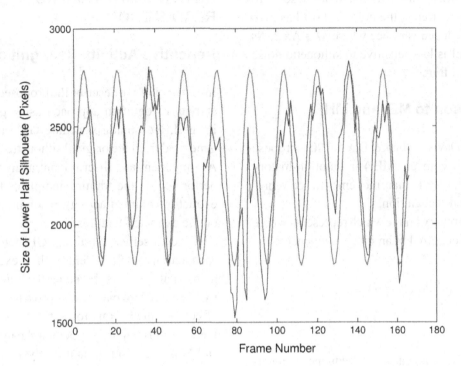

$$\sigma^2_{\eta_t(x,y)} = \sigma^2_{\eta_{1t}(x,y)} = \sigma^2_{\eta_{2t}(x,y)} = p(1-p) \tag{4}$$

Given a walking cycle with N frames where $f_t(x, y) = 1$ at a pixel (x, y) only in M frames, we have:

$$G(x,y) = \frac{1}{N}\sum_{t=1}^{N}B_t(x,y) = \frac{1}{N}\sum_{t=1}^{N}f_t(x,y) + \frac{1}{N}\sum_{t=1}^{N}\eta_t(x,y) = \frac{M}{N} + \bar{\eta}(x,y)$$

Therefore, the noise in GEI is:

$$E\{\bar{\eta}(x,y)\} = \frac{1}{N}\left[\sum_{t=1}^{M}E\{\eta_{1t}(x,y)\} + \sum_{t=M+1}^{N}E\{\eta_{2t}(x,y)\}\right]$$

$$= \frac{1}{N}[M(-p) + (N-M)p] = \frac{N=2M}{N}p$$

And

$$\sigma^2_{\bar{\eta}(x,y)} = E\{[\bar{\eta}(x,y) - E\{\bar{\eta}(x,y)\}]^2\} =$$

$$\frac{1}{N^2}E\left\{\left[\sum_{t=1}^{M}[\eta_{1t}(x,y) - E\{\eta_{1t}(x,y)\}] + \sum_{t=M+1}^{N}[\eta_{2t}(x,y) - E\{\eta_{2t}(x,y)\}]\right]^2\right\} =$$

$$\frac{1}{N^2}[M\sigma^2_{\eta_{1t}(x,y)} + (N-M)\sigma^2_{\eta_{2t}(x,y)}] = \frac{1}{N^2}\sigma$$

Therefore, the mean of the noise in GEI varies between Ip and p depending on M while its variability ($\sigma^2_{\bar{\eta}(x,y)}$) decreases. If $M = N$ at (x, y) (all $f_t(x, y) = 1$), $E\{\eta(x, y)\}$ becomes Ip; if $M = 0$ at (x, y) (all $f_t(x, y) = 0$), $E\{\eta(x, y)\}$ becomes p. At the location (x, y), the mean of the noise in GEI is the same as that in the individual silhouette image, but the noise variance reduces so that the probability of outliers is reduced. If M varies between 0 and N at (x, y), $E\{\eta(x, y)\}$ also varies between p and $-p$. Therefore, both the mean and the variance of the noise in GEI are reduced compared to the individual silhouette image at these locations. At the extreme, the noise in GEI has zero mean and reduced variance where $M = N = 2$. As a result, GEI is less sensitive to silhouette noise in individual frames.

Comparison to MEI and MHI

Bobick and Davis (Bobick & Davis, 2001) propose motion-energy image (MEI) and motion-history image (MHI) for human movement type representation and recognition.

MEI is a binary image which represents where motion has occurred in an image sequence:

$$E_\tau(x,y,t) = \bigcup_{i=0}^{\tau-1} D(x,y,t-i)$$

(5)

where $D(x, y, t)$ is a a binary sequence indicating regions of motion, τ is the duration of time, t is the moment of time, x and y are values of 2D image coordinates.

MHI is a grey-level image which represents how motion in the image is moving:

$$H\tau(x,y,t) = \begin{cases} \tau, & \text{if } D(x,y,t)=1; \\ \max\{0, H_\tau(x,y,t-1)-1\}, & \text{otherwise.} \end{cases}$$

(6)

Both MEI and MHI are vector-images where the vector value at each pixel is a function of the motion properties at this location in an image sequence. As compared to MEI and MHI, GEI targets the representation of repetitive activity, which has been successfully used in human identification by gait (Han & Bhanu, 2006).

ACTIVITY AND INDIVIDUAL RECOGNITION

Repetitive Activity Recognition

In this section, we describe the proposed repetitive activity recognition approach using gait energy image. In the training procedure, GEI templates are generated from the original silhouette sequences. A component and discriminant analysis is them performed on the training templates for feature extraction. Human activity recognition is based on the extracted features.

Given a series of training GEI templates for each activity, the problem of their excessive dimensionality occurs. To reduce their dimensionality, there are two classical approaches of finding effective linear transformations by combing features - Principal Component Analysis (PCA) and Multiple Discriminant Analysis (MDA). As described in (Duda, Hart & Stork, 2000), PCA seeks a projection that best represents the data in a least square sense, while MDA seeks a projection that best separates the data in a least-square sense. We combine PCA and MDA to achieve the best data representation and the best class separability simultaneously (Huang, Harris & Nixon, 1999).

Given n d-dimensional training templates $[\{x\}_1, x_2, ..., x_{12}\}$, PCA minimizes the criterion function

$$I_{d'} = \sum_{k=1}^{n} \left\| \left(m + \sum_{i=1}^{d'} a_{ki} e_i \right) - x_k \right\|^2$$

(7)

where $d' < d$, $m = \frac{1}{N} \sum_{k=1}^{n} x_k$, and $[\{e\}_1, e_2, ..., e_{d'}\}$ are a set of unit vectors. $J_{d'}$ is minimized when e_1, e_2, ..., and $e_{d'}$ are the d' eigenvectors of the scatter matrix S having the largest eigenvalues, where

$$S = \sum_{k=1}^{n} (x_k - m)(x_k - m)^T \tag{8}$$

The d'-dimensional principal component vector y_k is obtained from the d-dimensional GEI template x_k by multiplying the transformation matrix $[[e]_1, e_2, ..., e_{d'}]$:

$$y_k = [[a]_1, a_2, ..., a_{d'}]^T = [[e]_1, e_2, ..., e_{d'}]^T x_k, \qquad k = 1, ..., n \tag{9}$$

where n is the number of the expanded GEI templates from all people in the training dataset.

Although PCA finds components that are useful for representing data, there is no reason to assume that these components must be useful for discriminating between data in different classes because PCA does not consider the class label of training templates. Multiple discriminant analysis (MDA) seeks a projection that is efficient for discrimination. Suppose that the n d0-dimensional transformed training templates $[\{y\}_1, y_2, ..., y_n\}$, belong to c classes. MDA seeks a transformation matrix W that maximizes the ratio of the between-class scatter S_B to the within-class scatter S_W:

$$J(W) = \frac{|S_B|}{|S_W|} = \frac{|W^T S_B W|}{|W^T S_W W|} \tag{10}$$

The within-class scatter S_B is defined as

$$S_w = \sum_{i=1}^{c} S_i \tag{11}$$

where

$$S_i = \sum_{y \in D_i} (y - m_i)(y - m_i)^T \tag{12}$$

and

$$m_i = \frac{1}{n_i} \sum_{y \in D_i} y \tag{13}$$

where D_i is the training template set that belongs to the ith class and n_i is the number of templates in D_i. The within-class scatter S_B is defined as

$$S_B = \sum_{y \in D_i} n_i (m_i - m)(m_i - m)^T \tag{14}$$

where

$$m = \frac{1}{n} \sum_{y \in D} y \tag{15}$$

and D is the whole training template set. $J(W)$ is maximized when the columns of W are the generalized eigenvectors that correspond to the largest eigenvalues in

$$S_B W_i = \lambda_i S_W W_i \tag{16}$$

There are no more than $c-1$ nonzero eigenvalues, and the corresponding eigenvectors $v_1, ..., v_{c-1}$ form transformation matrix. The $(c-1)$-dimensional multiple discriminant vector z_k is obtained from the d'-dimensional principal component vector y_k by multiplying the transformation matrix $[v_1, ..., v_{c-1}]$:

$$z_k = [v_1, ..., v_{c-1}]^T y_k, \ k = 1, ..., n \tag{17}$$

The obtained multiple discriminant vectors compose the feature database for activity recognition. Assuming that the obtained feature vectors in each class are Gaussian distributed with the same covariance matrix, Bayesian classifier becomes minimum Euclidean distance classifier that is used for activity recognition.

Figure 3. Thermal images of the background at different times of a day, recorded using a thermal infrared sensor: noon, late afternoon and nigh. Each image is normalized by its temperature range individually

Noon   Late Afternoon   Night

Individual Recognition

The same framework as described in Section 4.1 is used for individual recognition during each of the activities (walking and running). In this case the training data consists of all the individuals for a given activity under a given contextual conditions (noon, late afternoon, night) and the testing is performed on the data acquired under different contextual conditions.

EXPERIMENTAL RESULTS

We have recorded real thermal image data of human activities by a FLIR SC2000 long-wave infrared camera in an outdoor environment. The image size is 240*320. The field-of-view of the camera is fixed during a human walking. Repetitive activities of five people are recorded at different time: noon (four people), late afternoon (three people) and night (two people). Each person was asked to slow walk, fast walk and run forward and backward along the fronto-parallel direction at each time. The corresponding backgrounds are shown in Figure 3. Each background is normalized by the temperature range individually.

For activity recognition three data sets recorded at noon are used for training, and other data sets are used for testing. Figure 4 shows GEI Examples of the 9 data sets (54 human motion sequences) used in our experiments. An observation from this

figure is that the silhouette extraction performance at late afternoon is better than that at noon and night. This means that the temperature contrast between the human object and the background is larger at late afternoon. The motion of trees in the background also contributes to the silhouette extraction performance in some frames.

The goal of our activity recognition here is to discriminate human walking or running regardless of their speed (slow or fast walking). In the recorded data, the speed in some fast walking sequences is equivalent or faster than that in some training sequences. Therefore, the speed is not appropriate for recognition of activity (walking or running). We employ the approach of combining PCA and MDA for feature extraction. The four-dimensional vectors obtained by PCA are used as the input of the MDA, and the final feature vectors are of one dimension. The recognition performance on training data and testing data are all 100%. This demonstrates that the proposed approach achieves good performance for human repetitive activity recognition in the limited dataset.

We do the recognition of only four (first 4 rows in Figure 4) individuals. Individuals are recognized for the same activity and the training/ testing data are appropriately chosen for the same/ different contextual conditions. The recognition of these individuals is quite simple as evidenced by different GEI images. Elsewhere we have done an extensive evaluation and comparison of individual recognition of 122 individuals in color

Figure 4. GEI Examples of the 54 human motion sequences used in our experiments. Training and test-ing data shown in the figure correspond to activity recognition experiments

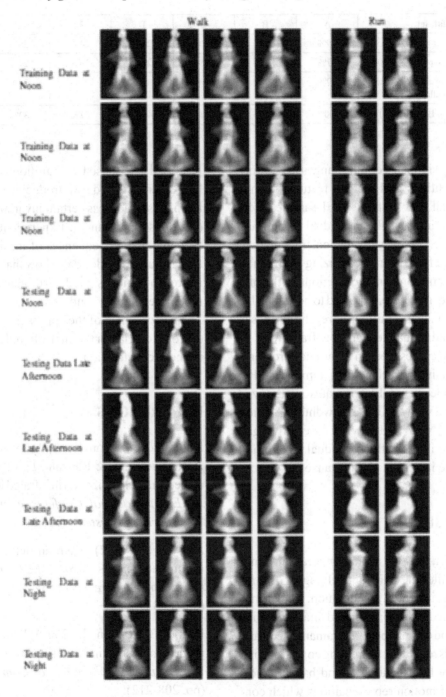

video imagery on DARPA HumanID Database and the results are briefly outlined in Table 1 (Han & Bhanu, 2006). Gait features generated from original GEI tem plates in a gait sequence may be dependent on certain environmental conditions. In [13], synthetic GEI samples were

Table 1. Comparison of Recognition Performance Using Different Approaches on USF HumanID gait database (Adapted from Sarkar et al., 2005)

dataset	A	B	C	D	E	F	G
USF (Sarkar et al., 2005)	79%	66%	56%	29%	24%	30%	10%
CMU (Collins, Gross & Shi, 2002)	87%	81%	66%	21%	19%	27%	23%
UMD (Sundaresan, RoyChowdhury & Chellappa, 2003)	99%	89%	78%	36%	29%	24%	18%
GEI (Han & Bhanu, 2006)	100%	90%	85%	47%	57%	32%	31%

generated to simulate certain changes in environmental conditions, and the gait features learned from original and synthetic GEI samples were combined to improve the individual recognition performance. These results demonstrate that our approach is effective in recognizing individuals in complex environmental conditions with color imagery, and, therefore, expected to be extensible to thermal imagery. Furthermore, the proposed GEI-base individual recognition framework is extensible to address certain invariance problems by synthesizing invariant GEI templates. For example, side-view GEI templates synthesized from various views (Kale, Chowdhury & Chellappa, 2003) may lead to view-insensitive gait features, and improve the individual recognition performance in certain circumstances.

CONCLUSION

In this chapter, we use a spatio-temporal gait representation, called the Gait Energy Image (GEI), for human repetitive activity recognition. Human motion is detected in thermal infrared imagery, which provides good contrast between human objects and backgrounds regardless of lighting conditions and colors of the human surfaces and backgrounds. Unlike other motion representations which consider gait as a sequence of templates (poses), GEI represents human motion sequence in a single image while preserving temporal information. A statistical approach is used to extract features from GEI for activity and individual recognition. The

proposed GEI-based recognition method could be further extended by introducing synthetic GEI templates to address certain invariance problems (e.g., pose invariance). Experimental results on 5 people and 54 sequences of infrared data and extensive color video data show that the proposed approach achieves good performance for human repetitive activity and individual recognition. The performance of the approach will be further explored on a larger thermal infrared dataset which is under construction.

REFERENCES

Andreone, L., Antonello, P., Bertozzi, M., Broggi, A., Fascioli, A., & Ranzato, D. (2002). Vehicle detection and localization in infrared images. *Proc. IEEE International Conference on Intelligent Transportation Systems* (pp. 141-146).

Arlowe, H. (1992). Thermal detection contrast of human targets. *Proc. IEEE International Carnahan Conference on Security Technology* (pp. 27-33).

Bhanu, B., & Han, J. (2002). Kinematic-based motion analysis in infrared sequences. *Proc. IEEE Workshop on Applications of Computer Vision* (pp. 208-212).

Bobick, A., & Davis, J. (2001). The recognition of human movement using temporal templates. *IEEE Transactions on Pattern Analysis and Machine Intelligence, 23*(3), 257–267. doi:10.1109/34.910878

Collins, R., Gross, R., & Shi, J. (2002). Silhouette-based human identification from body shape and gait. *Proc. IEEE Intl. Conf. on Automatic Face and Gesture Recognition* (pp. 351-356).

Cutler, R., & Davis, L. (2000). Robust real-time periodic motion detection, analysis, and applications. *IEEE Transactions on Pattern Analysis and Machine Intelligence, 22*(8), 781–796. doi:10.1109/34.868681

Davis, J. (2004). Sequential reliable-inference for rapid detection of human actions. *Proc. Conference on Computer Vision and Pattern Recognition* (pp. 111-118).

Duda, R., Hart, P., & Stork, D. (2000). *Pattern classification*. John Wiley & Sons.

Elgammal, A., Harwood, D., & Davis, L. (2000). Nonparametric model for background subtraction. *Proc. European Conf. on Computer Vision, II*, 751–767.

Fujiyoshi, H., & Lipson, A. (1998) Real-time human motion analysis by image skeletonization. *Proc. 4th IEEE Workshop on Applications of Computer Vision* (pp. 15-21).

Ginesu, G., Giusto, D., Margner, V., & Meinlschmidt, P. (2004). Detection of foreign bodies in food by thermal image processing. *IEEE Transactions on Industrial Electronics, 51*(2), 480–490. doi:10.1109/TIE.2004.825286

Guo, Y., & Tsuji, S. (1994). Understanding human motion patterns. *Proc. International Conference on Pattern Recognition, 2*, 325–329.

Han, J., & Bhanu, B. (2006). Individual recognition using gait energy image. *IEEE Transactions on Pattern Analysis and Machine Intelligence, 28*(2), 316–322. doi:10.1109/TPAMI.2006.38

Han, J., & Bhanu, B. (2007). Fusion of color and infrared video for moving human detection. *Pattern Recognition, 40*(6), 1771–1784. doi:10.1016/j.patcog.2006.11.010

Huang, P., Harris, C., & Nixon, M. (1999). Recognizing humans by gait via parameteric canonical space. *Artificial Intelligence in Engineering, 13*, 359–366. doi:10.1016/S0954-1810(99)00008-4

Kale, A., Chowdhury, A., & Chellappa, R. (2003). Towards a view invariant gait recognition algorithm. *Proc. of IEEE Conference on Advanced Video and Signal Based Surveillance* (pp. 143-150).

Little, J., & Boyd, J. (1998). Recognizing people by their gait: The shape of motion. *Videre: Journal of Computer Vision Research, 1*(2), 1–32.

Nadimi, S., & Bhanu, B. (2004). Physical models for moving shadow and object detection in video. *IEEE Transactions on Pattern Analysis and Machine Intelligence, 26*(8), 1079–1087. doi:10.1109/TPAMI.2004.51

Oliver, N., Rosario, B., & Pentland, A. P. (2000). A Bayesian computer vision system for modeling human interactions. *IEEE Transactions on Pattern Analysis and Machine Intelligence, 22*(8), 831–843. doi:10.1109/34.868684

Pavlidis, I., Levine, J., & Baukol, P. (2000). Thermal imaging for anxiety detection. *Proc. IEEE Workshop on Computer Vision beyond the Visible Spectrum: Methods and Applications* (pp. 104-109).

Polana, R., & Nelson, R. (1994). Low level recognition of human motion (or how to get your man without finding his body parts). *Proc. IEEE Workshop on Motion of Non-Rigid and Articulated Objects* (pp. 77-82).

Rajagopalan, A., & Chellappa, R. (2000). Higher-order spectral analysis of human motion. *Proc. International Conference on Image Processing, 3*, 230-233.

Sappa, A., Aifanti, N., Malassiotis, S., & Strintzis, M. (2000). Unsupervised motion classification by means of efficient feature selection and tracking. *Proc. International Symposium on 3D Data Processing, Visualization and Transmission* (pp. 912-917).

Sarkar, S., Phillips, P., Liu, Z., Vega, I., Grother, P., & Bowyer, K. (2005). The humanID gait challenge problem: Datasets, performance, and analysis. *IEEE Transactions on Pattern Analysis and Machine Intelligence, 27*(2), 162–177. doi:10.1109/TPAMI.2005.39

Sarkar, S., & Vega, I. (2001). Discrimination of motion based on traces in the space of probability functions over feature relations. *Proc. IEEE International Computer Society Conference Computer Vision and Pattern Recognition, 1*, 976-983.

Stauffer, C., & Grimson, W. (1999). Adaptive background mixture models for real-time tracking. *Proc. Computer Vision and Pattern Recognition* (pp. 246-252).

Sundaresan, A. RoyChowdhury, A., & Chellappa, R. (2003). A hidden Markov model based framework for recognition of humans from gait sequences. *Proc. ICIP, 2*, 93-96.

Wren, C., Azarbayejani, A., Darrell, T., & Pentland, A. (1996). Pfinder: Real-time tracking of the human body. *Proc. IEEE Conference on Automatic Face and Gesture Recognition* (pp. 51-56).

Yoshitomi, Y., Miyaura, T., Tomita, S., & Kimura, S. (1997). Face identification using thermal image processing. *Proc. IEEE International Workshop on Robot and Human Communication* (pp. 374-379).

Chapter 12
Gaze Based Personal Identification

Clinton Fookes
Queensland University of Technology, Australia

Anthony Maeder
CSIRO ICT Centre, Australia

Sridha Sridharan
Queensland University of Technology, Australia

George Mamic
Queensland University of Technology, Australia

ABSTRACT

This chapter describes the use of visual attention characteristics as a biometric for authentication or identification of individual viewers. The visual attention characteristics of a person can be easily monitored by tracking the gaze of a viewer during the presentation of a known or unknown visual scene. The positions and sequences of gaze locations during viewing may be determined by overt (conscious) or covert (subconscious) viewing behaviour. Methods to quantify the spatial and temporal patterns established by the viewer for both overt and covert behaviours are proposed. The former behaviour entails a simple PIN-like approach to develop an independent signature while the latter behaviour is captured through three proposed techniques: a principal component analysis technique ('eigenGaze'); a linear discriminant analysis technique; and a fusion of distance measures. Experimental results suggest that both types of gaze behaviours can provide simple and effective biometrics for this application.

INTRODUCTION

The ability to recognise or authenticate an individual is an important capability required in many security solutions and is employed in a range of diverse sectors including finance, healthcare, transportation, entertainment, law enforcement, access control and border control. Traditional modes for person authentication including knowledge-based and token-based systems have obvious disadvantages due to the likelihood of theft, forgotten information and fraudulent reproduction. Biometric person recognition, however, has the ability to identify or

DOI: 10.4018/978-1-60566-725-6.ch012

authenticate an individual with much stronger certainty and relies on a person's physiological or behavioural traits (Ratha et. al 2003). Current biometric systems may make use of fingerprint, iris, retina, face, hand geometry, and palm-print (all which can be classed as physiological traits), signature, typing style and gait (which are behavioural traits) as well as voice (which is a combination of both physiological and behavioural traits) (Alexandre 1997, Ashbourn 2000, Crowley 1997).

Despite the enormous promise and potential capability of biometric technology, the uptake within industry and the community has not been as prolific as expected. This is likely due to a number of reasons:

1. There are challenges with the human interface, supporting ICT systems, and business process models that must be addressed with a practical implementation of any biometric system.

2. There are still several problems which are limiting the technology including problems such as noise in the sensed data (eg: acquired voice may be corrupted by background noise in a voice-based biometric system), intra-class variation (eg: testing lighting conditions may be different to enrolment lighting conditions in face biometrics), distinctiveness (eg: two people may have very similar hand geometry), and non-universality (eg: certain people have very faint fingerprints which cannot be used to extract suitable features) (Jain 2007).

3. Finally, most biometrics are not secret – they are often freely available and easy to acquire and this makes them prone to spoof attacks (for example, a photo of a person's face, or a copy of their fingerprint can be used to foil a biometric system).

While biometrics are harder to violate than pure knowledge-based or token-based systems,

it is not impossible. Ideally, safer forms of biometrics would be based on non-visible and non-physiological information hidden deep within the person. Such a biometric could be based on behaviour or even thought processes. Gait recognition is an example of a behavioural biometric which is particularly hard to reproduce even though it is still visible. The downside for such biometrics is generally an increase in the intra-class variability, making the recognition process significantly harder and thus reducing recognition accuracies.

This chapter proposes to exploit the personal aspects of an individual's visual attention processes as a unique behavioural biometric which can be used for authentication or identification applications. The visual attention process of a person can easily be inferred through capturing their gaze (i.e. monitoring their viewing behaviour through measuring their eye movements). The approach relies on the principle that the human visual system requires the eye to rest motionless for short periods during its traversal of the viewing space, to assimilate detail at a given location in a visual scene. The assumption behind this biometric is that the viewing behaviour a person employs to gather information from a visual scene is inherently unique to that person. By detecting how and when the viewer looks at certain features in a presented scene, a signature for personal identification can be established and this is completely independent of other physiological measures of the viewer. The advantage of this approach is that it does not require physical contact between the viewer and a device, and at the same time it is difficult to detect by surveillance due to the close range nature of the monitoring required.

The viewing process can be directed overtly (consciously) or covertly (unconsciously). The later covert process is heavily related to the higher cognitive, psychological and neurological processes of that person. Thus, the process of utilising this information within a biometric system becomes one of identifying appropriate features to extract, which hopefully provide the ideal situation where intra-class variability is small and separation between classes (or inter-class variability) is large.

The specific objectives of this chapter include the following.

- **To propose two biometrics based on the visual attention processes of a person:** one biometric based on overt viewing behaviour which mimics the process of entering a simple PIN number but through a person's gaze pattern; and a second biometric (which is significantly more challenging) based on the covert (or unconscious) viewing behaviour of a person when presented with an image.

- **To investigate the effects of different features, their discriminability, and classification approaches to implement a viable biometric based on the covert gaze behaviour and thereby assess its feasibility.**

The remainder of this chapter will first provide some background on aspects of the human visual system and its association with gaze. The chapter will then describe a general approach to make use of gaze patterns for construction of PIN-like personal identification gaze signatures. A second biometric based on the covert viewing behaviour will then be presented. Three different approaches to implementing this second biometric are proposed and include an 'eigenGaze' technique, a linear discriminant analysis technique, and a fusion of distance measures. Experimental results suggest that both types of gaze behaviours can provide simple and effective biometrics for this application. The chapter then concludes with a brief discussion on possible future trends for this biometric measure and a conclusion which discusses the feasibility of the approaches followed by some recommendations concerning its general applicability.

BACKGROUND AND RELATED WORK

Knowledge of the eye and its behaviour conveys an abundance of information and this is reflected in the variety of research that employs the use of gaze and their resulting applications. Gaze can be employed in pre-processing stages of other biometrics such as iris recognition where the gaze can aid in identifying and compensating for any pose variations in the iris image capture (Schuckers et al. 2007). Gaze is often heavily utilised in intelligent vehicle applications such as the monitoring of driver vigilance where the gaze behaviour (including eye-lid movement, eye openness and gaze narrowness in the line of sight) will change with increasing driver fatigue (Ji & Yang 2002). Gaze information is particularly important for social interactions where the eyes support communication by indicating attention, intention or emotion (Hooker et. al 2003). This information can also be exploited and used in conjunction with other supporting information such as head pose within human-machine interaction applications where interfaces need to know the users intention and attention (Matsumoto et. al 2000). Understanding the visual search processes of human's in both bottom-up stimulus-driven, and top-down visual searches can be used to inform models of robotic visual systems (Belardinelli et. al 2007). Some also suggest that it is possible to make androids more "human" through the incorporation of appropriate gaze behaviours into their design (Minato et. al 2005).

It has been estimated that approximately 80% of the information a human receives comes from visual inputs (Roux & Coatrieux 1997). Visual information therefore plays a major role in our daily activities and also in our ability to make decisions based on this information. Visual attention is the name of the research field which investigates aspects of human vision and how it relates to higher cognitive, psychological and neurological processes. The concept of attention, or conscious selecting and directing of perceptual information intake, arises because finite physical human limitations prevent us from perceiving all things at once. This process makes efficient the serial searching and processing of areas for "visual processing" by using the *scan paths* of the eyes to simplify an image to extract relevant information based upon the task at hand (Noton & Stark 1971).

Over the past fifty years many hypotheses on selective attention have been proposed. Broadbent (1977) proposed that two stages were involved consisting firstly of a filtering stage which is aimed at computing simple visual features in parallel, and secondly a cognitive stage which makes higher level decisions such as object recognition. Treisman (1964) proposed a modification to Broadbent's theories stating that irrelevant information was not discarded but attenuated according to some specific features. This theory was later expanded (Treisman et. al 1980) by explaining that the initial 'simple' features are extracted in parallel across the entire visual field and separated by colour, orientation, spatial frequency, intensity, and direction of motion. This then gives rise to a saliency map of the visual scene. Braun and Sagi (1990), put forward the hypothesis of a "*focus of attention*" (*FOA*), which integrated the two main processes of volition controlled and saliency-driven visual attention. These hypotheses have been divided into two main groups:

1. **Top-down models** based on the knowledge related to the task that the user is performing;
2. **Bottom-up models** based on the work of Treisman (1964) where saliency maps are built.

From this body of work it is clear that the human visual system relies on positioning of the eyes to bring a particular component of the visible field of view into high resolution. This permits the person to view an object or region of interest near the centre of the field in much finer detail.

In this respect, visual attention acts as a "spotlight" effect (Itti & Koch 2001). The region viewed at high resolution is known as the foveal region and is much smaller than the entire field of view contained in the periphery. However, 50% of the primary visual cortex of the primate, for example, is devoted to processing input from this central 2% of the visual field (Wandell, 1995).

Viewing of a visual scene consists of a sequence of brief gaze periods (typically 100-500ms) of visual concentration (fixations) at specific locations in the field of view, interspersed with two distinct types of eye movements - saccades and vergence. This discovery was made by French ophthalmologist, Emile Javal in 1879 (Javal 1879). He discovered by direct observation that eyes move in a series of jumps (saccades) and pauses (fixations). Saccades are voluntary shifts (rapid eye movements) of the angle of gaze between different points of fixation while vergence movements are voluntary shifts of fixation points lying at different depths in the viewing space (Kumar et. al 2001). Saccades take less than 100ms for completion whereas vergence movements may require several seconds.

Numerous researchers have investigated the psychological aspects of covert and overt gaze shifting. The work of Rizzolatti (Rizzolatti et. al 1987) and Hoffman and Subramamian (1995) showed that covert shifts of attention consist of a shift in spatial attention alone, whilst overt shifts of attention consisted of a shift in spatial attention in conjunction with a shift in eye position. Beauchamp (Beauchamp et. al 2002) performed a functional imaging experiment to determine the common network of brain areas active when subjects performed shifts of attention (overt or covert). As the biometric experiments being conducted here are only concerned with gaze behaviour when viewing an image on a PC, the only movement of concern are those of saccadic movements.

Thus, the viewing process provides the brain with detailed visual information over a succession of fixation-saccade events covering a few comparatively small areas in the field of view. From this, a "conceptual" image of the visual scene is constructed by combining these with the large area of low resolution information gained from the periphery. The fixation-saccade events may be consciously directed by the viewer to visit a sequence of specific points in the scene (overt), or else may be allowed to be directed subconsciously by the brain according to its choice of points of interest (covert) (Itti & Koch 2000). The development of a person's subconscious viewing behaviour also begins early in life during infancy stages (Belardinelli et. al 2007), thus providing further evidence to the uniqueness of this process and giving further weight to its use as a biometric.

In order to understand visual attention processes better, methods have been devised to track gaze location through eye movements: a simple approach uses a video camera image to recover the 3D orientation of the eye. Using eye movements in this manner is an overt measure of where a viewer is directing their covert attention (Hooker et. al 2003). This method is based on the pre-motor theory of attention which advocates eye movements and shifts in attention are driven by the same internal mechanisms (Rizzolatti, et. al 1987). Thus, by observing where and when a person's gaze is directed, it is possible to establish the fixation-saccade path followed by the viewer. This provides insights about what the viewer found interesting (i.e. what captured their attention) and perhaps reveal how that person perceived the visual scene they were viewing (Duchowski 2003). This attentional guidance also does not only depend on local visual features; it also includes the effects of interactions among features (Peters et. al 2005). If the viewer is undertaking a defined task, such as following a prescribed sequence of gaze locations, this is equivalent to providing a password. If a task is not specified, the path denotes the pattern of visual interest for that individual, corresponding to the scene being

viewed. Either of these situations can provide a suitable foundation for a biometric, and both are explored in this chapter.

As described earlier, a viewer will build up a perception or "conceptual image" of the visual scene by a sequence of fixation-saccade events. The spatial and temporal pattern of these events for a given visual scene varies widely between different people and accordingly can be used to compute a visual attention "signature" of each individual. These signatures can be formulated by quantitative analysis of the individual's gaze data (Goldberg & Kotval 1999). Two possible ways that such signatures could be constructed are as follows.

1. The viewer could be presented with a known picture for which they had decided upon a personal sequence of fixation points, already informed to the authentication system in a training phase. The viewer would consciously (overtly) direct their gaze to these points in the order established, while the authentication system tracked the sequence of points, loosely mimicking the process of entering a PIN on a keypad.

2. The viewer could be presented with a known picture for which their unconscious (covert) pattern of gaze points when inspecting the picture had previously been captured by the authentication system in a training phase. The viewer would simply view the picture passively and allow the authentication system to collect the pattern of gaze points occurring naturally.

Both methods require some assumptions about the properties of eye movement and gaze tracking, as follows.

1. The operating characteristics of the tracking device need to be sufficient to allow the necessary detail in spatial and temporal resolution. A sampling rate of approximately

50-70ms or less will achieve the temporal requirement for detecting fixations generally. Spatial localisation to around 10% of the overall scene linear dimensions is judged sufficient to establish fixation points appropriate to this application.

2. A sufficient number of successive gaze points is required to allow unique characterisation of an individual within the population, and to override the effect of involuntary errors in gaze location and sequence, without requiring too many points or too long a gaze duration for practical purposes. A comfortable maximum viewing time for an image is approximately 20 secs, after which some fatigue/boredom effects typically occur. This normally allows for at least 40 fixations to be measured.

3. The gaze pattern followed by a viewer needs to be reasonably similar on different occasions. Substantial evidence from experiments with numbers of viewers indicates this expectation is realistic (Yarbus 1967).

4. The covert viewing gaze patterns for different viewers of the same scene need to differ significantly and consistently from each other to allow effective detection. Evidence in the literature (Duchowski 2003) suggests that this is the case.

5. An efficient and unbiased technique is needed to establish the distance between two gaze patterns, to allow easy decision-making for establishing similarity. A signature of relatively few numerical values representing a compacted form of the gaze pattern would be appropriate, and can be compared using ranking or matching type procedures.

6. A distance measure between gaze patterns also needs to make allowance for involuntary errors, such as sequence or duration variations. The signature should therefore be constructed to constrain the effects of same viewer variations.

For both the overt and covert approaches, the system may be considered to have two operating modes. The first mode consists of the off-line training wherein the library of gaze "signatures" is compiled for each individual. The second mode is the actual online operation of the authentication system. In this mode, an observer's gaze data is recorded online and compared against the database of signatures to identify or authenticate an individual.

Despite the widespread use of gaze behaviour, few researchers have attempted to exploit the human visual attention process as a source for a unique behavioural biometric (Maeder & Fookes 2003, Maeder et. al 2004, Kasprowski et. al 2004). Kasprowski presented a technique of performing human identification which is based on eye movements. The system measured human eye reaction to visual stimulation. Initial experiments showed that it was possible to identify people by means of that method. Silver and Biggs (2006) presented an Eye-Password system where a user entered a sensitive input (password, PIN, etc.) by selecting from an on-screen keyboard using only the orientation of their pupils. The results demonstrate that gaze-based password entry requires marginal additional time over using a keyboard; error rates are similar to those of using a keyboard; and subjects preferred the gaze-based password entry approach over traditional methods.

The approaches presented in this chapter for developing the overt and covert biometrics described above, and establishing their viability subject to the above assumptions, is described in the sections below. Experimental work to characterize different viewer behaviours and repeatability / robustness of the approach in both of these cases will be presented. This work was conducted using two images and a cohort of 10 and 5 viewers for the overt and covert methods respectively. All viewers were male and were aged in their 20s to 40s. Methods to systematically quantify the spatial and temporal patterns established by the viewer gaze sequences for particular cases will be described. Candidate classification techniques including an 'eigenGaze' technique, a linear discriminat analysis technique, and a fusion of distance measures will be proposed for use in identification applications.

Gaze-Tracking Device

Measuring the gaze of a person typically involves tracking specific optical characteristics such as the corneal reflection when the eyes are illuminated with a light source which is typically near infrared. Other methods, however, may include the use of appearance manifold models for example (Kar-Han et. al 2002). The device used to record eye movements during the following experiments was an EyeTech video-based corneal reflection eye tracker. This device is normally used for point-of-regard measurements, i.e. those that measure the position of the eye relative to 3D space rather than relative to the head (Young & Sheena 1975). The method of operation relies on tracking the corneal reflection from an infra-red light source, as it is invisible to the human eye and non-distracting. Although four separate reflections are formed during the reflection of a light source, referred to as Purkinje reflections (Crane 1994), only the first Purkinje reflection is utilized in the video-based tracker and is located relative to the location of the pupil centre using image processing techniques. A small amount of head movement is acceptable for stable gaze monitoring with this device, however, research is continuing to investigate robust methods for dealing with large head movements (Yoo & Chung 2004).

The gaze-tracker utilized operated in a default setting of 15 frames per second, resulting in a sample of the observer's gaze direction approximately every 67ms. The experiments were conducted using an image and screen resolution of 1024 x 768 pixels.

OVERT GAZE BIOMETRIC

Following the above principles, an experimental investigation was conducted to establish the accuracy, reliability, efficiency and useability of the proposed *overt* gaze-based user authentication method. A test image of the city of Prague (see Figure 1) was selected as a reasonably complex yet recognizably natural scene, for which viewers should have little difficulty selecting several distinctive and well separated gaze points. This figure also shows the six locations of interest (as squares) which were utilised in the experiments.

A grid of 3 horizontal cells and 3 vertical cells was also superimposed on the image and is shown in Figure 2. The individual cells in this 3 x 3 grid, (a total of 9 cells in all), can be encoded conceptually with the numbers 1-9 from left to right and top to bottom, analogous to a telephone keypad. This grid can also be customised to suit the image being viewed. In this case, the grid was made marginally non-uniform in order to separate some of the detail in the centre of the image more effectively, as seen in Figure 2(b).

Ten viewers were used in this experiment and all viewers were instructed to look at the six specific points of interest in the Prague image as illustrated in Figure 1. As only a small number of people were utilized, the same six points were used in each case, however, the viewing sequence was re-arranged for each person. This essentially provided a unique PIN sequence which could be used to distinguish very clearly between the different individuals. The viewers were instructed to follow their respective sequence of points with their eye movements, and to hold their gaze for an estimated duration of approximately 1 second at each location. Figure 2(a) illustrates an example gaze sequence recorded with the extracted fixations superimposed on the image in Figure 2(b).

Each of these six points are contained in a different cell in the 3 x 3 grid. As the eye movements of the viewer were recorded during this process, the gaze data was passed through a clustering al-

Figure 1. "Prague" test image used for the overt experiments with six highlighted locations of interest

Figure 2. (a) Example of gaze data, (b) Plot of extracted fixations

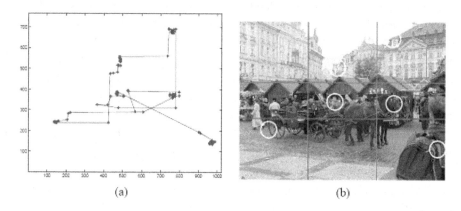

(a)   (b)

gorithm to extract fixations with a time constraint (or threshold) imposed on the fixation duration, T_{fix}. All fixations with a duration equal to or larger than this threshold were extracted and encoded according to the cell in the 3 x 3 grid in which it was contained. The experiment was repeated for the ten different viewers on 3 different occasions separated by several minutes, so as to simulate PIN entry on separate user authentication occasions.

The clustering method employed is summarised in Box 1.

For this overt approach to developing a biometric measure, the system may be considered to have two operating modes. The first mode consists of the off-line training wherein the library of PIN sequences is compiled for each individual. The second mode is the actual online operation of the authentication system. In this mode, an observer's

Box 1. Clustering algorithm

- Define threshold or radius for a cluster, initially 40 pixels
- Define cluster counter
- Assign first node into current cluster
- For all gaze sample points
    - Compute common mean location of samples in current cluster, and the next temporally sequential sample
    - Store the index of current points into current cluster
    - If new point is not within threshold from common mean, then the current cluster becomes an old cluster, and the new point becomes the current cluster.
- Check number of gaze sample points in each cluster to determine if a fixation
    - Determine Total Fixation Clusters. For all fixations
        - Find distances between fixations less than threshold and add those fixations to current one
        - If fixations identified within threshold, then add to current fixation, else make it a fixation by itself
    - Define boundaries for 3x3 grid
    - Define 9 Point Pin
    - Initialise block viewing sequence
    - Find all points in each bin
    - Find percentage of total points and store in Pin
    - Assign viewing sequence
- end

gaze data is first recorded online, then the PIN sequence is extracted by processing the gaze data, and compared against the database of PIN sequences to automatically identify or authenticate an individual.

For each of the ten viewers, the viewing of the six points of interest in the Prague image will result in a six PIN sequence that is unique for that individual. These sequences are recorded and stored in the database during offline training and are shown below as a sequence of six numbers in Table 1.

For the given Prague image, the observer was directed to gaze at each of the six specific points for approximately one second each and in their prescribed sequence. The gaze data (sampled at 15fps, or once every 0.067 secs) was then passed through the spatial clustering algorithm outlined earlier to extract any fixations with a duration equal to or larger than the fixation threshold T_{fix}. The threshold used for this first experiment was 0.67 secs, i.e. 10 gaze samples. These fixations were then encoded as a PIN sequence according to the cell in the 3 x 3 grid in which the fixation was located, and were finally compared against the database to authenticate the individual. Using the threshold $T_{fix} = 0.67$ secs, this experiment resulted in 100% authentication for all individuals. Thus, the extracted PIN sequences from the 3 repeat scans of all ten viewers exactly matched their respective PIN sequences stored in the database given by Table 1.

This first experiment resulted in a successful authentication in all cases. Figure 2(a) shows some example gaze data recorded during one of these experiments. After clustering these original gaze samples with a constraint on the time of fixation, only six fixations were obtained and are plotted against the Prague image in Figure 2(b). These fixations correspond to the six points the observer was directed to examine. Similar fixation plots were also obtained across the three repeat experiments from all viewers.

Table 1. PIN sequences for the ten observers

Person	PIN	Person	PIN
P1	962375	P6	792356
P2	672359	P7	963752
P3	327965	P8	293657
P4	523796	P9	572369
P5	257369	P10	736952

To determine the optimum threshold value for the fixation duration, previous work in (Maeder et. al 2004) generated plots of the recognition rate verses the threshold value in seconds which are shown in Figure 3. This figure shows the recognition rates for the three repeat experiments for each of the ten viewers. The recognition rate is a measure of the recognition accuracy and is computed as,

$$RR = \frac{\#P_c - \#P_i}{N} \, x100\%,$$

$$(1)$$

where $\#P_c$ is a count of the number of correct PINs recorded in the correct sequence, $\#P_i$ is the number of incorrect PINs in the sequence, and N is the total number of PINs in the correct sequence, (which is six in these experiments).

As can be seen from Figure 3, there is an empirical optimum for the fixation threshold. Values too low result in the generation of extra incorrect PINs in the sequence and hamper the recognition rate while values too high result in the loss of PINs being extracted and also degrade the recognition rate. The optimum value was found to be approximately $T_{fix} = 0.6$ secs for this experiment.

COVERT GAZE BIOMETRIC

For the covert biometric, the experimental methodology adopted consisted of recording gaze data of five different viewers for a particular image of an outdoor scene of a rock climb (see Figure 4). For each session, the viewer was directed to examine the scene without any consciously directed (or task specified) gaze pattern. That is, the viewer was free to examine the image in their natural manner, i.e. at the whim of their personal visual attention processes. The sequence of eye saccades and fixations was captured for a total duration of 10 secs. For each case, the gaze-tracking experiment

was repeated three times, each occasion being separated from the others by several days or by some other visual tasks to reduce the influence of repetition.

Comparing the recorded gaze signatures of a person with those in a database is a straight forward procedure for the overt experiments. A valid authentication is simply the case when the location of the clustered fixations, and their viewing sequence, matches those stored in the database. However, the comparison of the gaze patterns for the covert experiments is a much more complicated and problematic endeavour than the overt category. This is due to the inherent variations that exist not only between viewing patterns of different people, but more significantly, between different scans of the same person. This inter- and intra-variability makes the development of a simple authentication process extremely difficult. Consequently, more sophisticated measures need to be developed in order to truly identify commonalities, if any, that exist between different scans of the same observer and between observers.

The measures and data that will be discussed in this section are presented to ascertain if any patterns exist across the same observers and/or different observers. The existence of any such patterns will determine if a person's covert visual attention processes can in fact be used as a successful biometric. Three different approaches are proposed as possible candidate techniques to extract these biometric patterns. They consist of an 'eigenGaze' technique, a linear discriminant analysis technique, and a fusion of distance measures. All three approaches yield promising results and so provide possible avenues for future research.

Figure 5 presents some sample data for the covert experiments. Plots (a), (b) and (c) show fixations of Scan 1 for Person 1, Person 2, and Person 3 (out of the database of 5 people) respectively, plotted against the Rockclimb image. The variations between observers in these cases are quite apparent. Figures (d), (e) and (f) represent the

Figure 3. Recognition rates plotted against the fixation threshold T_{fix} for Scans 1, 2, and 3 of the 10 viewers respectively

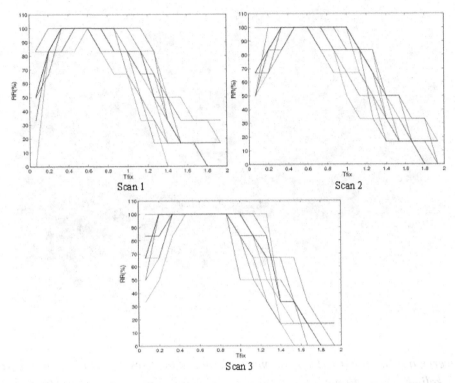

Scan 1

Scan 2

Scan 3

three repeated scans for Person 1 on the Rockclimb image. These three scans appear to have many similarities after a visual comparison, however, there is still obviously some diversity between them, i.e. intra-viewer variation. Moreover, the plots in Figure 5 do not contain any information about the sequence in which these points were viewed.

A supplementary experiment was conducted in parallel to the covert experiment outlined above. This second experiment was to investigate the hypothesis that certain categories of people with a highly trained gaze behaviour may yield more repeatable gaze sequences. This experiment was conducted on radiologists who routinely read screening mammogram images for the detection of cancer, lesions, calcifications, or tumors. A sample image utilised for these experiments is illustrated in Figure 6 along with some example gaze data captured. The idea behind conducting this test is

that these viewers have a highly structured gaze sequence when they read mammograms. This form of structured gaze sequence for a particular image type may be an easier source from which to extract a viable biometric compared with a regular human observer, whose viewing pattern may be more random.

'eigenGaze' Technique

One of the most common feature extraction techniques employed within the field of biometrics is based on Principal Component Analysis (PCA). This technique was first utilised in a fully automated face recognition system proposed by Turk & Pentland (1991). This work applied PCA to derive a set of face representations which were termed 'eigenFaces'. This technique has since become the gold standard for face verification and was utilised as the baseline system in the

Figure 4. "Rockclimb" image used in the covert experiments

Figure 5. Covert Gaze Data: Extracted fixations for Scan 1 of (a) Person 1, (b) Person 2, and (c) Person 3, for the Rockclimb image. Figures (d), (e) and (f) show all of the extracted fixations from the three repeated scans for Person 1

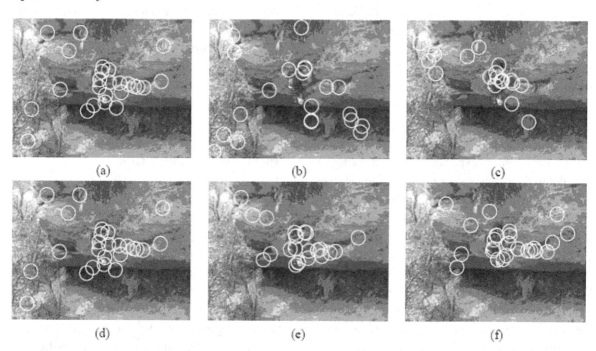

(a) (b) (c)

(d) (e) (f)

Figure 6. (a) Example image utilised in the mammogram covert experiment, (b) example gaze data

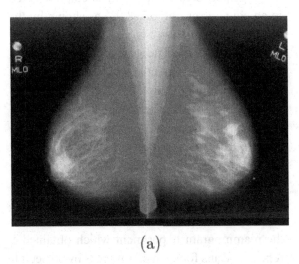

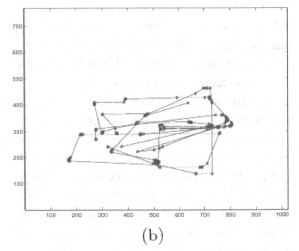

(a)

(b)

Face Recognition Grand Challenge (Phillips et. al 2005) evaluation. Since its introduction, similar techniques have been proposed for other biometric applications including 'eigenLips' for speech recognition (Bregler & Konig 1994), 'eigenEyes' (Campos et. al, 2000), and 'eigenPulse' for human identification from cardiovascular function (Irvine et. al 2008). This chapter proposes a similar 'eigenGaze' technique as a method for developing a biometric from a human's gaze behaviour.

This technique applies eigen-decomposition to the covariance matrix of a set of M vectorised training sequences of gaze. PCA is used to derive a set of eigenvectors which are ranked based on their eigenvalues λ. The D most relevant eigenvectors are retained to form a sub-space φ. The eigenvalues represent the variance of each eigenvector and so represent the relative importance of each of the eigenvectors with regards to minimising the reconstruction error in a least squares sense. Once the sub-space φ is obtained, a vectorised gaze sequence v_a can be projected into the space to obtain a feature vector $\mathbf{a}$ ($\mathbf{a} = (v_a - \omega) * \varphi$) where ω is the mean gaze vector.

This technique can be termed 'eigenGaze' as each eigenvector is representative of the most variant attributes of the training gaze sequences

(similar to eigenFaces for face recognition). For this approach, the gaze data was clustered into fixations in a similar manner to the overt experiment (using a cluster radius of 10 pixels, rather than a PIN cell) and the mean duration of clusters, the mean number of revists, cluster length and mean fixation durations, were used as features. To find the 'eigenGaze's, each gaze capture is converted into a vector of clustered fixations, Γn, of length 20. Multiple gazes per person are utilised as this sharply increases accuracy due to the increased information available on each known individual. This collection of gazes can be referred to as the "gaze space." As usual for the construction of a basis set, the mean of the observations is removed and a covariance matrix, C, for the dataset is computed. The 'eigenGaze's then are simply the eigenvectors of C. These 'eigenGaze's provide a small yet powerful basis for the gaze space. Using only a weighted sum of these 'eigenGaze's, it is possible to reconstruct each gaze in the dataset.

For each view of the Rockclimb image, the first eight 'eigenGaze's (which comprised 99.5% of the gaze space) were used to extract a feature vector of weights which were then passed to the classifier to evaluate the probability of the gaze belonging to a given individual. The similarity measure used in this case is the cosine of the angle between the projected 'eigenGaze' vectors. Table 2 presents the similarity measures calculated between all possible scan combinations (where Pi is the ith person being tested, and Vj is the jth viewing sequence for a given person).

As illustrated in Table 2, the intra-class similarity scores (highlighted) are generally much higher (close to unity) than the inter-class scores. Thus, based on this dataset it is clear that there is strong separation between classes which should yield reasonable classification rates. That is, intra-class scores of a person's gaze viewing sequence matching to another of their scans at a later period in time is higher than the score achieved from matching with any of the other four identities in the database. To illustrate the recognition ability of the 'eigenGaze' method, the scores in Table 2 were utilised to generate a Detection Error Trade-off plot (or DET plot). This is given in Figure 7 which shows the false alarm probability versus the miss probability for the 'eigenGaze' technique. This method resulted in an equal error rate of ~8.9% as shown by the black circle plotted in Figure 7.

Thus, this experiment does yield promising results that the 'eigenGaze' approach may be a worthy technique capable of classifying individuals using the clustering of their gaze data. Although this technique does certainly yield some potential, the true capability of this technique and the viability of 'eigenGaze' will not be clear until further research and experiments are conducted on much larger datasets.

A similar experiment was also conducted for the mammogram experiment which obtained 5 repeated scans for each of 8 images by 3 specialised radiologists who routinely engage in reading screening mammograms. The same 'eigenGaze' process as just outlined was conducted and the following results were obtained.

Intra-class matches: Person 1: range from 0.82 – 0.86

Person 2: range from 0.89 – 0.94

Table 2. Classification results generated by 5 people with 3 different viewing sequences when projected into the 'eigenGaze' space

	P1 V1	P1 V2	P1 V3	P2 V1	P2 V2	P2 V3	P3 V1	P3 V2	P3 V3	P4 V1	P4 V2	P4 V3	P5 V1	P5 V2	P5 V3
P1V1	1	0.99	0.85	-0.1	-0.0	0.3	-0.4	-0.4	-0.4	-0.4	-0.3	-0.4	-0.9	-0.4	-0.9
P1V2		1	0.81	-0.2	-0.1	0.2	-0.4	-0.4	-0.4	-0.5	-0.3	-0.4	-0.9	-0.5	-0.9
P1V3			1	0.4	0.4	0.7	-0.6	-0.6	-0.6	-0.5	-0.5	-0.5	-0.7	0.12	-0.7
P2V1				1	1	0.93	-0.2	-0.1	-0.1	0.11	-0.1	0.1	0.32	0.92	0.34
P2V2					1	0.93	-0.2	-0.2	-0.2	0.08	-0.1	0.1	0.30	0.92	0.33
P2V3						1	-0.2	-0.2	-0.1	0.09	-0.0	0.1	0.06	0.71	0.07
P3V1							1	1	1	0.97	0.99	0.96	0.66	-0.1	0.59
P3V2								1	1	0.46	0.45	0.45	0.67	-0.1	0.61
P3V3									1	0.97	0.99	0.97	0.68	-0.1	0.62
P4V1										1	0.97	1	0.75	0.12	0.70
P4V2											1	0.97	0.6	-0.1	0.53
P4V3												1	0.73	0.11	0.67
P5V1													1	0.54	1
P5V2														1	0.59
P5V3															1

Figure 7. Detection-Error-Trade-off plot for the 'eigenGaze' covert experiment yielding an equal error rate of ~8.9%

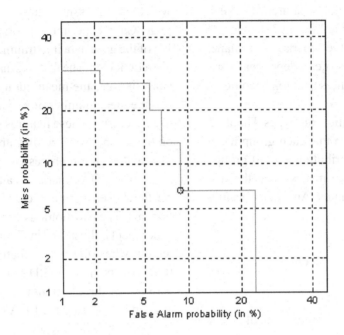

Person 3: range from 0.86 – 0.93

Inter-class matches: Person 1 – 2,3: range from 0.74 – 0.91

Person 2 – 1,3: range from 0.81 – 0.91

Person 3 – 1,2: range from 0.74 – 0.89

Thus, as can be seen from the above scores computed during this experiment, there is clearly not adequate separation between the classes. There is a significant overlap between classes and thus classification accuracy would be quite poor. There are many instances where a person's gaze will actually match more closely to another person's sequence. This result suggests that it is inherently harder to extract a biometric signature from the gaze sequence of a person who has a highly trained and structured viewing behaviour as is expected from radiologists who are trained to view images in a certain sequence.

Linear Discriminant Analysis Technique

The second method presented for classifying covert gaze sequences is based on Linear Discriminant Analysis (LDA) (Hastie et. al 2001) which is a statistical technique popular for classifying samples into mutually exclusive or exhaustive categories, particularly for face recognition (Robinson & Clarke 2007). The purpose of discriminant analysis is to classify objects into groups based on a set of features that describe the objects. The dependent variable, Y, is the group and the independent variables, X, are the object features that might describe the group. The dependent variable is always a categorical (nominal scale) variable while the independent variables can be of any measurement scale (i.e. nominal, ordinal, interval or ratio).

If the assumption is made that the groups are linearly separable, then a linear discriminant model can be employed. Linear separability means that the groups can be separated by a linear combination of features that describe the objects. If only two features are used, the separators between object groups will become lines in 2D space. If three features are used, the separator is a plane. If the number of features (i.e. independent variables) is more than 3, the separator becomes a hyper-plane.

With some manipulation of Bayes Theorem and under the assumption that each group has a multivariate Normal distribution and all groups have the same covariance matrix, then the following Linear Discriminant Analysis formula can be employed,

$$f_i = \mu_i C^{-1} x_k^T - \frac{1}{2} \mu_i C^{-1} \mu_i^T + \ln(p_i). \tag{2}$$

The second term ($\mu_i C^{-1} \mu_i^T$) is the Mahalanobis distance, which in this case quantifies the dissimilarity between several groups.

The LDA formulation was applied to the original data of the Rockclimb image viewings which was the same dataset outlined in the first 'eigenGaze' experiment. An appropriate partitioning of the gaze data into training and test sets was also conducted. The features that were tested in the analysis were the mean duration of each cluster and the mean number of revisits that were made to each cluster. These features were chosen based on the assumption that they are major indicators of visual attention processes.

For this LDA experiment and the same sample set, the chosen features yielded a 100% classification rate. The partitioning of the 2D space for this experiment is illustrated in Figure 8. This shows the regions where the chosen features for each of the five viewers map into 2D space. The boundaries between the three regions represent the separators as estimated during the LDA process.

Similarly to the 'eigenGaze' experiment earlier, a second test was conducted on the mammogram

Figure 8. LDA space partitioning of viewers

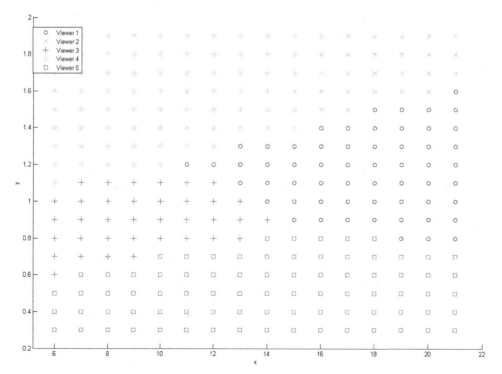

viewing sequences to test if a similar pattern was discovered. In this case, when the LDA experiment was conducted on the mammography data set using the same feature set of the mean fixation duration and the mean number of revisits, the experiment yielded a 45% classification rate. This result supports the findings that were discussed earlier and provides further evidence to indicate that the highly structured and trained viewing sequence actually removes the discriminable information inherent to a person that can be used as a biometric measure. However, given non-structured viewings of images (i.e. from a person who is not a trained or specialised domain specific viewer of images) then there is certainly potential to recognise the viewer based upon the time that they spend within each cluster and the number of times that they revisit a particular cluster. Further research is required to investigate whether these patterns will hold for much larger databases of gaze sequences.

Distance Measures

The third potential candidate technique proposed to extract a biometric measure from the covert gaze experiments is based on a set of distance measures, which were introduced in previous work (Maeder & Fookes 2003). This approach offers the advantage of computational simplicity and speed. The distance measures that were employed to determine the similarities between different scans in this experiment are outlined below.

1. **D**: is used to measure or count the number of common fixations between any two scans. A common fixation is one which coincides spatially (within a given threshold) with another fixation in the second scan.
2. **D***: is used quantify the difference in visit periods of the first five fixations in two scans. This is achieved by the computation of a SAD score (sum of absolute differences) between the number of gaze samples in each of the first five fixations,

$$D^* = \sum_{i=1}^{N} \left| p(F_i^1) - p(F_i^2) \right|, \tag{3}$$

where N=5, F_i^1 and F_i^2 are the ith fixations of scan 1 and scan 2, and p(.) is the number of gaze samples in each fixation.

3. **D⁺**: quantifies the difference between the number of revisits of each of the first five fixations. The revisits, similar to a feature used in the LDA experiment, is represented as a count of the number of times a viewer "revisits" one of the first five fixations during the entire viewing duration. This measure is implemented with another SAD score,

$$D^+ = \sum_{i=1}^{N} \left| r(F_i^1) - r(F_i^2) \right|, \tag{4}$$

where N=5, and r(.) is the number of revisits for each fixation.

The first distance measure is used to assess the commonality of the fixations between any two scans, i.e. **D** simply counts the number of common fixations. The second two distance measures described above are used to quantify slightly different aspects of the visual attention process. **D*** measures the difference between the period (or the number of sample points) of the first five fixations via a SAD score. Empirical evidence has shown that the most prominent of all fixations generally occur within the first five viewed. Later fixations as a general rule contain a much smaller period (this is the reason for only comparing the first five fixations). Note however, that these first five fixations can be revisited during the entire viewing duration (10 secs). Thus, **D*** computes the SAD score between the total number of sample points between the first five fixations obtained over the entire viewing sequence. The last distance measure **D⁺** quantifies the difference between the revisiting habits of the viewers. Different viewers will have different underlying psychological and cognitive process which direct them to revisit points or regions of interest to them in various manners. Thus, D^+ measures the differences in the number of revisits of the first five prominent fixations via another SAD score.

Table 3 presents the **D** distance measures calculated between all possible scan combinations (where Pi is the ith person being tested, and Vj is the jth viewing sequence for a given person). The larger the value, the more similar the scans as they share a larger number of common fixations. The diagonal values in this table signify comparison between a scan and itself, which simply yields the total number of fixations in that person's scan. From a simple visual inspection of the table, there is evidence that the **D** scores of intra-viewer comparisons (not including the diagonals) are generally larger than inter-viewer comparisons, but not for all cases. This measure however, is by no means sufficient enough to adequately distinguish between different viewers.

Table 4 presents the **D*** SAD scores which measure the difference in the visit period (or number of gaze samples) between the first five fixations of any two scans, whatever location those fixations

may be. This measure essentially compares how long a person views each of the first five fixations, which have been shown empirically to be the most prominent fixations. Similarly Table 5 presents the SAD scores between the number of revisits of the first five fixations. For the values in both Table 4 and 5, the smaller the score, the more similar the scans. Once again, from a visual inspection of both of these tables, there is an obvious trend where the intra-viewer comparisons are generally smaller than inter-viewer comparisons, except for a few cases.

From the preliminary results presented thus far, there are some obvious trends in the data to suggest that a scan from one person is in actual fact more similar to other scans from that same person than to scans from other people utilising these simple distance measures. Although no single distance measure provides a definitive answer and consequently could not be used solely for classification, a combination of these measures may provide greater discriminiability through the fusion of the complimentary information captured

Table 3. Quantitative measures: **D** *calculated between scans of all viewers*

	P1 V1	P1 V2	P1 V3	P2 V1	P2 V2	P2 V3	P3 V1	P3 V2	P3 V3	P4 V1	P4 V2	P4 V3	P5 V1	P5 V2	P5 V3
P1V1	14	9	9	5	5	3	6	8	7	5	5	5	7	8	6
P1V2		10	8	3	3	2	3	7	5	6	4	4	5	5	5
P1V3			11	4	4	3	3	5	5	5	5	6	7	4
P2V1				9	7	6	4	2	4	7	3	3	5	5	4
P2V2					10	5	3	2	5	6	6	5	6	7	5
P2V3						7	3	2	3	4	4	2	2	5	4
P3V1							15	7	9	4	3	5	4	10	3
P3V2								13	6	4	5	5	3	6	7
P3V3									13	5	3	4	7	7	6
P4V1										11	5	5	6	6	6
P4V2											8	5	6	8	5
P4V3												10	4	4	5
P5V1													13	8	5
P5V2														17	8
P5V3															12

Table 4. Quantitative measures: **D*** *calculated between scans of all viewers*

	P1 V1	P1 V2	P1 V3	P2 V1	P2 V2	P2 V3	P3 V1	P3 V2	P3 V3	P4 V1	P4 V2	P4 V3	P5 V1	P5 V2	P5 V3
P1V1	0	27	56	87	85	59	64	45	72	95	86	69	42	51	55
P1V2		0	53	80	78	48	80	54	81	112	93	86	49	62	56
P1V3			0	69	85	49	63	69	82	113	94	87	68	81	97
P2V1				0	36	44	76	78	95	128	111	106	105	104	124
P2V2					0	54	108	72	115	146	133	124	95	94	98
P2V3						0	82	68	83	114	83	80	79	64	82
P3V1							0	38	31	64	59	42	39	50	64
P3V2								0	51	82	69	60	33	30	52
P3V3									0	33	32	11	56	49	65
P4V1										0	39	34	87	72	96
P4V2											0	31	76	51	79
P4V3												0	61	40	62
P5V1													0	35	29
P5V2														0	38
P5V3															0

Table 5. Quantitative measures: **D⁺** *calculated between scans of all viewers*

	P1 V1	P1 V2	P1 V3	P2 V1	P2 V2	P2 V3	P3 V1	P3 V2	P3 V3	P4 V1	P4 V2	P4 V3	P5 V1	P5 V2	P5 V3
P1V1	**0**	**3**	**8**	**8**	**8**	**4**	**8**	**7**	**9**	**8**	**9**	**7**	**8**	**7**	**10**
P1V2		0	5	7	5	3	9	10	12	11	12	10	11	10	13
P1V3			0	8	6	4	10	11	13	12	13	11	12	11	14
P2V1				0	6	4	8	7	9	10	11	9	8	9	10
P2V2					0	4	8	9	11	10	11	9	6	7	8
P2V3						0	8	7	9	8	9	7	8	7	10
P3V1							0	3	3	4	7	3	4	5	4
P3V2								0	4	5	4	4	3	2	3
P3V3									0	1	4	2	5	6	5
P4V1										0	3	1	6	5	6
P4V2											0	4	7	4	7
P4V3												0	5	4	5
P5V1													0	3	2
P5V2														0	3
P5V3															0

from the multiple intrinsic features, (which are being measured implicitly through the distance measures). The following paragraphs will briefly outline a proposed fusion strategy.

The above three distance measures provide quantitative measures of the degree of similarity between any two gaze sequences. That is, each distance measure can provide a score or a measure of the likelihood that the gaze sequences are captured from the same person. As no single measure provides absolute certainty about the authentication or identification of a person, a fusion of the given measures may provide a more effective outcome (that is to perform classifier score fusion as opposed to classifier decision fusion). The assumption behind performing classifier score fusion is that complimentary information exists between the different distance measures being fused.

The fusion method employed here is a weighted linear fusion where the optimal weights utilised in the fusion are estimated using a linear logistic regression (LLR). The weighted fusion is of the form,

$$C_{Weight\_Sum} = \sum_{k=1}^{M} \beta_k C_k,$$

(5)

where β_k is the weight given to the kth classifier C_k.

The first stage in the fusion process is to normalise the distance scores using Z-score normalisation. This will set the mean and standard deviation of the score distributions to zero and unity respectively. This normalisation is a key stage as it ensures the creation of a consistent frame of reference from which the scores can be fused and is made under the assumption that the scores are normally distributed. The outputs of the normalisation are the scores with the same range of magnitude. Two properties of Z-score normalisation are exploited during the linear classifer score fusion. The first being that the resultant client scores will be displaced further from the imposter scores. The second is that there will be a reduction in the variance of the combined imposter scores.

Note that there exits a positive linear relationship between the value of the **D** distance measure and the likelihood that the gaze sequences are from the same person. For the remaining two distance measures, there is an inverse linear relationship. Thus, to bring all measures into the same behaviour, the **D** measure is adjusted as $1 - \mathbf{D}$.

The LLR method is chosen as it has a convex cost function and so will converge to a solution. The cost function which is to be minimised has the form,

$$C_{llr} = \frac{P}{K} \sum_{j=1}^{K} \log(1 + e^{-f_i - logitP}) + \frac{1-P}{L} \sum_{j=1}^{L} \log(1 + e^{-g_j - logitP})$$

(6)

where K is the number of true trials, L is the number of false trials, P is the synthetic prior (which by default is P = 0.5), f_i represents the fused true scores, g_i represents the fused false scores, and the logit function is of the form,

$$logit \quad P = \log \frac{P}{1-P}.$$

(7)

A package provided by Brummer (2005) is utilised for the implementation of this score fusion and the results of fusing the four distance measures together is provided in Table 6.

As illustrated in Table 6, there is once again a reasonably strong separation between the intra-class scores (highlighted) and the inter-class scores. This is further highlighted in Figure 9 which presents some simple box and whisker plots of the fused distance measures for both the intra-class variations and the inter-class variations. To demonstrate the recognition ability of this technique, a detection error trade-off plot is given in Figure 10. This method yielded an equal error rate of 13.33%. These results suggest that the fused use of simple distance measures offers another potential approach for identifying and

Table 6. Linear logistic regression results of the score fusion of the three distance measures

	P1 V1	P1 V2	P1 V3	P2 V1	P2 V2	P2 V3	P3 V1	P3 V2	P3 V3	P4 V1	P4 V2	P4 V3	P5 V1	P5 V2	P5 V3
P1V1	17.2	5.7	-3.0	-14.0	-13.5	-7.3	-7.6	-0.7	-8.9	-16.0	-14.0	-9.1	-0.9	-2.2	-5.5
P1V2		14.1	-2.2	-13.5	-12.5	-5.0	-14.0	-4.5	-13.5	-20.4	-17.3	-15.0	-5.0	-8.1	-7.3
P1V3			14.9	-10.1	-13.7	-4.8	-9.9	-10.1	-14.0	-21.7	-17.0	-14.7	-9.4	-11.7	-18.8
P2V1				13.4	1.1	-1.2	-11.9	-13.7	-17.1	-23.5	-22.4	-20.6	-18.6	-18.6	-24.7
P2V2					14.1	-4.5	-20.9	-12.7	-21.9	-28.8	-25.8	-23.7	-14.8	-14.0	-16.8
P2V3						11.8	-14.2	-11.2	-14.8	-21.7	-14.0	-14.3	-14.2	-7.9	-14.0
P3V1							18.0	1.4	4.7	-7.9	-8.1	-1.2	-1.5	0.1	-8.6
P3V2								16.4	-3.0	-12.7	-8.4	-6.1	-0.4	2.9	-2.2
P3V3									16.4	1.6	-0.4	6.2	-3.8	-2.2	-6.8
P4V1										14.9	-0.4	1.3	-12.7	-8.6	-15.0
P4V2											12.6	1.4	-10.2	-1.5	-11.7
P4V3												14.1	-7.3	-1.7	-6.8
P5V1													16.4	2.9	2.4
P5V2														19.5	2.1
P5V3															15.7

discriminating between viewers based on their gaze behaviour.

FUTURE TRENDS

The traditional biometric measures (such as fingerprint and face) can provide high recognition accuracies across large populations and databases. One of their biggest weaknesses, however, is that they are prone to spoof attacks due to their ease of artificial reproduction or counterfeiting. This is an unfortunate consequence of most biometrics being "non-secret". For example, a photo of a person's face can be easily used to foil a 2D facial recognition system, or a copy of a fingerprint can be used to foil a fingertip scanner. So although biometrics facilitate the identification or authentication of an individual with much stronger certainty, the consequence of identity theft involving biometrics is of much greater significance.

Perhaps one of the best applications for gaze in a biometric setting is its use within liveness detection. Liveness detection research is gaining much momentum recently due to its desirable property as an anti-spoofing measure for use in biometric applications (Kollreider et. al 2005). The gaze of a person has some strong properties which make it amenable to such a liveness test. There are also cases where the use of gaze as a liveness test in conjunction with other biometrics such as facial expression may provide strong motivations.

The properties usable for a liveness detection system can be categorised into three groups (Valencia & Horn 2003). These properties are discussed below along with their applicability to the use of gaze in a biometric system.

1. Intrinsic properties: are based on characteristics of a living biometric sample. In the context of a fingerprint, for example, one such possibility is to use the spectral characteristics of the skin such as its absorbance, transmittance and reflectance of electromagnetic radiation of different wavelengths (Drahansky 2008). Within

Figure 9. Box and whisker plots of the 5 intra-person fused scores and the total inter-person fused scores

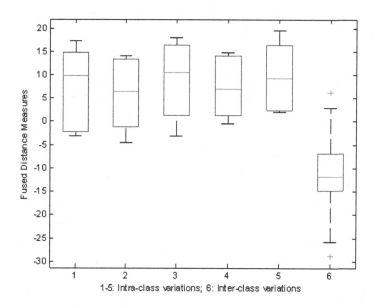

Figure 10. Detection-Error-Trade-off plot for the fusion of distance measures covert experiment yielding an equal error rate of 13.33%

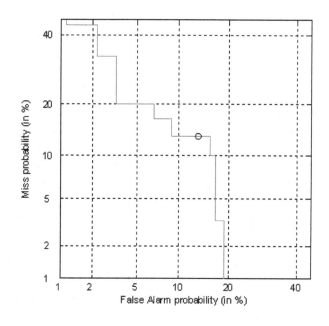

the context of gaze, the natural behaviour for viewing a scene or image consists of a sequence of brief gaze periods (typically 100-500ms) of visual concentration (fixations) at specific locations in the field of view, interspersed with two distinct types of eye movements - saccades and vergence. Depending on the environment of operation, if this typical fixation-saccade process (or fixation-saccade-vergence process) is not present or detected, or is abnormally removed from this typical process, then this may be a clear indication that the gaze is not from a living person.

2. Involuntarily generated signals: are spontaneously generated from a living body. A typical example is the pulse and this can be exploited as a biometric in its own right, such as the eigenPulse (Irvine et. al 2008), in addition to providing a liveness test. In the context of gaze, the existence of involuntarily generated signals are less clear. One possibility may include eye-blinking which is generally an involuntary (or unconscious) behaviour. However, this can be controlled consciously as well.

3. Responses to a stimulus: is perhaps the best opportunity for gaze to be utilised as a liveness test and there are several possibilities to achieve this: a moving object can be provided as a test for the gaze of a viewer to follow that object; a flash at a localised region in an otherwise static image can provide an opportunity to automatically direct the attention of a person's gaze to that location; a lighting source, either visible or infra-red, can be provided to test for some or all four of the Purkinje reflections (Crane 1994); an audio message can be provided to ask the person to direct their gaze in a certain manner; changing lighting conditions can also be used to measure the change in the iris of a person.

CONCLUSION

This chapter has presented how the use of visual attention characteristics of a person can be employed as a behavioural biometric for the authentication or identification of an individual. The visual attention characteristics of a person can be easily monitored by observing where and when a person's gaze is directed. Establishing this fixation-saccade path followed by the viewer through gaze tracking provides strong insights into a person's internal visual attention process through observing what captured their attention and how they perceive a visual scene they are viewing. It is also possible for these gaze behaviours to be directed by overt (conscious) or covert (subconscious) attentional processes. Both of these attentional processes have been exploited to create two different means of generating a gaze-based biometric for personal identification.

Methods to quantify the spatial and temporal patterns established by the viewer for both overt and covert behaviours were proposed. The former entailed a simple PIN-like approach to develop an independent gaze signature. The experiments reported validated the acceptable performance of the approach and demonstrated that it is comparable with conventional PIN based user authentication. Covert gaze viewing behaviours were captured through three proposed techniques: an 'eigenGaze' technique; a discriminant analysis technique; and a fusion of distance measures technique. These techniques were presented as three possible candidate techniques for classifying people's identity based on their covert gaze behaviour and represented three different methods of identifying and quantifying the commonalities that exist between different scans of the same observer and between observers.

The 'eigenGaze' technique involved a Principal Component Analysis or eigen-decomposition approach which was applied to clusters of gaze positions. The Linear Discriminant Analysis technique utilised features of the mean duration of each cluster and the mean number of revisits that were made to each cluster. The Fusion of Distance Measures technique involved three distance measures which aimed to assess and quantify the commonality of fixations and other characteristics of the visual attention process. These features were chosen based on the assumption that they are highly linked to a person's higher cognitive, neurological, and psychological processes (i.e. their visual attention processes) and thus could be utilised as a behavioural biometric.

Experimental results suggest that all three proposed techniques for covert gaze can provide a simple and effective biometric for classifying a small database of individuals. The discriminant analysis technique yielded perfect classification while the 'eigenGaze' and fusion of distance measures techniques yielded equal error rates of 8.9% and 13.33% respectively. Experimental results also reveal that the gaze of a highly trained specialised viewer (such as a radiologist) cannot be utilised for biometric recognition as the highly structured viewing process actually removes the variability required to recognise a person. All experimental results involved a small database of viewers. Further research is required to assess and confirm the true capability and behaviour of these proposed gaze biometrics for larger populations.

Future work in this area could examine the extension of the visual attention biometrics in a number of ways: firstly, experimental results could be enhanced through the testing and analysis of discriminability of gaze features of databases of a larger number of viewers and images to provide a richer set of base data; more sophisticated gaze signatures and metrics could be proposed which use more subtle and sophisticated features of gaze sequences; techniques could be investigated to cater for viewer behaviour changes over time and under stress; techniques to fuse gaze biometrics with other existing biometrics could be investigated; methods to effectively generate liveness tests based on gaze can also be pursued.

The covert viewing behaviour of a person certainly does not always comply with a set of known requirements. Thus, the intra-person variability of gaze behaviour makes the development of a stable behavioural biometric particularly challenging. Consequently, ongoing research into this biometric is likely to continue for some time to come.

REFERENCES

Alexandre, T. (1997). Biometrics on smart cards: An approach to keyboard behavioural signature. *Future Generation Computer Systems, 13*, 19–26. doi:10.1016/S0167-739X(97)00005-8

Ashbourn, J. (2000). *Biometrics: Advanced identity verification: The complete guide*. London: Springer.

Beauchamp, M. S., Lee, K. E., Haxby, J. V., & Martin, A. (2002). Parallel visual motrion processing streams for manipulable objects and human movements. *Neuron, 34*, 149–159. doi:10.1016/S0896-6273(02)00642-6

Belardinelli, A., Pirri, F., & Carbone, A. (2007). Bottom-up gaze shifts and fixations learning by imitation. *IEEE Transactions on Systems, Man, and Cybernetics . Part B, 37*(2), 256–271.

Braun, J., & Sagi, D. (1990, July). Vision outside the focus of attention. *Perception & Psychophysics, 48*(1), 45–58.

Bregler, C., & Konig, Y. (1994, April). "Eigenlips" for robust speech recognition. In . *Proceedings of the IEEE International Conference on Acoustics, Speech, and Signal Processing, 2*, 669–672.

Broadbent, D. E. (1977). The hidden preattentive process. *The American Psychologist, 32*, 109–118. doi:10.1037/0003-066X.32.2.109

Brummer, N. (2005). Tools for fusion and calibration of automatic speaker detection systems. Retrieved from http://www.dsp.sun.ac.za/.nbrummer/focal/index.htm

Campos, T. E., Feris, R. S., & Cesar, R. M. Jr. (2000, April). Eigenfaces vs. eigeneyes: First steps toward performance assessment of representarions for face recognition. ([]. Springer-Verlag Press.]. *LNAI, 1793*, 197–206.

Crane, H. (1994). The purkinje image eyetracker, image stabilization, and related forms of stimulus manipulation. In D. Kelly (Ed.), *Visual science and engineering: Models and applications* (pp. 13–89). New York: Marcel Dekker, Inc.

Crowley, J. (1997). Vision for man-machine interaction. *Robotics and Autonomous Systems, 19*, 347–358. doi:10.1016/S0921-8890(96)00061-9

Drahansky, M. (2008, August). Experiments with skin resistance and temperature for liveness detection. In *Proceedings of the International Conference on Intelligent Information Hiding and Multimedia Signal Processing* (pp. 1075–1079).

Duchowski, A. (2003). *Eye tracking methodology: Theory and practice*. London: Springer.

Goldberg, J., & Kotval, X. (1999). Computer interface evaluation using eye movements: Methods and constructs. *International Journal of Industrial Ergonomics, 24*, 631–645. doi:10.1016/S0169-8141(98)00068-7

Hastie, T., Tibshirani, R., & Friedman, J. H. (2001). *The elements of statistical learning: Data mining, inference, and prediction*. Springer.

Hoffman, J. E., & Subramaniam, B. (1995). The role of visual attention in saccadic eye movements. *Perception & Psychophysics, 57*, 787–795.

Hooker, C. I., Paller, K. A., Gitelman, D. R., Parrish, T. B., Mesulam, M.-M., & Reber, P. J. (2003, July). Brain networks for analyzing eye gaze. *Brain Research. Cognitive Brain Research, 17*(2), 406–418. doi:10.1016/S0926-6410(03)00143-5

Irvine, J. M., Israel, S. A., Scruggs, W. T., & Worek, W. J. (2008, November). EigenPulse: Robust human identification from cardiovascular function. *Pattern Recognition, 41*(11), 3427–3435. doi:10.1016/j.patcog.2008.04.015

Itti, L., & Koch, C. (2000). A saliency-based search mechanism for overt and covert shifts of visual attention. *Vision Research, 40*, 1489–1506. doi:10.1016/S0042-6989(99)00163-7

Itti, L., & Koch, C. (2001). Feature combination strategies for saliency-based visual attention systems. *Journal of Electronic Imaging, 10*(1), 161–169. doi:10.1117/1.1333677

Jain, A. K. (2007, November). Biometric recognition: Overview and recent advances. ([]. Heidelberg: Springer Berlin.]. *LNCS, 4756*, 13–19.

Javal, L. E. (1879). Essai sur la physiologie de la lecture. *Annales d'Oculistique, 82*, 242–253.

Ji, Q., & Yang, X. (2002, October). Real-time eye, gaze, and face pose tracking for monitoring driver vigilance. *Real-Time Imaging, 8*(5), 357–377. doi:10.1006/rtim.2002.0279

Kar-Han, T., Kriegman, D. J., & Ahuja, N. (2002, December). Appearance-based eye gaze estimation. In *Proceedings of the Sixth IEEE Workshop on Applications of Computer Vision* (pp. 191–195).

Kasprowski, P., & Ober, J. (2004). Eye movement in biometrics. In *Proceedings of Biometric Authentication Workshop, European Conference on Computer Vision in Prague 2004* (LNCS 3087). Berlin: Springer-Verlag.

Kollreider, K., Fronthaler, H., & Bigun, J. (2005, October). Evaluating liveness by face images and the structure tensor. In *Proceedings of the Fourth IEEE Workshop on Automatic Identification Advanced Technologies* (pp. 75–80).

Kumar, A. N., Leigh, R. J., & Ramat, S. (2001, October). The brainstem switch for gaze shifts in humans. In *Proceedings of the 23rd Annual International Conference of the IEEE Engineering in Medicine and Biology Society* (Vol. 1, pp. 869–872).

Maeder, A., & Fookes, C. (2003, December). A visual attention approach to personal identification. In *Proceedings of the Eighth Australian and New Zealand Intelligent Information Systems Conference,* Sydney, Australia (pp. 55–60).

Maeder, A., Fookes, C., & Sridharan, S. (2004, October). Gaze based user authentication for personal computer applications. In *Proceedings of the 2004 International Symposium on Intelligent Multimedia, Video, and Speech Processing*, Hong Kong (pp. 727–730).

Maeder, A. J. (2005, February). The image importance approach to human vision based image quality characterization. *Pattern Recognition Letters, 26*, 347–354. doi:10.1016/j.patrec.2004.10.018

Matsumoto, Y. Ogasawara, T., & Zelinsky, A. (2000, October). Behavior recognition based on head pose and gaze direction measurement. In *Proceedings of the IEEE/RSJ International Intelligent Robots and Systems* (Vol. 3, pp. 2127–2132).

Minato, T., Shimada, M., Itakura, S., Lee, K., & Ishiguro, H. (2005, July). Does gaze reveal the human likeness of an android? In *Proceedings of the 4th International Conference on Development and Learning* (pp. 106–111).

Noton, D., & Stark, L. (1971). Eye movements and visual perception. *Scientific American, 224*(6), 35–43.

Peters, R. J., Iyer, A., Itti, L., & Koch, C. (2005, August). Components of bottom-up gaze allocation in natural images. *Vision Research, 45*(18), 2397–2416. doi:10.1016/j.visres.2005.03.019

Phillips, J., Flynn, P., Scruggs, T., Bowyer, K., Chang, J., & Hoffman, K. (2005). Overview of the face recognition grand challenge. In . *Proceedings of IEEE Conference of Computer Vision and Pattern Recognition, 1*, 947–954.

Ratha, N., Connell, J., & Bolle, R. (2003). Biometrics break-ins and band-aids. *Pattern Recognition Letters, 24*, 2105–2113. doi:10.1016/S0167-8655(03)00080-1

Rizzolatti, G., Riggio, L., Dascola, I., & Umilta, C. (1987). Reorienting attention across the horizontal and vertical meridians-evidence in favor of a premotor theory of attention. *Neuropsychologia, 25*(1A), 31–40. doi:10.1016/0028-3932(87)90041-8

Robinson, P. E., & Clarke, W. A. (2007, March). Comparison of principal component analysis and linear discriminant analysis for face recognition. In *AFRICON* (pp. 1–6).

Roux, C., & Coatrieux, J.-L. (Eds.). (1997). *Contemporary perspectives in three-dimensional biomedical imaging* (Vol. 30 of Studies in Health Technology and Informatics). The Netherlands: IOS Press.

Schuckers, S. A. C., Schmid, N. A., Abhyankar, A., Dorairaj, V., Boyce, C. K., & Hornak, L. A. (2007, October). On techniques for angle compensation in nonideal iris recognition. *IEEE Transactions on Systems, Man, and Cybernetics . Part B, 37*(5), 1176–1190.

Silver, D. L., & Biggs, A. (2006). Keystroke and eye-tracking biometrics for user identification. In *IC-AI*, 344–348.

Treisman, A. (1964). Selective attention in man. *British Medical Bulletin, 20*, 12–16.

Treisman, A., & Gelade, G. (1980). A feature integration theory of attention. *Cognitive Psychology*, *12*, 97–136. doi:10.1016/0010-0285(80)90005-5

Turk, M., & Pentland, A. (1991). Eigenfaces for recognition. *Journal of Cognitive Neuroscience*, *3*(1), 71–86. doi:10.1162/jocn.1991.3.1.71

Valencia, V. S., & Horn, C. (2003). Biometric liveness testing. In *Biometrics* (pp. 139–149). Berkeley, CA: Osborne McGraw Hill.

Wandell, B. (1995). *Foundations of vision*. Sunderland, MA: Sinauer Associates.

Yarbus, A. (1967). *Eye movements and vision*. New York: Plenum Press.

Yoo, D. H., & Chung, M. J. (2004, May). Nonintrusive eye gaze estimation without knowledge of eye pose. In *Proceedings of the Sixth IEEE International Conference on Automatic Face and Gesture Recognition* (pp. 785–790).

Young, L., & Sheena, D. (1975). Survey of eye movement recording methods. *Behavior Research Methods and Instrumentation*, *7*(5), 397–439.

Chapter 13
Speaker Verification and Identification

Minho Jin
Korea Advanced Institute of Science and Technology, Republic of Korea

Chang D. Yoo
Korea Advanced Institute of Science and Technology, Republic of Korea

ABSTRACT

A speaker recognition system verifies or identifies a speaker's identity based on his/her voice. It is considered as one of the most convenient biometric characteristic for human machine communication. This chapter introduces several speaker recognition systems and examines their performances under various conditions. Speaker recognition can be classified into either speaker verification or speaker identification. Speaker verification aims to verify whether an input speech corresponds to a claimed identity, and speaker identification aims to identify an input speech by selecting one model from a set of enrolled speaker models. Both the speaker verification and identification system consist of three essential elements: feature extraction, speaker modeling, and matching. The feature extraction pertains to extracting essential features from an input speech for speaker recognition. The speaker modeling pertains to probabilistically modeling the feature of the enrolled speakers. The matching pertains to matching the input feature to various speaker models. Speaker modeling techniques including Gaussian mixture model (GMM), hidden Markov model (HMM), and phone n-grams are presented, and in this chapter, their performances are compared under various tasks. Several verification and identification experimental results presented in this chapter indicate that speaker recognition performances are highly dependent on the acoustical environment. A comparative study between human listeners and an automatic speaker verification system is presented, and it indicates that an automatic speaker verification system can outperform human listeners. The applications of speaker recognition are summarized, and finally various obstacles that must be overcome are discussed.

DOI: 10.4018/978-1-60566-725-6.ch013

INTRODUCTION

Speaker recognition can be classified into either 1) speaker verification or 2) speaker identification (Furui, 1997; J. Campbell, 1997; Bimbot et al., 2004). Speaker verification aims to verify whether an input speech corresponds to the claimed identity. Speaker identification aims to identify an input speech by selecting one model from a set of enrolled speaker models: in some cases, speaker verification will follow speaker identification in order to validate the identification result (Park & Hazen, 2002). Speaker verification is one case of biometric authentication, where users provide their biometric characteristics as passwords. Biometric characteristics can be obtained from deoxyribonucleic acid (DNA), face shape, ear shape, fingerprint, gait pattern, hand-vein pattern, hand-and-finger geometry, iris scan, retinal scan, signature, voice, etc. These are often compared under the following criteria (Jain, Ross, & Prabhakar, 2004):

- **Universality:** the biometric characteristic should be universally available to everyone.
- **Distinctiveness:** the biometric characteristics of different people should be distinctive.
- **Permanence:** the biometric characteristic should be invariant over a period of time that depends on the applications
- **Performance:** the biometric authentication system based on the biometric characteristic should be accurate, and its computational cost should be small.
- **Acceptability:** the result of a biometric authentication system based on certain biometric characteristic should be accepted to all users.

One additional criterion that should be included is circumvention which is given by

- **Circumvention:** biometric characteristics that are vulnerable to malicious attacks are leading to low circumvention.

High biometric characteristic scores on all above criteria except circumvention are preferable in real applications. As shown in Figure 1, voice is reported to have medium universality. However, in many cases, voice is the only biometric characteristic available: for example, when a person is talking over the phone. The distinctiveness of voice is considered low, and very often a speaker verification system can be fooled by an impostor mimicking the voice of an enrolled. For this, many features such as prosodic and idiosyncratic features have been incorporated to improve the speaker recognition system. The permanence of voice is low since a speaker's voice can vary under various situations, physical conditions, etc. By incorporating on-line speaker adaptation techniques that adapt a speaker's voice change on-line, the permanence of voice can be improved. We discuss the performance of a speaker recognition system in the latter part of this chapter.

Figure 1. Properties of voice: voice can be universally available for every person, and its authentication result is acceptable. However, its performance in terms of accuracy is known to be slightly inferior to that of other biometric characteristics

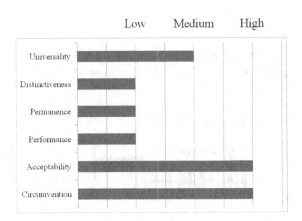

Figure 2. Conventional speaker verification system: the system extracts features from recorded voice, and it computes its matching score given the claimed speaker's model. Finally, an accept/reject decision is made based on the matching score

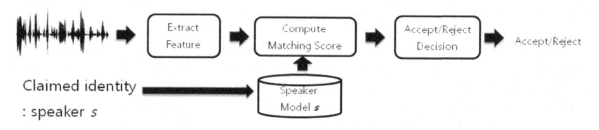

BACKGROUND

Common Tasks of Speaker Recognition

Speaker recognition system verifies or identifies a speaker's identity based on his/her speech. The length of speech data varies according to the application. For example, if an application is designed to identify a speaker when he/she tells his/her name, the input speech data will be 1-2 second long. The speech data is recorded using microphones in various environments. The types of microphone, environments (e.g., telephone communication, clean sound booth) can affect the speaker recognition performance. For this reason, several benchmark databases are collected to evaluate the performance of speaker recognition algorithms in various conditions: some examples of benchmark databases will be described in the latter of this chapter.

Speaker Verification

Figure 2 illustrates a conventional speaker verification system. A speaker verification system takes the speech of an unknown speaker with his/her claimed identity, and it determines whether the claimed identity matches the speech. The claimed identity can be fed into the system using various channels such as keyboard, identity card, etc. To verify whether the input speech matches the claimed identity, the claimed speaker's model must be enrolled beforehand as shown in Figure 3. As the amount of enrollment data increases, the performance of speaker verification system usually improves, but the speaker may feel uncomfortable with long enrollment process. Thus, in many applications, the enrollment is performed by adapting a speaker-independent model into an enrolled speaker's model using speaker adaptation techniques.

Figure 3. Enrollment of a target speaker model; each speaker's model is enrolled by training his/her model from features extracted from his/her speech data

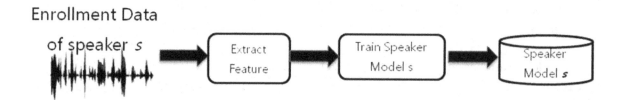

Speaker Identification

Figure 4 illustrates a conventional speaker identification system. A speaker identification system only takes the speech of an unknown speaker, and it determines which enrolled speaker best matches the speech. The speaker identification system finds the best matching speaker among the enrolled speakers, and it may be that the unknown speaker is not enrolled. For this reason, in many systems, speaker identification is followed by speaker verification. For example, the MIT-LCS ASR-based speaker recognition system first performs speaker identification and then performs speaker verification where the identification result is used as a claimed speaker identity (Hazen, Jones, Park, Kukolich, & Reynolds, 2003).

Operation Modes of Speaker Recognition

The speaker recognition system can operate in either a text-dependent (TD) mode or a text-independent (TI) mode. In the TD mode, the user speaks a pre-defined or prompted text transcription. In the TI mode, the user is allowed to speak freely. Since the TD mode provides the speaker recognition system with extra information, thus it generally performs better than in the TI mode. Various studies have been performed in order to reduce the performance gap between the two operation modes (Park & Hazen, 2002; Che, Lin, & Yuk, 1996; Newman, Gillick, Ito, Mcallaster, & Peskin, 1996; Weber, Peskin, Newman, Emmanuel, & Gillick, 2000).

Text-Dependent Speaker Recognition
In a TD mode, a speaker recognition system can be fooled by recording and play-back of pre-defined speech of an enrolled speaker. To

Figure 4. Conventional speaker identification system: the speaker identification system selects the best-matched speaker's model among enrolled speaker models

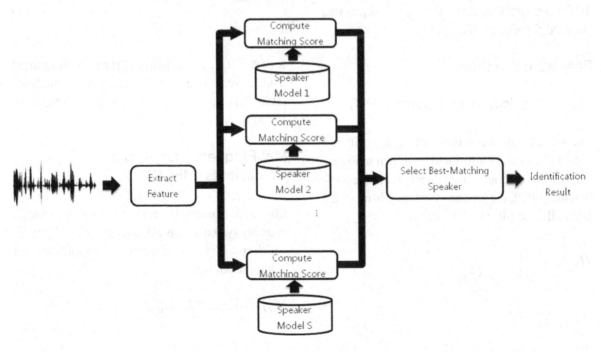

defend a speaker recognition system from such malicious attack, the system can request the user to utter a randomly prompted text. In most cases, a TD speaker recognition system outperforms a TI speaker recognition system since additional information (text transcription) is provided (Reynolds, 2002a). However, a TD speaker recognition system cannot be used when the true-underlying transcription is not provided, as in the situation when some is talking freely over the phone.

Text-Independent Speaker Recognition

A TI speaker recognition system does not require true-underlying transcription of an input speech. This may be useful for a forensic speaker recognition system such as identifying a speaker of a wiretapped conversation or in human-robot interface.

SPEAKER RECOGNITION SYSTEM

Both the speaker verification and identification system extract features from an input speech then computes matching score between enrolled speaker and the input speech. This section outlines the features and speaker modeling techniques that are used for speaker recognition.

Feature Extraction

Linear Predictive Coefficients (LPC)

The speech signal can be modeled as a filtered output of an excitation signal as shown in Figure 5. When computing P-order linear predictive coefficients (LPC), the human vocal tract is modeled as an all-pole filter as follows:

$$H(z) = \frac{S(z)}{E(z)} = \frac{1}{1 - \sum_{p=1}^{P} a_k z^{-k}},$$

(1)

where $S(z)$ and $E(z)$ are the z-transforms of the speech signal $s[n]$ and its excitation signal $e[n]$, respectively. For each frame of an input speech, the LPC parameters $\{a_k\}$ are computed and used for speaker recognition. Using the all-pole model, a speech signal $s[n]$ can be written as follows:

$$s[n] = \sum_{k=1}^{P} a_k s[n-k] + e[n].$$

(2)

Let $\hat{s}[n] = \sum_{k=1}^{P} a_k s[n-k]$ be the estimate of $s[n]$. Then, the mean squared error (MSE) of the estimate is given as follows:

$$E = \sum_n (s[n] - \hat{s}[n])^2$$

$$= \sum_n (s[n] - \sum_{k=1}^{P} a_k s[n-k])^2.$$

(3)

The MSE is convex function of a_k, and the minimum of equation (3) is achieved with a_k satisfying the following condition:

$$\sum_{k=1}^{P} a_k \sum_n s_{n-k} s_{n-i} = \sum_n s_n s_{n-i}$$

(4)

for $i = 1, 2, ..., P$. Equation (4) can be computed using covariance and autocorrelation methods (Huang, Acero, & Hon, 2001; Rabiner & Schafer, 1978)

Mel-Frequency Cepstrum Coefficients (MFCC)

Empirical studies have shown that the human auditory system resolves frequencies non-linearly, and the non-linear resolution can be approximated using the Mel-scale which is given by

$$M(f) = 1127.01048 \cdot \log_e f$$

(5)

Figure 5. Vocal tract modeling in linear predictive coefficients: the speech signal is modeled as a filtered output of a vocal chords excitation signal, where the filter is determined by the shape of his/her vocal tract

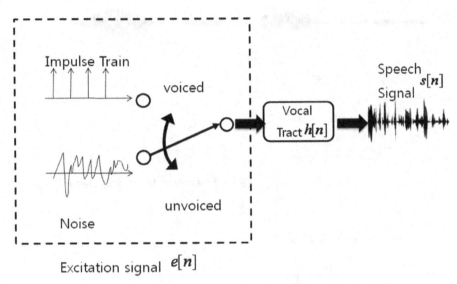

where f is a frequency (Volkman, Stevens, & Newman, 1937). This indicates that the human auditory system is more sensitive to frequency difference in lower frequency band than in higher frequency band. Figure 6 illustrates the process of extracting Mel-frequency cepstrum coefficients (MFCCs) with triangular filters that are equally-spaced in Mel-scale. An input speech is transformed using discrete Fourier transform, and the filter-bank energies are computed using triangular filters. The log-values of the filter-bank energies are transformed using discrete cosine transform (DCT). Finally, the M-dimensional MFCCs are extracted by taking M-DCT coefficients. Previous research has reported that using MFCCs is beneficial for both speaker and speech recognition (Davis & Mermelstein, 1980), and MFCCs are used in many speech and speaker recognition systems (Choi & Lee, 2002; Davis & Mermelstein, 1980; Hirsch & Pearce, 2000; Li, Chang, & Dai, 2002; Milner, 2002; Molla & Hirose, 2004; Pan & Waibel, 2000; Reynolds, Quatieri, & Dunn, 2000; Xiang & Berger, 2003; Zilca, 2002)

Prosodic Features

Prosodic features include pitch and its dynamic variations, inter-pause statistics, phone duration, etc. (Shriberg, 2007) Very often, prosodic features are extracted with larger frame size than acoustical features since prosodic features exist over a long speech segment such as syllables. Figure 7 illustrates the waveform, spectrum, pitch-contour and energy-contour from speaker A and B. Two speakers' prosodic features (pitch and energy-contours) are different even though two speakers are uttering the same sentence "she had your dark ...". The pitch and energy-contours change slowly compared to the spectrum, which implies that the variation can be captured over a long speech segment. Many literatures reported that prosodic features usually do not outperform acoustical features but incorporating prosodic features in addition to acoustical features can improve speaker recognition performance (Shriberg, 2007; Sönmez, Shriberg, Heck, & Weintraub, 1998; Peskin et al., 2003; Campbell, Reynolds, & Dunn, 2003; Reynolds et al., 2003).

Figure 6. Extraction of MFCCs: MFCCs are extracted based on the band-energy with triangular filters

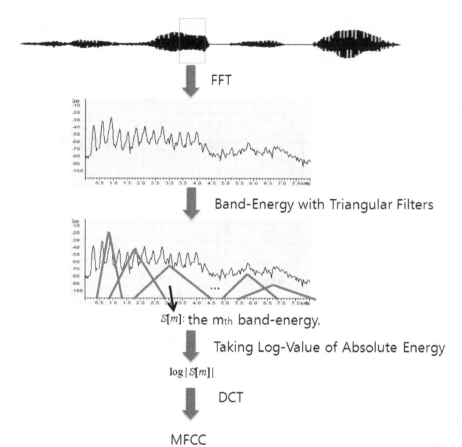

Idiolectal Features

The idiolectal feature is motivated by the fact that people usually use idiolectal information to recognize speakers. In telephone conversation corpus, Doddington (2001) reported enrolled speakers can be verified not using acoustical features that are extracted from a speech signal but using idiolectal feature that are observed in true-underlying transcription of speech. The phonetic speaker verification, motivated by Doddington (2001)'s work, creates a speaker using his/her phone n-gram probabilities that are obtained using multiple-language speech recognizers (Andrews, Kohler, & Campbell, 2001).

Speaker Model and Matching Score

Gaussian Mixture Model (GMM)

The speaker model can be trained as a Gaussian mixture model (GMM) with the expectation-maximization (EM) algorithm. When recognizing an input speech, the system extracts from a T-length input speech, and the matching score is computed as follows:

$$S_{GMM}(\mathbf{x_1}\mathbf{x_2}...\mathbf{x}_T, \Theta_s) = \prod_{t=1}^{T} p(\mathbf{x}_t \mid \Theta_s),$$

(6)

Figure 7. Waveform, spectrum, pitch-contour and energy-contour of the same sentence from different speakers: patterns from pitch or energy contour changes slowly compared to patterns from spectrum

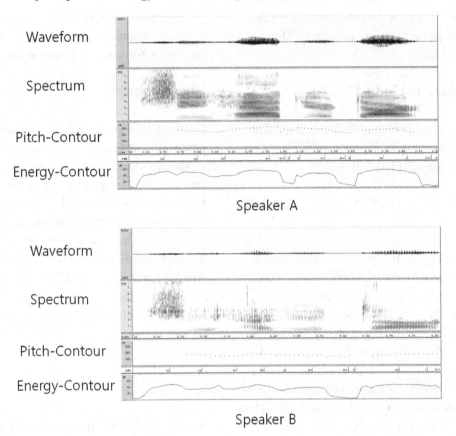

where Θ_s and x_t are a set of GMM parameters of speaker s and the tth feature vector of D dimension, respectively. The GMM parameter Θ_s includes the mean $\mu_{k,s}$ and variance vectors $\Sigma_{k,s}$ of the kth Gaussian kernel, and its weight $w_{k,s}$. Using this, the likelihood of a GMM can be computed as follows:

$$p(\mathbf{x}_t \mid \Theta_s) = \sum_{k=1}^{K} w_{k,s} \frac{1}{(2\pi)^{D/2} |\Sigma_{k,s}|^{1/2}} e^{-\frac{(\mathbf{x}_t - \mu_{k,s})^T \Sigma_{k,s}^{-1}(\mathbf{x}_t - \mu_{k,s})}{2}}$$

(7)

In the GMM-UBM (Gaussian Mixture Model – Universal Background Model) algorithm, the speaker model is adapted from the UBM which is a GMM trained using many speakers' speech (Reynolds, Quatieri, & Dunn, 2000). Mariethoz and Bengio (2002) compared the performances of GMM-UBM systems with various speaker adaptation techniques, where the maximum a posterior (MAP) adaptation performed the best: for detailed explanation on the MAP adaptation algorithm, please refer to (Gauvain & Lee, 1994). The GMM-UBM is a state of the art algorithm for TI speaker identification and verification. The GMM-UBM performs well with the small amount of enrollment data, say 2 minutes, and its computational cost is relatively small compared to other algorithms using a hidden Markov models (HMMs). The GMM-UBM is intrinsically well-fitted for a TI mode since the GMM is trained without transcription of speech data (Reynolds, et al, 2000). Nevertheless, it does not imply that the GMM cannot be used for a TD mode. For example, text-constrained GMM-UBM system incorporated GMMs trained on different word groups in order to improve the speaker verification performance (Sturim, Reynolds, Dunn, & Quatieri, 2002).

Hidden Markov Model (HMM)

The HMM is usually used to model each speaker's phonetic units or syllabic units. In a TD mode, the score is computed as follows:

$$S_{HMM,TD}(x_1 x_2 \ldots x_T, \Lambda_s) = p(x_1 x_2 \ldots x_T, Q \mid \Lambda_s) \quad (8)$$

where Λ_s and Q are the set of HMM parameters that are trained on the enrollment data of speaker s and a true-underlying transcription of $x_1 x_2 \ldots x_T$, respectively. The HMM can be trained using enrollment data with Baum-Welch algorithm, and the likelihood of $x_1 x_2 \ldots x_T$ and Q given Λ_s can be computed using forward, backward and Viterbi algorithms: for mathematical details, please refer to (Huang, et al., 2001; Rabiner & Schafer, 1978) for Baum-Welch algorithm and (Huang, et al., 2001; Rabiner & Schafer., 1978; Woodland, Leggetter, Odell, Valtchev, & Young, 1995) for likelihood computation. For a TI mode operation, researchers have used a large-vocabulary continuous speaker recognition (LVCSR) system to generate 1-best transcription Q_{1b}, and the matching score is computed as follows (Hazen, et al., 2003; Newman, Gillick, Ito, Mcallaster, & Peskin, 1996; Weber, et al., 2000):

$$S_{HMM,TI-1b}(x_1 x_2 \ldots x_T, \Lambda_s) = p(x_1 x_2 \ldots x_T, Q_{1b} \mid \Lambda_s) \quad (9)$$

Recently, it was reported that incorporating syllable lattice-decoding can be effective for speaker verification when Q_{1b} is highly erroneous (Jin, Soong, & Yoo, 2007). The syllable lattice from the LVCSR was incorporated in the matching score as follows:

$$S_{HMM,TI-L}(x_1 x_2 \ldots x_T, \Lambda_s) = p(x_1 x_2 \ldots x_T, L_X \mid \Lambda_s) \quad (10)$$

Where L_X is the syllable lattice decoded from $x_1 x_2 \ldots x_T$, where the likelihood is computed using the lattice forward-backward algorithm.

Phone n-grams

Unlike previous modeling techniques that are based on acoustical feature vector sequence $x_1 x_2 \ldots x_T$, speaker-dependent phone n-gram probabilities can be used for speaker verification (Andrews, Kohler, Campbell, & Godfrey, 2001). Very often, phone n-gram probabilities are computed using phone sequences created by phone recognizers that are trained on several languages. For example, Andrews et al. (2001) used six phone recognizers of English, German, Hindi, Japanese, Mandarin and Spanish. The enrolled speaker model is a set of phone n-gram probabilities which are given by

$$\Xi_s = \{\xi_{l,s}\} \quad (11)$$

where s and l are the indexes of speaker and language, respectively. Let Γ_l be the set of phone n-gram types in language l. Then, $\xi_{l,s}$ is defined as follows:

$$\xi_{l,s} = \{H_{l,s}(w) \mid w \in \Gamma_l\} \quad (12)$$

where $H_{l,s}(w)$ is given by

$$H_{l,s}(\mathbf{w}) = \frac{N_{l,s}(\mathbf{w})}{\sum_{\mathbf{w'} \in \Gamma_l} N_{l,s}(\mathbf{w'})}, \quad (13)$$

and where $N_{l,s}(w')$ is the number of phone n-gram w' in the recognition results of speaker s's enrollment data using the phone recognizer for language l. The matching score of speaker s can be computed as follows:

$$S_{PHN}(\mathbf{x_1 x_2}...\mathbf{x}_T, \Xi_s) = \sum_l \alpha_l \frac{\sum\limits_{\mathbf{w} \in \Gamma_l} c_l(\mathbf{x_1 x_2}...\mathbf{x}_T, \mathbf{w})^{1-d} H_{l,s}(\mathbf{w})}{\sum\limits_{\mathbf{w} \in \Gamma_l} c_l(\mathbf{x_1 x_2}...\mathbf{x}_T, \mathbf{w})^{1-d}},$$

(14)

where α_l and d are a weight for language l and a discounting factor between 0 and 1, respectively. In (0.13), $c_l(x_1 x_2 ... x_T, W)$ is a frequency count of w $\in \Gamma_l$ in the decoded result of $x_1 x_2 ... x_T$. Recently, it was reported that incorporating the phone-lattice decoding can improve the phonetic speaker recognition, where the phone n-grams are extracted not from the 1-best recognition result but from the phone lattice-decoding (Hatch, Barbara Peskin, & Stolcke, 2005).

Support-Vector Machine (SVM)

In a two-class SVM, an input feature vector is classified into either class 0 or class 1 using a discriminant function below

$$f(\mathbf{x}_i) = \sum_{l=0}^{L-1} \alpha_l t_l K(\mathbf{x}_i, \mathbf{u}_l) + d$$

(15)

where u_l and t_l are the lth support vector trained using training data and its label. Here, t_l is -1 if the support vector u_l is in class 0, and t_l is 1 if the support vector u_l is in class 1. The weight α_l is trained with constraints of $\alpha_l > 0$ and $\sum_{l=0}^{L-1} \alpha_l t_l = 0$: for detailed explanation on the SVM, please refer to (Scholkopf & Smola, 2002). The kernel $K(\cdot, \cdot)$ is a pre-defined kernel function. Schmidt and Gish (1996) proposed a speaker recognition system with speaker-dependent SVMs that are trained on enrolled speakers' acoustical features. Motivated by the extreme success of GMM-UBM in speaker recognition, Wan & Renals (2005) proposed to use

the Fisher-kernel for a GMM score $S_{GMM}(\mathbf{x_1 x_2}...\mathbf{x}_T, \Theta_s)$ and its derivatives with respect to Θ_s. Given the set of all input feature vectors X = [x_0, x_1, ..., x_{T-1}], the output of the SVM can be used as the likelihood of a target speaker s as follows:

$$S_{SVM,WAN}(\mathbf{X} | \{\alpha_l, t_l, \mathbf{u}_l\})$$
$$= f(\mathbf{X})$$
$$= \sum_{l=0}^{L-1} \alpha_l t_l K(\mathbf{X}, \mathbf{u}_l) + d,$$

(16)

where the kernel can be a Fisher kernel defined on the score space as follows:

$$K(X, u_l) = \psi_s(X) \bullet \psi_s(u_l)$$

(17)

and where

$$\psi_s(\mathbf{X}) = \begin{bmatrix} \nabla_{\Theta_s} \log p(\mathbf{X} | \Theta_s) \\ \log p(\mathbf{X} | \Theta_s) \end{bmatrix}$$

(18)

By using the Fisher kernel, the input feature vector is mapped into a hyper plane where the mapped feature vector is more sparsely distributed than that in the original feature vector space (Jaakkola & Haussler, 1998).

Figure 8 illustrates the system using the SVM for GMM parameters proposed by Campbell et al (2006). Given input feature vectors, the system first adapts the UBM; the UBM is trained as a GMM. The supervector of the adapted GMM, which is a concatenation of mean parameters of all Gaussian kernels in the adapted GMM, is used an input to the SVM. The experimental results have shown that incorporating the GMM parameters into the SVM can improve the speaker verification performance.

In the phonetic speaker recognition, where the speaker model is trained as phone n-grams, (W. Campbell, J. Campbell, Reynolds, Jones, & Leek,

Figure 8. SVM based on GMM supervector for speaker recognition

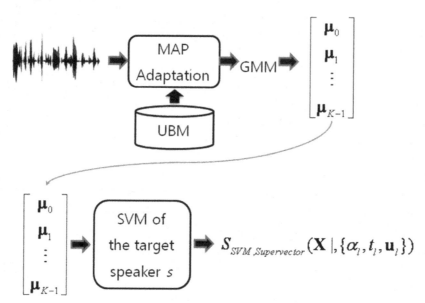

2004) demonstrated that the kernels constructed using vector of $H_{l,s}(w)$ in equation (13) can improve the speaker verification performance.

Neural Network

Speaker recognition can benefit from the neural network since the exact mapping between an input (speech features) and an output (speaker identity) is not known. Farrell et al (1994) have considered two kinds of neural netoworks for speaker recognition, multi-layer perceptron (MLP) (Haykin, 1999) and neural tree network (NTN) (Sankar & Mammone, 1991). The MLP can be trained for speech vectors such as pitch, LPC, etc. When training the MLP of a target speaker s, feature vectors from that speaker are labelled as 1, and feature vectors from non-target speakers are labelled as 0. Very often, the number of feature vectors from a target speaker is much smaller than those from non-target speakers. With such unbalanced label data, an MLP can be trained to alwaly output 0 (impostor). For this reason, Kevein et al (1994)

performed VQ on training data from non-target speakers, and only the codewords are used as training data for label 0. Figure 9 illustrates an MLP with 1 hidden layer. Let $x_i = [x_i[0], x_i[1], ..., x_i[D - 1]]$ be the input to the MLP. A weight w_{ij} corresponds to the weight of the arrowed line from a node i in the input layer to a node j in the hidden layer. The input to the hidden node j is a weighted sum of input nodes given by

$$v_j = \sum_{d=0}^{D-1} w_{dj} x_i[d]$$

(19)

Then, the output y_j of node j is computed as follows:

$$y_j = \varphi_j(v_j)$$

(20)

where $\varphi_j(\cdot)$ is the activation function of node j. Very often, the activation function is modeled as either logistic function

Figure 9. A Multi-Layer Perceptron Neural Network: this figure illustrates an example of MLP which consists 1 input, 1 hidden layer, and an output layer

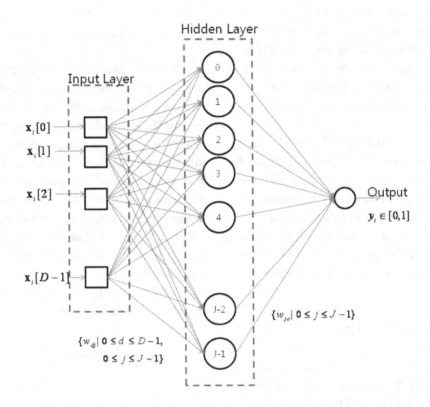

$$\varphi_j(v_j) = \frac{1}{1+\exp(-av_j)} \tag{21}$$

or hyperbolic tangent function

$$\varphi_j(v_j) = b\,\tanh(cv_j) \tag{22}$$

where a, b and c are preset parameters. Finally, the output of the MLP is obtained as follows:

$$y_i = \sum_{j=0}^{J-1} w_{jo}y_j \tag{23}$$

For binary classification, the output y_i is often compared to a preset threshold, and is mapped into either 0 or 1. The weights $\{w_{dj}, w_{jo}\}$ can be trained using the back-propagation algorithm: for details, please refer to (Haykin, 1999). The weights in the MLP can be trained by the back-propagation algorithm, but the number of layers and nodes must be pre-defined. For speaker recognition, Farrell et al. (1994) trained the MLP of each target speaker with following configuration:

- Input feature: 12th order LPC
- MLP structure: 64 hidden nodes within one hidden layer
- Activation function: Logistics function

Given a sequence of input feature $x_1 x_2 \ldots x_T$, the likelihood of a target speaker s can be computed as follows:

$$S_{MLP}(\mathbf{x_1 x_2}...\mathbf{x}_T, \Pi_s) = \frac{N_1}{N_1 + N_0} \tag{24}$$

where N_0 and N_1 are the number of feature vectors whose output is 0 (impostor) and 1 (target), respectively. The above function measures how many feature vectors are classified into a target speaker with its dynamic range normalized from 0 to 1. The normalized dynamic range can be beneficial to the speaker verification where it is important to set a proper threshold of an accept/reject decision.

In addition to the MLP, the NTN can be used for speaker recogntion. The NTN is a hybrid of a decision tree and a neural network, where the decision is made by the class of a leaf node that the input feature enters. Figure 10 illustrates an NTN using single-layer perceptron (SLP) neural network trained for a target speaker *s*. The hierarchical structure of NTN can be self-orgainzed as follows:

1. Create a root node, and assign entire training data to the root node
2. If there exists a node whose training data are not uniformly labeled (i. e., if there exists a node where both 0 and 1 training labels are observed in its training data)
   A. Train an SLP with its training data
   B. Let p and q be the set of training data whose SLP output is 0 and 1, respectively.
   C. Create two children nodes, and assign p and q to these children nodes.
   E. Go to 2.
3. Terminate.

The above procedure ends when all leaf nodes are uniformly labelled, i. e., all training data in each leaf node are either 0 or 1, respectively. In Figure 10, leaf nodes are assigned to either 0 for impostor or 1 for the target speaker. When classifying an input feature vector, at every non-leaf node (rectangular shaped), an input feature is classified into one of two child nodes. When the input feature enters a leaf node (oval shaped), the NTN outputs the class of that leaf node: in the speaker recognition considered in Figure 10, the output class is either a target speaker s or impostor for s. Similarly to the MLP, the likelihood of an input feature vector can be obtained as follows:

$$S_{NTN}(\mathbf{x}_1\mathbf{x}_2...\mathbf{x}_T,\Psi_s) = \frac{N_1}{N_1 + N_0} \tag{25}$$

Additionally, Kevin et al (1994) have used the following likelihood

Figure 10. An NTN trained for a target speaker s: the decision tree consists of several SLPs

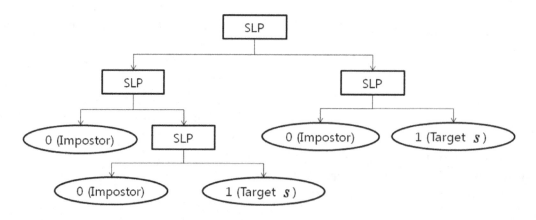

$$S_{MNTN}(\mathbf{x_1 x_2}...\mathbf{x}_T, \Pi_s) = \frac{\sum_{k=0}^{N_1-1} c_k^1}{\sum_{k=0}^{N_1-1} c_k^1 + \sum_{l=0}^{N_0-1} c_l^0} \quad (26)$$

where c_k^1 is the confidence score for output 1 obtained from the SLP for the kth input feature vector that is classified as the target speaker. Similarly, c_l^0 is the confidence score for output 0 obtained from the SLP for the lth input feature vector that is classified as an impostor. Farrell et al. (1994) reported that using the confidence score in equation (26) can significantly improve the performance compared to using equation (25).

Speaker Verification

The speaker verification system first extracts feature from input speech and computes the matching score of the claimed speaker model. The speaker verification system differs from the speaker identification system in that 1) it requests additional information of claimed identity and 2) the decision is an "Accept/Reject" decision. The accept/reject decision can be formulated as follows:

- H_0: The input speech is accepted as the claimed speaker s.
- H_1: The input speech is rejected.

$$\frac{S(\mathbf{x_1 x_2}...\mathbf{x}_T \mid H_0)}{S(\mathbf{x_1 x_2}...\mathbf{x}_T \mid H_1)} \underset{H_1}{\overset{H_0}{\underset{<}{>}}} \tau, \quad (27)$$

where τ, $S(x_1 x_2...x_T \mid H_0)$ and $S(x_1 x_2...x_T \mid H_1)$ are a preset threshold, the scores of H_0 and H_1, respectively. Let $S(\mathbf{x_1 x_2}...\mathbf{x}_T \mid s)$ be the matching score of the claimed speaker s: for example, equation (6), equation (8) and equation (14) can be used as $S(\mathbf{x_1 x_2}...\mathbf{x}_T \mid s)$. Very often, $S(x_1 x_2...x_T \mid s)$ is used as $S(x_1 x_2...x_T \mid H_0)$. In order to compute the score of

H_1, the UBM-based and cohort-based approaches can be used. In the UBM-based approach, the score $S(x_1 x_2...x_T \mid H_1)$ is approximated using the score of UBM. For example, in the GMM-UBM system, equation (27) is performed as follows:

$$\frac{S(\mathbf{x_1 x_2}...\mathbf{x}_T \mid H_0)}{S(\mathbf{x_1 x_2}...\mathbf{x}_T \mid H_1)} = \frac{S_{GMM}(\mathbf{x_1 x_2}...\mathbf{x}_T, \Theta_s)}{S_{GMM}(\mathbf{x_1 x_2}...\mathbf{x}_T, \Theta_{UBM})} \underset{H_1}{\overset{H_0}{\underset{<}{>}}} \tau, \quad (28)$$

where Θ_{UBM} is the set of GMM parameters that are trained on many speakers' development data: the development data is separate from the test and enrollment data. In the cohort model-based approach, cohort speakers are randomly selected speakers or most competitive speakers (Rosenberg, Lee, & Soong, 1990; Che et al., 1996; Higgins, Bahler, & Porter, 1991). Let $š_k$ be the kth cohort speaker of speaker s. Then, the score of H_1 is computed as follows:

$$S(x_1 x_2...x_T \mid H_1) = f(S(x_1 x_2...x_T \mid š_1), S(x_1 x_2...x_T \mid š_2), ..., S(x_1 x_2...x_T \mid š_k)) \quad (29)$$

Where f is a function that computes statistics of arguments $S(x_1 x_2...x_T \mid š_k)$ for $k = 1, 2, ..., K$: for example, f can be arithmetic, harmonic and geometric mean of $S(x_1 x_2...x_T \mid š_k)$ for $k = 1, 2, ..., K$.

The performance of the speaker verification system can be measured with various metrics such as equal-error rate (EER) and a detection error trade-off (DET) curve. The EER is the false alarm probability or the miss probability at the threshold τ where the false alarm probability equals the false rejection probability. Figure 11 illustrates the DET curve. Applications that require high security should have low false alarm probability, and applications that require high-convenience should have low miss probability. In this chapter, the EER is used to compare performances of speaker recognition systems.

Speaker Identification

The speaker identification system first extracts feature from an input speech, and it computes the matching scores of target speaker models. Then, the speaker s^* whose matching score is the largest is identified as a result as follows:

$$s^* = \arg\max_s S(\mathbf{x}_1\mathbf{x}_2...\mathbf{x}_T \mid s).$$

(30)

The performance of a speaker identification system can be measured in terms of the accuracy.

PERFORMANCE OF SPEAKER RECOGNITION SYSTEMS

The performance of speaker recognition system can be affected by many factors (Bimbot et al., 2004; Furui, 1997):

- Distortions in speech
    - ◦ Noise: speech can be collected in noisy environment
    - ◦ Channel distortions: speech can be collected via telephone and other channels, which can distort the speech signal.
- Speech variability
    - ◦ Physical condition of the user: the speech is affected by the physical condition of the user, especially by the condition of laryngitis.
    - ◦ Intersession variability: the difference between the enrollment environment and test environment can affect the speaker recognition performance.
    - ◦ Speaking style: the performance of

speaker recognition system varies with speaking styles.
- Amount of data
    - ◦ Amount of enrollment data: the amount of enrollment data affects the quality of enrolled speaker model
    - ◦ Amount of test data: the accuracy of speaker recognition system can be improved with long test speech.

In order to reduce the effect of distortions in speech, normalization in both the speech feature and scores have been proposed (Auckenthaler, Carey, & Lloyd-Thomas, 2000; Bimbot et al., 2004; D. A. Reynolds, 1995)

- Z-norm
    - ◦ Each speaker model has different dynamic range of matching scores. In order to normalize the matching scores of different models, the model-specific mean and the variance of the matching score are computed, and these parameters are used to normalize the matching score to follow a standard normal distribution.
- H-norm
    - ◦ The telephone speech is affected by the types of handset and microphone used. The effects of handset can be reduced by first recognizing which type of handsets is used for the input speech, and the matching score is normalized to follow a standard normal distribution using the handset-specific parameters (mean and variance).

Researchers have reported their experimental results of speaker recognition with different evaluation data, thus it is difficult to compare various experimental results. In the rest of this chapter, speaker recognition performance is evaluated with following criteria:

Figure 11. Detection Error Trade-off Curve: the horizontal and the vertical axis represent the false alarm and miss probabilities, respectively. The blue straight line intersects a DET curve at the EER operating point

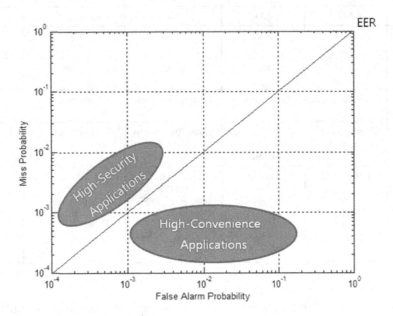

- Speaker Verification: EER
  - The amount of enrollment data
  - Operation mode: TD (fixed and variable text), TI
  - Acoustical environment: recorded in sound booth, telephone (land line and cellular)
- Speaker Identification: accuracy
  - The number of speakers to be identified
  - The amount of enrollment data
  - Operation mode: TD (fixed and variable text), TI

EER of Speaker Verification Systems

Table 1 summarizes the EERs for speaker verification systems that are reported for YOHO (Campbell, 1995), TIMIT (Garofolo, 1993), NTIMIT (Fisher et al., 1993), Switchboard (Godfrey, Holliman, & McDaniel, 1992) and Mercury dataset (Hazen et al., 2003). In the TIMIT and the YOHO database, where both enrollment and test data are recorded in sound-booth, the EER is less than 0.6%. The NTIMIT database is identical to the TIMIT database except that the speech is distorted with PSTN network, and it results in the verification performance degradation as shown in Table 1. According to Reynolds (2002), the accuracies of speaker verification systems are usually as follows:

- TD with combination lock: 0.1%-1%
  - Clean data
  - 3 min. enrollment data
  - 2 sec. test utterance
- TD with 10 digit strings: 1%-5%
  - Telephone data from multiple handset and multiple sessions
- TI with conversational speech: 7%-15%
  - Telephone data from multiple handset and multiple sessions
  - 2 min. enrollment data
  - 30 sec. test utterance

Table 1. EERs of speaker verification system in various tasks

	TIMIT	NTIMIT	YOHO	Switchboard I	Mercury
Mode	TI	TI	TD (variable)	TI	TI
# of speakers	630	630	138	500	38
Enrollment data / speaker	24sec	24sec	100sec	6min	30-90sec, variable
Length of Test Utterance	3sec	3sec	2.5sec	1min	2sec
Speaking Style	Read Sentence	Read Sentence	Combination Lock	Conversation	Conversation
Acoustical Environment	Clean, Recorded in Sound Booth	PSTN channel, Recorded in Sound Booth	Clean, Recorded in Sound Booth	Telephone	Telephone
EER	GMM: 0.24% (Reynolds, 1995) NTN: 1.9% (Farrell et al., 1994)	GMM: 7.19% (Reynolds, 1995)	HMM: 0.51% (Che et al., 1996)	GMM: 5.15% (Reynolds, 1995)	GMM&HMM: 4.83% (Hazen et al., 2003)

- TI with read sentences: 20%-35%
  - Noisy radio data from military radios
  - 30sec. enrollment data
  - 15sec. test utterance

The verification performances of various TI systems were reported in the SuperSID workshop (Reynolds et al., 2003). Various speaker modeling techniques are evaluated by NIST 2001 SRE Extended Task (Adami, Mihaescu, Reynolds, & Godfrey, 2003; Jin et al., 2003; Klusacek, Navratil, D. A. Reynolds, & J. P. Campbell, 2003; Navratil et al., 2003; Reynolds et al., 2003) .

- NIST 2001 SRE Extended Task
  - Data source: Switchboard I (Conversational speech on telephone line)
  - Enrollment data: Nominally 20 min. per each target speaker
  - Test data: 14-45 sec

Table 2 summarizes verification performances of a GMM-UBM with MFCCs, phone n-grams from speech recognizers of 5 different languages, word n-grams from English recognizers: for details, please refer to (Reynolds, et al., 2003). The GMM-UBM with MFCCs showed outstanding performance. Using other features such as prosodic features and phone n-gram features do not perform as well as the GMM-UBM with MFCCs, but it is shown that fusing the scores from different systems can reduce the EER. This implies that acoustical features, prosodic features, and phone and word n-gram features are complementary features for speaker recognition.

Accuracy of Speaker Identification Systems

Table 3 summarizes the speaker identification accuracies. As in speaker verification, the acoustical environment affects the accuracy. In speaker verification experiments, many studies have reported score and feature normalization techniques (Auckenthaler et al., 2000; Barras & Gauvain, 2003; Pelecanos & Sridharan, 2001). Applying these techniques to the NTIMIT da-

Table 2. EERs of various speaker verification systems in NIST SRE 2001 extended task (Reynolds et al., 2003)

Modeling	Feature	EER
GMM-UBM **(2,048 Kernels)**	MFCC	0.70%
GMM-UBM **(512 Kernels)**	Pitch + Energy Slopes + Duration + Phoneme Context	5.20%
Phone n-grams **(5 multiple languages)**	Phone n-grams from speech recognizers with 5 language phone models	4.80%
Word n-grams	Word n-grams from English speech recognizer	11.00%
Fusion	Matching scores of 8 different algorithms	0.20%

tabase could improve the accuracy of NTIMIT DB. The number of speakers to be identified in the Switchboard database is larger than that in the Mercury database, and the length of test utterance and the amount of enrollment data in the Switchboard database is also larger than those in the Mercury database. For this reason, the identification accuracies in the Switchboard and the Mercury database are similar.

Human and Machine Performance Comparison on Speaker Verification

Schmidt-Nielson and Crystal (2000) compared the speaker verification performances between human listeners and an automatic speaker verification (ASV) system, where the following restrictions are forced to human listeners and the ASV system:

Table 3. Accuracy of speaker identification system in various tasks

	TIMIT	NTIMIT	YOHO	Switchboard	Mercury
Mode	TI	TI	TD (variable)	TI	TI
# of speakers	630	630	138	500	38
Enrollment data / speaker	24sec	24sec	100sec	6min	30-90sec, variable
Length of Test Utterance	3sec	3sec	2.5sec	1min	2sec
Speaking Style	Read Sentence	Read Sentence	Combination Lock	Conversation	Conversation
Acoustical Environment	Clean, Recorded in Sound Booth	PSTN channel, Recorded in Sound Booth	Clean, Recorded in Sound Booth	Telephone	Telephone
Accuracy	GMM: 99.50% (Reynolds, 1995) MLP: 90% (Farrell et al., 1994) NTN: 96% (Farrell et al., 1994)	GMM: 60.70% (Reynolds, 1995)	GMM&HMM: 99.75% (Park & Hazen, 2002)	GMM: 82.80% (Reynolds, 1995)	GMM&HMM: 81.70% (Hazen et al., 2003)

Table 4. Comparison of human listeners and automatic speaker verification system

	16-individuals (Average EER)	Median of Scores from 16 individuals	Mean of Scores from 16 individuals	Machine (Hierarchical GMM)
EER	23%	12.50%	12.00%	12.00%
	(Schmidt-Nielsen & Crystal, 2000)	(Schmidt-Nielsen & Crystal, 2000)	(Schmidt-Nielsen & Crystal, 2000)	(Liu et al., 2002)

- The text-transcription of speech is unavailable for the ASV system.
- Human listeners are allowed to hear 2 min. enrollment data 3 times.
- The gender of speakers are provided for both human listeners and the ASV system
- The verification experiments of human listeners are performed by following procedures:
  - Listening to 2 min. enrollment data of target speakers
  - For each test sample
    - Listen to test sample twice.
    - Make 10-level scores on accept/reject decision

The experiments were performed using a database from NIST speaker recognition evaluation (SRE) 1998 (M. Przybocki & A. F. Martin, 2004). The number of human listeners participated in this experiment is 16. The average EER of these 16 human listeners is 23%, which is worse than the machine performance reported using the hierarchical GMM (Liu, Chang, & Dai, 2002). When matching scores from 16-individuals are available, the EERs of using the mean and the median are around 12%, which is similar to the EER of machine. The EERs of human listeners are reported to range from 10% to 25%, where the speaker verification performance is dependent on the human listener involved in the task. Human listeners did not outperform the ASV system in average, but they tend to outperform the ASV system for degraded speech as stated in Schmidt-Nielsen and Crystal (2000) as follows:

Both human and algorithm performance also went down when the signal was degraded by background noise, crosstalk, poor channel conditions, etc., but again the humans were more robust for the worst conditions.

APPLICATIONS

The major application of speaker recognition system is in an on-site or in a network-based access control. Since the speaker recognition system is not reliable enough for sensitive applications, very often, the speaker recognition system must be incorporated into a service that allows a certain level of verification/identification error. Applications to on-site access control for secured rooms can be considered. In such applications, a user claims his/her identity using ID card, badge, or personal identification number (PIN), and the claimed identity is verified using voice input. The voice signal is acquired in controlled environments, thus very often the speaker recognition system is reliable. The network-based access control differs from the on-site access control in that the voice is acquired through a remote terminal such as a telephone or a computer. Very often, the network-based access control applications are designed for customer relationship management (CRM), and various applications related to the CRM can be found in Markowitz (2002)'s survey. For example, the Union Pacific Railroad employed the speaker verification system. When a customer's goods are arrived, the customer calls the company to release empty railcars. Since the railcar number is complex, customers often mispronounce the railcar number. The speaker verification system determines whether the voice comes from the customer who is supposed to release the pronounced railcar number, which reduces the number of incorrectly released rail cars. Another CRM application is speaker verification based password reset system, which have been used by Volkswagen Financial Services. When a user forgets his/her password, the system resets the password only when the user's voice matches the enrolled speaker model. This can reduce many steps that are required to validate the user's identity.

The automatic speaker recognition techniques are also applicable to forensic speaker recognition which can be termed as follows:

Expert opinion is increasingly being sought in the legal process as to whether two or more recordings of speech are from the same speaker. This is usually termed forensic speaker identification, or forensic speaker recognition. (Rose 2002, p. 19)

In the forensic speaker recognition, the speaker model is often enrolled using limited data obtained from the questioning, and the voice evidence to be matched with the speaker model is usually distorted by acoustical noise and channel distortions. In addition, speakers are not cooperative and attempt to disguise their speaking style (Bimbot et al., 2004; Campbell, Reynolds, Campbell, & Brady, 2005; Kunzel, 1994; Meuwly & Drygajlo, 2001). Automatic speaker recognition systems have been evaluated on forensic speaker recognition tasks, but still, automatic speaker recognition systems do not achieve sufficient performance to be used in the forensic speaker recognition task (Nakasone & Beck, 2001).

CONCLUSION

In this chapter, we have considered basic concepts of speaker recognition and common speaker recognition techniques. The performances of speaker recognition systems are shown using experimental results from various tasks of YOHO,

TIMIT, NTIMIT, Switchboard, Mercury and NIST database. The performances of both speaker verification and identification are highly dependent on the acoustical environment and speaking styles. In order to compare performances of various speaker modeling techniques, the experimental results of super SID evaluation were presented. The GMM-UBM with MFCCs performed the best, and fusing scores from different systems improved the performance. Schmidt-Nielson and Crystal (2000)'s work was presented to compare the human listeners with the ASV system in speaker verification. The ASV system slightly outperformed human listeners, but human listeners were reported to be robust against distortions. This implies that more research on human listener's speaker recognition mechanism can improve the ASV system. The applications of speaker recognition were described. Many systems were designed for CRM applications using telephone. These applications have shown that the performance of speaker recognition system is not sufficient to be used for user authentication, but it can help the CRM system to reduce costs incurred by mistakes.

Currently, it is not sufficient for the speaker recognition system to be used as a stand-alone user authentication system. One alternative is to use the verbal information verification which incorporates speech recognition into speaker recognition (Li, Juang, Zhou, & Lee, 2000). With a properly defined confidence measure, the speaker recognition system can measure the reliability of the recognition results. If the reliability is smaller than a preset threshold, then the system may ask the speaker some private information which is enrolled beforehand, e.g., mother's maiden name, telephone number, etc. Then, the user's answer is recognized and determined to be correct or not by automatic speech recognition. By iterating this procedure until the system can make a reliable decision, the speaker recognition performance can be significantly improved (Li, Juang, Zhou, & Lee, 2000).

In addition, the multi-modal speaker recognition can be an alternative. Very often, speech, face and lip shapes are incorporated into the multimodal speaker recognition systems (Brunelli & Falavigna, 1995; Jourlin, Genound, & Wassner, 1997; Ben-Yacoub, Abdeljaoued, & Mayoraz, 1999; Chatzis, Bors, & Pitas, 1999; Wark & Sridharan, 2001; Sanderson & Paliwal, 2003). The face and lip recognition performance may also deteriorate under distortions in vision such as illumination change or head rotation. The probability that both the voice and the vision are degraded may be smaller than the probability that either the voice or the vision is degraded. In addition, recent development of information technology lowers the price of devices that can capture and process the face and lip shapes, which indicates that the speaker, face and lip recognition can be incorporated with a small increment in cost. Multi-modal systems extract features from considered biometric characteristics in the system. Some systems concatenate these features, and verify or identify a speaker by using a classifier trained with a concatenated feature (Bengio, Marcel & Mariethoz 2002). Other systems compute matching scores using these features, and verify or identify a speaker by using a classifier trained with these scores (Jourlin, Genound, & Wassner, 1997; Hazen et al., 2003b,;Erzin, Yemez, & Tekalp 2005). The multi-modal speaker recognition system performs well especially when the voice is contaminated under noisy conditions. In future, the advancement of speech recognition may provide accurate idiosyncratic features that can improve the speaker recognition performance. Relevant challenges to speaker recognition include the estimation of speaker's physical characteristics. Recently, some researchers have considered the estimation of speaker's physical characteristics (height, weight, vocal tract length) via voice. (Smith, & Nelson, 2004; Dusan 2005). The estimated speaker's physical characteristics can be used not only to profile unknown speaker but also to improve the speaker recognition performance.

REFERENCES

Adami, A., Mihaescu, R., Reynolds, D. A., & Godfrey, J. J. (2003). Modeling prosodic dynamics for speaker recognition. In *Proceedings of the International conference on Acoustics, Speech, and Signal Processing*.

Andrews, W. D., Kohler, M. A., & Campbell, J. P. (2001). Phonetic speaker recognition. In *Proceedings of the Eurospeech* (pp. 2517-2520).

Andrews, W. D., Kohler, M. A., Campbell, J. P., & Godfrey, J. J. (2001). Phonetic, idiolectal, and acoustic speaker recognition. In A *Speaker Odyssey-The Speaker Recognition Workshop*. ISCA.

Auckenthaler, R., Carey, M., & Lloyd-Thomas, H. (2000). Score normalization for text-independent speaker verification systems. *Digital Signal Processing, 10*, 42–54. doi:10.1006/dspr.1999.0360

Barras, C., & Gauvain, J. L. (2003). Feature and score normalization for speaker verification of cellular data. In *Proceedings of the International conference on Acoustics, Speech, and Signal Processing* (Vol. 2).

Ben-Yacoub, S., Abdeljaoued, Y., & Mayoraz, E. (1999). Fusion of face and speech data for person identity verification. *IEEE Transactions on Neural Networks, 10*(5), 1065–1074. doi:10.1109/72.788647

Bengio, S., Marcel, C., Marcel, S., & Mariethoz, J. (2002). Confidence measures for multimodal identity verification. *Information Fusion, 3*, 267–276. doi:10.1016/S1566-2535(02)00089-1

Bimbot, F., Bonastre, J. F., Fredouille, C., Gravier, G., Magrin-Chagnolleau, I., & Meignier, S. (2004). A tutorial on text-independent speaker verification. *EURASIP Journal on Applied Signal Processing*, (4), 430–451. doi:10.1155/S1110865704310024

Brunelli, R., & Falavigna, D. (1995). Person identification using multiple clues. *IEEE Transactions on Pattern Analysis and Machine Intelligence, 17*(10), 955–966. doi:10.1109/34.464560

Campbell, J. (1997). Speaker recognition: A tutorial. *Proceedings of the IEEE, 85,* 1437–1462. doi:10.1109/5.628714

Campbell, J. P., Jr. (1995). Testing with the YOHO CD-ROM voice verification corpus. In *Proceedings of the International conference on Acoustics, Speech, and Signal Processing, 1.*

Campbell, J. P., Reynolds, D. A., & Dunn, R. B. (2003). Fusing high-and low-level features for speaker recognition. In *Proceedings of the Eighth European Conference on Speech Communication and Technology.*

Campbell, W. M., Campbell, J. P., Reynolds, D. A., Jones, D. A., & Leek, T. R. (2004). Phonetic speaker recognition with support vector machines. *Advances in Neural Information Processing Systems, 16,* 57.

Campbell, W. M., Reynolds, D. A., Campbell, J. P., & Brady, K. J. (2005). Estimating and evaluating confidence for forensic speaker recognition. In *Proceedings of the International conference on Acoustics, Speech, and Signal Processing*

Campbell, W. M., Sturim, D. E., & Reynolds, D. A. (2006). Support vector machines using GMM supervectors for speaker verification. *IEEE Signal Processing Letters, 13*(5), 308. doi:10.1109/LSP.2006.870086

Chatzis, V., Bors, A. G., & Pitas, I. (1999). Multimodal decision-level fusion for person authentication *IEEE Transactions on System, Man . Cybernetics A, 29*(6), 674–680.

Che, C., Lin, Q., & Yuk, D. (1996). An HMM approach to text-prompted speaker verification. In *Proceedings of the International conference on Acoustics, Speech, and Signal Processing*

Choi, E., Hyun, D., & Lee, C. (2002). Optimizing feature extraction for English word recognition. In *Proceedings of the International conference on Acoustics, Speech, and Signal Processing.*

Davis, S., & Mermelstein, P. (1980). Comparison of parametric representations for monosyllabic word recognition in continuously spoken sentences. *IEEE Transactions on Acoustics, Speech, and Signal Processing, 28*(4), 357–366. doi:10.1109/TASSP.1980.1163420

Doddington, G. R., Przybocki, M. A., Martin, A. F., & Reynolds, D. A. (2000). The NIST speaker recognition evaluation-overview, methodology, systems, results, perspective. *Speech Communication, 31,* 225–254. doi:10.1016/S0167-6393(99)00080-1

Dusan, S. (2005). Estimation of speaker's height and vocal tract length from speech signal. In *Proceedings of INTERSPEECH.*

Erzin, E., Yemez, Y., & Tekalp, A. M. (2005). Multimodal speaker identification using an adaptive classifier cascade based on modality reliability. *IEEE Transactions on Multimedia, 7*(5), 840–852. doi:10.1109/TMM.2005.854464

Farrell, K. R., Mammone, R. J., & Assaleh, T. (1994). Speaker recognition using neural networks and conventional classifiers. *IEEE Transactions on Speech and Audio Processing, 2*(1), 194–205. doi:10.1109/89.260362

Fisher, W. M., Doddington, G. R., Goudie-Mashall, K. M., Jankowski, C., Kalyanswamy, A., Basson, S., et al. (1993). NTIMIT. *Linguistic Data Consortium.*

Furui, S. (1997). Recent advances in speaker recognition. *Pattern Recognition Letters, 18*(9), 859–872. doi:10.1016/S0167-8655(97)00073-1

Garofolo, J. S. (1993). TIMIT acoustic-phonetic continuous speech corpus. *Linguistic Data Consortium.*

Gauvain, J., & Lee, C. (1994). Maximum *a* posteriori estimation for multivariate Gaussian mixture observations of Markov chains. *IEEE Transactions on Audio, Speech, and Language Processing, 2*(2), 291–298. doi:10.1109/89.279278

Godfrey, J. J., Holliman, E. C., & McDaniel, J. (1992). SWITCHBOARD: Telephone speech corpus for research and development. In *Proceedings of the International Conference on Acoustics, Speech, and Signal Processing*

Hatch, A., Peskin, B., & Stolcke, A. (2005). Improved phonetic speaker recognition using lattice decoding. In *Proceedings of the International conference on Acoustics, Speech, and Signal Processing*.

Haykin, S. (1999). *Neural networks: A comprehensive foundation*. Upper Saddle River, NJ: Prentice-Hall, Inc.

Hazen, T. J., Jones, D. A., Park, A., Kukolich, L. C., & Reynolds, D. A. (2003a). Integration of speaker recognition into conversational spoken dialogue systems. In *Proceedings of the Eurospeech*.

Hazen, T. J., Weinstein, E., Kabir, R., Park, A., & Heisele, B. (2003b). Multimodal face and speaker identificaiton on a handheld device In *Proceedings of Workshop on Multimodal User Authentication* (pp. 113-120).

Higgins, A., Bahler, L., & Porter, J. (1991). Speaker verification using randomized phrase prompting. *Digital Signal Processing, 1*(2), 89–106. doi:10.1016/1051-2004(91)90098-6

Hirsch, H. G., & Pearce, D. (2000). The AURORA experimental framework for the performance evaluation of speech recognition systems under noisy conditions. In *ASR2000-Automatic Speech Recognition: Challenges for the new Millenium ISCA Tutorial and Research Workshop (ITRW)*. ISCA.

Huang, X., Acero, A., & Hon, H. (2001). *Spoken language processing*. Upper Saddle River, NJ: Prentice Hall PTR.

Jaakkola, T. S., & Haussler, D. (1998). Exploiting generative models in discriminative classifiers. *Advances in Neural Information Processing Systems, 11*.

Jain, A. K., Ross, A., & Prabhakar, S. (2004). An introduction to biometric recognition. *IEEE Transactions on Circuits and Systems for Video Technology, 14*(1), 4–20. doi:10.1109/TCSVT.2003.818349

Jin, M., Soong, F., & Yoo, C. (2007). A syllable lattice approach to speaker verification. *IEEE Transactions on Audio, Speech, and Language Processing, 15*(8), 2476–2484. doi:10.1109/TASL.2007.906181

Jin, Q., Navratil, J., Reynolds, D. A., Campbell, J. P., Andrews, W. D., & Abramson, J. S. (2003). Combining cross-stream and time dimensions in phonetic speaker recognition. In *Proceedings of the International conference on Acoustics, Speech, and Signal Processing*.

Jourlin, P., Luettin, J., Genoud, D., & Wassner, H. (1997). Acoustic-labial speaker veriifcaiton. *Pattern Recognition, 18*, 853–856. doi:10.1016/S0167-8655(97)00070-6

Klusacek, D., Navratil, J., Reynolds, D. A., & Campbell, J. P. (2003). Conditional pronunciation modeling in speaker detection. In *Proceedings of the International conference on Acoustics, Speech, and Signal Processing*.

Kunzel, H. J. (1994). Current approaches to forensic speaker recognition. In *Automatic Speaker Recognition, Identification and Verification*. ISCA.

Leeuwen, D. A. V., Martin, A. F., Przybocki, M. A., & Bouten, J. S. (2006). NIST and NFI-TNO evaluations of automatic speaker recognition. *Computer Speech & Language, 20,* 128–158. doi:10.1016/j.csl.2005.07.001

Li, Q., Juang, B.-H., Zhou, Q., & Lee, C.-H. (2000). Automatic verbal information verification for user authenticaion. *IEEE Transactions on Audio Processing, 8*(5), 585–596. doi:10.1109/89.861378

Li, X., Chang, E., & Dai, B. (2002). Improving speaker verification with figure of merit training. In *Proceedings of the International conference on Acoustics, Speech, and Signal Processing.*

Liu, M., Chang, E., & Dai, B. (2002). Hierarchical Gaussian mixture model for speaker verification. In *Seventh International Conference on Spoken Language Processing.* ISCA.

Markowitz, J. (2002). Speaker recognition. *Biometric Technology Today, 10*(6), 9–11. doi:10.1016/S0969-4765(02)00618-5

Meuwly, D., & Drygajlo, A. (2001). Forensic speaker recognition based on a Bayesian framework and Gaussian mixture modeling (GMM). In *A Speaker Odyssey-The Speaker Recognition Workshop.* ISCA.

Milner, B. (2002). A comparison of front-end configurations for robust speech recognition. In *Proceedings of the International conference on Acoustics, Speech, and Signal Processing.*

Molla, K., & Hirose, K. (2004). On the effectiveness of MFCCs and their statistical distribution properties in speaker identification. In *IEEE Symposium on Virtual Environments, Human-Computer Interfaces and Measurement Systems (VECIMS).*

Nakasone, H., & Beck, S. D. (2001). Forensic automatic speaker recognition. In *A Speaker Odyssey-The Speaker Recognition Workshop.* ISCA.

Navratil, J., Jin, Q., Andrews, W. D., & Campbell, J. P. (2003). Phonetic speaker recognition using maximum-likelihood binary-decision tree models. In *Proceedings of the International conference on Acoustics, Speech, and Signal Processing.*

Newman, M., Gillick, L., Ito, Y., Mcallaster, D., & Peskin, B. (1996). Speaker verification through large vocabulary continuous speech recognition. In *Proceedings International conference on Spoken Language Processing.*

Pan, Y., & Waibel, A. (2000). The effects of room acoustics on MFCC speech parameter. In *International conference on Spoken Language Processing.*

Park, A., & Hazen, T. J. (2002). ASR dependent techniques for speaker recognition. In *International Conference on Spoken Language Processing* (pp. 1337-1340).

Pelecanos, J., & Sridharan, S. (2001). Feature warping for robust speaker verification. In *A Speaker Odyssey-The Speaker Recognition Workshop.* ISCA.

Peskin, B., Navratil, J., Abramson, J., Jones, D., Klusacek, D., Reynolds, D., et al. (2003). Using prosodic and conversational features for high-performance speaker recognition: Report from JHU WS'02. In *Proceedings of the International conference on Acoustics, Speech, and Signal Processing*

Przybocki, M., & Martin, A. F. (2004). NIST speaker recognition evaluation chronicles. In *A Speaker Odyssey-The Speaker Recognition Workshop.* ISCA.

Rabiner, L. R., & Schafer, R. W. (1978). *Digital processing of speech signals.* Englewood Cliffs, NJ: Prentice-Hall.

Reynolds, D. (1995). Speaker identification and verification using Gaussian mixture speaker models. *Speech Communication, 17*(1-2), 91–108. doi:10.1016/0167-6393(95)00009-D

Reynolds, D. (2002). An overview of automatic speaker recognition technology. In *Proceedings of the International Conference on Acoustics, Speech, and Signal Processing.*

Reynolds, D., Andrews, W., Campbell, J., Navratil, J., Peskin, B., Adami, A., et al. (2003). The SuperSID project: Exploiting high-level information for high-accuracy speaker recognition. In *Proceedings of the International conference on Acoustics, Speech, and Signal Processing.*

Reynolds, D., Quatieri, T., & Dunn, R. (2000). Speaker verification using adapted Gaussian mixture models. *Digital Signal Processing, 10*, 19–41. doi:10.1006/dspr.1999.0361

Rosenberg, A. E., Lee, C., & Soong, F. K. (1990). Subword unit talker verification using hidden Markov models. In *Proceedings of the International conference on Acoustics, Speech, and Signal Processing.*

Sanderson, C., & Paliwal, K. K. (2003). Noise compensation in a person verification system using face and multiple speech features. *Pattern Recognition, 36*(2), 293–302. doi:10.1016/S0031-3203(02)00031-6

Sankar, A., & Mammone, R. J. (1991). *Neural tree networks in neural networks: Theory and applications.* San Diego, CA: Academic.

Schmidt-Nielsen, A., & Crystal, T. H. (2000). Speaker verification by human listeners: Experiments comparing human and machine performance using the NIST 1998 speaker evaluation data. *Digital Signal Processing, 10*(1-3), 249–266. doi:10.1006/dspr.1999.0356

Scholkopf, B., & Smola, A. J. (2002). *Learning with kernels.* Cambridge, London: The MIT Press.

Shriberg, E. (2007). Higher-level features in speaker recognition. In *Speaker classification I.*

Smith, L. H., & Nelson, D. J. (2004). An estimate of physical scale from speech. In *Proceedings of the International conference on Acoustics, Speech, and Signal Processing.*

Sönmez, K., Shriberg, E., Heck, L., & Weintraub, M. (1998). Modeling dynamic prosodic variation for speaker verification. In *the Proceedings of International conference on Spoken Language Processing.*

Sturim, D. E., Reynolds, D. A., Dunn, R. B., & Quatieri, T. F. (2002). Speaker verification using text-constrained Gaussian mixture models. In *Proceedings of the International conference on Acoustics, Speech, and Signal Processing.*

Volkmann, J., Stevens, S. S., & Newman, E. B. (1937). A scale for the measurement of the psychological magnitude pitch. *The Journal of the Acoustical Society of America, 8*(3), 208-208. doi:10.1121/1.1901999

Wan, V., & Renals, S. (2005). Speaker verification using sequence discriminant support vector machines. *IEEE Transactions on Speech and Audio Processing, 13*(2), 203–210. doi:10.1109/TSA.2004.841042

Wark, T., & Sridharan, S. (2001). Adaptive fusion of speech and lip information for robust speaker identification. *Digital Signal Processing, 11*(3), 169–186. doi:10.1006/dspr.2001.0397

Weber, F., Peskin, B., Newman, M., Emmanuel, A. C., & Gillick, L. (2000). Speaker recognition on single- and multispeaker data. *Digital Signal Processing, 10*, 75–92. doi:10.1006/dspr.1999.0362

Woodland, P. C., Leggetter, C. J., Odell, J. J., Valtchev, V., & Young, S. J. (1995). The 1994 HTK large vocabulary speech recognition system. In *Proceedings of the International conference on Acoustics, Speech, and Signal Processing*

Xiang, B., & Berger, T. (2003). Efficient text-independent speaker verification with structural Gaussian mixture models and neural network. *IEEE Transactions on Speech and Audio Processing, 11*(5), 447–456. doi:10.1109/TSA.2003.815822

Zilca, R. D. (2002). Text-independent speaker verification using utterance level scoring and covariance modeling. *IEEE Transactions on Speech and Audio Processing, 10*(6), 363–370. doi:10.1109/TSA.2002.803419

Chapter 14
Visual Attention for Behavioral Biometric Systems

Concetto Spampinato
University of Catania, Italy

ABSTRACT

The chapter is so articulated: the first section will tackle the state of art of the attention theory, with the third paragraph related to the computational models that implement the attention theories, with a particular focus on the model that is the basis for the proposed biometric systems. Such an algorithm will be used for describing the first biometric system. The following section will tackle the people recognition algorithms carried out by evaluating the FOAs distribution. In detail, two different systems are proposed: 1) a face recognition system that takes into account both the behavioral and morphological aspects, and 2) a pure behavioral biometric system that recognizes people according to their actions evaluated by a careful analysis of the extracted FOAs.

INTRODUCTION

With the establishment of the information society, personal identification systems have gained an increased interest, either for security or personalization purposes. Traditionally, computer systems have based identification procedures on something that one has (keys, magnetic cards or chip cards) or something that one knows (personal identification numbers and passwords) (Gamba, & Fred, 2004). These systems can easily fail to serve their objec-

tive in situations of loss or lent of a key or card, or in cases of forgotten passwords or disclosure of codes. Biometric authentication or identification systems use something one is, creating more reliable systems, with higher immunity to authorization theft, loss or lent.

Biometric techniques can be divided into *physiological* and *behavioral*. A physiological trait tends to be a more stable physical characteristic, such as finger print, hand silhouette, blood vessel pattern in the hand, face or back of the eye. A behavioral characteristic is a reflection of an individual's

DOI: 10.4018/978-1-60566-725-6.ch014

psychology. Because of the variability over time of most behavioral characteristics, a biometric system needs to be designed to be more dynamic and accept some degree of variability. On the other hand, behavioral biometrics are associated with less intrusive systems, conducing to a better acceptability by the users.

In this book chapter we propose novel behavioral biometric applications based on the *human visual attention* system. More in detail, we will discuss about two biometrics systems based on how humans recognize faces, bodies, postures, etc… according to the distribution of the *focuses of attention (FOAs*, that represent the most interesting parts in a visual scene) that are *fixations* reproducing the ability of humans in the interpretation of visual scenes. Indeed the pattern of these fixations and the choice of where to send the eye next are not random but appear to be guided (Rayner, K., & Pollatsek, A. (1989)).

In detail we will propose two approaches for behavioral biometrics: the first one uses a combination of *morphological features* with *behavioral features* by analyzing the FOAs distribution (*scanpath*) for recognizing faces and the second one uses just these *scanpaths*, suitably organized in *Information Path* (Boccignone et al., 2002), for recognizing people according to their actions.

As concern the face recognition system the analysis of the *FOAs*, allows us to integrate the face features (e.g., eyes, nose, mouth shape), the holistic features (the relations between the various parts of the face) and the facial expressions in the recognition task thus allowing us integration between physiological and behavioral features.

The same approach has been applied for recognizing people according to their actions and it is based just on spatial distribution of the FOAs and the saliency order of such a points.

The chapter is so articulated: the next section will tackle the state of art of the attention theories; the third paragraph is related to the computational models that implement the attention theories,

with a particular focus on the model that is the basis for the proposed biometric systems. Such an algorithm will be used for describing the first biometric system. The following section will tackle the people recognition algorithms carried out by evaluating the *FOAs* distribution. In detail two different systems are proposed: 1) A face recognition system that takes into account both the behavioral and morphological aspects and 2) A pure behavioral biometric system that recognizes people according to their actions evaluated by analyzing the extracted FOAs.

BACKGROUND OF ATTENTIONAL RESEARCH

Human vision system seems to apply serial computational strategy when inspecting complex visual scenes. Particular locations in scenes are selected based on their relevance from both the objective and subjective point of view, with reference to the observer, i.e. In notable study of 1967, Yarbus (Yarbus, A. L. (1967)) demonstrated that perception of complex scene involves complicated pattern of fixations, where the eye stands still, and saccades, where the eye moves to include in the fovea a part of the scene. Basically, fixations occur for zones that are salient to determine specific features of the scene under consideration. Therefore when humans look a face, they usually concentrate the attention (evidenced by the *saccadic movements*) to the main facial features like eyes, nose, mouth, etc. See Figure 1 for instance. The distributions of those movements are strongly connected to the personal psychology.

As is know the detection and the recognition of objects in a complex scene are difficult tasks for the artificial machines. Differently humans easily analyze and select interesting information in a generic scene according to a specific task.

In fact, humans have a remarkable ability to interpret scenes in real time, in spite of the limited speed of the neuronal hardware available for such

Figure 1. Saccadic movements when a person is looking a face during the experiment conducted by Yarbus, A. L. (1967)

tasks. The reason is that visual processes appear to select a subset of the available sensory information before further processing, most likely to reduce the complexity of scene analysis.

This ability to select useful information in an environment is called *Visual Attention,* which consists in solving the problem of visual object recognition and scene analysis by using a serial fashion with *scan paths* (Noton, D., & Stark, L. (1971)).

When humans analyze a visual scene, it is quite complex to fully model the acquired image. A typical example is a treed nature scene, where each tree has several branches and leaves. Completely modeling every scene detail as an internal process is practically impossible, indeed if humans should analyze all the information contained in an image by analyzing pixel per pixel, the computation complexity will grow in an exponential way.

The *selective attention* is a process, intrinsic in humans, that makes efficient the searching and the processing of a specific area for "the visual processing" by using the *scan paths* of the eyes

simplifying the image thus to contain only the most relevant information, where relevancy is often task-based.

Hence the selective attention is based on the hypothesis that not all parts of an image provide us useful information and analyzing only the relevant parts of the image in detail is sufficient for recognition and classification.

Hence, the selective attention, by directing focus to only a portion of the available information, works as a spotlight illuminating a small area with high resolution (Eriksen, C. W. W. and Hoffman, J. E. (1972); Treisman, A. M. & Gelade, G. (1980)).

Moreover, for the selection of the most spatial interesting regions, the attention controls information through the visual pathways and subsequently shifts focus between important parts of the scene (Tsotsos et al., 1995).

Many theories for understanding the selective attention have been developed and are following listed:

1. **Filter Theory (Broadbent, D. E., 1958):** Broadbent proposed a theory based on two main stages. The first one (*the filter*) aims at computing simple visual features in parallel, whereas the second one aims at making an higher level analysis such as object recognition. Such a level receives data (only a small portion of the whole acquired image) from the first level, which selects a data subset according to specific rules and discards the remaining information. This theory cannot fully explain the *cocktail party* (Conway, A. R. A et al. (2001)) *phenomenon*, hence it couldn't be used for modeling the selective attention.

2. **Attenuation Theory (Treisman, A., 1964):** This theory represents a modification of the filter theory, and it is based on the main hypothesis that all the not needed information are not cancelled but attenuated according to some specific features. By using this theory the *cocktail party* is explained, because the not needed information are attenuated and not cancelled and at the right time they could be retrieved.

3. **Later Theories (J. Deutsch & D. Deutsch, 1963):** Broadbent and Treisman's models proposed that the selection filter in attention occurs prior to selection, or pattern recognition stage. The Later theories by Deutsch and Deutsch (1963), and Norman (1968), aim to merge growing information regarding memory and the selection process of attention. According to these approaches the selection occurs after the pattern recognition stage differently that in the two previous models where the selection occurs at the beginning.

4. **Feature Integration Theory (Treisman, A. M. & Gelade, G., 1980):** This theory enhances the importance and method of preattentive features extraction. At the beginning simple features are extracted in parallel across the entire visual field and separated by color, orientation, spatial frequency, intensity, and direction of motion. The extracted features are further combined in a saliency map, which provides information about the more interesting zones of the visual scene.

5. **Binary Theory (Braun, J. & Sagi, D., 1990):** Braun and Sagi proposed a theory based on the idea that the selection is implemented in the form of a spatially circumscribed region of the visual field, called "*focus of attention*" (*FOA*), which scans the scene (by using sequence of eye movements, called *saccades*) both in a rapid, *bottom-up, saliency-driven*, and *task-independent* manner and in a slower, *top-down, volition-controlled*, and *task-dependent manner*. Bottom-up attention directs the gaze to salient regions (image-based saliency cues), while top-down attention enables goal directed visual search (task-dependent cues). Hence this theory is based on the integration theory between two main processes: one volition-controlled and one saliency-driven. More in detail the *bottom-up* mechanism provides information about *where* objects are, whereas *top-down* gives information about *what* the selected zones are.

COMPUTATIONAL MODELS FOR VISUAL ATTENTION

In this section the state of art of the most effective and common algorithms for implementing the visual attention will be reviewed. The approaches can be divided into two groups:

1. *Bottom-up models* based on the integration theory proposed by Treisman (Treisman, A. M. and Gelade, G. (1980)) and on the concept of saliency map and winner take all;

2. *Top-down models* based on the knowledge related to the task that the user is performing.

Bottom-Up Models

Most of the algorithms that implement a bottom-up architecture are based on two common elements: a *saliency map* that aims to detect the area potentially of interest and a mechanism for blocking or for routing the information flow toward fixed positions.

Saliency Maps provide a biologically reasonable model of visual attention based on color and orientations features.

According to the biological model proposed by Koch and Ullman (Koch, C. & Ullman, S. (1985)), the control of the visual attention is managed by using features map which are further integrated into a saliency map that codify how much is salient a point with respect to the neighboring zones. Furthermore a *"winner take all"* mechanism selects the region with the greatest saliency in the *saliency map.*

In this section an overview of such a methods is proposed, with a particular attention to the model proposed by Itti and Koch (Itti, L. et al (1998)) for implementing the saliency, thus is the method that most easily can be applied for implementing face recognition systems and more in general behavioral biometric methods.

Tsotsos et al. (Tsotsos et al. (1995)) propose a *selective tuning* model that aims to explain the computational and behavioral levels of visual attention in humans and primates. The proposed visual processing architecture is a pyramidal structure with nodes, which create a network, that has both feed-forward and feedback connections. There are two main contributions: 1) a new feed-forward motion processing hierarchy, 2) a new method for feature binding problem able to group the extracted features into well defined objects.

An interesting approach is the one proposed by Peters and Sullivan (Peters, C., & Sullivan, C. O. (2003)) where the authors propose a framework based on the interactions of several components: a vision model for perceiving the virtual world,

a model of bottom-up attention for early visual processing of perceived stimuli, a memory system for the storage of previously sensed data and a gaze controller for the generation of resultant behaviors. The bottom-up system is based on the saliency map extracted by the method proposed by Itti and Koch.

An interesting computation model for selective attention is the one proposed by Lee et al. (Lee, K., Buxton, H., & Feng, J. (2004)) where a general architecture which integrates top-down model and bottom-up model is developed.

In detail they propose a simple saliency-based attention system to model selective attention guided by top-down visual cues, which are dynamically integrated with the bottom-up information.

As enhanced in the introduction section all the biometric works proposed in this chapter are based on the Itti and Koch model that is following discussed.

Itti and Koch Bottom-Up Model

The Itti and Koch model describes a visual attention system, inspired by the neuronal topology of human visual system.

Such a model is based on a multi-scale image features that are combined into a saliency map. A *winner take all* algorithm then selects the most salient regions in order of decreasing saliency.

The model proposed by Itti and Koch is based on the biological architecture described by Koch and Ullman (Figure 2) according to the "feature integration theory," that explains human visual search strategies.

The input image is firstly decomposed into a set of topographic feature maps that provide us information about colors, intensity and objects orientation. Afterwards the identified spatial locations compete for the saliency. Hence all feature maps are integrated, in a purely bottom-up manner, into a "saliency map," which topographically codifies the most interesting zones of the image called *Focuses of Attention.*

Figure 2. Architecture of the Itti and Koch Model

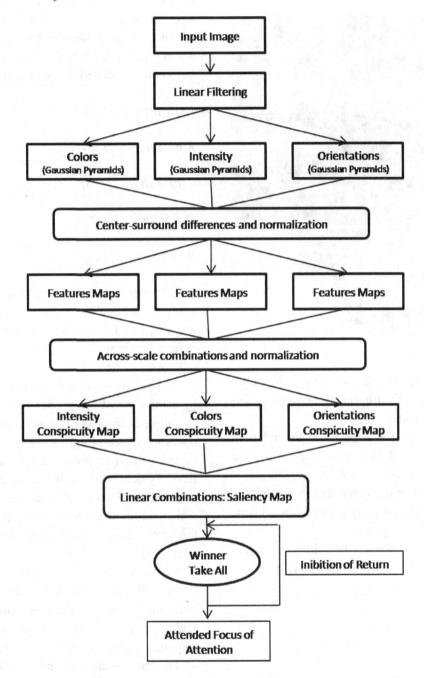

Let us analyze the Figure 2 that represents the proposed model. The input is a color image independent of the spatial resolution. The first step aims to reproduce the human vision cone by nine spatial levels obtained with the Gaussian pyramids (Greenspan et al. (1994)) obtaining the images shown in Figure 3.

The next step aims to extract the low-level vision features (colors, orientation and brightness) according to the bottom-up model creation. All

Figure 3. Gaussian Pyramids

the above features are processed at several spatial scales, using specific filtering operations as will be shown following.

Let us define *r, g, b* respectively the red, blue and green planes of the input image and *I* the intensity image obtained as $I = (r+g+b)/3$.

The red, blue and green channels are further normalized for the intensity image *I*, thus obtaining *r', g'* and *b'* images.

The final color images (the yellow channel is evaluated as well) are obtained by applying the following formulas:

$$R = r' - (g'+r')/2;$$

$$G = g' - (r'+b')/2;$$

$$B = b' - (r'+g')/2;$$

$$Y = (r'+g')/2 - |r'-g'|/2 - b'$$

For each of the extracted plane we have 8 images obtained by applying the Gaussian pyramids.

Hence after the low level features extraction we have 40 images, whose eight images for the red channel, eight for the blue channel, eight for the green one, eight for the yellow channel and the last eight are related to the intensity feature.

$$I(\sigma) \text{ with } \sigma \in [1..8]$$

$$R(\sigma) \text{ with } \sigma \in [1..8]$$

$$G(\sigma) \text{ with } \sigma \in [1..8]$$

$$Y(\sigma) \text{ with } \sigma \in [1..8]$$

$$B(\sigma) \text{ with } \sigma \in [1..8]$$

The orientation features have been evaluated by applying Gabor filters at the orientations $\theta \in [0°, 45°, 90°, 135°]$. For each orientation the Gaussian pyramids are applied, thus having the $O(\sigma, \theta)$, with $\sigma \in [1...8]$ and $\theta \in \{0°, 45°, 90°, 135°\}$.

The next step is to compute the '*feature maps*', by using a set of linear operations. Each feature is computed by a set of linear "*center-surround*" operations (according to the model shown in Figure 2) that reproduce the humans receptive field. Typical visual neurons are most sensitive in a small region of the visual space (the center), while stimuli presented in a broader, weaker antagonistic region concentric with the center (the surround) inhibit the neuronal response.

Center-surround is implemented in the model as the difference between fine and coarse levels of the Gaussian pyramids: the center is a pixel at scale $c \in \{2, 3, 4\}$, and the surround is the corresponding pixel at scale $s = c + \partial$, with $\partial \in \{3, 4\}$. The across-scale difference between two maps, denoted "Θ" below, is obtained by interpolation to the finer scale and point-by-point subtraction.

The first set of maps for the center-surround mechanism is related to the intensity $I(\sigma)$ that is the first set of maps perceived by out visual neuronal system (Leventhal, A.G. (1991)).

The intensity maps are computed by setting con

$c \in \{2, 3, 4\}$ e $s = c + \partial, \partial \in \{3, 4\}$ obtaining:

$$I(c, s) = |I(c) \Theta I(s)|$$

A second set of maps is similarly constructed for the color channels, which, in cortex, are represented using the "*color double-opponent*" system. In the center of their receptive fields, neurons are excited by one color (e.g., red) and inhibited by another (e.g., green), while the converse is true in the surround. Such spatial and color opponency has been proved existing for the red/green, green/red, blue/yellow, and yellow/blue color pairs in human primary visual cortex (Engel, S et al. (1997)). Hence the $RG(c,s)$ and the $BY(c,s)$ maps are created to account the red/green and blue/yellow double opponency:

$$RG(c, s) = |(R(c) - G(c)) \Theta (R(s) - G(s))|$$

$$BY(c, s) = |(B(c) - Y(c)) \Theta (Y(s) - B(s))|$$

Orientation information $O(c, s, \theta)$, that codify the contrast of the orientation with respect to the *surround*, are extracted by the following formula:

$$O(c, s, \theta) = |O(c, \theta) \Theta O(s, \theta)|$$

In total, 42 feature maps are computed: six for intensity, 12 for color, and 24 for orientation that will be further processed for evaluating the *saliency maps*.

An example of the *color double-opponent* mechanism is shown in Figure 4.

The computed features maps are combined for estimating the *conspicuity maps* that represent the conspicuity at every location in the visual field. A combination of the feature maps provides bottom-up input to the saliency map, modeled as a dynamical neural network.

An important step in the conspicuity maps computation is to combine the above feature maps that are a priori not comparable, because they are represented in different scales. Such a problem has been solved by applying a *normalization operator* $N(.)$ *(*Itti, L. et al. (1998)*)* that globally promotes the map where a small number of strong peaks

Figure 4. Color double-opponent Blue Yellow at different scales: (a) c = 2, s = 5, (b) c = 2, s = 6, (c) c = 3, s = 6 and (d) c = 3, s = 7

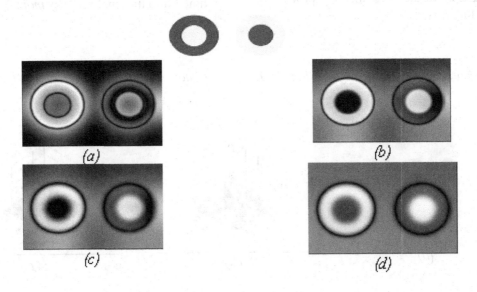

(a) (b) (c) (d)

of activity (conspicuous locations) is present, whereas it reduces the map where a numerous comparable of peaks is present.

Such a normalization is very simple to apply even if it is not biologically plausible, indeed it is known that cortical neurons are locally connected, hence they cannot make global operation, such as the global maximum computation.

Itti and Koch (Itti, L. & Koch, C. (2000)) for implementing such a behavior propose a new model based on the use of the Difference of Gaussian. The *DoG* is given by the formula:

$$DoG(x,y) = \frac{c_{ex}^2}{2\pi\sigma_{ex}^2} e^{-\frac{x^2+y^2}{2\sigma_{ex}^2}} - \frac{c_{ex}^2}{2\pi\sigma_{inh}^2} e^{-\frac{x^2+y^2}{2\sigma_{inh}^2}}$$

Where *ex* indicates excitatory distribution, whereas *inh* the inhibitory component. At each iteration of the normalization process a single map *M* is updated by using the following formula:

$$M \leftarrow \mid M + M \cdot DoG - C_{inh} \mid_{\geq 0}$$

where *DoG* is the filter whereas $|\cdot|_{\geq 0}$ takes into account just positive values. C_{inh} is an inhibition term that is set experimentally.

An example of the normalization process is shown in Figure 5.

The computed and normalized feature maps are further combined into three "*conspicuity maps*", $\bar{I}$ for intensity, $\bar{C}$ for color, and $\bar{O}$ for orientation at the scale ($\sigma = 4$). They are obtained through across-scale addition, "$\oplus$", which consists of reduction of each map to scale four and point-by-point addition:

$$\bar{I} = \oplus_{c=2}^4 \oplus_{s=c+3}^{c+4} N(I(c,s))$$

$$\bar{C} = \oplus_{c=2}^4 \oplus_{s=c+3}^{c+4} [N(RG(c,s)) + N(By(c,s))]$$

For orientation, four intermediary maps are first created by combination of the six feature maps for a given J and are then combined into a single orientation conspicuity map:

$$\bar{O} = \sum_{\vartheta \in \{0°,45°,90°,135°\}} N\left(\oplus_{c=2}^4 \oplus_{s=c+3}^{c+4} N(O(c,s,\vartheta))\right)$$

The motivation for the creation of three separate channels and their individual normalization is the hypothesis that similar features compete strongly for saliency, while different features contribute independently to the saliency map. The three conspicuity maps are, finally, normalized and summed into the final *saliency map*:

Figure 5. Normalization Process by using DoG: a) Input image, b) Intensity Map and c) Normalized map

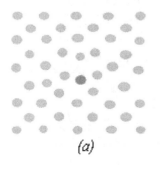 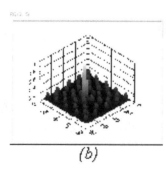 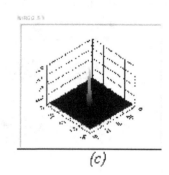

(a) (b) (c)

$$S = \frac{1}{3}(N(\bar{I}) + N(\bar{C}) + N(\bar{O}))$$

The maximum of the saliency map (*SM*) defines the most salient image location, to which the focus of attention (*FOA*) should be directed. We could now simply select the most active location as defining the point where the model should next attend by applying a winner take all algorithm.

Examples of the proposed system are shown in Figure 6.

BEHAVIORAL BIOMETRICS APPROACHES BY USING A PURE BOTTOM-UP COMPUTATIONAL VISUAL ATTENTION MODULE

The purpose of the approaches presented in this book chapter is to implement systems that allow us to recognize people according also to their behaviour by analysing the distribution of the focuses of attention. More in detail, the approaches memorize the *FOAs* distribution for various expressions of a person, for simplicity here we

Figure 6. Examples of outputs of the bottom-up model proposed by Itti and Koch

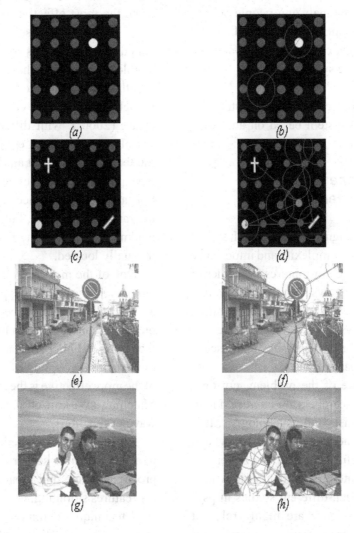

consider the facial expressions, but the model holds even for behavioural aspects of a person as harms movements or walking style.

Therefore, the approach proposed in this chapter uses the distribution of the *focuses of attention* (the most salient points) for identifying a person by analyzing its *facial expressions* and its *actions*. Indeed in these models a person is identified by a set of FOA distributions (*scan path*), each representing the specific person in a typical facial expression or in a specific action. The analysis of these two approaches starts from the analysis of the behavioural face recognition system where a pure bottom-up computational model is proposed and afterwards it will face a novel method based on the recognition by analyzing people actions where the bottom up model will be used..

Hence in this book chapter we will face two behavioural biometric systems:

1. A behavioural face recognition system;
2. A behavioural system based on analyzing people actions

A Behavioral Face Recognition System

As is known, face recognition is a research area of biometrics that for its complexity and importance is becoming one of the most interesting topics of study in the image analysis and understanding field. A general statement of the face recognition problem is as follows: given a video image of a scene, identify one or more persons in the scene using a stored database of faces.

Due to the nature of the problem, not only computer science researchers are interested in it, but also neuroscientists and psychologists. It is general opinion that advances in computer vision research provide useful insights to neuroscientists and psychologists into how human brain works, and vice versa. In fact, different studies in psychology and neuroscience are highly relevant for the design of these recognition systems. For

example, discoveries in psychology on the importance of some features for recognition (Graham, D. et al. (1981)) have influenced the engineering literature (Etemad, K, & Chellappa, R. (1997)); on the other hand, automated systems provide a significant support for studies in psychology. For example, a study on the lighting from bottom of the face (Johnston, A. et al. (1992)) has shown that if we use a lighting direction different by the one used normally, the recognition algorithm doesn't work.

Several approaches for automating the process of face recognition have been proposed in the last twenty years (Zhao, W. et al. (2003)).

Methods based on deformable templates seem to be the most effective. Yuille et al. (Yuille L. (1991)) describe the use of deformable templates called "*snakes*" (Kass et al., (1998)), based on simple geometrical shapes to locate eyes and mouth. Several methods use the active shape models (*ASMs*), (Jiao et al., (1998)) and (Wang et al., (2000)), with different approaches (e.g. wavelet, Gabor filter, etc.) for the detection of the features. Cootes et al. (Cootes et al., (1995)) have proposed an effective model for interpretation and coding of face images with results in the range [70%-97%], but in their approach the landmarks to detect the main facial features are manually located.

One of the most relevant algorithms for *face matching* is the eigenfaces proposed in (Pentlad et al., (1994)). The eigenfaces, based on the eigenpictures, remove the data redundancy within the face images. Other approaches have pointed out the structural coupling of the face features. One of the more effective is the Elastic Bunch Graphic Matching (Wiskott et al., (1997)) that uses the wavelet functions.

All the mentioned methods are not effective in all the possible scenarios, and require a high processing time and great amounts of memory for features storaging.

A techniques commonly used for features dimensionality reduction are Principal Components

Analysis (PCA) (Yang et al., (2004)) and Linear Discriminant Analysis (LDA) (Etemad, K, & Chellappa, R. (1997)). The main goal of PCA is to reduce the dimensionality of the while retaining as much as possible of the variation present in the original dataset. The reduction is obtained by selecting a set of orthogonal vectors maximizing the variance overall the samples.

Instead LDA seeks to find the direction in the dataset that maximizes between-class scatter and minimizes the within-class scatter.

Although these two methods reduce the space dimensionality, they face the computational difficulty when the dimension of the data is too huge. Moreover a critical issue of the LDA method is the singularity and instability of the within-class scatter matrix. Indeed, especially in face recognition problems, there are a large number of features available, while the total number of training patterns is limited and commonly less than the dimension of the features space. This implies that the within-class scatter matrix might be singular and instable (Jain et al, (1982)).

In order to overcome the singularity problem, an alternative method, called Fisherfaces (Belhumeur et al, (1997)), was proposed. Such method is a two stage dimensionally reduction technique carried out by: 1) performing PCA to project the *n-dimensional* image space onto a lower dimensional subspace and 2) applying LDA to the best linear discriminant features on such subspace.

Although Fisherfaces method partially solves the singularity problem, often the instability remains a huge drawback. Several methods, based on Fisherfaces, were proposed to bypass such limitation (Liu et al, (1993)), (Thomaz et al, (2003)). Some of the proposed methods are based on people behaviour analysis as for instance the PCA that stores in its model the facial expressions. Indeed the PCA-based systems can reliably extract and categorize facial cues to identity sex, race and expression, and simulate several face-perception phenomena, including distinctiveness effects, caricature effects,

etc. More recent works have shown that a PCA of facial expressions posed by different identities generated distinct sets of partially independent principal components (PCs) coding expression and identity. This partial independence of the PCs was sufficient to model the independent perception of facial expressions, even if the partial overlap in the PCs for facial identity and expressions offers unusual incidences in which facial identity and expression produced interference effects.

To overcome such a problems in the last years *behavioural* biometric approaches based on visual attention have been proposed as the one developed by A. A. Selah where a serial model for visual pattern recognition based on the primate selective attention mechanism by combining a feature integration scheme (Riesman, A. M. &Gelada, G. (1980)) with a Markov model (Ramey, R.D., & Brown, C.M. (1990).).

More in detail, the sequential approaches have received great interest, (Choir, V. & Desai, U. (1998), Selah, A.A. et al. (2002), Cicero, M. et al. (2003), Cicero, M. (2005)). These imitate the human visual system in its serial way of recognizing faces (see Figure 1) (Notion, D. &. Stark, L. (1971)), where the face image is explored with a scanning strategy, called a *scan path*, in order to collect a sequence of features.

The idea is that not all parts of an image give us information. If we can attend only to the relevant parts, we can recognize the image more quickly and using less resources.

The recognition system, proposed by Spampinato, C. et al. (2008), includes *behavioural* aspects and is based on the *hypothesis that in the recognition process humans memorize the distribution of some particular points, called "focuses of attention" (FOAs) that bind morphological and behavioural features*. Indeed as is shown in Figure 7 according to the facial expression the FOA distribution changes and it is representative of that person in that typical facial expression.

The approach proposed consists of four main parts:

Figure 7. FOA distribution in several face expressions

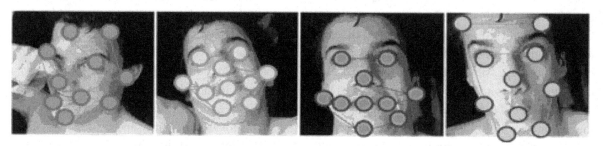

- **Target Detection:** by a suitable clustering algorithm based on colour processing. The detection can extract both a face and a whole person;
- **Visual Attention for Features Extraction:** where the points of interest are focused by a pure bottom-up attention module;
- **Features Extraction:** by a suitable analysis of the identified *FOAs*;
- **Target Matching:** where the features extracted by the previous module, are compared with the others stored in the database for face matching.

In Figure 8 the recognition system is proposed when the target object is a face. In this section a pure bottom-up attention model is proposed with the aim to extract the main interesting points according to the visual human model to analyze the scene. This model has been carried out for implementing an effective face recognition system and afterwards has been extended to the other proposed behavioural biometric system.

More in detail, the *FOA* extraction module modifies the architecture proposed by Koch and Pullman explained by the "feature integration theory" even if it is based on a *saliency map* that defines the relationships between the components of a scene depending on the importance that the components have for the generic observer.

The target detection process depends strongly from the illumination of the scene. For this reason in this algorithm the *HSL* (Hue, Saturation, and Loma) space colour has been chosen.

The target detection process uses an ad-hoc clustering algorithm based on the k-means model and consists of three steps:

- Identification of three clusters;
- Selection of the winner cluster;
- Filtering the input image with a mask obtained by a smoothing of the winner cluster.

More in details the clustering algorithm used is based on a modified version of the *k-means* algorithm. The first step aims to divide the *Hr* plane of the input image in a lot of clusters using the minimization of the Euclidean Distance between each one point value of the *Hr* plane and the centred value which represents the mean of the values of each one region of the image. A very great number of clusters produce an increasing of the *CPU* time and the merging problem, whereas few clusters could be not sufficient to separate the main parts of the *Hr* plane. In according to experimental test, three clusters have been chosen.

After the clustering algorithm the image is divided in clusters, thus to identify the **winner cluster,** which is the cluster with the major number of pixels whose *RGB* value is nearest at (195,145,155). By changing the value of the RGB is possible to select other target objects as a whole person while he/she is walking (see Figure 10).

Applying a suitable filtering the target mask,

Figure 8. The Overall Face Recognition System

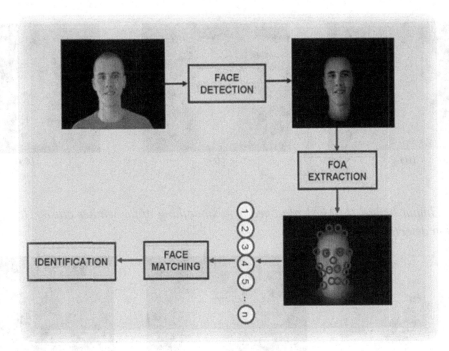

that allows us to detect the final target, is obtained as shown in Figure 9 and Figure 10.

The output image of the detection step is the input image for the algorithm that extracts features based on a visual attention system. The visual attention module proposed herein detects salient regions from a colour image simulating saccades of human vision using a saliency map. The differences in computing, with respect to the other methods based on the integration theory, the saliency map are: 1) it doesn't apply Gaussian pyramids, thus reducing the computational complexity and increasing the spatial resolution of the processed images and 2) it doesn't use the double colour opponent mechanism, and therefore the dependence of attention module on the illumination source is reduced, 3) the *HSL* space is the best representative of how the humans perceive colours.

The first step to compute the saliency map is to convert the image, obtained by the face detec-

tion module, in the *HrSL* space. Experimentally, it has been noticed that the saturation plane is unnecessary for the computation of the saliency map, while *Hr* and *L* planes are necessary, respectively, to detect the contours and the shapes of the face (e.g. eyes, nose, mouth, etc...). After having extracted the *Hr* and *L* planes, the following filters have been applied to the both planes, obtaining the images partially shown in Figure 11:

- Directional Prewitt filters (oriented at 0°, 45°, 90°, 135°) obtaining $Hr\_Prewitt^{0°}$, $Hr\_Prewitt^{45°}$, $Hr\_Prewitt^{90°}$, $Hr\_Prewitt^{135°}$ and $L\_Prewitt^{0°}$, $L\_Prewitt^{45°}$, $L\_Prewitt^{90°}$, $L\_Prewitt^{135°}$, features;
- Canny Filter to both planes, obtaining the Hr_Canny_map and L_Canny_map;

The images, processed with the above non-linear filters, are combined with the aim to obtain the *features maps* as follows:

Figure 9. (a) Imput Image, (b) Mask obtained by a smoothing of the winner cluster, (c) Final Image with tha face detected

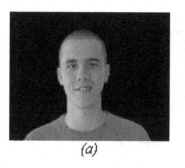  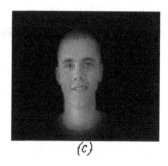

Figure 10. (a) Imput Image, (b) Mask obtained by a smoothing of the winner cluster, (c) Final Image with the person detected

 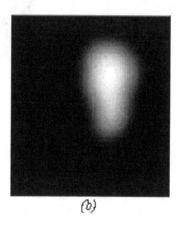 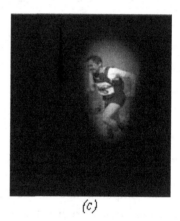

1. All the *Hr* images processed with Prewitt filters are summed obtaining the *Hr-Prewitt Features Map;*

2. All the *L* images processed with Prewitt filters are summed giving more weight to the 90° Map, obtaining the so called *L-Prewitt Features Map;*

3. The *Hr_Canny* map and *L_Canny* map are processed using a normalization function *N(·)* that implements the mechanism of *iterative spatial inhibition* by using the *DoG* (Difference of Gaussian) filter proposed in Itti, L., & Koch, C. (2000). The obtained maps are called respectively *Hr-Edge Map* and *L-Egde Map.*

Applying the normalization factor *N(·)* to both the *Hr-Prewitt Features Map* and *Hr- Egde-Map* and summing these two maps the *Hr-Saliency Map* is obtained (Figure 12(b)).

The same procedure is applied for *L-Saliency Map* (Figure 12(a)) which is obtained by summing the *L-Prewitt Features Map* and *L-Egde Map.* Finally, the *Saliency Map* (Figure 12(c)) is computed by summing the *L-Saliency* (with a greater weight) with the Hr-Saliency Map.

After having extracted the saliency map, the first *Focus of Attention* (*FOA*) is directed to the most salient region (the one with the highest grey level in Figure 12(c)).

Afterwards, this region is inhibited according to a mechanism called *inhibition of return (IOR),*

Figure 11. (a) Hr plane of the detected face, (b) L plane of the detected face, (c) Hr-Prewitt90° Map, (d) L-Prewitt90° Map, (e) Hr-Canny Map, (f) L-Canny Map

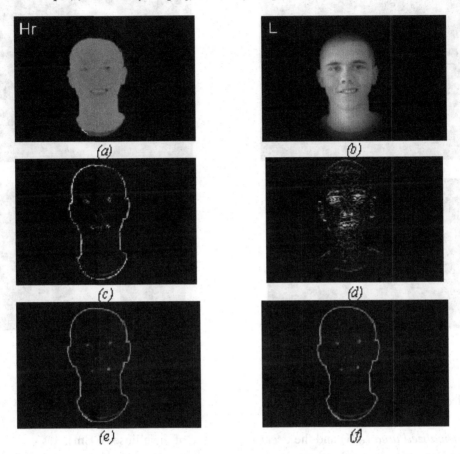

allowing the computation of the next *FOA*. The obtained *FOAs* are shown in Figure 12(d). In Figure 13 the *FOAs* for the previously detected person, while he is running, are shown. After the *FOAs* distribution extraction, a *FOAs* analysis has been carried out in order to identify both the morphological and the behavioural features. The type of approach is quite different for the person and for the face.

After having extracted the FOAs the features extraction and the target matching is quite different for the face with respect to the behaviour aspects such as walking, seating, etc....

As concern the face the first step aims to identity the ellipse surrounding the face and the mouth, thus for combining morphological with behavioural features. Afterwards the most two salient regions of the obtained *FOAs* distribution are considered for the eyes position detection.

For the ellipse identification the algorithm computes a set of distances from each extracted *FOA*. All the *FOAs*, which distance by the centre is greater than a suitable threshold, are considered as belonging to the face boundaries. By an interpolation of these *FOAs* we obtain the searched ellipse. By analyzing the remaining *FOAs*, it is possible to extract the mouth. After the face features extraction the holistic face features have been extracted.

The aim of the next module is to extract the *face features* and the *holistic features* starting from the most important *FOAs* previously identified.

Figure 12. (a) L_Saliency Map, (b) Hr_Saliency Map, (c) Saliency Map, (d) Some identified FOAs

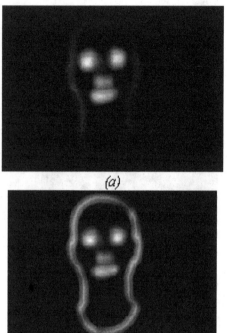

(a)

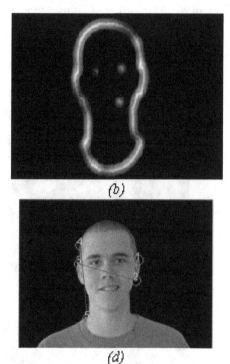

(b)

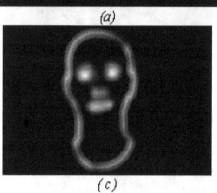

(c)

(d)

The identified *holistic features* are:

- The *normalized area* (**AN**) and the *eccentricity* (**E**) of the ellipse that best fits the contour *FOAs*, as described below:

$$E = 100 \cdot sign(A_y - A_x) \cdot \sqrt{1 - \frac{\min(A_x, A_y)^2}{\max(A_x, A_y)^2}}$$

$$A_N = \frac{A_x \cdot A_y}{\sqrt{A_x^2 + A_y^2}}$$

Where A_x and A_y are, respectively, the horizontal and the vertical axes of the ellipse;

- the distance between the central point of the *FOAs* eyes (**C0**) and the centre of the such ellipse (**CEm**);
- the focal distance between the eyes (**Cf**);

- the vertical distance (**Yb**) between the central point of the mouth (**Cm**) and the centre of the ellipse (**CEm**);
- the distance between the eyes and the mouth: computed as the distance between the central point of the eyes *FOAs***C0** and **Cm**;
- the distribution of the 20 most salient *FOAs*;

All the computed holistic features are shown in Figure 14.

The final step is to match the extracted features with the ones stored in the database. The considered features for the matching are:1) *FOAs* Distribution that takes into account the person behaviour, and 2) Morphological Features.

The target matching must be independent from the rotation, the scaling and the translation. For this reason the first step is to apply a Procrustes analysis (Bin, L. & Hancock, E.R. (1999)) to the

Figure 13. (a) Detected Target, (b) Some identified FOAs

FOAs distribution. After this transformation all the features are extracted and the *fitting value* computed as:

$$Fit = \alpha_1 \cdot T_1 + \alpha_2 \cdot T_2$$

Where T_1 is the fitting value of the distribution and T_2 the fitting value for the features extracted by using the *FOAs* distribution. The recognized person is the one with the max value of *Fit* if this one is greater than a threshold, otherwise nobody is recognized.

The proposed methods have been tested on a database of 114 subjects (*CVL and ŠCV, PTERŠ, Velenje face database*). Each subject is characterized by ten images taken for different face expressions, different distances from camera, and different background with five different facial expressions: smiling, sad, angry, crying and weariful. Each image is characterized by a spatial resolution of 640*480, with a uniform background and natural light. Subject's age is between 18 and 50 years.

The overall recognition rate is of about 93%. The classification performances are more than satisfying, especially if compared with other well-know and effective methods in literature.

Indeed Eigenfaces (Pentlad et al., (1994)) shows an average recognition rate of 88.0%, Fisherfaces (Belhumeur et al, (1997)) 86%, Liu Method (Liu et al, (1993)) 86.5%. The above results have been

Figure 14. Extracted holistic features

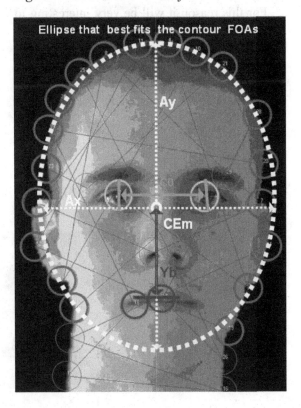

computed on the same set of images used in our experiments.

The system, proposed herein, proves effective due to the integration of the face, holistic and *behavioural* features. This integration is attained by applying both the *FOAs* distribution analysis and the algorithm proposed in (Etemad, K, & Chellappa, R. (1997)).

An important peculiarity of the systems is the independence from both the illumination source and the dimension of the face to be recognized.

One more advantage of these two systems is that they are very efficient and don't require huge quantity of memory for storing the people features.

An improvement that generalizes the system regards the integration of a top down module that includes the volition controlled task.

Although the features extraction and the face matching systems have shown good results, they should be tested especially with different face images with different orientation and non-uniform background.

For this reason it will be very interesting to develop a parallel system able to analyze at the same time different locations of the scene, especially for complex scenes with many faces and other objects.

A BEHAVIORAL RECOGNITION SYSTEM BY USING INFORMATION PATH APPROACH

According to the above proposed visual attention module, in this section the method for recognizing people from their "biometric behavioral characteristics" is proposed. Differently than the previous approach in this method we don't compute any morphological features, but it is based just on the analysis of the FOA distribution, both *temporal* and *spatial*.

For each person that will be further recognized we store in our database a set of FOA distributions, representing how he/she "*acts*" in particular events as shown in Figure 15. This allows us to recognize both the current person and its current action.

During the recognition phase the spatial distribution and the temporal distribution of the visual *scan paths* are evaluated.

The salient regions surrounding focus of attention points have been shaped as squared regions having dimensions equal to 1/16 of image's dimensions, roughly corresponding to biological FOA dimension. Each person is, therefore, represented through its FOA sequences, or *scan paths*, which can be organized into a sequential structure that contains spatial and saliency information. This structure image can be defined as *Information Path (IP)(Figure 16)*, which can be seen as a

Figure 15. FOA Distributions while a person is seating. All these distributions will be stored for the person X in the section "seating"

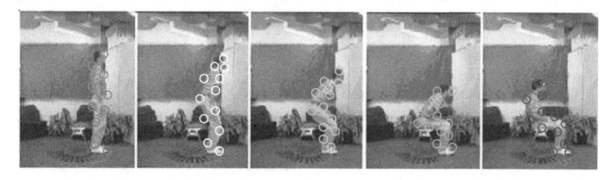

"signature" of a person.

A person X is recognized as *person Y (*already stored in our database*)* if its current *IP* has the major degree of *similarity* with all the IPs of the people stored in the database.

Let P_t be the person to be recognized and *IP_t* its current *Information Path (IP)*, and *IPi* the information path stored in the database, the similarity between the current *IP_t* and *IPi* is computed according the following formula:

$$M = \alpha \cdot M_{Content} + \beta \cdot M_{Spatial} + \gamma \cdot M_{Time}$$

where $M_{content}$ represents the content similarity, $M_{spatial}$ takes into account the similarity between the spatial coordinates of the extracted *scan path* and the stored one, whereas M_{time} considers the similarity in terms of saliency and:

$$\alpha + \beta + \gamma = 1$$

To evaluate the $M_{content}$, from each FOA belonging to the IP, some features relative to color, shape and texture are extracted. For what concerns color, a histogram is derived from each FOA in HSV color space. Evaluation of FOAs similarity is performed via histogram intersection. Given the color histograms of the person X *Hx* and the one stored in the database *Hy*, using the same number of bins $b = [0, ...,B]$, it is possible to define a similarity measure:

$$M_{col} = 1 - \frac{\sum_{b=0}^{B}(\min(H_x(b),H_y(b))}{\sum_{b=0}^{B}H_x(b)}$$

As regards shape and texture, we use feature descriptors based on intensity and oriented pyramids, which in this case can be thought as redundant wavelet representations (WT). We only take into account the details components of WT transform (high frequency), which contain shape and texture characterizations. Texture and shape are described via wavelet covariance signatures:

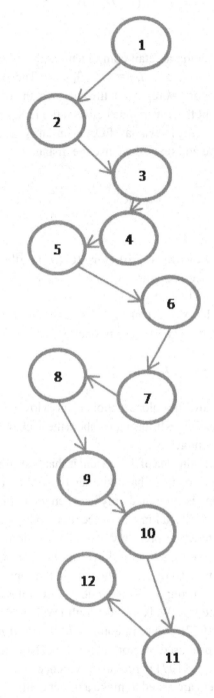

Figure 16.Information Path (IP)

$$Cov_{WT}(I) = \int D_{nk}^{X_j}(b) \cdot D_{nk}^{X_i}(b) \cdot db$$

D_l^X being a detail component, and $n = 0, \ldots,$ $d - 1$, $k = 1, 2, 3$, $i, j = 1, 2, 3$, $j \leq i$. These signatures for $j=k$ represent the energies; the others represent the covariance between the H,S, and V components. To evaluate FOA's similarity in terms of shape and texture we use the distance:

$$M_{text} = 1 - \sum_{j \in N(p,p')} \left| \frac{Cov_{WT}(C^X(p)) - Cov_{WT}(C^Y(p'))}{\min(abs(Cov_{WT}(C^X(p))), abs(Cov_{WT}(C^Y(p'))))} \right|$$

Where $Cov_{WT}(C^X(p))$, $Cov_{WT}(C^Y(p'))$ are the WT covariance signatures of target and test FOAs, respectively and p and p' are the considered FOAs. FOA's content similarity is given from the weighted mean of these two terms:

$$M_{content} = \mu_1 \cdot M_{col} + \mu_2 \cdot M_{tex}$$

Usually the color component has a low weight because it gives information about the background and clothing.

The main idea of the system is that two similar distributions must have similar IPs and that the matching is computed only between *homologous* FOAs, while taking into account node spatial position. More precisely, two IPs are similar if their homologous nodes have similar features in terms of saliency and if they are in the same image spatial region. This strategy resembles that suggested by Walker and Smith (Walker-Smith et al. (1977)), who, in contrast to the *scan path* theory proposed by Noton and Stark (Noton, D., & Stark, L. (1971)), provided evidence that when observers are asked to make a direct comparison between two simultaneously presented pictures, rather a repeated scanning, in the shape of a feature by feature comparison, occurs.

The similarity in terms of spatial position can be seen as an index of IPs overlay (suitably aligned by using Procrustes Method) as shown in Figure

17. More in detail, the homologous FOAs are the ones that have the biggest intersections when two IPs are overlapped.

To evaluate spatial similarity we use the *Euclidean distance* between homologous FOA's's centers:

$$d_{p,p'} = \sqrt{(x_2 - x_1)^2 + (y_2 - y_1)^2}$$

$p = (x_1, y_1)$ and $p' = (x_2, y_2)$ being FOA center coordinates. The distance is "penalized" if, for the two images, the movement between the current FOA and the next one is not in the same direction:

$$\hat{d}_{p,p'} = d_{p,p'} \cdot e^{-\Delta}$$

Where Δ is the difference of direction between two FOAs. After this normalization the similarity is given by $M_{Spatial} = 1 - \hat{d}_{p,p'}$

Clearly, due to variations of lighting conditions, pose, different background, we should expect certain variability in the feature range on similar FOA. Thus, a *fuzziness* degree is associated to the matching result between homologous FOAs. Thus the fuzzy horizon of the problem is subdivided into decision regions. These regions can be "certainty regions" *(CR)*, denoting high probability that FOAs distribution be similar or very different, or "uncertainty region" *(UR)*. The limits of *UR* and *CR* regions are represented by two thresholds experimentally determined: when the similarity value is greater than *thresholdMAX* or is less than *thresholdMIN* it falls in *CR*, otherwise in a *UR*.

After having identified $M_{spatial}$, we should take into account the difference of time that a human eye spend on two *FOAs* pertaining to two different images (*WTA fire times*), we introduce the distance $M_{time} = abs(t_C^q - t_C^i)$, t_C^q and t_C^i being the

Figure 17. a) IP of extracted from the current image, b) IP stored in the database for the Person X and c) Overlap of the two previous IP where it is possible to identify the homologous FOAs

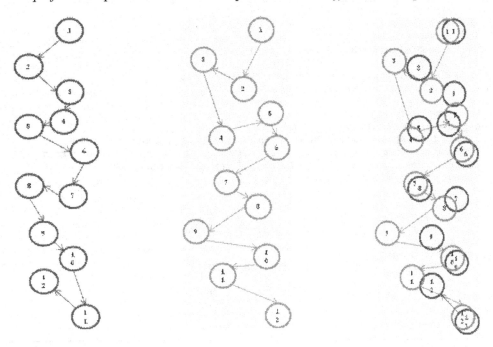

WTA fire times relative to homologous FOAs of the distribution IPq and IPi.

Hence the condition that must hold for the recognition of a person X as *Person Y* is: *the average of the similarities among its* IP_X *and the* IPs_Y *of the person Y must be the greatest value within our database and greater than a suitable threshold, otherwise no one is recognized.*

The similarity or matching M_{image} is obtained through the following matching algorithm. The algorithm compares the first k Target Image's FOAs, $k < K$ where K is the number of extracted FOAs, with the homologous FOAs of the various distributions in database. In the experiments, we set k = 3, the first FOAs being more important in a bottom-up process and in driving the Visual Attention search process. At the end of this first match we obtain a fuzzy IP similarity measure. For all images that have a fuzzy similarity value which falls in a CR the algorithm stops (see Box 1).

Finally we compute the average value of the vector M_{person} and if this value is greater than all the other average values computed for the other people and if it is greater than a suitable threshold the person is recognized.

After having recognized the person Y as X, the action is evaluated by considering the IPs similarities within the IPs of the person Y.

An example of the use of the algorithm is found in the following figures. Let us suppose that the target person is the one shown in Figure 18 with its related Information Path. A subset of the images stored in the database is the one show in Figure 19, where the similarity M between them and the target image is also shown.

M=0.759 represents the greatest value and it is also greater than the *recognizing threshold* (T_r) that has been experimentally evaluated to 0.7, hence the target person has been recognized as *Person 2,* which is correct. For detecting the action it is necessary to the IP of the current person with all the ones of the person who has been estimated to be similar and afterwards by computing the similarity it is possible to understand the action.

Box 1. Algorithm for IPs Matching

```
Compute the Information Path (IP_t) of the Target Person
j ←0
i ← 0
for (i=0; i < NumberFOADistributionPersonY; i++)
begin
current_IP = IP[i]; //IP contains all the IPs for the person Y
while (!stop && j < N°FOA Current Distribution)
begin
   current_FOA = current_IP[j]
   if(current_FOA is homologous to IP_t(j))
           Compute content similarity Mcontent between IP_t(j)and current_FOA;
           Compute spatial position similarity Mspatial between IP_t(j)and current_FOA;
          Compute time similarity Mtime between IP_t(j)and current_FOA;
          Compute FOA similarity M between Cq
          j ← j + 1
      if (j=k)
          Compute the mean similarity M
          if (M < thresholdMIN) AND (M > thresholdMAX) then stop
      if (j > k) then
          Compute the mean similarity M
          if (M < thresholdMIN) AND (M > thresholdMAX) then stop
      if (M >T) then
target FOA distribution is similar to the i FOA distribution
end
      Store computed M in M_person→ M_person[i]=M
end
```

The proposed methods were tested on a database of 150 subjects. Each subject is characterized by five images taken for different postures, with the same distances from camera, and same background. Each image is characterized by a spatial resolution of 640*480, with a uniform background and natural light.

The overall performances rate is of 88.6% that means that 133 subjects were correctly recognized over 150 subjects. For the 74.4% (99 subjects) of the subjects correctly identified, the current action was been correctly identified. The actions considered were five: 1) Walking, 2) Seating, 3) Dancing, 4) Moving Harms and 5) Running.

CONCLUSION

In this chapter we address the practical importance of using visual attention dynamics as a biometric for authenticating. *Visual Attention* consists in solving the problem of visual object recognition and scene analysis by using a serial fashion with *scan paths.*

We review the current state of visual attention systems for behavioral biometrics. We argue that although the use of a behavioral trait (rather than a physiological characteristic) has inherent limitations, when implemented in conjunction with physiological characteristic, as for instance the model proposed based on the analysis of the *FOAs* distribution for face recognition, it allows us a more robust authentication system.

We have presented a novel method for sequential face recognition, where a simple saliency-based *scan path* simulation guides feature extraction.

The performance of the proposed system is about 90%. Our results indicate that the advantages of employing a saliency-scheme over a raster scan are: 1) By associating a measure of informativeness with image patches, we are able to dedicate more resources to discriminative locations, and discard clutter. Thus, we are able to save time in

Figure 18. a) Target Image and its b) information path

 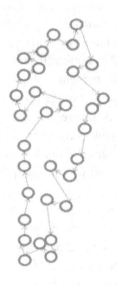

the classification phase by inspecting less than half of the image in detail, 2) the visual attention systems make the algorithms robust, thus the feature sampling follows salient locations instead of fixed points on the image plane.

Several directions are proposed for future work. Different saliency schemes must be tested to explore the trade-off between accuracy and computational complexity.

Finally a behavioral biometric system based on

Figure 19. Mean similarity values for testing images

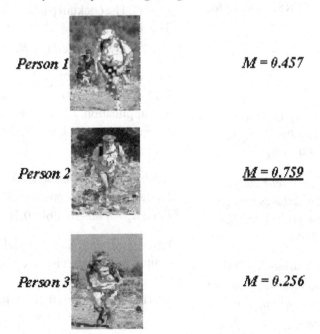

Person 1 $M = 0.457$

Person 2 $\underline{M = 0.759}$

Person 3 $M = 0.256$

analyzing the *scan paths* for recognizing people by using their actions has been discussed. This method is quite a challenging task in the biometric field, even if its reliability is still under study. The proposed method is quite efficient with respect to the other known methodologies because it doesn't use the whole image (as for instance in the motion history image) for the recognition. Moreover it has shown very good results reaching a *performances rate* of about 87% and it allows us also to understand which action the person is performing.

All the methods proposed are reliable solutions that avoid the computational costs inherent to a high features space dimensionality by using a restricted number of features face (such as EingenFace, LDA, etc...) and moreover they show a reasonable accuracy comparable with the best existing methods.

ACKNOWLEDGMENT

This paper has been partially supported by the project "Catania Territorio d'eccellenza - ICT " of the Catania municipality. Moreover we would to thank the CVL and ŠCV, PTERŠ, Velenje for the face database.

REFERENCES

Bartlett, J. C., & Searcy, J. (1993). Inversion and configuration of faces. *Cognitive Psychology, 25*, 281–316. doi:10.1006/cogp.1993.1007

Belhumeur, P. N., Hespandha, J. P., & Kriegman, D. J. (1997). Eigenfaces vs. fisherfaces recognition using class specific linear projection. *IEEE Trans. on PAMI, 19*(7), 711–729.

Bicego, M., Castellani, U., & Murino, V. (2003). Using hidden Markov models and wavelets for face recognition. In *IEEE. Proc. of Int. Conf on Image Analysis and Processing* (pp. 52–56).

Bicego, M., Grosso, E., & Tistarelli, M. (2005). Probabilistic face authentication using hidden Markov models. *Proc. of SPIE Int. Workshop on Biometric Technology for Human Identification*.

Bin, L., & Hancock, E. R. (1999). Matching point-sets using procrustes alignment and the EM algorithm. *Proc. of BMV99*, Manchester, UK.

Boccignone, G. Picariello, A., Moscato, V., & Albanese, M. (2002). Image similarity based on animate vision: Information path matching. *Multimedia Information Systems 2002* (pp. 66-75).

Braun, J., & Sagi, D. (1990). Vision outside the focus of attention. *Perception & Psychophysics, 48*, 45–58.

Broadbent, D. E. (1958). *Perception and communication*. London: Pergamon.

Bruce, V., Hancock, P., & Burton, A. (1998). *Human face perception and identification*. In Wechsler, Philips, Bruce, Fogelman-Soulie & Huang (Eds.), *Face recognition: From theory to applications* (pp. 51-72). Springer-Verlag.

Conway, A. R. A., Cowan, N., & Bunting, M. F. (2001). The cocktail party phenomenon revisited: The importance of working memory capacity. *Psychonomic Bulletin & Review, 8*, 331–335.

Cootes, T. F., Taylor, C. J., Cooper, D. H., & Graham, J. (1995). Active shape model-their training and application. *Computer Vision Graphics and Image Understanding, 61*, 38–59. doi:10.1006/cviu.1995.1004

Deutsch, J., & Deutsch, D. (1963). Attention: Some theoretical considerations. *Psychological Review, 70*, 80–90. doi:10.1037/h0039515

Engel, S., Zhang, X., & Wandell, B. (1997). Colour tuning in human visual cortex measured with functional magnetic resonance imaging. *Nature, 388*(6), 68–71. doi:10.1038/40398

Eriksen, C. W. W., & Hoffman, J. E. (1972). Temporal and spatial characteristics of selective encoding from visual displays. *Perception & Psychophysics*, *21*, 201–204.

Etemad, K., & Chellapa, R. (1997). Discrimant analysis for recognition of human face images. *Journal of the Optical Society of America. A, Optics, Image Science, and Vision*, *14*(8), 1724–1733. doi:10.1364/JOSAA.14.001724

Etemad, K., & Chellappa, R. (1997). Discriminant analysis for recognition of human face images. *Proc AVBPA . Lecture Notes in Computer Science*, *99*, 127–142.

Gamboa, H., & Fred, A. (2004). A Behavioral Biometric System based on Human Computer Interaction. Proc. of SPIE, Vol. 5404.

Graham, D., Hadyn, E., & Shepherd, J. (1981). *Perceiving and remembering faces*. New York & London: Academic Press.

Greenspan, H., Belongie, S., Goodman, R., Perona, P., Rakshit, S., & Anderson, C. H. (1994). Over complete steer able pyramid filters and rotation invariance. *Proc. IEEE Computer Vision and Pattern Recognition*, Seattle, WA (pp. 222-228).

Itti, L., & Koch, C. (2000). A saliency-based search mechanism for overt and covert shifts of visual attention. *Vision Research*, *40*, 1489–1506. doi:10.1016/S0042-6989(99)00163-7

Itti, L., Koch, C., & Niebur, E. (1998). A model of saliency-based visual attention for rapid scene analysis. *IEEE Transactions on Pattern Analysis and Machine Intelligence*, *20*(11), 1254-1259. doi:10.1109/34.730558

Jain, A. K., & Chandrasekaran, B. (1982). Dimensionality and sample size consideration in pattern recognition practice. In P.R. Krishnaiah & L.N. Kanal (Eds.), *Handbook of statistics* (Vol. 2, pp.835-855). North Holland.

Jiao, F., Li, S., Shum, H., & Schuurmans, D. (2003). Face allignment using statistical models and wavelet features. *Proc. of CVPR'03 IEEE* (pp. 1063–1069).

Johnston, A., Hill, H., & Carman, N. (1992). Recognizing faces: Effects of lighting direction, inversion, and brightness reversal. *Perception*, *21*, 365–375. doi:10.1068/p210365

Kass, M., Witkin, A., & Terzopoulos, D. (1998). Snakes: Active countorn models. *International Journal of Computer Vision*, ***, 321–331.

Koch, C., & Ullman, S. (1985). Shifts in selective visual attention: Towards the underlying neural circuitry. *Human Neurobiology*, *4*(4): 219–227.

Kohir, V., & Desai, U. (1998). Face recognition using DCT-HMM approach. In *Proc. Workshop on Advances in Facial Image Analysis and Recognition Technology (AFIART)*, Freiburg, Germany.

Lee, K., Buxton, H., & Feng, J. (2004). Cueguided search: A computational model of selective attention. *IEEE Transactions on Neural Networks*, *16*(4), 910–924. doi:10.1109/TNN.2005.851787

Leventhal, A. G. (1991). *The neural basis of visual function: Vision and visual dysfunction*. Boca Raton, FL: CRC Press.

Liu, K., Cheng, Y. Q., & Yang, J. Y. (1993). Algebraic feature extraction for image recognition based on an optimal discriminant criterion. *Pattern Recognition*, *26*(6), 903–911. doi:10.1016/0031-3203(93)90056-3

Noton, D., & Stark, L. (1971). Scanpaths in eye movements during pattern perception. *Science*, *171*(3968), 308–311. doi:10.1126/science.171.3968.308

Pentlad, A., Moghaddam, B., Starner, T., Oliyide, O., & Turk, M. (1994). *View based and modular eigeispaces for face recognition.* (Tech. Rep. 245). MIT Media Laboratory, Percentual Computing Section.

Peters, C., & Sullivan, C. O. (2003). Bottom-up visual attention for virtual human animation. In *Computer animation for social agents.*

Rayner, K., & Pollatsek, A. (1989). *The psychology of reading.* Englewood Cliffs, NJ: Prentice Hall.

Rimey, R. D., & Brown, C. M. (1990). *Selective attention as sequential behavior: Modeling eye movements with an augmented hidden Markov model.* (Tech. Rep. TR-327). Computer Science, University of Rochester.

Salah, A. A., Alpaydın, E., & Akarun, L. (2002). A selective attention-based method for visual pattern recognition with application to handwritten digit recognition and face recognition. *IEEE Transactions on Pattern Analysis and Machine Intelligence, 24*(3), 420–425. doi:10.1109/34.990146

Spampinato, C., Nicotra, M., & Travaglianti, A. (2008). Analysis of focuses of attention distribution for a novel face recognition system. *Proc. of BIOSTEC 2008,* Madeira, Portugal.

Thomaz, C. E., & Gillies, D. F. (2003). *A new Fisher-based method applied to face recognition.* (. *LNCS, 2756,* 596–605.

Treisman, A. (1964). Selective attention in man. *British Medical Bulletin, 20,* 12–16.

Treisman, A. M., & Gelade, G. (1980). A feature-integration theory of attention. *Cognitive Psychology, 12,* 97–136. doi:10.1016/0010-0285(80)90005-5

Tsotsos, J., Culhane, M., Wai, W. Y. K., Lai, Y., Davis, N., & Nuflo, F. (1995). Modeling visual attention via selective tuning. *Artificial Intelligence, 78*(1-2): 507–545. doi:10.1016/0004-3702(95)00025-9

Walker-Smith, G. J., Gale, A. G., & Findlay, J. M. (1977). Eye movement strategies involved in face perception. *Perception, 6*(3): 313–326. doi:10.1068/p060313

Wang, W., Shan, S., Gao, W., Cao, B., & Baocai, Y. (2000). An improved active shape model for face alignment. *Vision Research, 40,* 1489–1506. doi:10.1016/S0042-6989(99)00163-7

Wiskott, L., Fellous, J.-M., & von der Malsburg, C. (1997). Face recognition by elastic bunch graph matching. *IEEE Trans. on PAMI, 19,* 775–779.

Yang, J., Zhang, D., Frangi, A. F., & Yang, J. Y. (2004). Two dimensional PCA: A new approach to appearance-based face representation and recognition. *IEEE Trans. on PAMI, 26*(1), 131–137.

Yarbus, A. L. (1967). *Eye movements and vision.* New York: Plenum.

Yuille, A. L. (1991). Deformable templates for face detection. *Journal of Cognitive Neuroscience, 3*(1), 59–70. doi:10.1162/jocn.1991.3.1.59

Zhao, W., Chellappa, R., Phillips, P., & Rosenfeld, A. (2003). Face recognition: A literature survey. *ACM Computing Surveys, 35,* 399–458. doi:10.1145/954339.954342

Chapter 15
Statistical Features for Text-Independent Writer Identification

Zhenan Sun
NLPR, CAS, China

Bangyu Li
NLPR, CAS, China

Tieniu Tan
NLPR, CAS, China

ABSTRACT

Automatic writer identification is desirable in many important applications including banks, forensics, archeology, and so forth. A key and still open issue in writer identification is how to represent the distinctive and robust features of individual handwriting. This chapter presents three statistical feature models of handwritings in paragraph-level, stroke-level, and point-level, respectively, for text-independent writer identification. The three methods evolve from coarse to fine, showing the technology roadmap of handwriting biometrics. The proposed methods are evaluated on CASIA handwriting databases and perform well in both Chinese and English handwriting datasets. And the experimental results show that fine scale handwriting primitives are advantageous in text-independent writer identification. The best performing method adopts the probability distribution function and the statistical dynamic features of tripoint primitives for handwriting feature representation, achieving 95% writer identification accuracy on CASIA-HandwritingV2 with 1,500 handwritings from more than 250 subjects. And a demo system of online writer identification is developed to demonstrate the potential of current algorithms for real world applications.

DOI: 10.4018/978-1-60566-725-6.ch015

INTRODUCTION

Handwriting has been widely accepted as a unique characteristic of individuals for a long history. So the identity of a subject has been associated with his handwriting in both forensic and civilian applications. Traditional writer identification relies on manual efforts, which greatly limits the applicability of handwriting biometrics. With fast development of computer, sensor and pattern recognition, automatic writer identification has become possible and attracted great interests from researchers. However, accurate writer authentication is still a very challenging task because handwriting as a behavioral biometrics is less stable and distinctive than biological biometric traits such as iris and fingerprint.

The approaches for automatic writer authentication can be classified into two broad categories based on their requirements on the textual contents of handwriting. One category of approaches are named as *text-dependent* because they require the characters or words of the handwriting samples used for match should be similar or even identical, e.g. signature verification. In contrary, the other category of approaches are named as *text-independent* because they need no prior knowledge on the text contents of handwriting and the probe and gallery handwritings may be totally different in contents. Text-dependent approaches may align the corresponding text elements between two handwritings for precise one-to-one match, which is advantageous in pattern recognition. However, text-dependent approaches are limited in specific texts and easier to be cracked with forgery. In contrary, **text-independent writer identification** (TIWI) is insensitive to text content but it needs to find the similarity of two intra-class handwritten documents with different contents. So TIWI is a more challenging task but it is more resistant to forgery and has much broader applications.

Digital handwriting can be acquired into computer through off-line or on-line methods. Off-line methods scan the text blocks on handwritten documents to digital images. So image processing and analysis are the main technical tools of off-line writer identification. With fast development of pen-enabled electronic devices such as smart phone, PDA and Tablet PCs, temporal handwriting signals including pen-position, pen-down or pen-up, pen-pressure, pen-altitude, pen-azimuth at each sampling time can be recorded online. So online handwriting is in a higher dimensional signal format (6D or even higher), which contains much more information than two-dimensional image of off-line handwriting.

Automatic writer identification has a long history in pattern recognition and references of traditional methods can be found in the review paper of (Plamondon, & Lorette, 1989). This paper addresses the problem of text-independent writer identification (TIWI) from both off-line and on-line handwritings. Firstly the recent research works in text-independent writer identification are surveyed as follows.

Typical off-line TIWI methods proposed in literature are based on texture analysis (Said, Tan, & Baker, 2000; Said, Peake, Tan, & Baker, 1998), graphemes (Bensefia, Paquet, & Heutte, 2005a & 2005b), text line (Marti, Messerli, & Bunke, 2001; Hertel, & Bunke, 2003), Hidden Markov Model (Schlapbach, & Bunke, 2004), edge-based directional probability distributions (Bulacu, Schomaker, & Vuurpijl, 2003), hinge transform (Bulacu, & Schomaker, 2007), allographic fraglet codebooks (Bulacu, & Schomaker, 2007; Schomaker, & Bulacu, 2004). Said et al. (1998; 2000) globally regarded the handwriting image as a texture rather than a collection of text elements (Said, Tan, & Baker, 2000; Said, Peake, Tan, & Baker, 1998). So well-developed texture analysis methods such as Gabor filtering and gray-scale co-occurrence matrix can be directly used for handwriting feature representation. Texture-based methods have the advantage of robustness to noisy handwriting documents but they lose the local features for accurate identification. In a database of 40 writers, the texture methods (Said,

Tan, & Baker, 2000; Said, Peake, Tan, & Baker, 1998) correctly classify 96% samples. Bensefia et al. (2005) proposed to segment the graphemes for handwriting feature representation and information retrieval models were used for writer identification (Bensefia, Paquet, & Heutte, 2005a & 2005b). The approach achieved 95% correct identification on the PSI_DataBase and 86% on the IAM_DataBase. Similarly, Bulacu et al. (2004; 2007) clustered the grapheme codebook and the PDF of visual primitives was used to describe handwriting (Bulacu, & Schomaker, 2007; Schomaker, & Bulacu, 2004). Since handwriting primitives segmentation in offline documents is sensitive to noise and the clustering results rely on training database, grapheme or clustering codebook based methods are limited in generalization ability and not desirable in practical applications. The most promising feature model in writer identification is PDF or joint PDF of directional features (Bulacu, Schomaker, & Vuurpijl, 2003; Bulacu, & Schomaker, 2007). Directional PDF denotes slant angle information and joint directional PDF describe curvature information of handwriting. So statistics of directional handwriting primitives is both stable and distinctive feature and achieves state-of-the-art performance (EER=3.2% in a database of 250 writers and EER=2.6% in a database of 900 writers) in offline text-independent writer identification (Bulacu, & Schomaker, 2007).

Comparatively, on-line text-independent writer identification techniques are not well developed and only a few papers have been published on this subject (Thumwarin, & Matsuura, 2004; Namboodiri, & Gupta, 2006; Liwicki et al., 2006). Most research of text-independent writer identification is on off-line handwriting for the applications in forensic and historic documents where online data are not available. Thumwarin and Matsuura (2004) proposed to use velocity barycenter of pen-point movement for online writer recognition, with a result of FRR=1.5% when FAR=0.65% on a database of 6,642 samples from 81 writers in Thai scripts (Thumwarin, & Matsuura, 2004).

Namboodiri et al. (2006) proposed a text independent writer identification framework that uses a specified set of primitives of online handwritten data to ascertain the identity of the writer (Namboodiri, & Gupta, 2006). Accuracy of 87% was reported using only single primitive. Liwicki et al. (2006) used two sets of features extracted to train the GMM models: point-based features and stroke-based features (Liwicki et al., 2006). The method achieved a writer identification rate of 94.75% for writer sets with up to 200 writers.

This chapter describes the databases, algorithms and working systems of our research group for text-independent writer identification. We attempt to find the answer of the following questions:

- What are the stable and distinctive features of individual handwriting?
- How to integrate multiple handwriting features for better biometrics performance?
- How much handwritten text is needed for reliable text-independent writer identification?
- What is the similarity and dissimilarity between twins' handwritings?
- Is it possible to achieve cross-language writer identification?
- When does the research of text-independent writer identification come to real-world applications?

Many writer identification methods have been reported but these questions remain open and intriguing. This chapter can only provide the very first information of these problems to inspire readers to approach nearer the goal with new ideas.

The rest of this chapter is organized as follows. Text-independent writer identification algorithms, CASIA handwriting databases along with the experimental results, and a demo system for online writer authentication are presented in the Section 2, Section 3 and Section 4 respectively. Section 5 finally concludes this chapter.

TEXT-INDEPENDENT WRITER IDENTIFICATION

A core problem in text-independent writer identification is how to represent the stable and distinctive features of individual handwriting. On one hand, the feature representation should be robust against intra-class variations of handwriting. Handwriting is a behavioral biometric that is influenced by physical and emotional conditions of the writer. Thus no one writes exactly in the same way twice. For text-independent writer identification, changes in textual contents and length are another important source of variations in the handwriting. So it is challenging to derive stable features from variable handwriting samples. On the other hand, the uniqueness of handwriting can not be guaranteed since many people write in similar style. In addition, professional forgers may be able to reproduce indistinguishable handwritings that fool the system. So the most challenging issue in handwriting feature representation is to achieve sensitivity to inter-class differences and at the same time to maintain robustness against intra-class variations.

A handwriting sample is a hierarchical structure constituted by multi-level components: paragraph, sentence, word, character, stroke, and point. So the uniqueness of the handwriting biometric is believed to be shown at multiple scales of features. For example, some handwritten documents are often visually distinctive at the first look, which demonstrates the effectiveness of global features. In contrast, forensic experts usually pay more attention to local features of handwriting for identity verification. In this section, three text-independent writer identification methods that operate the handwritten document at paragraph-level, stroke-level and point-level respectively will be presented. A common characteristic of these methods is to decompose handwriting into primitives (HP, handwriting primitives) and use the statistics associated with the HP for feature representation. We think HP is critical to the success of text-independent writer identification because the character-independent primitives are the only commonly shared features between the within-class handwritings with different contents. So the core problem of TIWI is how to define the HP and derive stable statistical features on HP.

It should be noted that our research group has published the paragraph-level and stroke-level writer identification methods in (Zhu, Tan, & Wang, 2000) and (Li, Sun, & Tan, 2007) respectively. They are briefly described in the Section 2.1 and 2.2 again for the purpose of showing the technology roadmap of handwriting biometrics. Interested readers are suggested to read these two papers for more details.

Paragraph-Level Feature Representation for Text-Independent Writer Identification

The most salient paragraph-level features in handwriting are the texture-like appearance inter-weaved by ink-trace and uniform background. So the handwriting can be seen as an image containing some special texture and writer identification is regarded as a problem of texture analysis and identification (Said, Peake, Tan, & Baker, 1998). The idea of global texture analysis based TIWI method is described as the following diagram.

There are two stages in a writer identification system, i.e. enrollment and identification. In enrollment stage, each page of handwriting is preprocessed and compressed to form a compact image block of texture, with a balance between black (foreground) and white (background). Then the normalized handwritten image is analyzed with an appropriate texture operator and the resultant feature vector is stored as a template. In identification stage, the input handwriting will be processed with the same preprocessing and feature extraction methods in enrollment stage. Moreover, a matching module is needed to compare the input feature vector with all templates. When the match score is higher than a given threshold, the identity of the matched template is returned as the writer identification result. In our previous paper (Zhu, Tan, & Wang, 2000), the preprocessing is based on text line localization and space normalization. The multi-channel Gabor filters (MCGF) are used for handwriting feature extraction because Gabor filters are biologically inspired image analysis operators with proven excellent performance in texture analysis. The Gabor filter response on the normalized handwriting image of Figure 1 is shown in Figure 2. It is clear that handwriting texture is illustrated at different orientations and scales. The matching engine for Gabor-based handwriting features is a Weighted Euclidean Classifier.

The texture based handwriting features have been proven to have good performance in both English and Chinese writer identification. Results of 96.0% accuracy on the classification of 1,000 test documents from 40 writers are very promising in English writer identification (Said,, Tan, & Baker, 2000; Said, Peake, Tan, & Baker, 1998). And results of 95.7% accuracy on the classification of 34*25 test documents from 17 writers are very encouraging in Chinese writer identification

(Zhu, Tan, & Wang, 2000). The method is shown to be robust to noise and independent of textual contents. However, the multi-channel Gabor filtering is time-consuming and global texture features, i.e. overall statistics on response images of Figure 2, are less distinctive than local ones.

Stroke-level Feature Representation for Text-Independent Writer Identification

Each language of script is constituted by a set of basic units. As the building blocks of characters, these basic units always frequently occur in handwriting, no matter the content of text. So characterizing the personalized features of the basic units of handwriting is an effective method for text-independent writer identification. For English script, the basic unit set is the letters from '*a*' to '*z*'. In contrast, the basic unit of Chinese characters is stroke. The primary stroke types of Chinese characters are listed in Figure 3. So the main tasks in Chinese writer identification are segmentation of strokes from handwriting and description of strokes with appropriate features.

Figure 1. Diagram of global texture analysis based writer identification

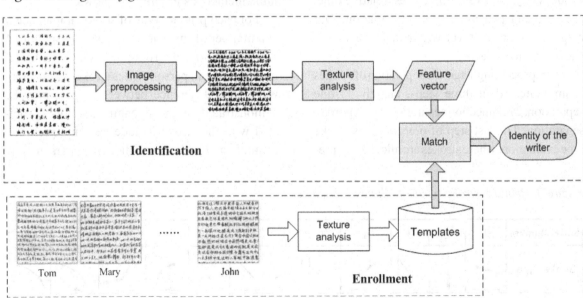

Figure 2. Gabor energy features with variations of orientation and frequency parameters

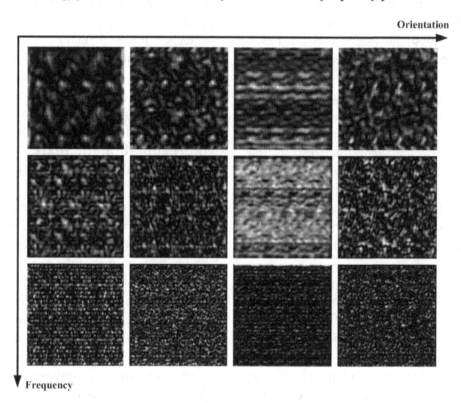

In this Sub-Section we discuss personal identification based on online handwriting acquired by a WACOM tablet. On-line handwriting samples are obtained as a sequence of parameterized dots, inside which involves coordinates, relative time, pressure and pen inclination information. Our diagram for stroke-level writer identification is shown in the Figure 4.

In preprocessing stage, the separation of strokes is implemented in three steps, namely 1) line separation, 2) connection separation, and 3) stroke separation. The last step of preprocess is stroke type evaluation, where strokes are allocated to pre-defined stroke types. The raw data collected from the tablet includes many fake strokes and noises, as Figure 5(a) shows. After the preprocessing to wipe off fake strokes, the separation of strokes is implemented, as Figure 5(b) shows.

For each primary type of stroke, it may occur at a number of times in a handwriting sample. A basic assumption in stroke-level writer identification is that each person writes strokes in different ways. The difference between writers may be demonstrated in the dynamic features associated with the stroke include velocity, pressure, azimuth and altitude. Although a person may

Figure 3. Primary stroke types of Chinese characters

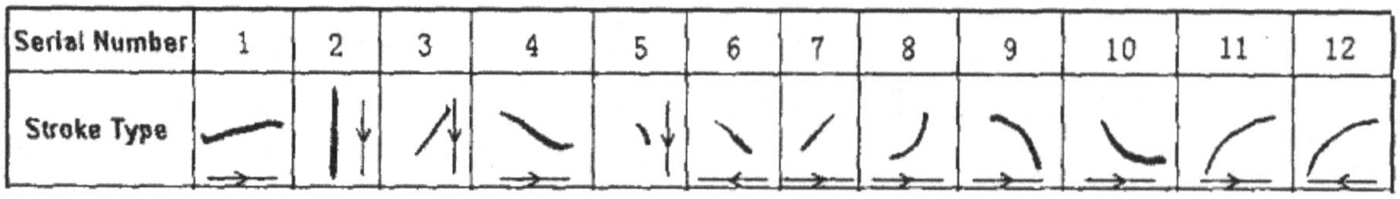

Serial Number	1	2	3	4	5	6	7	8	9	10	11	12
Stroke Type												

Figure 4. Diagram of stroke-level writer identification method

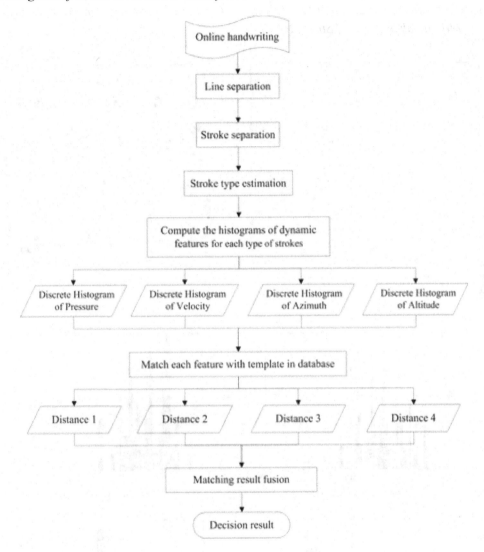

write a single stroke arbitrarily, the statistics of the dynamic stroke features should be stable as a behavioral biometrics. So we propose to adopt the probability distribution function (PDF) of the four dynamic features (velocity, pressure, azimuth and altitude) in a whole handwriting sample to characterize writer individuality (see Figure 5c). The tablet WACOM intuos2 I-620 has 1,024 levels of pressure sensitivity. For the purpose of robust representation of the PDF of dynamic features, the pressure signal is coarsely quantized into 64-level to ensure the amount of samples in each

bin is averagely sufficient. Similarly, the velocity feature is quantized into 30-level, azimuth into 18-level and altitude into 18-level. In summary, an overview of all the features used in our study is given in Table 1. In feature matching, the matching score between two handwriting samples can be measured by a similarity or distance function of histogram or signature. The candidates for this task include χ^2 distance, Euclidean distance, nominal distance, ordinal distance, modulo distance, etc (Serratosa, & Sanfeliu, 2006).

Figure 5. Example of stroke separation and feature description. (a)Original online text. (b)Stroke separation, where the black dots represent the starting and end points of a segment. (c)Pressure, velocity, azimuth and altitude histograms of Stroke type 1

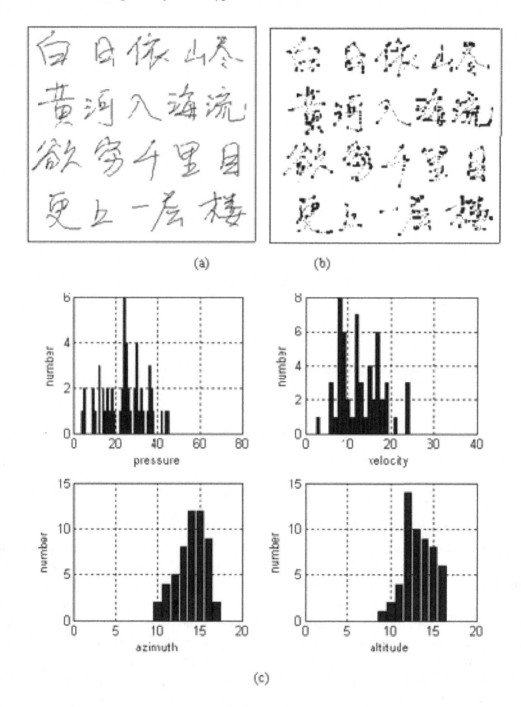

(a) (b)

(c)

Point-Level Feature Representation for Text-Independent Writer Identification

When you write on WACOM Intuos2 tablet, the online handwriting data are collected and encoded as time-varying parameters such as x and y components concerning the pen-position at time t, the status of pen-down or pen-up s, the pen-pressure pr, the pen-altitude ϕ and pen-azimuth φ at a sampling frequency of 200 points per second. So the raw handwritten data are represented as a seven dimensional feature vector $\{x, y, t, s, pr, \phi, \varphi\}$ at each sampling point.

Local image features are proven to be very effective in object recognition (Zhang, Marszałek, Lazebnik, & Schmid, 2007), which motivates the proposal of local point set based handwriting primitives. For the example shown in Figure 6, given two connected sampling points $P_k(x_k, y_k)$ and $P_{k+1}(x_{k+1}, y_{k+1})$, we can define $(P_k P_{k+1})$ as the di-point handwriting primitive (or Di-HP for short) and the direction θ, velocity V and pressure P as the attributes of this HP, where the definition of θ, V and P is shown as follows.

$$\theta = \arctan((y_{k+1} - y_k)/(x_{k+1} - x_k)) \tag{3}$$

$$V = \sqrt{(y_{k+1} - y_k)^2 + (x_{k+1} - x_k)^2} \tag{4}$$

$$P = (pr(P_k) + pr(P_{k+1}))/2 \tag{5}$$

Table 1. Overview of the dynamic features in stroke-level writer identification

Feature label	Feature meaning	Quantization level	Feature dimension
f_1	Pressure-PDF	64	768
f_2	Velocity-PDF	30	360
f_3	Azimuth-PDF	18	216
f_4	Altitude-PDF	18	216

Similarly, the tri-point handwriting primitives can be defined as Tri-HP $(P_k P_{k+1} P_{k+2})$, with the associated attributes θ_1 $\theta_2 V_1$, V_2, dP (see Figure 7). Here dP is developed to describe the average pressure changes in Tri-HP.

$$\theta_1 = \arctan((y_{k+1} - y_k)/(x_{k+1} - x_k)) \tag{6}$$

$$\theta_2 = \arctan((y_{k+2} - y_{k+1})/(x_{k+2} - x_{k+1})) \tag{7}$$

$$V_1 = \sqrt{(y_{k+1} - y_k)^2 + (x_{k+1} - x_k)^2} \tag{8}$$

$$V_2 = \sqrt{(y_{k+2} - y_{k+1})^2 + (x_{k+2} - x_{k+1})^2} \tag{9}$$

$$dP = (|pr(P_{k+1}) + pr(P_k)| + |pr(P_{k+2}) + pr(P_{k+1})|)/2 \tag{10}$$

Therefore a large number of Tri-HP can be derived from each handwriting sample when every three connected points form a Tri-HP. To efficiently represent the statistical features of a handwritten document, these Tri-HPs should be grouped into a limited number of categories. Inspired by the success of Hinge features (Bulacu, & Schomaker, 2007) in off-line writer identification, we propose to use the joint distribution of θ_1 and θ_2 as the categorization features of Tri-HP. Here the angle value of θ_1 or θ_2 is coarsely quantized into 12 sectors (see Figure 8, the angle quantization parameter 12 is chosen based on experiences). So there are totally 144 types of Tri-HPs (Figure 9).

We propose two kinds of statistical features on the basis of Tri-HP vocabulary. The first one aims to model the geometric shape of handwriting trajectory based on the PDF of Tri-HP, i.e. a 12×12 histogram (see Figure 10). Shape feature encodes both direction and curvature information of handwriting, which have been proven to be effective for off-line writer identification (Bulacu, & Schomaker, 2007). In this chapter we extend it to on-line handwriting feature representation. From Figure 10 we can observe that the shape feature is

Figure 6. Di-point handwriting primitives

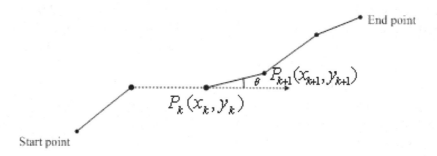

Figure 7. Tri-point handwriting primitives

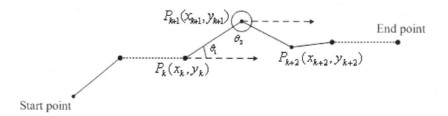

both stable across intra-class variations including changes of text contents and discriminating in different writers. The other one aims to represent the dynamic features of online handwriting using the mean and variance values of V_1, V_2, dP for each type of Tri-HP, which denotes the statistics of speed and pressure when a person writes a given type of handwriting primitive. In feature matching step, of course there is significant difference in recognition performance for the 144 Tri-HPs. So it is unreasonable to treat all these Tri-HPs evenly in classification. It is commonly acknowledged that individuality of each writer is more demonstrated in complex handwriting patterns. So here we assume that Tri-HP with higher curvature is more discriminating. To emphasize the contribution of high curvature Tri-HPs in writer authentication, we classify the 144 Tri-HPs into two groups, basic Tri-HPs and key Tri-HPs (Eqn. 11). θ^* is set to be 45° in our experiment. Then different weights w_1 and w_2 are associated with the two groups of dynamic features during feature matching. In the

experiment, we set $w_1 = 0.35$ and $w_2 = 0.65$ for basic Tri-HPs and key Tri-HPs respectively. The values of parameters θ^*, w_1 and w_2 are chosen based on experimental results.

$$\begin{cases} |\theta_2 - \theta_1| < \theta^*, & \text{basic Tri-HP} \\ |\theta_2 - \theta_1| \geq \theta^*, & \text{key Tri-HP} \end{cases} \tag{11}$$

Figure 8. Quantization of directional features

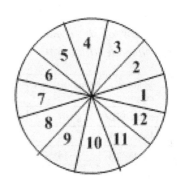

Figure 9. Examples of Tri-HPs

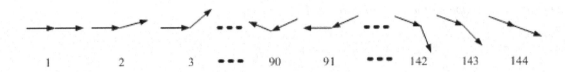

In summary, all the point-level handwriting features for a handwritten document are listed in Table 2.

In feature matching stage, the shape and dynamic features of handwriting samples can be compared separately (see Figure 11).

We try five different measures to compute the distance between histogram-based shape features $h_1(x)$ and $h_2(x)$ (Serratosa, & Sanfeliu, 2006).

- *L1* distance: $L1(h_1, h_2) = \sum\limits_{i=1}^{144} |h_1(i) - h_2(i)|$
- *L2* distance:
$$L2(h_1, h_2) = \sqrt{\sum\limits_{i=1}^{144} [h_1(i) - h_2(i)]^2}$$
- Cosine angle distance:
$$CA(h_1, h_2) = \arccos(h_1 \cdot h_2 / \sqrt{\|h_1\| \|h_2\|})$$
- Chi-square distance:
$$CS(h_1, h_2) = \sum\limits_{i=1}^{144} [h_1(i) - h_2(i)]^2 / [h_1(i) + h_2(i)]$$
- Diffusion distance: $DF(h_1, h_2)$ (Ling, & Okada, 2006)

For dynamic feature, basic Tri-HP and key Tri-HP are matched separately using Euclidean distance and then their weighted sum is computed as the dissimilarity between two dynamic features.

Finally, the overall distance between two handwritten documents is determined by the fusion output of the matching results of shape feature and dynamic feature based on weighted Sum-Rule. Based on one-to-one match result, the final decision of both writer identification and writer verification can be made (see Figure 11).

EXPERIMENTAL RESULTS

Handwriting database is important to technical evaluation of writer identification methods. However, there were no common online handwriting databases of a reasonable size in the public domain. We therefore constructed two handwriting databases namely CASIA-HandwritingV1 and CASIA-HandwritingV2 using WACOM Intuos2 tablet as illustrated in Figure 12. To make handwriting biometrics research possible to more people, we have released to the public domain the CASIA-HandwritingV2 (CASIA Handwriting Database, 2008). This section reports the experimental results of texture-level, stroke-level and point-level online handwriting feature representation methods on CASIA-HandwritingV2. In addition, stroke-level method is also evaluated on CASIA-HandwritingV1 and SVC2004 database (Yeung et al., 2004).

Table 2. Overview of the point-level handwriting features

Feature type	Feature meaning	Feature dimension
Shape feature	Occurrence frequency of Tri-HP	144
Dynamic feature	Mean and variance of speed and pressure for each type of Tri-HP	144×3×2=864

Figure 10. Illustration of the shape feature of handwriting (a) Two handwriting samples written by writer A, along with their shape feature, i.e. PDF of Tri-HP. (b) Two handwriting samples written by writer B, along with their shape feature, i.e. PDF of Tri-HP

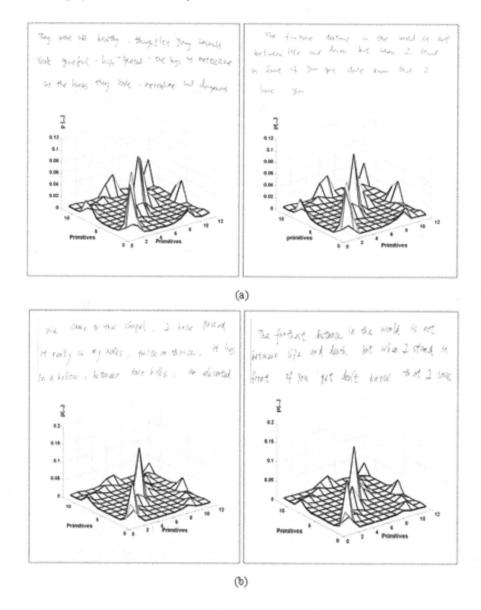

(a)

(b)

Experimental Results of Stroke-Level Handwriting Feature Representation Method on CASIA-HandwritingV1 and SVC2004 Database

CASIA-HandwritingV1 (Figure 13) includes 165 pages of Chinese handwriting from 55 subjects, i.e. 3 pages/subject. Each subject writes less than 200 Chinese characters on each page. The content of the handwriting is determined by the writers freely, so the database collected by this manner is text-independent handwriting. To test stroke-level handwriting feature representation method, the first two pages of handwriting are

Figure 11. Feature matching scheme for point-level handwriting feature representation method

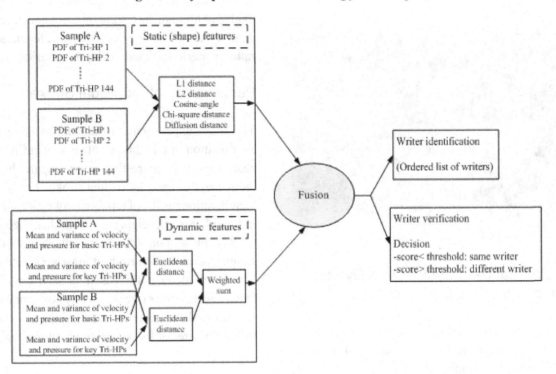

used for training and the last one (approximately 160 characters) is used for testing.

Performance of Individual Stroke-Level Dynamic Feature

Firstly, individual stroke-level dynamic feature such as Pressure-PDF, Velocity-PDF, Azimuth-PDF, Altitude-PDF is evaluated on CASIA-HandwritingV1 separately. The Correct Classification Rate (CCR) of writer identification as a function of the number of text lines is shown in Figure 14.

From experimental results we can conclude that 1) velocity is the most effective dynamic feature for online text-independent writer identification, followed by pressure, azimuth, and altitude; 2) writing more leads to more accurate identification results when the number of text lines are less than 7, and the statistical dynamic features of handwriting become stable when the number of text lines are larger than 7.

Combination of all Stroke-Level Dynamic Features

When we combine all dynamic features for writer identification, significant improvement of CCR can be achieved (see Figure 15). Here the matching results of four types of dynamic features are combined in score level using weighted Sum-rule and the min-max rule is used for score normalization. The writer identification results with five different distance functions for PDF feature matching respectively are compared in Figure 15. The result shows that ordinal distance is the best performing measure for histogram-based dynamic feature matching. From Figure 15 we can observe that when the number of text lines exceeds 5, the top-1 writer identification accuracy CCR is higher than 90%, which demonstrates the success of stroke-level dynamic features for TIWI.

Figure 12. Illustration of online handwriting data collection

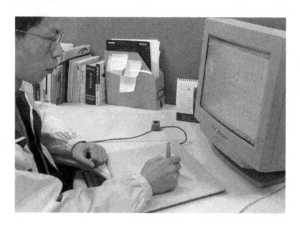

Performance of Stroke-Level Dynamic Features on the SVC Database

The proposed method is also evaluated on SVC2004 database (Yeung et al., 2004). Since SVC2004 is designed for signature verification, we regard each signature as a stroke. There are totally 800 genuine signatures from 40 subjects in our test. The EER (Equal Error Rate) results using different distance measures are shown in Table 3. Although the results are not excellent, they demonstrate that stroke-level dynamic features are rather generic for handwriting biometrics.

Performance of Individual Stroke

The above experimental results are based on the combination of all 12 types of strokes in Chinese characters. It is interesting to investigate the effectiveness of each individual stroke. The writer identification results of top four strokes are shown in Table 4. For other eight types of strokes, the top-1 CCR is only around 40%. The results show that the simplest strokes perform best in writer identification. We think the main reason for such a result is that subjects write more frequently horizontal and vertical strokes in Chinese handwriting so the statistical features of these strokes are more stable.

Figure 13. Handwriting samples in the CASIA-HandwritingV1

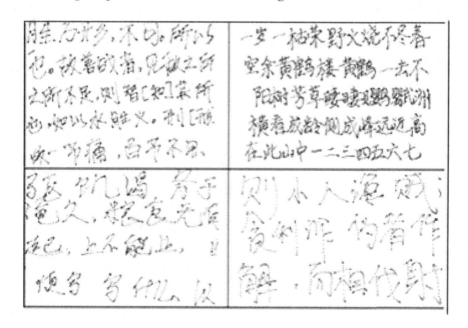

Figure 14. Performance of individual dynamic feature as a function of the number of handwriting lines

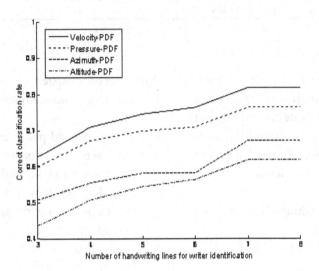

Figure 15. The identification results when four types of dynamic features are combined

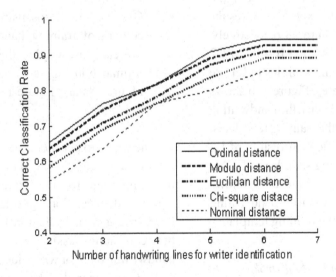

Experimental Results of Point-Level Handwriting Feature Representation Method

CASIA-HandwritingV2 contains more than 1,500 online handwritten documents from more than

250 subjects (Figure 16). The handwriting data are collected in two sessions. In the first session, each subject is required to write six pages of handwriting, i.e. one for fixed content in Chinese (C1), two for free content in Chinese (C2 and C3), one for fixed content in English (E1), and two for

Table 3. Performance of stroke-level dynamic features on the SVC database

Distance measure	Euclidean distance	Chi-square distance	Nominal distance	Ordinal distance	Modulo distance
EER	11.4%	11.8%	15.0%	9.7%	10.4%

free content in English (E2 and E3). In the second session, each subject is required to freely write one page of Chinese (C4) and one page of English (E4) respectively. There are about 50 words in each page. The handwriting data can be used to design two subsets for performance evaluation:

- Subset 1 contains all Chinese handwriting pages in the first session.
- Subset 2 contains all English handwriting pages in the first session.

The point-level handwriting feature representation methods with different distance measures in shape feature matching are tested on Subset 1 and Subset 2 respectively, with the experimental results shown in Figure 17 and Figure 18 respectively. Figure 17a shows the verification results of C2 and C3 when the handwriting samples in C1 are used as the training templates. Figure 17b shows the verification results of C3 when the handwriting samples in C2 are used as the training templates. Figure 18a shows the verification results of E2 and E3 when the handwriting samples in E1 are used as the training templates. Figure 18b shows the verification results of E3 when the handwriting samples in E2 are used as the training templates.

Table 4. Performance of individual stroke

Type of stroke	Top-1 CCR	Top-5 CCR
The horizontal stroke (type 1)	70%	92%
The vertical stroke (type 2)	68%	90%
The left-falling stroke (type 3)	60%	73%
The right-falling stroke (type 4)	63%	74%

A number of consistent conclusions can be drawn from the experimental results.

- The proposed point-level handwriting feature representation methods perform well in both Chinese and English handwriting datasets, which demonstrates that our writer identification method is generic and independent of language.
- Chi-square distance and diffusion distance are the most effective histogram distance measure for shape feature matching and the performance difference between Chi-square distance and diffusion distance is very small.
- Our method is insensitive to the textual content of training handwriting samples. We can observe that the recognition performance in Figure 17a and Figure 17b or Figure 18a and Figure 18b is approximately identical.

The above experiments compare handwriting samples collected in the same session and it is more important to investigate the effectiveness of writer identification algorithm in cross-session handwriting data. To demonstrate the difference between same session and different session handwriting data for writer identification, C1, C2 and C3 is compared with C4 respectively and the experimental results are shown in Figure 19. It demonstrates that the performance of cross-session handwriting authentication is much worse than the same-session results.

To put the proposed method in the context of state-of-the-art, our method is compared with the widely used online text-independent writer iden-

Figure 16. Example handwriting pages in CASIA-HandwritingV2

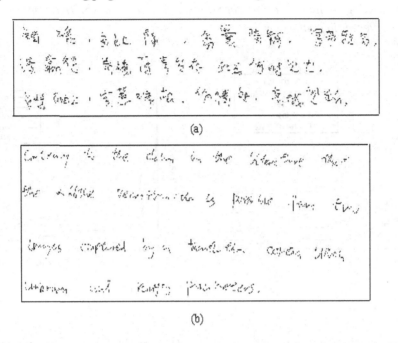

(a)

(b)

tification approaches in literature, i.e. (Liwicki et al., 2006) and (Namboodiri, & Gupta, 2006). The results are shown in Figure 20, demonstrating that our method is much better than the other two best performing methods in literature.

In this chapter, we have proposed three handwriting feature representation methods operating at different level of handwriting. So it is interesting to compare these methods on the same dataset. Because CASIA-HandwritingV2 contains only online

Figure 17. ROC curves of point-level handwriting feature representation method on Subset 1 (Chinese). (a) Training handwriting samples of all writers are same in content. (b) Training handwriting samples of all writers are different in content

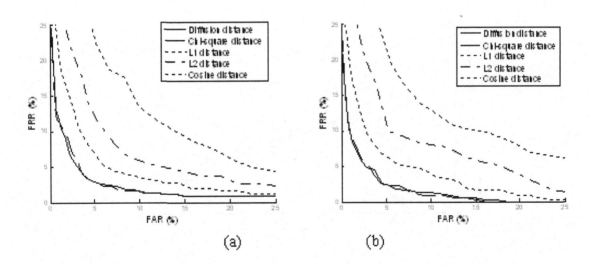

(a)   (b)

Figure 18. ROC curves of point-level handwriting feature representation method on Subset 2 (English). (a) Training handwriting samples of all writers are same in content. (b) Training handwriting samples of all writers are different in content

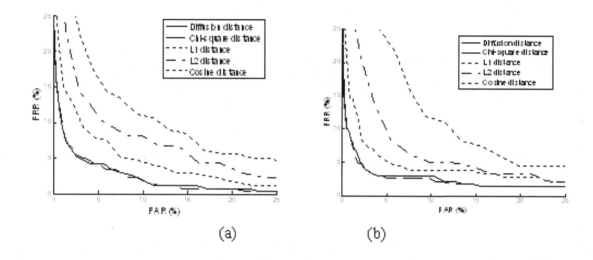

(a)   (b)

handwriting documents but texture-level features are designed for handwriting images, the sampling points in online data are connected into continuous handwriting trajectory, constructing an image

(Figure 21). The comparative experimental results are shown in Figure 22 and Figure 23. The results demonstrate that finer the scale of handwriting primitives, better the recognition performance.

Figure 19. ROC of cross-session handwriting authentication

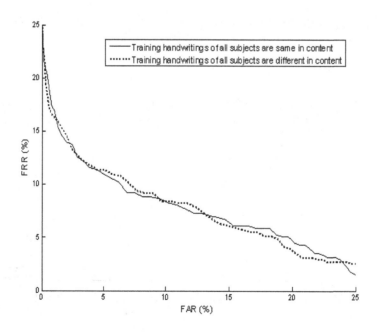

Figure 20. Comparison of the proposed writer identification method with state-of-the-art approaches. (a) ROCs in the Subset 1 (Chinese). (b) ROCs in the Subset 2 (English)

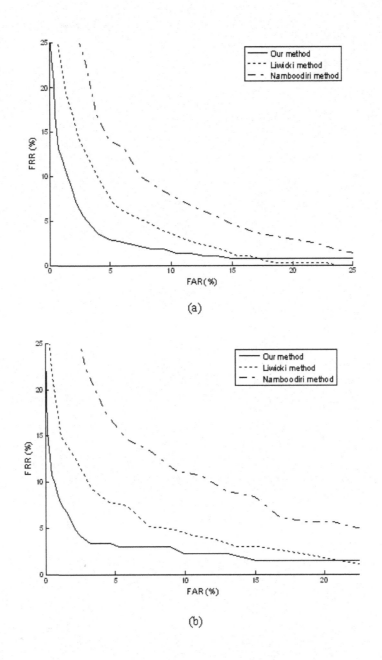

(a)

(b)

A REAL-TIME WRITER IDENTIFICATION SYSTEM

To the best of our knowledge, there is no report of real-time, online, text-independent writer identification system in literature. All our research efforts are trying to make handwriting biometrics work in practical applications. Based on the point-level handwriting feature representation method proposed in the Section 3.3, we developed a demo writer identification system. WACOM Intuos2 tablet is the input device of the system and users

Figure 21. Transform of online handwriting data into offline image data. (a) Sampling points in online handwriting data; (b) Image transformed from (a); (c) Sampling points in online handwriting data; (d) Image transformed from (c)

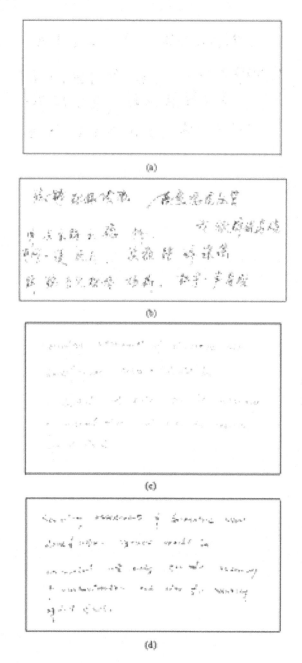

can write any text for enrolment or recognition (see Figure 24). A continuous online handwriting data block with more than twenty words is enough for enrolment. In the demo, there are more than 200 users enrolled into the database. When the system is performed in the recognition mode, the dynamic top-5 identities of the writer are automatically recognized and listed on the status bar

Figure 22. Correct recognition rate of point, stroke and texture based writer identification methods as a function of number of characters used for handwriting biometrics

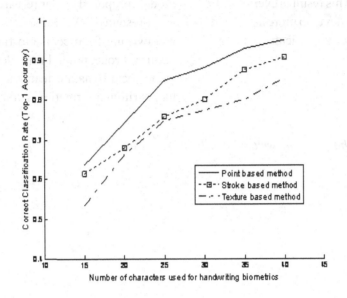

of the software interface when the user is writing. As shown in Figure 25a, the correct identification result "zhongcheng" is listed in the third rank even after the user writes only six English words. Figure 25b shows that after "zhongcheng" writes 14 words his identity is correctly recognized by the system

Figure 23. Receiver operation curves of point, stroke and texture based writer identification methods

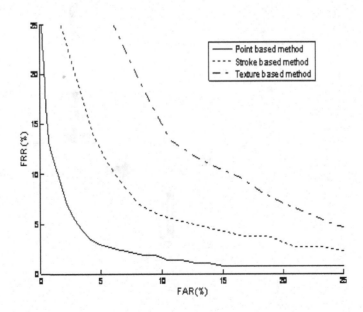

as the first candidate. More than 100 users have experienced our system and the success rate of returning correct query result in the top-5 list after 20 words is about 95%. This result is every exciting and encourages us to develop more advanced working system for writer identification.

CONCLUSION

In this chapter a variety of statistical feature models proposed by our research group for TIWI are presented. We represent text-independent handwriting from coarse to fine in three levels: texture, stroke, point. From global texture analysis to local dynamic features, from single type handwriting information to multiple handwriting

Figure 24. Diagram of the real-time writer identification system

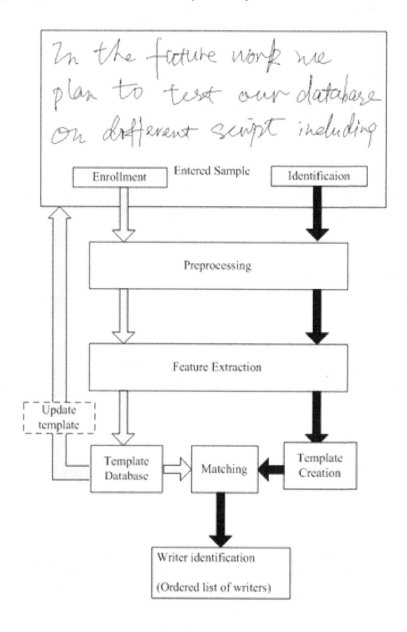

Figure 25. Demos of the writer identification system

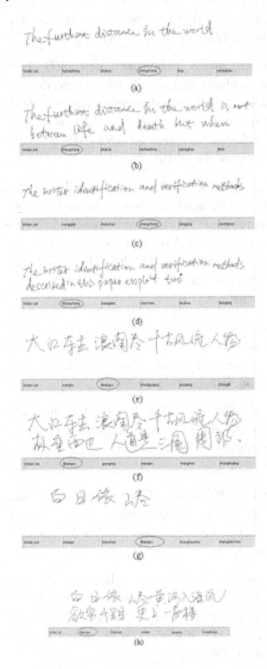

feature integration, the evolution of these feature representation methods shows the technology roadmap of handwriting biometrics. The major contributions of this chapter include:

1. A general framework of text-independent writer identification based on statistical handwriting feature representation is proposed. The core concept of this framework is the handwriting primitive. To demonstrate the effectiveness of this framework, texture-level, stroke-level and point-level handwriting primitives along with the total solutions to TIWI problem are proposed with promising performance in CASIA handwriting databases.

2. This chapter demonstrates that fine scale handwriting primitive is better than coarse one in text-independent writer identification. This result is consistent to the popularity of local features in object recognition. So further research in handwriting biometrics should focus on the micro feature representation.

3. This chapter compared different histogram matching methods for statistical handwriting features and the results show that Chi-square and diffusion distances are the recommended choices.

4. Fusion of statistical shape and dynamic features of point-level handwriting primitives achieves state-of-the-art performance in online TIWI problem.

5. A working system for real-time writer identification is developed. The most compelling feature of this system is online learning of writing style so it can generate dynamic recognition results as the increase of handwriting characters.

Although promising results have been obtained in this chapter, there are many open questions deserving further investigation:

- *How to select better handwriting primitives for statistical feature representation?* Although the tri-point handwriting primitive based method performs well, we think more and more advanced handwriting primitives will be proposed in the future.

- *How to develop a ensemble method to combine handwriting features at multiple scales?* Although texture and stroke based handwriting features do not perform as well as point based ones, they provide complementary information to point-level features.
- *How to propose an interactive writer identification system?* The current text-independent writer identification systems do not limit the textural content in handwriting to unknown subjects in practice. Random handwriting content is disadvantageous to feature modeling and writer authentication. So it is possible to propose an interactive writer identification system so that the most discriminative textural content can be adaptively selected online to test the identity of writers.

ACKNOWLEDGMENT

This work is supported by the National Basic Research Program of China (Grant No. 2004CB318100), the National Natural Science Foundation of China (Grant No. 60736018, 60702024, 60723005), the National Hi-Tech Research and Development Program of China (Grant No.2006AA01Z193, 2007AA01Z162), and the Chinese Academy of Sciences.

REFERENCES

Bensefia, A., Paquet, T., & Heutte, L. (2005a). A writer identification and verification system. *Pattern Recognition Letters*, *26*(13, 2080–2092. doi:10.1016/j.patrec.2005.03.024

Bensefia, A., Paquet, T., & Heutte, L. (2005b). Handwritten document analysis for automatic writer recognition. *Electronic Letters on Computer Vision and Image Analysis*, *5*(2), 72–86.

Bulacu, M., & Schomaker, L. (2007). Text-independent writer identification and verification using textural and allographic features. *IEEE Trans. on Pattern Analysis and Machine Intelligence, Special Issue-Biometrics . Progress and Directions*, *29*(4), 701–717.

Bulacu, M., Schomaker, L., & Vuurpijl, L. (2003). Writer identification using edge-based directional features. *Proc. Seventh International Conference on Document Analysis and Recognition*, 937–941. CASIA Handwriting Database. Retrieved from http://www.cbsr.ia.ac.cn/english/Handwriting Databases.asp

Hertel, C., & Bunke, H. (2003). A set of novel features for writer identification. *Proc. Fourth Int'l Conf. Audio and Video-Based Biometric Person Authentication*, 679-687.

Li, B., Sun, Z., & Tan, T. (2007). Online text-independent writer identification based on stroke's probability distribution function. (. *LNCS*, *4642*, 201–210.

Ling, H., & Okada, K. (2006). Diffusion distance for histogram comparison. *IEEE Conference on Computer Vision and Pattern Recognition*, 246–253.

Liwicki, M., Schlapbach, A., Bunke, H., Bengio, S., Mariéthoz, J., & Richiardi, J. (2006). Writer identification for smart meeting room systems. *Seventh IAPR Workshop on Document Analysis Systems*, 186-195.

Marti, U., Messerli, R., & Bunke, H. (2001). Writer identification using text line based features. *Proc. Sixth Int'l Conf. Document Analysis and Recognition (ICDAR)*, 101-105.

Namboodiri, A., & Gupta, S. (2006). Text independent writer identification from online handwriting. *Tenth International Workshop on Frontiers in Handwriting Recognition*, 131–147.

Plamondon, R., & Lorette, G. (1989). Automatic signature verification and writer identification—the state of the art. *Pattern Recognition, 22*(2), 107–131. doi:10.1016/0031-3203(89)90059-9

Said, H., Peake, G., Tan, T., & Baker, K. (1998). Writer identification from nonuniformly skewed handwriting images. *Proc. Ninth British Machine Vision Conference*, 478-487.

Said, H., Tan, T., & Baker, K. (2000). Personal identification based on handwriting. *Pattern Recognition, 33*(1), 149–160. doi:10.1016/S0031-3203(99)00006-0

Schlapbach, A., & Bunke, H. (2004). Using HMM-based recognizers for writer identification and verification. *Proc. Ninth Int'l Workshop Frontiers in Handwriting Recognition*, 167-172.

Schomaker, L., & Bulacu, M. (2004). Automatic writer identification using connected-component contours and edge-based features of upper-case western script. *IEEE Transactions on Pattern Analysis and Machine Intelligence, 26*(6), 787–798. doi:10.1109/TPAMI.2004.18

Serratosa, F., & Sanfeliu, A. (2006). Signatures versus histograms: Definitions, distances, and algorithms. *Pattern Recognition, 39*(5), 921–934. doi:10.1016/j.patcog.2005.12.005

Thumwarin, P., & Matsuura, T. (2004). Online writer recognition for Thai based on velocity of barycenter of pen-point movement. *Proc. of IEEE International Conference on Image Processing*, 889–892.

Yeung, D., Chang, H., Xiong, Y., George, S., Kashi, R., Matsumoto, T., & Rigoll, G. (2004). SVC 2004: First international signature verification competition. In D. Zhang & A. K. Jain (Eds.), *Proc. ICBA 2004.* (LNCS, 3072, pp. 16–22).

Zhang, J., Marszałek, M., Lazebnik, S., & Schmid, C. (2007). Local features and kernels for classification of texture and object categories: A comprehensive study. *International Journal of Computer Vision, 73*(2), 213–238. doi:10.1007/s11263-006-9794-4

Zhu, Y., Tan, T., & Wang, Y. (2000). Biometric personal identification based on handwriting. *Proceedings of the 15th International Conference on Pattern Recognition, 2*, 797-800.

KEY TERMS AND DEFINITIONS

Text-Independent Writer Identification: Recognizing the identity of a writer no matter the content of his handwriting.

Chapter 16
Keystroke Biometric Identification and Authentication on Long–Text Input

Charles C. Tappert
Pace University, USA

Mary Villani
Pace University, USA

Sung-Hyuk Cha
Pace University, USA

ABSTRACT

A novel keystroke biometric system for long-text input was developed and evaluated for user identification and authentication applications. The system consists of a Java applet to collect raw keystroke data over the Internet, a feature extractor, and pattern classifiers to make identification or authentication decisions. Experiments on over 100 subjects investigated two input modes–copy and free-text input–and two keyboard types–desktop and laptop keyboards. The system can accurately identify or authenticate individuals if the same type of keyboard is used to produce the enrollment and questioned input samples. Longitudinal experiments quantified performance degradation over intervals of several weeks and over an interval of two years. Additional experiments investigated the system's hierarchical model, parameter settings, assumptions, and sufficiency of enrollment samples and input-text length. Although evaluated on input texts up to 650 keystrokes, we found that input of 300 keystrokes, roughly four lines of text, is sufficient for the important applications described.

INTRODUCTION

This chapter describes the development and evaluation of a keystroke biometric system for long-text input. The system has user-identification and user-authentication internet applications that are of increasing importance as the population of application participants continues to grow. An example authentication application is verifying the identity of students taking online quizzes or tests, an application

DOI: 10.4018/978-1-60566-725-6.ch016

becoming more important with the student population of online classes increasing and instructors becoming concerned about evaluation security and academic integrity. Similarly, in a business setting employees can be required to take online examinations in their training programs and the companies would like the exam-takers authenticated. An example identification application is a small company environment (a closed system of known employees) in which there has been a problem with the circulation of inappropriate (unprofessional, offensive, or obscene) e-mail, and it is desirable to identify the perpetrator. Because the inappropriate email is being sent from computers provided by the company for employees to send email and surf the internet during lunch and coffee breaks, there are no ethical issues in capturing users' keystrokes. Finally, with more businesses moving to e-commerce, the keystroke biometric in internet applications can provide an effective balance between high security and customer ease-of-use (Yu & Cho, 2004).

Keystroke biometric systems measure typing characteristics believed to be unique to an individual and difficult to duplicate (Bolle, Connell, Pankanti, Ratha, & Senior, 2004; Jin, Ke, Manuel, & Wilkerson, 2004). The keystroke biometric is one of the less-studied behavioral biometrics. Most of the systems developed previously have been experimental in nature. However, several companies, such as AdmitOne (2008) and Bio-Chec (2008), have recently developed commercial products for hardening passwords (short input) in computer security schemes.

The keystroke biometric is appealing for several reasons. First, it is not intrusive and computer users type frequently for both work and pleasure. Second, it is inexpensive since the only hardware required is a computer with keyboard. Third, keystrokes continue to be entered for potential subsequent checking after an authentication phase has verified a user's identity (or possibly been fooled) since keystrokes exist as a mere consequence of users using computers (Gunetti

& Picardi, 2005). This continuing verification throughout a computer session is sometimes referred to as dynamic verification (Leggett & Williams, 2005; Leggett, Williams, Usnick, & Longnecker, 1991).

Most of the previous work on the keystroke biometric has dealt with user authentication, and while some studies used long-text input (Bergadano, Gunetti, & Picardi, 2002; Gunetti & Picardi, 2005; Leggett & Williams, 2005), most used passwords or short name strings (Bender & Postley, 2007; Bolle et al., 2004; Brown & Rogers, 1993; Monrose, Reiter, & Wetzel, 2002; Monrose & Rubin, 2000; Obaidat & Sadoun, 1999). Fewer studies have dealt with user identification (Gunetti & Picardi, 2005; Peacock, Ke, & Wilkerson, 2004; Song, Venable, & Perrig, 1997). Gunetti and Picardi (2005) focused on long free-text passages, similar to this research, and also attempted the detection of uncharacteristic patterns due to fatigue, distraction, stress, or other factors. Song et al. (1997) touched on the idea of detecting a change in identity through continuous monitoring.

Researchers tend to collect their own data and no known studies have compared techniques on a common database. Nevertheless, the published literature is optimistic about the potential of keystroke dynamics to benefit computer system security and usability (Woodward, Orlans, & Higgins, 2002). Gunetti and Picardi (2005) suggest that if short inputs do not provide sufficient timing information, and if long predefined texts entered repeatedly are unacceptable, we are left with only one possible solution, using users' normal interactions with computers, *free text*, as we do in this research.

Generally, a number of measurements or features are used to characterize a user's typing pattern. These measurements are typically derived from the raw data of key press times, key release times, and the identity of the keys pressed. From key-press and key-release times a feature vector, often consisting of keystroke duration times and keystroke transition times, can be created

(Woodward et al., 2002). Such measurements can be collected from all users of a system, such as a computer network or web-based system, where keystroke entry is available, and a model that attempts to distinguish an individual user from others can be established. For short input such as passwords, however, the lack of sufficient measurements presents a problem because keystrokes, unlike other biometric features, convey only a small amount of information. Moreover, this information tends to vary for different keyboards, different environmental conditions, and different entered texts (Gunetti & Picardi, 2005).

The keystroke biometric system reported here is unique in several respects. First, it collects raw keystroke data over the internet, which is desirable for internet security applications such as those described above. Second, it focuses on long-text input where sufficient keystroke data are available to permit the use of powerful statistical feature measurements – and the number, variety, and strength of the measurements used in the system are much greater than those used by earlier systems reported in the literature. Third, it focuses on applications using arbitrary text input because copy texts are unacceptable for most applications of interest. However, because of the statistical nature of the features and the use of arbitrary text input, special statistical fallback procedures were incorporated into the system to handle the paucity of data from infrequently used keyboard keys.

This chapter extends two previous studies on the *identification* application of a long-text keystroke biometric system. The first previous study showed the feasibility of an early version of the identification system on a text copy task (Curtin et al., 2006). The second showed the effectiveness of an improved system under ideal conditions of a fixed text and keyboard, and under less favorable conditions of arbitrary texts and different keyboard types for enrollment and testing (Villani et al., 2006). This chapter extends the earlier studies, essentially the second one, in

several ways. First, it presents the results of the second study in a clearer manner, separating the presentation of results into ideal and non-ideal conditions. Second, it extends the system to include an authentication component and presents authentication results to complement the earlier identification results. Third, it collects new data and performs longitudinal studies on data collected over intervals of several weeks and over an interval of two years to quantify performance degradation over time. Finally, it conducts additional experiments to investigate the hierarchical model, the parameter settings, the normal distribution assumption for the primary feature measurements, and the sufficiency of the number of enrollment samples and input text length.

The organization of the remainder of the chapter is straightforward: methodology, results, and conclusions. The next section describes the long-text keystroke biometric system, which has components for data capture, feature extraction, and classification. The following section describes the experimental design and data collection. The next section describes the experimental results on identification, on authentication, on the longitudinal studies, and on the system model and parameters. The final section presents the conclusions and suggestions for future work.

KEYSTROKE BIOMETRIC SYSTEM

The keystroke biometric system consists of four components: raw keystroke data capture, feature extraction, classification for identification, and classification for authentication.

Raw Keystroke Data Capture

A Java applet collects keystroke data over the internet (Figure 1). The user is required to type in his/her name, but no data is captured on this entry. The submission number is automatically incremented after each sample submission, so the subject can immediately start typing the next sample. If the user is interrupted during data entry, the "Clear" button blanks all fields, except name and submission number, allowing the user to redo the current entry.

Upon pressing submit, a raw-data text file is generated, which is delimited by the '~' character. Figure 2 shows the aligned version of the "Hello World!" raw data file. The raw data file contains the following information for each entry: 1) entry sequence number, 2) key's character, 3) key's code text equivalent, 4) key's location (1 = standard, only one key location; 2 = left side of keyboard; 3 = right side of keyboard), 5) time the key was pressed (milliseconds), 6) time the key was released (milliseconds). The number of left-mouse-click, right-mouse-click, and double left-mouse-click events during the session (these are events in contrast to key presses) are listed at the end of the file.

Figure 1. Java applet for data collection, (© 2006 IEEE. Used with permission.)

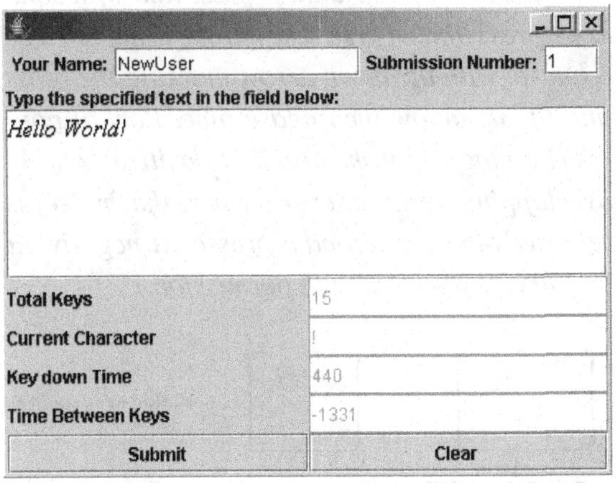

Feature Extraction

The system extracts a feature vector from the information in a raw data file. The features are statistical in nature and designed to characterize an individual's keystroke dynamics over writing samples of 200 or more characters. Most of the features are averages and standard deviations of key press duration times and of transition times

Figure 2. Aligned raw data file for "Hello World!" (© 2006 IEEE. Used with permission.)

NewUser	Submission 1				
Entry #	Key	Keycode	Location	Press	Release
Num 1	?	Shift	2	1114450735680	1114450736962
Num 2	H	H	1	1114450735991	1114450736311
Num 3	e	E	1	1114450737653	1114450738144
Num 4	l	L	1	1114450738735	1114450739256
Num 5	l	L	1	1114450739786	1114450740277
Num 6	o	O	1	1114450740998	1114450741399
Num 7		Space	1	1114450742090	1114450742420
Num 8	?	Shift	2	1114450743542	1114450745004
Num 9	W	W	1	1114450743872	1114450744263
Num 10	o	O	1	1114450745755	1114450746216
Num 11	r	R	1	1114450747017	1114450747437
Num 12	l	L	1	1114450748138	1114450748549
Num 13	d	D	1	1114450749310	1114450749771
Num 14	?	Shift	2	1114450751373	1114450753776
Num 15	!	1	1	1114450752445	1114450752885
Left Clicks	0				
Right Clicks	0				
Double Clicks	0				

Figure 3. A two-key sequence (th) shows the two transition measures:t_1 = press time of second key – release time of first, and t_2 = press time of second key – press time of first. A keystroke is depicted as a bucket with the down arrow marking the press and the up arrow the release time. Part a) non-overlapping keystroke events (t_1 positive), and b) overlapping keystroke events where the first key is released after the second is pressed (t_1 negative). (© 2006 IEEE. Used with permission.)

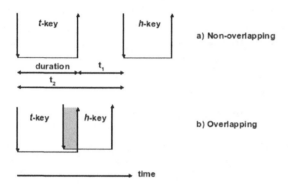

between keystroke pairs, such as digraphs (Obaidat & Sadoun, 1999; Peacock et al., 2004). Figure 3 shows the transition between keystrokes measured in two ways: from the release of the first key to the press of the second, t_1, and from the press of the first to the press of the second, t_2. While the second measure, t_2, is always positive because this sequence determines the keyboard output, the first measure, t_1, can be negative. We refer to these two measures of transition time as type-1 and type-2 transition features.

While key press duration and transition times are typically used as features in keystroke biometric studies, our use of the statistical measures of means and standard deviations of the key presses and transitions is uncommon and only practical for long text input. As additional features, we use percentages of key presses of many of the special keys. Some of these percentage features are designed to capture the user's preferences for using certain keys or key groups – for example, some users do not capitalize or use much punctuation.

Other percentage features are designed to capture the user's pattern of editing text since there are many ways to locate (using keys – Home, End, Arrow keys – or mouse clicks), delete (Backspace or Delete keys, or Edit-Delete), insert (Insert, shortcut keys, or Edit-Paste), and move (shortcut keys or Edit-Cut/Edit-Paste) words and characters.

This study used 239 feature measurements (a complete list is presented in the Appendix). These features make use of the letter and digraph frequencies in English text (Gaines, 1956), and the definitions of left-hand-letter keys as those normally struck by fingers of a typist's left hand (q, w, e, r, t, a, s, d, f, g, z, x, c, v, b) and right-hand-letter keys as those struck by fingers of the right hand (y, u, i, o, p, h, j, k, l, n, m). The features characterize a typist's key-press duration times, transition times in going from one key to the next, the percentages of usage of the non-letter keys and mouse clicks, and the typing speed. The granularity of the duration and transition features is shown in the hierarchy trees of Figures 4 and 5. For each of these trees, the granularity increases from gross features at the top of the tree to fine features at the bottom. The least frequent letter in the duration tree is "g" with a frequency of 1.6%, and the least frequent letter pair in the transition tree is "or" with a frequency of 1.1% (Gains, 1956). The six least frequent letters are grouped under "other" and the infrequent digraphs are also grouped. The 239 features are grouped as follows:

- 78 duration features (39 means and 39 standard deviations) of individual letter and non-letter keys, and of groups of letter and non-letter keys (Figure 4)
- 70 type-1 transition features (35 means and 35 standard deviations) of the transitions between letters or groups of letters, between letters and non-letters or groups thereof, between non-letters and letters or groups thereof, and between non-letters and non-letters or groups thereof (Figure 5)

- 70 type-2 transition features (35 means and 35 standard deviations) identical to the type-1 transition features except for the method of measurement (Figure 5)
- 19 percentage features that measure the percentage of use of the non-letter keys and mouse clicks
- 2 keystroke input rates: the unadjusted input rate (total time to enter the text / total number of keystrokes and mouse events) and the adjusted input rate (total time to enter the text minus pauses greater than ½ second / total number of keystrokes and mouse events)

The computation of a keystroke-duration mean (μ) or standard deviation (σ) requires special handling when there are few samples. For this we use a fallback procedure which is similar to the "*backoff*" procedures used in natural language processing (Jurafsky & Martin, 2000). To compute μ for few samples – that is, when the number of samples is less than $k_{fallback\text{-}threshold}$ (an experimentally-optimized constant) – we take the weighted average of μ of the key in question and μ of the appropriate fallback as follows:

$$\mu'(i) = \frac{n(i) \cdot \mu(i) + k_{fallback-weight} \cdot \mu(fallback)}{n(i) + k_{fallback-weight}} \quad (1)$$

where $\mu'(i)$ is the revised mean, $n(i)$ is the number of occurrences of key i, $\mu(i)$ is the mean of the $n(i)$ samples of key i, $\mu(fallback)$ is the mean of the fallback, and $k_{fallback\text{-}weight}$ is the weight (an experimentally-optimized constant) applied to the fallback statistic. The appropriate fallback is determined by the next highest node in the hierarchy tree. For example, the "m" falls back to "least frequent consonants", which falls back to "all letters", which falls back to "all keys". Because we are dealing with long-text input,

fallback is necessary for only infrequently used keys; thus, it is based primarily on frequency of use, and fallback of more than one level is rare. The $\sigma(i)$ are similarly computed, as are the means and standard deviations of the transitions. Thus, we ensure computability (no zero divides) and obtain reasonable values for all feature measurements.

Two preprocessing steps are performed on the feature measurements, outlier removal and feature standardization. Outlier removal consists of removing any duration or transition time that is far (more than $k_{outlier\text{-}\sigma}$ standard deviations) from the subject's $\mu(i)$ or $\mu(i, j)$, respectively. After outlier removal, averages and standard deviations are recalculated. The system can perform outlier removal a fixed number of times, recursively, or not at all, and this parameter, $k_{outlier\text{-}pass}$, is experimentally optimized. Outlier removal is particularly important for these features because a keyboard user could pause for a phone call, for a sip of coffee, or for numerous other reasons, and the resulting outliers (usually overly long transition times) could skew the feature measurements. Using a hill-climbing method, the four parameters – $k_{fallback\text{-}threshold}$, $k_{fallback\text{-}weight}$, $k_{outlier\text{-}\sigma}$, and $k_{outlier\text{-}pass}$ – were optimized on different data from an earlier study (Curtin et al., 2006).

After performing outlier removal and recalculation, we standardize the measurements by converting raw measurement x to x' by the formula,

$$x' = \frac{x - x_{min}}{x_{max} - x_{min}} \quad (2)$$

where min and max are the minimum and maximum of the measurement over all samples from all subjects (Dunn & Everitt, 2004). This provides measurement values in the range 0-1 to give each measurement roughly equal weight.

Figure 4. Hierarchy tree for the 39 duration categories (each oval)(© 2006 IEEE. Used with permission.)

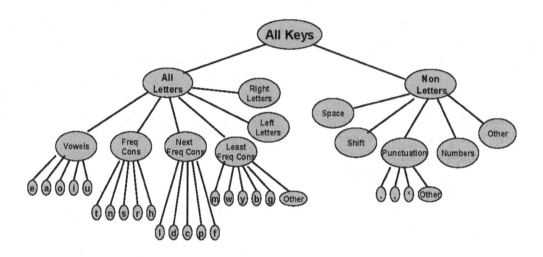

Figure 5. Hierarchy tree for the 35 transition categories (each oval) for type 1 and type 2 transitions(© 2006 IEEE. Used with permission.)

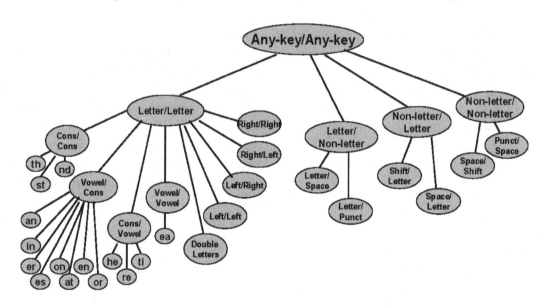

Classification for Identification

For identification, a Nearest Neighbor classifier, using Euclidean distance, compares the feature vector of the test sample in question against those of the samples in the training (enrollment) set. The author of the training sample having the smallest Euclidean distance to the test sample is identified as the author of the test sample. The Nearest Neighbor classifier is a non-parametric technique applied to this multidimensional (239 feature) problem.

Figure 6. Authentication transformation from (a) Feature space to (b) Feature distance space.(© 2005 ICGST-GVIP Journal. Used with permission.)

Transformation to Dichotomy

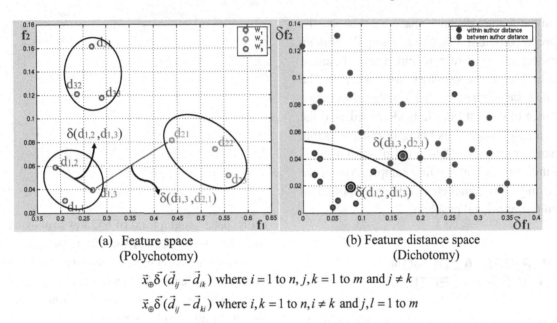

(a) Feature space
    (Polychotomy)

(b) Feature distance space
    (Dichotomy)

$$\vec{x}_\oplus \vec{\delta}\,(\vec{d}_{ij} - \vec{d}_{ik}) \text{ where } i=1 \text{ to } n,\, j,k=1 \text{ to } m \text{ and } j \neq k$$

$$\vec{x}_\oplus \vec{\delta}\,(\vec{d}_{ij} - \vec{d}_{ki}) \text{ where } i,k=1 \text{ to } n,\, i \neq k \text{ and } j,l=1 \text{ to } m$$

Classification for Authentication

For authentication, a vector-difference model, found to be particularly effective for multidimensional feature-space problems, transforms a multiclass (polychotomy) problem into a two-class (dichotomy) problem (Figure 6) (Cha & Srihari, 2000; Choi, Yoon, Cha, & Tappert, 2004; Srihari, Cha, Arora, & Lee, 2002; Yoon, Choi, Cha, Lee, & Tappert, 2005). The resulting two classes are "you are verified" and "you are not verified."

To explain the dichotomy transformation process, take an example of three people $\{P_1, P_2, P_3\}$ where each person supplies three biometric samples. Figure 6 (a) plots the biometric sample data for these three people in the feature space, exemplifying the polychotomy model. This feature space is transformed into a distance vector space by calculating vector distances between pairs of samples of the *same* person (*intra-person distances*, denoted by $x_\oplus$) and distances between

pairs of samples of *different* people (*inter-person distances*, denoted by $x_\oslash$). Let d_{ij} represent the feature vector of the ith person's jth biometric sample, then $x_\oplus$ and $x_\oslash$ are calculated as follows:

$$x_\oplus = |d_{ij} - d_{ik}| \text{ where } i=1 \text{ to } n, \text{ and } j,k=1 \text{ to } m, j \neq k \tag{3}$$

$$x_\oslash = |d_{ij} - d_{kl}| \text{ where } i,k=1 \text{ to } n, i \neq k \text{ and } j,l=1 \text{ to } m$$

where n is the number of people and m is the number of samples per person. Figure 6 (b) shows the transformed feature distance space for the example problem.

Yoon et al. (2005) derive the numbers of the inter- and intra-person distances. If n people provide m biometric samples each, the numbers of intra-person and inter-person distance samples, respectively, are:

$$n_{\oplus} = \frac{m \times (m-1) \times n}{2} \quad \text{and} \quad n_{\varnothing} = m \times m \times \frac{n \times (n-1)}{2}$$

$$(4)$$

In the feature distance space we then use the Nearest Neighbor classifier, using Euclidean distance, to compare a feature vector distance against those in the training (enrollment) set. The training sample having the smallest Euclidean distance to the test sample is identified, and the test sample assigned as being intra-class (same person) or inter-class (different people) according the truth of that training sample. Again, we are using a non-parametric technique applied on a multidimensional problem.

EXPERIMENTAL DESIGN AND DATA COLLECTION

In this study, we vary two independent variables – keyboard type and input mode – to determine their effect on both identification and authentication performance. The keyboard types were desktop and laptop PC keyboards. The input modes were a copy task and free (arbitrary) text input. By varying these independent variables, we determined the distinctiveness of keystroke patterns when training and testing on long-text input under ideal conditions (same input mode and keyboard type for enrollment and testing) and under non-ideal conditions (different input mode, different type of keyboard, or both, for enrollment and testing).

All the desktop keyboards were manufactured by Dell and the data obtained primarily in classroom environments; over 90% of the smaller laptop keyboards (mostly individually owned) were also by Dell, and the others were a mix of IBM, Compaq, Apple, HP, and Toshiba keyboards.

We used two input modes: a copy-task in which subjects copied a predefined text of 652 keystrokes (515 characters with no spaces, 643

Figure 7. Experimental design showing the subject pool, (adapted with permission from Villani, 2006)

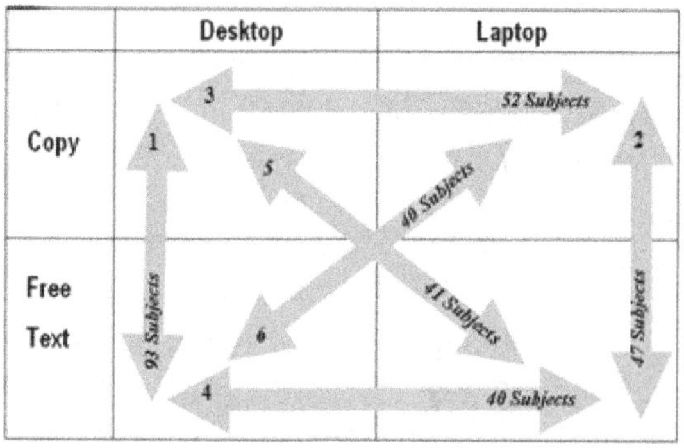

with spaces, and a total of 652 keystrokes when including 9 shift-key presses for uppercase), and free-text input in which subjects typed arbitrary emails of at least 650 keystrokes. The subjects were instructed to correct errors, further increasing the number of keystrokes.

Figure 7 summarizes the experimental design and shows the subject pool. The two independent variables – the two keyboard types and the two input modes – yield four data quadrants. Data were collected in each quadrant: desktop copy, laptop copy, desktop free text, and laptop free text. There are four ideal (optimal) conditions – enrollment and testing on data within each of the four quadrants.

There are six non-ideal experimental groups corresponding to the six arrows in Figure 7 – training on data at one end of the arrow and testing on data at the other end (and since either end of an arrow can be the starting point, there are a total of 12 non-ideal experimental conditions). Groups 1 and 2 compare the two input modes on the desktop and laptop keyboards, respectively. Groups 3 and 4 compare the two keyboard types on the copy-task and free-text inputs, respectively. Finally, groups 5 and 6 compare the two possible ways of having different keyboard types and different input modes for enrollment and testing. Note that although there are six experimental groups (arrows), there are three major experimental groupings – training and testing on different input modes (the two vertical arrows), different keyboard types (the two horizontal arrows), and both different input modes and different keyboard types (the two diagonal arrows).

For data collection, the subjects were asked to complete a minimum of two of the four quadrants as indicated by the two horizontal and two vertical arrows in Figure 7. A subject completes a quadrant by typing a minimum of 5 samples of that category. Data samples were obtained from students in introductory computer classes (accounting for the majority of the data samples); from students in classes at the masters and doctoral levels; and from friends, family, work colleagues, and fellow academics.

Although all subjects were invited to participate in all four quadrants of the experiment, due to time or equipment limitations some opted for two (minimum) while others participated in three or four quadrants of the experiment. A total of 118 subjects supplied five entries in at least two quadrants of the experiment (incomplete sample sets were discarded), and 36 completed all four quadrants of the experiment (Figure 7, Table 1).

Data on the 118 subjects were collected in 2006. To collect reasonable amounts of data quickly the timing of the input samples was not controlled, and about half of the subjects input all their keystroke data samples in one sitting, while the others input their samples over several days or weeks. Similar data were collected in 2008 for the longitudinal studies, and the recording times of these data were accurately controlled.

For the copy and free-text tasks on a desktop keyboard (group 1), the subjects typed a copy of the predefined passage five times and then typed five arbitrary emails on a desktop keyboard. For the copy and free-text tasks on a laptop keyboard (group 2), the typing was similar but on a laptop keyboard. These two experimental groupings were most suited for subjects having access to

Table 1. Summary of subject demographics, adapted with permission from Villani (2006)

Age	Female	Male	Total
Under 20	15	19	34
20-29	12	23	35
30-39	5	10	15
40-49	7	11	18
50+	11	5	16
All	50	68	118

only one keyboard. Groups 3 and 4 required the subjects to type in the same mode but on different keyboards. Finally, groups 5 and 6 required the subjects to type in different input modes and on different keyboard types.

EXPERIMENTAL RESULTS

Experimental results are presented here for biometric identification, for biometric authentication, for longitudinal studies on both identification and authentication, and for an investigation of the system hierarchical model and parameter settings.

Identification Experimental Results

The identification results of the study are summarized in Tables 2 and 3, and corresponding Figures 8 and 9, respectively. Table 2 and Figure 8 present the results under the *ideal conditions* of training (enrollment) and testing on data obtained using the same keyboard type and the same input mode. Since training and testing were under the same conditions, the leave-one-out procedure was used in order to test on data different from that used for training. As anticipated, performance (accuracy) is high under these ideal conditions – greater than 98% when the population of users is relatively small (36-subject experiment), and decreasing for larger numbers of subjects. This performance decrease as the number of subjects

Table 2. Identification performance under ideal conditions

Conditions	36-Subject		Full-Subject	
Train and Test	Subjects	Accuracy	Subjects	Accuracy
DeskCopy	36	99.4%	93	99.1%
LapCopy	36	100.0%	47	99.2%
DeskFree	36	98.3%	93	93.3%
LapFree	36	99.5%	47	97.9%
Average	**36**	**99.3%**	**70**	**97.4%**

Table 3. Identification performance under non-ideal conditions

Group	Conditions		36-Subject		Full-Subject	
	Train	Test	Subjects	Accuracy	Subjects	Accuracy
1	DeskCopy	DeskFree	36	89.3%	93	73.7%
	DeskFree	DeskCopy	36	91.7%	93	81.1%
2	LapCopy	LapFree	36	86.2%	47	80.2%
	LapFree	LapCopy	36	91.0%	47	87.7%
3	DeskCopy	LapCopy	36	60.8%	52	54.6%
	LapCopy	DeskCopy	36	60.6%	52	51.9%
4	DeskFree	LapFree	36	59.0%	40	59.1%
	LapFree	DeskFree	36	61.0%	40	62.4%
5	DeskCopy	LapFree	36	51.6%	41	51.4%
	LapFree	DeskCopy	36	58.0%	41	51.4%
6	DeskFree	LapCopy	36	52.1%	40	44.2%
	LapCopy	DeskFree	36	50.3%	40	51.4%

increases is highlighted in the average of the four cases at the bottom of Table 2, which indicates that doubling the number of subjects increases the error rate by about a factor of four (from 0.7% to 2.6%). The graphs of the four ideal-condition cases in Figure 8 also show the large effect of population increase on performance.

Under ideal conditions in the 36-subject experiment, accuracy varied somewhat from quadrant to quadrant. For example, accuracy was a little higher on the copy task compared to free-text input – 99.4% compared to 98.3% on desktop keyboards, and 100.0% compared to 99.5% on laptop keyboards. These differences, however, were not statistically significant – for example, the first difference yielded a null hypothesis $p =$

0.3 (Chi-square was used for all tests of statistical significance). Higher copy task accuracy is understandable since the copy samples were of the same text whereas the free-text samples were of different texts. Also, other variables being equal, accuracy was a little higher on the laptop keyboards compared to the desktop keyboards – 100.0% compared to 99.4% for the copy task, and 99.5% compared to 98.3% for free-text input. These differences were also not statistically significant. The reason for higher laptop accuracy is likely the greater variety of laptop keyboards used in the experiments and the subject's greater familiarity with the laptops since they were usually owned by the subjects.

Table 3 and Figure 9 present the results under

Figure 8. Identification performance under ideal conditions, graphs of results from Table 2

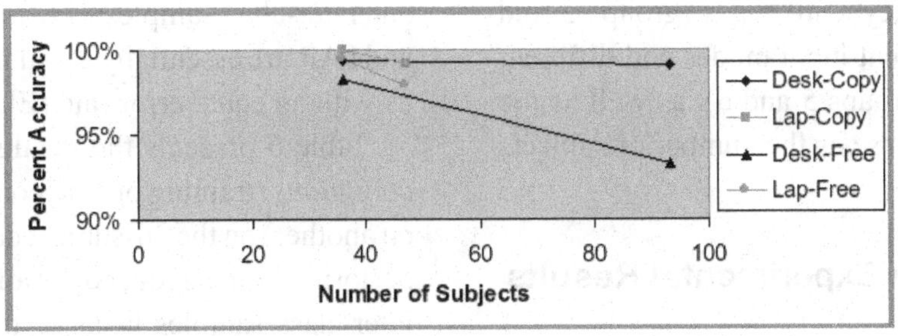

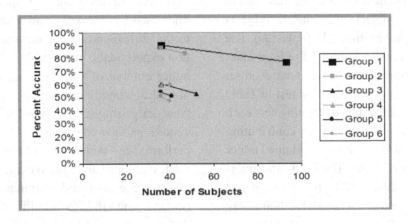

Figure 9. Identification performance under non-ideal conditions, graphs of averaged group results from Table 3

the *non-ideal conditions* of training and testing under different conditions – different input modes, different keyboard types, or both different input modes and different keyboard types. The graphs of Figure 9, which average the two cases in each of the six groups of Table 3, clearly show the degradation in performance as the conditions for training and testing go from different input modes (groups 1 and 2), to different keyboard types (groups 3 and 4), and finally to both different input modes and different keyboard types (groups 5 and 6). They also show the decrease in performance as the population increases.

Under non-ideal conditions in the 36-subject experiment, accuracy decreased from about 99% under ideal conditions to about 90% when the subjects used the same keyboard type but different input modes (the four cases in groups 1 and 2).

For example the accuracy decrease in going from the ideal-condition DeskCopy/DeskCopy (99.4%) to the non-ideal- condition DeskCopy/DeskFree (89.3%) was statistically significant (p < 0.0001). Accuracy dropped even more significantly (from about 99% to about 60%) when the subjects used the same copy or free-text input mode but different keyboard types for enrollment and testing (groups 3 and 4). Finally, accuracy decreased most significantly, from about 99% to about 53%, when the subjects used different input modes and different keyboard types (groups 5 and 6). These results suggest that an individual's keystroke patterns differ for the different input modes and the different keyboard types, and differ more for different keyboard types than for different input modes. Figure 9 graphically shows the performance on the three major conditions of training and testing on different input modes (groups 1 and 2), different keyboard types (groups 3 and 4), and both different input modes and different keyboard types (groups 5 and 6), as well as the performance decrease as the number of subjects increase.

Authentication Experimental Results

The authentication results are presented in Tables 4, 5, and 6. Tables 4 and 5 (summarized in Figures 10 and 11, respectively) present the results under *ideal conditions* (same conditions for training and testing) on the 36-subject data, using 18 subjects for training and the remaining 18 for testing. The experiments in Table 4 used all the inter-class samples and those in Table 5 used a reduced set of inter-class samples. For the first test in Table 4, for example, the training and testing sets each consisted of 90 samples (18 subjects contributing 5 samples each), with all samples obtained under the DeskCopy conditions. The intra- and inter-class sizes were 180 and 3825, respectively, and the tests in this case were run on all the dichotomy data without reducing the sample size of the inter class data (in the third test the smaller intra-inter class size is due to a few missing samples).

Table 5 repeated the ideal-conditions experiments of Table 4 but used a reduced set of randomly selected 500 inter-class data samples. With fewer enrollment samples system performances decreased from roughly 95% to 90%, a doubling

of the error rate, but because the numbers of intra and inter-class samples were more balanced FRR and FAR are essentially equal in value, providing us with an equal error rate (EER) point.

Table 6 presents the results under *non-ideal conditions* (training on one condition and testing on another) on the 36-subject data. The tests were performed on a reduced set of 500 randomized inter-class samples because the full number of inter-class samples was over 15,000. Interestingly, the authentication results under non-ideal conditions only decreased from an average of 90.2% to 87.4% (Tables 5 and 6, respectively, on 500 inter-class samples), a small decrease compared to the corresponding decrease in the identification experiments, but partially explained by the larger number of intra-class samples under the non-ideal conditions. Furthermore, and somewhat surprisingly, the three different primary conditions showed essentially the same average performance – same keyboard type/different input modes (groups 1 and 2) an average performance of 87.0%, same input mode/different keyboard types (groups 3 and 4) 87.5%, and different input modes/different keyboard types (groups 5 and 6) 87.7%. Thus, although average performance dropped from 90.2% under ideal conditions to 87.4% under non-ideal conditions, the performance does not change significantly among the three different non-ideal primary conditions. We attribute these strong non-ideal results to the robustness of the authentication system.

Table 4. Authentication performance under ideal conditions, train 18 and test 18 different subjects using all inter-class samples.

| Conditions | Intra-Inter Class Sizes | | FRR | FAR | Performance |
	Train	Test			
DeskCopy	180-3825	180-3825	11.1%	6.0%	93.8%
LapCopy	180-3825	180-3825	7.8%	4.4%	95.5%
DeskFree	171-3570	176-3740	28.4%	1.4%	97.4%
LapFree	180-3825	180-3825	15.6%	3.7%	95.7%
Average			15.7%	3.9%	95.6%

Table 5. Authentication performance under ideal conditions, train 18 and test 18 different subjects using 500 random inter-class samples

Conditions	Intra-Inter Class Sizes		FRR	FAR	Performance
	Train	Test			
DeskCopy	180-500	180-500	10.0%	13.4%	87.5%
LapCopy	180-500	180-500	1.7%	10.2%	92.1%
DeskFree	171-500	176-500	18.8%	5.0%	91.4%
LapFree	180-500	180-500	9.4%	10.8%	89.6%
Average			10.0%	9.9%	90.2%

Table 6. Authentication performance under non-ideal conditions, 36 subjects, using 500 random inter-class samples

	Conditions		Intra-Inter Class Sizes		FRR	FAR	Performance
	Train	Test	Train	Test			
1	DeskCopy	DeskFree	360-500	347-500	8.1%	17.8%	86.2%
	DeskFree	DeskCopy	347-500	360-500	3.3%	13.0%	91.0%
2	LapCopy	LapFree	360-500	360-500	3.6%	40.4%	75.0%
	LapFree	LapCopy	360-500	360-500	5.8%	3.4%	95.6%
3	DeskCopy	LapCopy	360-500	360-500	5.3%	6.8%	93.8%
	LapCopy	DeskCopy	360-500	360-500	4.7%	18.0%	87.6%
4	DeskFree	LapFree	347-500	360-500	3.1%	38.8%	76.2%
	LapFree	DeskFree	360-500	347-500	8.9%	6.8%	92.3%
5	DeskCopy	LapFree	360-500	360-500	5.8%	22.2%	84.7%
	LapFree	DeskCopy	360-500	360-500	5.3%	8.8%	92.7%
6	DeskFree	LapCopy	347-500	360-500	1.7%	14.4%	90.9%
	LapCopy	DeskFree	360-500	347-500	3.2%	27.6%	82.4%
Average					4.9%	18.2	87.4

LONGITUDINAL STUDY RESULTS

In order to study the accuracy of identification and authentication over time, we performed studies at two-week intervals and at a two-year interval. The two-week interval study used 13 subjects who had not participated in the earlier experiments, and the two-year interval study brought back 8 of the participants of the earlier 36-subject study for additional data samples. All the longitudinal experimental results were obtained under *non-ideal conditions*

– different keyboard type, different input mode, or both, for training (enrollment) and testing.

The identification and authentication results of the two-week-interval study are presented in the Tables 7 and 8, respectively. Baseline results were obtained by training and testing on data from the same week – week 0 (W0-W0), week 2 (W2-W2), and week 4 (W4-W4), and these three sets of results were combined to obtain overall "Same-Week" performance. For the two-week interval, results were obtained by training on week 0 and

Figure 10. Authentication performance under ideal conditions,graph of results from Table 4

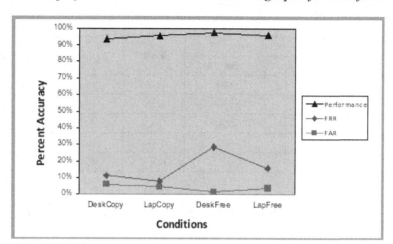

Figure 11. Authentication performance under ideal conditions (500 random inter-class samples), graph of results from Table 5

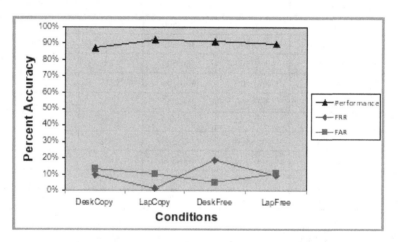

testing on week 2 (W0-W2) and by training on week 2 and testing on week 4 (W2-W4), and these two sets of results were combined for the overall "Two-Week Interval" performance. For the "Four-Week Interval", results were obtained by training on week 0 and testing on week 4 (W0-W4). Five samples were collected from each subject in each quadrant, for a total of 65 samples per file (with the exception of the week-4 laptop copy file, which was missing one sample for a total of 64 samples). Percentages shown are the percent of the samples correctly identified. The identification

results (Table 7) shows the degree of performance degradation over time, summarized by the average performance (bottom line of table).

The authentication results (Table 8) showed less performance degradation than the identification results over the two- and four-week intervals.

For the two-year interval study, we contacted each of the subjects who participated in the earlier 36-subject study in 2006 (Y0), and asked them to enter new complete data sets (5 samples in each of the four quadrants). New data sets were obtained from 8 of these individuals in 2008 (Y2), ap-

Table 7. Identification performance on 13 subjects over two-week intervals

	Conditions		Same Week	Two Week Interval	Four Week Interval
	Train	Test			
1	DeskCopy	DeskFree	94.3	77.7	78.5
	DeskFree	DeskCopy	97.5	87.7	90.8
2	LapCopy	LapFree	94.3	93.1	90.8
	LapFree	LapCopy	91.7	89.1	89.1
3	DeskCopy	LapCopy	90.2	89.2	87.5
	LapCopy	DeskCopy	96.9	97.7	87.7
4	DeskFree	LapFree	85.7	79.2	76.9
	LapFree	DeskFree	96.4	91.6	87.7
5	DeskCopy	LapFree	81.7	74.2	70.7
	LapFree	DeskCopy	89.7	80.0	83.1
6	DeskFree	LapCopy	74.7	77.5	75.0
	LapCopy	DeskFree	85.1	86.2	81.5
Average Performance			**89.9**	**85.3**	**83.3**

Table 8. Authentication performance on 13 subjects over two-week intervals

	Conditions		Same Week		Two-Week Interval		Four-Week Interval	
	Train	Test	FAR/FRR	Perf.	FAR/FRR	Perf.	FAR/FRR	Perf.
1	DeskCopy	DeskFree	2.8/4.1	96.1	3.0/4.3	95.9	3.8/4.4	95.7
	DeskFree	DeskCopy	3.9/7.6	92.9	3.1/10.8	90.1	3.1/16.1	85.4
2	LapCopy	LapFree	9.6/8.0	83.0	6.9/24.1	77.9	5.4/34.9	68.5
	LapFree	LapCopy	4.1/9.3	91.3	3.1/9.4	91.3	2.3/10.5	90.4
3	DeskCopy	LapCopy	2.1/3.3	96.8	2.3/4.2	96.1	6.9/1.8	97.6
	LapCopy	DeskCopy	6.7/25.1	77.0	5.8/33.4	69.8	4.6/35.6	68.0
4	DeskFree	LapFree	5.6/7.0	93.2	2.3/7.8	92.9	10.0/9.6	90.4
	LapFree	DeskFree	7.2/6.8	93.2	1.9/10.2	90.8	1.5/21.2	81.1
5	DeskCopy	LapFree	4.4/6.6	93.7	5.0/7.9	92.5	2.3/7.1	93.5
	Lap Free	DeskCopy	3.3/4.2	87.0	3.5/15.6	85.8	2.3/26.4	76.4
6	DeskFree	LapCopy	3.3/9.3	91.4	3.1/7.0	93.5	7.7/2.9	96.5
	LapCopy	DeskFree	6.5/9.7	81.8	5.8/30.1	72.7	7.1/21.6	80.0
Average Performance				**89.8**		**87.4**		**85.3**

proximately two years after obtaining their earlier data. Since each of the 8 subjects submitted five samples in each of four quadrants, there were a total of 40 samples in each quadrant.

Both the Y0 and Y2 data from these 8 subjects were run through the system. The results of training and testing on data recorded in the same year, Y0-Y0 and Y2-Y2, were averaged. Table 9 shows the percent of the samples (80 samples in the "Same Year", half in Y0 and half in Y2; and 40 in the "Two-Year Interval") accurately identified. The resulting substantial degradation in performance

Table 9. Identification performance on 8 subjects over a two-year interval

Group	Conditions		Same Year	Two-Year Interval
	Train	**Test**		
1	DeskCopy	DeskFree	97.5	57.5
	DeskFree	DeskCopy	92.5	75.0
2	LapCopy	LapFree	98.8	60.0
	LapFree	LapCopy	100.0	57.5
3	DeskCopy	LapCopy	87.5	67.5
	LapCopy	DeskCopy	76.3	65.0
4	DeskFree	LapFree	80.0	80.0
	LapFree	DeskFree	76.3	80.0
5	DeskCopy	LapFree	80.0	65.0
	LapFree	DeskCopy	72.5	52.5
6	DeskFree	LapCopy	76.3	57.5
	LapCopy	DeskFree	75.0	82.5
Average Performance			**84.4**	**66.7**

Table 10. Authentication performance on 8 subjects over a two-year interval

	Conditions		Same Year		Two-Year Interval	
	Train	**Test**	**FAR/FRR**	**Performance**	**FAR/FRR**	**Performance**
1	DeskCopy	DeskFree	8.75 / 7.50	92.4	10.00/12.00	88.2
	DeskFree	DeskCopy	5.13 / 10.61	89.9	2.63 / 9.37	91.3
2	LapCopy	LapFree	0.00 / 2.86	97.4	0.00 / 3.71	96.7
	LapFree	LapCopy	1.25 / 3.29	96.9	0.00 / 7.28	93.5
3	DeskCopy	LapCopy	5.00 / 8.29	92.1	5.00 / 9.71	90.8
	LapCopy	DeskCopy	1.25 / 4.14	96.2	0.00 / 8.42	92.4
4	DeskFree	LapFree	0.64 / 8.33	92.4	3.94 / 5.82	94.4
	LapFree	DeskFree	1.56 / 2.21	97.7	2.50 / 3.42	96.7
5	DeskCopy	LapFree	5.63 / 10.29	90.2	6.25 / 12.85	87.8
	Lap Free	DeskCopy	3.13 / 8.86	91.7	2.50 / 9.00	91.7
6	DeskFree	LapCopy	0.00 / 10.40	90.6	1.31 / 13.49	87.7
	LapCopy	DeskFree	5.00 / 5.00	95.0	1.25 / 6.57	94.0
Average Performance				**93.5**		**92.1**

indicates that one's keystroke patterns change significantly over a two-year interval.

Authentication results (Table 10) are better, with an average accuracy of 92% with a two-year interval between the training and test sets.

Although this performance is better than that obtained over two- and four-week intervals, this is likely due to the smaller number of subjects in the two-year study.

SYSTEM HIERARCHICAL MODEL AND PARAMETER EXPERIMENTS

The hierarchical model was investigated and alternative models were evaluated. The system parameters were analyzed by measuring accuracy as a function of the outlier removal parameters (the number of outlier passes and the outlier distance), accuracy as a function of the number of enrollment samples, and accuracy as a function of input text length. The parameter experiments were performed on the identification system using the full-subject ideal DeskFree condition, or both the DeskFree and DeskCopy conditions – the conditions having the largest number of 93 subjects. Finally, the normal distribution assumption of the statistical features was verified.

Hierarchical Fallback Model

We investigated the fallback aspect of the hierarchical model by comparing the hierarchical fallback as described above to simply falling back to the top nodes of the hierarchy trees as was done in an earlier study (Curtin et al., 2006). For the desktop-free condition the hierarchical fallback procedure increased accuracy from 91.0% to 93.3% (a 26% decrease in error rate). For the desktop-copy condition, identification accuracy increased from 98.1% to 99.1% (a 53% decrease in error rate). Using the hierarchical model for fallback is therefore highly beneficial.

An analysis of the fallback model showed that fallback never occurred more than one level up from the leaf nodes and that most of the one-level-up nodes were essentially never used (vowel, frequent consonant, all letters, non-letters) because their leaf nodes were sufficiently frequent to not require fallback. Thus, the original fallback model was essentially a frequency of use model with the infrequent letters falling back to a group average of the infrequent letters.

Two new fallback models were investigated (Ritzmann, in preparation). The first, a touch-type model, was based on the fingers used to strike keys by touch typists (Figures 12 and 13), thinking that this model should be superior to the one described above that is frequency oriented but not particu-

Figure 12. Touch-type hierarchy tree for durations, (adopted with permission from Ritzmann (in preparation))

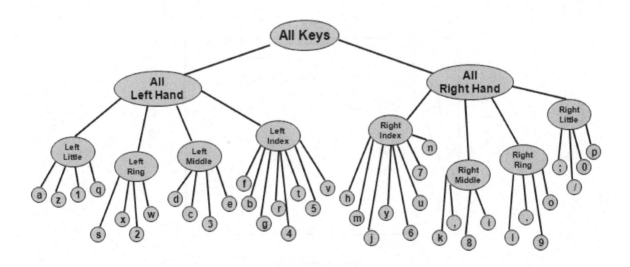

Figure 13. Touch-type hierarchy tree for transitions, (adopted with permission from Ritzmann (in preparation))

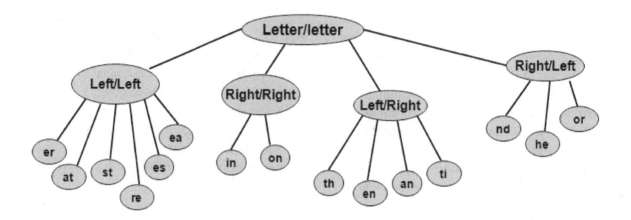

larly relevant to typing. The second was a statistical model that groups keys displaying similar key-strike statistics. The results of the touch-type model were similar to those obtained above but not significantly different. The statistical model was significantly poorer than the other two.

Outlier Parameters

We verified the method of performing outlier removal recursively – that is, continuing to remove outliers until a complete pass through the data resulted in no further outliers being removed (Figure 14). We then measured accuracy as a function of the outlier removal distance (in terms of the number of σ from the μ), finding that the

Figure 14. Identification accuracy versus outlier removal passes, (adapted with permission from Villani, 2006)

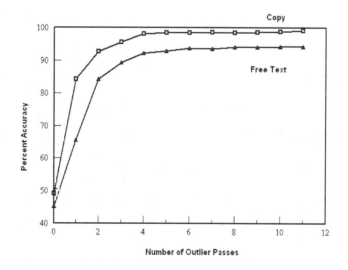

Figure 15. Identification accuracy versus outlier removal distance σ, (adapted with permission from Villani, 2006)

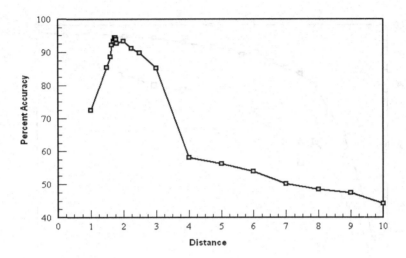

2σ distance used in the experiments was close to the optimal value of 1.75σ (Figure 15). Note that the parameter settings used in this study were established on different data from an earlier study (Curtin et al., 2006).

Number of Enrollment Samples

In order to check the sufficiency of the number of enrollment samples, we obtained accuracy as the number of enrollment samples varied from one to four (Figure 16). Because each subject supplied five data samples per quadrant, the leave-one-out procedure left a maximum of four enrollment samples to match against. The results indicate that two enrollment samples per user might suffice for this application.

Input Text Length

We obtained accuracy as a function of input text length (Figure 17). We found that our choice of 650

Figure 16. Identification accuracy versus enrollment samples, (adapted with permission from Villani, 2006)

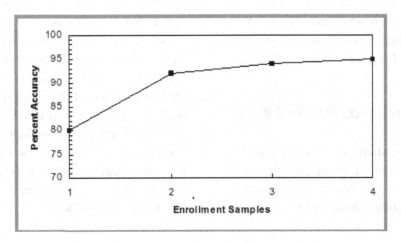

Figure 17. Identification accuracy versus input text length, (adapted with permission from Villani, 2006)

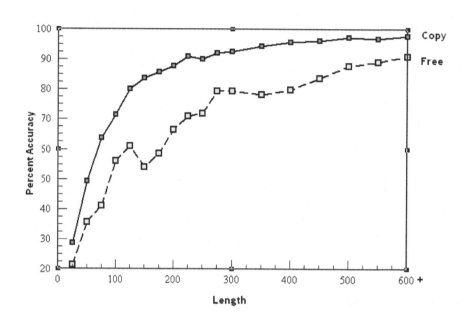

keystrokes was in the region where the curve levels off, but that reasonable accuracy can be obtained on shorter text lengths of about 300 keystrokes. The accuracy curve of the copy task is considerably smoother than that of the free text input, perhaps because all copy samples were of the same text but the free text samples were all of different texts.

Probability Distributions of Statistical Features

We verified the normal distribution assumption for the duration and transition times. Figure 18, for example, shows the distributions of the key-press durations for the letter *u* for each entry mode.

CONCLUSIONS AND FUTURE WORK

The results of this study are both important and timely as more people become involved in the applications of interest. Online test-taking is being used more frequently in both academic and busi-

ness environments, and the test-takers need to be authenticated. And, as problems with the circulation of inappropriate (unprofessional, offensive, or obscene) e-mail become more prevalent, so does the need to identify the perpetrators. We also found that about 300 keystrokes (four lines of text) yields sufficient accuracy in these applications, thereby reducing the text input requirement to less than half of that used in the experiments. Furthermore, because we eliminate long-duration outliers, there is no problem if the keyboard user pauses during text input for a phone call, a sip of coffee, or other reasons.

We found that the keystroke biometric can be useful for identification and authentication applications if two or more enrollment samples are available and if the same type of keyboard is used to produce both the enrollment and the questioned samples. The keystroke biometric was significantly weaker for the identification and authentication applications when enrollment and testing used different input modes (copy or free-text), different keyboard types (desktop or

Figure 18. Distributions of "u" duration times for each entry mode, (adapted with permission from Villani, 2006)

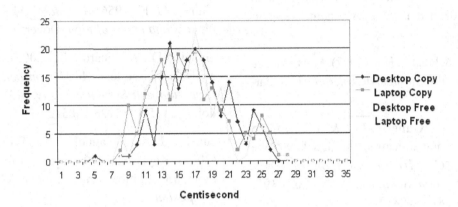

laptop), or both different input modes and different keyboard types. Additional findings include the degree of performance degradation as the number of subjects increases and as the time interval between enrollment and testing increases.

The identification application of interest was to identify the sender of inappropriate email in a closed system of n people (1-of-n problem). Most such perpetrators will likely be novices not trying to disguise their typing, and not knowing that their keystrokes are being captured. For the studies described here, using first-choice accuracy as the evaluation criterion, we achieved high accuracies under ideal conditions – an average of 97.4% for the 36-subject experiments.

In this work we have applied the non-parametric, nearest-neighbor classifier to a multidimensional 239-feature problem. Because the error rate of the nearest-neighbor is limited to twice the Bayes rate as the quantity of data increases (Duda, Hart, & Stork, 2001), it is considered a robust technique and one that is often used in early work on a problem. A downside of using this non-parametric technique, however, is that it is not easy to obtain receiver operating characteristic (ROC) curves. ROC curves are typically obtained in studies that estimate probability distributions,

making it possible to vary a threshold and obtain the FAR/FRR tradeoff. Nevertheless, we were able to obtain the equal error rate (EER) value (that is, where FAR = FRR) in the authentication study under ideal conditions (using 500 random inter-class samples), and we anticipate obtaining ROC curves in future studies.

Future work could also involve experiments using the system in an actual internet security situation, like verifying the identity of online test takers. More sophisticated classification techniques might be explored, such as Support Vector Machines (SVM). Finally, although it is likely difficult to mimic another person's keystroke pattern, imposter performance might be investigated.

ACKNOWLEDGMENT

We thank the student teams in the masters-level projects course that contributed to this effort over the past several years.

REFERENCES

AdmitOne Security Inc. (2008). Retrieved in October 2008, from http://www.admitonesecurity.com/

Bender, S. S. & Postley, H. J. (2007). *Key sequence rhythm recognition system and method.* U.S. Patent 7,206,938.

Bergadano, F., Gunetti, D., & Picardi, C. (2002). User authentication through keystroke dynamics. *ACM Transactions on Information and System Security, 5*(4), 367–397. doi:10.1145/581271.581272

BioChec. (2008). Retrieved in October 2008, from http://www.biochec.com/

Bolle, R., Connell, J., Pankanti, S., Ratha, N., & Senior, A. (2004). *Guide to biometrics.* New York: Springer.

Brown, M., & Rogers, S. J. (1993). User identification via keystroke characteristics of typed names using neural networks. *International Journal of Man-Machine Studies, 39*(6), 999–1014. doi:10.1006/imms.1993.1092

Cha, S., & Srihari, S. N. (2000). Writer identification: Statistical analysis and dichotomizer. *Proc. SPR and SSPR 2000, LNCS - Advances in Pattern Recognition, 1876,* 123-132.

Choi, S.-S., Yoon, S., Cha, S.-H., & Tappert, C. C. (2004). Use of histogram distances in iris authentication. *Proc. MSCE-MLMTA,* Las Vegas. (LNCS Image Analysis and Recognition, pp. 1118-1124). New York: Springer.

Curtin, M., Tappert, C., Villani, M., Ngo, G., Simone, J., St. Fort, H., & Cha, S.-H. (2006). Keystroke biometric recognition on long-text input: A feasibility study. *Proc. Int. MultiConf. Engineers & Computer Scientists (IMECS),* Hong Kong.

Duda, R. O., Hart, P. E., & Stork, D. G. (2001). *Pattern classification.* New York: Wiley.

Dunn, G., & Everitt, B. S. (2004). *An introduction to mathematical taxonomy.* Dover.

Gaines, H. F. (1956). *Cryptanalysis: A study of ciphers and their solution.* Dover.

Gunetti, D., & Picardi, C. (2005). Keystroke analysis of free text. *ACM Transactions on Information and System Security, 8*(3), 312–347. doi:10.1145/1085126.1085129

Jin, L., Ke, X., Manuel, R., & Wilkerson, M. (2004). Keystroke dynamics: A software based biometric solution. *Proc. 13th USENIX Security Symposium.*

Jurafsky, D., & Martin, J. H. (2000). *Speech and language processing.* NJ: Prentice.

Leggett, J., & Williams, G. (1988). Verifying identity via keystroke characteristics. *International Journal of Man-Machine Studies, 28*(1), 67–76. doi:10.1016/S0020-7373(88)80053-1

Leggett, J., Williams, G., Usnick, M., & Longnecker, M. (1991). Dynamic identity verification via keystroke characteristics. *International Journal of Man-Machine Studies, 35*(6), 859–870. doi:10.1016/S0020-7373(05)80165-8

Monrose, F., Reiter, M. K., & Wetzel, S. (2002). Password hardening based on keystroke dynamics. *International Journal of Information Security, 1*(2), 69–83. doi:10.1007/s102070100006

Monrose, F., & Rubin, A. D. (2000). Keystroke dynamics as a biometric for authentication. *Future Generation Computer Systems, 16*(4), 351–359. doi:10.1016/S0167-739X(99)00059-X

Obaidat, M. S., & Sadoun, B. (1999). Keystroke dynamics based authentication. In A. K. Jain, R. Bolle & S. Pankanti (Eds.), *Biometrics: Personal identification in networked society* (pp. 213-230). New York: Springer.

Peacock, A., Ke, X., & Wilkerson, M. (2004). Typing patterns: A key to user identification. *IEEE Security & Privacy*, *2*(5), 40–47. doi:10.1109/MSP.2004.89

Ritzmann, M. (in preparation). *Strategies for managing missing or incomplete data in biometric and business applications*. Unpublished doctoral dissertation, Pace University, New York.

Song, D., Venable, P., & Perrig, A. (1997). User recognition by keystroke latency pattern analysis. Retrieved in May 2005, from http://citeseer.ist.psu.edu/song97user.html

Srihari, S. N., Cha, S., Arora, H., & Lee, S. (2002). Individuality of handwriting. *Journal of Forensic Sciences*, *47*(4), 1–17.

Villani, M. (2006). Keystroke biometric identification studies on long text input. Unpublished doctoral dissertation, Pace University, New York.

Villani, M., Tappert, C., Ngo, G., Simone, J., St. Fort, H., & Cha, S.-H. (2006). Keystroke biometric recognition studies on long-text input under ideal and application-oriented conditions. *Proc. 2006 Conference on Computer Vision and Pattern Recognition, Workshop on Biometrics*, New York (pp. 39-46). Washington: IEEE Computer Society.

Woodward, J. D., Jr., Orlans, N. M., & Higgins, P. T. (2002). *Biometrics* (p. 107). New York: McGraw-Hill.

Yoon, S., Choi, S.-S., Cha, S.-H., Lee, Y., & Tappert, C. C. (2005). On the individuality of the iris biometric. *Proc. Int. J. Graphics . Vision & Image Processing*, *5*(5), 63–70.

Yu, E., & Cho, S. (2004). Keystroke dynamics identity verification–its problems and practical solutions. *Computers & Security*, *23*(5), 428–440. doi:10.1016/j.cose.2004.02.004

APPENDIX: SUMMARY OF THE 239 FEATURES.

Feature	Measure	Feature Measured	Feature	Measure	Feature Measured
1-2	μ & σ	dur all keystrokes	131-32	μ & σ	tran1 letter/non-letter
3-4	μ & σ	dur all alphabet letters	133-34	μ & σ	tran1 letter/space
5-6	μ & σ	dur vowels	135-36	μ & σ	tran1 letter/punct
7-8	μ & σ	dur vowels a	137-38	μ & σ	tran1 non-letter/letter
9-10	μ & σ	dur vowels e	139-40	μ & σ	tran1 shift/letter
11-12	μ & σ	dur vowels i	141-42	μ & σ	tran1 space/letter
13-14	μ & σ	dur vowels o	143-44	μ & σ	tran1 non-letter/non-letter
15-16	μ & σ	dur vowels u	145-46	μ & σ	tran1 space/shift
17-18	μ & σ	dur freq cons	147-48	μ & σ	tran1 punct/space
19-20	μ & σ	dur freq cons t	149-50	μ & σ	tran2 any-key/any-key
21-22	μ & σ	dur freq cons n	151-52	μ & σ	tran2 letter/letter
23-24	μ & σ	dur freq cons s	153-54	μ & σ	tran2 top cons pairs
25-26	μ & σ	dur freq cons r	155-56	μ & σ	tran2 top cons pairs th
27-28	μ & σ	dur freq cons h	157-58	μ & σ	tran2 top cons pairs st
29-30	μ & σ	dur next freq cons	159-60	μ & σ	tran2 top cons pairs nd
31-32	μ & σ	dur next freq cons l	161-62	μ & σ	tran2 vowel/cons
33-34	μ & σ	dur next freq cons d	163-64	μ & σ	tran2 vowel/cons an
35-36	μ & σ	dur next freq cons c	165-66	μ & σ	tran2 vowel/cons in
37-38	μ & σ	dur next freq cons p	167-68	μ & σ	tran2 vowel/cons er
39-40	μ & σ	dur next freq cons f	169-70	μ & σ	tran2 vowel/cons es
41-42	μ & σ	dur least freq cons	171-72	μ & σ	tran2 vowel/cons on
43-44	μ & σ	dur least freq cons m	173-74	μ & σ	tran2 vowel/cons at
45-46	μ & σ	dur least freq cons w	175-76	μ & σ	tran2 vowel/cons en
47-48	μ & σ	dur least freq cons y	177-78	μ & σ	tran2 vowel/cons or
49-50	μ & σ	dur least freq cons b	179-80	μ & σ	tran2 cons/vowel
51-52	μ & σ	dur least freq cons g	181-82	μ & σ	tran2 cons/vowel he
53-54	μ & σ	dur least freq cons other	183-84	μ & σ	tran2 cons/vowel re
55-56	μ & σ	dur all left hand letters	185-86	μ & σ	tran2 cons/vowel ti
57-58	μ & σ	dur all right hand letters	187-88	μ & σ	tran2 vowel/vowel
59-60	μ & σ	dur non-letters	189-90	μ & σ	tran2 vowel/vowel ea
61-62	μ & σ	dur space	191-92	μ & σ	tran2 double letters
63-64	μ & σ	dur shift	193-94	μ & σ	tran2 left/left
65-66	μ & σ	dur punctuation	195-96	μ & σ	tran2 left/right
67-68	μ & σ	dur punctuation period .	197-98	μ & σ	tran2 right/left
69-70	μ & σ	dur punctuation comma,	199-200	μ & σ	tran right/right
71-72	μ & σ	dur punctuation apost '	201-02	μ & σ	tran2 letter/non-letter
73-74	μ & σ	dur punctuation other	203-04	μ & σ	tran2 letter/space
75-76	μ & σ	dur numbers	205-06	μ & σ	tran2 letter/punct
77-78	μ & σ	dur other	2070-8	μ & σ	tran2 non-letter/letter

Feature	Measure	Feature Measured	Feature	Measure	Feature Measured
79-80	μ & σ	tran1 any-key/any-key	209-10	μ & σ	tran2 shift/letter
81-82	μ & σ	tran1 letter/letter	211-12	μ & σ	tran2 space/letter
83-84	μ & σ	tran1 top cons pairs	213-14	μ & σ	tran2 non-letter/non-letter
85-86	μ & σ	tran1 top cons pairs th	215-16	μ & σ	tran2 space/shift
87-88	μ & σ	tran1 top cons pairs st	217-18	μ & σ	tran2 punct/space
89-90	μ & σ	tran1 top cons pairs nd	219	%	shift
91-92	μ & σ	tran1 vowel/cons	220	%	caps lock
93-94	μ & σ	tran1 vowel/cons an	221	%	space
95-96	μ & σ	tran1 vowel/cons in	222	%	backspace
97-98	μ & σ	tran1 vowel/cons er	223	%	delete
99-100	μ & σ	tran1 vowel/cons es	224	%	insert
101-02	μ & σ	tran1 vowel/cons on	225	%	home
103-04	μ & σ	tran1 vowel/cons at	226	%	end
105-06	μ & σ	tran1 vowel/cons en	227	%	enter
107-08	μ & σ	tran1 vowel/cons or	228	%	ctl
109-10	μ & σ	tran1 cons/vowel	229	%	four arrow keys combined
111-12	μ & σ	tran1 cons/vowel he	230	%	sentence ending punct .?!
113-14	μ & σ	tran1 cons/vowel re	231	%	other punct
115-16	μ & σ	tran1 cons/vowel ti	232	%	left shift
117-18	μ & σ	tran1 vowel/vowel	233	%	right shift
119-20	μ & σ	tran1 vowel/vowel ea	234	%	left mouse click
121-22	μ & σ	tran1 double letters	235	%	right mouse click
123-24	μ & σ	tran1 left/left	236	%	double left mouse click
125-26	μ & σ	tran1 left/right	237	%	left shift to right shift
127-28	μ & σ	tran1 right/left	238	rate	input rate with pauses
129-30	μ & σ	tran1 right/right	239	rate	input rate w/o pauses

Chapter 17
Secure Dynamic Signature–Crypto Key Computation

Andrew Teoh Beng Jin
Yonsei University, Korea

Yip Wai Kuan
Multimedia University, Malaysia

ABSTRACT

Biometric-key computation is a process of converting a piece of live biometric data into a key. Among the various biometrics available today, the hand signature has the highest level of social acceptance. The general masses are familiar with the use of handwritten signature by means of verification and acknowledgement. On the other hand, cryptography is used in multitude applications present in technologically advanced society. Examples include the security of ATM cards, computer networks, and e-commerce. The signature crypto-key computation is hence of highly interesting as it is a way to integrate behavioral biometrics with the existing cryptographic framework. In this chapter, we report a dynamic hand signatures-key generation scheme which is based on a randomized biometric helper. This scheme consists of a randomized feature discretization process and a code redundancy construction. The former enables one to control the intraclass variations of dynamic hand signatures to the minimal level and the latter will further reduce the errors. Randomized biometric helper ensures that a signature-key is easy to be revoked when the key is compromised. The proposed scheme is evaluated based on the 2004 signature verification competition (SVC) database. We found that the proposed methods are able to produce keys that are stable, distinguishable, and secure.

INTRODUCTION

With widespread information exchange and access to resources over public network, cryptography has become an important and necessary mechanism for

DOI: 10.4018/978-1-60566-725-6.ch017

secure channel access and authentication. According to Schneier (1996), the aim of cryptography is to provide secure transmission of messages, in the sense that two or more persons can communicate in a way that guarantees to meet the desired subset of the following four goals - confidentiality, data integrity, authentication and non-repudiation.

However, there are some practical problems associated with the use of cryptosystem since the current methods authenticate the key instead of the user. The need for a proper and reliable key management mechanism is required in order to confirm that the listed keys actually belong to the given entities.

Currently, a manual method of authentication using identification card, company number or license, is required for enrolment of keys. In addition, the security depends on the large size of a cryptographic secret key generated, and it is not feasible to require user to remember such a long key. Thus a simple password is still required for key encryption which in turn leads to continuing potential hacker attack on the password to retrieve the cryptographic keys. Both passwords and cryptographic keys do not necessarily require the user to be present, leading to identity frauds.

Biometrics is the science of using unique human characteristics for personal authentication based on a person's biological and behavioral characteristics (Jain, A. K., Hong, L. & Pankanti, S. 2000). By incorporating biometrics technologies which utilize the uniqueness of personal characteristics, the keys can be placed in a secure storage and be protected by biometrics, instead of password. The keys will be released if a query biometrics matches the stored template. The security of cryptosystems could be strengthened as authentication now requires the presence of the user. Traditionally, biometrics based authentication for access into systems has always been yes/no decision model depending on how "close" the test biometrics is to a stored template. The decision is determined empirically and entails tuning of a threshold. This may open to systematic attack where a test biometrics is repeatedly presented to retrieve system threshold and hence leads to keys disclosure. This is more vulnerable to behavioral biometrics such as hand signature, due to existence of skilled forgery which is unlikely found in physiological biometric. To avoid the storage of the template, one alternative solution is biometrics on-the-fly using the help of some information about the biometrics. An unique and compact bit string of the biometric input can be used instead of just a simple threshold-based decision. Keys that could be generated directly from biometrics data are crucial for seamless integration between biometrics and cryptography.

Motivations and Contributions

In reality, direct biometrics to key transformation is not favorable. This is because biometrics suffers from privacy invasion and it is not replaceable. To make the matter worse, a new template cannot be assigned when compromised, and the only solution is to replace with another biometric feature. Yet, a person has only a limited number of biometric features which can be utilized, and thus, the replacement of biometric feature is not a feasible solution. Furthermore, inherent high variability of biometric data hinders it to be directly transformed into deterministic bit strings. Hence new frameworks and formalisms related to integrating biometrics into cryptosystems need to be considered.

Among various biometrics available today, hand signature is an ideal candidate for biometric-key computation. This is of particular important as wide array of cryptographic applications are remote and unattended over an unsecure public network. Hand signature has several advantages such as socially and generally well-accepted, more cost effective in terms of capturing equipment (e.g. PDAs, smartphones and mouse-pen) and non-intrusive. In online applications, dynamic hand signatures is preferable than just offline hand signatures due to higher security concern. Dynamic hand signatures are more difficult to copy as they require the capture of timing information from the signing action and other behavioral characteristics such as the pressure imposed, altitude of the pen and azimuth.

In this chapter, a dynamic hand signatures crypto-key computation scheme is discussed.

Figure 1. Biometric-key generation

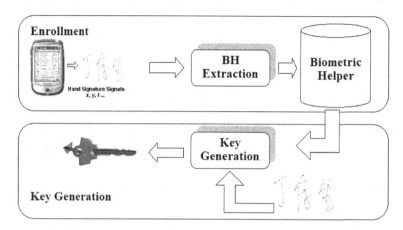

Signature-crypto key computation is referred to as a process of converting the dynamic hand signatures into a stable bit-string representation (key) by using auxiliary information, which we coin as biometrics helper (BH). BH is learned from the enrolled hand signature signal and stored in a local device while the latter can be discarded. BH should reveal no or minimal information regarding the biometric data or key. During key computation, BH is used together with the query hand signature to generate a key as shown in Figure 1. We outline seven criteria for reliable signature-key computation and we specifically addressed the inherent difficulties of using hand signature as crypto-key, for instance high variability of signature representation and the skilled forgery attacks. Hence, hybrid Discrete Fourier Transform - Discrete Wavelet Transform (DFT-DWT) and BioPhasoring discretization are devised for this purpose.

In section 2, we discuss a handful of existing biometric-key computation schemes. We then propose several requirements and the solutions to realize the dynamic hand signatures crypto-key computation in section 3. The numerical evaluation and the security analysis of the proposed technique are then reported in section 4 and 5 respectively. Finally, a concluding remark is given in section 6.

BACKGROUND

There are a handful of reports in biometric-key generation scheme. Davida et al (1999) made the first attempt by adopting an error correction code for iris biometrics. In their technique, parity checksum was first calculated from an enrolled IrisCode (Daugman, 2003) and stored. During authentication, an IrisCode was extracted from several query samples through a majority decoding scheme. The parity checksum was used to correct the test data. However, no empirical results were reported. Another work based on error correction was done by Hao et al. (2006). In this work, an IrisCode, which is ready in the form of a 2048-bit string and a concatenated Error Correction Code, namely Reed-Solomon code and Hadamard code were used to encode and decode the key. Their algorithm showed remarkably good performance with FRR =0.47% at 0% FAR for a 140-bit key based on iris data. This approach has its restriction since most of the biometric features are not ready in binary representation.

In Tuyls et al.(2005), the authors proposed to binarize face features by extracting user-specific reliable components based on the highest Signal-to-Noise ratio. This is followed by a conversion from real biometric to binary representation with a simple threshold scheme based on the distribution mean. Error correction code such as BCH is then performed. Based on experiments conducted on two fingerprint datasets, the error rates of about 4.5% and 4.2% were obtained. However, the binarization degrades the original performances ie. 1.4% and 1.6% for first and second datasets respectively. Same group of researchers implemented a similar technique in face biometrics by using a challenging database such as FERET, the false reject rate was reported to be about 35%, which was considered unacceptable in practice (Kevenaar et al. 2005).

Vielhauer et al. (2002, 2004) proposed a technique which used a 50-feature-parameter set from dynamic hand signature and an interval matrix to store the upper and lower thresholds permissible for correct verification. The technique has FAR of 0% and FRR of 7.05% using the best parameter setting in a dataset with 11 users, thus it is difficult to assess the accuracy of the model for large database. Chang et al. (2004) utilized user-dependent transforms to generate multiple bits which allow the generation of a more compact and distinguishable bit string. The idea behind this scheme relies on the distribution of the user biometric feature elements. The element feature space is divided into multiple segments allowing more than one bit to be assigned depending on the number of segments specified by tuning the segment width and boundaries. The main advantage of this technique is its efficiency as it only involves basic operations, such as mean and standard deviation computations. Since the thresholds are user-specific, it could produce accurate separation of genuine-imposter distribution, which contributed to FAR = 0.09% and FRR=0.74% in a 30 users and simple face dataset. Another scheme that is similar to Vielhauer et al. and Chang et al. using the same principle - user specific boundaries can be found in Feng et al (2002). The scheme uses 43 features (but not all are published) and reported 8% EER. However, this group of techniques is lack of key stability property and no security analysis was reported. Most recently, Chen et al. (2007)

proposed a user-specific, likelihood ratio based quantizer (LQ) that allows to extract multiple bits from a single feature. Experiments are carried out on both fingerprint data (FVC2000) and face data (FRGC). Results showed the method achieves good performance in terms of FAR/FRR (when FAR is 10^{-4}, the corresponding FRR are 16.7% and 5.77% for FVC2000 and FRGC, respectively).

Previous methods of Davida et al. (1999), Feng and Chan (2002), Vielhauer et al. (2002, 2004) and Chang et al. (2004), Chen et al. (2007) derive keys directly from biometrics data as keys to be used in various cryptosystems. Again, in the event of compromised keys, the user has to change his biometrics, which is not feasible for biometrics like face, iris, fingerprint and even hand signatures. Keys that can be replaced in the event of key compromise will be an important consideration for integration into cryptographic protocols.

SYSTEM OVERVIEW

The review of the previous works in section 2 suggested that there are much room for improvement. In general, we require that the proposed dynamic hand signature to key transformation technique should have the following traits:

1.   No signature template storage
     2. Keys revocability
          3.   **Keys diversity:** Different user keys should be sufficiently different from each other.
          4.   **Keys stability:** Since every capture of the hand-signatures is not exact, a tolerable application of correction is needed to ensure that the keys are stable enough to be used as cryptographic keys.
          5.   **Biometric helper secrecy:** Throughout the transformation

process, no information can be used for biometric data reconstruction.

6. **Unpredictable key space:** It should not be possible for an adversary to perform a statistical extraction of key space patterns based on intercepting multiple keys. The keys should be sufficiently different in terms of bits from non-genuine keys, and should be uniformly distributed.

7. **One-way transformation:** The transformation from dynamic signature to cryptographic key should not be reversible to thwart attempts in recovering the biometric.

Since bio-crypto key computation was designed to be free from the template storage, condition 1 is automatically fulfilled. However, hand-signature verification system typically engaged feature extraction and classifiers for optimum performance. In this regard, classifier is not allowed in the key computation framework as classifiers require a reference for comparison. Hence, the reliability of a feature extractor becomes more prominent in key computation. In our work, we propose to compress the signature signal using a hybrid of Discrete Fourier Transform (DFT) with Discrete Wavelet Transform (DWT) for this purpose. Such approach would also benefit the solution to condition 8 as longer and more features could be obtained.

Besides that, keys revocability, diversity and stability requirements (condition 2-4) are another major culprits in designing a feasible bio-key computations. The keys revocability and keys diversity are interrelated in such a way that the revoke keys must has no correlation to the old keys, and hence this problem can be tackled in one scoop. Keys stability is of much more critical as the transformation of the fuzziness of biometric

representation (real space) into the deterministic format (integer or binary space) is not a trivial problem. This can be conceived as a lossy process as some useful information might be discarded in the transformation. Compare to other physiological biometrics such as fingerprint, iris etc, the high degree of dynamic hand signature varying and the skilled forged signature (forgery who tries to simulate the genuine signature to enter into the system) scenario exaggerate the problem. However, if this problem can be handled gracefully, condition 6 to 7 can be satisfied easily by applying cryptographic hash function, such as MD5, SHA etc (Schneier 1996). This will be touched in much more detail later. In a nutshell, seven requirements can be squeezed into three major ones, ie. stability, revocability and BH secrecy.

To address the above three conditions, we propose a two-stage approach for biometric key generation based on the dynamic hand signatures. At the first stage, a secure randomized feature discretization (RFD) is applied. RFD uses randomized BH and serves for two purposes. First is to enable the revocability of hand signatures by incorporating randomness via external tokens which are independent from the biometric data and could be stored in tamper-proof storages e.g. password protected thumb drives or smart cards. Secondly, to alleviate intra-class variations of hand signatures to the minimal level. The randomized BH is calculated by minimizing a user-specific objective function with respect to randomly projected feature vector. At the second stage, a code-redundancy construction for the Hamming metric is adopted. As the first stage construction had already trimmed down a great amount of errors; then second stage only has to deal with small number of them.

RFD consists two steps: (1) random projection via BioPhasoring (Teoh et al. 2006b) and (2) feature discretization for real-to-binary conversion (Teoh et al. 2007). The BioPhasoring can be seen as a secure and robust projection method based on user token. By implementing this method in the real-space (as with the biometric feature), we disallow an adversary from recovering the original biometric exactly but can be revoked when the key is compromised. Injecting randomness into the bio-keys also has the positive effect of increasing the entropy of the final keys, making them suitable for use as cryptographic keys.

An outline of our key computation method is shown in Figure 2. First, we obtain the dynamic hand signature input from pen-based tablets or personal data assistants. Using non-pressure sensitive pens, we could capture time-stamped positional signals and derive higher derivatives such as velocity and acceleration information. Using higher-end devices such as pressure-sensitive pens, we could obtain more dynamic features such as pressure, azimuth or altitude (angle between pen and the tablet surface). This information was then pre-processed using by aligning to the centre and/ or normalized to have almost the same signature size. The pre-processed signals are then used for feature extraction using DWT-DFT methods. Each of these signals are then compressed and concatenated to form one single feature vector. Some population-wide normalization may be required to standardize the feature space size. Randomized projection is then done on the feature vector to obtain a random projected based on user token input and followed by discretization process. Error correction codes are used to reduce intra-variations amongst same user bit strings.

Feature Extraction

We applied a hybrid technique of Discrete Wavelet Transform (DWT) and Discrete Fourier Transform (DFT) for the signature signal extraction. DWT was chosen due to its good localization feature which gave a more accurate model for compression without losing important information such as sudden peaks or stops as shown by Silva, A.V., and Freitas, D.S (2002), Deng et al. (1999), Lejtman and George (2001) and Nakanishi et al. (2003). Then DFT threshold based compression as by

Lam and Kamins (1989) was performed on the DWT-compressed vector to further remove high-frequency coefficients, resulting in a compact representation of the dynamic signature features. We assume a pressure-sensitive pen and tablet for capturing the online signature signals in terms of x, y coordinates (x, y), pressure information (p), pen altitude (a), and azimuth (az) for each point. In addition to that, several derivative features also can be obtained such as the distance signal from the positional signals, $d = \sqrt{x^2 + y^2}$. the first derivatives of the x and y positional signals - the velocity components x' and y', computed as the sequential difference of the positional signals. The velocity is computed as $v = \sqrt{x'^2 + y'^2}$. The acceleration components are also computed the same way. Since the points are sampled consistently (10 milliseconds), no re-sampling was performed and the pen-down segments (detected as points between two pen downs) are concatenated to form one single signal. Each signal is then compressed with the DWT-DFT method described below.

The DWT involves the selection of dyadic (powers of two) scales and positions, and applying them to the mother wavelet. In particular, a function $f(t) \in L^2(R)$ that defines space of square integrable functions can be represented as

$$f(t) = \sum_{j=1}^{L} \sum_{k=-\infty}^{\infty} d(j,k) y(2^{-j}t - k) + \sum_{k=-\infty}^{\infty} a(L,k) f(2^{-L}t - k)$$

with $\psi(t)$ the mother wavelet, $\varphi(t)$ the scaling function, and the orthonormal basis for $L^2(R)$ defined by the set of functions $\{\sqrt{2^{-l}} f(2^{-L}t - k), \sqrt{2^{-j}} y(2^{-j}t - k) \mid j \leq L, j,k,L \in \mathbb{Z}\}$

The approximation coefficients at scale L are given as $a(L, k) = \dfrac{1}{\sqrt{2^L}} \int_{-\infty}^{\infty} f(t)\phi(2^{-L}t - k)dt$ while the detail coefficients at scale j are $d(j,k)$ $= \dfrac{1}{\sqrt{2^j}} \int_{-\infty}^{\infty} f(t)y(2^{-j}t - k)dt$.

From (1), the wavelet decomposition at any level $L, f_L(t)$ can be obtained from approximation

Figure 2. The progression of the proposed signature-key generation

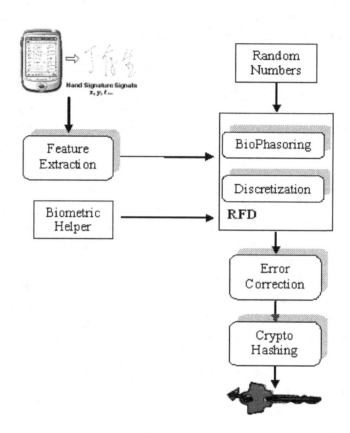

coefficient $a(L, k)$ and layers of detail coefficients $\{d(j, k)| j \leq L\}$. As the signal is discretized, the decomposed signal in L level can be represented in the vector format such as $w = [a_L | d_L | d_{L-1} | d_{L-2} |...|d_1]$. The selection of the optimal L relies on the experimental data used. In our case, we are also interested in compressing the dynamic hand signature signal by zeroing wavelet coefficients below a certain threshold, to obtain the most compact representation as the feature vector. The global threshold compression method which kept the largest absolute value coefficients and set the others to zero is used. Each compressed wavelet w_t can then be transformed using FFT, g=FFT(w_t) and each signal is then normalized via multiplication with $\frac{1}{\sqrt{\sum g_i^2}}$. Each signal is further truncated

using a global thresholding method to obtain a truncated g, g_t. The first τ significant amplitudes of the transforms are selected based on the lowest error rates between genuine and forgery signature distributions. In our experiments, we selected the real, imaginary, and magnitude components of g_t that associated with α signature features, ie. x, y p, a, az etc. Finally, all the DWT-FFT compressed vectors are concatenated and normalized again to form a feature feature, s with length n. In our experiment, $n = 3\alpha\tau$. 3 refers to three FFT components ie. real, imaginary, and magnitude.

Note that each original dynamic feature signal is varying in length due to the signing speed. Using this threshold DWT-DFT based compression, the input signal is padded with zeros to up to the power of two large enough to cover all the number of points captured. The reason for setting the number of points to power of two is to enable the efficient computation of FFT. From the SVC (2004) database, most samples have 200-300 points, so the nearest power of two FFT input size of 512 points is selected.

Randomized Feature Discretization (RFD)

Randomized Feature Discretization (RFD) consists of two components: randomized projection through BioPhasoring and discretization.

For BioPhasoring, the process is carried out based on the iterated assimilation between the tokenised pseudo-random number (PRN) and the signature feature vector that derived from section 3.1, $s \in R^n$. The PRN is generated from an external input, such as a password or a token which is *specific* to each user. The objectives of the proposed method are twofold: (1) to inject randomness into biometric features, and (2) to enable the changeability of biometric features by altering the external secret, r_{ij}. Specifically, formulation of the *j*th user is given as

$$\alpha_{ij} = \frac{1}{n} \sum_{k=1}^{n} \tan^{-1}(\frac{s_k^j}{r_{ik}^j}), i=1,...,m, m \leq n \quad (1)$$

where r_{ik} is a PRN that is independently drawn from $N(0, 1)$. The output is a set of m phasor values $\{\alpha_i | i=1,...,m\}$ with range $[-\pi, \pi]$ where m can be set either equal to or smaller than the original biometric feature length, n.

One potential issue of random phasoring is that if an adversary obtains the genuine tokenised PRN and uses it to claim as the genuine user with an adversary biometric feature. Here we will consider whether the adversary can impersonate the genuine in this scenario (stolen-token scenario) (Teoh et al. 2006a). In this case, the false accept rate will increase. This is based on the intuition that token may overpower biometrics due to random phasoring's direct mixing process, and leads to a situation whereby token determines the decision. We shall show experimentally in section 4 that random phasoring is resistant to this threat.

Discretization is to convert the randomly transformed feature's *i*th element of user k, $\alpha = \{\alpha_{ik} | i=1,...,m\}$ into a binary bit. In the simplest form, this can be a two-state decision based on the mean of vector elements, $b_{jk} = \begin{cases} 0 & if\, 0 \leq \alpha_{jk} < \pi \\ 1 & if -\pi < \alpha_{jk} < 0 \end{cases}$.
However, too much information will be lost when each element is crudely quantized.

Alternatively, we extract sort of user-specific information, which we name it as Biometric Helper (BH) from α to aid the discretization process. With BH, α can be discretized without introducing significant information lost. Our discretization technique learns the BH by minimizing a user-specific objective function, ψ so that intra-class variations of randomized feature α can be minimized while maximizing the inter-class variations by increasing the disparity between the features of the two subjects.

For each feature element's j of user k, $\alpha_{jk} \in R$, we take r samples from the training set and expect all α_{jk} to line in the interval $[\mu_{jk}-\sigma_{jk}, \mu_{jk}+\sigma_{jk}]$, where μ_{jk} and σ_{jk} are the sample mean and standard deviation calculated from the training samples. Thus, the interval width of α_{jk} is given by $2\sigma_{jk}$. On the other hand, the feature space of α_{jk} with range $[-\pi, \pi]$ can be partitioned into 2^{Mjk} segments. The widths of the segments are defined as:

$$\Delta_{jk} = \frac{2\pi}{2^{M_{jk}}} \text{ where } M_{jk} \in Z^+. \quad (2)$$

A choice to determine the correct segment interval, Δ_{jk} of each v_{jk} is to minimize the cost function ψ as follow:

$$M_{jk}^* = \arg \min_{M_{jk}} \psi = \arg \min_{M_{jk}} \left(\frac{R-L}{2^{M_{jk}}} - 2g\sigma_{jk} \right) \quad (3)$$

Figure 3. Feature weights learning through minimization of a cost function. From the figure above, M^*_{jk} =2 gives the smallest error in ψ

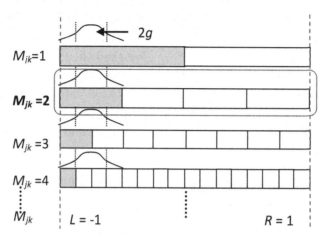

where g is a tunable parameter that can be chosen to be any arbitrarily large values. Small g will lead to a problem that BH could be over corrected for the imposter features.

Figure 3 illustrates the idea of how the user-dependent interval width, Δ_{jk} can be determined by minimizing the ψ in equation (3)

Specifically, the randomized BH, M^*_{jk} can be obtained as follows:

1). Given a set of r training samples α_{jk}
   a) Compute the standard deviation of α_j
   ofuser k, $\tilde{A}_{jk} = \sqrt{\left(\sum_{t=1}^{r}(\alpha_{jkt} - \bar{\alpha}_{jk})^2\right)/r}$
   , j =1, ..., m where $\bar{\alpha}_{jk}$ is the mean of α_{jk}.
   b) For each calculated σ_{jk}, M^*_{jk} is calculated based on equation (3) and then they are stored in the device, such as smart card.

2) For discretization, given a fresh v_k and the corresponding M_k^*, the *genuine segment index* d_{jk} can be obtained from $d_{jk} = \left| \left(\frac{\alpha_{jk} + \pi}{2\pi}\right) 2^{M^*_{jk}} \right|$. The binary representation of α_k is rendered by Gray Coding, $b_{jk} =$

gray(d_{jk}). Gray Coding enables α_k to render multiple numbers of bits instead of one bit. The number of bits is determined by M^*_{jk}. Therefore, the resultant bit string with length

$$\gamma_j = \sum_{i=1}^{m} M^*_{ij}$$ can be generated by cascading

all Gray encoded indices of genuine segments from α_j. In this paper, the maximum value of M_{jk} is limited to 10 (i.e M_{jk} = [1, ..., 10]) to avoid too many bits being used for one representative. This indicates the minimum and maximum bits lengths that can be rendered from RFD are m and mM_{jk}, respectively. Anyway, the exact γ_j has to be determined empirically.

Code-Redundancy Construction

We adopt the linear algebraic error correcting code, e: $\{0, 1\}^\gamma \rightarrow \{0, 1\}^\gamma$ (Pulsar 1995). In general e(K, S, t)$_q$ is a code of K-symbols codewords with S the number of information digits over finite field q, and d the minimum distance of the code, which can correct up to t errors. The additional ρ = (K-S) symbols are often known as the parity as they are used to check and correct the S information symbols.

Let the generated signature bit string of user j denoted as $\boldsymbol{b}_j = \{b_{jk} | k=1,\ldots, \gamma\}$. $e(K, S, t)_q$ consists of two parts, namely an Encoder, e_e: $\{0, 1\}^\gamma \rightarrow \{0, 1\}^l$ and a Decoder, e_d: $\{0, 1\}^l \rightarrow \{0, 1\}^\gamma$, where $l > \gamma$.

1). e_e: Given a set of h number of $\boldsymbol{b}$ where h is an odd number, $b_{ij}, j = 1,.., h$ from a user,

    (a) we perform a majority voting to compute $\hat{b} = \{ \hat{b}_g | g=1,\ldots,k\}$ where $\hat{b}_g$ = majority $(b_{g1}, \ldots, b_{gh})$ ie. $\hat{b}_g$ is the majority of 0's or 1's of bit g from each of the h bit strings.

    (b) a parity checksum, ρ is generated based on $\hat{b}$ and stored.

2). e_d: Given a fresh bit string and ρ, the user corrects the errors to recover $\hat{b}$.

In this paper, we opt for a Reed-Solomon code due to its powerful error correction capacity, especially for burst and random errors. The Reed-Solomon code is denoted as $RS(n_b, k_b, t_b)$ where $n_b \leq -1$ and $2t_b \leq n_b - k_b$. k_b is the number of blocks after encoding, n_b represents the number of blocks before encoding, t_b the number of error blocks that can be corrected and m_b the bits number per block. We denote the RS parity as $\rho_b = n_b - k_b$. In this work, ρ_b is also a BH besides M^*_{jk}.

The nature of a biometric system offers two possible error outcomes known as false accept rate (FAR) and false reject rate (FRR). The interdependency of FAR and FRR is regulated by a threshold value τ as indicated in Figure 4. As $\hat{b}$ is represented in bit string, we use normalized Hamming distance, $(\hat{b}_i \oplus \hat{b}_j)/\gamma$ to quantify τ, where $i \neq j$, $\oplus$ denotes XOR operation and γ is the bit length.

In ECC theory, we have $\gamma = m_b k_b$ and $\hat{b}_i \oplus \hat{b}_j = m_b t_b$, hence $\tau = t_b/k_b$. In order to achieve the best error recovery rate, an optimum t_b/k_b can be estimated from the maximum value in genuine distribution. Note that if intra-variations of biometric features (genuine distribution) are large, a high t_b/k_b is required to correct the errors. This leads to the danger that it may wrongly correct the imposter bit strings as well. Therefore, it is preferably to have large or complete separation in genuine-imposter distribution before ECC is applied.

STABILITY EVALUATIONS

In this section, we shall focus on the stability requirement in keys computation. We tested the proposed algorithm with datasets from signature

Figure 4. The relation between the biometric decision profile (genuine-imposter distribution) and RS(n_b, k_b, t_b)

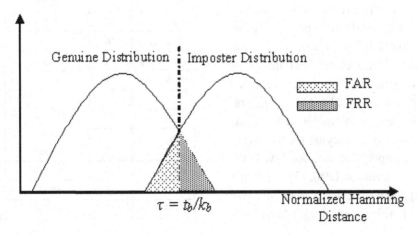

verification competition2004 (SVC 2004). The SVC 2004 databases are chosen as they are currently the most widely used benchmark for online signatures. There are two databases available based on the information captured from normal PDA and pressure-sensitive pens on digitizing tablets. The first database - Task 1 database, consists of coordinate information only, with corresponding timestamp for each sampling point. The second database - Task 2 database, consists of pen orientation, namely altitude and azimuth, and pen pressure. Each datasets consists of 40 users with 20 genuine and 20 skilled forgery samples per user. The accuracy measurement of the SVC 2004 results is based on Equal Error Rate (EER) which can be seen as a compromised between FAR and FRR. The EER is the rate where the FAR is equals to the FRR. We will also adopt this measurement in our presentation of the experiment results. Since there are two types of forgery, we denote EER_S and EER_R for Skilled forgery and Random forgery, respectively.

In section 4.1, we will first discuss the selection of the best signature feature representation and its optimal configuration in DWT-DFT technique. In section 4.2, the performance after applying RFD will be investigated. Section 4.3 reports the overall stability performance after ECC.

Optimal Signature Representation Features

Firstly, we utilize *x, y* positional signals as they can be obtained easily compare to pressure information etc. For the DWT, we chose to work on the mother wavelet Daubechies (DB) order 6 as it models hand signature signals well, as reported in Lejtman and George (2001). The configuration of DWT-DFT feature extraction method was determined empirically by varying the following parameters: (1) compression rate for DWT, (2) the decomposition level for DB6, (3) the first τ significant component to be selected in DFT. We report only the significant results for high-level

tuning of the proposed DWT-DFT method. From the experiments, DFT threshold $\tau = 18$, decomposition level 2 and compression rate 0.60 for DWT are chosen. These configurations are selected because they provided the lowest EER, indicating that feature vectors are most distinguishable.

Using the selected configuration, we investigate the EER for each individual feature. We observed that the complex x, y features have the lowest EERs as shown in Table 1. Also, when higher derivatives (velocity, followed by acceleration) are taken, the performance deteriorates.

Table 2 shows the EER of the combinations of different dynamic features. It is generally shown that the error rate decreases when more features are used.

Next, we consider the use of pressure and pen information on top of the existing features with

Table 1. DWT-DFT extracted features using task 1 database

Features	Size, *n*	EER$_R$ (%)	EER$_S$ (%)
imag(x, y)	**36**	**6.335**	**17.750**
real(x, y)	**36**	**6.331**	**18.444**
mag(x, y)	36	7.228	20.416
mag(d)	18	15.117	22.211
real(d)	18	14.519	23.361
imag(d)	18	14.519	23.361
ang(x, y)	36	14.408	26.694
real(v)	17	25.783	39.055
imag(a)	16	28.722	39.416
imag(v)	17	26.529	39.527
real(a)	16	28.562	40.000
imag(x',y')	34	30.269	41.944
real(x',y')	34	32.491	42.111
mag(v)	17	32.230	43.305
mag(a)	16	37.025	44.277
imag(x'', y'')	32	39.997	44.666
mag(x', y')	34	40.459	44.972
real(x'', y'')	32	40.467	45.500
mag(x'', y'')	32	47.502	49.055

Table 2. DWT-DFT extracted features combination using task 1 database

Features	Size, n	EER_R (%)	EER_S (%)
real,imag(x-y)	72	5.601	16.611
real,imag,mag(x-y)	108	5.329	16.250
real,imag,mag(x-y), real, imag, mag(d)	162	5.433	15.778
real(x-y), imag(x-y), mag(x-y), mag(x'-y'), real(x'-y'), imag(x'-y'), real(d), imag(d), mag(d), real(v), imag(v), mag(v)	**186**	**5.023**	**15.410**

the hope to obtain lower EERs especially for the more difficult case of skilled forgery. From Table 3, we notice that the EERs decreased significantly for the skilled forgery case, but increased for the random forgery case. This unexpected result shows that the pressure and pen information are important for distinguishing the skilled forgery from the genuine users. One possible reason for the higher random forgery however, is that the pressure and pen information is not normalized as with the positional signals. Normalization to standardize the size of all the signals tends to make the forgery samples more similar to the genuine ones. One possible way to reduce the random forgery error rate is to incorporate some "helper" data to correct specific users as will be discussed in the next section. For the sequel discussion, we shall only concentrate on Task 1 Database evaluation as x–y positional information is the more practical features (commonly available in signature acquisition devices) compare to pen orientations and pen pressure information.

Randomized Feature Discretization (RFD)

We examine the effect of using RFD on Task 1 database in this subsection. From Table 4, the best configuration is obtained when $g = 2$, with $EER_R = 0\%$ and $EER_S = 14.5\%$ for stolen-token scenario (refer to section 3.2). Compared with only hand signature feature (Table 2), there is a 1% decrease in the EER, which shows that discretisation is able to improve the performance of the recognition slightly in stoken-token scenario. For the genuine token scenario (a genuine user holds his own specific token), both EERs are 0% as expected.

The side-by-side genuine, skilled forgery and random forgery distributions for the best configurations ($g = 2$) in stolen-token and genuine-token scenarios are graphically illustrated in Figure 5. The clear separation of genuine and random imposter distribution suggests that the error rate is zero, which is also reflected in Table 4. For genuine-token scenario, both genuine-random imposter and genuine-skilled imposter distribu-

Table 3. DWT-DFT extracted features combination using task 2 database

Feature	Size	EER_R (%)	EER_S (%)
real(pr), imag(pr), mag(pr), real(z), imag(z), mag(z), real(l), imag(l), mag(l)	144	11.780	10.833
real(pr), imag(pr), mag(pr), real(z), imag(z), mag(z), real(l), imag(l), mag(l), real(x-y), imag(x-y), mag(x-y)	240	11.504	13.222
real(pr), imag(pr), mag(pr), real(z), imag(z), mag(z), real(l), imag(l), mag(l), real(x-y), imag(x-y), mag(x-y) - all range normalized	240	12.947	15.917
real(pr), imag(pr), mag(pr), real(z), imag(z), mag(z), real(l), imag(l), mag(l), real(x-y)/10, imag(x-y)/10, mag(x-y)/10	**240**	**10.090**	**10.278**

Table 4. EERs of RFD features from Task 1 database

Scenario	g	bits, γ	EER$_R$ (%)	EER$_S$ (%)
Bio + stolen token	0.2	809	0.012	15.138
	0.4	644	0.006	15.222
	0.6	540	0.000	15.444
	0.8	479	0.000	15.083
	1	413	0.000	14.888
	2	**254**	**0.000**	**14.583**
	3	197	0.000	14.944
	4	173	0.000	15.694
	5	169	0.000	15.888
	6	165	0.000	16.638
	7	165	0.006	17.388
Bio + genuine token	0.2	798	0.025	0.027
	0.4	633	0.006	0.027
	0.6	543	0.000	0.000
	0.8	468	0.000	0.000
	1	417	0.000	0.000
	2	**257**	**0.000**	**0.000**
	3	200	0.000	0.000
	4	179	0.000	0.000
	5	168	0.000	0.000
	6	166	0.000	0.000
	7	165	0.000	0.000

tions are clear separated. These distributions can be characterized by two simple statistic measures such as mean and standard deviation as shown in Table 5.

For the implementation of bio-key generation, an exact reproduction of bit string is required whenever auxiliary information such as the number bits per segment M_k^*, parity ρ and genuine signature are presented. This is equivalent to the case where the mean and standard of genuine distribution are equal to zero or when the system threshold, τ (normalized Hamming distance) is set to 0 in the conventional biometric authentication system. This harsh requirement could be satisfied by using ECC.

Effect of Error Correction Code

Theoretically, applying ECC should only affect the genuine distribution, to help the extracted bit strings can be reproduced exactly. What this means is that ECC should transform the genuine distribution into a stage where both mean and standard deviation are zero. However, if the genuine-imposter distribution has no near or clear separation, some of the imposter bit strings will inevitably be corrected also. The best configuration would be the one that reduces the genuine

Figure 5. Graphical illustration of the distribution of the genuine, skilled forgery and random forgery for (a) stolen token and (b) genuine-token scenarios

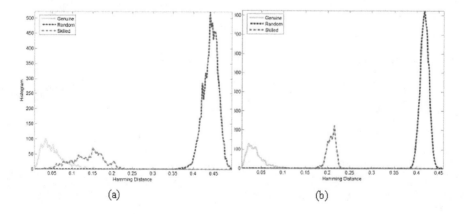

(a)　　　　　　　　　(b)

Table 5. Statistics for genuine (G), random (R) and skilled (S) imposter distributions

Scenario	g	γ	Mean$_G$	Std$_G$	Mean$_R$	Std$_R$	Mean$_S$	Std$_S$
Bio + stolen token	2	254	0.060	0.025	0.444	0.020	0.116	0.027
Bio + genuine token	2	257	0.057	0.024	0.424	0.012	0.201	0.008

bit string distribution while retaining the skilled forgery bit string distribution. The exact calculation has been given in section 3.3.

We redefine the FAR and FRR in terms of the bio-key generation context. Here, FRR$_b$ is defined as the error rate when a genuine user's key failed to be generated from his/her biometrics, and the FAR$_b$ is defined as the error rate that a legitimate user's key is produced from an imposter's biometrics. FAR$_b$ can be further divided into FAR$_{br}$ and FAR$_{bs}$ for random and skilled imposters. Note that for the stolen-token scenario, FAR$_b$ is the only indicator as we do not allow an adversary to generate the genuine-user's key by using his own biometric and the stolen token. In this section, we use these measures as the performance indicator instead of EER.

In the experiments, we try $m_b = 5$ and $m_b = 6$, hence $n_b = 2^5 - 1 = 31$ and $n_b = 2^6 - 1 = 63$ blocks. Table 6 shows the list of possible RS codes that can be used. From Table 5, the mean values of genuine score for both stolen-token and genuine-token are about 0.06. We may choose a suitable RS(n_b, k_b, t_b) where $t_b/k_b \geq 0.06$. From Table 6, we notice that there are many codes can be selected since they all fulfilled the condition, ie. $t_b/k_b \geq 0.06$. However, we should choose the one which offers a sufficiently long bit string $m_b k_b$, as well as good performance. In this case, a moderate t_b/k_b such as RS(63, 41, 10) could be a good candidate. From this code, the key length is large, ie. 246 (41x6) bits. This implies that the genuine key can be recovered correctly with high probability 99.9% (FRR$_b$=0.01%) but that is impossible for random and skilled forgers to regenerate the genuine key (FAR$_{br}$ = FAR$_{bs}$ = 0%). However, there are 2.12% and 4.01% chances for random and skilled forgers

to recover the genuine key when the genuine token is stolen. Nevertheless, the stolen-token case is the worst scenario that less likely to happen. It should be noted that this simulation is done on SVC Task 1 dataset and we do not generalize these results to all circumstances.

BIOMETRIC HELPER (BH) SECURITY

The security of signature-key can be measured by using the discrete Entropy, which is defined as $H(x) = -\Sigma Pr(x)\log_2 Pr(x)$ where $Pr(x)$ denotes bit probability and maximum bit unit entropy is 1 (Joy and Thomas 1991). For key with length γ, $H(key) = \gamma$. If $H(key) < \gamma$, an adversary can guess a key by trying the combination of bit strings less than 2^γ. Practically, γ should not be less than 80 due to the fact that a total search space of 2^{80} is believed still out of the capabilities of modern computer. In this section we evaluate the security impact of two BHs used in our scheme.

We examine the case when an adversary manages to acquire the stored information of RFD such as the segment bits number M_k^*, where the information leakage due to M_k^*. In other words, the conditional entropy $H(key|M_k^*)$ is considered. If this is a leakage, then $H(key|M_k^*) < H(key)$ where $H(key)$ is the empirical entropy of key. However, no information is leaked from M_k^* since we do not store the statistics of feature elements, which may reveal the probable location of the genuine segment. Hence $H(key|M_k^*) = H(key) \approx 250$ bits (the lower computed entropy bound).

Another concern is the information leakage due to EEC parity checksum, ρ_b. According to Tulys et al. (2005), the conditional entropy of key given

Table 6. Performances of ECC in FAR_b and FRR_b with $m_b=5$ and $m_b=6$

n_b	k_b	t_b	t_b/k_b	Bit length	FRR_b (%)	FAR_{br} (%)	FAR_{bs} (%)	FAR_{br}(%) (stolen -token)	FAR_{bs}(%) (stolen -token)
31	11	10	0.91	55	0.00	1.31	3.12	11.4	14.13
	15	8	0.53	75	0.00	0.73	0.86	7.30	9.12
	21	4	0.19	105	2.45	0.01	0.03	3.73	6.02
	27	2	0.07	135	5.87	0.00	0.00	0.17	3.63
63	21	20	0.95	126	0.00	1.28	1.92	9.64	13.81
	31	16	0.51	186	0.00	0.51	0.08	6.21	8.64
	41	**10**	**0.24**	**246**	**0.01**	**0.00**	**0.00**	**2.12**	**4.01**
	51	6	0.11	306	1.01	0.00	0.00	1.01	2.62

the ECC parity checksum is defined as $H(key|\rho_b)$ = H(key) - $m_b\rho_b$. However, due to the two-stage formulation of our technique. The formula should be modified to as:

$$H(key|\rho_b) = H(key| M_k^*) - m_b\rho_b \qquad (1)$$

Equation (4) indicates that if an adversary knows ρ_b, he may exploit ρ_b to deduce the search space of key. For example, if $H(key| M_k^*) = \gamma$, the adversary just need to try $\gamma - m_b\rho_b$ combinations to recover the key without any other information. As the relation between t_b and ρ_b is a linearly proportional one, ie. $2t_b \leq \rho_b$, this justifies why t_b has to be small. For a smaller ρ_b, the entropy loss is lesser and this increases the difficulty to be guessed. For instance, based on the data in section 4.3 and assume no leakage in RFD stage. We have $H(key|\rho) = 246 - 6(63-41) = 114$ bits. Nevertheless, even if an adversary accesses ρ, the length of bit string is still sufficiently large (114 bits) to prevent a brute-force attack.

CONCLUSION

We propose a secure and robust method for extracting replaceable biometric keys using dynamic hand signature and random token. The motivation for our work is fuelled by the need to overcome inherent security weakness in conventional biometric authentication systems which disallows easy integration into cryptographic protocols and did not address the issue of biometric key management. In particular, our key generation method should not require storage of the template hand signature or leak the original biometric information. The keys must be replaceable in the event of key compromise, sufficiently long, secure, distinguishable between different users, and reproducible exactly. The experimental results and security proofs have demonstrated that the proposed method using the sequence of DWT-DFT biometric extraction, random feature discretization (RFD) and error correction code (ECC) is able to fulfill the required objective without compromising the biometric while providing sufficiently good recognition rates.

ACKNOWLEDGMENT

This work was supported by the Korea Science and Engineering Foundation (KOSEF) through the Biometrics Engineering Research Center (BERC) at Yonsei University (Grant Number:R112002105080020(2008)).

REFERENCES

Chang, Y. C., Zhang, W., & Chen, T. (2004). Biometric-based cryptographic key generation. *IEEE Conference on Multimedia and Expo 2004*, Taiwan.

Chen, C., Veldhuis, R. N. J., Kevenaar, T. A. M., & Akkermans, A. H. M. (2007, September 27-29). Multibits biometric string generation based on the likelihood ratio. *IEEE Conference on Biometrics: Theory, Applications and Systems*, Washington, D.C. (pp. 1-6).

Daugman, J. (2003). The important of being random: Statistical principles of iris recognition. *Pattern Recognition, 36*, 279–291. doi:10.1016/S0031-3203(02)00030-4

Davida, G., Frankel, Y., Matt, B. J., & Peralta, R. (1999, January). On the relation of error correction and cryptography to an offline biometric based on identification scheme. *Workshop on Coding and Cryptography (WCC)*.

Deng, P. S., Liao, H. Y. M., Chin, W. H., & Tyan, H. R. (1999). Wavelet-based offline signature verification. *Computer Vision and Image Understanding, 76*, 173–190. doi:10.1006/cviu.1999.0799

Feng, H., & Chan, C. W. (2002). Private key generation from online handwritten signatures. *Information Management & Computer Security, 10*(4), 159–164. doi:10.1108/09685220210436949

Hao, F., Anderson, R., & Daugman, J. (2006). Combining crypto with biometrics effectively. *IEEE Transactions on Computers, 55*(9), 1081–1088. doi:10.1109/TC.2006.138

Jain, A. K., Hong, L., & Pankanti, S. (2000). Biometric identification. *Communications of the ACM, 43*(2), 90–98. doi:10.1145/328236.328110

Joy, T. M., & Thomas, J. A. (1991). *Elements of information theory* (2nd ed.). John Wiley & Sons Inc.

Kevenaar, T. A. M., Schrijen, G. J., van der Veen, M., & Akkermans, A. H. M. (2005, October 17-18). Face recognition with renewable and privacy preserving binary templates. *4th IEEE Workshop on Automatic Identification Advanced Technologies (AutoID '05)*, Buffalo, NY (pp. 21-26).

Lam, C. F., & Kamins, D. (1989). Signature recognition through spectral analysis. *Pattern Recognition, 22*(1), 39–44. doi:10.1016/0031-3203(89)90036-8

Lejtman, D. Z., & George, S. E. (2001). Online handwritten signature verification using wavelets and back-propagation neural networks. *6th International Conference on Document Analysis and Recognition (ICDAR)* (pp. 992-996).

Nakanishi, I., Nishiguchi, N., Itoh, Y., & Fukui, Y. (2003). Online signature verification method utilizing feature extraction based on DWT. *Proceedings of the 2003 International Symposium on Circuits and Systems (ISCAS 2003), IV* (pp. 73-76).

Purser, M. (1995). *Introduction to error-correcting codes*. Boston: Artech House.

Schneier, B. (1996). *Applied cryptography: Protocols algorithms and source code*. John Wiley and Sons, Inc.

Silva, A. V., & Freitas, D. S. (2002). Wavelet-based compared to function-based online signature verification. *Proceedings of the XV Brazilian Symposium on Computer Graphics and Image Processing (SIBGRAPI 02)* (pp. 218-225).

SVC 2004. (n.d.). First international signature verification competition [online]. Retrieved from http://www.cs.ust.hk/svc2004/

Teoh, A. B. J., & Ngo, D. C. L. (2006b). Cancellable biometrics realization through BioPhasoring. *Proc. of 9th International Conference on Control, Automation, Robotics and Vision, ICARCV 2006*, Singapore.

Teoh, A. B. J., Ngo, D. C. L., & Goh, A. (2006a). Quantized multispace random mapping for two-factor identity. *IEEE Transaction on Pattern Recognition and Machine Intelligence, 28*(12), 1892–1901. doi:10.1109/TPAMI.2006.250

Teoh, A. B. J., Toh, K. A., & Yip, W. K. (2007, August 27-29). 2^N discretisation of BioPhasor in cancellable biometrics. *2nd International Conference on Biometrics*, Seoul Korea. (LNCS 4642, pp. 435-444).

Tuyls, P., Akkermans, A. H. M., Kevenaar, T. A. M., Schrijen, G.-J., Bazen, A. M., & Veldhuis, R. N. J. (2005). Practical biometric authentication with template protection. AVBPA 2005. (*. LNCS, 3546*, 436–446.

Vielhauer, C., & Steinmetz, R. (2004). Handwriting: Feature correlation analysis for biometric hashes. *EURASIP Journal of Applied Signal Processing . Special Issue on Biometric Signal Processing, 4*, 542–558.

Vielhauer, C., Steinmetz, R., & Mayerhorf, A. (2002). Biometric hash based on statistical features of online signatures. *16th International Conference on Pattern Recognition (ICPR 2002)*, 1, 123-126.

Chapter 18
Game Playing Tactic as a Behavioral Biometric for Human Identification

Roman V. Yampolskiy
University of Louisville, USA

Venu Govindaraju
University at Buffalo, USA

ABSTRACT

This chapter expends behavior based intrusion detection approach to a new domain of game networks. Specifically, our research shows that a behavioral biometric signature can be generated based on the strategy used by an individual to play a game. We wrote software capable of automatically extracting behavioral profiles for each player in a game of poker. Once a behavioral signature is generated for a player, it is continuously compared against player's current actions. Any significant deviations in behavior are reported to the game server administrator as potential security breaches. In this chapter, we report our experimental results with user verification and identification, as well as our approach to generation of synthetic poker data and potential spoofing approaches of the developed system. We also propose utilizing techniques developed for behavior based recognition of humans to the identification and verification of intelligent game bots. Our experimental results demonstrate feasibility of such methodology.

INTRODUCTION TO BEHAVIORAL BIOMETRICS

Behavioral biometrics are a valuable tool in many security tasks, which require identification or verification of an individual. Behavioral biometrics are often employed because they can be easily collected non-obtrusively and are particularly useful in situations, which do not provide an opportunity for collection of stronger - more reliable biometric data. We investigated strategy used while playing a game as a type of a behavioral biometric (Yampolskiy & Govindaraju, 2008b). The game of poker is used as an example of a game with a clearly identifiable player strategy. The profile produced for each player is used as the person's behavioral-biometric profile. This chapter is based on "Strategy-Based Behavioral Biometric a Novel Approach to Automatic Identi-

DOI: 10.4018/978-1-60566-725-6.ch018

fication" by R. Yampolskiy and V. Govindaraju, which appeared in the International Journal of Computer Applications in Technology, Special Issues on Automated Identification Technology. The chapter presents a new comprehensive view of research results previously published in a number of venues including: (Yampolskiy, 2006, 2007a, 2007b, 2008) and (Yampolskiy & Govindaraju, 2006a, 2006b, 2007, 2008a, 2008b).

Our approach can be used by online casinos to detect a masquerader who is utilizing a stolen account on a game server or a player trying to cheat by using an AI bot in order to win more money. Both are currently big problems in the world of online gaming and a successful solution is beneficial not just from theoretical but also from a practical point of view. Advantages of the developed solution are listed below:

- No special hardware required
- No noticeable enrolment period
- Provides continuous player verification
- Identifies user not the system or geographic location

ON THE GAME OF POKER

In our experiments we used a variant of poker known as Texas Hold'em. It is a game of incomplete information with rules which are easy for beginners to understand, but the game takes years to master. The rules are simple; each player (number of players can be between 2 and 10) gets two private cards from a standard deck of 52. A round of betting takes place after which only players who wish to play their hand remain in the game. The rest of the players give up their claims to the money in the process known as Folding. Poker is played for money and the amount to bet can either be structured (Limit) or unstructured (No Limit). The process of increasing the amount of money necessary to play is known as Betting or Raising, if another player has already engaged in Betting.

After the first round of betting 3 community cards are revealed known as the flop. Another round of betting takes place. This is followed by another revealed card known as the Turn. After another round of betting the final card, known as the River, is revealed and a final round of betting takes place. The remaining players go to the Showdown in which all still participating players open their private cards to examination by other players and the player with the best Hand (2 private cards) wins all the money contributed to the Pot (bank) in this hand. The ranking of hands is based on the five best cards out of 7 available (2 private and 5 community cards). The ranks are: Straight Flush, 4-of a kind, Full House, Flush, Straight, Set, 2 pair, 1 pair and finally the weakest is the high card. A straight is 5 cards in a raw based on the rank. Flush is 5 cards of the same suit. Full House is a pair and a Set. A set is 3-of a kind.

Players also take turns being the Dealer or the person who distributes the cards and is the last one to act in latter betting rounds. The player to the left of the dealer is known as the Small Blind because he has to contribute a small forced Bet to the pot pre-Flop. The person to the left of the Small Blind is known as the Big Blind and has to contribute a large forced Bet pre-Flop. This is done to encourage active participation by players instead of conservative waiting for the best possible hand pre-flop such as AA (two aces). In case of a draw (same card combination is displayed at showdown by multiple players) money in the pot is equally divided among such players. If a player runs out of money he has an option of limiting his loses by going All-In, which means only contributing his remaining money to the pot, regardless of the contribution amount from other players. In this case the player who goes All-In can only win a portion of the Pot proportional to his All-In bet.

Overall, Poker game strategy is heavily influenced by the nature of your opponents, amount of money at the table, your position around the table and tendency of players to Bluff (deceive others about the strength of their hand) or go All-In. A good player has a good understanding of statistics involved as well as ability to psychologically profile/model other players and to read their body language. As of this writing, best humans are still beating best computer players at poker, but this is likely to change in the near future.

PREVIOUS WORK

A wide range of both software and hardware solutions are available to address the player verification problem. Unfortunately each approach has its problems such as difficulty of implementation or high costs of operation (Nevadaigtf.org, 2005; Yampolskiy & Govindaraju, 2006b).

User Name-Password

A combination of user name and password is probably the most popular player verification and identification solution, but it does have its shortcomings. Anyone with the password can claim to be a legitimate account owner, but the password can be lost, stolen or accidentally given away. It can also be guessed or hacked by an intelligent thief or simply forgotten by not so intelligent owner. Another drawback of passwords is that they are often stored in the application itself, which simplifies the log in process but is a security nightmare (Nevadaigtf.org, 2005).

BioPassword

BioPassword is a patented software-only authentication system based on the keystroke dynamics biometric. While the user enters his password the system captures information about just how the user types, including any pauses between the pressings of different keys. Essentially the software observes the typing rhythm, pace and syncopation. This information is used to create a statistically reliable profile for an individual. In combination with the user's password BioPassword creates a so-called hardened password. It is no longer enough to know the password itself, it is also important to enter it in precisely the same way as the true account owner. This is a great improvement over traditional passwords, but unfortunately it still has some shortcomings, such as that it does not provide continuous player verification after the initial log in. It can also be bypassed with the auto-login feature and BioPassword also requires an enrolment period. Another important factor is the cost associated with purchasing a BioPassword license which for a large number of user can be relatively expensive (Nevadaigtf.org, 2005).

IP Filtering

This is a way to identify the location from which the user is connecting to the server, an assumption is made that if the service provider and/or geographic location associated with the IP address has not changed from the last login, neither did the user identity. This is a questionable assumption and so the technology is mostly used to tell if a user is located in a locality where gambling is legal, not to identify or verify users. ``Where direct broadband connections such as cable modem, DSL, or T1 services are used, this mechanism is virtually foolproof. Where dialup to the ISP is used, these filtering systems lack an ability to accurately identify location. These systems can be used to allow connections through known ISP's where the final hop is hard wired. In general where this cannot be ascertained admittance is denied. As a result this is a coarse selection mechanism that will deny many users who are in fact geographically acceptable, but assures that anyone permitted within the filter is within the jurisdiction" (Nevadaigtf.org, 2005).

GeoBio Indicator

A device consisting of an integrated GPS based geographical indicator and biometric-based smart card that attaches to a personal computer via the Universal Serial Bus port. As with any standard USB plug in it is self-installing. GeoBio indicator can be used for player identification and border control, but has significant implementation costs and distribution barriers associated with hardware purchasing and distribution as well as with the enrolment process. Among other problems with this approach is privacy issues inevitable raised by integration of biometric and geographic information in one data-system (Nevadaigtf.org, 2005).

Phone Call Verification

Represents a method utilizing a synchronized phone call with a web session to identify user's geographic location. It even works for users with a single phone line. ``During the synchronized call, casino employs data matching and telephone provisioning information to determine who owns the phone and its location. A voice recording and voice biometric is captured to ensure acceptance of a transaction and limit use of an account. Country code, area code, and local exchange information can be matched to IP address providing strong location assurance. This approach offers a way to verify user's ... location, in real time, without installing hardware or software on the end users computer'' (Nevadaigtf.org, 2005). This approach works well for geographical location based restriction of access to the casino but it only identifies geographic location not the user, requires knowledge of English language from the user and is time consuming.

Face Recognition Via Web-Cam

Another biometrics-based approach is to use a web-camera that would constantly monitor the player sitting at the computer. The constant visual recognition would ensure that only the player who has signed up continues playing. Problems with such an approach include a hardware requirement for a web-cam of high quality. Additionally

it would limit user's mobility and can easily be spoofed. Finally, it generates some serious privacy concerns, as most people would feel unease about allowing a security camera to be pointed at them in their own home (Nevadaigtf.org, 2005).

OUR APPROACH TO THE PLAYER VERIFICATION PROBLEM

Based on the idea of using strategy followed while playing a game as a type of a behavioral biometric we propose a complete system for player verification. First a player profile is generated either by data mining an existing database of poker hands or by observing a live game of poker. Next a similarity measure is obtained between the feature vector generated based on the recently collected player data and the data for the same player obtained in previous sessions. A score is generated indicating how similar the current style of play is to the historically shown style of play for a particular player. If a score is above a certain threshold, it might indicate that a different user from the one who has originally registered is using the account and so the administrator of the casino needs to be alerted to that fact. If the score is below some threshold, the system continues collecting and analyzing the player data.

As can be seen from the figure below using a previously generated database of poker hands does not provide an option of continuous monitoring and so is an inferior alternative, which might be valuable in terms of initial experimentation, but which must be replaced by live data collection for the completed product.

Data

Data for poker related experiments could be obtained in several ways: by observing real games played by human opponents in casinos, home games and at online gambling sites or by utilizing existing poker-hand databases.

Figure 1. A diagram of the developed system (©2009 Inderscience Publishers Ltd. Used with permission)

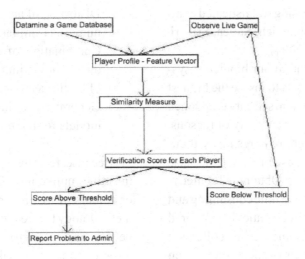

Internet Relay Chat Poker Dataset

Long before online casinos became prevalent on the Internet, there exists the Internet Relay Chat (IRC) poker server. Michael Maurer developed a program he called the Observer that resided on the IRC poker channels and monitored and logged the details of every game it observed. This resulted in the collection of the more than 10 million complete poker hands (from 1995-2001) that comprise the IRC Poker Database (Maurer, 2005).

Data from Monitoring Human Play

Additional data for poker related experiments could be obtained by observing many real games played by human opponents in casinos, home games and at online gambling sites.

Data from Observing Online Human Play. This is probably the best source of data since the games are multiple in number, stakes and quality of players. The data is same as the data potentially generated in the desired field of application of the final algorithm. The data can also be easily collected automatically by creating a simple observer bot or even easier collected by the online casino

itself if it desires to do so, perhaps for security reasons. In fact most casinos already do collect some game data if not the complete information about every hand played.

Data from Observing Off-Line Human Play. Another alternative is to attempt to collect data from real brick and mortar casinos, home games and tournaments. This approach is interesting because many additional factors may be collected which are not available in an online setting and are generally referred to as tells. But this information is neither objective nor useful for our purposes since it will not be possible to obtain similar data while employing our algorithm online. Finally it is a daunting manual task to collect data from real life human play, which results in expensive and potentially full of errors set of statistics.

SYNTHESIS OF ARTIFICIAL PROFILES

Many biometric technologies are still in their infancy and do not yet have large reliable data sets which are needed for further development of such systems. One solution to the problem of insufficient availability of training and testing biometric data is the creation of the so-called simulated or synthetic biometric data using sophisticated computer algorithms (Yanushkevich, Stoica, Srihari, Shmerko, & Gavrilova, 2004).

While ideally we want all our biometric systems to be tested on real data to insure the highest standard of quality and system security is obtained it is not always possible for a variety of reasons. Testing a biometric system requires many thousands of samples in order to establish system's false reject and false accept rates. Obtaining biometric data in sufficient quantity is a time consuming and expansive process. Volunteers quickly get bored with a repetitive task of biometric data collection and paying people for their cooperation is often beyond the budget of many research centres. Also dealing with real biometric data brings up issues with privacy of individuals providing their data and with security of biometric databases (Sumi & Matsuyama, 2005).

Synthetic data addresses many of the concerns presented above. Once a system for producing simulated data is developed it is fast and cheap to produce large quantities of high quality biometric data which adheres to statistical distributions desired by the investigator without any privacy or security concerns to worry about. Such data can be used for testing newly developed biometric systems, benchmarking well developed security systems, testing scalability of authentication systems or for certification of commercially available packages. Production of synthetic biometrics allows researchers to better understand individuality of biometric patterns and allows parametric sensitivities of algorithms to be investigated in greater detail (Ma, Schuckers, & Cukic, 2005; Makthal & Ross, 2005); (Orlans, Buettner, & Marques, 2004).

A number of approaches exist for the generation of the artificial biometric data. Most of them are concerned with the creation of a simulated image depicting a particular physical biometric such as a fingerprint, face or iris. The existing approaches

can be grouped into the following categories:

- Distortion of an existing image to generate numerous similar images
- Combination of multiple images to produce a novel image with partial properties of all the seed images
- Generation of images based on physical models for the biometric in question

Because features of a strategic profile have meaning, unlike minutiae points of fingerprints or colours of iris, it is possible to apply a fourth methodology for creation of synthetic game-based behavioural biometrics, namely parameterized design. It may not make any sense to design a synthetic fingerprint with all the minutiae points located in just the left half of the fingerprint but it makes sense to have a strategic profile for a player who is only aggressive in the first two rounds of the game. A fifth and final option we are not really considering here is generation of a synthetic-behavioural-biometric based on purely random approach. Such simulated data would correspond to unrealistic strategies not encountered at real world poker tables and as such would be completely useless for our purposes of generating realistic artificial biometric data possessing all properties of the authentic samples.

The first approach to the creation of the synthetic behavioural biometric we have implemented is based on taking an existing player profile and modifying it to make numerous additional profiles similar to the given one (Yampolskiy & Govindaraju, 2008a). Poker is a game of high variance and so even by following the same exact strategy it is possible for a player to play a slightly different number of cards at every stage based on the actual cards being dealt to him. We have estimated poker variance for a reasonably large number of played hands to be around 3 percent. By taking all the feature points in a given profile and replacing them with new randomly generated values in the range of +/-3% of the given ones we are able to obtain multiple artificial profiles for the same player which are representative of the authentic profiles which could be produced by the same player due to the degree of natural variance in the game of poker. Any resulting values outside of the range from zero percent to hundred percent are changed to the closest values falling in the range. Obviously it is also possible to adjust the variance rate to accommodate different playing styles and types of poker games. An example of one profile generated in such a way based on a temporal-seed-profile from player Bob is shown in Table 1.

This methodology is best for generation of multiple profiles for the same individual which can be used for testing of verification or even identification abilities of strategy based behavioral biometric systems.

Second approach to the generation of artificial behavioural biometric data we implemented is based on combining feature points from two or more different seed profiles. This can be done in two different ways either simply picking one of the profiles as providing a particular data point for the profile being created or taking average of the values in the seed profiles to serve as the new value. This methodology is similar to the crossover operations used in genetic algorithms for production of the next generation of solutions from the currently available distribution of genetic

strings (Goldberg, 1989; Yampolskiy, Anderson, Arney, Misic, & Clarke, 2004).

In case of strategic profiles this approach leads to the production of profiles representing somewhat averaged strategies. For example, combining an overly aggressive and a passive profile results in a solid profile typical of many good players at low level tables. This methodology is best for generation of multiple profiles needed to make sure our database is sufficiently large to make verification of particular individuals of interest a non-trivial task. It also works well for generation of novel strategic profiles not yet encountered during the collection of authentic data and so insures diversity of strategies encountered by the biometric processing system.

An approach corresponding to the generation of synthetic biometrics based on physical models with respect to poker strategies is achieved by creation of realistically behaving artificial poker players. It is up to the poker experts to develop multiple strategically interesting poker bots. Typically a number of basic strategies are used for the initial design and by adding some behavioural variation at particular stages of the game new strategies are introduced. Most popular basic profiles are Solid, Rock, Maniac, Fish, and Typical (Pokerinspector.com, 2006). Once such players are created they are allowed to play

Table 1. A sample profile generated from a seed profile (©2009 Inderscience Publishers Ltd. Used with permission)

Player Name: Synthetic Bob		Hands Dealt: n/a		
	Pre-Flop	Flop	Turn	River
# of Hands Played	n/a	n/a	n/a	n/a
Folded	68.4%	26.7%	23.8%	20.1%
Checked	5.7%	52.3%	51.8%	53.8%
Called	21.3%	32.1%	28.2%	33.4%
Raised	4.9%	3.5%	4.4%	5.7%
Check-Raised	2.2%	2.9%	2.0%	2.7%
Re-Raised	1%	0.2%	0.0%	0.4%
All-In	1.5%	3.4%	4.9%	39.5%

against each other or against human opponents while the system generates corresponding strategy based behavioural profiles for them which also include the contextual information about the flop, player's position and stages of the hand. Profiles produced in such a way show a very high degree of over time consistency as computerized players are not subject to psychological swings so typical of human players commonly referred to as going on tilt (Schoonmaker, 2005).

Our implementation of poker bots was done using the statistical package called Online Hold'em Inspector version 2.26d4 (Pokerinspector.com, 2006). By specifying such conditions as tendency of our bots to bluff, slow play, check raise and their aggressiveness level as well as their pre-flop card selection we were able to generate numerous valid poker strategies. Validity of our poker bots was tested at low-stakes real-money online poker tables against human opponents where our bots consistently scored around 3 big bets per hour in profits (Yampolskiy & Govindaraju, 2008a). Figures 2 and 3 demonstrate bot's characteristics, which we were able to manipulate.

By manipulating hundreds of variables associated with our bots playing strategy and combining them in numerous ways we were able to generate a multitude of realistically behaving poker players and as a result collected behavioral biometric data on all such strategies. Also by statistically analyzing our bot's strategy we were able to predict some characteristics of the bot's behavioral profile as shown in Figure 4.

Finally we get to an approach we call parameterized design. Because we are not generating a raw biometric image but rather a set of feature measurements we are able to declare with statistical parameters in which ranges we wish all feature points to reside. This is a somewhat inverted approach from the one utilizing artificially intelligent poker playing programs. Instead of designing a poker strategy which can be observed to produce a statistical profile describing player's behavior we are directly generating the statistical feature vector which is parameterized with the intention of representing a valid game strategy. This is a less tedious approach as instead of prescribing particular actions to each one of the thousands

Figure 2. Flop playing strategy menu (©2009 Inderscience Publishers Ltd. Used with permission)

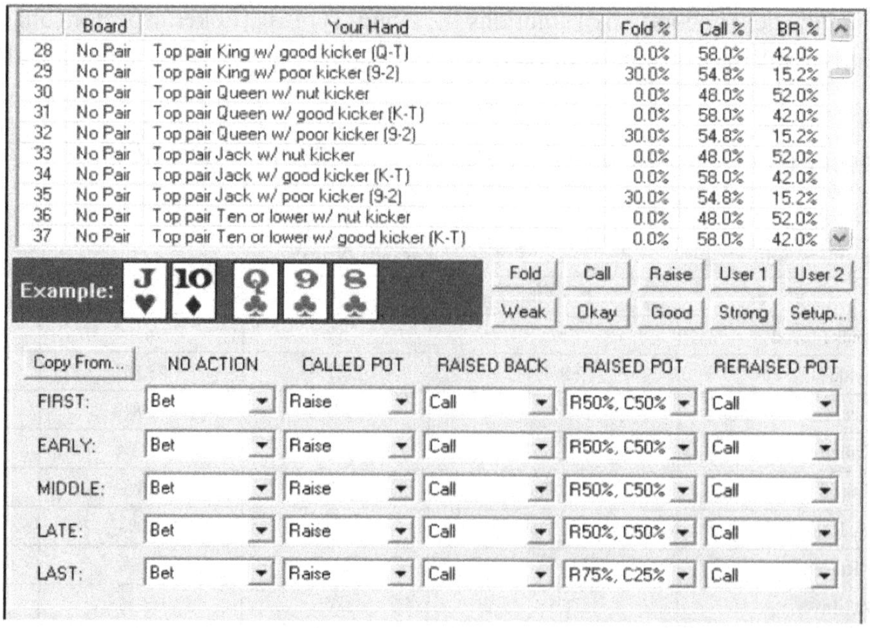

Figure 3. Pre-flop hand selection strategy menu (©2009 Inderscience Publishers Ltd. Used with permission)

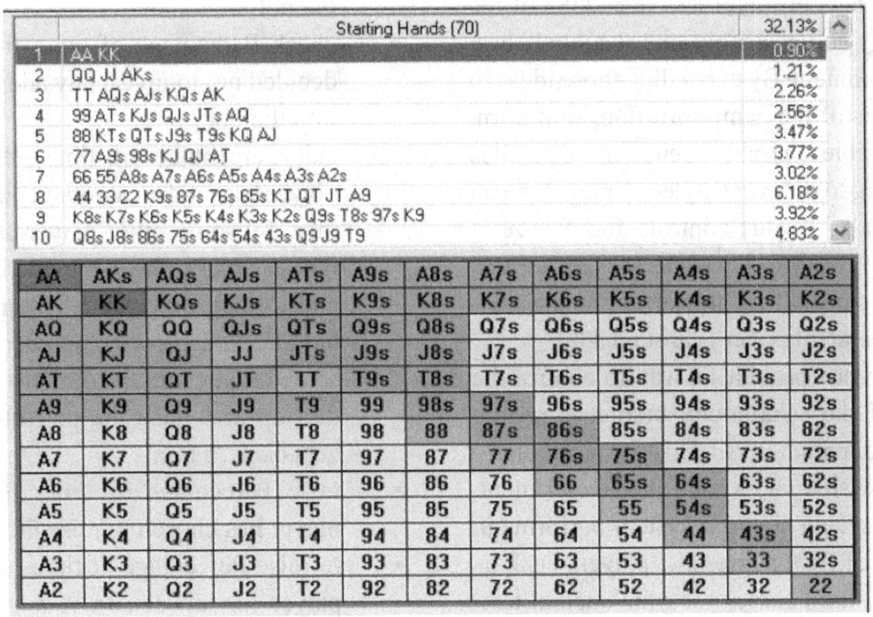

	Starting Hands (70)	32.13%
1	AA KK	0.90%
2	QQ JJ AKs	1.21%
3	TT AQs AJs KQs AK	2.26%
4	99 ATs KJs QJs JTs AQ	2.56%
5	88 KTs QTs J9s T9s KQ AJ	3.47%
6	77 A9s 98s KJ QJ AT	3.77%
7	66 55 A8s A7s A6s A5s A4s A3s A2s	3.02%
8	44 33 22 K9s 87s 76s 65s KT QT JT A9	6.18%
9	K8s K7s K6s K5s K4s K3s K2s Q9s T8s 97s K9	3.92%
10	Q8s J8s 86s 75s 64s 54s 43s Q9 J9 T9	4.83%

AA	AKs	AQs	AJs	ATs	A9s	A8s	A7s	A6s	A5s	A4s	A3s	A2s
AK	KK	KQs	KJs	KTs	K9s	K8s	K7s	K6s	K5s	K4s	K3s	K2s
AQ	KQ	QQ	QJs	QTs	Q9s	Q8s	Q7s	Q6s	Q5s	Q4s	Q3s	Q2s
AJ	KJ	QJ	JJ	JTs	J9s	J8s	J7s	J6s	J5s	J4s	J3s	J2s
AT	KT	QT	JT	TT	T9s	T8s	T7s	T6s	T5s	T4s	T3s	T2s
A9	K9	Q9	J9	T9	99	98s	97s	96s	95s	94s	93s	92s
A8	K8	Q8	J8	T8	98	88	87s	86s	85s	84s	83s	82s
A7	K7	Q7	J7	T7	97	87	77	76s	75s	74s	73s	72s
A6	K6	Q6	J6	T6	96	86	76	66	65s	64s	63s	62s
A5	K5	Q5	J5	T5	95	85	75	65	55	54s	53s	52s
A4	K4	Q4	J4	T4	94	84	74	64	54	44	43s	42s
A3	K3	Q3	J3	T3	93	83	73	63	53	43	33	32s
A2	K2	Q2	J2	T2	92	82	72	62	52	42	32	22

of possible situations in a game of poker we only have to specify some general trends such as aggression and card selection at different phases of the game.

Generally a style of a poker player is represented as a point on a 2-dimensional styles grid. The y dimension represents the tight/loose score and the x dimension stands for the passive/aggressive behaviour of the player. Players are measured on each dimension from 1 to 9 (Schoonmaker, 2005). This gives us up to 81 different playing styles which is sufficient for production of baseline profiles for testing of verification systems. The resulting baseline profiles can later be used to generate additional profiles using methods presented above.

Our algorithm takes an (x,y) pair and produces a behavioural profile which confirms to a statistically predicted action frequency distribution for this particular playing style. For example a loose and passive player commonly refereed to as a "Calling Station" is represented by a point (9,1)

Figure 4. Estimates of a statistical profile for a bot's strategy (©2009 Inderscience Publishers Ltd. Used with permission)

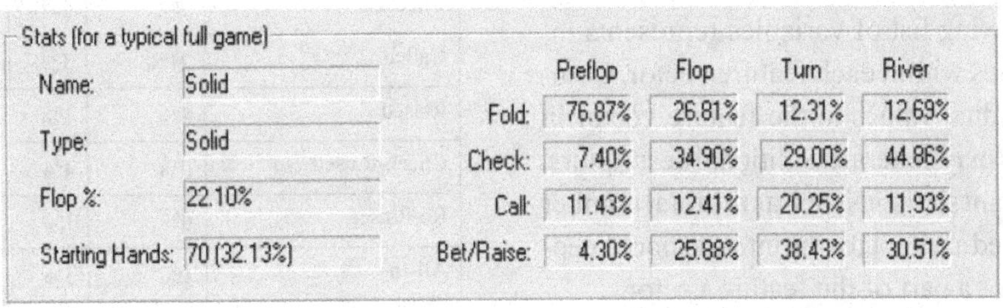

Stats (for a typical full game)

			Preflop	Flop	Turn	River
Name:	Solid	Fold:	76.87%	26.81%	12.31%	12.69%
Type:	Solid	Check:	7.40%	34.90%	29.00%	44.86%
Flop %:	22.10%	Call:	11.43%	12.41%	20.25%	11.93%
Starting Hands:	70 (32.13%)	Bet/Raise:	4.30%	25.88%	38.43%	30.51%

on a playing styles grid and would correspond to a behavioural profile which looks at over 89% of flops and bets or raises less than 11% of the time basically only if he holds the absolutely best cards at the moment. By expanding those ideas to all four stages of the game (pre-flop, flop, turn, river) we are able to produce behavioural profiles corresponding to different styles of play. We can see that each grid value controls about 11% of style space and so different styles are very easy to distinguish using statistical analyzer as the variance in the game of poker is around 3%.

This approach provides a way to control the properties of the behavioural biometric profile via specified parameters. This is particularly useful if we wish to run a controlled experiment, for example seeing how our system performs in a large field of tight/aggressive players such as found at high limit games for which actual testing of the system may be beyond the means for many researchers.

Statistical Measurement of Player's Style

If we are going to study the game of poker and more particularly the style of our opponents scientifically, we will need to quantify and statistically analyze our opponents' behavior. In order to do so we propose and define a number of variables associated with actions of our opponents. The parameters chosen are selected because they can be easily tracked by relatively straightforward methodologies and more importantly they are believed to accurately describe the long-term model of behavior of our opponents (Brandt, 2005; poker-edge.com, 2006; ultimatebet.com, 2005).

The following list of variables represents individual values within each feature vector. Combining individual values in the feature vector in varying ways may generate additional descriptors. Some important statistics such as the total number of hands played are kept for the internal bookkeeping but are not a part of the feature vector.

- fold Percentage of times this particular player has decided to give up his claims to the pot.
- check Percentage of times this player has decided not to invest any additional money into the pot
- call Percentage of times this particular player has paid an amount equivalent to the raise by some other player ahead in position in order to keep playing this hand
- check-raise Percentage of times a player has checked allowing another player to put some money into the pot, just to come over the top and raise the pot after the action gets back to him.
- raise Percentage of times this particular player has chosen to raise the stakes.
- re-raise Percentage of times this particular player has chosen to re-raise somebody-else's raise. This would include a re-re-raise and re-re-re-raise so on.
- all-in Percentage of times this particular player has chosen to invest all his money in the current hand.

A combination of such statistical variables taken together produces a feature vector which

Table 2. Temporal strategy profile (Yampolskiy & Govindaraju, 2006b)

Player Name: Bob	Hands Dealt: 224			
	Pre-Flop	Flop	Turn	River
# of Hands Played	224	68	46	33
Folded	67%	28%	24%	18%
Checked	7%	54%	52%	52%
Called	21%	32%	28%	33%
Raised	4%	1%	4%	6%
Check-Raised	0%	4%	0%	0%
Re-Raised	0%	1%	0%	0%
All-In	1%	3%	4%	39%

Table 3. Spatial strategy profile (©2009 Inderscience Publishers Ltd. Used with permission)

Action	Small	Big	3rd	4th	5th	6th	7th	8th	9th	Dealer
Folded	77	73	71	69	67	64	61	59	57	51
Checked	55	53	50	49	48	44	41	39	37	34
Called	14	16	19	22	26	29	33	37	43	53
Raised	2	3	4	6	8	11	13	15	17	20
Check-Raised	31	28	23	19	17	15	12	9	6	4
Re-Raised	0	1	2	4	6	10	14	18	25	30
All-In	37	39	41	43	47	51	55	59	62	65

is used by a pattern recognition algorithm to determine if a current profile is consistent with that previously seen one from this particular player or if a possible intruder has taken the control of the account.

Descriptive accuracy of a behavioural profile can be greatly increased if additional information is included. We have utilized a profile structure which separates player's actions into the four stages of the hand, making temporal information available, and as a result, description of player's strategy more meaningful. Table 2 is an example of such temporal profile.

Profiles can be further enhanced with the inclusion of spatial information, essentially making a separate profile for each of the ten positions a player can have around the table. Such profiles clearly demonstrate dependence of player's strategy on position and are shown in Table 3.

Finally with the addition of contextual information about the cards revealed at the flop divided into 7 flop types described in the poker literature (as shown in Table 4) (Badizadegan, 1999) we have a 3D information space, which for every stage of the game, every position and every flop provides frequency counts of player's actions as illustrated in Figures 5 and 6.

Dimensionality of such a profile could be extremely high, compared to the basic profiles (Yampolskiy & Govindaraju, 2006a). Table 5 summarizes different possible profile types which can be used with strategy based behavioral bio-

metrics along with the information they include and lists the profile's dimensionality. Ideally any similarity measure function we propose to utilize should be flexible enough to handle any of the presented profile types (Yampolskiy & Govindaraju, 2006a).

As the amount of contextual information increases so does the dimensionality of the behavioural profile. This results in what is known as the "curse of dimensionality". The matching algorithm needs a large number of feature measurements to account for all the different possibilities of potential situations. The complexity of a high-dimensional space increases exponentially with the number of features. This large collection

Table 4. Flop types and number of variations for each type (Badizadegan, 1999)

Flop Type	Number of Variations	Example
Three cards of the same rank	1	2♣ 2♠ 2♦
Pair plus a 0-3 gapped card	2	J♦ J♣ 10♦
Pair plus a 4+ gapped card	2	K♥ K♠ 7♣
Three cards 0-2 gaps apart	3	9♠ 10♦ J♥
Two cards 0-3 gapped and a third card 4+	3	K♠ 7♣ 8♥
Three cards 3-6 gapped	3	J♥ 10♦ 6♣
Three cards with 4+ gaps between all cards	3	K♠ 8♣ 3♥

Table 5. Profile types by information included and dimensionality (©2009 Inderscience Publishers Ltd. Used with permission)

Profile Type	Information Included	Profile Dimensionality
Basic	Frequency counts for actions	7
Temporal	Frequency counts for actions at different stages of the game	$7 \times 4 = 28$
Contextual	Frequency counts for actions with respect to the flop type	$7 \times 7 = 49$
Spatial	Frequency counts for actions at different positions around the table	$7 \times 10 = 70$
Temporal-Spatial	Frequency counts for actions with respect to the stage of the game and relative position around the table	$7 \times 10 \times 4 = 280$
Temporal-Contextual-Spatial	Frequency counts for actions with respect to the stage of the game and relative position around the table and the flop	$7 \times 10 \times 4 + 3 \times 7 \times 7 = 427$

Figure 5. Poker table with the flow of information (©2009 Inderscience Publishers Ltd. Used with permission)

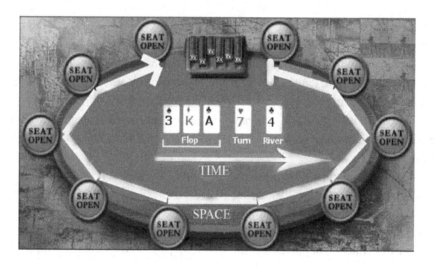

of features forms a high-dimensional space, in which it is very difficult to find the best decision boundary (Baggenstoss, 2004). One of the similarity measure functions, 2D style measure, examined in this paper is specifically designed to avoid the complications presented by the curse of dimensionality.

Similarity Measure Functions

When a new biometric data sample is presented to a security system, it is necessary to measure how closely it resembles template data (Yampolskiy & Govindaraju, 2006a). A good similarity measure takes into account statistical characteristics of the data distribution assuming enough data is available to determine such properties (Lee & Park, 2003). Alternatively expert knowledge about the data can be used to optimize a similarity measure function, for example a weighted Euclidean distance function can be developed if it is known that certain features are more valuable than others.

Figure 6. 3D profile structure (©2009 Inderscience Publishers Ltd. Used with permission)

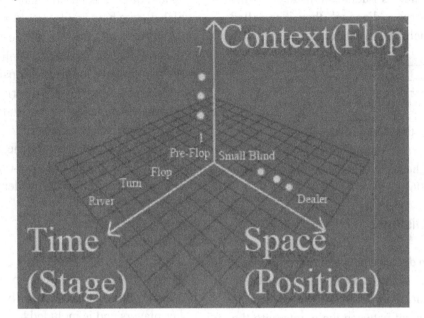

Euclidean Distance

One of the most popular similarity distance functions is the Euclidean distance. It is just the square root of the sum of the squared distance between the element of the n-dimensional vectors (x_i, y_i) (Sturn, 2000):

$$d_E = \sqrt{\sum_{i=1}^{n}(x_i - y_i)^2}$$

Euclidean distance is variant to both adding and multiplying all elements of a vector by a constant factor. It is also variant to the dimensionality of the vectors, for example if missing values reduce the dimension of certain vectors produced output will change. In general the value of Euclidean similarity measure may fall in the range from zero indicating a perfect match to sqrt(*n*) (where normalized n-dimensional vector is used) indicating maximum dissimilarity of playing styles. Obviously both of those extreme cases don't occur in real life and represent only theoretical possibilities not related to any viable playing style. In experiments with real life data Euclidean Similarity measure is always in between the two extremes (Yampolskiy & Govindaraju, 2006a, 2006b).

Mahalanobis Distance

Mahalanobis distance is defined as (Yampolskiy & Govindaraju, 2006a):

$$d_M = \sqrt{\left(x - \mu\right)^T \sum\nolimits^{-1}\left(x - \mu\right)}$$

with mean $\mu = (\mu_1, \mu_2, \mu_3, \ldots, \mu_n)$ and covariance matrix Σ for a multivariate vector $x = (x_1, x_2, x_3, \ldots, x_n)$. Mahalanobis distance can also be defined as dissimilarity measure between two random vectors X and Y of the same distribution with the covariance matrix Σ:

$$d_M = \sqrt{\left(x_i - y_i\right)^T \sum\nolimits^{-1}\left(x_i - y_i\right)}.$$

If the covariance matrix is the identity matrix

then it is the same as Euclidean distance. If the covariance matrix is diagonal, then it is called normalized Euclidean distance:

$$d_{NE} = \sqrt{\sum_{i=1}^{n} \frac{(x_i - y_i)^2}{\sigma_i^2}} \, ,$$

where σ_i is the standard deviation of the x_i over the sample set. Mahalanobis distance is not dependent on the scale of measurements (Wikipedia.com, 2006).

Manhattan Distance

The Manhattan distance between two points, in a Euclidean space with fixed Cartesian coordinate system, is the sum of the lengths of the projections of the line segment between the points onto the coordinate axes. In other terms, Manhattan distance is the absolute differences of the elements of the two vectors (x_i, y_i) (Sturn, 2000; Yampolskiy & Govindaraju, 2006a)

$$d_{Man} = \sum_{i=1}^{n} |x - y| .$$

Weighted Euclidean Distance

Performance of the Euclidean similarity measure function can be greatly improved if an expert knowledge about the nature of the data is available. If it is known that some values in the feature vector hold more discriminatory information with respect to others, it is possible to assign proportionally higher weights to such vector components and as a result influence the final outcome of the similarity function (Yampolskiy & Govindaraju, 2006a).

In the case of the poker domain, it is believed by the experts in the field, that the style of the poker player is particularly evident in the pre-flop card selection. Before the flop cards are revealed the player has relatively little information to ana-

lyze and often acts based on a small set of rules, which dictate how hands should be played based on the hand itself, position of the player and betting action so far observed. Application of such rules is relatively long-term consistent by most players and so has higher discrimination value as compared to action at the later rounds in the game. In such later rounds additional information about communal cards and opponent reading skills become more important than pre-established rules and so are more situation dependent (Yampolskiy & Govindaraju, 2006a).

2D Style Measure

This is a similarity measure approach used by human poker experts to classify and compare poker players and is included here to investigate feasibility of using such approaches by computerized systems. Generally a style of a poker player is represented as a point on a 2-dimensional styles grid shown in Figure 7. The y dimension represents the tight/loose score and the x dimension stands for the passive/aggressive behavior of the player. Players are measured on each dimension from 1 to 9 (Schoonmaker, 2005). For example a loose and passive player, commonly known as a "Calling Station", is represented by a point (9,1) on a playing styles grid and would correspond to a behavioral profile which looks at over 89% of flops and bets or raises less than 11% of the time basically only if he holds the absolutely best cards at the moment. This gives us only 81 different playing styles, however mathematically we are not restricted to only integer values for expressing the players' style and so in theory the number of styles can be infinite.

The proposed 2D style measure only takes into account the pre-flop selectiveness of the player and the overall aggressiveness expressed in raising, re-raising and going all-in. The two style descriptors chosen (tightness and aggressiveness) are selected because they are least dependent on elements of chance such as the cards revealed by

Figure 7. The 2-dimenstinal styles (Schoonmaker, 2005)

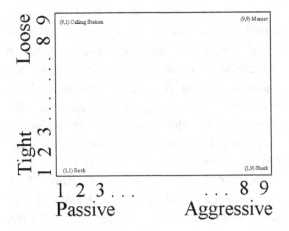

the board and the playing style of the opposing players. The proposed descriptors are computationally easy to obtain.

tightness = % of cards folded pre-flop

aggressiveness = average(% raised + % check raised + % re-raised + % all-in)

Aggressiveness value is determined over all stages of the hand, all possible positions and flop types depending on the type of the behavioral profile used to represent the player's strategy and the availability of the contextual information.

ARTIMETRICS: A NEW FIELD

Artificially Intelligent (AI) programs are quickly becoming a part of our everyday life. Virtual assistants, shopping bots, and smart search engines to give just some examples are used daily by millions of people. As such programs become closer in their abilities and intelligence to human beings the need arises to verify and recognize such artificially intelligent software just like it is often necessary to authenticate and confirm identity of people. With respect to human beings

identification and verification is mostly done for security reasons, to prevent certain people from unauthorized access to some resources and to allow it to the authorized personal.

Similarly, with respect to artificially intelligent programs reasons exist for determining the "identity" of a program or to verify the program is what it claims to be. Such reasons include but are not limited to:

- Finding out which program has actually performed a given task in case a number of possible agents exist, either for assigning blame or reward.
- Determining who has the authorship rights to the results of computation and creative output produced by AI software.
- Securing interaction between different pieces of intelligent software or between a human being and an instance of intelligent software.
- Preventing malicious intelligent software from obtaining access to information or system resources and granting it to authorized intelligent agents.
- Indirectly proving possession of unlicensed software on a system or network based on the observed capabilities of the system.

We are particularly interested in game playing programs which are commonly known as bots. Bots are a source of problems for many game networks from first person shooter games to online casinos. They are used by unscrupulous players to automate tedious tasks, to allow for longer play hours, and to defeat human opponents in games where AI-based players are clearly dominating their human opponents (chess, checkers). Basically bots are used as cheating tools in online games and some research has already been done on both detecting their use and to counteract such detection (Yampolskiy, 2007b). Our ability to verify and recognize intelligent game playing agents can be directly transformed into an ability to limit their use or restrict their application all together.

We propose applying techniques developed for behaviour based recognition of humans to the identification and verification of intelligent programs. Those techniques are commonly called behavioural biometrics. The paper is organized as follows: first we provide an overview of existing behavioural biometric technologies and other approaches aimed at player verification. Next we review existing AI software to which we can apply such techniques and cover previous work in the field. This is followed by presentation of a strategy based behavioural biometric used to verify identities of poker players. Finally, we report results of our experiments with automatic verification and recognition of artificially intelligent poker players.

Previous Work Related to Artimetrics

Existing research can be classified into three groups: recognizing patterns in the output of software and behavior of robots, distinguishing between people and computers, and identifying people (biometrics). To the best of our knowledge no research in output-based bot recognition or verification exists; some work has been done in program recognition (Ourston, 1989) and program understanding (Quilici, Yang, & Woods, 1998), in which the source code of the program is analyzed with the purpose of understanding the original purpose behind the creation of such software. Others have researched possibility of robot's behavior prediction and recognition never applying discovered trends to the recognition of robots exhibiting the observed behavior (Barrios-Aranibar & Alsina, 2005; Han & Veloso, 1999). Same thing can be said about the field of opponent modeling which is clearly related to our research but does not take the extra step of applying its findings to recognition of the opponent.

In 1950 Alan Turing published his most famous work "Computing Machinery and Intelligence" in which he proposes evaluation of abilities of an artificially intelligent machine based on how closely it can mimic human behaviour (Turing, 1950). The test, which is now commonly known as the Turing test is structured as a conversation and can be used to evaluate multiple behavioural parameters, such as agent's knowledge, skills, preferences, and strategies. In essence it is the ultimate multimodal behavioural biometric, which was postulated to make it possible to detect differences between man and machine.

In 2000 Luis von Ahn et al. (Ahn, Blum, Hopper, & Langford, 2003; Ahn, Blum, & Langford, 2004) proposed the concept of CAPTCHA (Completely Automated Public Turing test to tell Computers and Humans Apart). It is a type of challenge-response test used in computing to determine whether or not the user is human. It relies on ability of human beings to perform pattern recognition at a level which is beyond that currently achievable by artificially intelligent programs. Both the Turing test and CAPTCHAs take advantage of the differences in abilities between human beings and intelligent machines to identify to which group an agent being tested belongs. Majority of previous research falls under the heading of biometric research and it is the utilization of biometric methodologies for recognition of AI software which forms the cornerstone of our research.

Existing Intelligent Software and Robots

The artificially intelligent programs we currently have are still years away from being as intelligent as human beings, but there are some programs to which we can attempt to apply our verification/identification techniques. Some examples are provided below, but the list will unquestionably grow as our success with AI technologies progresses and we obtain programs which are as creative and unique as human beings. We already have programs capable of composing inspiring music (Cope, 2001), drawing beautiful paintings

(Cohen, 1988), and writing poetry (Boyd-Graber, 2006) and no limits are known to the abilities which a machine can eventually obtain. Table 6 lists some well developed artificially intelligent programs and behavioral biometrics we can apply to their verification (Yampolskiy, 2007a).

Biometrics refer to biological measurements collected for the purpose of identifying human beings, however this name is not appropriate with respect to non-biological agents. We propose that the research aimed at recognition and verification of software programs, robots and other non-biological agents be known as *Artimetrics* after the word "artilect", which is a shortened version of "artificial intellect" (Garis, 2005).

Artificially Intelligent Bots-Poker Players

Historically games were a sandbox used for testing novel AI theories and tools. It is a restricted domain, which allows techniques, which are not yet ready for the real world to be examined under controlled conditions. From the AI perspective game of Poker provides opportunities for working with Neural Networks, Genetic Algorithms, Fuzzy Logic, and Distributed Agents to solve problems with probabilistic knowledge, risk assessment, deception, and other real world situations. Ideas from game theory, pattern recognition, simulation and modeling are also come into play, not even mentioning mathematics, statistics, probability

and other areas of mathematics (Billings, Papp, Schaeffer, & Szafron, 1998a; Schaeffer, 2000). As a result research of artificial poker players enjoys a long and fruitful history. We will begin with a short overview of existing work in the field of developing artificially intelligent poker players. Our approach to the creation of AI poker players used as subjects in our experiments on AI player verification and recognition is presented in the prior section on Generation of Synthetic Profiles.

Full Scale Texas Hold'em Poker Billings et al. (Billings, et al., 2003; Billings, et al., 1998a; Billings, Papp, Schaeffer, & Szafron, 1998b; Billings, Pena, Schaeffer, & Szafron, 1999, 2001; Davidson, 2005; Davidson, Billings, Schaeffer, & Szafron, 2000) have investigated development of a complete poker playing program for the game of Texas Hold'em. They use opponent modelling, statistical analysis, semi-optimal pre-flop strategy and even neural-network-based opponent's action prediction to construct a world-class poker-playing program. Their research is still in progress, but their best program Poki has already proven itself as a reasonable strength opponent against both computers and people. It has been playing online and consistently winning, but since the games were not real money games the quality of opponents remains questionable.

Bayesian Poker Korb et al. are developing a Bayesian Poker (BP) program which uses a

Table 6. AI software and behavioral biometrics we can apply (©2009 Inderscience Publishers Ltd. Used with permission)

AI software	Behavioral biometric we can apply
Game Playing Software (Chess, Poker, Go)	Profile of the game strategy, frequently used moves, openings, aggression level, etc.
Chat Bots	Linguistic profile based on frequently used words, common phrases, topics of conversation.
Text-to-Speech Software	Voice recognition, based on acoustic features such as voice pitch and speaking style.
Translation Software	Linguistic profile based on frequently used phrases, idioms, etc.
Speech Recognition	Text authorship combined with error rate analysis.

Bayesian network to model the program's poker hand, the opponent's hand and the opponent's playing behaviour based on the hand, and betting curves which govern play given a probability of winning. The history of play with opponents is used to improve program's understanding of their behaviour (Korb, Nicholson, & Jitnah, 1999). BP is written to play a two-player five-card stud poker game and is still a work in progress.

Evolved Poker Players Genetic algorithms provide an automated way to solve complex problems without explicitly solving every particular sub-instance of the problem. Many researchers have attempted to evolve good players for the game of poker, typically for one of the simplified versions, making search space more reasonable.

Barone and While Barone et al. (Barone & While, 1998, 1999a, 1999b) use a simple poker variant where each player has two private cards, access to five community cards and there is only one round of betting. Their solution takes into account hand strength, betting position and risk management. The approach shows how a player that has evolved using evolutionary strategies can adapt its style to two types of game: loose or tight.

Noble and Watson Noble et al. (Noble, 2002; Noble & Watson, 2001) use Pareto co-evolution on the full scale game of Texas Hold'em and show that as compared to the traditional genetic algorithm their approach shows promise. Pareto co-evolution treats players as dimensions and attempts to find optimal playing strategies for a multidimensional space of potential strategies.

Kendall and Willdig Kendall et al. (Kendall & Willdig, 2001) have also attempted to evolve a good poker player and showed that a simple reward system of adjusting weights is sufficient to produce a player capable of beating its opponents after playing them for some time and adapting to their style of play.

PERFORMED EXPERIMENTS

In this section we present results of our experiments with user verification and identification as well as our approach to validation of synthetic poker data and results of a spoofing attack on the developed system.

User Verification (Euclidean on Temporal Profiles)

In a databank of 30 player signatures each one was compared with one profile taken from the same player as the one who generated the original signature and with another profile taken from a randomly chosen player. Giving us an experimental set up in which intruders and legitimate users are equal in number. Using Euclidean similarity measure and a threshold of 75 the original algorithm has positively verified 46.66% (28) users. The False Accept Rate (FAR) was 13.33% (8 users) and False Reject Rate (FRR) was only 8.33% (5 users). This gives us player verification with overall 78.33% accuracy.

We hoped to obtain some improvement in performance of our algorithm as a result of including slow-playing as a part of the feature vector. But possibly because slow-playing is an advanced technique which is not practiced by many players (and even those who do practice it only rarely get the best possible hand to do so), only a small improvement in performance was obtained over previous result (Yampolskiy & Govindaraju, 2006b). This outcome might also be a result of relatively small data set we were working with. It is possible that including other advanced features such as bluffing in addition to slow-playing will produce better results. Using Euclidean measure and a threshold of 75 the algorithm has achieved an accuracy of 80.0%. The False Accept Rate (FAR) was 11.66% (7 users) and False Reject Rate (FRR) was only 8.33% (5 users).

Intruder Identification (Euclidean on Temporal Profiles)

Once the difference between an expected user's behavior and the observed behavior goes over a pre-established threshold a network administrator is notified that an attack may be taking place. While many such occurrences are just false alarms, some do represent accurately detected intrusions. If the network administrator does believe that a real attack took place, he is interested in finding out the identity of the perpetrator. In some instances it may be the case that someone from within the organization performed an attack, and so the intruder himself has a legitimate account on the same network, probably with fewer privileges (funds) as compared to the compromised account. We investigated the feasibility of determining intruder's identity by comparing the signature for detected deviant behavior against the database of behavioral signatures from all the users in the system.

For this experiment we used a databank of 30 players. Each player's record contains an original signature from the enrolment period and a second signature from the testing period. Each testing signature was compared against all original signatures in the databank, for a total of 30 comparisons each. The highest matching profile with respect to the similarity measure was recorded as either belonging to the same player (a successful identification) or to a different player (a false identification). From the total of 30 highest matching profiles 5 were correctly identified and 25 were false matches. This gives us intruder identification with overall 16.66% accuracy. These results are obviously below acceptable industry standards but clearly indicate feasibility of behaviour-based intruder identification. This methodology might give us a certain edge in the fight for network security, but also explains why behavioural biometrics are not typically used for user identification but only for verification.

Similarity Measure Function Experiments

Experiments were conducted with a 100 authentic user profiles and a 100 impostor profiles used in each. Three different experiments were conducted; in each one a different type of behavioral profile representation was used. Specifically a 28-dimensional temporal profile, a 280-dimensional temporal-spatial profile and a 427-dimensional temporal-spatial-contextual profile were chosen as this allowed us to observe the influence of increasing the amount of environmental information available to the security system on systems performance. We also had an opportunity to observe the effect of the curse of dimensionality with respect to the performance of our similarity measure functions.

For each similarity function a continuously varying threshold curve was generated demonstrating the relationship between False Accept Rate (FAR) and a False Reject Rate (FRR). Changing threshold trades the FAR off against the FRR, so the error rates can be adjusted according to the requirements of the security application (Lee & Park, 2003). For our experiments the value of the threshold which makes FRR equal to FAR was selected for each similarity measure function and is used as the representative accuracy of the utilized similarity measure function.

We compared three general similarity measure functions (Euclidean, Mahalanobis, Manhattan) with two domain specific functions developed by us (Weighted Euclidean, 2D Style). The Weighted Euclidean distance measure we have utilized in our experiments assigns a weight of 3 to all pre-flop features of the vector and weight of 1 to all other features. The weight of 3 has been experimentally established by trial and error of different weights in the range from 1 to 10. The weight is incorporated into the formula by dividing the difference between corresponding values in the two feature vectors by the selected weight.

The 2D style measure approach was designed

to counteract the problems with the "curse of dimensionality" which become particularly taxing with the use of contextual information within the profile. Tightness value is easy to compute as it is simply the average percentage of cards folded pre-flop from all possible positions. Aggressiveness value is slightly more involved but is essentially the average percentage of raised, check raised, re-raised and all in actions from all possible positions at all stages of the game and for each possibly flop type.

As can be seen from Table 7 general similarity measure functions (Euclidean, Mahalanobis and Manhattan) showed a very similar performance, with Mahalanobis distance being slightly inferior to Euclidean and Manhattan distances which showed identical performance of 12% Equal Error Rate (EER). Best performance was shown by a task specific Weighted Euclidean distance which had a 10% EER. 2D Style measure performed poorly in case of temporal profiles, probably because some of the discriminatory power is lost in the averaging process.

A great improvement in performance of the strategy based behavioral biometric system was observed with the inclusion of spatial information into the profiles as demonstrated in the Table 7. Once again the Weighted Euclidean distance function was the best matching algorithm obtaining 7% EER with general similarity measure functions performing in the range of 9-10% EER. However, performance of the 2D style measure actually

became worse to the level of 25% EER.

Improvement in the performance of most similarity measure functions can be explained by a more refined capture of the player's strategy associated with inclusion of information about the spatial location of the player. Decreased performance of the 2D style matcher probably resulted from the influence of zero-value variables on the overall profile average. Zero-value variables are a consequence of not having enough data points in a high-dimensionality profile such as 280-dimensional spatial-temporal profile.

With the inclusion of the contextual information the dimensionality of behavioural profile has ballooned to 427D and the influence of the "curse of dimensionality" became apparent. Performance of all similarity measures has significantly decreased, with that of 2D style measure to almost the point of random guessing. With such a high-dimensionality-behavioural-profile the number of zero-value variables becomes overwhelming as the amount of time needed to collect sufficient data is unreasonable for any real-life security system.

Validation of Synthetic Data

We have also performed testing using our biometric verification system which uses a Weighted Euclidean distance measure with an experimentally determined optimal threshold (Yampolskiy & Govindaraju, 2007). For each experiment 100 artificial baseline player profiles have been

Table 7. Verification results using temporal profiles (©2009 Inderscience Publishers Ltd. Used with permission)

Similarity Measure	Equal Error Rate
Euclidean Distance	12%
Mahalanobis Distance	13%
Manhattan Distance	12%
Weighted Euclidean Distance	10%
2D Style Measure	14%

Table 8. Verification results using temporal-spatial profiles (©2009 Inderscience Publishers Ltd. Used with permission)

Similarity Measure	Equal Error Rate
Euclidean Distance	9%
Mahalanobis Distance	10%
Manhattan Distance	9%
Weighted Euclidean Distance	7%
2D Style Measure	25%

Table 9. Verification using temporal-spatial-contextual profiles (©2009 Inderscience Publishers Ltd. Used with permission)

Similarity Measure	Equal Error Rate
Euclidean Distance	33%
Mahalanobis Distance	36%
Manhattan Distance	33%
Weighted Euclidean Distance	29%
2D Style Measure	46%

generated using one of the developed methodologies along with a 100 of testing profiles. In each experiment the number of legitimate users and impostors was equal with no overlap between testing and baseline profiles. Impostor profiles were randomly chosen from profiles unrelated to the baseline one.

Table 10 compares EER obtained on artificial data with that reported from the original experiments on genuine data (Yampolskiy & Govindaraju, 2008a). As can be seen, with some data generation methodologies, we have obtained accuracy levels statistically indistinguishable from those originally produced by the system on genuine data. In particular, approaches based on modifying seed profile, parameterized design and observation of AI players showed the best results. Also the ROC curves of those methods were an almost exact match with the ones from the experiments on genuine data. This leads us to believe that both intra-class and inter-class variation of strategy-based profiles is well simulated with those approaches.

Crossover-based approach did not show good results, which can be explained by the random nature in which multiple profiles are combined during the crossover process.

Spoofing Experiments

Approaches to spoofing behavioral biometrics are similar to those for physical biometrics but with some domain specific variability. Replay attacks are very popular since it is easy to record an individual's voice or copy a signature. Human mimicking or forgery is also a very powerful technique with experts consistently breaching security of signature-based or voice-based authentication systems.

Additionally in the domain of behavioural biometrics it is possible for a parameterized computer generated model to perform the mimicking/forgery of the biometric sample. Such computer produced models of behaviour parameterized with observed target user data steadily improve in their performance.

In order to create an artificial poker player with the strategy of a particular user a number of steps need to be followed. First a long term statistical profile for a large number of players needs to be obtained. We have written special software which observes the game and records every player's action in an individual behavioural profile.

Alternatively this can be easily accomplished as services exist which sell such information for a fee, examples being poker-edge.com (poker-edge.com, 2006) and pokerprophecy.com (Pokerprophecy.com, 2006). These companies have special purpose computers monitoring online casinos around the clock recording every hand of poker played along with actions of individual players and financial outcome. By analyzing statistical data provided by poker-edge.com we were able to reverse engineer the strategy employed by differ-

Table 10. EER comparison for genuine and synthetic data (©2009 Inderscience Publishers Ltd. Used with permission)

Data Type	Equal Error Rate
Genuine Data	7%
Modified Seed Profile	8%
Multi-profile Crossover	19%
AI Players	7%
Parameterized Design	9%

ent human poker players. Table 11 demonstrates the sample of statistics collected by poker-edge.com alongside the analysis of usefulness for those strategy descriptors.

A target player's percent of hands for which he voluntarily puts money into the pot is one of best indicators as to what type of player he is. By interpreting this number it can be determined how tight or loose the player is, and what types of cards he is likely to play. To get an idea of what types of hands correspond to what percentage level we can utilize Table 12.

A player's strategy can be reversed engineered from statistical observations. We will use an example from poker-edge.com's statistical analysis page. Suppose we have a player with VP$IP of 18%, and a PreFlop Raise of 3.5%. To make 18% for VP$IP, this player is likely playing Big Pocket Pairs, Big Cards, Other Broadway Cards (suited), and half of the Other Broadway Cards (unsuited). If we add the percentages together, we get 2.26+6.03+1.51+2.26 =12.06%. Assuming this player calls about half of the small blinds,

that adds another 5%. We arrive at 17.06% which is very close to his VP$IP of 18%. His PreFlop Raise of 3.5% indicates that he is probably only raising Big Pockets, and AK (Poker-edge.com, Retrieved June 7, 2006).

After obtaining statistical measurements of the player's style and performing analysis similar to the one just described we were able to obtain information sufficient to program an artificial poker player with a strategy similar to that used by the target player. For each human player we had two statistical profiles collected from separate game sets. One was used for training artificial player and the other was used for verification experiments. The two data sets were completely different and had no overlap of any kind.

Our implementation of poker bots was once again done using the statistical package known as Online Hold'em Inspector (Pokerinspector.com, 2006). We were able to generate a set of 50 artificially intelligent poker players with observable actions mimicking those of human poker players participating in our study.

Table 11. Description of key statistics (poker-edge.com, 2006)

Statistic	Description	Analysis
VP$IP	The percent of hands a player voluntarily puts money into the pot (PreFlop). Small blind completions count, Big Blind checks do not count. Roughly PreFlop Call%+Raise%	This stat is the number one indicator for how loose or tight a player is. Higher than 33% loose, and lower than 18% as tight.
PreFlop Raise	The percent of time a player raises pre flop.	PreFlop Aggression/Passiveness. 5% is a median. The higher a player is above 5% the more aggressive, and the lower below 5%, the more passive.
PostFlop Aggression	The player's combined aggression rating for the Flop, Turn and River. (Bet% + Raise%) / Call%	1.5 is a median for PostFlop Aggression. Players that are much higher than this are very aggressive, and players that are much lower are very passive.
Flops Seen	The percent of hands a player sees the Flop. (FLseen/HandsPlayed)*100	Another indicator for PreFlop tightness/looseness.
Turns Seen	The percent of hands a player sees the Turn. (TUseen/HandsPlayed)*100	An indicator for Flop tightness/looseness.
Rivers Seen	The percent of hands a player sees the river. (RIseen/HandsPlayed)*100	An indicator for Turn tightness/looseness.
Showd-owns Seen	The percent of hands a player sees a showdown. (SDseen/HandsPlayed)*100	An indicator for River tightness/looseness.

Table 12. Pre-Flop indicators analyzed (poker-edge.com, 2006)

Group	Hands	Number of Combinations	% seen
Big Pocket Pairs	AA, KK, QQ, JJ, TT	6+6+6+6+6=30	2.26
Big Cards	AK, AQ, AJ, KQ, AT	16+16+16+16+16=80	6.03
Other Broadway Cards (suited)	KJs, KTs, QJs, QTs, JTs	4+4+4+4+4=20	1.51
Other Broadway Cards (un-suited)	KJ, KT, QJ, QT, JT	12+12+12+12+12=60	4.52
Mid Pocket Pairs	99, 88, 77, 66	6+6+6+6=24	1.81
A-x suited	A9s, A8s, A7s, A6s, A5s, A4s, A3s, A2s	4+4+4+4+4+4+4+4=32	2.41
Suited Connectors	T9s, 98s, 87s, 76s, 65s	4+4+4+4+4=20	1.51
Low Pocket Pairs	55, 44, 33, 22	6+6+6+6=24	1.81
A-x (not suited)	A9, A8, A7, A6, A5, A4, A3, A2	12+12+12+12+12+12+12+12=96	7.24
Small Blind Calls	N/A	N/A	10.0

Because we have adjusted each artificial poker player to act just like its human counterpart the resulting statistical profiles look almost identical to a human eye. We have essentially stolen the behavioural identity of our human poker players and have given it to artificially intelligent programs to mimic. In other words we have obtained a set of parameters for a strategic behaviour and have passed it on to a generative model to synthesize the desired behaviour. Not surprisingly we have obtained very good results for our verification experiments.

To get the desired statistical profiles from artificially intelligent poker players we had them play against each other for a minimum of 10000 poker hands, which is probably equivalent to 100 of hours of human play. This was done so we could obtain the long term statistically consistent behavioural profiles. With a set of 50 genuine players and 50 spoofed profiles we performed 100 verification comparisons.

We used a decision threshold obtained in finding the best possible FAR on true identity and random (non-spoofed) impostor tests (Yampolskiy, 2006; Yampolskiy & Govindaraju, 2006b, 2007). Similarity of each artificial profile was compared to that of a human profile it was modelled after and against another human profile which was randomly chosen from the set. All 50 artificial profiles were positively verified as profiles of target users they were spoofing, giving us 100% FAR if we keep in mind that we are comparing profiles from a human and a bot. 5 profiles were incorrectly positively verified than compared to a randomly chosen human profile. This can be explained by a significant degree of similarity between playing styles of some people. The system used in the experiment gives a FRR of about 8 percent if only real human profiles are submitted. Our experiments show that spoofing behavioural biometrics is a definite possibility (Yampolskiy, 2008).

Our experiments show that with respect to strategy-based biometrics it is possible to secretly observe the target user during play, generate a statistical profile of his actions and train a behaviour generating model to mimic target's behaviour. This is equivalent to stealing of the individual's behavioural identity and some measures need to be taken to prevent this from happening, particularly as similar approach can be used in domains beyond game networks.

Artimetrics Experiments

For our experimental set of artificially intelligent poker players we have taken a number of built-in profiles which came standard with the Hold'em Inspector namely: Solid, Rock, Maniac, Fish, and Typical. We have also included some profiles available via Internet poker forums particularly: Vixen70, GoldenEagle, BettyBot v1.1, and poker_champ (Cyberloonies.com, 2006). Finally we have programmed in an additional artificial poker player, called AIbot, based on the game theory research presented by Sklansky et al. (Sklansky & Malmuth, 2004). Validity of our poker bot was tested at low-stakes real-money online poker tables against human opponents where our bot consistently scored around 3 big bets per hour in profits. In total we ended up with 10 artificial poker players which is representative of the current number of competing programs in many AI sub-fields such as character recognition, chess, translation software, etc.

Each artificially intelligent poker player had played two long poker games, each one of at least 150 hands, against a mixture of human and artificial opponents. First game was played to establish the biometric template for the player and second one to perform the verification and identification experiments.

Artimetrics: Verification

In a databank of 10 AI player's signatures each one was compared with one profile taken from the same player as the one who generated the original signature and with another profile taken from a randomly chosen player, for a total of 20 comparisons. This gave us an experimental set up in which authentic users and imposters are equal in number. Using Euclidian distance similarity measure and an experimentally established threshold of 75 the algorithm has positively verified 90.00% of users. The only false verification was the positive verification of the Solid bot as the Rock bot,

which could be explained by the fact that both bots are programmed to play a conservative type of poker strategy.

Artimetrics: Identification

For this experiment we used a databank of 10 AI player signatures. Each player's record contains an original signature from the enrollment period and a second signature from the testing period. Each testing signature was compared against all original signatures in the databank, for a total of 100 comparisons. The highest matching profile with respect to the similarity measure was recorded as either belonging to the same player (a successful identification) or to a different player (a false identification). From the total of 10 highest matching profiles 3 were correctly identified and 7 were false matches. This gives us artificial player identification with overall 30.00% accuracy, which is a good result considering we are using a soft behavioral biometric technique, which are typically only used for verification not for identification purposes.

CONCLUSIONS AND FUTURE DIRECTIONS

A number of conclusions can be drawn from the results of our experiments. First the poker player style measure used by human experts, 2D style measure, is not well suited for use in behavioral biometric systems. It is not capable of coping with insufficient amount of data in high-dimensionality behavioral profiles and is really only suitable for describing the four basic types of poker players encountered in the poker literature (Schoonmaker, 2005). Regardless of the type of profile representation used in the experiments it was the worst performing similarity measure outperformed even by the general similarity measure functions.

Examined general similarity measure functions showed an acceptable profile verification performance with Euclidean and Manhattan distances being indistinguishable from each other in terms of their accuracy. Mahalanobis distance function performed slightly worse possibly as a result of the normalization procedure which took into account variance of the data in each profile. Since the degree of variance in each user profile is different it is possibly that normalization was not evenly distributed and so produced a slight decrease in the performance of this general similarity measure function.

Customized Weighted Euclidean measure function specifically designed for the domain of poker-based behavioural profiles showed the best performance on all types of data representation. Heavier consideration for pre-flop player's actions allowed this similarity measure function to pick out the fundamental tendencies of the player's strategy and as a result improve algorithms verification accuracy to as low as the 7% EER for the behavioural profiles enhanced with temporal and spatial information (Yampolskiy & Govindaraju, 2006a).

The use of biometric technologies is growing at an increasing rate. In order to properly test such systems we need a consistent supply of readily available biometric data. Synthetic data generation provides a time and cost effective way of obtaining benchmark and test data not just for biometric systems but also for security and intrusion detection systems in general (Barse, Kvarnström, & Jonsson, 2003; Chinchani, Muthukrishnan, Chandrasekaran, & Upadhyaya, 2004; Debar, Dacier, Wespi, & Lampart, 1998; Garg, Sankaranarayanan, Upadhyaya, & Kwiat, 2006; Kayacik & Zincir-Heywood, 2005; Lundin, Kvarnström, & Jonsson, 2002; Rossey, et al., 2002).

Our spoofing experiments demonstrate that with respect to game-strategy biometrics it is possible to secretly and automatically monitor the target user during play in an online casino, generate an accurate statistical profile of his actions and train an artificially intelligent poker playing program to mimic target player's behaviour.

This is equivalent to stealing of the individual's behavioural online identity and is a matter of serious concern for both privacy advocates and security specialists.

Our artimetrics research shows possibility of using strategy-based behavioural biometrics for accurate verification of intelligent game bots. We further believe that it is feasible to apply other behavioural biometric techniques to additional domains in which artificially intelligent programs are becoming a major force. In the field of output authorship recognition of AI software we expect a lot of progress as such programs become capable of many tasks usually only attributed to humans such as telling a joke (Ritchie, 2001), composing music (Cope, 2001), painting (Cohen, 1988), or creating poetry (Boyd-Graber, 2006).

As AI technologies become more commonplace in our society it will be necessary to determine which program has actually performed a given task, assign the authorship rights to software, secure interaction between different pieces of intelligent software, and prevent malicious software from accessing certain information. We have demonstrated that it is possible to verify and even identify artificially intelligent game bots based on their observable behaviour. We further propose that the research aimed at recognition and verification of software programs, industrial and personal robots and other non-biological agents be known as *Artimetrics* to distinguish it from the traditional biology centred research in biometrics.

REFERENCES

Ahn, L. v., Blum, M., Hopper, N., & Langford, J. (2003, May). *CAPTCHA: Using hard AI problems for security.* Paper presented at the Eurocrypt-Advances in Cryptology (pp. 294-311).

Ahn, L. v., Blum, M., & Langford, J. (2004). How lazy cryptographers do AI. *Communications of the ACM, 47*(2), 56–60. doi:10.1145/966389.966390

Badizadegan, M. (1999). *Texas hold'em flop types*. Los Angeles, CA: Goldstar Books.

Baggenstoss, P. M. (2004, January). *Class-specific classifier: Avoiding the curse of dimensionality*. Paper presented at the Aerospace and Electronic Systems Magazine (pp. 37-52).

Barone, L., & While, L. (1998). *Evolving computer opponents to play a game of simplified poker*. Paper presented at the International Conference on Evolutionary Computation (ICEC'98) (pp. 108-113).

Barone, L., & While, L. (1999a). *An adaptive learning model for simplified poker using evolutionary algorithms*. Paper presented at the Congress of Evolutionary Computation (GECCO-1999) (pp. 153-160).

Barone, L., & While, L. (1999b). *Evolving adaptive play for simplified poker*. Paper presented at the IEE International Conference on Computational Intelligence (ICEC-98) (pp. 108-113).

Barrios-Aranibar, D., & Alsina, P. J. (2005, December 6-9). *Recognizing behaviors patterns in a microrobot soccer game*. Paper presented at the Fifth international Conference on Hybrid Intelligent Systems, Washington, D.C.

Barse, E. L., Kvarnström, H., & Jonsson, E. (2003, December 8-12). *Synthesizing test data for fraud detection systems*. Paper presented at the 19th Annual Computer Security Applications Conference (ACSAC 2003), Las Vegas, NV.

Billings, D., Burch, N., Davidson, A., Holte, R., Schaeffer, J., Schauenberg, T., et al. (2003). *Approximating game-theoretic optimal strategies for full-scale poker*. Paper presented at the IJCAI-03.

Billings, D., Papp, D., Schaeffer, J., & Szafron, D. (1998a). *Opponent modeling in poker*. Paper presented at the 15th National Conference on Artificial Intelligence (AAAI-98), Madison, WI (pp. 493-498).

Billings, D., Papp, D., Schaeffer, J., & Szafron, D. (1998b). *Poker as testbed for AI research*. Paper presented at the 12th Biennial Conference of the Canadian Society for Computational Studies of Intelligence on Advances in Artificial Intelligence, London, UK (pp. 228-238).

Billings, D., Pena, L., Schaeffer, J., & Szafron, D. (1999). *Using probabilistic knowledge and simulation to play poker*. Paper presented at the In AAAI/IAAI (pp. 697-703).

Billings, D., Pena, L., Schaeffer, J., & Szafron, D. (2001). *Learning to play strong poker*. Paper presented at the Machines that Learn to Play Games, Commack, NY (pp. 225-242).

Boyd-Graber, J. (2006). *Semantic poetry creation using lexicographic and natural language texts*. Retrieved on July 2, 2006, from http://www.cs.princeton.edu/~jbg/documents/poetry.pdf

Brandt, K. (2005). *Player profiling in texas holdem*. Retrieved on May 29, 2005, from http://www.soe.ucsc.edu/~kbrandt/pubs/prof.pdf

Chinchani, R., Muthukrishnan, A., Chandrasekaran, M., & Upadhyaya, S. (2004, December 6-10). *RACOON: Rapidly generating user command data for anomaly detection from customizable templates*. Paper presented at the 0th Annual Computer Security Applications Conference, Tucson, AZ.

Cohen, H. (1988). *How to draw three people in a botanical garden*. Retrieved from http://crca.ucsd.edu/~hcohen/cohenpdf/how2draw3people.pdf

Cope, D. (2001). *Virtual music: Computer synthesis of musical style*. Cambridge, MA: The MIT Press.

Cyberloonies.com. (2006). *Texas holdem poker. Cyber loonies.* Retrieved in May 2006, from http://cyberloonies.com/poker.html

Davidson, A. (2005). *Using artificial neural networks to model opponents in Texas hold'em.* Retrieved on May 25, 2005, from http://citeseer.ist.psu.edu/460830.html

Davidson, A., Billings, D., Schaeffer, J., & Szafron, D. (2000). *Improved opponent modeling in poker.* Paper presented at the International Conference on Artificial Intelligence (ICAI'2000) Las Vegas, NV (pp. 1467-1473).

Debar, H., Dacier, M., Wespi, A., & Lampart, S. (1998). *An experimentation workbench for intrusion detection systems* (No. RZ2998). IBM Research Report

Garg, A., Sankaranarayanan, V., Upadhyaya, S., & Kwiat, K. (2006, April 2-6). *USim: A user behavior simulation framework for training and testing IDSs in GUI based systems.* Paper presented at the 39th Annual Simulation Symposium (ANSS 06), Huntsville, AL.

Garis, H. d. (2005). *The artilect war.* Palm Springs, CA: ETC Publications.

Goldberg, D. E. (1989). *Genetic algorithms in search, optimization, and machine learning.* Addison-Wesley Pub. Co.

Han, K., & Veloso, M. (1999). *Automated robot behavior recognition.* Paper presented at the Workshop on Team Behaviors and Plan Recognition.

Kayacik, G. H., & Zincir-Heywood, A. N. (2005, May). *Generating representative traffic for intrusion detection system benchmarking.* Paper presented at the *IEEE CNSR 2005*, Halifax, Canada (pp. 112-117).

Kendall, G., & Willdig, M. (2001, December 10-14). *An investigation of an adaptive poker player.* Paper presented at the 14th Australian Joint Conference on Artificial Intelligence, Adelaide, Australia (pp. 189-200).

Korb, K., Nicholson, A., & Jitnah, N. (1999). *Bayesian poker.* Paper presented at the 15th Annual Conference on Uncertainty in Artificial Intelligence (UAI-99), San Francisco, CA (pp. 343-335).

Lee, K., & Park, H. (2003). A new similarity measure based on intraclass statistics for biometric systems. *ETRI Journal, 25*(5), 401–406. doi:10.4218/etrij.03.0102.0017

Lundin, E., Kvarnström, H., & Jonsson, E. (2002, December 9-12). *A synthetic fraud data generation methodology.* Paper presented at the 4th International Conference on Information and Communications Security (ICICS 2002), Singapore (pp. 265-277).

Ma, Y., Schuckers, M., & Cukic, B. (2005), October. *Guidelines for appropriate use of simulated data for bio-authentication research.* Paper presented at the 4th IEEE Workshop on Automatic Identification Advanced Technologies (AUTO ID), Buffalo, NY (pp. 251-256).

Makthal, S., & Ross, A. (2005, September). *Synthesis of iris images using Markov random fields.* Paper presented at the 13th European Signal Processing Conference (EUSIPCO), Antalya, Turkey.

Maurer, M. (2005). *IRC database.* Retrieved on May 19, 2005, from http://games.cs.ualberta.ca/poker/IRC

Nevadaigtf.org. (2005). Player id, age verification, and border control technology forum. *Nevada Interactive Gaming Task Force.* Retrieved on October 23, 2005, from http://www.nevadaigtf.org/TechnologyForum.html

Noble, J. (2002). *Finding robust Texas hold'em poker strategies using pareto coevolution and deterministic crowding.* Paper presented at the International Conference on Machine Learning and Applications (ICMLA'02).

Noble, R. A., & Watson, J. (2001). *Pareto co-evolution: Using performance against coevolved opponents in a game as dimensions for pareto selection.* Paper presented at the Genetic and Evolutionary Computation Conference, GECCO-2001 (pp. 493-500).

Orlans, N. M., Buettner, D. J., & Marques, J. (2004). *A survey of synthetic biometrics: Capabilities and benefits.* Paper presented at the International Conference on Artificial Intelligence (IC-AI'04) (pp. 499-505).

Ourston, D. (1989). Program recognition. *IEEE Expert, 4*(4), 36–49. doi:10.1109/64.43284

poker-edge.com. (2006). *Stats and analysis.* Retrieved on June 7, 2006, from http://www.poker-edge.com/stats.php

Poker-edge.com. (n.d.). *Stats and analysis.* Retrieved on June 7, 2006, from http://www.poker-edge.com/stats.php

Pokerinspector.com. (2006). *Online holdem inspector.* Retrieved on May 2, 2006, from http://www.pokerinspector.com/

Pokerprophecy.com. (2006). *Pokerprophecy.* Retrieved on September 26, 2006, from http://www.pokerprophecy.com

Quilici, A., Yang, Q., & Woods, S. (1998). Applying plan recognition algorithms to program understanding. *Automated Software Engineering: An International Journal, 5*(3), 347–372. doi:10.1023/A:1008608825390

Ritchie, G. (2001). Current directions in computational humor. *Artificial Intelligence Review, 16-2,* 119-135.

Rossey, L. M., Cunningham, R. K., Fried, D. J., Rabek, J. C., Lippmann, R. P., Haines, J. W., et al. (2002). *LARIAT: Lincoln adaptable real-time information assurance testbed.* Paper presented at the Aerospace Conference 6-2671- 2676-2682.

Schaeffer, J. (2000). *The games computers (and people) play.* Paper presented at the AAAI/IAAI, 1179-.

Schoonmaker, A. N. (2005). *The psychology of poker* (first ed.). Henderson, NV: Two Plus Two Publishing.

Sklansky, D., & Malmuth, M. (2004). *Hold'em poker for advanced players.* Henderson, NV: Two Plus Two Publishing.

Sturn, A. (2000, December 20). *Cluster analysis for large scale gene expression studies.* Paper presented at the Masters thesis, The Institute for Genomic Research, Rockville, MD.

Sumi, K., & Matsuyama, T. (2005, January). *Privacy protection of biometric evaluation database–a preliminary study on synthetic biometric database.* Paper presented at the Japan-Korea Joint Workshop on Frontiers of Computer Vision (pp. 189-194).

Turing, A. (1950). Computing machinery and intelligence. *Mind, 59*(236), 433–460. doi:10.1093/mind/LIX.236.433

ultimatebet.com. (2005). *Software-statistics.* Retrieved on May 4, 2005, from http://www.ultimatebet.com

Wikipedia.com. (2006). *Mahalanobis distance.* Retrieved on August 22, 2006, from http://en.wikipedia.org/wiki/Mahalanobis_distance

Yampolskiy, R., Anderson, P., Arney, J., Misic, V., & Clarke, T. (2004, September 24). *Printer model integrating genetic algorithm for improvement of halftone patterns.* Paper presented at the Western New York Image Processing Workshop (WNYIPW)-IEEE Signal Processing Society, Rochester, NY.

Yampolskiy, R. V. (2006, February 24). *Behavior based identification of network intruders.* Paper presented at the 19th Annual CSE Graduate Conference (Grad-Conf2006), Buffalo, NY.

Yampolskiy, R. V. (2007a, April 13). *Behavioral biometrics for verification and recognition of AI programs.* Paper presented at the 20th Annual Computer Science and Engineering Graduate Conference (GradConf2007), Buffalo, NY.

Yampolskiy, R. V. (2007b, September 10-12). *Online poker security: Problems and solutions.* Paper presented at the EUROSIS North American Simulation and AI in Games Conference (GAMEON-NA2007), Gainesville, FL.

Yampolskiy, R. V. (2008, April 7-9). *Mimicry attack on strategy-based behavioral biometric.* Paper presented at the 5th International Conference on Information Technology: New Generations (ITNG2008), Las Vegas, NV (pp. 916-921).

Yampolskiy, R. V., & Govindaraju, V. (2006a, December 16-18). *Similarity measure functions for strategy-based biometrics.* Paper presented at the International Conference on Signal Processing (ICSP 2006), Vienna, Austria.

Yampolskiy, R. V., & Govindaraju, V. (2006b, April 17-22). *Use of behavioral biometrics in intrusion detection and online gaming.* Paper presented at the Biometric Technology for Human Identification III, SPIE Defense and Security Symposium, Orlando, FL.

Yampolskiy, R. V., & Govindaraju, V. (2007, April 9-13). *Dissimilarity functions for behavior-based biometrics.* Paper presented at the Biometric Technology for Human Identification IV, SPIE Defense and Security Symposium, Orlando, FL.

Yampolskiy, R. V., & Govindaraju, V. (2008a, March 16-20). *Generation of artificial biometric data enhanced with spatialtemporal and environmental information.* Paper presented at the Biometric Technology for Human Identification V. SPIE Defense and Security Symposium, Orlando, FL.

Yampolskiy, R. V., & Govindaraju, V. (2008b). Strategy-based behavioral biometric a novel approach to automated identification. *International Journal of Computer Applications in Technology (IJCAT), Special Issue on: Automated Identification Technology.*

Yanushkevich, S., Stoica, A., Srihari, S., Shmerko, V., & Gavrilova, M. (2004). *Simulation of Biometric Information: The new generation of biometric systems.* Paper presented at the Int'l Workshop on Biometric Technologies, Calgary, AB, Canada (pp. 87-98).

Chapter 19
Multimodal Biometrics Fusion for Human Recognition in Video

Xiaoli Zhou
University of California - Riverside, USA

Bir Bhanu
University of California - Riverside, USA

ABSTRACT

This chapter introduces a new video based recognition system to recognize noncooperating individuals at a distance in video, who expose side views to the camera. Information from two biometric sources, side face and gait, is utilized and integrated for recognition. For side face, an enhanced side face image (ESFI), a higher resolution image compared with the image directly obtained from a single video frame, is constructed, which integrates face information from multiple video frames. For gait, the gait energy image (GEI), a spatiotemporal compact representation of gait in video, is used to characterize human walking properties. The features of face and gait are extracted from ESFI and GEI, respectively. They are integrated at both of the match score level and the feature level by using different fusion strategies. The system is tested on a database of video sequences, corresponding to 45 people, which are collected over several months. The performance of different fusion methods are compared and analyzed. The experimental results show that (a) the idea of constructing ESFI from multiple frames is promising for human recognition in video and better face features are extracted from ESFI compared to those from the original side face images; (b) the synchronization of face and gait is not necessary for face template ESFI and gait template GEI; (c) integrated information from side face and gait is effective for human recognition in video. The feature level fusion methods achieve better performance than the match score level methods fusion overall.

INTRODUCTION

Biometrics is the study of methods for uniquely recognizing humans based upon one or more intrinsic physical or behavioral traits, such as fingerprint, face, voice, gait, iris, signature, hand geometry and ear. The biometric trait of an individual is characterized by a set of discriminatory features or attributes. Therefore, the performance of a single biometric system is constrained by the intrinsic fac-

DOI: 10.4018/978-1-60566-725-6.ch019

tors of a trait. However, this inherent limitation of a single biometric can be alleviated by fusing the information presented by multiple sources. A system that consolidates the evidence presented by multiple biometric sources are expected to be more reliable.

It has been found to be difficult to recognize a person from arbitrary views when one is walking at a distance. For optimal performance, a system should use as much information as possible from the observations. Based on the different inherent characteristic, a fusion system, which combines face and gait cues from video sequences, is a potential approach to accomplish the task of human recognition at a distance. The general solution to analyze face and gait video data from arbitrary views is to estimate 3-D models. However, the problem of building reliable 3-D models for non-rigid face, with flexible neck and the articulated human body from low resolution video data remains a hard one. In this chapter, integrated face and gait recognition approaches without resorting to 3-D models is addressed. Experiment results show the effectiveness of the proposed system for human recognition at a distance in video. The contributions of this chapter are as follows:

- A system that integrates side face and gait information from video data in a single camera scenario is presented. The experimental results demonstrate the feasibility and effectiveness of the proposed system for human recognition at a distance.
- Both face and gait recognition systems integrate information over multiple frames in a video sequence for improved performance. To overcome the problem of the limited resolution of a face at a distance, a Enhanced Side Face Image (ESFI), a higher resolution image compared with the image directly obtained from a single video frame, is constructed to fuse the information of face from multiple video frames. Experiments show that better face features

can be extracted from constructed ESFI compared to those from original side face images. For Gait, the Gait Energy Images (GEI), a spatio-temporal compact representation of gait in video, is used to characterize human working properties.

- The fusion of side face and gait biometrics is explored at both the match score level and the feature level. The match score level fusion schemes includes Sum and Max rules. The performance characterization is analyzed using the Q statistic. The feature level fusion schemes are implemented in two ways. In the first approach, feature concatenation is conducted directly on the features of face and gait, which are obtained using PCA and MDA combined method from ESFI and GEI, respectively. In the second approach, MDA is applied after, not before, the concatenation of face and gait features that are obtained using PCA from ESFI and GEI, respectively.
- Various experiments are performed on 45 people with data from 100 video sequences collected over several months. Performance comparisons between different biometrics and different fusion methods are presented. The experimental results demonstrate the effectiveness of the fusion at the feature level in comparison to the match score level. Besides the recognition rates, the performance is also compared using CMC curves. They further demonstrate the strength of the proposed fusion system.

The chapter is organized as follows. Section 2 gives a review of recent work about the integration of face and gait. Section 3 presents the overall technical approach. It introduces the construction of Enhanced Side Face Image (ESFI) and Gait Energy Image (GEI). It describes feature extraction from ESFI and GEI. It explains the proposed schemes to fuse side face and gait at both the match score level and the feature level fusion for human recognition. A number of dynamic video sequences are tested using the approaches presented. Experimental results are compared and analyzed. Section 4 concludes the chapter.

RELATED WORK

In recent years, integrated face and gait recognition approaches without resorting to 3-D models have achieved some success. Most current gait recognition algorithms rely on the availability of the side view of the subject since human gait or the style of walking is best exposed when one presents a side view to the camera. For face recognition, on the other hand, it is preferred to have frontal views. These conflicting requirements pose some challenges when one attempts to integrate face and gait biometrics in real world applications. In the previous fusion systems (Shakhnarovich & Darrell, 2002) (Shakhnarovich et al., 2001) (Kale et al., 2004), the side view of gait and the frontal view of face are used. Shakhnarovich et al. (Shakhnarovich et al., 2001) (Shakhnarovich & Darrell, 2002) compute an image-based visual hull from a set of monocular views of multiple cameras. It is then used to render virtual canonical views for tracking and recognition. They discuss the issues of cross-modal correlation and score transformations for different modalities, and present the cross-modal fusion. In their work, four monocular cameras are used to get both the side view of gait and the frontal view of face simultaneously. Kale et al. (Kale et al., 2004) present a gait recognition algorithm and a face recognition algorithm based on sequential importance sampling. The database contains video sequences for 30 subjects walking in a single camera scenario. For face recognition, only the final segment of the database presents a nearly frontal view of face and it is used as the probe. The gallery consists of static faces for the 30 subjects. Therefore, they perform still-to-video face recognition. Zhou *et*

al. (Zhou et al., 2005) propose a system which combines cues of face profile and gait silhouette from the video sequences taken by a single camera. It is based on the fact that a side view of a face is more likely to be seen than a frontal view of a face when one exposes the best side view of the gait to the camera. The data are collected for 14 people with two video sequences per person. Even though the face profile in the work of Zhou *et al.* is used reasonably, it only contains shape information of the side view of a face and misses the intensity distribution on the face.

In this chapter, information from two biometrics sources, side face and gait, from the single-camera video sequence, is combined aiming at recognizing non-cooperating individuals at a distance. We distinguish a side face from a face profile. A face profile refers to the outline of the shape of a face as seen from the side. A side face includes not only the outline of the side view of a face, but also the entire side view of the eye, nose, and mouth, possessing both shape and intensity information. Therefore, a side face has more discriminating power for recognition than a face profile. It is very natural to integrate information of the side face view and the side gait view in a single camera scenario. Table 1 presents a summary of related work and compares it with the work presented in this chapter.

Compared with the abundance of research work related to fusion at the match score level, fusion at the feature level is a relatively understudied problem because of the difficulties in practice. Multiple modalities may have incompatible feature sets and the relationship between different feature spaces may not be known (Ross et al., 2006). Moreover, the concatenated feature vectors may lead to the problem of curse of dimensionality and it may contain noisy or redundant data, thus leading to a decrease in the performance of the classifier. However, computer vision and pattern recognition systems that integrate information at an early stage of processing are believed to be more effective than those systems that perform

Table 1. The related work for integrating face and gait for human recognition vs. this work

Authors	Modalities	Fusion Methods	Data
(Shakhnarovich et al., 2001)	Frontal face an gait	Sum rule	12 subjects and 2 to 6 sequences per person
(Shakhnarovich & Darrell, 2002)	Frontal face an gait	Min, Max, Sum and Product rules	26 subjects and 2 to 14 sequences per person
(Kale et al., 2004)	Frontal face an gait	Hierarchical fusion and Sum/Product rule	30 subjects and static images as the face gallery
(Zhou et al., 2005)	Face profile and gait	Hierarchical fusion, Sum and Product rules	14 subjects and 2 sequences per person
This work (Zhou & Bhanu, June, 2007) (Zhou & Bhanu, 2008)	Side face and gait	• Sum and Max rules • Feature concatenation after MDA and PCA combined method • MDA after concatenation of PCA- based features of side face and gait	45 subjects and 2 to 3 video per person

integration at a later stage. Therefore, while it is relatively difficult to achieve in practice, fusion at the feature level has drawn more attention in recent years. Among the existing research work, feature concatenation is the most popular feature level fusion methodology. Some of schemes perform feature concatenation after dimensionality reduction (Kumar, Wong, Shen, & Jain, 2003) (Feng, Dong, Hu, & Zhang, 2004) (Kinnunen, Hautamaki, & Franti, 2004) (Zhou & Bhanu, 2006) while others perform feature concatenation before feature selection or transformation (Yang, Yang, Zhang, & Lu, 2003) (Ross & Govindarajan, 2005).

Most of the fusion schemes based on the integrated face and gait information have focused on the fusion of face and gait at the match score level and the experimental results demonstrate improved performance after fusion. However, since the feature set contains richer information about the input biometrics pattern than the match score, integration at this level is expected to provide better recognition result than the match score level. Therefore, the fusion of face and gait at the feature level deserves a closer study and performance comparison between different fusion schemes needs to be done. In this chapter, information of side face and gait is combined at both of the match score level (Zhou & Bhanu, June, 2007) and the

feature level (Zhou & Bhanu, 2008). Besides two match score level fusion methods, we present two approaches that are based on feature level fusion of face and gait. Furthermore, a closer study and performance comparison among different fusion schemes are conducted on a video database with 100 sequences from 45 people. The experimental results also show the performance improvement compared with the single biometrics.

TECHNICAL APPROACH

Enhanced Side Face Image (ESFI) Construction

It is difficult to get reliable information of a side face directly from a video frame for recognition task because of the limited resolution. To overcome this problem, we construct an Enhanced Side Face Image (ESFI), a higher resolution image compared with the image directly obtained from a single video frame, to fuse the information of face from multiple video frames. The low-resolution images used in multiframe resolution enhancement must be of the same object, taken from slightly different angles, but not so much as to change the overall appearance of the object in the image. The idea of constructing ESFI relies on the fact that the temporally adjacent frames in a video sequence, in which one is walking with a side view to the camera, contain slightly different, but unique information about a side face. The process of construction includes the alignment of the low-resolution side face images, the combination of the low-resolution side face images and the normalization of the enhanced side face images.

We use a simple background subtraction method (Han & Bhanu, 2005) for human body segmentation. A human body is divided into two parts according to the proportion of its parts (Hewitt & Dobberfuhl, 2004): from the top of the head to the bottom of the chin, and then from the bottom of the chin to the bottom of the foot. A head tall is defined as the length from the top of the head to the bottom of the chin. We regard the adult human body as 7.75 head tall. Another 0.25 of one head length is added when the height of hair and the length of neck are considered. So the human head cut from the human body in the image should be 1.25 head tall. The ratio of human head (1.25 head) to human body (7.75 head) is 0.16. Therefore, we assume that the upper 16% of the segmented human body includes the human head. In this work, original low-resolution side face images are first localized and extracted by cutting the upper 16% of the segmented human body obtained from multiple video frames.

Side Face Image Alignment

Before multiple low-resolution face images can be fused to construct a high-resolution image, motion estimates must be computed to determine pixel displacements between them. It is very important since the quality of a high-resolution image relies on the correctness of low-resolution image alignment. In this work, the side face images are aligned using a two step procedure. In the first step, an elastic registration algorithm (Periaswamy & Farid, 2003) is used for motion estimation in low-resolution side face images. In the second step, a match statistic is introduced to detect and discard images that are poorly aligned. Hence, the quality of constructed high-resolution images can be improved by rejecting such errors.

Elastic Registration Method

Denote $f(x, y, t)$ and $f(\hat{x}, \hat{y}, t-1)$ as the reference side face image and the image to be aligned, respectively. Assuming that the image intensities are conserved at different times, the motion between images is modeled locally by an affine transform:

$$f(x, y, t) = f(m_1 x + m_2 y + m_5, m_3 x + m_4 y + m_6, t-1)$$

where m_1, m_2, m_3, and m_4 are the linear affine parameters, and m_5 and m_6 are the translation parameters. To account for intensity variations, an explicit change of local contrast and brightness is incorporated into the affine model. Specifically, the initial model takes the form:

$$m_7 f(x, y, t) + m_8 = f(m_1 x + m_2 y + m_5, m_3 x + m_4 y + m_6, t-1) \tag{1}$$

where m_7 and m_8 are two new (spatially varying) parameters that embody a change in contrast and brightness, respectively. In order to estimate these parameters, the following quadratic error function is minimized:

$$E(\mathbf{m}) = \sum_{x,y \in \Omega} [m_7 f(x, y, t) + m_8 - f(m_1 x + m_2 y + m_5, m_3 x + m_4 y + m_6, t-1)]^2 \tag{2}$$

where $\mathbf{m} = (m_1 m_2 \ldots m_8)^T$, and Ω denotes a small spatial neighborhood around (x, y). Since this error function is nonlinear in its unknowns, it cannot be minimized analytically. To simplify the minimization, this error function is approximated by using a first-order truncated Taylor series expansion. It now takes the form below.

$$E(\mathbf{m}) = \sum_{x,y \in \Omega} (k - c^T \mathbf{m})^2 \tag{3}$$

where the scalar k and vector $\mathbf{c}$ are given as:

$$k = f_t - f + x f_x + y f_y$$

$$c = (x f_x \ y f_x \ x f_y \ y f_y \ f_x \ f_y \ -f \ -1) \tag{4}$$

where $f_x(\cdot), f_y(\cdot)$, and $f_t(\cdot)$ are the spatial/temporal derivatives of $f(\cdot)$. Minimization of this error function is accomplished by differentiating $E(\mathbf{m})$, setting the result equal to zero and solving for $\mathbf{m}$. The solution is,

$$\mathbf{m} = (\sum_{x,y \in \Omega} \mathbf{c} \mathbf{c}^T)^{-1} (\sum_{x,y \in \Omega} \mathbf{c}k) \tag{5}$$

Intensity variations are typically a significant source of error in differential motion estimation. The addition of the contrast and brightness terms allows us to accurately register images in the presence of local intensity variations. Another important assumption on the model is that the model parameters $\mathbf{m}$ vary smoothly across space. A smoothness constraint on the contrast/brightness parameters has the added benefit of avoiding a degenerate solution where a pure brightness modulation is used to describe the mapping between images.

To begin, the error function $E(\mathbf{m})$ in (3) is augmented as follows:

$$\hat{E}(\mathbf{m}) = E_b(\mathbf{m}) + E_s(\mathbf{m}) \tag{6}$$

where $E_b(\mathbf{m})$ is defined without the summation:

$$E_b(\mathbf{m}) = (k - \mathbf{c}^T \mathbf{m})^2 \tag{7}$$

with k and $\mathbf{c}$ as in Equation (4). The new quadratic error term $E_s(\mathbf{m})$ embodies the smoothness constraint:

$$E_s(\mathbf{m}) = \sum_{i=1}^{8} \lambda_i \left[\left(\frac{\partial m_i}{\partial x} \right)^2 + \left(\frac{\partial m_i}{\partial y} \right)^2 \right] \tag{8}$$

where λ_i is a positive constant that controls the relative weight given to the smoothness constraint on parameter m_i. This error function is again minimized by differentiating with respect to the model parameters, setting the result equal to zero and solving $\dfrac{d\hat{E}(\mathbf{m})}{dm} = \dfrac{dE_b(\mathbf{m})}{dm} + \dfrac{dE_s(\mathbf{m})}{dm} = 0$. Since solving for $\mathbf{m}$ at each pixel location yields an enormous linear system which is intractable to solve, an iterative scheme is used to solve for $\mathbf{m}$ (Horn, 1986). Now $\mathbf{m}$ is expressed as the following iterative equation:

$$\mathbf{m}^{(j+1)} = (\mathbf{c}\mathbf{c}^T + \mathbf{L})^{-1}(\mathbf{c}k + \mathbf{L}\bar{\mathbf{m}}^{(j)}) \tag{9}$$

Where $\bar{\mathbf{m}}$ is the component-wise average of $\mathbf{m}$ over a small spatial neighborhood, and $\mathbf{L}$ is an 8x8 diagonal matrix with diagonal elements λ_i, and zero off the diagonal. On each iteration j, $\bar{\mathbf{m}}^{(j)}$ is estimated from the current $\mathbf{m}^{(j)}$. The initial estimate $\mathbf{m}^{(0)}$ is estimated from Equation (5).

In this chapter, a two-level Gaussian pyramid is constructed for both the reference side face image and the side face image to be aligned. The global parameters $\mathbf{m}$ are first estimated at each pyramid level as in Equation (5) for the entire image. Then, the local parameters $\mathbf{m}$ are estimated with $\Omega = 5 \times 5$ as in Equation (5) using the least square algorithm. This estimate of $\mathbf{m}$ is used to bootstrap the iterations in Equation (9). At each iteration, λ_i,

i=1,...,8, is constant for all **m** components and its value is set to 10^{11}. $\bar{m}_i$ is computed by convolving with the 3×3 kernel (1 4 1; 4 0 4; 1 4 1)/20. The number of iterations is 10. This process is repeated at each level of the pyramid. The values of these parameters are chosen empirically and based on the previous motion estimation work (Periaswamy & Farid, 2003). Although the contrast and brightness parameters, m_7 and m_8, are estimated, they are not used when the side face image is aligned to the reference side face image.

Match Statistic

A match statistic is designed to indicate how well a transformed image aligns with the reference image. It is used to select or reject a low-resolution image during alignment. If the size of the reference image is $M \times N$, the mean square error (MSE) between the aligned image and the reference image is

$$E = \sum_{x=1}^{M}\sum_{y=1}^{N}[f(x,y,t) -$$

$$f(m_1 x + m_2 y + m_5, m_3 x + m_4 y + m_6, t-1)]^2 \, / \, MN$$

The match statistic of the aligned image is defined as

$$S = 1 - \frac{E}{[\sum_{x=1}^{M}\sum_{y=1}^{N} f^2(x,y,t)]/MN} \tag{10}$$

If the value of S is close to 1, the image at time $t-1$ is well aligned with the image at time t. A very low value indicates misalignment. A perfect match is 1. However, even images that are very well aligned typically do not achieve 1 due to error in the transformation and noise. For improving image quality, the resolution enhancement method discussed next works most effectively when the match values of aligned images are close to 1. A match threshold is specified and any aligned image, whose match statistic falls below the threshold, will not be subsequently used.

The pseudo code for the low-resolution image alignment is shown in Box 1. Two alignment results with the match statistic S are shown in Figure 1. The reference images and the images to be aligned are from a video sequence, in which a person is walking and exposes a side view to the camera. The reference images in both Figures 1(a) and 1(b) are the same. The time difference between the image to be aligned in Figure 1(a) and the reference image is about 0.033 seconds, and the time difference between the image to be aligned in Figure 1(b) and the reference image is about 0.925 seconds. The S values are 0.95 and 0.86 for Figures 1(a) and 1(b), respectively. Note the differences in the bottom right part of each of the aligned images. We specify the match threshold at 0.9. For 28 out of 100 video sequences used in our experiments, one or two low-resolution images are discarded from each of the sequences during the image alignment process.

Resolution Enhancement Algorithm

An iterative method (Irani & Peleg, 1993) is used to construct a high-resolution side face image from aligned low-resolution side face images, whose match statistics are above the specified threshold. The details are as follows.

The Imaging Model

The imaging process, yielding the observed side face image sequence f_k, is modeled by:

$$f_k(m, n) = \sigma_k(h(T_k(F(x, y))) + \eta_k(x, y)) \tag{11}$$

where

- f_k is the sensed image of the tracked side face in the kth frame.
- F is a high-resolution image of the tracked side face in a desired reconstruction view. Finding F is the objective of the super-

Figure 1. Two examples of alignment results with the match statistic S. (a) and (b): the reference image (left), the image to be aligned (middle) and the aligned image (right)

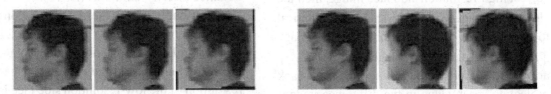

(a) A well aligned image with S = 0.95.   (b) A bad aligned image with S = 0.86.

Box 1. Pseudo code for low-resolution image alignment

> **Align the low-resolution side face image with the reference side face image**
> **Input:** *the reference side face image and the side face image to be aligned.*
> **Output:** *the motion vector **m** and the match statistic S of the aligned image.*
> *1. For each pyramid level in global registration*
> *1.1 Estimate **m** between the newest warped image and the reference image using Equation (5)*
>   *1.2 Warp the image to the next level of the pyramid using the newest estimate*
> *2. For each pyramid level in local registration*
> *2.1 Estimate **m** between the newest warped image and the reference image using Equation (5) with*
> *$\Omega = 5 \times 5$*
>   *2.2 Warp the image using the newest estimate*
>   *2.3 For each iteration*
>   *2.3.1 Estimate **m** between the newest warped image and the reference image using Equation (9)*
>   *2.3.2 Warp the image using the newest estimate*
>   *2.4 Warp the image to the next level of the pyramid using the newest estimate*
> *3. Compute the match statistic S of the aligned image*
> *4. If $S \geq$ threshold, keep the low-resolution image; otherwise, discard it*

resolution algorithm.

- T_k is the 2-D geometric transformation from F to f_k, determined by the 2-D motion parameters **m** of the tracked side face in the image plane. T_k is assumed to be invertible and does not include the decrease in the sampling rate between F and f_k.

- h is a blurring operator, determined by the Point Spread Function (PSF) of the sensor. We use a circular averaging filter with radius 2 as PSF.

- η_k is an additive noise term.

- σ_k is a down sampling operator which digitizes and decimates the image into pixels and quantizes the resulting pixel values.

The receptive field (in F) of a detector whose output is the pixel $f_k(m, n)$ is uniquely defined by its center (x, y) and its shape. The shape is determined by the region of the blurring operator h, and by the inverse geometric transformation T_k^{-1}. Similarly, the center (x, y) is obtained by $T_k^{-1}(m, n)$. The resolution enhancement algorithm aims to construct a higher resolution image $\hat{F}$, which approximates F as accurately as possible, and surpasses the visual quality of the observed images in $\{f_k\}$.

Algorithm for Resolution Enhancement

The algorithm for creating higher resolution images is iterative. Starting with an initial guess $F^{(0)}$ for the high-resolution side face image, the imaging process is simulated to obtain a set of low-resolution side face images $\{f_k^{(0)}\}_{k=1}^{K}$ corresponding to the observed input images $\{f_k\}_{k=1}^{K}$. If $F^{(0)}$ were the correct high-resolution side face image, then the simulated images $\{f_k^{(0)}\}_{k=1}^{K}$ should be identical to the observed low-resolution side face image $\{f_k\}_{k=1}^{K}$. The difference images $\{f_k - f_k^{(0)}\}_{k=1}^{K}$ are used to improve the initial guess by "back projecting" each value in the difference images onto its receptive field in $F^{(0)}$, yielding an improved high-resolution side face image $F^{(1)}$. This process is repeated iteratively to minimize the error function:

$$e^{(n)} = \sqrt{\frac{1}{K}\sum_{k=1}^{K} \| f_k - f_k^{(n)} \|^2}$$

(12)

The imaging process of f_k at the nth iteration is simulated by:

$$f_k^{(n)} = T_k(F^{(n)}) * h) \downarrow s$$

(13)

where $\downarrow s$ denotes a down sampling operator by a factor s, and $*$ is the convolution operator. The iterative update scheme of the high-resolution image is expressed by:

$$F(n+1) = F(n) + \frac{1}{K}\sum_{k=1}^{K} T_k^{-1}(((f_k - f_k^{(n)}) \uparrow s) * p)$$

(14)

where K is the number of low-resolution side face images. $\uparrow s$ is an up sampling operator by a factor s, and p is a "back projection" kernel, determined by h. T_k is 2-D motion parameters. The averaging process reduces additive noise.

In this chapter, we use a sampling factor $s=2$. An initial guess $F^{(0)}$ for the high resolution image is obtained by up sampling a low-resolution image using bilinear interpolation. Ten low-resolution side face images contribute to a high-resolution side face image. The high-resolution image is obtained after 10 iterations ($N=10$).

The pseudo code for the high-resolution image construction is shown in Box 2. Figure 2 shows four examples of low-resolution face images and reconstructed high-resolution face images. The resolution of the low-resolution side face images is 68×68 and the resolution of the high-resolution side face images is 136×136. For comparison, we resize the low-resolution face images using bilinear interpolation. From this figure, we can see that the quality of the reconstructed high-resolution images is much better than the resized low-resolution images.

Side Face Normalization

Before feature extraction, all high-resolution side face images are normalized. The normalization is based on the locations of nasion, pronasale and throat on the face profile. These three fiducial points are identified by using a curvature based fiducial extraction method (Bhanu & Zhou, 2004). It is explained as follows.

We apply a canny edge detector to the side face image. After edge linking and thinning, the profile of a side face is extracted as the leftmost points different from background, which contain fiducial points like nasion, pronasale, chin and throat. The profile consists of a set of points $T=(x,y)$, where x is a row index and y is a column index of a pixel. Then, a Gaussian scale-space filter is applied to this $1D$ curve to reduce noise. The convolution between Gaussian kernel $g(x,\sigma)$ and signal $f(x)$ depends both on x, the signal's independent variable, and on σ, the Gaussian's standard deviation. It is given by

$$F(x,\sigma) = f(x) \otimes g(x,\sigma) = \int_{-\infty}^{\infty} f(u)\frac{1}{\sigma\sqrt{2\pi}}e^{\frac{-(x-u)^2}{2\sigma^2}} du$$

(15)

Figure 2. Four examples of resized low-resolution face images (top) and constructed high-resolution face images (bottom)

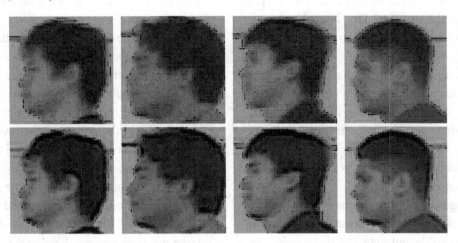

Box 2. Pseudo code for high-resolution image construction

> **Construct the high-resolution side face image from the low-resolution side face images**
>
> **Input:** *the observed input images* $\{f_k\}_{K=1}^{K}$ and the corresponding motion vectors $\{m_k\}_{K=1}^{K}$
> **Output:** *the high-resolution image F .*
> *1. Start with iteration n = 0*
> *2. Obtain an initial guess $F^{(0)}$ for the high-resolution image using bilinear interpolation*
> *3. Obtain a set of low-resolution images $\{f_k^{(n)}\}_{K=1}^{K}$ using Equation (13)*
> *4. Obtain an improved high-resolution image $F^{(n+1)}$ using Equation (14)*
> *5. Let n = n + 1*
> *6. If n <= N, go to step 3; otherwise, stop*

where $\oplus$ denotes convolution with respect to x. The bigger the σ, the smoother the $F(x,\sigma)$. The curve T is parameterized as $T(u)=(x(u),y(u))$ by the arc length parameter u. An evolved version of T is $T\sigma(u) = (X(u, \sigma), Y(u, \sigma))$, where $X(u, \sigma) = x(u) \oplus g(u, \sigma))$ and $Y(u, \sigma) = y(u) \oplus g(u, \sigma)$.

Curvature κ on $T\sigma$ is computed as:

$$\kappa(x,\sigma) = \frac{X_u(u,\sigma)Y_{uu}(u,\sigma) - X_{uu}(u,\sigma)Y_u(u,\sigma)}{(X_u(u,\sigma)^2 + Y_u(u,\sigma)^2)^{1.5}}$$

(16)

where the first and second derivatives of X and Y can be computed as:

$$X_u(u, \sigma) = x(u) \oplus g_u(u, \sigma) \quad X_{uu}(u, \sigma) = x(u) \oplus g_{uu}(u, \sigma)$$

$$Y_u(u, \sigma) = y(u) \oplus g_u(u, \sigma) \quad Y_{uu}(u, \sigma) = y(u) \oplus g_{uu}(u, \sigma)$$

$g_u(u, \sigma)$ and $g_{uu}(u, \sigma)$ are the first derivative and the second derivative of Gaussian Kernel.

To localize the fiducial points, the curvature of a profile is first computed at an initial scale and the locations, where the local maxima of the absolute values occur, are chosen as corner candidates. These locations are tracked down and the fiducial points are identified at lower scales. The initial scale must be large enough to remove noise and small enough to retain the real corners. Our method has advantages in that it does not depend on too many parameters and not require any thresholds. It is also fast and simple. The complete process to find the fiducial points is described as follows:

Step 1: Compute the curvature of a profile at an initial scale, find all points with the large absolute curvature values as corner candidates and track them down to lower scales.

Step 2: Regard the rightmost point in the candidate set as the throat.

Step 3: Regard the pronasale as one of the two leftmost candidate points in the middle part of the profile and then identify it using the curvature value around this point.

Step 4: Assume that there are no candidate points between pronasale and nasion and identify the first candidate point above the pronasale as nasion.

Figure 3 shows the extracted face profile and the absolute values of curvature. We amplify the absolute values of curvature 20 times in order to show them more clearly. It is clear that the locations of the fiducial points, including nasion, pronasale and throat, have large curvature values. Given a set of high-resolution images and the three fiducial points of each face image, affine transformations are computed between the first image and all the other images. Subsequently, images are cropped as follows: the highest point is defined as the point six pixels above nasion; the lowest point is defined as the throat; the leftmost point is defined as the point 4 pixels to the left of pronasion; and the rightmost point is defined as the one, which is half of the height of the cropped image and is to the right of the leftmost point. All cropped images are further normalized to the size of 64 × 32. We call these images as Enhanced Side Face Images (ESFIs). Similarly, Original Side Face Image (OSFI) is a subimage from the normalized version of the low-resolution side face image. It is obtained by the similar process explained above. The size of OSFI is 34 × 18. Examples of resized OSFIs and ESFIs for four people are shown for comparison in Figure 4. Clearly, ESFIs have better quality than OSFIs.

Figure 3. The extracted face profile and the absolute values of curvature

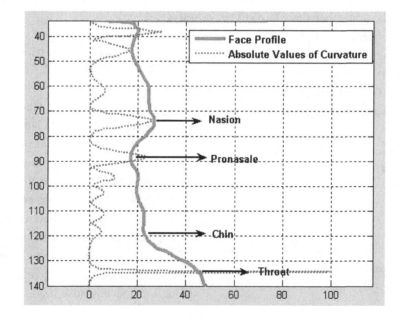

Gait Energy Image (GEI) Construction

In recent years, various approaches have been proposed for human motion understanding. These approaches generally fall under two major categories: model-based approaches and model-free approaches. When people observe human walking patterns, they not only observe the global motion properties, but also interpret the structure of the human body and detect the motion patterns of local body parts. The structure of the human body is generally interpreted based on their prior knowledge. Model-based gait recognition approaches focus on recovering a structural model of human motion, and the gait patterns are then generated from the model parameters for recognition. Model-free approaches make no attempt to recover a structural model of human motion. The features used for gait representation includes: moments of shape, height and stride/width, and other image/shape templates. In this work, we focus on a model-free approach that does not recover a structure model of human motion. We only consider individual recognition by activity-specific human motion, i.e., regular human walk-

Figure 4. Examples of 4 people: (a) Resized OSFIs (b) ESFIs

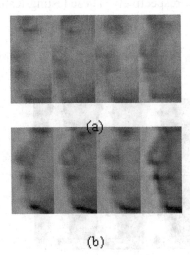

(a)

(b)

ing, which is used in most current approaches of individual recognition by gait.

Silhouette Extraction and Processing

Regular human walking can be considered as a cyclic motion where human motion repeats at a stable frequency. Therefore, it is possible to divide the entire gait sequence into cycles. Since the human body segmentation is performed on the original human-walking sequences, we begin with the extracted binary silhouette image sequences. The raw silhouettes are extracted by a simple background subtraction method. The silhouette preprocessing includes size normalization (proportionally resizing each silhouette image so that all silhouettes have the same height) and horizontal alignment (centering the upper half silhouette part with respect to its horizontal centroid). In a preprocessed silhouette sequence, the time series signal of lower half silhouette size from each frame indicates the gait frequency and phase information. We estimate the gait frequency and phase by a maximum entropy spectrum estimation (Little & Boyd, 1998) from the obtained time series signal.

Representation Construction

Given the preprocessed binary gait silhouette image $B_t(x, y)$ at time t in a sequence, the grey-level gait energy image (GEI) is defined as follows (Han & Bhanu, 2006):

$$G(x, y) = \frac{1}{N} \sum_{t=1}^{N} B_t(x, y)$$

(17)

where N is the number of frames in the complete cycle(s) of a silhouette sequence, t is the frame number of the sequence (moment of time), and x and y are values in the 2D image coordinate. Figure 5 shows the sample silhouette images in a gait cycle from 2 people and the right most images are the corresponding GEIs. As expected, GEI reflects major shapes of silhouettes and their changes over the gait cycle. It accounts for human walking at different speeds. It is referred as the gait energy image because: (a) each silhouette image is the space-normalized energy image of human walking at this moment; (b) GEI is the time-normalized accumulative energy image of human walking in the complete cycle(s); (c) a pixel with higher intensity value in GEI means that human walking occurs more frequently at this position (i.e., with higher energy). GEI has several advantages over the gait representation of binary silhouette sequence. GEI is not sensitive to incidental silhouette errors in individual frames. Moreover, with such a 2D template, we do not need to consider the time moment of each frame, and the incurred errors can be, therefore, avoided. Controlled experiments are performed to verity that GEI is not sensitive to errors in individual frames. For the same person, we construct the first GEI using all the silhouette images in a complete walking cycle. We construct the second GEI using the left silhouette images after discarding two silhouette images, the first one and the last one, in a complete walking cycle. We construct the third GEI using the left silhouette images after discarding three silhouette images, the first one, the middle one and the last one, in a complete walking cycle. For each of 16 people, three

different GEIs are constructed using the above method. Correspondingly, three experiments for gait recognition are performed using these three different types of GEIs. The result demonstrates that with the removal of frames, there is no effect on gait-recognition performance, i.e., all three experiments achieve the same recognition rate. Note that it is different from ESFI construction where the removal of misaligned images is necessary.

Match Score Level Fusion for Video-based Human Identification

We construct Enhanced Side Face Image (ESFI) as the face biometrics template using the process presented in Section 3.1 and Gait Energy Image (GEI) as the gait biometrics template from video sequences using the process presented in Section 3.2. The match score level fusion scheme for integrating side face and gait is shown in Figure 6. During the training procedure, we perform a component and discriminant analysis separately on ESFI and GEI obtained from all training videos. As a result, transformation matrices and features that form feature gallery are obtained. During the recognition procedure, each testing video is processed to generate both face templates and gait templates, which are then transformed by the transformation matrices obtained during the training procedure to extract face features and gait features, respectively. These testing features are

Figure 5. Two examples of normalized and aligned silhouette images in a gait cycle. The right most images are the corresponding gait energy images (GEIs)

compared with gallery features in the database, and then different fusion strategies are used to combine the results of face classifier and gait classifier to improve recognition performance.

Feature Learning Using PCA and MDA

In the match score level fusion, PCA and MDA combined method (Belhumeur, Hespanha, & Kriegman, 1997) is applied to face templates, ESFIs, and gait templates, GEIs, separately to get low dimensional feature representation for side face and gait. PCA reduces the dimension of feature space, and MDA automatically identifies the most discriminating features.

Let $\{\mathbf{x}_1, \mathbf{x}_2, ..., \mathbf{x}_n\}$, $\mathbf{x}_k \in R^N$ be n random vectors representing n ESFIs or n GEIs, where N is the dimensionality of the image. The covariance matrix is defined as $\Sigma_{\mathbf{x}} = E([\mathbf{x} - E(\mathbf{x})][\mathbf{x} - E(\mathbf{x})]T)$, where $E(\cdot)$ is the expectation operator and T denotes the transpose operation. The covariance matrix $\Sigma_{\mathbf{x}}$ can be factorized into the following form:

$$\Sigma_{\mathbf{x}} = \Phi \Lambda \Phi \qquad (18)$$

where $\Phi = [\Phi_1 \Phi_2 ... \Phi_N] \in R^{N \times N}$ is the orthogonal eigenvector matrix of $\Sigma_{\mathbf{x}}$; $\Lambda = [\Lambda_1 \Lambda_2 ... \Lambda_N] \in R^{N \times N}$ is the diagonal eigenvalue matrix of $\Sigma_{\mathbf{x}}$ with diagonal elements in descending order. One important property of PCA is its optimal signal

reconstruction in the sense of minimum mean square error (MSE) when only a subset of principal components are used to represent the original signal. An immediate application of this property is the dimensionality reduction:

$$\mathbf{y}_k = \mathbf{P}_{pca}^T[\mathbf{x}_k - E(\mathbf{x})]k = 1,...,n. \qquad (19)$$

where $\mathbf{P}_{pca} = [\Phi_1 \Phi_2 ... \Phi_m]$, $m < N$. The lower dimensional vector $\mathbf{x}_k \in R^m$ captures the most expressive features of the original data $\mathbf{x}_k$.

MDA seeks a transformation matrix $\mathbf{W}$ that maximizes the ratio of the between-class scatter matrix $\mathbf{S}_B$ to the within-class scatter matrix $\mathbf{S}_W$:

$$J(\mathbf{W}) = \frac{|\mathbf{W}^T \mathbf{S}_B \mathbf{W}|}{|\mathbf{W}^T \mathbf{S}_w \mathbf{W}|}.$$ Suppose that $\mathbf{w}_1$, $\mathbf{w}_2$, ...,

$\mathbf{w}_c$ and n_1, n_2, ..., n_c denote the classes and the number of images within each class, respectively, with $n = n_1, n_2, ..., n_c$ and $\mathbf{w} = \mathbf{w}_1 \cup \mathbf{w}_2 \cup ... \cup \mathbf{w}_c$. c is the number of classes. The within-class scatter matrix is $\mathbf{S}_\mathbf{w} = \sum_{i=1}^{c} \sum_{\mathbf{y} \in w_i} (\mathbf{y} - \mathbf{M}_i)(\mathbf{y} - \mathbf{M}_i)^T$ and the between-class scatter matrix is $\mathbf{S}_B = \sum_{i=1}^{c} ni(\mathbf{M}_i - \mathbf{M})(\mathbf{M}_i - \mathbf{M})^T$, where $\mathbf{M}_i = \frac{1}{n_i} \sum_{\mathbf{y} \in w_i} \mathbf{y}$ and $\mathbf{M} = \frac{1}{n} \sum_{\mathbf{y} \in w} \mathbf{y}$ are the means of the class i and the grand mean, respectively.

$J(\mathbf{W})$ is maximized when the columns of $\mathbf{W}$

Figure 6. The match score level fusion scheme for integrating side face and gait in video.

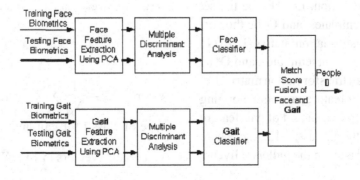

are the generalized eigenvectors of $\mathbf{S}_B$ and $\mathbf{S}_W$ corresponding to the largest generalized eigenvalues in

$$\mathbf{S}_B\Psi_i = \lambda_i\mathbf{S}_W\Psi_i \qquad (20)$$

There are no more than $c-1$ nonzero eigenvalues λ_i and the corresponding eigenvectors Ψ_i. The transformed feature vector is obtained as follows:

$$\mathbf{z}_k = \mathbf{P}_{mda}^T\mathbf{y}_k = \mathbf{P}_{mda}^T\mathbf{P}_{pca}^T[\mathbf{x}_k - E(\mathbf{x})] = \mathbf{Q}[\mathbf{x}_k - E(\mathbf{x})]k = 1,...,n.$$

$$(21)$$

where $\mathbf{P}_{mda} = [\Psi_1\Psi_2...\Psi_r]$, $r < c$ and $\mathbf{Q}$ is the overall transformation matrix. We can choose r to perform feature selection and dimensionality reduction. The choice of the range of PCA and the dimension of MDA reflects the energy requirement. On the one hand, we hope to lose as little representative information of the original data as possible. On the other hand, the small eigenvalues mainly correspond to the high-frequency noise, which may lead to decreased performance for recognition. We choose the threshold of 99% in eigenvalue energy for eigenvector selection. The lower dimensional vector $z^k \in R^r$ captures the most expressive and discriminating features of the original data $\mathbf{x}_k$.

Generation and Classification of Synthetic Match Score

We train face templates and gait templates separately for feature extraction. Let $\{\mathbf{F}\}$ be the set of all training face templates, and $\mathbf{Q}^f$ be the corresponding face transformation matrix. Let $\{\mathbf{G}\}$ be the set of all training gait templates, and $\mathbf{Q}^g$ be the corresponding gait transformation matrix. Let $\{\mathbf{f}_i\}$ be the set of face feature vectors belonging to the ith class, and $\{\mathbf{g}_i\}$ be the set of gait feature vectors belonging to the ith class, i=1,2,...,c, where c is the number of classes in the gallery. Given a

testing video P, we follow the procedure explained in Section 3.1 and Section 3.2 to generate the set of testing face templates $\{\hat{\mathbf{F}}_p\}$ and the set of testing gait templates $\{\hat{\mathbf{G}}_p\}$, respectively. The corresponding face and gait feature vector sets are obtained using Equation (21) as follows:

$$\{\hat{\mathbf{f}}_P\} : \hat{\mathbf{f}}_{Pj} = \mathbf{Q}^f\hat{\mathbf{F}}_{pj} \qquad j = 1,2,...,n_f$$
$$\{\hat{\mathbf{g}}_P\} : \hat{\mathbf{g}}_{Pj} = \mathbf{Q}^g\hat{\mathbf{G}}_{pj} \qquad j = 1,2,...,n_g \qquad (22)$$

where n_f is the number of testing face templates and n_g is the number of testing gait templates.

The Euclidean distance is used as the similarity measure for the face classifier and the gait classifier. From the classifier based on face templates, we obtain

$$D(\hat{\mathbf{f}}_{Pj},\mathbf{f}_i) = \|\hat{\mathbf{f}}_{Pj} - \mathbf{m}_{fi}\| \quad i = 1,2,...,c \quad j = 1,2,...,n_f$$

$$(23)$$

where $\mathbf{m}_{fi} = \frac{1}{N_{fi}}\sum_{\mathbf{f}\in\mathbf{f}_i}\mathbf{f}$, i=1,2,...,c, is the prototype of class i for face and N_{fi} is the number of face feature vectors in $\{\mathbf{f}_i\}$. We assign the testing video P to class k if

$$D(\hat{\mathbf{f}}_P,\mathbf{f}_k) = min_{i=1}^c min_{j=1}^{n_f}D(\hat{\mathbf{f}}_{Pj},\mathbf{f}_i) \qquad (24)$$

From the classifier based on gait templates, we obtain

$$D(\hat{\mathbf{g}}_{Pj},\mathbf{g}_i) = \|\hat{\mathbf{g}}_{Pj} - \mathbf{m}_{gi}\| \quad i = 1,2,...,c \quad j = 1,2,...,n_g$$

$$(25)$$

where $\mathbf{m}_{gi} = \frac{1}{N_{gi}}\sum_{\mathbf{g}\in\mathbf{g}_i}\mathbf{g}$, i=1,2,...,c, is the prototype of class i for gait and N_{gi} is the number of gait feature vectors in $\{\mathbf{g}_i\}$. We assign the testing video P to class k if

$$D(\hat{\mathbf{g}}_P, \mathbf{g}_k) = min_{i=1}^{c} min_{j=1}^{n_g} D(\hat{\mathbf{g}}_{Pj}, \mathbf{g}_i) \qquad (26)$$

Before combination of the results of face classifier and the results of gait classifier, it is necessary to map distances obtained from the different classifiers to the same range of values. We use exponential transformation here. Given that the distance for a probe X are $D_1, D_2, ..., D_c$, we obtain the normalized match scores as

$$S'_i = \frac{exp(-D_i)}{\sum_{i=1}^{c} exp(-D_i)} \quad i = 1, 2, ..., c \qquad (27)$$

After normalization, the match scores of face templates and the match scores of gait templates from the same class are fused using different fusion methods. Since face and gait can be regarded as two independent biometrics in our scenario, synchronization is totally unnecessary for them. To take advantage of information for a walking person in video, we use all the possible combinations of face match scores and gait match scores to generate new match scores, which encode information from both face and gait. The new match scores are called synthetic match scores, defined as

$$S_t(\{\hat{\mathbf{f}}_p, \hat{\mathbf{g}}_p\}, \{\mathbf{f}_l, \mathbf{g}_l\}) = R\{S'(\hat{\mathbf{f}}_{Pi}, \mathbf{f}_i), S'(\hat{\mathbf{g}}_{pj}, \mathbf{g}_i)\}$$
$$i = 1, 2, ..., n_f, j = 1, 2, ..., n_g, t = 1, 2, ..., n_f n_g, l = 1, 2, ..., c \qquad (28)$$

where S' means the normalized match score of the corresponding distance D, and $R\{,\}$ means a fusion method. In this chapter, we use Sum and Max rules. It is reasonable to generate synthetic match scores using Equation (28), since ESFI is built from multiple video frames and GEI is a compact spatio-temporal representation of gait in video. In this chapter, we use 2 face match scores

and 2 gait match scores to generate 4 synthetic match scores for one person from each video.

Distances representing dissimilarity become match scores representing similarity by using Equation (27), so the unknown person should be classified to the class for which the synthetic match score is the largest. We assign the testing video P to class k if

$$S(\{\hat{\mathbf{f}}_P, \hat{\mathbf{g}}_P\}, \{\mathbf{f}_k, \mathbf{g}_k\}) = max_{l=1}^{c} max_{t=1}^{n_f n_g} S_t(\{\hat{\mathbf{f}}_P\}, \hat{\mathbf{g}}_P\}, \{\mathbf{f}_l, \mathbf{g}_l\}$$
$$(29)$$

Since we obtain more than one synthetic match scores after fusion for one testing video sequence, Equation (29) means the unknown person is classified to the class which gets the maximum synthetic match score out of all the synthetic match scores corresponding to all the classes.

Feature Level Fusion for Video-based Human Recognition

In this section, as compared to the approach based on the match score level fusion, we present two approaches that are based on the feature level fusion of face and gait. We also construct Enhanced Side Face Image (ESFI) as the face biometrics template and Gait Energy Image (GEI) as the gait biometrics template from video sequences. In the first approach, feature concatenation is conducted based on the features of face and gait, which are obtained separately using Principal Component Analysis (PCA) and Multiple Discriminant Analysis (MDA) combined method from ESFI and GEI. In the second approach, MDA is applied after, not before, the concatenation of face and gait features that are obtained separately using Principal Component Analysis (PCA) from ESFI and GEI. The performance of the feature level fusion schemes are compared with the match score level fusion schemes in Section 3.5.

Feature Level Fusion Scheme I

The feature level fusion scheme I for integrating side face and gait is shown in Figure 7. In the training procedure, we perform a Principle Component Analysis (PCA) and Multiple Discriminant Analysis (MDA) combined transformation separately on face biometrics templates (ESFI) and gait biometrics templates (GEI) obtained from all training videos to obtain lower dimensional face features and gait features. These features is then concatenated to generate the synthetic features. As a result, PCA and MDA combined transformation matrices and synthetic features that form feature gallery are obtained. In the recognition procedure, each testing video is processed to generate both face templates and gait templates. These templates are transformed by PCA and MDA combined transformation matrices to obtain face features and gait features, which are then concatenated. Finally, these testing synthetic features are compared with the training synthetic features to evaluate the performance of the proposed approach.

PCA and MDA combined method as explained in Section 3.3 is applied to face templates (ESFIs) and gait templates (GEIs) separately to get side face features **f'** and gait features **g'**. Before they are combined, the individual face features **f'** and gait features **g'** are normalized to have their values lie within similar ranges. We use a linear method (Theodorids & Koutroumbas, 1998), which provides a normalization via the respective estimates of the mean and variance. For the jth feature value in the ith feature vector w_{ij}, we have

$$\hat{w}_{ij} = \frac{w_{ij} - \bar{w}_j}{\sigma_j} \qquad i = 1, 2, \ldots I \qquad j = 1, 2, \ldots L$$

(30)

where $\bar{w}_j = (1/I)\sum_{i=1}^{I} w_{ij}$ and $\sigma_j^2 = (1/(I-1))\sum_{i=1}^{I}(w_{ij} - \bar{w}_j)^2$. I is the number of available feature vectors and L is the number of features for each feature vector. The resulting normalized features have zero mean and unit variance.

Assume that $\hat{\mathbf{f}}$ and $\hat{\mathbf{g}}$ are face features and gait features after normalization using Equation (30), respectively. They are concatenated to form the synthetic features as follows

$$\mathbf{p} = [\hat{\mathbf{f}} \ \hat{\mathbf{g}}] \tag{31}$$

where $\mathbf{p} \in \Re^{m_1+m_2}$, m_1 and m_2 are the feature dimensions of face and gait, respectively. We use all possible combinations of side face features and gait features to generate the maximum number of concatenated feature vectors. Specifically, 4 concatenated features are constructed based on 2 face features and 2 gait features for one person from each video. It is reasonable to concatenate face and gait feature vectors in this way, since ESFI is built from multiple video frames and GEI is a compact spatio-temporal representation of gait in video.

Let $\mathbf{V}_i$, $i = 1, 2, \ldots c$, the mean of the training synthetic features of class i, be the prototype of class i. The unknown person is classified to class K to whom the synthetic feature $\mathbf{p}$ is the nearest neighbor.

$$\|\mathbf{p} - \mathbf{V}_K\| = min\|\mathbf{p} - \mathbf{V}_i\| \tag{32}$$

When multiple synthetic features are obtained for one person, Equation (32) means that the unknown person is classified to the class which has the minimum distance out of all the distances corresponding to all the classes.

Feature Level Fusion Scheme II

The feature level fusion scheme II for integrating side face and gait is shown in Figure 8. In the training procedure, we perform a Principle

Figure 7. The feature level fusion scheme I for integrating side face and gait in video

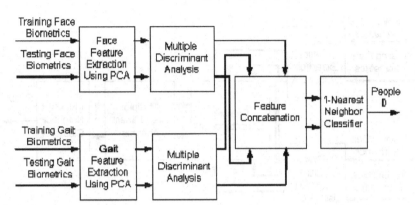

Component Analysis (PCA) separately on face biometrics templates (ESFI) and gait biometrics templates (GEI) obtained from all training videos to obtain lower dimensional face features and gait features. Multiple Discriminant Analysis (MDA) is then applied to the concatenated features of face and gait to generate the synthetic features. As a result, PCA transformation matrices and synthetic features that form feature gallery are obtained. In the procedure, each testing video is processed to generate both face templates and gait templates, which are transformed by PCA transformation matrices to obtain face features and gait features. The concatenated features are then transformed by MDA to obtain the synthetic features. Finally, these testing synthetic features are compared with the training synthetic features to evaluate the performance of the proposed approach.

PCA transformation is first applied separately to face template ESFI and gait template GEI to get side face feature $\mathbf{f'}$ and gait feature $\mathbf{g'}$ using Equation (19). $\mathbf{f'} \in \Re^{m_1}$, $\mathbf{g'} \in \Re^{m_2}$, and m_1 and m_2 are the dimensionality of the reduced face feature space and gait feature space, respectively. Before they are combined, the individual face features $\mathbf{f'}$ and gait features $\mathbf{g'}$ are normalized to have their values lie within similar ranges. Assume that $\hat{\mathbf{f}}$ and $\hat{\mathbf{g}}$ are face features and gait features after normalization using Equation (30), respectively.

They are concatenated to form the features as follows

$$\mathbf{h}=[\,\hat{\mathbf{f}}\ \hat{\mathbf{g}}] \tag{33}$$

where $\mathbf{h} \in \Re^{m_1+m_2}$. We use all possible combinations of side face features and gait features to generate the maximum number of vectors $\mathbf{h}$. Specifically, 4 concatenated features $\mathbf{h}$ is generated based on 2 feature vectors of side face and 2 feature vectors of gait for one person from one video. It is reasonable to concatenate face and gait feature vectors in this way, since ESFI is built from multiple video frames and GEI is a compact spatio-temporal representation of gait in video. MDA transformation is then applied to the concatenated feature vector $\mathbf{h}$ to obtain the synthetic feature vector as follows:

$$\mathbf{z}_k = \mathbf{P}_{mda}^T \mathbf{h}_k \, k = 1,2...\hat{n} \tag{34}$$

where $\mathbf{P}_{mda}$ is the MDA transformation matrix and $\hat{n}$ is the number of the concatenated feature vectors. The synthetic feature $z_k \in \mathrm{R}^{c-1}$ is a lower dimensional vector, which captures the most discriminating power of the face and gait. c is the number of classes.

Let $\mathbf{U}_i$, $i = 1, 2, ...c$, the mean of the training synthetic features of class i, be the prototype of

Figure 8. The feature level fusion scheme II for integrating side face and gait in video

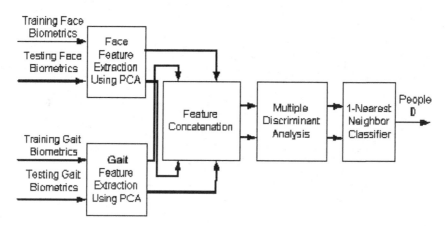

class *i*. The unknown person is classified to class *K* to which the synthetic feature **z** is the nearest neighbor.

$$\|\mathbf{z} - \mathbf{U}_K\| = min\|\mathbf{z} - \mathbf{U}_i\| \qquad (35)$$

When multiple synthetic features are obtained for one person, Equation (35) means that the unknown person is classified to the class which has the minimum distance out of all the distances corresponding to all the classes.

Experimental Results

Experiments and Parameters

We perform two experiments to test different fusion methods at both of the match score level and the feature level. The data are obtained by a Sony DCR-VX1000 digital video camera recorder operating at 30 frames per second. We collect video sequences of 45 people, who are walking in outdoor condition and expose a side view to the camera. The number of sequences per person varies from 2 to 3. The resolution of each frame is 720x480. The distance between people and the video camera is about 10 feet. Each video sequence includes only one person. Figure 9 shows some examples of the data

In Experiment 1, the data consists of 90 video sequences of 45 people. Each person has two video sequences, one for training and the other one for testing. For the same person, the clothes are the same in the training sequence and the testing sequence. In Experiment 2, the data consists of 90 video sequences of 45 people. Each person has two video sequences, one for training and the other one for testing. For 10 of 45 people, the clothes are different in the training sequences and the testing sequences, and the data are collected

Figure 9. Two examples of video sequences

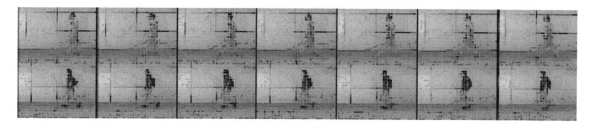

on two separate days about one month apart. For the other 35 people, the clothes are the same in the training sequences and the testing sequences. Table 2 summaries the key features of the two experiments.

For gait, we obtain 2 complete walking cycles from a video sequence according to the gait frequency and gait phase. Each walking cycle includes about 20 frames. We construct 2 GEIs corresponding to 2 walking cycles from one video sequence. The resolution of each GEI is 300x200. For face, we also construct 2 high-resolution side face images from one video sequence. The match threshold (the match statistic S) for aligned low-resolution side face images is specified at 0.9. Each high-resolution side face image is built from 10 low-resolution side face images that are extracted from adjacent video frames. The resolution of low-resolution side face images is 68x68 and the resolution of reconstructed high-resolution side face images is 136x136. After normalization, the resolution of ESFI is 64x32. Recognition performance is used to evaluate our method in the two experiments. For a video sequence, it is defined as the ratio of the number of the correctly recognized people to the number of all the people. To analyze the performance of our method more insightfully, we provide the error index that gives the numbers of misclassified sequences. For comparison, we also show the performance using face features from the Original Side Face Images (OSFIs) to demonstrate the performance

Table 2. Summary of two experiments

Data	Experiments	
	1	2
Number of subjects	45	45
Number of subjects with changed clothes	0	10
Number of GEIs for testing per video	2	2
Number of ESFIs for testing per video	2	2

improvement by using constructed ESFIs. The resolution of OSFI is 34x18. The procedures of feature extraction and classification are the same for ESFI and OSFI.

Besides the recognition rate and the error, Cumulative Match Characteristic (CMC) curve is used to further evaluate the performance of the systems. The CMC curve returns identities associated with the K highest-scoring biometrics samples from the training data. For x axis, K rank means the K nearest neighbors are considered for the recognition results. For y axis, the accuracy rate means the frequency when the genuine identities are included in the K nearest neighbors. The lower the rank of the genuine matching biometrics in the training data, the better the performance of identification system. Improved algorithms would result in a better CMC curve, one that would run more toward the upper left corner of the plot. The fusion schemes, including two feature level fusion methods and two match score level fusion methods, are compared with the single biometrics scheme where MDA is applied to the PCA features of the single biometrics.

The selection of eigenvectors after PCA transformation is based on both the observation and the energy criteria. Figure 10 and 11 show the top 70 eigenvectors of face and gait, respectively. The order of eigenvectors corresponds to the descending order of the eigenvalues. The higher numbered eigenvectors seem more blotchy and it becomes more and more difficult to discern the semantics of what they are encoding. This indicates that eliminating these eigenvectors from the eigenspace should have a minimal effect on performance (Yambor, Draper, & Beveridge, 2002). Meanwhile, the remaining eigenvectors should satisfy the requirement that the corresponding eigenvalues have 99% of the total energy. Furthermore, we decide to keep no more than two-thirds of the total eigenvectors to reduce the problem of curse of dimensionality. In both experiments, we retain eigenvectors corresponding to the top 59 eigenvalues as face features and the top 56 eigenvalues as gait features. After MDA transformation, the dimensionality of the features is 44 ($c-1$).

Experiment 1

We name 45 people from 1 to 45 and each person has 2 video sequences. For each of the 45 people, some frames of the training sequence and the testing sequence are shown. Since we construct 2 GEIs and 2 ESFIs for each sequence, we totally obtain 90 ESFIs and 90 GEIs as the gallery and another 90 ESFIs and 90 GEIs as the probe. For the match score level fusion, 4 synthetic match scores are generated based on 2 face match scores and 2 gait match scores for one person from each video; for the feature level fusion, 4 synthetic features are generated based on 2 face features and 2 gait features for one person from each video. Table 3 shows the performance of single biometric. Table 4 shows the performance of fusion using different schemes. In Table 3 and Table 4, the error index gives the number of misclassified sequence.

From Table 3, we can see that 73.3% people are correctly recognized by OSFI (12 errors out of 45 people), 91.1% people are correctly recognized by

ESFI (4 errors out of 45 people) and 93.3% people are correctly recognized by GEI (3 errors out of 45 people). Among the three people misclassified by GEI, the person (26) has a backpack in the testing sequence but not in the training sequence. The difference causes the body shape to change enough to make a recognition error. The changes of the walking style for the other two people (4, 15) also cause the recognition errors. We show GEIs of people who are misclassified by the gait classifier in Figure 12. Face is sensitive to noise as well as facial expression. We show ESFIs of people who are misclassified by the face classifier in Figure 13.

Among fusion performance of ESFI and GEI in Table 4, the two feature fusion approaches has the same performance at the best recognition rate of 100%, followed by the Max rule at 97.8% and the Sum rule at 95.6%. Figure 14 shows people (video sequences) misclassified by integrating ESFI and GEI using the different fusion rules. It is clear that both of the match score level fusion schemes using Sum and Max rules misclassify the person (26), but both of the feature level fusion schemes recognize the person correctly. For fusion

Figure 10. The Top 70 eigenvectors of face (from left to right and top to bottom)

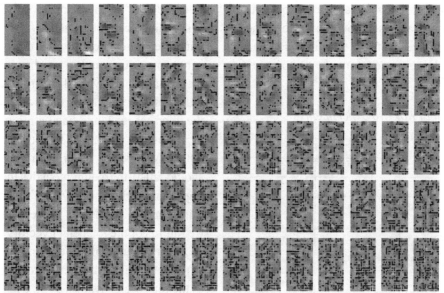

Figure 11. The top 70 eigenvectors of gait (from left to right and top to bottom)

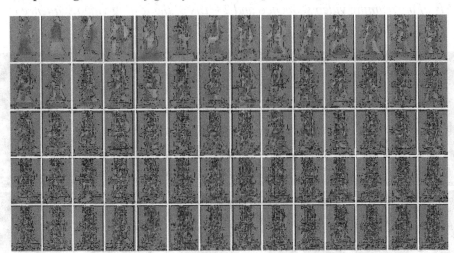

Table 3. Experiment 1: single biometric performance and error index of individuals

Performance	Biometric		
	Original Face (OSFI)	**Enhanced Face (ESFI)**	**Gait (GEI)**
Recognition Rate	73.3%	91.1%	93.3%
Error Index	1, 6, 10, 12, 14, 18, 20, 22, 26, 28, 42, 43	13, 16, 21, 35	4, 15, 26

based on OSFI and GEI, the best performance is also achieved by the two proposed feature fusion approach at 97.8%, followed by the Sum rule and the Max rule at 93.3%. It is clear that fusion based on ESFI and GEI has better performance than fusion based on OSFI and GEI.

Figure 15 shows the CMC curves of Experiment 1. The CMC curves of the two proposed feature fusion schemes overlaps. Both of them are more toward the upper left corner of the plots compared with that of the match score fusion schemes. It is clear that the feature level fusion schemes are more effective than the match score level fusion schemes. Fusion based on ESFI and GEI always has better performance than fusion based on OSFI and GEI using the same fusion scheme. It also demonstrates that the synthetic match scores and the synthetic features carry more discriminating power than the individual biometrics features.

Table 4. Experiment 1: fused biometric performance and error index of individuals

Fusion Method		Match Score Level		Feature Level	
		Sum Rule	Max Rule	Scheme I	Scheme II
OSFI & GEI	Recognition Rate	93.3%	93.3%	97.8%	97.8%
	Error Index	4, 10, 26	4, 10, 26	26	6
ESFI & GEI	Recognition Rate	95.6%	97.8%	100%	100%
	Error Index	4, 26	26	None	None

Figure 12. Experiment 1: GEIs of people misclassified by the gait classifier (see Table 3). For each person, 2 GEIs of the training video sequence and 2 GEIs of the testing video sequence are shown for comparison

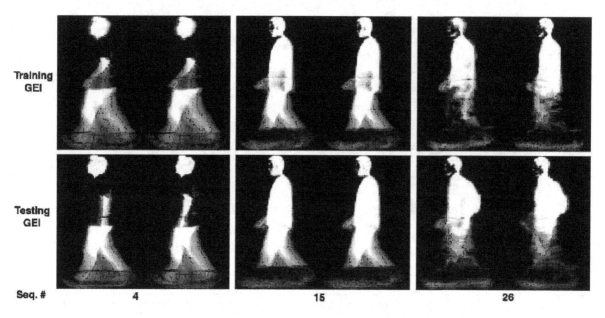

Experiment 2

The data used in Experiment 2 are obtained by substituting 10 testing video sequences of Experiment 1 with the other 10 testing video sequences. We use the same order as in Experiment 1 to name 45 people. Compared with the data in Experiment 1, the 10 replaced testing video sequences are {1,2,5,6,8,9,10,13,19,40}. Therefore, 10 out of 45 people in Experiment 2 wear different clothes in the training sequences and the testing sequences, and for each of the 10 people, two video sequences are

collected on two separate days about one month apart. We construct 2 GEIs and 2 ESFIs from each sequence, so we totally obtain 90 ESFIs and 90 GEIs as the gallery and another 90 ESFIs and 90 GEIs as the probe for 45 people. For the match score level fusion, 4 synthetic match scores are generated based on 2 face match scores and 2 gait match scores for one person from each video; for the feature level fusion, 4 synthetic features are generated based on 2 face features and 2 gait features for one person from each video. Table 5

Figure 13. Experiment 1: ESFIs of people misclassified by the face classifier (see Table 3). For each person, 2 ESFIs of the training video sequence and 2 ESFIs of the testing video sequence are shown for comparison

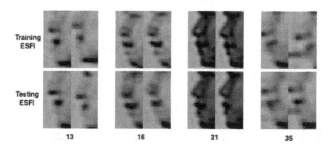

Figure 14. Experiment 1: People misclassified by the integrated classifier based on ESFI and GEI using different fusion rules (see Table 11). For each person, one frame of the training video sequence and one frame of the testing video sequence are shown for comparison. Two feature level fusion schemes achieve the recognition rate of 100%

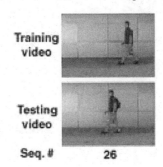

shows the performance of single biometric. Table 6 shows the performance of fusion using different schemes. In Table 5 and Table 6, the error index gives the number of misclassified sequence.

From Table 5, we can see that 64.4% people are correctly recognized by OSFI (16 errors out of 45 people), 80% people are correctly recognized by ESFI (9 errors out of 45 people) and 82.2% people are correctly recognized by GEI (8 errors out of 45 people). Compared with the performance of individual biometric in Experiment 1 in Table 3, all the performance of individual biometric in Experiment 2 decreases to some extent. It is reasonable since gait recognition based on GEI is not only affected by the walking style of a person, but also by the shape of a human body. Changing clothes causes the difference in the shape of the training sequence and the testing sequence for the same person. Also, the lighting condition and the color of clothes cause human body segmentation inaccurate. Figure 16 shows GEIs of people who are misclassified by the gait classifier. Meanwhile, since face is sensitive to noise as well as facial expressions, the different condition in the two video sequences that are taken one month apart brings face recognition errors. Figure 17 shows ESFIs of people who are misclassified by the face

classifier. Note the differences in the training and testing GEIs and ESFIs in Figure 16 and 17.

For the fusion performance based on ESFI and GEI in Table 6, the feature fusion scheme II achieves the best performance at 91.1%. The feature fusion scheme I has the same performance as the Sum rule and the Max rule at 88.9%. We can see that a larger improvement of fusion performance is achieved by the feature level fusion scheme II compared with the other fusion schemes. Figure 18 shows the people (video sequences) misclassified by integrating ESFI and GEI using different fusion rules. For fusion based on OSFI and GEI, the best performance is also achieved by the feature fusion scheme II at 86.7%, followed by the feature fusion scheme I at 84.4%, and the Sum rule and the Max rule at 82.2%.

Figure 19 shows the CMC curves of Experiment 2. In Figure 21(a), it is clear that the CMC curve of the proposed feature fusion scheme II has the better performance than any other scheme. In Figure 19(b), the accuracy rate of the feature fusion scheme II is lower than that of the Max rule fusion scheme at rank 4 and 5, but for the other ranks, the accuracy rate of the feature fusion scheme II is higher than or equal to that of the Max rule fusion scheme. Specifically, the highest accuracy

Figure 15. Experiment 1: (a) CMC curves of the classifiers using GEI and OSFI. (b) CMC curves of the classifiers using GEI and ESFI

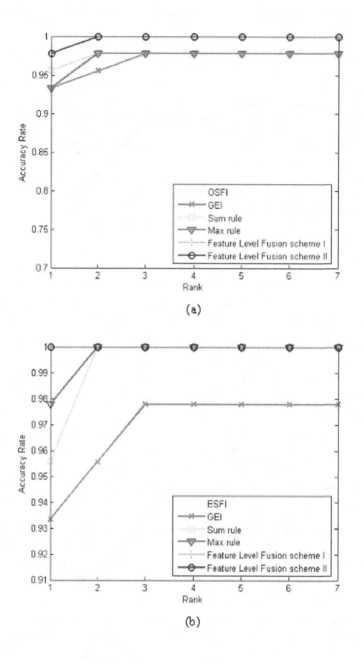

(a)

(b)

rates are achieved by the feature fusion scheme II at rank 1 and 2, which demonstrates the better performance than other fusion schemes since the accuracy rates at low ranks are more important for a recognition system.

Performance Analysis

Discussion on Experiments

The experimental results in Experiment 1 and 2 clearly demonstrate the importance of constructing ESFI. From ESFI, we can extract face features

Table 5. Experiment 2: single biometric performance and error index of individuals

Performance	Biometric		
	Original Face (OSFI)	**Enhanced Face (ESFI)**	**Gait (GEI)**
Recognition Rate	64.4%	80%	82.2%
Error Index	1, 2, 5, 6, 8, 9, 13, 18, 19, 20, 26, 28, 34, 40, 42, 43	1, 2, 5, 8, 11, 13, 30, 35, 42	2, 5, 6, 8, 13, 19, 26, 40

Table 6. Experiment 2: fused biometric performance and error index of individuals

Fusion Method		Match Score Level		Feature Level	
		Sum Rule	**Max Rule**	**Scheme I**	**Scheme II**
OSFI & GEI	Recognition Rate	82.2%	82.2%	84.4%	86.7%
	Error Index	2, 5, 6, 8, 13, 19, 26, 40	2, 5, 6, 8, 13, 19, 26, 40	1, 2, 5, 8, 13, 19, 40	1, 2, 5, 6, 8, 19
ESFI & GEI	Recognition Rate	88.9%	88.9%	88.9%	91.1%
	Error Index	2, 5, 6, 8, 13	2, 5, 6, 8, 13	2, 5, 8, 13, 19	2, 5, 6, 13

with more discriminating power. Therefore, better performance is achieved when ESFI instead of OSFI is used for all of the fusion schemes. For example, in Experiment 2, OSFI has bad performance at 64.4%, but ESFI still achieves the recognition rate of 80%. The feature fusion scheme II based on ESFI and GEI achieves the performance improvement of 8.9% (from 82.2% to 91.1%), while the improvement is 4.5% (from 82.2% to 86.7%) for fusion of OSFI and GEI. The results demonstrate that ESFI serves as a better face template than OSFI. The features obtained from ESFI capture more discriminating power than that from OSFI. Consequently, the fusion based on ESFI and GEI always has better performance than fusion based on OSFI and GEI using the same fusion scheme.

When we compare Experiment 1 and Experiment 2, it can be seen that the recognition rates in Experiment 2 decrease compared with Experiment 1 since 10 out of 45 people change their clothes in the testing sequences. As explained before, gait recognition based on GEI is not only affected by the walking style of a person, but also by the shape of human body. Face is sensitive to noise as well

as facial expressions, so the different condition in the training sequence and the testing sequence affects its reliability. All these factors contribute to recognition errors of the individual classifiers. However, the fusion system based on side face and gait overcomes this problem to some extent. In Experiment 2, there are some people who are not correctly recognized by gait, but when side face information is integrated, the recognition rate is improved. It is because the clothes or the walking style of these people are much different between the training and testing video sequences, so the gait classifier cannot recognize them correctly. However, the side face of these people does not change so much in the training and testing sequences, and it brings useful information for the fusion system and corrects some errors. For example, in Experiment 2, the gait classifier misclassifies 8 people {2, 5, 6, 8, 13, 19, 26, 40}. After fusion with ESFI, Sum rule and Max rule correct 3 errors {19, 26, 40}; the feature level fusion scheme I corrects 3 errors {6, 26, 40}; the feature level fusion scheme II corrects four errors {8, 19, 26, 40}. On the other hand, since the face classifier is comparatively sensitive to the variation of facial expressions

Figure 16. Experiment 2: GEIs of people misclassified by the gait classifier (see Table 5). For each person, 2 GEIs of the training video sequence and 2 GEIs of the testing video sequence are shown for comparison

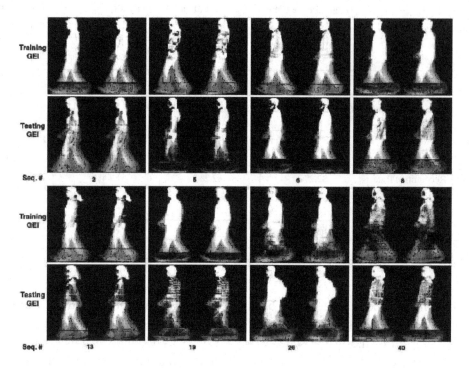

Figure 17. Experiment 2: ESFIs of people misclassified by the face classifier (see Table 5). For each person, 2 ESFIs of the training video sequence and 2 ESFIs of the testing video sequence are shown for comparison

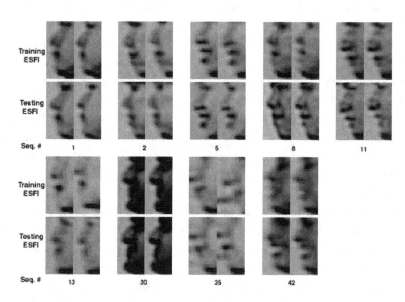

Figure 18. Experiment 2: people misclassified by the integrated classifier based on ESFI and GEI using different fusion rules (see Table 13). For each person, one frame of the training video sequence and one frame of the testing video sequence are shown for comparison

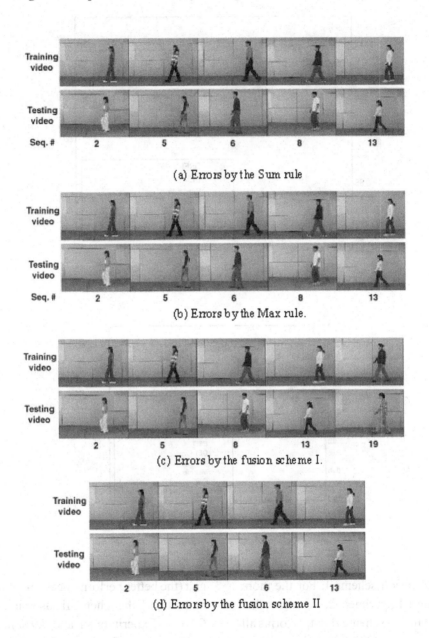

(a) Errors by the Sum rule

(b) Errors by the Max rule.

(c) Errors by the fusion scheme I.

(d) Errors by the fusion scheme II

and noise, it cannot get a good recognition rate by itself. When gait information is combined, the better performance is achieved. Our experimental results demonstrate that the fusion system using side face and gait has potential since face and gait are two complementary biometrics. Consequently, our fusion system is relatively robust compared with the system using only one biometrics in the same scenario.

In Experiment 1, the feature level fusion scheme II outperforms the match score level fusion schemes but has the same performance as

Figure 19. Experiment 2: (a) CMC curves of the classifiers using GEI and OSFI. (b) CMC curves of the classifiers using GEI and ESFI

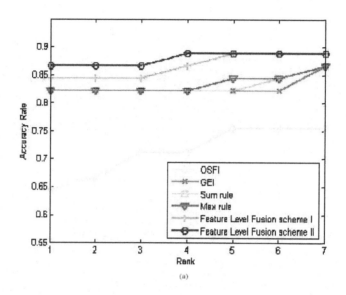

(a)

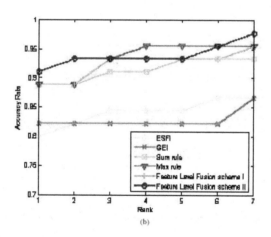

(b)

the feature level fusion scheme I. For the more difficult database in Experiment 2, we can see that the feature level fusion scheme II outperforms all the other fusion schemes. The feature level fusion scheme I does not perform better than the match score level fusion schemes. Moreover, the feature level fusion scheme II achieves a larger performance improvement in Experiment 2 compared with the improvement in Experiment 1. Specifically, compared with the performance achieved by

gait (the better performance of the two individual biometrics), the scheme II has an improvement of 6.7% in Experiment 1 and 8.9% in Experiment 2. All these results demonstrate the effectiveness of integrating face and gait information for human recognition using the feature level fusion scheme II since it outperforms the other fusion schemes and even achieves a larger improvement for the more challenging database. Furthermore, the results in both experiments indicate that the feature level fusion scheme II does not depend on specific features since it achieves the best fusion performance in both of cases: fusion of OSFI and GEI, and fusion of ESFI and GEI.

These results also demonstrate that the match score fusion cannot rectify the misclassification conducted by both of the face classifier and the gait classifier. For the match score fusion, people misclassified by the individual classifiers are likely to be classified correctly after fusion on the condition that there is at least one of the two classifiers that work correctly. For example, in Table 5, there are 4 misclassified people {2, 5, 8, 13} overlapped between classification using ESFI only and GEI only. From Table 6, we can see that the set of misclassified people {2, 5, 8, 13} are always a subset of the error indices when ESFI and GEI are combined by Sum and Max rules. However, the classifier using the synthetic features can rectify the misclassification conducted by both of the individual classifier. For example, the feature level fusion scheme II based on ESFI and GEI correctly recognizes the person (8) who is misclassified by both the face classifier and the gait classifier individually. It is clear that the performance of the feature level fusion mainly depends on the fused feature set while the performance of the match score level fusion mainly depends on the results of the individual biometrics classifiers. Since the fused feature set contains richer information about the input biometrics pattern than the match score, the feature level fusion is more effective than the match score level fusion when individual biometrics features are appropriately combined.

Performance Characterization Statistic Q for the Match Score Level Fusion

Although the feature level fusion methods are expected to achieve better performance than the match score level fusion methods, it is difficult to access the relationship between different feature spaces before fusion. It is one of the unsolved problems in practice for fusion at the feature level fusion. For the match score level fusion, we can use a statistic to demonstrate the potential of the performance improvement after fusion. Initiatively, if the different classifiers misclassify features for the same person, we do not expect as much improvement as in the case where they complement each other (Kinnunen et al.., 2004). There are several methods to assess the interrelationships between the classifiers in a classifier ensemble (Shipp & Kuncheva, 2002)(Brown, Wyatt, Harris, & Yao, 2005). Given classifiers i and j corresponding to feature vectors f_i and f_j from the same person, respectively, we compute Q statistic:

$$Q_{i,j} = \frac{N^{11}N^{00} - N^{01}N^{10}}{N^{11}N^{00} + N^{01}N^{10}} \qquad (36)$$

where N^{00} is the number of misclassification by both i and j; N^{11} is the number of correct classification by both i and j; N^{10} and N^{01} are the number of misclassification by i or j, but not by both. It can be easily verified that $-1 \le Q \le 1$. The Q value can be considered as a correlation measure between the classifier decisions. The best combination is the one that minimizes the value of Q statistic, which means the smaller the Q value is, the greater the potential for performance improvement by fusion.

Table 7 and 8 show the Q values in Experiment 1 and 2. N^{01} is defined as the number of people misclassified by the face classifier but correctly recognized by the gait classifier. N^{10} is defined as the number of people misclassified by the gait classifier but correctly recognized by the face classifier. The Q value based on OSFI and GEI in Experiment 2 is 1, which means the performance improvement by fusion will be zero. The experimental results in Table 6 verify it. When we compare the Q values between fusion of OSFI and GEI, and fusion of ESFI and GEI, the results show that the Q values based on ESFI and GEI are always smaller than the Q values based on OSFI and GEI in both of the experiments. It indicates that the expected performance improvement using ESFI and GEI is higher than using OSFI and GEI. For example, in Experiment 1, the Q value based on fusion of ESFI and GEI is -1 and the Q value based on fusion of OSFI and GEI is 0.1698. The maximum performance increase is 4.5% (from 93.3% to 97.8%) by fusion of ESFI and GEI, while the performance increase by fusion of OSFI and GEI is only 2.3% (from 93.3% to 95.6%). On the other hand, even though the Q value of 0.7297 for fusion performance of ESFI and GEI, are smaller than the Q value of 1 for fusion performance of OSFI and GEI in Experiment 2, it is positive and relatively high. This indicates that many times the gait classifier and the face classifier are both performing correct classification and incorrect classification for the same person. In spite of this, Sum rule and Max rule based on ESFI and GEI always achieves better performance than either of the individual classifier.

CONCLUSION

Our research work has demonstrated that the proposed video-based fusion system is effective for human identification. The fusion of face and gait is promising in real world application because of their individual characteristics. Compared

with gait, face images are readily interpretable by humans, which allows people to confirm whether a biometrics system is functioning correctly, but the appearance of a face depends on many factors: incident illumination, head pose, facial expressions, moustache/beard, eyeglasses, cosmetics, hair style, weight gain/loss, aging, and so forth. Although gait images can be easily acquired from a distance, the gait recognition is affected by clothes, shoes, carrying status and specific physical condition of an individual. The fusion system is relatively more robust compared with the system that uses only one biometrics. For example, face recognition is more sensitive to low lighting conditions, whereas gait is more reliable under these conditions. Similarly, when the walker is carrying a heavy baggage or he/she is injured, the captured face information may contribute more than gait. We believe that the integration of face and gait biometrics will be highly useful in the future.

Furthermore, the experimental results demonstrate that the feature level fusion methods achieve better performance than the match score level methods fusion overall. The representations of face and gait, ESFI and GEI, which both fuse information from multiple video frames, are promising in real-world applications. Although the video-based fusion system we have developed achieved a good performance in human recognition at a distance,

Table 7. Experiment 1: Q statistics

Fused Templates	N^{11}	N^{00}	N^{01}	N^{10}	Q Statistic
OSFI & GEI	31	1	11	2	0.1698
ESFI & GEI	38	0	4	3	-1

Table 8. Experiment 2: Q statistics

Fused Templates	N^{11}	N^{00}	N^{01}	N^{10}	Q Statistic
OSFI & GEI	29	8	8	0	1
ESFI & GEI	32	4	5	4	0.7297

we believe that some problems need to be worked on to make face- and gait- fusion system more effective and efficient in the future. We list the possible directions as follows.

- Gait recognition based on GEI is affected by the shape of human body to some extent. For gait recognition, some static features, such as the length of arms and torso, could be used to improve performance.
- For better face recognition, the camera could track the whole human body first and then zoom in to get to get face images with as high quality as possible. Moreover, other biometrics, such as ear, can be obtained and combined so that the integrated system could be used in the high security applications.
- The side face contains less information compared with the frontal face and it is sensitive to noise as well as facial expressions. Multiple cameras could be used to capture different views of a person since an integrated system based on different views could be more favorable in real-world applications.
- Currently, our database is of reasonable size with 100 video sequences of 45 people. Experiments focus on demonstrating that side face is a useful biometrics, and the integration of side face and gait can achieve promising recognition performance at a distance in video without using 3D model. It discusses the influence of changes of clothes and time. A larger database with more variety, such as variation of lighting conditions, backgrounds and head orientation, could be collected to further evaluate the performance of the fusion system.
- The construction of ESFI and GEI is time consuming compared with other processes during the implementation of the fusion system. The efficiency of these processes could be improved so that our system can operate in real time.

REFERENCES

Belhumeur, P. N., Hespanha, J. P., & Kriegman, D. J. (1997). Eigenfaces vs. fisherfaces: Recognition using class specific linear projection. *IEEE Transactions on Pattern Analysis and Machine Intelligence, 19*(7), 711–720. doi:10.1109/34.598228

Bhanu, B., & Zhou, X. (2004). Face recognition from face profile using dynamic time warping. In *Proc. int'l conf. on pattern recogntion* (Vol. 4, pp. 499-502).

Brown, G., Wyatt, J., Harris, R., & Yao, X. (2005). Diversity creation methods: A survey and categorisation. *Information Fusion, 6*(1), 5–20. doi:10.1016/j.inffus.2004.04.004

Feng, G., Dong, K., Hu, D., & Zhang, D. (2004). When faces are combined with palmprints: A novel biometric fusion strategy. In *Int'l Conf. on Biometric Authentication* (pp. 701-707).

Gao, Y., & Maggs, M. (2005). Feature-level fusion in personal identification. In *Proc. IEEE Conf. on Computer Vision and Pattern Recognition.*

Gonzalez, R. C., & Woods, R. E. (1992). *Digital image processing.* Addison Wesley Publishing Company.

Han, J., & Bhanu, B. (2005). Performance prediction for individual recognition by gait. *Pattern Reconition, 2005*(5), 615-624.

Han, J., & Bhanu, B. (2006). Individual recognition using gait energy image. *IEEE Transactions on Pattern Analysis and Machine Intelligence, 28*(2), 316–322. doi:10.1109/TPAMI.2006.38

Hewitt, P. A., & Dobberfuhl, D. (2004). The science and art of proportionality. *Science Scope,* •••, 30–31.

Horn, B. K. P. (1986). *Robot vision.* Cambridge, MA: MIT Press.

Irani, M., & Peleg, S. (1993). Motion analysis for image enhancement: Resolution, occlusion, and transparency. *Journal of Visual Communication and Image Representation, 4*, 324–335. doi:10.1006/jvci.1993.1030

Kale, A., Roy-chowdhury, A., & Chellappa, R. (2004). Fusion of gait and face for human identification. In *Proc. of Acoustics, Speech, and Signal Processing* (Vol. 5, pp. 901-904).

Kinnunen, T., Hautamaki, V., & Franti, P. (2004, September). Fusion of spectral feature sets for accurate speaker identification. In *Proc. Int'l Conf. Speech and Computer* (pp. 361-365).

Kittler, J., Hatef, M., Duin, R., & Matas, J. (1998). On combining classifiers. *IEEE Transactions on Pattern Analysis and Machine Intelligence, 20*, 226–239. doi:10.1109/34.667881

Kong, A., Zhang, D., & Kamel, M. (2006). Palmprint identification using feature-level fusion. *Pattern Recognition, 39*(3), 478–487. doi:10.1016/j.patcog.2005.08.014

Kumar, A., Wong, D. C. M., Shen, H. C., & Jain, A. K. (2003). Personal verification using palmprint and hand geometry biometric. In *Proc. Audio- and Video-based Biometric Person Authentication* (pp. 668-678).

Li, Q., & Qiu, Z. (2006). Handmetric verification based on feature-level fusion. *J. of Computer Science and Network Security, 6*(2A).

Little, J. J., & Boyd, J. E. (1998). Recognizing people by their gait: The shape of motion. *Videre: J. Computer Vision Research, 1*(2), 1–32.

Moon, Y. S., Yeung, H. W., Chan, K. C., & Chan, S. O. (2004). Template synthesis and image mosaicking for fingerprint registration: An experimental study. In *IEEE Int'l Conf. on Acoustics, Speech, and Signal Processing* (Vol. 5, pp. 409-412).

Periaswamy, S., & Farid, H. (2003). Elastic registration in the presence of intensity variations. *IEEE Transactions on Medical Imaging, 22*(7), 865–874. doi:10.1109/TMI.2003.815069

Ross, A. A., & Govindarajan, R. (2005, March). Feature level fusion of hand and face biometrics. In *Proc. Spie Conf. on Biometric Technology for Human Identification II* (pp. 196-204).

Ross, A. A., Nandakumar, K., & Jain, A. K. (2006). *Handbook of multibiometrics*. Springer.

Shakhnarovich, G., & Darrell, T. (2002). On probabilistic combination of face and gait cues for identification. In *Proc. of Automatic Face and Gesture Recognition* (Vol. 5, pp. 169-174).

Shakhnarovich, G., Lee, L., & Darrell, T. (2001). Integrated face and gait recognition from multiple views. In *Proc. of Computer Vision and Pattern Recognition* (Vol. 1, pp. 439-446).

Shipp, C. A., & Kuncheva, L. I. (2002). Relationships between combination methods and measures of diversity in combining classifiers. *Information Fusion, 3*, 135–148. doi:10.1016/S1566-2535(02)00051-9

Theodorids, S., & Koutroumbas, K. (1998). *Pattern recongnition*. Academic Press.

Yambor, W. S., Draper, B. A., & Beveridge, J. R. (2002). Analyzing PCA-based face recognition algorithms: Eigenvector selection and distance measures. In H. Christensen & J. Phillips (Eds.), *Empirical evaluation method in computer vision*. World Scientific Press.

Yang, J., Yang, J. Y., Zhang, D., & Lu, J. F. (2003). Feature fusion: Parallel strategy vs. serial strategy. *Pattern Recognition, 38*(6), 1369–1381. doi:10.1016/S0031-3203(02)00262-5

Zhou, X., & Bhanu, B. (2006). Feature fusion of face and gait for human recognition at a distance in video. In *Proc. IEEE Int'l Conf. Pattern Recognition.*

Zhou, X., & Bhanu, B. (2007, June). Integrating face and gait for human recognition at a distance in video. *IEEE Transactions on Systems, Man, and Cybernetics. Part B, Cybernetics, 37*(3).

Zhou, X., & Bhanu, B. (Manuscript submitted for publication). Feature fusion of side face and gait for video-based human identification. *Pattern Recognition.*

Zhou, X., Bhanu, B., & Han, J. (2005). Human recognition at a distance in video by integrating face profile and gait. In *Proc. Audio- and Video-based Biometric Person Authentication* (pp. 533-543).

Compilation of References

Abdelkader, C. B., Cutler, R., et al. (2002). View-invariant estimation of height and stride for gait recognition. *Proceedings of the ECCV 2002 Workshop Copenhagen on Biometric Authentication* (pp. 155-167).

Abdelkader, C. B., Cutler, R., Nanda, H., & Davis, L. (2001). Eigengait: Motion-based recognition using image self-similarity. (LNCS 2091, pp. 284–294). Berlin: Springer.

Abut, H., Hansen, J. H. L., & Takeda, K. (2005). Is our driving behavior unique? *DSP for In-Vehicle and Mobile Systems*, 257-274.

Adami, A., Mihaescu, R., Reynolds, D. A., & Godfrey, J. J. (2003). Modeling prosodic dynamics for speaker recognition. In *Proceedings of the International conference on Acoustics, Speech, and Signal Processing*.

Adler, A., & Suckers, M. E. (2007). Comparing human and automatic face recognition performance. *IEEE Transactions on Systems, Man, and Cybernetics, 37*, 1248–1255. doi:10.1109/TSMCB.2007.907036

Adler, A., Youmaran, R., & Loyka, S. (2006). *Towards a measure of biometric information*. Retrieved on August 2, 2006, from http://www.sce.carleton.ca/faculty/adler/publications/2006/youmaran-ccece2006-biometric-entropy.pdf

AdmitOne Security Inc. (2008). Retrieved in October 2008, from http://www.admitonesecurity.com/

Ahmadi1, H., Pousaberi, A., Azizzadeh, A., & Kamarei, M. (2007). *An efficient iris coding based on Gauss-Laguerre wavelets*. (LNCS 4642, pp. 917–926).

Ahmed A. A. E., & Traore I. (2003). System and method for determining a computer user profile from a motion-based input device. Priority Date 2 May 2003, PCT Filling Date 3 May 2004, PCT/CA2004/000669. USPTO Application No. 10/555408, 1 Nov 2005. CIPO Application No. 2535542, 1 Nov 2005.

Ahmed, A. A. E., & Traore, I. (2005). Anomaly intrusion detection based on biometrics. *IAW, 05*, 452–453.

Ahmed, A. A. E., & Traore, I. (2005). Detecting computer intrusions using behavioral biometrics. *Proc. of 3rd Ann. Conf. on Privacy, Security, and Trust*, Canada (pp. 91-98).

Ahmed, A. A. E., & Traore, I. (2005, June). *Anomaly intrusion detection based on biometrics*. Paper presented at the Workshop on Information Assurance, United States Military Academy, West Point, NY.

Ahmed, A. A. E., & Traore, I. (2007). A new biometric technology based on mouse dynamics. *IEEE Transactions on Dependable and Secure Computing, 4*(3), 165–179. doi:10.1109/TDSC.2007.70207

Ahn, L. v., Blum, M., & Langford, J. (2004). How lazy cryptographers do AI. *Communications of the ACM, 47*(2), 56–60. doi:10.1145/966389.966390

Ahn, L. v., Blum, M., Hopper, N., & Langford, J. (2003, May). *CAPTCHA: Using hard AI problems for security*. Paper presented at the Eurocrypt-Advances in Cryptology (pp. 294-311).

Al-Zubi, S., Brömme, A., & Tönnies, K. (2003, September 10-12). *Using an active shape structural model for biometric sketch recognition.* Paper presented at the DAGM, Magdeburg, Germany (pp. 187-195).

Anderson, J. P. (1980). *Computer security threat monitoring and surveillance.* Fort Washington, PA: James P. Anderson Company.

Andrea, C. (2001). Dynamic time warping for offline recognition of a small gesture vocabulary. *International Conference on Recognition, Analysis and Tracking of Faces and Gestures in Real-Time Systems* (pp. 82-89).

Andreone, L., Antonello, P., Bertozzi, M., Broggi, A., Fascioli, A., & Ranzato, D. (2002). Vehicle detection and localization in infrared images. *Proc. IEEE International Conference on Intelligent Transportation Systems* (pp. 141-146).

Andrews, W. D., Kohler, M. A., & Campbell, J. P. (2001). Phonetic speaker recognition. In *Proceedings of the Eurospeech* (pp. 2517-2520).

Andrews, W. D., Kohler, M. A., Campbell, J. P., & Godfrey, J. J. (2001). Phonetic, idiolectal, and acoustic speaker recognition. In A *Speaker Odyssey-The Speaker Recognition Workshop.* ISCA.

Angle, S., Bhagtani, R., & Chheda, H. (2005, March 27-30). *Biometrics: A further echelon of security.* Paper presented at the First UAE International Conference on Biological and Medical Physics.

Apap, F., Honig, A., Hershkop, S., Eskin, E., & Stolfo, S. (2002). *Detecting malicious software by monitoring anomalous windows registry accesses.* Paper presented at the Fifth International Symposium on Recent Advances in Intrusion Detection (pp. 16-18).

Arlowe, H. (1992). Thermal detection contrast of human targets. *Proc. IEEE International Carnahan Conference on Security Technology* (pp. 27-33).

Ashbourn, J. (2000). *Biometrics: Advanced identity verification: The complete guide.* London: Springer.

Auckenthaler, R., Carey, M., & Lloyd-Thomas, H. (2000). Score normalization for text-independent speaker verification systems. *Digital Signal Processing, 10,* 42–54. doi:10.1006/dspr.1999.0360

Australian Biometrics Institute. (2008). *Biometric vulnerability: A principled assessment methodology.* White paper.

Australian Defence Signals Directorate. (2003). *EAL2 certification report for Iridian technologies KnoWho authentication server and private ID.* Certification Report 2003/31.

Awad, A., & Traore, I. (2005). Detecting computer intrusions using behavioral biometrics. *3rd Annual Conference on Privacy, Security, and Trust,* St. Andrews, New Brunswick, Canada (pp. 91-98).

Badizadegan, M. (1999). *Texas hold'em flop types.* Los Angeles, CA: Goldstar Books.

Baggenstoss, P. M. (2004, January). *Class-specific classifier: Avoiding the curse of dimensionality.* Paper presented at the Aerospace and Electronic Systems Magazine (pp. 37-52).

Ballard, L., Lopresti, D., & Monrose, F. (2006, October). *Evaluating the security of handwriting biometrics.* Paper presented at the 10th International Workshop on Frontiers in Handwriting Recognition (IWFHR06), La Baule, France (pp. 461-466).

Ballard, L., Monrose, F., & Lopresti, D. P. (2006, July-August). *Biometric authentication revisited: Understanding the impact of wolves in sheep's clothing.* Paper presented at the Fifteenth USENIX Security Symposium, Vancouver, BC, Canada.

Banikazemi, M., Poff, D., & Abali, B. (2005, April 11-14). *Storage-based intrusion detection for storage area networks (SANs).* Paper presented at the 22nd IEEE/13th NASA Goddard Conference on Mass Storage Systems and Technologies (pp. 118- 127).

Barone, L., & While, L. (1998). *Evolving computer opponents to play a game of simplified poker.* Paper presented at the International Conference on Evolutionary Computation (ICEC'98) (pp. 108-113).

Barone, L., & While, L. (1999). *An adaptive learning model for simplified poker using evolutionary algorithms.* Paper presented at the Congress of Evolutionary Computation (GECCO-1999) (pp. 153-160).

Barone, L., & While, L. (1999). *Evolving adaptive play for simplified poker.* Paper presented at the IEE International Conference on Computational Intelligence (ICEC-98) (pp. 108-113).

Barras, C., & Gauvain, J. L. (2003). Feature and score normalization for speaker verification of cellular data. In *Proceedings of the International conference on Acoustics, Speech, and Signal Processing* (Vol. 2).

Barrios-Aranibar, D., & Alsina, P. J. (2005, December 6-9). *Recognizing behaviors patterns in a microrobot soccer game.* Paper presented at the Fifth international Conference on Hybrid Intelligent Systems, Washington, D.C.

Barse, E. L., Kvarnström, H., & Jonsson, E. (2003, December 8-12). *Synthesizing test data for fraud detection systems.* Paper presented at the 19th Annual Computer Security Applications Conference (ACSAC 2003), Las Vegas, NV.

Bartlett, J. C., & Searcy, J. (1993). Inversion and configuration of faces. *Cognitive Psychology, 25,* 281–316. doi:10.1006/cogp.1993.1007

Bartolacci, G., Curtin, M., Katzenberg, M., Nwana, N., Cha, S.-H., & Tappert, C. C. (2005). *Long-text keystroke biometric applications over the Internet.* Paper presented at the MLMTA (pp. 119-126).

Bazin, A. I., Middleton, L., & Nixon, M. S. (2005). Probabilistic fusion of gait features for biometric verification. In *. Proceedings of International Conference on Information Fusion, 2,* 1211–1217.

Beauchamp, M. S., Lee, K. E., Haxby, J. V., & Martin, A. (2002). Parallel visual motrion processing streams for manipulable objects and human movements. *Neuron, 34,* 149–159. doi:10.1016/S0896-6273(02)00642-6

Belardinelli, A., Pirri, F., & Carbone, A. (2007). Bottom-up gaze shifts and fixations learning by imitation. *IEEE Transactions on Systems, Man, and Cybernetics . Part B, 37*(2), 256–271.

Belhumeur, P. N., Hespanha, J. P., & Kriegman, D. J. (1997). Eigenfaces vs. fisherfaces: Recognition using class specific linear projection. *IEEE Transactions on Pattern Analysis and Machine Intelligence, 19*(7), 711–720. doi:10.1109/34.598228

Bella, S. D., & Palmer, C. (2006). Personal identifiers in musicians' finger movement dynamics. *Journal of Cognitive Neuroscience, 18.*

Ben, C., Kader, A. & Davis, L. S. (2002). Detection of people carrying objects: A motion-based recognition approach. *FG'02,* 378-383.

BenAbdelkader, C., Cutler, R. G., & Davis, L. S. (2004). Gait recognition using image self-similarity. *EURASIP Journal on Applied Signal Processing, 4,* 1–14.

BenAbdelkader, C., Cutler, R., & Davis, L. (2002). *Person identification using automatic height and stride estimation.* Paper presented at the IEEE International Conference on Pattern Recognition.

BenAbdelkader, C., Davis, L. S., & Cutler, R. (2002). Stride and cadence as a biometric in automatic person identification and verification. In *Proceedings of the Fifth IEEE International Conference on Automatic Face and Gesture Recognition* (pp. 372-377).

Bender, S. S. & Postley, H. J. (2007). *Key sequence rhythm recognition system and method.* U.S. Patent 7,206,938.

Bengio, S., Marcel, C., Marcel, S., & Mariethoz, J. (2002). Confidence measures for multimodal identity verification. *Information Fusion, 3,* 267–276. doi:10.1016/S1566-2535(02)00089-1

Bensefia, A., Paquet, T., & Heutte, L. (2005). A writer identification and verification system. *Pattern Recognition Letters*, 26(13, 2080–2092. doi:10.1016/j.patrec.2005.03.024

Bensefia, A., Paquet, T., & Heutte, L. (2005). Handwritten document analysis for automatic writer recognition. *Electronic Letters on Computer Vision and Image Analysis*, 5(2), 72–86.

Ben-Yacoub, S., Abdeljaoued, Y., & Mayoraz, E. (1999). Fusion of face and speech data for person identity verification. *IEEE Transactions on Neural Networks*, 10(5), 1065–1074. doi:10.1109/72.788647

Bergadano, F., Gunetti, D., & Picardi, C. (2002). User authentication through keystroke dynamics. *ACM Transactions on Information and System Security*, 5(4), 367–397. doi:10.1145/581271.581272

Berger, H. (1929). Über das Elektroenkephalogram des Menschen . *Arch. f. Psychiat.*, 87, 527–570.

Betkowska, A., Shinoda, K., & Furui, S. (2006). FHMM for robust speech recognition in home environment. In *Proceedings of Symposium on Large-Scale Knowledge Resources* (pp. 129-132).

Beveridge, J. R., She, K., Draper, B. A., & Givens, G. H. (2001). Parametric and nonparametric methods for the statistical evaluation of human ID algorithms. In *Proceedings of the Third Workshop on Empirical Evaluation Methods in Computer Vision* (pp. 535-542).

Bhanu, B., & Han, J. (2002). Individual recognition by kinematic-based gait analysis. In *Proceedings of ICPR02*, 3, 343–346.

Bhanu, B., & Han, J. (2002). Kinematic-based motion analysis in infrared sequences. *Proc. IEEE Workshop on Applications of Computer Vision* (pp. 208-212).

Bhanu, B., & Zhou, X. (2004). Face recognition from face profile using dynamic time warping. In *Proc. int'l conf. on pattern recogntion* (Vol. 4, pp. 499-502).

Bhatkar, S., Chaturvedi, A., & Sekar, R. (2006, May). *Dataflow anomaly detection.* Paper presented at the IEEE Symposium on Security and Privacy.

Bicego, M., Castellani, U., & Murino, V. (2003). Using hidden Markov models and wavelets for face recognition. In *IEEE. Proc. of Int. Conf on Image Analysis and Processing* (pp. 52–56).

Bicego, M., Grosso, E., & Tistarelli, M. (2005). Probabilistic face authentication using hidden Markov models. *Proc. of SPIE Int. Workshop on Biometric Technology for Human Identification.*

Biel, L., Pettersson, O., Philipson, L., & Wide, P. (2001). ECG analysis: A new approach in human identification. *IEEE Transactions on Instrumentation and Measurement*, 50(3), 808–812. doi:10.1109/19.930458

Billings, D., Burch, N., Davidson, A., Holte, R., Schaeffer, J., Schauenberg, T., et al. (2003). *Approximating game-theoretic optimal strategies for full-scale poker.* Paper presented at the IJCAI-03.

Billings, D., Papp, D., Schaeffer, J., & Szafron, D. (1998). *Opponent modeling in poker.* Paper presented at the 15th National Conference on Artificial Intelligence (AAAI-98), Madison, WI (pp. 493-498).

Billings, D., Papp, D., Schaeffer, J., & Szafron, D. (1998). *Poker as testbed for AI research.* Paper presented at the 12th Biennial Conference of the Canadian Society for Computational Studies of Intelligence on Advances in Artificial Intelligence, London, UK (pp. 228-238).

Billings, D., Pena, L., Schaeffer, J., & Szafron, D. (1999). *Using probabilistic knowledge and simulation to play poker.* Paper presented at the In AAAI/IAAI (pp. 697-703).

Billings, D., Pena, L., Schaeffer, J., & Szafron, D. (2001). *Learning to play strong poker.* Paper presented at the Machines that Learn to Play Games, Commack, NY (pp. 225-242).

Bimbot, F., Bonastre, J. F., Fredouille, C., Gravier, G., Magrin-Chagnolleau, I., & Meignier, S. (2004). A tutorial on text-independent speaker verification. *EURASIP Journal on Applied Signal Processing*, (4), 430–451. doi:10.1155/S1110865704310024

Bin, L., & Hancock, E. R. (1999). Matching point-sets using procrustes alignment and the EM algorithm. *Proc. of BMV99*, Manchester, UK.

BioApi Consortium. (2005). Retrieved from http://www.bioapi.org/

BioChec. (2008). Retrieved in October 2008, from http://www.biochec.com/

Bioprivacy.org. (2005a). *FAQ. BioPrivacy Initiative.* Retrieved on July 22, 2005, from http://www.bioprivacy.org/faqmain.htm

Bioprivacy.org. (2005b). *FAQ's and definitions.* International Biometric Group, LLC. Retrieved on October 2, 2005, from http://www.bioprivacy.org/bioprivacy_text.htm

Birbaumer, N., Ghanayim, N., Hinterberger, T., Iversen, I., Kotchoubey, B., & Kubler, A. (1999). A spelling device for the paralysed. *Nature, 398*, 297–298. doi:10.1038/18581

Bobick, A. F., & Davis, J. W. (2001). The recognition of human movement using temporal templates. *IEEE Transactions on Pattern Analysis and Machine Intelligence, 23*(3), 257–267. doi:10.1109/34.910878

Bobick, A. F., & Johnson, A. Y. (2001). Gait recognition using static, activity specific parameters. *Proceedings of the IEEE Conference on Computer Vision and Pattern Recognition, CVPR* (pp. 423-430).

Boles, W. W., & Boashash, B. (1998). A human identification technique using images of the iris and wavelet transform. *IEEE Trans. SP, 46*(4), 1185–1188. doi:10.1109/78.668573

Bolle, R., Connell, J., Pankanti, S., Ratha, N., & Senior, A. (2004). *Guide to biometrics.* New York: Springer.

Bouchrika, I., & Nixon, M. (2008). Exploratory factor analysis of gait recognition. In *Proc. of the 8ᵗʰ IEEE International Conference on Automatic Face and Gesture Recognition.*

Boulgouris, N. V., & Chi, Z. X. (2007). Gait recognition using radon transform and linear discriminant analysis. *IEEE Transactions on Image Processing, 16*, 731–740. doi:10.1109/TIP.2007.891157

Boulgouris, N. V., Hatzinakos, D., & Plataniotis, K. N. (2005). Gait recognition: A challenging signal processing technology for biometric identification. *IEEE Signal Processing Magazine, 22*, 78–90. doi:10.1109/MSP.2005.1550191

Boutsidis, C., Gallopoulos, E., Zhang, P., & Plemmons, R. J. (2006). PALSIR: A new approach to nonnegative tensor factorization. In *Proc. of the 2ⁿᵈ Workshop on Algorithms for Modern Massive Datasets (MMDS).*

Boyd, J. E. (2004). Synchronization of oscillations for machine perception of gaits. *Computer Vision and Image Understanding, 96*, 35–59. doi:10.1016/j.cviu.2004.04.004

Boyd-Graber, J. (2006). *Semantic poetry creation using lexicographic and natural language texts.* Retrieved on July 2, 2006, from http://www.cs.princeton.edu/~jbg/documents/poetry.pdf

Braithwaite, R., & Bhanu, B. (1994). Hierarchical Gabor filters for object detection in infrared images. *IEEE Conf. Com. Vision Pattern Recognition*, 628–631.

Brandt, K. (2005). *Player profiling in texas holdem.* Retrieved on May 29, 2005, from http://www.soe.ucsc.edu/~kbrandt/pubs/prof.pdf

Braun, J., & Sagi, D. (1990, July). Vision outside the focus of attention. *Perception & Psychophysics, 48*(1), 45–58.

Brause, R., Langsdorf, T., & Hepp, M. (1999). *Neural data mining for credit card fraud detection.* Paper presented at the 11ᵗʰ IEEE International Conference on Tools with Artificial Intelligence (pp. 103-106).

Bregler, C., & Konig, Y. (1994, April). "Eigenlips" for robust speech recognition. In . *Proceedings of the IEEE International Conference on Acoustics, Speech, and Signal Processing, 2*, 669–672.

Broadbent, D. E. (1958). *Perception and communication.* London: Pergamon.

Broadbent, D. E. (1977). The hidden preattentive process. *The American Psychologist, 32,* 109–118. doi:10.1037/0003-066X.32.2.109

Bromme, A. (2003, July 6-9). *A classification of biometric signatures.* Paper presented at the International Conference on Multimedia and Expo (ICME '03) (pp. 17-20).

Brömme, A., & Al-Zubi, S. (2003, July 24). *Multifactor biometric sketch authentication.* Paper presented at the BIOSIG, Darmstadt, Germany (pp. 81-90).

Broun, C. C., Zhang, X., Mersereau, R. M., & Clements, M. A. (2002). Automatic speechreading with applications to speaker verification. *ICASSP '02, 1,* 685-688.

Brown, G., Wyatt, J., Harris, R., & Yao, X. (2005). Diversity creation methods: A survey and categorisation. *Information Fusion, 6*(1), 5–20. doi:10.1016/j.inffus.2004.04.004

Brown, M., & Rogers, S. J. (1993). User identification via keystroke characteristics of typed names using neural networks. *International Journal of Man-Machine Studies, 39*(6), 999–1014. doi:10.1006/imms.1993.1092

Bruce, V., Hancock, P., & Burton, A. (1998). *Human face perception and identification.* In Wechsler, Philips, Bruce, Fogelman-Soulie & Huang (Eds.), *Face recognition: From theory to applications* (pp. 51-72). Springer-Verlag.

Brummer, N. (2005). Tools for fusion and calibration of automatic speaker detection systems. Retrieved from http://www.dsp.sun.ac.za/.nbrummer/focal/index.htm

Brunelli, R., & Falavigna, D. (1995). Person identification using multiple clues. *IEEE Transactions on Pattern Analysis and Machine Intelligence, 17*(10), 955–966. doi:10.1109/34.464560

Bulacu, M., & Schomaker, L. (2007). Text-independent writer identification and verification using textural and allographic features. *IEEE Trans. on Pattern Analysis and Machine Intelligence, Special Issue-Biometrics . Progress and Directions, 29*(4), 701–717.

Bulacu, M., Schomaker, L., & Vuurpijl, L. (2003). Writer identification using edge-based directional features. *Proc. Seventh International Conference on Document Analysis and Recognition,* 937–941. CASIA Handwriting Database. Retrieved from http://www.cbsr.ia.ac.cn/english/Handwriting Databases.asp

Cacioppo, J. T., Berntson, G. G., Larsen, J. T., & Poehlmann, K. M. (2000). The psychophysiology of emotion. In M. Lewis & J. M. Haviland-Jones (Eds.), *The handbook of emotion,* 2nd edition (pp. 173-191). New York: Guilford Press.

Cahill, M., Lambert, D., Pinheiro, J., & Sun, D. (2000). *Detecting fraud in the real world.* (Tech. Rep.). Bell Labs, Lucent Technologies.

Campbell, F. W., & Robson, J. G. (1968). Application of Fourier analysis to the visibility of gratings. *The Journal of Physiology, 197,* 551–566.

Campbell, J. P. (1997). Speaker recognition: A tutorial. *Proceedings of the IEEE, 85*(9), 1437–1462. doi:10.1109/5.628714

Campbell, J. P., Jr. (1995). Testing with the YOHO CD-ROM voice verification corpus. In *Proceedings of the International conference on Acoustics, Speech, and Signal Processing, 1.*

Campbell, J. P., Reynolds, D. A., & Dunn, R. B. (2003). Fusing high-and low-level features for speaker recognition. In *Proceedings of the Eighth European Conference on Speech Communication and Technology.*

Campbell, W. M., Campbell, J. P., Reynolds, D. A., Jones, D. A., & Leek, T. R. (2004). Phonetic speaker recognition with support vector machines. *Advances in Neural Information Processing Systems, 16,* 57.

Campbell, W. M., Reynolds, D. A., Campbell, J. P., & Brady, K. J. (2005). Estimating and evaluating confidence for forensic speaker recognition. In *Proceedings of the International conference on Acoustics, Speech, and Signal Processing*

Campbell, W. M., Sturim, D. E., & Reynolds, D. A. (2006). Support vector machines using GMM supervectors for speaker verification. *IEEE Signal Processing Letters, 13*(5), 308. doi:10.1109/LSP.2006.870086

Campos, T. E., Feris, R. S., & Cesar, R. M. Jr. (2000, April). Eigenfaces vs. eigeneyes: First steps toward performance assessment of representarions for face recognition. ([]. Springer-Verlag Press.]. *LNAI, 1793,* 197–206.

Canadian Communications Security Establishment. (2001). *EAL2 certification report for Bioscrypt^{TM} Enterprise for NT logon version 2.1.3.* Certification Report 383-4-8.

Canny, J. (1986). A computational approach to edge detection. *IEEE Trans. Pattern Analysis and. Machine Intelligence (PAM)I, 8*(6), 679-698.

Cappelli, R., Maio, D., & Maltoni, D. (2002). Synthetic fingerprint-database generation. *16th International Conference on Pattern Recognition (ICPR), 3.*

Cappelli, R., Maio, D., Maltoni, D., Wayman, J. L., & Jain, A. K. (2006). Performance evaluation of fingerprint verification systems. *IEEE Transactions on Pattern Analysis and Machine Intelligence, 28*(1), 3–18. doi:10.1109/TPAMI.2006.20

Caslon.com.au. (2005). *Caslon-analytics.* Retrieved on October 2, 2005, from http://www.caslon.com.au/biometricsnote8.htm

Cattin, P. C., Zlatnik, D., et al. (2001). Biometric system using human gait. *Proc. of Mechatronics and Machine Vision in Practice (M2VIP),* Hong Kong.

Cha, S., & Srihari, S. N. (2000). Writer identification: Statistical analysis and dichotomizer. *Proc. SPR and SSPR 2000, LNCS - Advances in Pattern Recognition, 1876,* 123-132.

Chan, A., Lau, R. W. H., & Si, A. (2001). A motion prediction method for mouse-based navigation. *Proc. IEEE Computer Graphics International 2001 (CGI'01)* (pp. 139-146).

Chang, C. K. (2005). *Human identification using one lead ECG.* M.S. thesis, Department of Computer Science and Information Engineering, Chaoyang University of Technology, Taiwan.

Chang, K., Bowyer, K. W., Sarkar, S., & Victor, B. (2003). Comparison and combination of ear and face images in appearance-based biometrics. *IEEE Trans. PAMI, 25*(9), 1160–1165.

Chang, Y. C., Zhang, W., & Chen, T. (2004). Biometric-based cryptographic key generation. *IEEE Conference on Multimedia and Expo 2004,* Taiwan.

Chatzis, V., Bors, A. G., & Pitas, I. (1999). Multimodal decision-level fusion for person authentication *IEEE Transactions on System, Man . Cybernetics A, 29*(6), 674–680.

Che, C., Lin, Q., & Yuk, D. (1996). An HMM approach to text-prompted speaker verification. In *Proceedings of the International conference on Acoustics, Speech, and Signal Processing*

Chen, C., Veldhuis, R. N. J., Kevenaar, T. A. M., & Akkermans, A. H. M. (2007, September 27-29). Multibits biometric string generation based on the likelihood ratio. *IEEE Conference on Biometrics: Theory, Applications and Systems,* Washington, D.C. (pp. 1-6).

Chen, Y., Dass, S. C., & Jain, A. K. (2006). Localized iris image quality using 2-D wavelets. (. *LNCS, 3832,* 373–381.

Cheng, M., Ho, M., et al. (2007). Gait analysis for human identification through manifold learning and HMM. *Proc. of IEEE Workshop on Motion and Video Computing (WMVC'07).*

Chinchani, R., Muthukrishnan, A., Chandrasekaran, M., & Upadhyaya, S. (2004, December 6-10). *RACOON: Rapidly generating user command data for anomaly detection from customizable templates.* Paper presented at the 0th Annual Computer Security Applications Conference, Tucson, AZ.

Choi, E., Hyun, D., & Lee, C. (2002). Optimizing feature extraction for English word recognition. In *Proceedings of the International conference on Acoustics, Speech, and Signal Processing.*

Choi, S.-S., Yoon, S., Cha, S.-H., & Tappert, C. C. (2004). Use of histogram distances in iris authentication. *Proc. MSCE-MLMTA,* Las Vegas. (LNCS Image Analysis and Recognition, pp. 1118-1124). New York: Springer.

Cichocki, A., Zdunek, R., Plemmons, R., & Amari, S. (2007). Novel multilayer nonnegative tensor factorization with sparsity constraints. (. *LNCS, 4432,* 271–280.

Ciota, Z. (2004). Speaker verification for multimedia application. *IEEE Int. Conf. SMC, 3,* 2752–2756.

Clark, A. F., & Clark, C. (n.d.). *Performance characterization in computer vision: A tutorial.* Retrieved from http://peipa.essex.ac.uk/benchmark/tutorials/essex/tutorial.pdf

Clark, M., Bovik, A. C., & Geisler, W. S. (1987). Texture segmentation using Gabor modulation/ demodulation. *Pattern Recognition Letters, 6,* 261–267. doi:10.1016/0167-8655(87)90086-9

Clarke, N. L., & Furnell, S. M. (2007). Advanced user authentication for mobile devices. *Computers & Security, 26,* 109–119. doi:10.1016/j.cose.2006.08.008

Clynes, D. M. (1977). *Sentics: The touch of the emotions.* Anchor Press/Doubleday.

Coetzer, J., Herbst, B. M., & du Preez, J. A. (2004). Offline signature verification using the discrete radon transform and a hidden Markov model. *EURASIP Journal on Applied Signal Processing, 4,* 559–571. doi:10.1155/S1110865704309042

Cohen, H. (1988). *How to draw three people in a botanical garden.* Retrieved from http://crca.ucsd.edu/~hcohen/cohenpdf/how2draw3people.pdf

Collins, R., Gross, R., & Shi, J. (2002). Silhouette-based human identification from body shape and gait. *Proc. IEEE Intl. Conf. on Automatic Face and Gesture Recognition* (pp. 351-356).

Colombi, J., Ruck, D., Rogers, S., Oxley, M., & Anderson, T. (1996). *Cohort selection and word grammar effects for speaker recognition.* Paper presented at the IEEE International Conference on Acoustics, Speech, and Signal Processing, Atlanta, GA (pp. 85-88).

Common Criteria Biometric Evaluation Methodology Working Group. (2002). *Biometric evaluation methodology.* Version 1.0.

Conway, A. R. A., Cowan, N., & Bunting, M. F. (2001). The cocktail party phenomenon revisited: The importance of working memory capacity. *Psychonomic Bulletin & Review, 8,* 331–335.

Cootes, T. F., Taylor, C. J., Cooper, D. H., & Graham, J. (1995). Active shape model-their training and application. *Computer Vision Graphics and Image Understanding, 61,* 38–59. doi:10.1006/cviu.1995.1004

Cope, D. (2001). *Virtual music: Computer synthesis of musical style.* Cambridge, MA: The MIT Press.

Crane, H. (1994). The purkinje image eyetracker, image stabilization, and related forms of stimulus manipulation. In D. Kelly (Ed.), *Visual science and engineering: Models and applications* (pp. 13–89). New York: Marcel Dekker, Inc.

Crompton, M. (2003). *Biometrics and privacy: The end of the world as we know it or the white knight of privacy?* Paper presented at the 1st Biometrics Institute Conference.

Crowley, J. (1997). Vision for man-machine interaction. *Robotics and Autonomous Systems, 19,* 347–358. doi:10.1016/S0921-8890(96)00061-9

Cunado, D., & Nixon, M. S. (2003). Automatic extraction and description of human gait models for recognition purposes. *Computer Vision and Image Understanding, 90*(1), 1–41. doi:10.1016/S1077-3142(03)00008-0

Cunado, D., Nash, J. M., Nixon, M. S., & Carter, J. N. (1999). Gait extraction and description by evidence-gathering. In . *Proceedings of, AVBPA99*, 43–48.

Curtin, M., Tappert, C., Villani, M., Ngo, G., Simone, J., St. Fort, H., & Cha, S.-H. (2006). Keystroke biometric recognition on long-text input: A feasibility study. *Proc. Int. MultiConf. Engineers & Computer Scientists (IMECS)*, Hong Kong.

Cutler, R., & Davis, L. (2000). Robust real-time periodic motion detection, analysis, and applications. *IEEE Transactions on Pattern Analysis and Machine Intelligence, 22*(8), 781–796. doi:10.1109/34.868681

Cutting, J., & Kozlowski, L. (1977). Recognizing friends by their walk: Gait perception without familiarity cues. *Bulletin of the Psychonomic Society, 9*, 353–356.

Cutting, J., Prott, D., & Kozlowski, L. (1978). A biomechanical invariant for gait perception. *Journal of Experimental Psychology. Human Perception and Performance, 4*(3), 357–372. doi:10.1037/0096-1523.4.3.357

Cyberloonies.com. (2006). *Texas holdem poker. Cyber loonies.* Retrieved in May 2006, from http://cyberloonies.com/poker.html

Dahel, S. K., & Xiao, Q. (2003, June 18-20). *Accuracy performance analysis of multimodal biometrics.* Paper presented at the IEEE Information Assurance Workshop on Systems, Man, and Cybernetics Society (pp. 170-173).

Dailey, M. N., Cottrell, G. W., Padgett, C., & Adolphs, R. (2002). EMPATH: A neural network that categorizes facial expressions. *Journal of Cognitive Neuroscience, 14*(8), 1158–1173. doi:10.1162/089892902760807177

Dao, V., & Vemuri, V. (2000, December 11-15). *Profiling users in the UNIX OS environment.* Paper presented at the International ICSC Conference on Intelligent Systems and Applications, University of Wollongong Australia.

Darwin, C. (1859). *On the origin of species by means of natural selection, or the preservation of favoured races in the struggle for life.* London: John Murray, 1st edition.

Das, S. R., Wilson, R. C., Lazarewicz, M. T., & Finkel, L. H. (2006). Two-stage PCA extracts spatiotemporal features for gait recognition. *Journal of Multimedia, 1*(5), 9–17.

Daubechies, I. (1992). Ten lectures on wavelets. *61 of CBMS-NSF Regional Conference Series in Applied Mathematics.*

Daugman, J. (2003). The important of being random: Statistical principles of iris recognition. *Pattern Recognition, 36*, 279–291. doi:10.1016/S0031-3203(02)00030-4

Daugman, J. G. (1980). Two-dimensional spectral analysis of cortical receptive field profiles. *Vision Research, 20*, 847–856. doi:10.1016/0042-6989(80)90065-6

Daugman, J. G. (1985). Uncertainty relation for resolution in space, spatial frequency, and orientation optimized by two-dimensional visual cortical filters. *Journal of the Optical Society of America, 2*(7), 1160–1169. doi:10.1364/JOSAA.2.001160

Daugman, J. G. (1988). Complete discrete 2-D Gabor transforms by neural networks for image analysis and compression. *IEEE Trans. ASSP, 36*(7), 1169–1179. doi:10.1109/29.1644

Daugman, J. G. (1993). High confidence visual recognition of persons by a test of statistical independence. *IEEE Trans. PAMI, 15*, 1148–1161.

Daugman, J. G. (1993). Quadrature-phase simple-cell pairs are appropriately described in complex analytic form. *Journal of the Optical Society of America, 10*(7), 375–377.

Daugman, J. G. (2003). Demodulation by complex-valued wavelets for stochastic pattern recognition. *International Journal of Wavelets, Multresolution, and Information Processing, 1*(1), 1–17. doi:10.1142/S0219691303000025

Daugman, J. G. (2006). Probing the uniqueness and randomness of iris codes: Results from 200 billion iris pair comparisons. *Proceedings of the IEEE, 94*(11), 1927–1935. doi:10.1109/JPROC.2006.884092

Daugman, J. G., & Downing, C. J. (1995). Demodulation, predictive coding, and spatial vision. *Journal of the Optical Society of America, 12*, 641–660. doi:10.1364/JOSAA.12.000641

Daugman, J. G., & Downing, C. J. (2001). Epigenetic randomness, complexity, and singularity of human iris patterns. *Proceedings of the Royal Society of London, 268*, 1737–1740. doi:10.1098/rspb.2001.1696

Davida, G., Frankel, Y., Matt, B. J., & Peralta, R. (1999, January). On the relation of error correction and cryptography to an offline biometric based on identification scheme. *Workshop on Coding and Cryptography (WCC)*.

Davidson, A. (2005). *Using artificial neural networks to model opponents in Texas hold'em*. Retrieved on May 25, 2005, from http://citeseer.ist.psu.edu/460830.html

Davidson, A., Billings, D., Schaeffer, J., & Szafron, D. (2000). *Improved opponent modeling in poker*. Paper presented at the International Conference on Artificial Intelligence (ICAI'2000) Las Vegas, NV (pp. 1467-1473).

Davis, J. (2004). Sequential reliable-inference for rapid detection of human actions. *Proc. Conference on Computer Vision and Pattern Recognition* (pp. 111-118).

Davis, J. W., & Bobick, A. F. (1997). The representation and recognition of action using temporal templates. In *Proceedings of the IEEE Computer Society Conference on Computer Vision and Pattern Recognition* (pp. 928-934).

Davis, J. W., & Gao, H. (2004). *Gender recognition from walking movements using adaptive three-mode PCA*. Washington, D.C.: IEEE Computer Society.

Davis, S., & Mermelstein, P. (1980). Comparison of parametric representations for monosyllabic word recognition in continuously spoken sentences. *IEEE Transactions on Acoustics, Speech, and Signal Processing, 28*(4), 357–366. doi:10.1109/TASSP.1980.1163420

De Lathauwer, L., De Moor, B., & Vandewalle, J. (2000). A multilinear singular value decomposition. *SIAM Journal on Matrix Analysis and Applications, 21*(4).

Debar, H., Dacier, M., Wespi, A., & Lampart, S. (1998). *An experimentation workbench for intrusion detection systems* (No. RZ2998). IBM Research Report

Delac, K., & Grgic, M. (2004, June 16-18). *A survey of biometric recognition methods*. Paper presented at the 46th International Symposium Electronics in Marine, ELMAR-2004, Zadar, Croatia (pp. 184-193).

Democraticmedia.org. (2001). *TV that watches you: The prying eyes of interactive television. A report by the Center for Digital Democracy*. Retrieved June 11, 2001, from www.democraticmedia.org/privacyreport.pdf

Dempster, A. P., Laird, N. M., & Rubin, D. B. (1977). Maximum likelihood from incomplete data via the EM algorithm. *Journal of the Royal Statistical Society. Series B. Methodological, 39*(1), 1–38.

Deng, P. S., Liao, H. Y. M., Chin, W. H., & Tyan, H. R. (1999). Wavelet-based offline signature verification. *Computer Vision and Image Understanding, 76*, 173–190. doi:10.1006/cviu.1999.0799

Denning, D. E. (1987). An intrusion-detection model. *IEEE Transactions on Software Engineering, 13*(2), 222–232. doi:10.1109/TSE.1987.232894

Deshpande, S., Chikkerur, S., & Govindaraju, V. (2005, October 17-18). *Accent classification in speech*. Paper presented at the Fourth IEEE Workshop on Automatic Identification Advanced Technologies (pp. 139-143).

Deutsch, J., & Deutsch, D. (1963). Attention: Some theoretical considerations. *Psychological Review, 70*, 80–90. doi:10.1037/h0039515

DeValois, R. L., & DeValois, K. K. (1988). *Spatial vision.* New York: Oxford Univ. Press.

DeValois, R. L., Yund, E. W., & Hepler, N. (1982). The orientation and direction selectivity of cells in macaque visual cortex. *Vision Research, 22*, 531–544. doi:10.1016/0042-6989(82)90112-2

Doddington, G. R., Przybocki, M. A., Martin, A. F., & Reynolds, D. A. (2000). The NIST speaker recognition evaluation-overview, methodology, systems, results, perspective. *Speech Communication, 31*, 225–254. doi:10.1016/S0167-6393(99)00080-1

Doddington, G., Liggett, W., Martin, A., Przybocki, M., & Reynolds, D. (1998). Sheep, goats, lambs, and wolves: A statistical analysis of speaker performance in the NIST 1998 speaker recognition evaluation. In *International Conference on Spoken Language Processing*, Sydney, Australia.

Donato, G., Bartlett, M. S., Hager, J. C., Ekman, P., & Sejnowski, T. J. (1999). Classifying facial actions. *IEEE Trans. PAMI, 21*(10), 974–989.

Draft European Standard prEN 14890-1. (2007). *Application interface for smart cards used as secure signature creation devices–part 1: Basic services.*

Drahansky, M. (2008, August). Experiments with skin resistance and temperature for liveness detection. In *Proceedings of the International Conference on Intelligent Information Hiding and Multimedia Signal Processing* (pp. 1075–1079).

Duchowski, A. (2003). *Eye tracking methodology: Theory and practice.* London: Springer.

Duda, R. O., Hart, P. E., & Stork, D. G. (2001). *Pattern classification.* New York: Wiley.

Duda, R., Hart, P., & Stork, D. (2000). *Pattern classification.* John Wiley & Sons.

Dugelay, J.-L., Junqua, J.-C., Kotropoulos, C., Kuhn, R., Perronnin, F., & Pitas, I. (2002, May). *Recent advances in biometric person authentication.* Paper presented at the IEEE Int. Conf. on Acoustics Speech and Signal Processing (ICASSP), Special Session on Biometrics, Orlando, FL.

Dunn, G., & Everitt, B. S. (2004). *An introduction to mathematical taxonomy.* Dover.

Dusan, S. (2005). Estimation of speaker's height and vocal tract length from speech signal. In *Proceedings of INTERSPEECH.*

Ekinci, M., Aykut, M., & Gedikli, E. (2007). Gait recognition by applying multiple projections and kernel PCA. In *Proceedings of MLDM 2007* (LNAI 4571, pp. 727–741.

Electroencephalography. (n.d.). Retrieved on August 1, 2008, from http://butler.cc.tut.fi/~malmivuo/bembook/13/13.html

Elgammal, A., & Lee, C. S. (2004). Separating style and content on a nonlinear manifold. In . *Proceedings of of IEEE Conference on Computer Vision and Pattern Recognition, 1*, 478–485.

Elgammal, A., Harwood, D., & Davis, L. (2000). Nonparametric model for background subtraction. *Proc. European Conf. on Computer Vision, II*, 751–767.

Elissetche, M. M. (2005). *Social science dictionary.* Retrieved on October 6, 2005, from http://www.elissetche.org/dico/p.htm

Elliot, R., Aggoun, L., & Moore, J. (1995). *Hidden Markov models: Estimation and control.* Springer Verlag.

Engel, S., Zhang, X., & Wandell, B. (1997). Colour tuning in human visual cortex measured with functional magnetic resonance imaging. *Nature, 388*(6), 68–71. doi:10.1038/40398

Erdogan, H., Ercil, A., Ekenel, H., Bilgin, S., Eden, I., & Kirisci, M. (2005a). Multimodal person recognition for vehicular applications. *LNCS, 3541*, 366–375.

Erdogan, H., Ozyagci, A. N., Eskil, T., Rodoper, M., Ercil, A., & Abut, H. (2005b, September). *Experiments on decision fusion for driver recognition.* Paper presented at the Biennial on DSP for in-vehicle and mobile systems, Sesimbra, Portugal.

Eriksen, C. W. W., & Hoffman, J. E. (1972). Temporal and spatial characteristics of selective encoding from visual displays. *Perception & Psychophysics, 21*, 201–204.

Erzin, E., Yemez, Y., & Tekalp, A. M. (2005). Multimodal speaker identification using an adaptive classifier cascade based on modality reliability. *IEEE Transactions on Multimedia, 7*(5), 840–852. doi:10.1109/TMM.2005.854464

Erzin, E., Yemez, Y., Tekalp, A. M., Erçil, A., Erdogan, H., & Abut, H. (2006). Multimodal person recognition for human-vehicle interaction. *IEEE MultiMedia, 13*, 18–31. doi:10.1109/MMUL.2006.37

Etemad, K., & Chellapa, R. (1997). Discrimant analysis for recognition of human face images. *Journal of the Optical Society of America. A, Optics, Image Science, and Vision, 14*(8), 1724–1733. doi:10.1364/JOSAA.14.001724

Farrell, K. R., Mammone, R. J., & Assaleh, T. (1994). Speaker recognition using neural networks and conventional classifiers. *IEEE Transactions on Speech and Audio Processing, 2*(1), 194–205. doi:10.1109/89.260362

Farzin, H., Abrishami-Moghaddam, H., & Moin, M.-S. (2008). A novel retinal identification system. *J. Advances in Signal Processing*, 1-10.

Fawcett, T., & Provost, F. (1997). Adaptive fraud detection. *Data Mining and Knowledge Discovery, 1*(3), 291–316. doi:10.1023/A:1009700419189

Felzenszwalb, P. F. (2001). Learning models for object recognition. *Proceedings of the IEEE Conference on Computer Vision and Pattern Recognition* (pp. 1056-1062).

Feng, G., Dong, K., Hu, D., & Zhang, D. (2004). When faces are combined with palmprints: A novel biometric fusion strategy. In *Int'l Conf. on Biometric Authentication* (pp. 701-707).

Feng, H. H., Kolesnikov, O. M., Fogla, P., Lee, W., & Gong, W. (2003b). *Anomaly detection using call stack information.* Paper presented at the IEEE Symposium on Security and Privacy (pp. 62-78).

Feng, H., & Chan, C. W. (2002). Private key generation from online handwritten signatures. *Information Management & Computer Security, 10*(4), 159–164. doi:10.1108/09685220210436949

Feng, H., Kolesnikov, O., Fogla, P., Lee, W., & Gong, W. (2003a, May 11-14). *Anomaly detection using call stack information.* Paper presented at the IEEE Security and Privacy, Oakland, CA.

Ferisa, R. S., Kruegerb, V., & Cesar, R. M. Jr. (2004). A wavelet subspace method for real-time face tracking. *Real-Time Imaging, 10*, 339–350. doi:10.1016/j.rti.2004.06.002

Final Committee Draft ISO/IEC 19792. (2008). *Information technology–security techniques–security evaluation of biometrics.*

Fisher, W. M., Doddington, G. R., Goudie-Mashall, K. M., Jankowski, C., Kalyanswamy, A., Basson, S., et al. (1993). NTIMIT. *Linguistic Data Consortium.*

Fodor, J. (2001). The modularity of mind. Cambridge, MA: MIT Press. (12th ed.).

Forsen, G., Nelson, M., & Staron. (1977). *Personal attributes authentication techniques.* Rome Air Development Center, Report RADC-TR-77-1033, ed. A.F.B. Griffis, RADC, New York.

Frantzeskou, G., Gritzalis, S., & MacDonell, S. (2004, August). *Source code authorship analysis for supporting the cybercrime investigation process.* Paper presented at the 1st International Conference on E-Business and Telecommunication Networks-Security and Reliability in Information Systems and Networks Track, Setubal, Portugal (pp. 85-92).

Frischholz, R., & Dieckmann, U. (2000). BioID: A multimodal biometric identification system. *IEEE Computer, 33*(2), 64–68.

Frosini, P. (1991). Measuring shape by size functions. In *. Proceedings of SPIE on Intelligent Robotic Systems, 1607,* 122–133.

Fu, Y., & Shih, M. (2002, June). *A framework for personal Web usage mining.* Paper presented at the International Conference on Internet Computing (IC'2002), Las Vegas, NV (pp. 595-600).

Fujiyoshi, H., & Lipson, A. (1998) Real-time human motion analysis by image skeletonization. *Proc. 4th IEEE Workshop on Applications of Computer Vision* (pp. 15-21).

Furui, S. (1997). Recent advances in speaker recognition. *Pattern Recognition Letters, 18*(9), 859–872. doi:10.1016/S0167-8655(97)00073-1

Gabor, D. (1946). Theory of communication. *J. Institute of Electronic Engineers, 93,* 429–457.

Gafurov, D. (2007). A survey of biometric gait recognition: Approaches, security, and challeges. In *Proceedings of NIK-2007.*

Gaines, H. F. (1956). *Cryptanalysis: A study of ciphers and their solution.* Dover.

Gait Database, C. A. S. I. A. (2004). Retrieved from http://www.cbsr.ia.ac.cn/english/Database.asp

Gamboa, H., & Fred, A. (2003). *An identity authentication system based on human computer interaction behaviour.* Paper presented at the 3rd Intl. Workshop on Pattern Recognition in Information Systems (pp. 46-55).

Gamboa, H., & Fred, A. (2004). *A behavioral biometric system based on human computer interaction.* Paper presented at the SPIE (pp. 5404-5436).

Gan, J., & Liang, Y. (2006). Applications of wavelet packets decomposition in iris recognition. (. *LNCS, 3832,* 443–449.

Gao, Y., & Maggs, M. (2005). Feature-level fusion in personal identification. In *Proc. IEEE Conf. on Computer Vision and Pattern Recognition.*

Garg, A., Rahalkar, R., Upadhyaya, S., & Kwiat, K. (2006, June 21-23). *Profiling users in GUI based systems for masquerade detection.* Paper presented at The 7th IEEE Information Assurance Workshop (IAWorkshop 2006), West Point, NY.

Garg, A., Sankaranarayanan, V., Upadhyaya, S., & Kwiat, K. (2006, April 2-6). *USim: A user behavior simulation framework for training and testing IDSs in GUI based systems.* Paper presented at the 39th Annual Simulation Symposium (ANSS 06), Huntsville, AL.

Garis, H. d. (2005). *The artilect war.* Palm Springs, CA: ETC Publications.

Gauvain, J., & Lee, C. (1994). Maximum *a* posteriori estimation for multivariate Gaussian mixture observations of Markov chains. *IEEE Transactions on Audio, Speech, and Language Processing, 2*(2), 291–298. doi:10.1109/89.279278

Geng, X., Zhou, Z., & Smith-Miles, K. (2007). Automatic age estimation based on facial aging patterns. *IEEE Trans. PAMI, 29*(12), 2234–2240.

German Federal Office for Information Security. (2008). *Biometric verification mechanisms protection profile (BVMPP).* Common Criteria Protection Profile BSI-CC-PP-0043.

German Government. (2001). *Ordinance on electronic signatures.*

Ghahramani, Z., & Jordan, M. I. (1997). Factorial hidden Markov models. *Machine Learning, 29,* 245–273. doi:10.1023/A:1007425814087

Ghosh, A. K., Schwatzbard, A., & Shatz, M. (1999b, April). *Learning program behavior profiles for intrusion detection.* Paper presented at the 1st USENIX Workshop on Intrusion Detection and Network Monitoring, Santa Clara, CA (pp. 51-62).

Giffin, J., Jha, S., & Miller, B. (2004, February). *Efficient context-sensitive intrusion detection.* Paper presented at the 11th Annual Network and Distributed Systems Security Symposium (NDSS), San Diego, CA.

Ginesu, G., Giusto, D., Margner, V., & Meinlschmidt, P. (2004). Detection of foreign bodies in food by thermal image processing. *IEEE Transactions on Industrial Electronics, 51*(2), 480–490. doi:10.1109/TIE.2004.825286

Godfrey, J. J., Holliman, E. C., & McDaniel, J. (1992). SWITCHBOARD: Telephone speech corpus for research and development. In *Proceedings of the International Conference on Acoustics, Speech, and Signal Processing*

Godfrey, J., & Graff, D. (1994). Public databases for speaker recognition and verification. *ECSA Workshop Automat. Speaker Recognition, 10,* 39–42.

Godil, A., Grother, P., & Ressler, S. (2003). Human identification from body shape. *3DIM'03,* 386-391.

Goecks, J., & Shavlik, J. (2000). *Learning users' interests by unobtrusively observing their normal behavior.* Paper presented at the International Conference on Intelligent User Interfaces, New Orleans, LA (pp. 129-132).

Goh, K. G., Hsu, W., & Lee, M. L. (2000). An automatic diabetic retinal image screening system. *Medical Data Mining and Knowledge Discovery,* 181–210.

Goldberg, D. E. (1989). *Genetic algorithms in search, optimization, and machine learning.* Addison-Wesley Pub. Co.

Goldberg, J., & Kotval, X. (1999). Computer interface evaluation using eye movements: Methods and constructs. *International Journal of Industrial Ergonomics, 24,* 631–645. doi:10.1016/S0169-8141(98)00068-7

Goldring, T. (2003). User profiling for intrusion detection in windows NT. *Computing Science and Statistics, 35.*

González, I., Déjean, S., Martin, P. G. P., & Baccini, A. (2008). CCA: An R package to extend canonical correlation analysis. *Journal of Statistical Software, 23*(12).

Gonzalez, R. C., & Woods, R. E. (1992). *Digital image processing.* Addison Wesley Publishing Company.

Graham, D., Hadyn, E., & Shepherd, J. (1981). *Perceiving and remembering faces.* New York & London: Academic Press.

Gray, A., Sallis, P., & MacDonell, S. (1997). *Software forensics: Extending authorship analysis techniques to computer programs.* Paper presented at the In Proc. 3rd Biannual Conf. Int. Assoc. of Forensic Linguists (IAFL'97).

Greenspan, H., Belongie, S., Goodman, R., Perona, P., Rakshit, S., & Anderson, C. H. (1994). Over complete steer able pyramid filters and rotation invariance. *Proc. IEEE Computer Vision and Pattern Recognition,* Seattle, WA (pp. 222-228).

Griffin, J. L., Pennington, A. G., Bucy, J. S., Choundappan, D., Muralidharan, N., & Ganger, G. R. (2003). *On the feasibility of intrusion detection inside workstation disks.* (Tech. Rep. CMU-PDL-03-106). Carnegie Mellon University.

Gross, R., & Shi, J. (2001). *The CMU motion of body (MoBo) database.* (Tech. Rep. 01-18). Robotics Institute, Carnegie Mellon University.

Grosser, H., Britos, H., & García-Martínez, R. (2005). *Detecting fraud in mobile telephony using neural networks.* (LNAI, pp. 613-615).

Gunetti, D., & Picardi, C. (2005). Keystroke analysis of free text. *ACM Transactions on Information and System Security, 8*(3), 312–347. doi:10.1145/1085126.1085129

Gunetti, D., Picardi, C., & Ruffo, G. (2005). *Keystroke analysis of different languages: A case study.* Paper presented at the Proc. of the Sixth Symposium on Intelligent Data Analysis (IDA 2005), Madrid, Spain (pp. 133-144).

Gunn, S. R. (1998). *Support vector machines for classification and regression.* (Tech. Rep. No. 6459). Image, Speech, and Intelligent Systems Research Group, University of Southampton.

Guo, A., & Siegelmann, H. (2004). Time-warped longest common subsequence algorithm for music retrieval. *Proc of the Fifth International Conference on Music Information Retrieval (IS-MIR)* (pp. 10-14).

Guo, Y., & Tsuji, S. (1994). Understanding human motion patterns. *Proc. International Conference on Pattern Recognition*, 2, 325–329.

Gupta, G., Mazumdar, C., & Rao, M. S. (2004). Digital forensic analysis of e-mails: A trusted e-mail protocol. *International Journal of Digital Evidence*, 2(4).

Guyton, A. C., & Hall, J. E. (2000). *Textbook of medical physiology*. Saunders Company, 10th edition.

Halteren, H. v. (2004). *Linguistic profiling for author recognition and verification*. Paper presented at the ACL-2004.

Han, J., & Bhanu, B. (2004). Statistical feature fusion for gait-based human recognition. In . *Proceedings of IEEE Computer Society Conference on Computer Vision and Pattern Recognition*, 2, 842–847.

Han, J., & Bhanu, B. (2005). Performance prediction for individual recognition by gait. *Pattern Recognition Letters*, 26(5), 615–624. doi:10.1016/j.patrec.2004.09.011

Han, J., & Bhanu, B. (2006). Individual recognition using gait energy image. *IEEE Transactions on Pattern Analysis and Machine Intelligence*, 28(2), 316–322. doi:10.1109/TPAMI.2006.38

Han, J., & Bhanu, B. (2007). Fusion of color and infrared video for moving human detection. *Pattern Recognition*, 40(6), 1771–1784. doi:10.1016/j.patcog.2006.11.010

Han, J., Bhanu, B., & Roy-Chowdhury, A. K. (2005). Study on view-insensitive gait recognition. In *Proceedings of ICIP'05* (Vol. 3, pp. 297–300).

Han, J., Bhanu, B., et al. (2005). A study on view-insensitive gait recognition. *Proc. of IEEE International Conference on Image Processing (ICIP 2005)*, III (pp. 297-300).

Han, K., & Veloso, M. (1999). *Automated robot behavior recognition*. Paper presented at the Workshop on Team Behaviors and Plan Recognition.

Hanley, J. A., & McNeil, B. J. (1982). The meaning and use of the area under a receiver operating characteristic (ROC) curve. *Radiology*, 143, 29–36.

Hao, F., Anderson, R., & Daugman, J. (2006). Combining crypto with biometrics effectively. *IEEE Transactions on Computers*, 55(9), 1081–1088. doi:10.1109/TC.2006.138

Haritaoglu, I., Cutler, R., Harwood, D., & Davis, L. (2001). Backpack: Detection of people carrying objects using silhouettes. *J. CVIU*, 6(3), 385–397.

Hastie, T., Tibshirani, R., & Friedman, J. H. (2001). *The elements of statistical learning: Data mining, inference, and prediction*. Springer.

Hatch, A., Peskin, B., & Stolcke, A. (2005). Improved phonetic speaker recognition using lattice decoding. In *Proceedings of the International conference on Acoustics, Speech, and Signal Processing*.

Haykin, S. (1999). *Neural networks: A comprehensive foundation*. Upper Saddle River, NJ: Prentice-Hall, Inc.

Hazen, T. J., Jones, D. A., Park, A., Kukolich, L. C., & Reynolds, D. A. (2003a). Integration of speaker recognition into conversational spoken dialogue systems. In *Proceedings of the Eurospeech*.

Hazen, T. J., Weinstein, E., Kabir, R., Park, A., & Heisele, B. (2003b). Multimodal face and speaker identificaiton on a handheld device In *Proceedings of Workshop on Multimodal User Authentication* (pp. 113-120).

He, Q., & Debrunner, C. H. (2000). Individual recognition from periodic activity using hidden markov models. *Proceedings IEEE Workshop on Human Motion*, (pp. 47-52).

He, X., Cai, D., & Niyogi, P. (2005). Tensor subspace analysis. In *Advances in Neural Information Processing Systems 18 (NIPS)*.

Hemery, B., Rosenberger, C., & Laurent, H. (2007). The ENSIB database: A benchmark for face recognition. *International Symposium on Signal Processing and Its Applications (ISSPA), Special Session on Performance Evaluation and Benchmarking of Image and Video Processing.*

Hemery, B., Rosenberger, C., Toinard, C., & Emile, B. (2006). Comparative study of invariant descriptors for face recognition. *8ᵗʰ International IEEE Conference on Signal Processing (ICSP).*

Henderson, N. J., White, N. M., Veldhuis, R. N. J., Hartel, P. H., & Slump, C. H. (2002). *Sensing pressure for authentication.* Paper presented at the 3ʳᵈ IEEE Benelux Signal Processing Symp. (SPS), Leuven, Belgium (pp. 241-244).

Henderson, N. Y., Papakostas, T. V., White, N. M., & Hartel, P. H. (2001). *Polymer thick-film sensors: Possibilities for smartcard biometrics.* Paper presented at the Sensors and Their Applications XI (pp. 83-88).

Herbst, B., & Coetzer, H. (1998). *On an offline signature verification system.* Paper presented at the 9ᵗʰ Annual South African Workshop on Pattern Recognition (pp. 39-43).

Hertel, C., & Bunke, H. (2003). A set of novel features for writer identification. *Proc. Fourth Int'l Conf. Audio and Video-Based Biometric Person Authentication,* 679-687.

Hewitt, P. A., & Dobberfuhl, D. (2004). The science and art of proportionality. *Science Scope,* 30–31.

Higgins, A., Bahler, L., & Porter, J. (1991). Speaker verification using randomized phrase prompting. *Digital Signal Processing, 1*(2), 89–106. doi:10.1016/1051-2004(91)90098-6

Hilas, C., & Sahalos, J. (2005, October 15-16). *User profiling for fraud detection in telecommunication networks.* Paper presented at the 5ᵗʰ International Conference on Technology and Automation (ICTA 2005), Thessaloniki, Greece (pp. 382-387).

Hill, R. B. (1999). Retinal identification. In A. Jain, R. Bolle & S. Pankati (Eds.), *Biometrics: Personal identification in networked society.* Berlin: Springer.

Hirsch, H. G., & Pearce, D. (2000). The AURORA experimental framework for the performance evaluation of speech recognition systems under noisy conditions. In *ASR2000-Automatic Speech Recognition: Challenges for the new Millenium ISCA Tutorial and Research Workshop (ITRW).* ISCA.

Hocquet, S., Ramel, J. Y., & Cardot, H. (2004). Users authentication by a study of human computer interactions. *8ᵗʰ Annual (Doctoral) Meeting on Health, Science, and Technology.*

Hocquet, S., Ramel, J.-Y., & Cardot, H. (2007). User classification for keystroke dynamics authentication. *International Conference on Biometrics (ICB)* (LNCS 4642, pp. 531-239). Berlin Heidelberg: Springer-Verlag.

Hoffman, J. E., & Subramaniam, B. (1995). The role of visual attention in saccadic eye movements. *Perception & Psychophysics, 57,* 787–795.

Hofmeyr, S. A., Forrest, S., & Somayaji, A. (1998). Intrusion detection using sequences of system calls. *Journal of Computer Security, 6,* 151–180.

Honggui, L., & Xingguo, L. (2004). Gait analysis using LLE. *Proceedings of ICSP'04.*

Hooker, C. I., Paller, K. A., Gitelman, D. R., Parrish, T. B., Mesulam, M.-M., & Reber, P. J. (2003, July). Brain networks for analyzing eye gaze. *Brain Research. Cognitive Brain Research, 17*(2), 406–418. doi:10.1016/S0926-6410(03)00143-5

Horn, B. K. P. (1986). *Robot vision.* Cambridge, MA: MIT Press.

Hu, M. (1962). Visual pattern recognition by moment invariants. *I.R.E. Transactions on Information Theory, IT-8,* 179–187.

Hu, W. M., Tan, T. N., Wang, L., & Maybank, S. (2004). A survey of visual surveillance of object motion and behaviors. *IEEE Trans. SMC-C, 34*(3), 334–352.

Huang, P., Harris, C., & Nixon, M. (1999). Recognizing humans by gait via parameteric canonical space. *Artificial Intelligence in Engineering, 13*, 359–366. doi:10.1016/S0954-1810(99)00008-4

Huang, X., & Boulgouris, N. V. (2008). Human gait recognition based on multiview gait sequences. *EURASIP Journal on Advances in Signal Processing.*

Huang, X., Acero, A., & Hon, H. (2001). *Spoken language processing.* Upper Saddle River, NJ: Prentice Hall PTR.

Humm, A., Hennebert, J., & Ingold, R. (2006, July 10-12). *Scenario and survey of combined handwriting and speech modalities for user authentication.* Paper presented at the 6th International Conference on Recent Advances in Soft Computing (RASC'06), Canterbury, UK (pp. 496-501).

Hurley, D. J., Arbab-Zavar, B., & Nixon, M. S. (2007). *The ear as a biometric.* Retrieved from http://www.eurasip.org/Proceedings/Eusipco/Eusipco2007/Papers/A1L-B02.pdf

Hurley, D. J., Nixon, M. S., & Carter, J. N. (2005). Force field feature extraction for ear biometrics. *J. CVIU, 98*, 491–512.

Huttenlocher, D. P., Klanderman, G. A., & Rucklidge, W. J. (1993). Comparing images using the Hausdorff distance. [PAMI]. *IEEE Transactions on Pattern Analysis and Machine Intelligence, 15*(9), 850–863. doi:10.1109/34.232073

Hwang, S., Lee, H., & Cho, S. (2006). Improving authentication accuracy of unfamiliar passwords with pauses and cues for keystroke dynamics-based authentication. *WISI* (LNCS 3917, pp. 73-78). Berlin Heidelberg: Springer-Verlag.

Igarashi, K., Miyajima, C., Itou, K., Takeda, K., Itakura, F., & Abut, H. (2004). *Biometric identification using driving behavioral signals.* Paper presented at the Proc. 2004 IEEE International Conference on Multimedia and Expo (pp. 65-68).

Ilgun, K., Kemmerer, R. A., & Porras, P. A. (1995). State transition analysis: A rule-based intrusion detection approach. *Software Engineering, 21*(3), 181–199.

Ilonen, J. (2006). *Keystroke dynamics.* Retrieved on July 12, 2006, from www.it.lut.fi/kurssit/03-04/010970000/seminars/ilonen.pdf

Ilonen, J. (2008). *Keystroke dynamics.* Retrieved from www.it.lut.fi/kurssit/03-04/010970000/seminars/Ilonen.pdf

International Standard ISO 19092. (2008). *Financial services–biometrics–security framework.*

International Standard ISO/IEC 15408-1. (2005). *Information technology–security techniques–evaluation criteria for IT security–part 1: Introduction and general model.*

International Standard ISO/IEC 15408-2. (2008). *Information technology–security techniques–evaluation criteria for IT security–part 2: Security functional components.*

International Standard ISO/IEC 15408-3. (2008). *Information technology–security techniques–evaluation criteria for IT security–part 3: Security assurance components.*

International Standard ISO/IEC 18045. (2008). *Information technology–security techniques–methodology for IT security evaluation.*

International Standard ISO/IEC 19795-1. (2006). *Information technology–biometric performance testing and reporting–part 1: Principles and framework.*

Irani, M., & Peleg, S. (1993). Motion analysis for image enhancement: Resolution, occlusion, and transparency. *Journal of Visual Communication and Image Representation, 4*, 324–335. doi:10.1006/jvci.1993.1030

Irvine, J. M., Israel, S. A., Scruggs, W. T., & Worek, W. J. (2008, November). EigenPulse: Robust human identification from cardiovascular function. *Pattern Recognition, 41*(11), 3427–3435. doi:10.1016/j.patcog.2008.04.015

ISO International Standard. (2006). Information technology—biometric performance testing and reporting. ISO/IEC 19795-1.

Israel, S., Irvine, J., Cheng, A., Wiederhold, M., & Wiederhold, B. (2005). ECG to identify individuals. *Pattern Recognition*, *38*(1), 133–142. doi:10.1016/j.patcog.2004.05.014

Ito, A., Wang, X., Suzuki, M., & Makino, S. (2005). *Smile and laughter recognition using speech processing and face recognition from conversation video.* Paper presented at the International Conference on Cyberworlds (pp. 437-444).

Itti, L., & Koch, C. (2000). A saliency-based search mechanism for overt and covert shifts of visual attention. *Vision Research*, *40*, 1489–1506. doi:10.1016/S0042-6989(99)00163-7

Itti, L., & Koch, C. (2001). Feature combination strategies for saliency-based visual attention systems. *Journal of Electronic Imaging*, *10*(1), 161–169. doi:10.1117/1.1333677

Itti, L., Koch, C., & Niebur, E. (1998). A model of saliency-based visual attention for rapid scene analysis. *IEEE Transactions on Pattern Analysis and Machine Intelligence*, *20*(11), 1254-1259. doi:10.1109/34.730558

Jaakkola, T. S., & Haussler, D. (1998). Exploiting generative models in discriminative classifiers. *Advances in Neural Information Processing Systems*, 11.

Jacob, B. A., & Levitt, S. D. (2004). *To catch a cheat.* Paper presented at the Education Next Retrieved from www.educationnext.org

Jafri, R., & Arabnia, H. R. (2008). Fusion of face and gait for automatic human recognition. In *Proc. of the Fifth International Conference on Information Technology.*

Jain, A. K. (2007, November). Biometric recognition: Overview and recent advances. ([]. Heidelberg: Springer Berlin.]. *LNCS*, *4756*, 13–19.

Jain, A. K., & Chandrasekaran, B. (1982). Dimensionality and sample size consideration in pattern recognition practice. In P.R. Krishnaiah & L.N. Kanal (Eds.), *Handbook of statistics* (Vol. 2, pp.835-855). North Holland.

Jain, A. K., & Farrokhnia, F. (1991). Unsupervised texture segmentation using Gabor filters. *Pattern Recognition*, *24*(12), 1167–1186. doi:10.1016/0031-3203(91)90143-S

Jain, A. K., Bolle, R., & Pankanti, S. (Eds.). (1999). *Biometrics: Personal identification in networked society.* Kluwer Academic Publishers.

Jain, A. K., Dass, S. C., & Nandakumar, K. (2004). *Can soft biometric traits assist user recognition?* Paper presented at the SPIE Defense and Security Symposium, Orlando, FL, April 2004.

Jain, A. K., Dass, S. C., & Nandakumar, K. (2004, July). *Soft biometric traits for personal recognition systems.* Paper presented at the International Conference on Biometric Authentication (ICBA), Hong Kong (pp. 731-738).

Jain, A. K., Duin, R. P. W., & Mao, J. (2000). Statistical pattern recognition: A review. *IEEE Trans. PAMI*, *22*(1), 4–37.

Jain, A. K., Griess, F., & Connell, S. (2002). Online signature verification. *Pattern Recognition*, *35*, 2963–2972. doi:10.1016/S0031-3203(01)00240-0

Jain, A. K., Hong, L., & Pankanti, S. (2000). Biometric identification. *Communications of the ACM*, *43*(2), 90–98. doi:10.1145/328236.328110

Jain, A. K., Hong, L., Pankanti, S., & Bolle, R. (1997). An identity authentication system using fingerprints. *Proceedings of the IEEE*, *85*(9), 1365–1388. doi:10.1109/5.628674

Jain, A. K., Pankanti, S., Prabhakar, S., Hong, L., & Ross, A. (2004, August). *Biometrics: A grand challenge.* Paper presented at the International Conference on Pattern Recognition, Cambridge, UK.

Jain, A. K., Ross, A., & Prabhakar, S. (2004). An introduction to biometric recognition. *IEEE Transactions on Circuits and Systems for Video Technology, 14*(1), 4–20. doi:10.1109/TCSVT.2003.818349

Jain, A., Griess, F., & Connell, S. (2002). Online signature verification. *Pattern Recognition, 35*, 2963–2972. doi:10.1016/S0031-3203(01)00240-0

Jain, K., Nandakumar, K., & Ross, A. (2005). Score normalization in multimodal biometric systems. *Pattern Recognition, 38*(12), 2270–2285. doi:10.1016/j.patcog.2005.01.012

Janakiraman, R., & Sim, T. (2007). Keystroke dynamics in a general setting. *International Conference on Biometrics (ICB)* (LNCS 4642, pp. 584-593). Berlin Heidelberg: Springer-Verlag.

Jansen, A. R., Dowe, D. L., & E., G. (2000). *Farr inductive inference of chess player strategy.* Paper presented at the 6th Pacific Rim International Conference on Artificial Intelligence (PRICAI'2000) (pp. 61-71).

Javal, L. E. (1879). Essai sur la physiologie de la lecture. *Annales d'Oculistique, 82*, 242–253.

Jermyn, I., Mayer, A., Monrose, F., Reiter, M. K., & Rubin, A. D. (1999, August 23-26). *The design and analysis of graphical passwords.* Paper presented at the 8th USENIX Security Symposium, Washington, D.C.

Ji, Q., & Yang, X. (2002, October). Real-time eye, gaze, and face pose tracking for monitoring driver vigilance. *Real-Time Imaging, 8*(5), 357–377. doi:10.1006/rtim.2002.0279

Jiao, F., Li, S., Shum, H., & Schuurmans, D. (2003). Face allignment using statistical models and wavelet features. *Proc. of CVPR'03 IEEE* (pp. 1063–1069).

Jie, Y., Yi fang, Y., Renjie, Z., & Qifa, S. (2006). Fingerprint minutiae matching algorithm for real time system. *Pattern Recognition, 39*(1), 143–146. doi:10.1016/j.patcog.2005.08.005

Jin, L., Ke, X., Manuel, R., & Wilkerson, M. (2004). Keystroke dynamics: A software based biometric solution. *Proc. 13th USENIX Security Symposium.*

Jin, M., Soong, F., & Yoo, C. (2007). A syllable lattice approach to speaker verification. *IEEE Transactions on Audio, Speech, and Language Processing, 15*(8), 2476–2484. doi:10.1109/TASL.2007.906181

Jin, Q., Navratil, J., Reynolds, D. A., Campbell, J. P., Andrews, W. D., & Abramson, J. S. (2003). Combining cross-stream and time dimensions in phonetic speaker recognition. In *Proceedings of the International conference on Acoustics, Speech, and Signal Processing.*

Jng, X., Wong, H., & Zhang, D. (2006). Face recognition based on 2D fisherface approach. *Pattern Recognition, 39*(4), 707–710. doi:10.1016/j.patcog.2005.10.020

Johansson, G. (1975). Visual motion perception. *Scientific American, 232*(6), 76–88.

Johnson, A. Y., & Bobick, A. F. (2001). A multiview method for gait recognition using static body parameters. *Proc. of 3rd International Conference on Audio and Video Based Biometric Person Authentication* (pp. 301-311).

Johnston, A., Hill, H., & Carman, N. (1992). Recognizing faces: Effects of lighting direction, inversion, and brightness reversal. *Perception, 21*, 365–375. doi:10.1068/p210365

Jones, J. P., & Palmer, L. A. (1987). An evaluation of the two-dimensional Gabor filter model of simple receptive fields in the cat striate cortex. *Journal of Neurophysiology, 58*, 1233–1258.

Jourlin, P., Luettin, J., Genoud, D., & Wassner, H. (1997). Acoustic-labial speaker verification. *Pattern Recognition Letters, 18*(9), 853–858. doi:10.1016/S0167-8655(97)00070-6

Joy, T. M., & Thomas, J. A. (1991). *Elements of information theory* (2nd ed.). John Wiley & Sons Inc.

Juola, P., & Sofko, J. (2004). *Proving and improving authorship attribution.* Paper presented at the CaSTA-04 The Face of Text.

Jurafsky, D., & Martin, J. H. (2000). *Speech and language processing.* NJ: Prentice.

Kale, A., & Sundaresan, A. RoyChowdhury, A., & Chellappa, R. (2005). Gait-based human identification from a monocular video sequence. In *Handbook on pattern recognition and computer vision*. World Scientific Publishing Company.

Kale, A., Chowdhury, A., & Chellappa, R. (2003). Towards a view invariant gait recognition algorithm. *Proc. of IEEE Conference on Advanced Video and Signal Based Surveillance* (pp. 143-150).

Kale, A., Cuntoor, N., & Chellappa, R. (2002). A framework for activity-specific human identification. In *Proc. the Int. Conf. on Acoustics, Speech and Signal Processing* (Vol. 4, pp. 3660-3663).

Kale, A., Rajagopalan, A., et al. (2002). Gait-based recognition of humans using continuous HMMs. *Proc. of 5th IEEE International Conference on Automatic Face and Gesture Recognition* (pp. 336-341).

Kale, A., Roy, A. K., et al. (2003). Towards a view invariant gait recognition algorithm. *Proc. of IEEE Conference on Advanced Video and Signal Based Surveillance* (pp. 143-150).

Kale, A., Roy-chowdhury, A., & Chellappa, R. (2004). Fusion of gait and face for human identification. In *Proc. of Acoustics, Speech, and Signal Processing* (Vol. 5, pp. 901-904).

Kale, A., Sundaresan, A., Rajagopalan, A. N., & Cuntoor, N., RoyChowdhury, A., Kruger, V., et al. (2004). Identification of humans using gait. *IEEE Transactions on Image Processing, 13*(9). doi:10.1109/TIP.2004.832865

Kalyanaraman, S. (2006). *Biometric authentication systems a report*. Retrieved from http://netlab.cs.iitm.ernet.in/cs650/2006/termpapers/sriramk.pdf

Kar-Han, T., Kriegman, D. J., & Ahuja, N. (2002, December). Appearance-based eye gaze estimation. In *Proceedings of the Sixth IEEE Workshop on Applications of Computer Vision* (pp. 191–195).

Kasprowski, P., & Ober, J. (2004). Eye movement in biometrics. In *Proceedings of Biometric Authentication Workshop, European Conference on Computer Vision in Prague 2004* (LNCS 3087). Berlin: Springer-Verlag.

Kass, M., Witkin, A., & Terzopoulos, D. (1998). Snakes: Active countorn models. *International Journal of Computer Vision*, 321–331.

Kauffman, J. A., Bazen, A. M., Gerez, S. H., & Veldhuis, R. N. J. (2003). *Grip-pattern recognition for smart guns*. Paper presented at the 14th Annual Workshop on Circuits, Systems, and Signal Processing (ProRISC), Veldhoven, The Netherlands (pp. 379-384).

Kaufman, K., Cervone, G., & Michalski, R. S. (2003). *An application of symbolic learning to intrusion detection: Preliminary results from the LUS methodology* (No. MLI 03-2). Fairfax, VA: George Mason University.

Kayacik, G. H., & Zincir-Heywood, A. N. (2005, May). *Generating representative traffic for intrusion detection system benchmarking*. Paper presented at the *IEEE CNSR 2005*, Halifax, Canada (pp. 112-117).

Kaziska, D., & Srivastava, A. (2006). Cyclostationary processes on shape spaces for gait-based recognition. *Proc. of the 9th European Conference on Computer Vision*, Graz, Austria (pp. 442-453).

Kendall, G., & Willdig, M. (2001, December 10-14). *An investigation of an adaptive poker player*. Paper presented at the 14th Australian Joint Conference on Artificial Intelligence, Adelaide, Australia (pp. 189-200).

Kevenaar, T. A. M., Schrijen, G. J., van der Veen, M., & Akkermans, A. H. M. (2005, October 17-18). Face recognition with renewable and privacy preserving binary templates. *4th IEEE Workshop on Automatic Identification Advanced Technologies (AutoID'05)*, Buffalo, NY (pp. 21-26).

Kholmatov, A. (2003). *A biometric identity verification using online and offline signature verification*. MSc Thesis, Sabanci University, Turkey.

Kiers, H. A. L. (2000). Towards a standardized notation and terminology in multiway analysis. *Journal of Chemometrics, 14*(3), 105–122. doi:10.1002/1099-128X(200005/06)14:3<105::AID-CEM582>3.0.CO;2-I

Kim, Y., Jo, J.-Y., & Suh, K. (2006, April). *Baseline profile stability for network anomaly detection.* Paper presented at the IEEE ITNG 2006, Internet and Wireless Network Security Track, Las Vegas, NV.

Kinnunen, T., Hautamaki, V., & Franti, P. (2004, September). Fusion of spectral feature sets for accurate speaker identification. In *Proc. Int'l Conf. Speech and Computer* (pp. 361-365).

Kittler, J., Hatef, M., Duin, R., & Matas, J. (1998). On combining classifiers. *IEEE Transactions on Pattern Analysis and Machine Intelligence, 20*, 226–239. doi:10.1109/34.667881

Kleinschmidt, M. (2002). *Robust speech recognition based on spectrotemporal processing.* Unpublished doctoral dissertation, University of Oldenburg. Retrieved from http://docserver.bis.uni-oldenburg.de/publikationen/dissertation/2002/klerob02/pdf/klerob02.pdf

Klusacek, D., Navratil, J., Reynolds, D. A., & Campbell, J. P. (2003). Conditional pronunciation modeling in speaker detection. In *Proceedings of the International conference on Acoustics, Speech, and Signal Processing.*

Ko, C., Fink, G., & Levitt, K. (1994, December). *Automated detection of vulnerabilities in privileged programs by execution monitoring.* Paper presented at the 10th Annual Computer Security Applications Conference (pp. 134-144).

Koch, C., & Ullman, S. (1985). Shifts in selective visual attention: Towards the underlying neural circuitry. *Human Neurobiology, 4*(4): 219–227.

Kohir, V., & Desai, U. (1998). Face recognition using DCT-HMM approach. In *Proc. Workshop on Advances in Facial Image Analysis and Recognition Technology (AFIART)*, Freiburg, Germany.

Kolda, T. G. (2001). Orthogonal tensor decompositions. *SIAM Journal on Matrix Analysis and Applications, 23*(1), 243–255. doi:10.1137/S0895479800368354

Kollreider, K., Fronthaler, H., & Bigun, J. (2005, October). Evaluating liveness by face images and the structure tensor. In *Proceedings of the Fourth IEEE Workshop on Automatic Identification Advanced Technologies* (pp. 75–80).

Kong, A., Zhang, D., & Kamel, M. (2006). Palmprint identification using feature-level fusion. *Pattern Recognition, 39*(3), 478–487. doi:10.1016/j.patcog.2005.08.014

Koppel, M., & Schler, J. (2004, July). *Authorship verification as a one-class classification problem.* Paper presented at the 21st International Conference on Machine Learning, Banff, Canada (pp. 489-495).

Koppel, M., Schler, J., & Mughaz, D. (2004, January). *Text categorization for authorship verification.* Paper presented at the Eighth International Symposium on Artificial Intelligence and Mathematics, Fort Lauderdale, FL.

Korb, K., Nicholson, A., & Jitnah, N. (1999). *Bayesian poker.* Paper presented at the 15th Annual Conference on Uncertainty in Artificial Intelligence (UAI-99), San Francisco, CA (pp. 343-335).

Korotkaya, Z. (2003). Biometrics person authentication: Odor. Retrieved on October 12, 2008, from http://www.it.lut.fi/kurssit/03-04/010970000/seminars/korotkaya.pdf

Koychev, I., & Schwab, I. (2000). *Adaptation to drifting user's interests.* Paper presented at the Workshop: Machine Learning in New Information Age, Barcelona, Spain.

Kronfeld, P. C. (1962). Gross anatomy and embryology of the eye. In *The eye.*

Kuge, N., Yamamura, T., & Shimoyama, O. (1998). *A driver behavior recognition method based on driver model framework.* Paper presented at the Society of Automotive Engineers.

Kulikowski, J. J., & Bishop, P. O. (1981). Fourier analysis and spatial representation in the visual cortex. *Experientia, 37,* 160–163. doi:10.1007/BF01963207

Kullback, S., & Leibler, R. A. (1951). On information and sufficiency. *Annals of Mathematical Statistics, 22,* 79–86. doi:10.1214/aoms/1177729694

Kumar, A. N., Leigh, R. J., & Ramat, S. (2001, October). The brainstem switch for gaze shifts in humans. In *Proceedings of the 23rd Annual International Conference of the IEEE Engineering in Medicine and Biology Society* (Vol. 1, pp. 869–872).

Kumar, A., Wong, D. C. M., Shen, H. C., & Jain, A. K. (2003). Personal verification using palmprint and hand geometry biometric. In *Proc. Audio- and Video-based Biometric Person Authentication* (pp. 668-678).

Kunzel, H. J. (1994). Current approaches to forensic speaker recognition. In *Automatic Speaker Recognition, Identification and Verification.* ISCA.

Kurakake, S., & Nevatia, R. (1994). Description and tracking of moving articulated objects. *Systems and Computers in Japan, 25*(8), 16–26. doi:10.1002/scj.4690250802

Lades, M., Vorbruggen, J. C., Buhmann, J., Lange, J., Von Der Malsburg, C., Wurtz, R. P., & Konen, W. (1993). Distortion invariant object recognition in the dynamic link architecture. *IEEE Transactions on Computers, 42,* 300–311. doi:10.1109/12.210173

Lam, C. F., & Kamins, D. (1989). Signature recognition through spectral analysis. *Pattern Recognition, 22*(1), 39–44. doi:10.1016/0031-3203(89)90036-8

Lam, L.-c., Li, W., & Chiueh, T.-c. (2006, June). *Accurate and automated system call policy-based intrusion prevention.* Paper presented at the International Conference on Dependable Systems and Networks (DSN 2006).

Lam, T., Lee, R., & Zhang, D. (2007). Human gait recognition by the fusion of motion and static spatiotemporal templates. *Pattern Recognition, 40*(9), 2563–2573. doi:10.1016/j.patcog.2006.11.014

Lane, T., & Brodley, C. E. (1997). *An application of machine learning to anomaly detection.* Paper presented at the 20th Annual National Information Systems Security Conference (pp. 366-380).

Lane, T., & Brodley, C. E. (1997). *Detecting the abnormal: Machine learning in computer security* (No. ECE-97-1). West Lafayette: Purdue University

Lawrence, N. (2004). *Probabilistic nonlinear principal component analysis with Gaussian process latent variable models.* (Tech. Rep. CS-04-8). Dept. of Computer Science, Univ. of Sheffield.

Lawson, W. (2002). *The new wave ("Biometric access & neural control").* Retrieved on November 24, 2008, from http://www.icdri.org/biometrics/new_wave.htm

Leclerc, F., & Plamondon, R. (1994). Automatic signature verification: The state of the art. *J. PRAI, 8*(3), 643–660.

Lee, C.-S., & Elgammal, A. (2004). Gait style and gait content: bilinear models for gait recognition using gait resampling. In . *Proceedings of AFGR, 04,* 147–152.

Lee, C.-S., & Elgammal, A. (2005). Towards scalable view-invariant gait recognition: Multilinear analysis for gait. (. *LNCS, 3546,* 395–405.

Lee, H. C., & Gaensslen, R. E. (Eds.). (1991). *Advances in fingerprint technology.* New York: Elsevier.

Lee, H., Kim, Y.-D., Cichocki, A., & Choi, S. (2007). Nonnegative tensor factorization for continuous EEG classifcation. *International Journal of Neural Systems, 17*(4), 305–317. doi:10.1142/S0129065707001159

Lee, K., & Park, H. (2003). A new similarity measure based on intraclass statistics for biometric systems. *ETRI Journal, 25*(5), 401–406. doi:10.4218/etrij.03.0102.0017

Lee, K., Buxton, H., & Feng, J. (2004). Cue-guided search: A computational model of selective attention. *IEEE Transactions on Neural Networks, 16*(4), 910–924. doi:10.1109/TNN.2005.851787

Lee, L., & Grimson, W. E. L. (2002). Gait analysis for recognition and classification. *Proc. of 5ᵗʰ IEEE International Conference on Automatic Face and Gesture Recognition* (pp. 155-162).

Lee, S., Liu, Y., & Collins, R. (2007). Shape variation-based frieze pattern for robust gait recognition. In *Proceedings of IEEE International Conference on Computer Vision and Pattern Recognition* (pp.1-8).

Lee, T. K. M., Ranganath, S., & Sanei, S. (2006). Fusion of chaotic measure into a new hybrid face-gait system for human recognition. In . *Proceedings of International Conference on Pattern Recognition, 4,* 541–544.

Lee, T. S. (1996). Image representation using 2D Gabor wavelets. *IEEE Trans. PAMI, 18*(10), 1–13.

Lee, W., Stolfo, S. J., & Mok, K. W. (1999). *A data mining framework for building intrusion detection models.* Paper presented at the IEEE Symposium on Security and Privacy, Oakland, CA.

Leeuwen, D. A. V., Martin, A. F., Przybocki, M. A., & Bouten, J. S. (2006). NIST and NFI-TNO evaluations of automatic speaker recognition. *Computer Speech & Language, 20,* 128–158. doi:10.1016/j.csl.2005.07.001

Leggett, J., & Williams, G. (1988). Verifying identity via keystroke characteristics. *International Journal of Man-Machine Studies, 28*(1), 67–76. doi:10.1016/S0020-7373(88)80053-1

Leggett, J., Williams, G., Usnick, M., & Longnecker, M. (1991). Dynamic identity verification via keystroke characteristics. *International Journal of Man-Machine Studies, 35*(6), 859–870. doi:10.1016/S0020-7373(05)80165-8

Lei, H., Palla, S., & Govindaraju, V. (2004). *ER2: An intuitive similarity measure for online signature verification.* Paper presented at the Ninth International Workshop on Frontiers in Handwriting Recognition (IWFHR'04) (pp. 191-195).

Lejtman, D. Z., & George, S. E. (2001). Online handwritten signature verification using wavelets and back-propagation neural networks. *6ᵗʰ International Conference on Document Analysis and Recognition (ICDAR)* (pp. 992-996).

Leventhal, A. G. (1991). *The neural basis of visual function: Vision and visual dysfunction.* Boca Raton, FL: CRC Press.

lexandre, T. (1997). Biometrics on smart cards: An approach to keyboard behavioural signature. *Future Generation Computer Systems, 13,* 19–26. doi:10.1016/S0167-739X(97)00005-8

Li, B., & Chellappa, R. (2001). Face verification through tracking facial features. *Journal of the Optical Society of America, 18*(12), 2969–2981. doi:10.1364/JOSAA.18.002969

Li, B., Sun, Z., & Tan, T. (2007). Online text-independent writer identification based on stroke's probability distribution function. (. *LNCS, 4642,* 201–210.

Li, Q., & Qiu, Z. (2006). Handmetric verification based on feature-level fusion. *J. of Computer Science and Network Security, 6*(2A).

Li, Q., Juang, B.-H., Zhou, Q., & Lee, C.-H. (2000). Automatic verbal information verification for user authenticaion. *IEEE Transactions on Audio Processing, 8*(5), 585–596. doi:10.1109/89.861378

Li, S. Z., Chu, R. F., Liao, S. C., & Zhang, L. (2007). Illumination invariant face recognition using near-infrared images. *IEEE Trans. PAMI, 29*(4), 1–13.

Li, X. L., Maybank, S. J., Yan, S. J., Tao, D. C., & Xu, D. J. (2008). Gait components and their application to gender recognition. *IEEE Trans. SMC-C, 38*(2), 145–155.

Li, X., Chang, E., & Dai, B. (2002). Improving speaker verification with figure of merit training. In *Proceedings of the International conference on Acoustics, Speech, and Signal Processing.*

Li, Y., Wu, N., Jajodia, S., & Wang, X. S. (2002). *Enhancing profiles for anomaly detection using time granularities.* Paper presented at the Journal of Computer Security (pp. 137-157).

Liang, T. P., & Lai, H.-J. (2002). *Discovering user interests from Web browsing behavior.* Paper presented at the Hawaii International Conference on Systems Sciences, HI.

Lien, C. C., Tien, C. C., et al. (2007). Human gait recognition for arbitrary view angles. *Proc. on the Second International Conference on Innovative Computing, Information and Control, (ICICIC 2007)* (pp. 303-303).

Lin, X., & Simske, S. (2004, November 7-10). *Phoneme-less hierarchical accent classification.* Paper presented at the Thirty-Eighth Asilomar Conference on Signals, Systems, and Computers (pp. 1801- 1804).

Ling, H., & Okada, K. (2006). Diffusion distance for histogram comparison. *IEEE Conference on Computer Vision and Pattern Recognition*, 246–253.

Little, J., & Boyd, J. (1998). Recognizing people by their gait: The shape of motion. *Videre: Journal of Computer Vision Research*, *1*(2), 1–32.

Liu, A., & Salvucci, D. (2001, August 5-10). *Modeling and prediction of human driver behavior.* Paper presented at the 9th HCI International Conference, New Orleans, LA (pp. 1479-1483).

Liu, C. (2002). Gabor feature based classification using the enhanced fisher linear discriminant model for face recognition. *IEEE Trans. IP.*, *11*(4), 467–476.

Liu, C. (2004). Gabor-based kernel PCA with fractional power polynomial models for face recognition. *IEEE Trans. PAMI*, *26*(5), 572–581.

Liu, C., & Wechsler, H. (2003). Independent component analysis of Gabor features for face recognition. *IEEE Trans. NN.*, *14*(4), 919–928.

Liu, D., & Huebner, F. (2002, November 6-8). *Application profiling of IP traffic.* Paper presented at the 27th Annual IEEE Conference on Local Computer Networks (pp. 220-229).

Liu, F., & Picard, R. W. (1998). Finding periodicity in space and time. *Proceedings of the IEEE Sixth International Conference on Computer Vision* (pp. 376-382).

Liu, J., & Zheng, N. (2007). Gait history image: A novel temporal template for gait recognition. In *Proceedings of IEEE International Conference on Multimedia and Expo* (pp. 663-666).

Liu, K., Cheng, Y. Q., & Yang, J. Y. (1993). Algebraic feature extraction for image recognition based on an optimal discriminant criterion. *Pattern Recognition*, *26*(6), 903–911. doi:10.1016/0031-3203(93)90056-3

Liu, M., Chang, E., & Dai, B. (2002). Hierarchical Gaussian mixture model for speaker verification. In *Seventh International Conference on Spoken Language Processing*. ISCA.

Liu, Y. X., Collins, R. T., & Tsin, Y. H. (2002). Gait sequence analysis using frieze patterns. In *Proceedings of European Conference on Computer Vision* (pp. 659-671).

Liu, Z. Y., & Sarkar, S. (2006). Improved gait recognition by gait dynamics normalization. *IEEE Trans. PAMI*, *28*(6), 863–876.

Liu, Z., & Bridges, S. M. (2005, April 4-6). *Dynamic learning of automata from the call stack log for anomaly detection.* Paper presented at the International Conference on Information Technology: Coding and Computing (ITCC 2005) (pp. 774-779).

Liu, Z., & Sarkar, S. (2004). Simplest representation yet for gait recognition: Averaged silhouette. *IEEE Int'l Conf. Pattern Recognition*, *4*, 211–214.

Liu, Z., & Sarkar, S. (2007). Outdoor recognition at a distance by fusing gait and face. *Image and Vision Computing*, *25*, 817–832. doi:10.1016/j.imavis.2006.05.022

Liwicki, M., Schlapbach, A., Bunke, H., Bengio, S., Mariéthoz, J., & Richiardi, J. (2006). Writer identification for smart meeting room systems. *Seventh IAPR Workshop on Document Analysis Systems*, 186-195.

Logan, B., & Moreno, P. J. (1997). *Factorial hidden Markov models for speech recognition: Preliminary experiments.* (Tech. Rep. CRL-97-7). Cambrige Research Laboratory.

Logan, B., & Moreno, P. J. (1998). Factorial HMMs for acoustic modeling. In *Proceedings of IEEE International Conference on Acoustics, Speech and Signal Processing* (Vol. 2, pp. 813-816).

Lu, H., Plataniotis, K. N., & Venetsanopoulos, A. N. (2006). Multilinear principal component analysis of tensor objects for recognition. In *Proc. of the 18th International Conference on Pattern Recognition (ICPR'06)* (Vol. 2, pp. 776–779).

Lu, J. W., & Zhang, E. (2007). Gait recognition for human identification based on ICA and fuzzy SVM through multiple views fusion. *Pattern Recognition Letters, 28*(16), 2401–2411. doi:10.1016/j.patrec.2007.08.004

Lu, J., Plataniotis, K. N., Venetsnopulos, A. N., & Li, S. Z. (2006). Ensemble-based discriminant learning with bosting for face recognition. *IEEE Trans. NN., 17*(1), 1–13.

Luck, S. J. (2005). An introduction to the event related potential technique. Cambridge, MA: MIT Press.

Luettin, J., Thacker, N. A., & Beet, S. W. (1996). *Speaker identification by lipreading.* Paper presented at the 4th International Conference on Spoken Language Processing (ICSLP'96).

Lundin, E., Kvarnström, H., & Jonsson, E. (2002, December 9-12). *A synthetic fraud data generation methodology.* Paper presented at the 4th International Conference on Information and Communications Security (ICICS 2002), Singapore (pp. 265-277).

Lunt, T. (1993). *Detecting intruders in computer systems.* Paper presented at the Conference on Auditing and Computer Technology.

Lyons, M. J., Budynek, J., & Akamatsu, S. (1999). Automatic classification of single facial images. *IEEE Trans. PAMI, 21*(12), 1357–1362.

Lyons, M. J., Budynek, J., Plante, A., & Akamatsu, S. (2000). Classifying facial attributes using a 2-D Gabor wavelet representation and discriminant analysis. *FG'02*, 202-207.

Lyu, S., Rockmore, D., & Farid, H. (2004). A digital technique for art authentication. *Proceedings of the National Academy of Sciences of the United States of America, 101*(49), 17006–17010. doi:10.1073/pnas.0406398101

Ma, Q., Wang, S., Nie, D., & Qiu, J. (2007). Recognizing humans based on gait moment image. In *Proceedings of Eighth ACIS International Conference on Software Engineering, Artificial Intelligence, Networking and Parallel Distributed Computing, 2*, 606–610.

Ma, Y., Schuckers, M., & Cukic, B. (2005), October. *Guidelines for appropriate use of simulated data for bio-authentication research.* Paper presented at the 4th IEEE Workshop on Automatic Identification Advanced Technologies (AUTO ID), Buffalo, NY (pp. 251-256).

Maclennan, B. (1991). *Gabor representations of spatiotemporal visual images.* Retrieved from www.cs.utk.edu/~mclennan/papers/GRSTVI.ps

Maeder, A. J. (2005, February). The image importance approach to human vision based image quality characterization. *Pattern Recognition Letters, 26*, 347–354. doi:10.1016/j.patrec.2004.10.018

Maeder, A., & Fookes, C. (2003, December). A visual attention approach to personal identification. In *Proceedings of the Eighth Australian and New Zealand Intelligent Information Systems Conference,* Sydney, Australia (pp. 55–60).

Maeder, A., Fookes, C., & Sridharan, S. (2004, October). Gaze based user authentication for personal computer applications. In *Proceedings of the 2004 International Symposium on Intelligent Multimedia, Video, and Speech Processing,* Hong Kong (pp. 727–730).

Maffei, L., & Fiorentini, A. (1973). The visual cortex as a spatial frequency analyzer. *Vision Research, 13,* 1255–1267. doi:10.1016/0042-6989(73)90201-0

Mahier, J., Pasquet, M., Rosenberger, C., & Cuozzo, F. (2008). Biometric authentication. In *IGI encyclopedia of information science and technology, 2nd edition*

Mainguet, J.-F. (2006). *Biometrics,* Retrieved on July 28, 2006, from http://perso.orange.fr/fingerchip/biometrics/biometrics.htm

Makihara, Y., Sagawa, R., Mukaigawa, Y., Echigo, T., & Yagi, Y. (2006). Gait recognition using a view transformation model in the frequency domain. In *Proceedings of ECCV* (Vol. 3, pp. 151–163).

Makthal, S., & Ross, A. (2005, September). *Synthesis of iris images using Markov random fields.* Paper presented at the 13th European Signal Processing Conference (EUSIPCO), Antalya, Turkey.

Maltoni, M. (2004). Generation of synthetic fingerprint image databases. In N. Ratha & R. Bolle (Eds.), *Automatic fingerprint recognition systems.* Springer.

Mansfield, A. J., & Wayman, J. L. (2002). *Best practices in testing and reporting performance of biometric devices.* NPL Report CMSC 14/02.

Marceau, C. (2000, September 19-21). *Characterizing the behavior of a program using multiple-length n-grams.* Paper presented at the New Security Paradigms Workshop, Cork, Ireland.

Marcel, S., & Millan, J. (2007). Person authentication using brainwaves (EEG) and maximum a posteriori model adaptation. *IEEE Transactions on Pattern Analysis and Machine Intelligence, 29*(4), 743–752. doi:10.1109/TPAMI.2007.1012

Marcelja, S. (1980). Mathematical description of the responses of simple cortical cells. *Journal of the Optical Society of America, 70,* 1297–1300. doi:10.1364/JOSA.70.001297

Marin, J., Ragsdale, D., & Surdu, J. (2001). *A hybrid approach to the profile creation and intrusion detection.* Paper presented at the DARPA Information Survivability Conference and Exposition (DISCEX II'01).

Markowitz, J. (2002). Speaker recognition. *Biometric Technology Today, 10*(6), 9–11. doi:10.1016/S0969-4765(02)00618-5

Marti, U., Messerli, R., & Bunke, H. (2001). Writer identification using text line based features. *Proc. Sixth Int'l Conf. Document Analysis and Recognition (ICDAR),* 101-105.

Mason, J. S. D., Brand, J., Auckenthaler, R., Deravi, F., & Chibelushi, C. (1999). *Lip signatures for automatic person recognition.* Paper presented at the In IEEE Workshop, MMSP (pp. 457-462).

Matsumoto, Y. Ogasawara, T., & Zelinsky, A. (2000, October). Behavior recognition based on head pose and gaze direction measurement. In *Proceedings of the IEEE/RSJ International Intelligent Robots and Systems* (Vol. 3, pp. 2127–2132).

Maurer, M. (2005). *IRC database.* Retrieved on May 19, 2005, from http://games.cs.ualberta.ca/poker/IRC

Maxion, R. A., & Townsend, T. N. (2002, June 23-26). *Masquerade detection using truncated command lines.* Paper presented at the International Conference of Dependable Systems and Networks, Washington, D.C.

McCraty, R., Atkinson, M., Tiller, W. A., Rein, G., & Watkins, A. D. (1995). The effects of emotions on short-term power spectrum analysis of heart rate variability. *The American Journal of Cardiology, 76*(14), 1089–1093. doi:10.1016/S0002-9149(99)80309-9

Mehta, S. S., & Lingayat, N. S. (2004). Comparative study of QRS detection in single lead and 12-lead ECG based on entropy and combined entropy criteria using support vector machine. *Journal of Theoretical and Applied Information Technology, 3*(2), 8–18.

Meuwly, D., & Drygajlo, A. (2001). Forensic speaker recognition based on a Bayesian framework and Gaussian mixture modeling (GMM). In *A Speaker Odyssey-The Speaker Recognition Workshop*. ISCA.

Michael, C. C. (2003, April 22-24). *Finding the vocabulary of program behavior data for anomaly detection*. Paper presented at the DARPA Information Survivability Conference and Exposition (pp. 152-163).

Michael, C. C., & Ghosh, A. (2000, October). *Using finite automata to mine execution data for intrusion detection: A preliminary report*. Paper presented at the Third International Workshop in Recent Advances in Intrusion Detection, Toulouse, France.

Mildner, V., Goetze, S., Kammeyer, K. D., & Mertins, A. (2007). Optimization of Gabor features for text-independent speaker identification. *ISCAS, 07*, 3932–3935.

Milner, B. (2002). A comparison of front-end configurations for robust speech recognition. *Proceedings of the International conference on Acoustics, Speech, and Signal Processing*.

Minato, T., Shimada, M., Itakura, S., Lee, K., & Ishiguro, H. (2005, July). Does gaze reveal the human likeness of an android? In *Proceedings of the 4th International Conference on Development and Learning* (pp. 106–111).

Mitra, S., Mitra, M., & Chaudhuri, B. B. (2006). A rough-set-based inference engine for ECG classification. *IEEE Transactions on Instrumentation and Measurement, 55*(6), 2198–2206. doi:10.1109/TIM.2006.884279

Mohammadi, G., Shoushtari, P., Ardekani, B. M., & Shamsollahi, B. (2006, February 11). Person identification by using AR model for EEG signals. *Proceedings of the World Academy of Science, Engineering, and Technology* (pp. 281-285).

Mok, L., Lau, W. H., Leung, S. H., Wang, S. L., & Yan, H. (2004, October 24-27). *Person authentication using ASM based lip shape and intensity information*. Paper presented at the International Conference on Image Processing (pp. 561-564).

Molla, K., & Hirose, K. (2004). On the effectiveness of MFCCs and their statistical distribution properties in speaker identification. In *IEEE Symposium on Virtual Environments, Human-Computer Interfaces and Measurement Systems (VECIMS)*.

Monrose, F., & Rubin, A. D. (2000). Keystroke dynamics as a biometric for authentication. *Future Generation Computer Systems, 16*(4), 351–359. doi:10.1016/S0167-739X(99)00059-X

Monrose, F., Reiter, M. K., & Wetzel, S. (2002). Password hardening based on keystroke dynamics. *International Journal of Information Security, 1*(2), 69–83. doi:10.1007/s102070100006

Moon, Y. S., Yeung, H. W., Chan, K. C., & Chan, S. O. (2004). Template synthesis and image mosaicking for fingerprint registration: An experimental study. In *IEEE Int'l Conf. on Acoustics, Speech, and Signal Processing* (Vol. 5, pp. 409-412).

Morup, M., Hansen, L. K., Herrmann, C. S., Parnas, J., & Arnfred, S. M. (2006). Parallel factor analysis as an exploratory tool for wavelet transformed event-related EEG. *NeuroImage, 29*(3), 938–947. doi:10.1016/j.neuroimage.2005.08.005

Movellan, J. R. (2008). *Tutorial on Gabor filters*. Retrieved from http://mplab.ucsd.edu/wordpress/tutorials/gabor.pdf

Mowbray, S. D., & Nixon, M. S. (2003). Automatic gait recognition via Fourier descriptors of deformable objects. *Proc. of 4th International Conference on Audio- and Video-based Biometric Person Authentication* (pp. 566-573).

Muller, H., Muller, W., Squire, D. M., Marchand-Maillet, S., & Pun, T. (2001). Performance evaluation in content-based image retrieval: Overview and proposals. *Pattern Recognition Letters, 22*, 593–601. doi:10.1016/S0167-8655(00)00118-5

Muralidharan, N., & Wunnava, S. (2004, June 2-4). *Signature verification: A popular biometric technology.* Paper presented at the Second LACCEI International Latin American and Caribbean Conference for Engineering and Technology (LACCEI'2004), Miami, FL.

Muramatsu, D., & Matsumoto, T. (2007). Effectiveness of pen pressure, azimuth, and altitude features for online signature verification. *Proceedings of the International Conference on Advances in Biometrics (ICB)* (LNCS 4642, pp. 503-512). Springer.

Murase, H., & Sakai, R. (1996). Moving object recognition in eigenspace representation: Gait analysis and lip reading. *Pattern Recognition Letters, Elsevier Science, 17*(2), 155–162. doi:10.1016/0167-8655(95)00109-3

Murray, M. P. (1967). Gait as a total pattern of movement. *American Journal of Physical Medicine, 46*(1), 290–332.

Murray, M. P., & Drought, A. B. (1964). Walking patterns of normal men. *Journal of Bone and Joint Surgery, 46-A*(2), 335–360.

Nadimi, S., & Bhanu, B. (2004). Physical models for moving shadow and object detection in video. *IEEE Transactions on Pattern Analysis and Machine Intelligence, 26*(8), 1079–1087. doi:10.1109/TPAMI.2004.51

Nakanishi, I., Nishiguchi, N., Itoh, Y., & Fukui, Y. (2003). Online signature verification method utilizing feature extraction based on DWT. *Proceedings of the 2003 International Symposium on Circuits and Systems (ISCAS 2003), IV* (pp. 73-76).

Nakasone, H., & Beck, S. D. (2001). Forensic automatic speaker recognition. In *A Speaker Odyssey-The Speaker Recognition Workshop.* ISCA.

Nalwa, V. S. (1997). Automatic online signature verification. *Proceedings of the IEEE, 85*, 215–239. doi:10.1109/5.554220

Namboodiri, A., & Gupta, S. (2006). Text independent writer identification from online handwriting. *Tenth International Workshop on Frontiers in Handwriting Recognition*, 131–147.

Navratil, J., Jin, Q., Andrews, W. D., & Campbell, J. P. (2003). Phonetic speaker recognition using maximum-likelihood binary-decision tree models. In *Proceedings of the International conference on Acoustics, Speech, and Signal Processing.*

Nayar, S. K., Murase, M., & Nene, S. A. (1986). Parametric appearance representation. In *Early visual learning.* Oxford: Oxford University Press.

Nazar, A., Traore, I., & Ahmed, A. A. E. (2008). Inverse biometrics for mouse dynamics. [IJPRAI]. *International Journal of Pattern Recognition and Artificial Intelligence, 22*(3), 461–495. doi:10.1142/S0218001408006363

Nevadaigtf.org. (2005). Player id, age verification, and border control technology forum. *Nevada Interactive Gaming Task Force.* Retrieved on October 23, 2005, from http://www.nevadaigtf.org/TechnologyForum.html

Newman, M., Gillick, L., Ito, Y., Mcallaster, D., & Peskin, B. (1996). Speaker verification through large vocabulary continuous speech recognition. In *Proceedings International conference on Spoken Language Processing.*

Nguyen, N., Reiher, P., & Kuenning, G. H. (2003, June 18-20). *Detecting insider threats by monitoring system call activity.* Paper presented at the IEEE Systems, Man, and Cybernetics Society Information Assurance Workshop (pp. 45-52).

Nixon, M. S., & Carter, J. N. (2004). On gait as a biometric: Progress and prospects. *EUSIPCO, 04*, 1401–1404.

Nixon, M. S., & Carter, J. N. (2006). Automatic recognition by gait. *Proceedings of the IEEE, 94*(11), 2013–2024. doi:10.1109/JPROC.2006.886018

Nixon, M. S., Tan, T. N., & Chellappa, R. (2005). *Human identification based on gait.* New York: Springer.

Nixon, M., Carter, J., Nash, J., Huang, P., Cunado, D., & Stevenage, S. (1999). Automatic gait recognition. *Proceedings of the IEE Colloquium on Motion Analysis and Tracking* (pp. 31-36).

Niyogi, S., & Adelson, E. (1994). Analyzing and recognizing walking figures in XYT. In . *Proceedings of CVPR, 94*, 469–474.

Noble, J. (2002). *Finding robust Texas hold'em poker strategies using pareto coevolution and deterministic crowding.* Paper presented at the International Conference on Machine Learning and Applications (ICMLA'02).

Noble, R. A., & Watson, J. (2001). *Pareto coevolution: Using performance against coevolved opponents in a game as dimensions for pareto selection.* Paper presented at the Genetic and Evolutionary Computation Conference, GECCO-2001 (pp. 493-500).

Noton, D., & Stark, L. (1971). Eye movements and visual perception. *Scientific American, 224*(6), 35–43.

Noton, D., & Stark, L. (1971). Scanpaths in eye movements during pattern perception. *Science, 171*(3968), 308–311. doi:10.1126/science.171.3968.308

Novikov, D. (2005). *Neural networks to intrusion detection.* Unpublished MS thesis, Rochester Institute of Technology, Rochester, NY.

Novikov, D., Yampolskiy, R. V., & Reznik, L. (2006, April 10-12). *Anomaly detection based intrusion detection.* Paper presented at the Third International Conference on Information Technology: New Generations (ITNG 2006), Las Vegas, NV (pp. 420-425).

Novikov, D., Yampolskiy, R. V., & Reznik, L. (2006, May 5). *Artificial intelligence approaches for intrusion detection.* Paper presented at the Long Island Systems Applications and Technology Conference (LISAT 2006), Long Island, NY (pp. 1-8).

Obaidat, M. S., & Sadoun, B. (1999). Keystroke dynamics based authentication. In A. K. Jain, R. Bolle & S. Pankanti (Eds.), *Biometrics: Personal identification in networked society* (pp. 213-230). New York: Springer.

Oel, P., Schmidt, P., & Shmitt, A. (2001). Time prediction of mouse-based cursor movements. *Proc. of Joint AFIHM-BCS Conf. on Human-Computer Interaction IHM-HCI, 2*, 37–40.

Oliver, N., & Pentland, A. P. (2000). *Graphical models for driver behavior recognition in a SmartCar.* Paper presented at the IEEE Intelligent Vehicles Symposium.

Oliver, N., Rosario, B., & Pentland, A. P. (2000). A Bayesian computer vision system for modeling human interactions. *IEEE Transactions on Pattern Analysis and Machine Intelligence, 22*(8), 831–843. doi:10.1109/34.868684

Orlans, N. M., Buettner, D. J., & Marques, J. (2004). *A survey of synthetic biometrics: Capabilities and benefits.* Paper presented at the International Conference on Artificial Intelligence (IC-AI'04) (pp. 499-505).

Orozco, M., Asfaw, Y., Adler, A., Shirmohammadi, S., & Saddik, A. E. (2005, May 17-19). *Automatic identification of participants in haptic systems.* Paper presented at the IEEE Instrumentation and Measurement Technology Conference, Ottawa, Canada.

Orozco, M., Asfaw, Y., Shirmohammadi, S., Adler, A., & El Saddik, A. (2006). Haptic-based biometrics: A feasibility study. *Symposium on Haptic Interfaces for Virtual Environment and Teleoperator Systems (HAPTICS)* (pp. 265-271).

Orozco, M., Asfaw, Y., Shirmohammadi, S., Adler, A., & Saddik, A. E. (2006, March 25-29). *Haptic-based biometrics: A feasibility study.* Paper presented at the IEEE Virtual Reality Conference, Alexandria, VA.

Ortega, M., Marino, C., Penedo, M. G., Blanco, M., & Gonzalez, F. (2006). Biometric authentication using digital retinal images. *ACOS, 06*, 422–427.

Ortega-Garcia, J., Fiérrez-Aguilar, J., Simon, D., Gonzalez, J., Faundez-Zanuy, M., & Espinosa, V. (2003). MCYT baseline corpus: A bimodal biometric database. *IEEE Proceedings Visual Image Processing, 150*(6), 395–401. doi:10.1049/ip-vis:20031078

Ourston, D. (1989). Program recognition. *IEEE Expert, 4*(4), 36–49. doi:10.1109/64.43284

Palaniappan, R. (2005). Multiple mental thought parametric classification: A new approach for individual identification. *International Journal of Signal Processing, 2*(1), 222–225.

Palaniappan, R., & Mandic, D. P. (2007). Biometrics from brain electrical activity: A machine learning approach. *The Journal of VLSI Signal Processing, 29*(4), 738–742.

Pamudurthy, S., Guan, E., Mueller, K., & Rafailovich, M. (2005). Dynamic approach for face recognition using digital image skin correlation. In *Audio and video-based biometrics person authentication.* New York.

Pan, Y., & Waibel, A. (2000). The effects of room acoustics on MFCC speech parameter. In *International conference on Spoken Language Processing.*

Pankanti, S., & Jain, A. K. (2008). Beyond fingerprinting. *Scientific American,* 79–81.

Park, A., & Hazen, T. J. (2002). ASR dependent techniques for speaker recognition. In *International Conference on Spoken Language Processing* (pp. 1337-1340).

Park, S. W., & Savvides, M. (2006). Estimating mixing factors simultaneously in multilinear tensor decomposition for robust face recognition and synthesis. In *Proceedings of the 2006 Conference on Computer Vision and Pattern Recognition Workshop (CVPRW'06).*

Pavlidis, I., Levine, J., & Baukol, P. (2000). Thermal imaging for anxiety detection. *Proc. IEEE Workshop on Computer Vision beyond the Visible Spectrum: Methods and Applications* (pp. 104-109).

Peacock, A., Ke, X., & Wilkerson, M. (2004). Typing patterns: A key to user identification. *IEEE Security & Privacy, 2*(5), 40–47. doi:10.1109/MSP.2004.89

Pelecanos, J., & Sridharan, S. (2001). Feature warping for robust speaker verification. In *A Speaker Odyssey-The Speaker Recognition Workshop.* ISCA.

Pennington, A. G., Strunk, J. D., Griffin, J. L., Soules, C. A. N., Goodson, G. R., & Ganger, G. R. (2002). *Storage-based intrusion detection: Watching storage activity for suspicious behavior.* (No. CMU--CS-02-179). Carnegie Mellon University.

Pentlad, A., Moghaddam, B., Starner, T., Oliyide, O., & Turk, M. (1994). *View based and modular eigeispaces for face recognition.* (Tech. Rep. 245). MIT Media Laboratory, Percentual Computing Section.

Periaswamy, S., & Farid, H. (2003). Elastic registration in the presence of intensity variations. *IEEE Transactions on Medical Imaging, 22*(7), 865–874. doi:10.1109/TMI.2003.815069

Peskin, B., Navratil, J., Abramson, J., Jones, D., Klusacek, D., Reynolds, D., et al. (2003). Using prosodic and conversational features for high-performance speaker recognition: Report from JHU WS'02. In *Proceedings of the International conference on Acoustics, Speech, and Signal Processing*

Peters, C., & Sullivan, C. O. (2003). Bottom-up visual attention for virtual human animation. In *Computer animation for social agents.*

Peters, R. J., Iyer, A., Itti, L., & Koch, C. (2005, August). Components of bottom-up gaze allocation in natural images. *Vision Research, 45*(18), 2397–2416. doi:10.1016/j.visres.2005.03.019

Petrovska-Delacretaz, D., El Hannani, A., & Chollet, G. (2007). Text-independent speaker verification: State of the art and challenges. ([). *Progress in nonlinear speech processing*]. *LNCS, 4391,* 135–169.

Phillips, J., Flynn, P., Scruggs, T., Bowyer, K., Chang, J., & Hoffman, K. (2005). Overview of the face recognition grand challenge. In . *Proceedings of IEEE Conference of Computer Vision and Pattern Recognition, 1,* 947–954.

Phillips, P. J., Moon, H., Rizvi, S. A., & Rauss, P. J. (2000). The FERET evaluation methodology for face-recognition algorithms. *IEEE Transactions on Pattern Analysis and Machine Intelligence Archive, 22*(10), 1090–1104. doi:10.1109/34.879790

Phillips, P. J., Sarkar, S., et al. (2002). The gait identification challenge problem: Data sets and baseline algorithm. *Proc. of International Conference on Pattern Recognition* (pp. 385-388).

Phua, K., Dat, T. H., Chen, J., & Shue, L. (2006). *Human identification using heart sound.* Paper presented at the Second International Workshop on Multimodal User Authentication, Toulouse, France.

Picard, R. W., Vyzas, E., & Healey, J. (2001). Toward machine emotional intelligence: Analysis of affective physiological state. *IEEE Transactions on Pattern Analysis and Machine Intelligence, 23*(10), 1175–1191. doi:10.1109/34.954607

Plamondon, R., & Lorette, G. (1989). Automatic signature verification and writer identification: The state of the art. *Pattern Recognition, 22*(2), 107–131. doi:10.1016/0031-3203(89)90059-9

poker-edge.com. (2006). *Stats and analysis.* Retrieved on June 7, 2006, from http://www.poker-edge.com/stats.php

Poker-edge.com. (n.d.). *Stats and analysis.* Retrieved on June 7, 2006, from http://www.poker-edge.com/stats.php

Pokerinspector.com. (2006). *Online holdem inspector.* Retrieved on May 2, 2006, from http://www.pokerinspector.com/

Pokerprophecy.com. (2006). *Pokerprophecy.* Retrieved on September 26, 2006, from http://www.pokerprophecy.com

Polana, R., & Nelson, R. (1993). Detecting activities. In *Proceedings of the IEEE Computer Society Conference on Computer Vision and Pattern Recognition* (pp. 2-7).

Polana, R., & Nelson, R. (1994). Low level recognition of human motion (or how to get your man without finding his body parts). *Proc. IEEE Workshop on Motion of Non-Rigid and Articulated Objects* (pp. 77-82).

Polemi, D. (1997). *Biometric techniques: Review and evaluation of biometric techniques for identification and authentication, including an appraisal of the areas where they are most applicable.* (Tech. Rep.). Retrieved from ftp://ftp.cordis.lu/pub/infosec/docs/biomet.doc

Pollen, D. A., & Ronner, S. F. (1981). Phase relationships between adjacent simple cells in the visual cortex. *Science, 212,* 1409–1411. doi:10.1126/science.7233231

Pollen, D. A., Lee, J. R., & Taylor, J. H. (1971). How does the striate cortex begin the reconstruction of the visual world? *Science, 173,* 74–77. doi:10.1126/science.173.3991.74

Porat, M., & Zeevi, Y. (1988). The generalized Gabor scheme of image representation in biological and machine vision. *IEEE Trans. PAMI, 10*(4), 452–468.

Porteus, I., Bart, E., & Welling, M. (2008). Multi-HDP: A nonparametric Bayesian model for tensor factorization. In *Proc. of AAAI 2008* (pp. 1487–1490).

Prabhakar, S., Pankanti, S., & Jain, A. K. (2003). Biometric recognition: Security and privacy concerns. *IEEE Security & Privacy*, March/April, 33–42

Prassas, G., Pramataris, K. C., & Papaemmanouil, O. (2001, June). *Dynamic recommendations in Internet retailing.* Paper presented at the 9th European Conference on Information Systems (ECIS 2001).

Pratheepan, Y., Prasad, G., & Condell, J. V. (2008). Style of action based individual recognition in video sequences. *Proceeding of the IEEE International Conference on Systems, Man, and Cybernetics (SMC)* (pp. 1237-1242).

Pratheepan, Y., Torr, P. H. S., Condell, J. V., & Prasad, G. (2008). Body language based individual identification in video using gait and actions. *The Third International Conference on Image and Signal Processing (ICISP)* (pp. 368-377).

Preez, J., & Soms, S. H. (2005). *Person identification and authentication by using "the way the heart beats."* Paper presented at the ISSA 2005 New Knowledge Today Conference, Sandton, South Africa.

Przybocki, M., & Martin, A. F. (2004). NIST speaker recognition evaluation chronicles. In *A Speaker Odyssey-The Speaker Recognition Workshop*. ISCA.

Purser, M. (1995). *Introduction to error-correcting codes*. Boston: Artech House.

Pusara, M., & Brodley, C. E. (2004). *User reauthentication via mouse movements*. Paper presented at the ACM Workshop on Visualization and Data Mining for Computer Security, Washington, D.C. (pp. 1-8).

Quilici, A., Yang, Q., & Woods, S. (1998). Applying plan recognition algorithms to program understanding. *Automated Software Engineering: An International Journal, 5*(3), 347–372. doi:10.1023/A:1008608825390

Rabiner, L. R., & Schafer, R. W. (1978). *Digital processing of speech signals*. Englewood Cliffs, NJ: Prentice-Hall.

Rafael, C. G., & Richard, E. W. (2003). *Digital image processing*. Pearson Education, second edition.

Rainville, R., Bechara, A., Naqvi, N., & Damasio, A. R. (n.d.). Basic emotions are associated with distinct patterns of cardiorespiratory activity. *International Journal of Psychophysiology*.

Rajagopalan, A., & Chellappa, R. (2000). Higher-order spectral analysis of human motion. *Proc. International Conference on Image Processing, 3*, 230-233.

Ramann, F., Vielhauer, C., & Steinmetz, R. (2002). Biometric applications based on handwriting. *IEEE ICME'02, 2*, 573–576.

Ramon, J., & Jacobs, N. (2002). *Opponent modeling by analysing play*. Paper presented at the Computers and Games workshop on Agents in Computer Games, Edmonton, Albera, Canada.

Ratha, N. K., Connell, J. H., & Bolle, R. M. (2001). Enhancing security and privacy in biometrics-based authentication systems. *IBM Systems Journal, 40*(3).

Ratha, N. K., Senior, A., & Bolle, R. M. (2001, March). *Automated biometrics*. Paper presented at the International Conference on Advances in Pattern Recognition, Rio de Janeiro, Brazil.

Ratha, N., Connell, J., & Bolle, R. (2003). Biometrics break-ins and band-aids. *Pattern Recognition Letters, 24*, 2105–2113. doi:10.1016/S0167-8655(03)00080-1

Rayner, K., & Pollatsek, A. (1989). *The psychology of reading*. Englewood Cliffs, NJ: Prentice Hall.

Renaud, K. (2003). Quantifying the quality of Web authentication mechanisms. A usability perspective. *Journal of Web Engineering, 0*(0). Retrieved from http://www.dcs.gla.ac.uk/~karen/papers/j.pdf

Rentfrow, P. J., & Gosling, S. D. (2003). The do-re-mi's of everyday life: The structure and personality correlates of music preferences. *Journal of Personality and Social Psychology, 84*, 1236–1256. doi:10.1037/0022-3514.84.6.1236

Revett, K. (2008). *Behavioral biometrics: A remote access approach*. Chichester, UK: Wiley.

Revett, K., Gorunescu, F., Gorunescu, G., Ene, M., Sérgio Tenreiro de Magalhães, S., & Santos, H. M. D. (2006, April 20-22). Authenticating computer access based on keystroke dynamics using a probabilistic neural network. *International Conference on Global E-Security*, London, UK (pp. 65- 71).

Reynold, D. A., & Rose, R. C. (1995). Robust text-independent speaker identification using Gaussian mixture speaker models. *IEEE Trans. SAP, 3*(1), 72–83.

Reynolds, D. (1995). Speaker identification and verification using Gaussian mixture speaker models. *Speech Communication, 17*(1-2), 91–108. doi:10.1016/0167-6393(95)00009-D

Reynolds, D. (2002). An overview of automatic speaker recognition technology. In *Proceedings of the International Conference on Acoustics, Speech, and Signal Processing*.

Reynolds, D., Andrews, W., Campbell, J., Navratil, J., Peskin, B., Adami, A., et al. (2003). The SuperSID project: Exploiting high-level information for high-accuracy speaker recognition. In *Proceedings of the International conference on Acoustics, Speech, and Signal Processing*.

Reynolds, D., Quatieri, T., & Dunn, R. (2000). Speaker verification using adapted Gaussian mixture models. *Digital Signal Processing, 10*, 19–41. doi:10.1006/dspr.1999.0361

Richards, E. P. (2008). *Phenotype vs. genotype: Why identical twins have different fingerprints?* Retrieved from http://www.forensic-evidence.com/site/ID Twins.html

Riera, A., Dunne, S., Cester, I., & Ruffini, G. (2007a). *STAFAST: A wireless wearable EEG/ECG biometric system based on the ENOBIO sensor*.

Riera, A., Soria-Frisch, A., Caparrini, M., Grau, C., & Ruffini, G. (2007b). Unobtrusive biometric system based on electroencephalogram analysis. *EURASIP Journal on Advances in Signal Processing*.

Riha, Z., & Matyas, V. (2000). *Biometric authentication systems*. Paper presented at the FI MU Report Series.

Rimey, R. D., & Brown, C. M. (1990). *Selective attention as sequential behavior: Modeling eye movements with an augmented hidden Markov model*. (Tech. Rep. TR-327). Computer Science, University of Rochester.

Ritchie, G. (2001). Current directions in computational humor. *Artificial Intelligence Review, 16-2*, 119-135.

Ritzmann, M. (in preparation). *Strategies for managing missing or incomplete data in biometric and business applications*. Unpublished doctoral dissertation, Pace University, New York.

Rizzolatti, G., Riggio, L., Dascola, I., & Umilta, C. (1987). Reorienting attention across the horizontal and vertical meridians-evidence in favor of a premotor theory of attention. *Neuropsychologia, 25*(1A), 31–40. doi:10.1016/0028-3932(87)90041-8

Robinson, P. E., & Clarke, W. A. (2007, March). Comparison of principal component analysis and linear discriminant analysis for face recognition. In *AFRICON* (pp. 1–6).

Rogez, G., Guerrero, J. J., Martinez del Rincon, J., & Orrite-Uranela, C. (2006). Viewpoint independent human motion analysis in man-made environments. In *Proceedings of BMVC '06*.

Rosenberg, A. E., Lee, C., & Soong, F. K. (1990). Subword unit talker verification using hidden Markov models. In *Proceedings of the International conference on Acoustics, Speech, and Signal Processing*.

Ross, A. A., & Govindarajan, R. (2005, March). Feature level fusion of hand and face biometrics. In *Proc. Spie Conf. on Biometric Technology for Human Identification II* (pp. 196-204).

Ross, A. A., Nandakumar, K., & Jain, A. K. (2006). *Handbook of multibiometrics*. Springer.

Ross, A., & Jain, A. (2003). Information fusion in biometrics. *Pattern Recognition Letters, 24*(13), 2115–2125. doi:10.1016/S0167-8655(03)00079-5

Rossey, L. M., Cunningham, R. K., Fried, D. J., Rabek, J. C., Lippmann, R. P., Haines, J. W., et al. (2002). *LARIAT: Lincoln adaptable real-time information assurance testbed*. Paper presented at the Aerospace Conference 6-2671- 2676-2682.

Roux, C., & Coatrieux, J.-L. (Eds.). (1997). *Contemporary perspectives in three-dimensional biomedical imaging* (Vol. 30 of Studies in Health Technology and Informatics). The Netherlands: IOS Press.

Ruggles, T. (2007). *Comparison of biometric techniques*. Retrieved on May 27, 2007, from http://www.bio-tech-inc.com/bio.htm

Said, H., Peake, G., Tan, T., & Baker, K. (1998). Writer identification from nonuniformly skewed handwriting images. *Proc. Ninth British Machine Vision Conference*, 478-487.

Said, H., Tan, T., & Baker, K. (2000). Personal identification based on handwriting. *Pattern Recognition, 33*(1), 149–160. doi:10.1016/S0031-3203(99)00006-0

Salah, A. A., Alpaydın, E., & Akarun, L. (2002). A selective attention-based method for visual pattern recognition with application to handwritten digit recognition and face recognition. *IEEE Transactions on Pattern Analysis and Machine Intelligence, 24*(3), 420–425. doi:10.1109/34.990146

Sanchez-Avila, C., Sanchez-Reil, R., & Martin-Roche, D. (2002). Iris-based biometric recognition using dyadic wavelet transform. *IEEE AESS Systems Magazine*, 3-6.

Sanderson, C., & Paliwal, K. K. (2001). *Information fusion for robust speaker verification.* Paper presented at the 7th European Conference on Speech Communication and Technology (EUROSPEECH'01), Aalborg.

Sanderson, C., & Paliwal, K. K. (2003). Noise compensation in a person verification system using face and multiple speech features. *Pattern Recognition, 36*(2), 293–302. doi:10.1016/S0031-3203(02)00031-6

Sankar, A., & Mammone, R. J. (1991). *Neural tree networks in neural networks: Theory and applications.* San Diego, CA: Academic.

Sappa, A., Aifanti, N., Malassiotis, S., & Strintzis, M. (2000). Unsupervised motion classification by means of efficient feature selection and tracking. *Proc. International Symposium on 3D Data Processing, Visualization and Transmission* (pp. 912-917).

Sarkar, S., & Phillips, P. J. (2005). The humanID gait challenge problem: Data sets, performance, and analysis. *IEEE Transactions on Pattern Analysis and Machine Intelligence, 27*(2), 162–177. doi:10.1109/TPAMI.2005.39

Sarkar, S., & Vega, I. (2001). Discrimination of motion based on traces in the space of probability functions over feature relations. *Proc. IEEE International Computer Society Conference Computer Vision and Pattern Recognition, 1*, 976-983.

Sarkar, S., Phillips, P., Liu, Z., Vega, I., Grother, P., & Bowyer, K. (2005). The humanID gait challenge problem: Datasets, performance, and analysis. *IEEE Transactions on Pattern Analysis and Machine Intelligence, 27*(2), 162–177. doi:10.1109/TPAMI.2005.39

Schlapbach, A., & Bunke, H. (2004). Using HMM-based recognizers for writer identification and verification. *Proc. Ninth Int'l Workshop Frontiers in Handwriting Recognition*, 167-172.

Schmidt-Nielsen, A., & Crystal, T. H. (2000). Speaker verification by human listeners: Experiments comparing human and machine performance using the NIST 1998 speaker evaluation data. *Digital Signal Processing, 10*(1-3), 249–266. doi:10.1006/dspr.1999.0356

Schneier, B. (1996). *Applied cryptography: Protocols algorithms and source code.* John Wiley and Sons, Inc.

Scholkopf, B., & Smola, A. J. (2002). *Learning with kernels.* Cambridge, London: The MIT Press.

Schomaker, L., & Bulacu, M. (2004). Automatic writer identification using connected-component contours and edge-based features of upper-case western script. *IEEE Transactions on Pattern Analysis and Machine Intelligence, 26*(6), 787–798. doi:10.1109/TPAMI.2004.18

Schonlau, M., DuMouchel, W., Ju, W.-H., Karr, A. F., Theus, M., & Vardi, Y. (2001). Computer intrusion: Detecting maquerades. *Statistical Science, 16*(1), 1–17.

Schoonmaker, A. N. (2005). *The psychology of poker* (first ed.). Henderson, NV: Two Plus Two Publishing.

Schuckers, S. A. C. (2002). Spoofing and antispoofing measures. *Information Security, 7*(4), 56–62.

Schuckers, S. A. C., Schmid, N. A., Abhyankar, A., Dorairaj, V., Boyce, C. K., & Hornak, L. A. (2007, October). On techniques for angle compensation in nonideal iris recognition. *IEEE Transactions on Systems, Man, and Cybernetics . Part B, 37*(5), 1176–1190.

Seleznyov, A., & Puuronen, S. (1999). *Anomaly intrusion detection systems: Handling temporal relations between events.* Paper presented at the 2nd International Workshop on Recent Advances in Intrusion Detection (RAID'99).

Serratosa, F., & Sanfeliu, A. (2006). Signatures versus histograms: Definitions, distances, and algorithms. *Pattern Recognition, 39*(5), 921–934. doi:10.1016/j. patcog.2005.12.005

Shakhnarovich, G., & Darrell, T. (2002). On probabilistic combination of face and gait cues for identification. In *Proc. of Automatic Face and Gesture Recognition* (Vol. 5, pp. 169-174).

Shakhnarovich, G., Lee, L., & Darrel, T. I. (2001). Integrated face and gait recognition from multiple views. In *Proceeding of Computer Vision and Pattern Recognition* (Vol. 1, pp. 439–446).

Shashua, A., & Hazan, T. (2005). Non-negative tensor factorization with applications to statistics and computer vision. In *Proceedings of the 22nd International Conference on Machine Learning* (pp. 792–799).

Shen, T. W., Tompkins, W. J., & Hu, Y. J. (2002, October 23-26). One-lead ECG for identity verification. *Proceedings of the Second Joint EMBS/BMES Conference*, Houston, TX (pp. 62-63).

Shipilova, O. (2006). *Person recognition based on lip movements.* Retrieved on July 15, 2006, from http://www. it.lut.fi/kurssit/03-04/010970000/seminars/shipilova. pdf

Shipp, C. A., & Kuncheva, L. I. (2002). Relationships between combination methods and measures of diversity in combining classifiers. *Information Fusion, 3*, 135–148. doi:10.1016/S1566-2535(02)00051-9

Shriberg, E. (2007). Higher-level features in speaker recognition. In *Speaker classification I.*

Shutler, J. D., Grant, M. G., et al. (2002). On a large sequence-based human gait database. *Proc. of 4th International Conference on Recent Advances in Soft Computing* (pp. 66-71).

Silva, A. V., & Freitas, D. S. (2002). Wavelet-based compared to function-based online signature verification. *Proceedings of the XV Brazilian Symposium on Computer Graphics and Image Processing (SIBGRAPI 02)* (pp. 218-225).

Silva, H. H. P., Gamboa, H. F. S., & Fred, A. L. N. (2007, April). Applicability of lead V_2 ECG measurements in biometrics. *Proc International Educational and Networking Forum for eHealth, Telemedicine, and Health ICT-Med-e-Tel*, Luxembourg.

Silva, L. S., Santos, A. F. d., Silva, J. D. d., & Montes, A. (2004). A neural network application for attack detection in computer networks. *Instituto Nacional de Pesquisas Espanciais.*

Silver, D. L., & Biggs, A. (2006). Keystroke and eye-tracking biometrics for user identification. In *IC-AI*, 344–348.

Simon, C., & Goldstein, I. (1935). A new scientific method of identification. *New York State Journal of Medicine, 35*(18), 901–906.

Sirovich, L., & Kirby, M. (1987). Low dimensional procedure for the characterization of human faces. *Journal of the Optical Society of America. A, Optics, Image Science, and Vision, 4*(3), 519–524. doi:10.1364/ JOSAA.4.000519

Sklansky, D., & Malmuth, M. (2004). *Hold'em poker for advanced players.* Henderson, NV: Two Plus Two Publishing.

Smith, L. H., & Nelson, D. J. (2004). An estimate of physical scale from speech. In *Proceedings of the International conference on Acoustics, Speech, and Signal Processing.*

Soares, J. V. B., Leandro, J. J. G., Cesar, R. M. Jr, Jelinek, H. F., & Cree, M. J. (2006). Retinal vessel segmentation using the 2-D Gabor wavelet and supervised classification. *IEEE Trans. MI., 25*(9), 1214–1222.

Solayappan, N., & Latifi, S. (2006). *A survey of unimodal biometric methods.* Paper presented at the Security and Management, Las Vegas, NV (pp. 57-63).

Sommer, R., & Paxson, V. (2003). *Enhancing byte-level network intrusion detection signatures with context.* Paper presented at the 10th ACM Conference on Computer and Communications Security.

Song, D., Venable, P., & Perrig, A. (1997). User recognition by keystroke latency pattern analysis. Retrieved in May 2005, from http://citeseer.ist.psu.edu/song97user.html

Sönmez, K., Shriberg, E., Heck, L., & Weintraub, M. (1998). Modeling dynamic prosodic variation for speaker verification. In *the Proceedings of International conference on Spoken Language Processing.*

Spafford, E. H., & Weeber, S. A. (1992, October). *Software forensics: Can we track code to its authors?* Paper presented at the 15th National Computer Security Conference (pp. 641-650).

Spampinato, C., Nicotra, M., & Travaglianti, A. (2008). Analysis of focuses of attention distribution for a novel face recognition system. *Proc. of BIOSTEC 2008,* Madeira, Portugal.

Spencer, N. M., & Carter, J. N. (2002). Viewpoint invariance in automatic gait recognition. *Proc. of AutoID* (pp. 1–6).

Srihari, S. N., Cha, S., Arora, H., & Lee, S. (2002). Individuality of handwriting. *Journal of Forensic Sciences, 47*(4), 1–17.

Stamatatos, E., Fakotakis, N., & Kokkinakis, G. (1999, June). *Automatic authorship attribution.* Paper presented at the Ninth Conf. European Chap. Assoc. Computational Linguistics, Bergen, Norway (pp. 158-164).

Standring, S. (2004). *Gray's anatomy: The anatomical basis of medicine and surgery.*

Stanton, P. T., Yurcik, W., & Brumbaugh, L. (2005, June 15-17). *FABS: File and block surveillance system for determining anomalous disk accesses.* Paper presented at the Sixth Annual IEEE Information Assurance Workshop (pp. 207-214).

Statham, P. (2005). Threat ananlysis–how can we compare different authentication methods? In *Biometric Consortium Conference*, Arlington, VA.

Stauffer, C., & Grimson, W. (1999). Adaptive background mixture models for real-time tracking. *Proc. Computer Vision and Pattern Recognition* (pp. 246-252).

Stecklow, S., Singer, J., & Patrick, A. (2005). Watch on the Thames. *The Wall Street Journal.* Retrieved on October 4, 2005, from http://online.wsj.com/public/article/sb112077340647880052-ckyzgab0t3asu4udfvnpwroaqcy_20060708.html

Stein, E. M., & Weiss, G. (1971). *Introduction to Fourier analysis on Euclidean spaces.* Princeton University Press.

Stolfo, S. J., Hershkop, S., Wang, K., Nimeskern, O., & Hu, C.-W. (2003, September). *A behavior-based approach to securing e-mail systems.* Paper presented at the Mathematical Methods, Models, and Architectures for Computer Networks Security.

Stolfo, S. J., Hu, C.-W., Li, W.-J., Hershkop, S., Wang, K., & Nimeskern, O. (2003). *Combining behavior models to secure e-mail systems* (No. CU Tech. Rep.). Retrieved from www1.cs.columbia.edu/ids/publications/EMT-weijen.pdf

Sturim, D. E., Reynolds, D. A., Dunn, R. B., & Quatieri, T. F. (2002). Speaker verification using text-constrained Gaussian mixture models. *Proceedings of the International conference on Acoustics, Speech, and Signal Processing.*

Sturn, A. (2000). *Cluster analysis for large scale gene expression studies.* Unpublished Masters thesis, The Institute for Genomic Research, Rockville, MD.

Sumi, K., & Matsuyama, T. (2005, January). *Privacy protection of biometric evaluation database–a preliminary study on synthetic biometric database.* Paper presented at the Japan-Korea Joint Workshop on Frontiers of Computer Vision (pp. 189-194).

Sundaresan, A., Roy-Chowdhury, A. K., & Chellappa, R. (2003). A hidden Markov model based framework for recognition of humans from gait sequences. In *Proceedings of ICIP'03* (Vol. 2, pp. 93–96).

Sutton, S., Braren, M., Zubin, J., & John, E. R. (1965). Evoked-potential correlates of stimulus uncertainty. *Science, 150*(3700), 1187–1188. doi:10.1126/science.150.3700.1187

SVC 2004. (n.d.). First international signature verification competition [online]. Retrieved from http://www.cs.ust.hk/svc2004/

Swets, D. L., & Weng, J. (1996). Using discriminant eigenfeatures for image retrieval. *IEEE Trans. PAMI, 18*(8), 831–836.

Tan, D. L., Huang, K. Q., Yu, S. Q., & Tan, T. N. (2007). Orthogonal diagonal projections for gait recognition. In *Proceedings of ICIP'07* (Vol. 1, pp. 337–340).

Tan, D., Huang, K., et al. (2007). Uniprojective feature for gait recognition. *Proc. of The 2nd International Conference on Biometrics*, Seoul, Korea (pp. 673-682).

Tan, D., Yu, S., et al. (2007). Walker recognition without gait cycle estimation. *Proc. of The 2nd International Conference on Biometrics*, Seoul, Korea (pp. 222-231).

Tan, X., & Bhanu, B. (2005). Fingerprint classification based on learned features. *IEEE Trans. SMC-C., 35*(3), 287–300.

Tanawongsuwan, R., & Bobick, A. (2001). Gait recognition from time-normalized joint-angle trajectories in the walking plane. In *Proceeding of IEEE Computer Vision and Pattern Recognition* (Vol. 2, pp. 726–731).

Tao, D. (2006). Discriminative linear and multilinear subspace methods. Unpublished doctoral dissertation, University of London Birkbeck.

Tao, D., & Li, X. (2007). General tensor discriminant analysis and Gabor features for gait recognition. *IEEE Transactions on Pattern Analysis and Machine Intelligence, 29*(10), 1700-1715. doi:10.1109/TPAMI.2007.1096

Tao, D., Li, X., Wu, X., & Maybank, S. J. (2007). General tensor discriminant analysis and Gabor features for gait recognition. *IEEE Transactions on Pattern Analysis and Machine Intelligence, 29*(10), 1700–1715. doi:10.1109/TPAMI.2007.1096

Technical Report ISO/IEC 19795-3. (2007). *Information technology–biometric performance testing and reporting–part 3: Modality-specific testing.*

Tenenbaum, J. B., & Freeman, W. T. (2000). Separating style and content with bilinear models. *Neural Computation, 12*(6), 1247–1283. doi:10.1162/089976600300015349

Teoh, A. B. J., & Ngo, D. C. L. (2006). Cancellable biometrics realization through BioPhasoring. *Proc. of 9th International Conference on Control, Automation, Robotics and Vision, ICARCV 2006*, Singapore.

Teoh, A. B. J., Ngo, D. C. L., & Goh, A. (2006). Quantized multispace random mapping for two-factor identity. *IEEE Transaction on Pattern Recognition and Machine Intelligence, 28*(12), 1892–1901. doi:10.1109/TPAMI.2006.250

Teoh, A. B. J., Toh, K. A., & Yip, W. K. (2007, August 27-29). 2^N discretisation of BioPhasor in cancellable biometrics. *2nd International Conference on Biometrics*, Seoul Korea. (LNCS 4642, pp. 435-444).

Thacker, N. A., Clark, A. F., Barron, J. L., Ross Beveridge, J., Courtney, P., & Crum, W. R. (2008). Performance characterization in computer vision: A guide to best practices. *Computer Vision and Image Understanding, 109*, 305–334. doi:10.1016/j.cviu.2007.04.006

Theodorids, S., & Koutroumbas, K. (1998). *Pattern recongnition.* Academic Press.

Thomaz, C. E., & Gillies, D. F. (2003). *A new Fisher-based method applied to face recognition.* (. *LNCS, 2756*, 596–605.

Thompson, K., Miller, G., & Wilder, R. (1997). Wide area Internet traffic patterns and characteristics. *IEEE Network, 11*, 10–23. doi:10.1109/65.642356

Thorpe, J., Oorschot, P. C., & Somayaji, A. (2005). Passthoughts: Authenticating with our minds. In *Proceedings of New Security Paradigms Workshop*, Lake Arrowhead (pp. 45-56).

Thumwarin, P., & Matsuura, T. (2004). Online writer recognition for Thai based on velocity of barycenter of pen-point movement. *Proc. of IEEE International Conference on Image Processing*, 889–892.

Tolliver, D., & Collins, R. (2003). Gait shape estimation for identification. In *Proc. of AVBPA'03* (pp. 734–742).

Tootell, R., Silverman, M., & DeValois, R. L. (1981). Spatial frequency columns in primary visual cortex. *Science, 214*, 813–815. doi:10.1126/science.7292014

Treisman, A. (1964). Selective attention in man. *British Medical Bulletin, 20*, 12–16.

Treisman, A., & Gelade, G. (1980). A feature integration theory of attention. *Cognitive Psychology, 12*, 97–136. doi:10.1016/0010-0285(80)90005-5

Trujillo, M. O., Shakra, I., & Saddik, A. E. (2005). *Haptic: The new biometrics-embedded media to recognizing and quantifying human patterns.* Paper presented at the 13th Annual ACM International Conference on Multimedia, Hilton, Singapore (pp. 387-390).

Tsai, W.-H., & Wang, H.-M. (2006, January). Automatic singer recognition of popular music recordings via estimation and modeling of solo vocal signals. *IEEE Transactions on Audio, Speech, and Language Processing, 14*(1), 330–341. doi:10.1109/TSA.2005.854091

Tsotsos, J., Culhane, M., Wai, W. Y. K., Lai, Y., Davis, N., & Nuflo, F. (1995). Modeling visual attention via selective tuning. *Artificial Intelligence, 78*(1-2): 507–545. doi:10.1016/0004-3702(95)00025-9

Tsymbal, A. (2004). *The problem of concept drift: Definitions and related work* (No. TCD-CS-2004-15). Dublin, Ireland: Trinity College.

Turing, A. (1950). Computing machinery and intelligence. *Mind, 59*(236), 433–460. doi:10.1093/mind/LIX.236.433

Turk, M., & Pentland, A. (1991). Eigenfaces for recognition. *Journal of Cognitive Neuroscience, 3*(1), 71–86. doi:10.1162/jocn.1991.3.1.71

TÜViT. (2005). *EAL2 certification report for authentication engine of VOICE.TRUST server version 4.1.2.0.* Certification Report TUViT-DSZ-CC-9224.

Tuyls, P., Akkermans, A. H. M., Kevenaar, T. A. M., Schrijen, G.-J., Bazen, A. M., & Veldhuis, R. N. J. (2005). Practical biometric authentication with template protection. AVBPA 2005. (. *LNCS, 3546*, 436–446.

Tyagi, A., Davis, J., & Keck, M. (2006). Multiview fusion for canonical view generation based on homography constraints. *ACM-MM Work. on Video Surveillance and Sensor Networks*, 61-69.

U.S. Information Assurance Directorate. (2007). *U.S. government biometric verification mode protection profile for basic robustness environments.* Version 1.1.

UK CESG. (2001). *Biometric device protection profile (BDPP).* Draft issue 0.82.

ultimatebet.com. (2005). *Software-statistics.* Retrieved on May 4, 2005, from http://www.ultimatebet.com

Uludag, U., Pankanti, S., Prabhakar, S., & Jain, A. K. (2004). Biometric cryptosystems: Issues and challenges. *Proceedings of the IEEE, 92*(6). doi:10.1109/JPROC.2004.827372

Urtasun, R., & Fua, P. (2004). *3D tracking for gait characterization and recognition.* (Tech. Rep. No. IC/2004/04). Lausanne, Switzerland: Swiss Federal Institute of Technology.

Valencia, V. S., & Horn, C. (2003). Biometric liveness testing. In *Biometrics* (pp. 139–149). Berkeley, CA: Osborne McGraw Hill.

Varenhorst, C. (2004). *Passdoodles: A lightweight authentication method.* Retrieved on July 27, 2004, from http://people.csail.mit.edu/emax/papers/varenhorst.pdf

Vasilescu, M. A. O., & Terzopoulos, D. (2005). Multilinear independent component analysis. In *Proceedings of the 2005 IEEE Computer Society Conference on Computer Vision and Pattern Recognition (CVPR'05)* (Vol. 1, pp. 547–553).

Vel, O. D., Anderson, A., Corney, M., & Mohay, G. (2001). *Mining e-mail content for author identification forensics.* Paper presented at the SIGMOD: Special Section on Data Mining for Intrusion Detection and Threat Analysis.

Veldhuis, R. N. J., Bazen, A. M., Kauffman, J. A., & Hartel, P. H. (2004). *Biometric verification based on grip-pattern recognition.* Paper presented at the Security, Steganography, and Watermarking of Multimedia Contents (pp. 634-641).

Veres, G. V., Nixon, M. S., Middleton, L., & Carter, J. N. (2005). Fusion of dynamic and static features for gait recognition over time. In *Proceedings of the Eighth International Conference on Information Fusion* (Vol. 2, pp. 1211-1217).

Vielhauer, C., & Steinmetz, R. (2004). Handwriting: Feature correlation analysis for biometric hashes. *EURASIP Journal of Applied Signal Processing. Special Issue on Biometric Signal Processing, 4,* 542–558.

Vielhauer, C., Steinmetz, R., & Mayerhorf, A. (2002). Biometric hash based on statistical features of online signatures. *16ᵗʰ International Conference on Pattern Recognition (ICPR 2002), 1,* 123-126.

Villani, M. (2006). Keystroke biometric identification studies on long text input. Unpublished doctoral dissertation, Pace University, New York.

Villani, M., Tappert, C., Ngo, G., Simone, J., St. Fort, H., & Cha, S.-H. (2006). Keystroke biometric recognition studies on long-text input under ideal and application-oriented conditions. *Proc. 2006 Conference on Computer Vision and Pattern Recognition, Workshop on Biometrics,* New York (pp. 39-46). Washington: IEEE Computer Society.

Vlasic, D., Brand, M., Pfister, H., & Popovic, J. (2005). Face transfer with multilinear models. (Tech. Rep. No. TR2005-048). Cambridge, MA: Mitsubishi Electric Research Laboratory.

Volkmann, J., Stevens, S. S., & Newman, E. B. (1937). A scale for the measurement of the psychological magnitude pitch. *The Journal of the Acoustical Society of America, 8*(3), 208-208. doi:10.1121/1.1901999

Wagner, D., & Dean, D. (2001). *Intrusion detection via static analysis.* Paper presented at the IEEE Symposium on Security and Privacy.

Walker-Smith, G. J., Gale, A. G., & Findlay, J. M. (1977). Eye movement strategies involved in face perception. *Perception, 6*(3): 313–326. doi:10.1068/p060313

Waller, A. D. (1887). A demonstration on man of electromotive changes accompanying the heart's beat. [London.]. *The Journal of Physiology, 8,* 29–234.

Wan, V., & Renals, S. (2005). Speaker verification using sequence discriminant support vector machines. *IEEE Transactions on Speech and Audio Processing, 13*(2), 203–210. doi:10.1109/TSA.2004.841042

Wandell, B. (1995). *Foundations of vision.* Sunderland, MA: Sinauer Associates.

Wang, H., & Ahuja, N. (2003). Facial expression decomposition. *Proceedings of, ICCV,* 958–965.

Wang, J., Plataniotis, K. N., & Venetsanopoulos, A. N. (2005). Selecting discriminant eigenfaces for face recognition. *Pattern Recognition Letters, 26*(10), 1470–1482. doi:10.1016/j.patrec.2004.11.029

Wang, J., Plataniotis, K. N., Lu, J., & Venetsanopoulos, A. N. (2006). On solving the face recognition problem with one training sample per subject. *Pattern Recognition, 39,* 1746–1762. doi:10.1016/j.patcog.2006.03.010

Wang, L. (2006). Abnormal walking gait analysis using silhouette-masked flow histograms. In *Proceedings of ICPR'06* (Vol. 3, pp. 473–476).

Wang, L., & Ning, H. (2004). Fusion of static and dynamic body biometrics for gait recognition. *IEEE Transactions on Circuits and Systems for Video Technology, 14*(2), 149–158. doi:10.1109/TCSVT.2003.821972

Wang, L., & Tan, T. (2003). Automatic gait recognition based on statistical shape analysis. *IEEE Transactions on Image Processing, 12*(9), 1120–1131. doi:10.1109/TIP.2003.815251

Wang, L., & Tan, T. (2003). Silhouette analysis-based gait recognition for human identification. *IEEE Transactions on Pattern Analysis and Machine Intelligence, 25*(12), 1505–1518. doi:10.1109/TPAMI.2003.1251144

Wang, L., Ning, H., Tan, T., & Hu, W. (2004). Fusion of static and dynamic body biometrics for gait recognition. *IEEE Transactions on Circuits and Systems for Video Technology, 14*(2), 149–158. doi:10.1109/TCSVT.2003.821972

Wang, L., Tan, T. N., Hu, W. M., & Ning, H. Z. (2003). Automatic gait recognition based on statistical shape analysis. *IEEE Transactions on Image Processing, 12*(9), 1120–1131. doi:10.1109/TIP.2003.815251

Wang, W., Shan, S., Gao, W., Cao, B., & Baocai, Y. (2000). An improved active shape model for face alignment. *Vision Research, 40*, 1489–1506. doi:10.1016/S0042-6989(99)00163-7

Wang, Y., Agrafioti, F., Hatzinakos, D., & Plataniotis, K. N. (2008, January). Analysis of human electrocardiogram for biometric recognition. *EURASIP Journal on Advances in Signal Processing.*

Wang, Y., Yu, S., Wang, Y., & Tan, T. (2006). Gait recognition based on fusion of multiview gait sequences. In *Proceedings of the International Conference on Biometrics* (pp. 605-611).

Wark, T., & Sridharan, S. (2001). Adaptive fusion of speech and lip information for robust speaker identification. *Digital Signal Processing, 11*(3), 169–186. doi:10.1006/dspr.2001.0397

Wark, T., Thambiratnam, D., & Sridharan, S. (1997). *Person authentication using lip information.* Paper presented at the IEEE 10th Annual Conference, Speech and Image Technologies for Computing and Telecommunications (pp. 153-156).

Warrender, C., Forrest, S., & Pearlmutter, B. (1999, May 9-12). *Detecting intrusions using system calls: Alternative data models.* Paper presented at the IEEE Symposium on Security and Privacy Oakland, CA (pp. 133-145).

Weber, F., Peskin, B., Newman, M., Emmanuel, A. C., & Gillick, L. (2000). Speaker recognition on single- and multispeaker data. *Digital Signal Processing, 10*, 75–92. doi:10.1006/dspr.1999.0362

Welling, M., & Weber, M. (2001). Positive tensor factorization. *Pattern Recognition Letters, 22*(12), 1255–1261. doi:10.1016/S0167-8655(01)00070-8

Wespi, A., Dacier, M., & Debar, H. (2000). *Intrusion detection using variable-length audit trail patterns.* Paper presented at the Recent Advances in Intrusion Detection (RAID).

Westeyn, T., & Starner, T. (2004). *Recognizing song-based blink patterns: Applications for restricted and universal access.* Paper presented at the Sixth IEEE International Conference on Automatic Face and Gesture Recognition (p. 717).

Westeyn, T., Pesti, P., Park, K., & Starner, T. (2005, July). *Biometric identification using song-based eye blink patterns.* Paper presented at the Human Computer Interaction International (HCII), Las Vegas, NV.

Whisenand, T. G., & Emurian, H. (1996). Effects of angle of approach on cursor movement with a mouse: Consideration of Fitts' law. *Computers in Human Behavior, 12*(3), 481–495. doi:10.1016/0747-5632(96)00020-9

Whisenand, T. G., & Emurian, H. H. (1999). Analysis of cursor movements with a mouse. *Computers in Human Behavior, 15*(1), 85–103. doi:10.1016/S0747-5632(98)00036-3

WHO. (2006). *Neurological disorders: Public health challenges.* report published by the World Health Organization. ISBN: 92 4 156336 2.

Wikipedia.com. (2006). *Mahalanobis distance.* Retrieved on August 22, 2006, from http://en.wikipedia.org/wiki/Mahalanobis_distance

Wikipedia.org. (2005). *Behavioural sciences.* Retrieved on October 6, 2005, from http://en.wikipedia.org/wiki/behavioral_sciences

Winter, D. (1991). *The biomechanics and motor control of human gait: normal, elderly, and pathological*. Waterloo Biomechanics.

Wiskott, L., Fellous, J.-M., & von der Malsburg, C. (1997). Face recognition by elastic bunch graph matching. *IEEE Trans. on PAMI, 19*, 775–779.

Wolpaw, J. R., Birbaumer, N., Mcfarland, D. J., Pfurtscheller, G., & Vaughan, T. M. (2002). Brain-computer interfaces for communication and control. *Clinical Neurophysiology, 113*, 767–791. doi:10.1016/S1388-2457(02)00057-3

Woodland, P. C., Leggetter, C. J., Odell, J. J., Valtchev, V., & Young, S. J. (1995). The 1994 HTK large vocabulary speech recognition system. In *Proceedings of the International conference on Acoustics, Speech, and Signal Processing*

Woodward, J. D., Jr., Orlans, N. M., & Higgins, P. T. (2002). *Biometrics* (p. 107). New York: McGraw-Hill.

Wren, C., Azarbayejani, A., Darrell, T., & Pentland, A. (1996). Pfinder: Real-time tracking of the human body. *Proc. IEEE Conference on Automatic Face and Gesture Recognition* (pp. 51-56).

Wu, X., & Bhanu, B. (1997). Gabor wavelet representation for 3-D object recognition. *IEEE Trans. IP, 6*(1), 47–63.

Xiang, B., & Berger, T. (2003). Efficient text-independent speaker verification with structural Gaussian mixture models and neural network. *IEEE Transactions on Speech and Audio Processing, 11*(5), 447–456. doi:10.1109/TSA.2003.815822

Xu, D., Yan, S., Tao, D., Lin, S., & Zhang, H.-J. (2007). Marginal Fisher analysis and its variants for human gait recognition and content-based image retrieval. *IEEE Transactions on Image Processing, 16*(11), 2811–2821. doi:10.1109/TIP.2007.906769

Xu, D., Yan, S., Tao, D., Zhang, L., Li, X., & Zhang, H. (2006). Human gait recognition with matrix representation. *IEEE Transactions on Circuits and Systems for Video Technology, 16*(7), 896–903. doi:10.1109/TCSVT.2006.877418

Xu, Z.-W., Guo, X.-X., Hu, X.-Y., & Cheng, X. (2005). The blood vessel recognition of ocular fundus. *ICMLC, 05*, 4493–4498.

Yam, C. Y., Nixon, M. S., et al. (2002). On the relationship of human walking and running: Automatic person identification by gait. *Proc. of International Conference on Pattern Recognition* (pp. 287-290).

Yam, C., Nixon, M., & Carter, J. (2004). Automated person recognition by walking and running via model-based approaches. *Pattern Recognition, 37*(5), 1057–1072. doi:10.1016/j.patcog.2003.09.012

Yambor, W. S., Draper, B. A., & Beveridge, J. R. (2002). Analyzing PCA-based face recognition algorithms: Eigenvector selection and distance measures. In H. Christensen & J. Phillips (Eds.), *Empirical evaluation method in computer vision*. World Scientific Press.

Yampolskiy, R. V. (2006, February 24). *Behavior based identification of network intruders*. Paper presented at the 19th Annual CSE Graduate Conference (Grad-Conf2006), Buffalo, NY.

Yampolskiy, R. V. (2007, April 11-12). *Motor-skill based biometrics*. Paper presented at the 6th Annual Security Conference, Las Vegas, NV.

Yampolskiy, R. V. (2007, April 13). *Behavioral biometrics for verification and recognition of AI programs*. Paper presented at the 20th Annual Computer Science and Engineering Graduate Conference (GradConf2007), Buffalo, NY.

Yampolskiy, R. V. (2007, April 2-4). *Human computer interaction based intrusion detection*. Paper presented at the 4th International Conference on Information Technology: New Generations (ITNG 2007), Las Vegas, NA (pp. 837-842).

Yampolskiy, R. V. (2007, April 2-4). *Secure network authentication with passtext*. Paper presented at the 4th International Conference on Information Technology: New Generations (ITNG 2007), Las Vegas, NA (pp. 831-836).

Yampolskiy, R. V. (2007, October 9-11). *Indirect human computer interaction-based biometrics for intrusion detection systems*. Paper presented at the 41st Annual IEEE International Carnahan Conference on Security Technology (ICCST2007), Ottawa, Canada (pp. 138-145).

Yampolskiy, R. V. (2007, September 10-12). *Online poker security: Problems and solutions*. Paper presented at the EUROSIS North American Simulation and AI in Games Conference (GAMEON-NA2007), Gainesville, FL.

Yampolskiy, R. V. (2008). Behavioral modeling: An overview. *American Journal of Applied Sciences*, 5(5), 496–503.

Yampolskiy, R. V. (2008). *Computer security: From passwords to behavioral biometrics*. London: New Academic Publishing.

Yampolskiy, R. V. (2008, April 7-9). *Mimicry attack on strategy-based behavioral biometric*. Paper presented at the 5th International Conference on Information Technology: New Generations (ITNG2008), Las Vegas, NV (pp. 916-921).

Yampolskiy, R. V., & Govindaraju, V. (2006, April 17-22). *Use of behavioral biometrics in intrusion detection and online gaming*. Paper presented at the Biometric Technology for Human Identification III, SPIE Defense and Security Symposium, Orlando, FL.

Yampolskiy, R. V., & Govindaraju, V. (2006, December 16-18). *Similarity measure functions for strategy-based biometrics*. Paper presented at the International Conference on Signal Processing (ICSP 2006), Vienna, Austria.

Yampolskiy, R. V., & Govindaraju, V. (2007). Direct and indirect human computer interaction based biometrics. *Journal of Computers*, 2(8), 76–88.

Yampolskiy, R. V., & Govindaraju, V. (2007, April 9-13). *Dissimilarity functions for behavior-based biometrics*. Paper presented at the Biometric Technology for Human Identification IV, SPIE Defense and Security Symposium, Orlando, FL.

Yampolskiy, R. V., & Govindaraju, V. (2008). Behavioral biometrics: A survey and classification. [IJBM]. *International Journal of Biometric*, 1(1), 81–113. doi:10.1504/IJBM.2008.018665

Yampolskiy, R. V., & Govindaraju, V. (2008). Strategy-based behavioral biometric a novel approach to automated identification. *International Journal of Computer Applications in Technology (IJCAT), Special Issue on: Automated Identification Technology.*

Yampolskiy, R. V., & Govindaraju, V. (2008, March 16-20). *Generation of artificial biometric data enhanced with spatialtemporal and environmental information*. Paper presented at the Biometric Technology for Human Identification V. SPIE Defense and Security Symposium, Orlando, FL.

Yampolskiy, R., Anderson, P., Arney, J., Misic, V., & Clarke, T. (2004, September 24). *Printer model integrating genetic algorithm for improvement of halftone patterns*. Paper presented at the Western New York Image Processing Workshop (WNYIPW)-IEEE Signal Processing Society, Rochester, NY.

Yang, J., Yang, J. Y., Zhang, D., & Lu, J. F. (2003). Feature fusion: Parallel strategy vs. serial strategy. *Pattern Recognition*, 38(6), 1369–1381. doi:10.1016/S0031-3203(02)00262-5

Yang, J., Zhang, D., Frangi, A. F., & Yang, J. Y. (2004). Two dimensional PCA: A new approach to appearance-based face representation and recognition. *IEEE Trans. on PAMI*, 26(1), 131–137.

Yanushkevich, S., Stoica, A., Srihari, S., Shmerko, V., & Gavrilova, M. (2004). *Simulation of Biometric Information: The new generation of biometric systems*. Paper presented at the Int'l Workshop on Biometric Technologies, Calgary, AB, Canada (pp. 87-98).

Yarbus, A. (1967). *Eye movements and vision*. New York: Plenum Press.

Ye, N. (2000). *A Markov chain model of temporal behavior for anomaly detection*. Paper presented at the IEEE Systems, Man, and Cybernetics Information Assurance and Security Workshop.

Yeung, D. Y., & Ding, Y. (2001). (n.d.) Host-based intrusion detection using dynamic and static behavioral models. *Pattern Recognition, 36*, 229–243. doi:10.1016/S0031-3203(02)00026-2

Yeung, D., Chang, H., Xiong, Y., George, S., Kashi, R., Matsumoto, T., & Rigoll, G. (2004). SVC 2004: First international signature verification competition. In D. Zhang & A. K. Jain (Eds.), *Proc. ICBA 2004.* (LNCS, 3072, pp. 16–22).

Yokouchi, H., Yamamoto, S., Suzuki, T., Matsui, M., & Kato, K. (1974). Fundus pattern recognition. *Japanese J. Med. Electronics and Biological Engineering, 12*(3), 123–130.

Yoo, D. H., & Chung, M. J. (2004, May). Nonintrusive eye gaze estimation without knowledge of eye pose. In *Proceedings of the Sixth IEEE International Conference on Automatic Face and Gesture Recognition* (pp. 785–790).

Yoo, J. H., Hwang, D., et al. (2005). Gender classification in human gait using support vector machine. *Proceedings of Advanced Concepts for Intelligent Vision Systems 2005*, Antwerp, Belgium (pp. 138-145).

Yoon, S., Choi, S.-S., Cha, S.-H., Lee, Y., & Tappert, C. C. (2005). On the individuality of the iris biometric. *Proc. Int. J. Graphics . Vision & Image Processing, 5*(5), 63–70.

Yoshitomi, Y., Miyaura, T., Tomita, S., & Kimura, S. (1997). Face identification using thermal image processing. *Proc. IEEE International Workshop on Robot and Human Communication* (pp. 374-379).

Young, L., & Sheena, D. (1975). Survey of eye movement recording methods. *Behavior Research Methods and Instrumentation, 7*(5), 397–439.

Yu, E., & Cho, S. (2004). Keystroke dynamics identity verification–its problems and practical solutions. *Computers & Security, 23*(5), 428–440. doi:10.1016/j.cose.2004.02.004

Yu, S., Tan, D., et al. (2006). A framework for evaluating the effect of view angle, clothing, and carrying condition on gait recognition. *Proc. of the 18ᵗʰ International Conference on Pattern Recognition (ICPR06)* (pp. 441-444).

Yu, S., Wang, L., et al. (2004). Gait analysis for human identification in frequency domain. *Proc. of the 3ʳᵈ International Conference on Image and Graphics* (pp. 282-285).

Yuille, A. L. (1991). Deformable templates for face detection. *Journal of Cognitive Neuroscience, 3*(1), 59–70. doi:10.1162/jocn.1991.3.1.59

Yutaka, K. (2005). *Behaviormetrics.* Retrieved on October 6, 2005, from http://koko15.hus.osaka-u.ac.jp/

Zeeuw, P. M. (2002). *A toolbox for the lifting scheme on quincunx grids (LISQ).* (Tech. Rep. PNA-R0224). Centrum voor Wiskunde en Informatica.

Zhang, D. (2004). Palmprint authentication system. In P. Wang (Ed.), *Handbook of pattern recognition and computer vision* (pp. 431-444).

Zhang, J., Marszałek, M., Lazebnik, S., & Schmid, C. (2007). Local features and kernels for classification of texture and object categories: A comprehensive study. *International Journal of Computer Vision, 73*(2), 213–238. doi:10.1007/s11263-006-9794-4

Zhang, R., & Vogler, C. (2007). Human gait recognition at sagittal plane. *Image and Vision Computing, 25*(3), 321–330. doi:10.1016/j.imavis.2005.10.007

Zhang, R., Vogler, C., & Metaxas, D. (2004). Human gait recognition. In . *Proceedings of IEEE Computer Vision and Pattern Recognition, 2*, 342–349.

Zhang, Y., & Wang, D. (2006, July 12-15). *Research on object-storage-based intrusion detection.* Paper presented at the 12ᵗʰ International Conference on Parallel and Distributed Systems (ICPADS) (pp. 68- 78).

Zhang, Z., & Manikopoulos, C. (2003, August 11-13). *Investigation of neural network classification of computer network attacks.* Paper presented at the International Conference on Information Technology: Research and Education (pp. 590- 594).

Zhao, G., Liu, G., Li, H., & Pietikäinen, M. (2006). 3D gait recognition using multiple cameras. In *Proceedings of the 7th IEEE International Conference on Automatic Face and Gesture Recognition* (pp. 529–534).

Zhao, W., Chellappa, R., Phillips, P. J., & Rosenfeld, A. (2003). Face recognition: A literature survey. *ACM Computing Surveys*, *35*(4), 399–458. doi:10.1145/954339.954342

Zhou, X., & Bhanu, B. (2007). Integrating face and gait for human recognition at a distance in video. *IEEE Transactions on Systems, Man, and Cybernetics. Part B, Cybernetics*, *37*(5), 1119–1137. doi:10.1109/TSMCB.2006.889612

Zhou, X., & Bhanu, B. (2008). Feature fusion of side face and gait for video-based human identification. *Pattern Recognition*, *41*, 778–795. doi:10.1016/j.patcog.2007.06.019

Zhou, X., & Bhanu, B. (Manuscript submitted for publication). Feature fusion of side face and gait for video-based human identification. *Pattern Recognition*.

Zhou, X., Bhanu, B., & Han, J. (2005). Human recognition at a distance in video by integrating face profile and gait. In *Proc. Audio- and Video-based Biometric Person Authentication* (pp. 533-543).

Zhu, G. Y., Zheng, Y. F., Doermann, D., & Jaeger, S. (2007). Multiscale structural saliency for signature detection. *IEEE Int'l Conf. Computer Vision and Pattern Recognition*, 1-8.

Zhu, Y., Tan, T., & Wang, Y. (2000). Biometric personal identification based on handwriting. *Proceedings of the 15th International Conference on Pattern Recognition*, *2*, 797-800.

Zilca, R. D. (2002). Text-independent speaker verification using utterance level scoring and covariance modeling. *IEEE Transactions on Speech and Audio Processing*, *10*(6), 363–370. doi:10.1109/TSA.2002.803419

About the Contributors

Dr. Liang Wang obtained the B. Eng and M. Eng degrees in electronic engineering from Anhui University and PhD in pattern recognition and intelligent system from National Laboratory of Pattern Recognition, Institute of Automation, Chinese Academy of Sciences. From July 2004 to January 2007, he worked in Imperial College London, UK, and in Monash University, Australia, respectively. He is currently working as a Research Fellow in The University of Melbourne, Australia. His main research interest includes pattern recognition, machine learning, computer vision, data mining, etc. He has widely published at IEEE TPAMI, TIP, TKDE, TCSVT, TSMC, CVIU, PR, CVPR, ICCV, ICDM, etc. He serves for many major international journals and conferences as AE, reviewer or PC member. He is currently an associate editor of IEEE TSMC-B, IJIG and Signal Processing. He is a co-editor of four books to be published by IGI Global and Springer, and a guest editor of three special issues in the international journals of PRL, IJPRAI and IEEE TSMC-B, as well as co-chairing a special session and three workshops, e.g., VM'08, MLVMA'08 and THEMIS'08.

Dr. Xin Geng received the B.Sc. and M.Sc. degrees in computer science from Nanjing University, China, and the Ph.D degree in computer science from Deakin University, Australia. He is currently an associate professor in the School of Computer Science and Engineering, Southeast University, China. His research interests include computer vision, pattern recognition, and machine learning. He has published over twenty refereed papers in these areas, including those published in prestigious journals and top international conferences. He has been a Guest Editor of several international journals, such as PRL and IJPRAI. He has served as a Program Committee Member for a number of international conferences, such as PRICAI'08, AI'08, MMSP'08, CIT'08, IEEE IRI'09, etc. He is also a frequent reviewer for various international journals and conferences.

***

Ahmed Awad E. Ahmed is a Postdoctoral Researcher at the Electrical and Computer Engineering Department, University of Victoria. He is a member of the Security and Object Technology (ISOT) Research Laboratory at the University of Victoria and the principal investigator of Biotracker, a new intrusion detection system based on biometrics (http://www.isot.ece.uvic.ca/projects/biotracker). Dr. Ahmed worked as a Software Design Engineer, Project Manager, and Quality Assurance Consultant in a number of leading software firms. He received a Ph.D. in Electrical and Computer Engineering from the University of Victoria, Victoria, BC, Canada in 2008. His Ph.D. dissertation presents a number of new trends in security monitoring through human computer interaction devices. Dr. Ahmed completed his B.Sc. and M.Sc degrees at the Electrical and Computer Engineering Department, Ain Shams University, Cairo, Egypt in 1992, and 1997 respectively.

M. Ashraful Amin received his B. Sc. degree in Computer Science from North South University of Bangladesh in 2002, the M.Sc. degree in Computer Science from Asian Institute of Technology, Thailand in 2005, and now pursuing doctoral studies in the department of Electrical Engineering at City University of Hong Kong. His research interests include Facial Recognition and Biometrics.

Bir Bhanu is Professor of EECS and Director of VISLab and the Center for Research in Intelligent Systems (CRIS) at the University of California, Riverside (UCR). Previously he was a Senior Honeywell Fellow at Honeywell Inc. He has been on the faculty of the Department of Computer Science, University of Utah, and has worked with Ford Aerospace & Communications Corporation, INRIA-France and IBM San Jose Research Laboratory. He has been the Principal Investigator of various programs from NSF, DARPA, NASA, AFOSR, ARO, ONR and other agencies and industries in the areas of object recognition, learning and vision, image understanding, image/video databases and machine vision applications. Dr. Bhanu's current research interests are Computer Vision, Machine Learning for Computer Vision, Multimedia Databases, Pattern Recognition, Image Processing, Graphics/Visualization, Robotics, Human-Computer Interactions, Biometrics, Commercial, Defense and Medical applications. Dr. Bhanu is a Fellow of IEEE, AAAS, IAPR and SPIE.

Dr. Sung-Hyuk Cha received his Ph.D. in Computer Science from State University of New York at Buffalo in 2001 and B.S. and M.S. degrees in Computer Science from Rutgers, the State University of New Jersey in 1994 and 1996, respectively. During his undergraduate years, he became a member of Phi Beta Kappa and Golden Key National Honor Society. He graduated with High Honors and received High Honors in Computer Science. From 1996 to 1998, he was working in the area of medical information systems such as PACS, teleradiology, and telemedicine at Information Technology R&D Center, Samsung SDS. During his PhD years, he was affiliated with the Center of Excellence for Document Analysis and Recognition (CEDAR). Major contribution made at CEDAR includes dichotomy model to establish the individuality of handwriting supervised by Prof. Sargur N. Srihari. He has been a faculty member of Computer Science department at Pace University since 2001. His main interests include computer vision, data mining, pattern matching & recognition.

Changhong Chen received the B.S. degree from the Yantai University, Shandong, China, in 2004. She is pursuing her Ph.D degree in the school of electronic engineering, Xidian University, Shannxi, China. Her research focuses on biometric recognition.

Fouad Cherifi is a Master student in the GREYC laboratory. He obtained his Master of Science in 2008 from the University of Caen. His research interests the evaluation of biometric systems.

Dr Joan Condell is a Lecturer at the School of Computing & Intelligent Systems, Faculty of Computing & Engineering, University of Ulster, Magee. She completed her Ph.D. in Mathematics and Theoretical Computer Science at the University of Ulster, Coleraine in 2002, a Master's of Science degree in Industrial Mathematics (M.Sc.) at the University of Strathclyde in 1997 and her Bachelor's of Science degree in Mathematics, Statistics and Computing (B.Sc., Hons.) at University of Ulster, Jordanstown in 1996.

She has published numerous papers in international conferences, journals, and research books. Her primary research interests are in Computer Vision (motion analysis), Image Processing and Robotics.

Fabio Cuzzolin was born in Jesolo, Italy. He received the laurea degree magna cum laude from the University of Padova, Italy, in 1997 and the Ph.D. degree from the same institution in 2001, with a thesis entitled "Visions of a generalized probability theory". He has been researcher at the Politecnico di Milano, Italy, post-doctoral fellow with the UCLA Vision Lab at the University of California at Los Angeles, and Marie Curie fellow at INRIA Rhone-Alpes, Grenoble, France. He is now Lecturer with the Department of Computing of Oxford Brookes University. His research spans computer vision applications such as action recognition, pose estimation and identity recognition from gait. His main field of investigation remains however that of generalized and imprecise probabilities. In particular, he has formulated a geometric approach to uncertainty measures and studied the notion of independence in abstract algebra.

Dr Clinton Fookes is a Senior Research Fellow with the Speech, Audio, Image and Video Technologies group within the Faculty of Built Environment and Engineering and the Information Security Institute at the Queensland University of Technology. He has a BEng (Aerospace/Avionics) and a PhD in the area of medical image registration. His current areas of research include computer vision, biometrics, super-resolution, intelligent surveillance, aviation security, visual attention and other machine learning and pattern recognition areas. He is a member of the IEEE, the Systems, Man and Cybernetics Society, the International Council of Systems Engineering, and the Australian Pattern Recognition Society.

Romain Giot is a research engineer in the GREYC laboratory. He obtained his Master of Science in 2008 from ENSICAEN. His research interests biometrics, especially the definition of keystroke dynamics biometric systems.

Venu Govindaraju is a Professor of Computer Science and Engineering at the University at Buffalo (SUNY Buffalo). He received his B-Tech (Honors) from the Indian Institute of Technology (IIT), Kharagpur, India in 1986, and his Ph.D. from UB in 1992. He has co-authored more than 230 scientific papers. He has been the PI/Co-PI of projects funded by government and industry for over 50 million dollars in the last 15 years. He is the founding director of the Center for Unified Biometrics and Sensors (CUBS) and the associate director of the Center for Document Analysis and Recognition (CEDAR).He has served on the editorial boards of five premier journals in his area including the IEEE Transactions on Pattern Analysis and Machine Intelligence. He has served as the general chair of the IEEE AutoID 2005 and is the program co-chair of the First IEEE Conference on Biometrics.

Ju Han received his Ph.D. degree in the Electrical Engineering Department from the University of California, Riverside in 2005. Since December of 2005, he has been a specialist at the Imaging and Informatics Lab with joint appointment at U.C. Berkeley and Lawrence Berkeley National Laboratory. His research interests include biological image understanding, computational biology, and biometrics.

Baptiste Hemery is a PhD student in the GREYC laboratory. He obtained his Master of Science in 2006 from the University of Orleans. His research interests the evaluation of image interpretation systems and biometric systems.

Olaf Henniger obtained his Dipl.-Ing. degree in automation engineering from the Otto-von-Guericke University Magdeburg, Germany, in 1991, and his Ph.D. in computer science from the Brandenburg University of Technology in Cottbus, Germany, in 2003. He is working as a research fellow at the Fraunhofer Institute for Secure Information Technology in Darmstadt, Germany. His research interests include software engineering, especially model-based testing, and security engineering, especially smart cards and biometrics. He is editor of the International Standard ISO/IEC 19794-7 "Information technology – Biometric data interchange formats – Part 7: Signature/sign time series data". He lectures on smart-card systems at the University of Applied Sciences in Darmstadt.

Haihong Hu received the B.S. degree in image processing and transmission from Beijing University of Post and Telecommunication in 1994, and M.S. degree in signal processing from Xidian University in 2001. Currently, she is a Ph.D. student in pattern recognition and intelligent system and works in the Life Science Research Center, School of Electronic Engineering, Xidian University. Her research interests include computer vision, machine learning, and pattern recognition.

Jin, Minho He received the B.S. and M.S. degrees from Korea Advanced Institute of Science and Technology in 2002 and 2004, respectively, all in electrical engineering. He is currently pursuing his Ph. D. degree in the Department of Electrical Engineering, Korea Advanced Institute of Science and Technology. During 2005, he visited Microsoft Research Asia as an intern where he developed speaker verification systems. His research interests include speech processing, utterance verification, speaker verification, speech recognition, graphical model, stereo matching, multimedia retrieval and machine learning.

Bangyu Li received the BSE degree from Hefei University of Technology in 1998 and the MS degree from Jiangsu University of Science and Technology in 2005. He is currently a Ph.D. candidate at National Laboratory of Pattern Recognition, Institute of Automation, Chinese Academy of Sciences. His research interests include data minding and pattern recognition, online handwriting recognition, and computer vision.

Jimin Liang received the B.S. in 1992, M.S. in 1995 and Ph.D in 2000 from Xidian University, Xi'an, China, all majored in electronic engineering. He joined the Xidian University in 1995, where he is currently a professor in the Life Science Research Center (LSRC), School of Electronic Engineering. In the year of 2002, he was a research associate professor at the Electrical and Computer Engineering Department, University of Tennessee, Knoxville, USA. His general areas of research are in biometric recognition, biometric encryption, information fusion, and image processing.

Anthony Maeder was appointed as Professor in Health Informatics in the School of Computing and Mathematics at UWS in July 2008. He was previously Research Director of the CSIRO eHealth Research Centre in Brisbane, from 2004. Prior to that, he followed an academic career as Head of School in Engineering at University of Ballarat and subsequently at QUT Electrical and Electronic Systems Engineering. His earlier appointments were at Monash University in the Department of Computer Science, where he also undertook his PhD in Software Engineering. He is a Fellow of the Institution of Engineers, Australia, a Member of ACM, IEEE and SPIE, and was the founding President of the Australian Pattern Recognition Society in 1990.

Dr George Mamic was appointed a Senior Research Fellow at the School of Electrical and Electronic Systems Engineering at Queensland University of Technology in 2005. He was previously employed as a software engineer with CSIRO after completing his PhD in 3D Object Recognition. His research interests include: Pattern/Object Recognition, Applied Statistics and Image Processing.

Marc PASQUET is an assistant professor at ENSICAEN, France. He obtained his Master degree from ENSAM (Ecole Nationale Supérieure des Arts et Métiers) in 1977. He worked for 13 years for different companies belonging to the signal transmission field and 15 years for the banking sector in the field of electronic payment. He joined ENSICAEN (National Engineer School of Caen in France) in 2006 where he is now leading research in the field of electronic payment.

Girijesh Prasad received the B.Tech. degree in electrical engineering from Regional Engineering College, Calicut, India, in 1987, the M.Tech. degree in computer science and technology from the University of Roorkee, Roorkee, India, in 1992, and the Ph.D. degree from Queen's University, Belfast, U.K., in 1997. He has been a member of academic staff in the Faculty of Computing and Engineering at the University of Ulster, Magee Campus, Londonderry, U.K., since 1999 and holds the post of Reader. He is an executive member of Intelligent Systems Research Centre at Magee Campus where he leads the Brain-Computer Interface and Assistive Technology team. Previously, he worked as a Digital Systems Engineer, as a Power Plant Engineer, and finally, as a Research Fellow on an UK EPSRC/industry project. His research focus is on self-organising hybrid intelligent systems involving innovative fusion of neural computation, fuzzy neural networks, type-1 and type-2 fuzzy logic, local model networks, evolutionary algorithms, adaptive predictive modeling and control with applications in complex industrial and biological systems including brain-computer interface (BCI), intelligent surveillance systems, autonomic computing and assistive robotic systems. He has published over 80 peer reviewed academic papers in international journals, books, and conference proceedings. Dr. Prasad is a Chartered Engineer, a Member of the IET and a Senior Member of IEEE.

Kenneth Revett received his PhD in neuroscience from the University of Maryland, College Park in 1999. His research interests include behavioral biometrics and computational modeling. He has authored a text on behavioral Biometrics: Behavioral Biometrics: A Remote Access Approach and has a UK patent on an implementation of keystroke dynamics. He regularly lectures in biometrics and related topics and has published numerous articles in the field. His current interest in behavioral biometrics lie in biosignal analysis, examining the role of emotive states on authentication using EEG and ECG. In addition, novel authentication approaches other than textual and graphical based passwords will be explored - investigating the utility of deploying game-like authentication mechanisms within a 3D environment.

Christophe Rosenberger is a Full Professor at ENSICAEN, France. He obtained his Master of Science in 1996 and its Ph.D. degree in 1999 from the University of Rennes I. He works at the GREYC Laboratory and is the leader of computer security research unit. His research interests include computer security and biometrics. He is particularly interested in the evalaution of biometric systems.

Concetto Spampinato received the degree in Informatics Engineering from University of Catania, in 2003 with Academic Laude. Afterward he pursued the Ph.D in the Department of Informatics and Telecomunications of the Catania University, Italy, where, currently, he is assistant professor. His research interests include image and signal processing, cognitive informatics and bioengineering applications.

Professor Sridha Sridharan has a BSc (Electrical Engineering) degree and obtained a MSc (Communication Engineering) degree from the University of Manchester Institute of Science and Technology, UK and a PhD degree in the area of Signal Processing from University of New South Wales, Australia. He is a Senior Member of the Institute of Electrical and Electronic Engineers - IEEE (USA). He is currently with the Queensland University of Technology where he is a full Professor in the School of Engineering Systems. Professor Sridharan is the Deputy Director of the Information Security Institute and the Leader of the Research Program in Speech, Audio, Image and Video Technologies at QUT. He has published over 300 papers consisting of book chapters and publications in journals and in refereed international conferences in the areas of Speech and Image technologies during the period 1990-2008.

Zhenan Sun is an Assistant Professor at Institute of Automation, Chinese Academy of Sciences (CASIA). He received the B.E. degree in industrial automation from Dalian University of Technology, the M.S. degree in system engineering from Huazhong University of Science and Technology, and Ph.D. degree in Pattern Recognition and Intelligent Systems from CASIA in 1999, 2002 and 2006, respectively. Since March 2006, Dr. Sun has joined the Center of Biometrics and Security Research (CBSR) in the National Laboratory of Pattern Recognition (NLPR) of CASIA as a faculty. He has published more than 40 research papers in refereed journals and conferences in the areas of iris, palmprint and face recognition. Dr. Sun is a member of the IEEE and the IEEE Computer Society. His current research focuses on biometrics, pattern recognition and computer vision.

Tieniu Tan received his B.Sc. degree in electronic engineering from Xi'an Jiaotong University, China, in 1984, and his M.Sc. and Ph.D. degrees in electronic engineering from Imperial College of Science, Technology and Medicine, London, U.K., in 1986 and 1989, respectively. In October 1989, he joined the Computational Vision Group at the Department of Computer Science, The University of Reading, Reading, U.K., where he worked as a Research Fellow, Senior Research Fellow and Lecturer. In January 1998, he returned to China to join the National Laboratory of Pattern Recognition (NLPR), Institute of Automation of the Chinese Academy of Sciences (CAS), Beijing, China, where is currently Professor and Director of the NLPR, and a former Director-General of the Institute (2000-2007). He is also a Deputy Secretary-General of the CAS and the Head of the Department of Automation, The University of Science and Technology of China (USTC). He has published more than 250 research papers in refereed journals and conferences in the areas of image processing, computer vision and pattern recognition. His current research interests include biometrics, image and video understanding, information hiding and information forensics. Dr Tan is a Fellow of the IEEE and the IAPR (the International Association of Pattern Recognition).

Dr. Charles Tappert is a Computer Science Professor at Pace University with over 40 years experience in the computing profession. He researched pen computing and speech recognition at IBM Research for 26 years, concurrently doing adjunct teaching at several institutions. He then taught full-time in the EE&CS Department at West Point for 7 years before joining the Pace faculty in 2000. Dr. Tappert has extensive experience in computer science, specializing in pen computing, pattern recognition, algorithms, graphics, artificial intelligence, and more recently biometrics and security. He has taught graduate and undergraduate courses, supervised doctoral and masters' theses, and secured government contracts. He has over 100 publications: book chapters, journals articles, conference papers, and patents.

Andrew Beng Jin Teoh obtained his BEng (Electronic) in 1999 and Ph.D degree in 2003 from National University of Malaysia. He is currently an assistance professor in EE Department, College Engineering of Yonsei University. He was an associate dean and Senior Lecturer in Multimedia University Malaysia. His research interest is in biometrics security, watermarking and pattern recognition. He had published around 130 international journal and conference papers in his area.

Jie Tian received the Ph.D. degree (with honors) in artificial intelligence from the Institute of Automation, Chinese Academy of Sciences, Beijing, in 1992. From 1994 to 1996, he was a Postdoctoral Fellow with the medical image processing group, University of Pennsylvania, Philadelphia. Since 1997, he has been a Professor with the Institute of Automation, Chinese Academy of Sciences. From 2007, he has been the Chair Professor of the Cheung Kong Scholars in Xidian University. His research interests include pattern recognition, machine learning, image processing and their applications in biometrics, etc.

Issa Traore received an Aircraft Engineer degree from Ecole de l'Air in Salon de Provence (France) in 1990, and successively two Master degrees in Aeronautics and Space Techniques in 1994, and in Automatics and Computer Engineering in 1995 from Ecole Nationale Superieure de l'Aeronautique et de l'Espace (E.N.S.A.E), Toulouse, France. In 1998, Dr. Traore received a Ph.D. in Software Engineering from Institute Nationale Polytechnique (INPT)-LAAS/CNRS, Toulouse, France. From June - Oct. 1998, he held a post-doc position at LAAS-CNRS, Toulouse, France, and Research Associate (Nov. 1998 - May 1999), and Senior Lecturer (June-Oct. 1999) at the University of Oslo. Since Nov. 1999, he has joined the faculty of the Department of ECE, University of Victoria, Canada. He is currently an Associate Professor. His research interests include Behavioral biometrics systems, intrusion detection systems, software security metrics, and software quality engineering. He is the founder and coordinator of the Information Security and Object Technology (ISOT) Research Lab (http://www.isot.ece.uvic.ca).

Dr. Mary Villani is an Assistant Professor in the Computer Systems Department at the State University of New York (SUNY) at Farmingdale. She holds a Doctor of Professional Studies degree from Pace University. Her dissertation topic was Keystroke Biometric Identification Studies on Long-Text Input. Publications in this area include three peer-reviewed external conference papers, three peer-reviewed internal Pace University conference papers and one peer-reviewed paper at SUNY Farmingdale. She continues to conduct research in Keystroke Biometrics at Pace University to streamline research and data collection methods as well as to widen the scope of the research and analysis. Prior to joining SUNY Farmingdale, Dr. Villani had a fifteen year computer consulting career in the insurance industry. She authored articles and papers in the area of Risk Management Information Systems and as a recognized expert made several invited presentations at conferences in the discipline.

Roman V. Yampolskiy holds a PhD degree from the department of computer science and engineering at the University at Buffalo. There he was a recipient of a four year National Science Foundation IGERT fellowship. After graduating, Roman served as an Affiliate Academic at the University of London, College of London until finally accepting an assistant professor position at the University of Louisville in the August of 2008. He had previously worked at the Laboratory for Applied Computing at the Rochester Institute of Technology and at the Center for Unified Biometrics and Sensors at the University at Buffalo. Dr. Yampolskiy's main areas of interest are computer security, artificial intelligence, behavioral biometrics and intrusion detection. Dr. Yampolskiy is an author of over 40 publications including multiple books.

Hong Yan received his Ph.D. degree from Yale University. He was a professor in electrical and information engineering at the University of Sydney and is currently a professor in electronic engineering at City University of Hong Kong. His research interests include image processing, pattern recognition and bioinformatics and he has over 300 journal and conference publications in these areas. Professor Yan is a fellow of the Institute of Electrical and Electronics Engineers (IEEE), the International Association of Patten Recognition (IAPR) and the Institution of Engineers, Australia (IEAust).

Wai Kuan Yip received her B.S. and M.S. degrees in computer science from University Science of Malaysia in 1999 and 2003, respectively. Currently, she is completing her Ph.D. degree in information technology from Multimedia University, Malaysia in the areas of dynamic hand signatures, signal processing, and information security. Previously, she worked as an Analytic Solutions Development Engineer in Intel Malaysia developing data mining solutions for manufacturing use.

Pratheepan Yogarajah received his B.Sc. Honours degree in Computer Science from University of Jaffna, Sri Lanka in 2001. He completed his M.Phil. in Computer Vision at Oxford Brookes University, UK in 2006. He is currently a part-time PhD student at the School of Computing & Intelligent Systems, Faculty of Computing and Engineering, University of Ulster, UK. He worked as an Instructor in Computer Science and then as an Assistant Lecturer in Computer Science at University of Jaffna, Sri Lanka. He also worked as Lecturer (Probationary) in Information Communication Technology (ICT) at Eastern University, Sri Lanka. His research interests include image processing, machine learning and computer vision. He is an associate member of BCS.

Yoo, Chang D. He received the B.S. degree in Engineering and Applied Science from California Institute of Technology in 1986, the M.S. degree in Electrical Engineering from Cornell University in 1988 and the Ph.D. degree in Electrical Engineering from Massachusetts Institute of Technology in 1996. From January 1997 to March 1999 he worked at Korea Telecom as a Senior Researcher. He joined the Department of Electrical Engineering at Korea Advanced Institute of Science and Technology in April 1999. From March 2005 to March 2006, he was with Research Laboratory of Electronics at MIT. His current research interests are in the application of machine learning and digital signal processing in multimedia. He is a member of Tau Beta Pi and Sigma Xi. He is currently a technical committee member of IEEE Machine Learning for Signal Processing.

Shiqi Yu received his B.S. degree in computer science and engineering from Chu Kochen Honors College, Zhejiang University in 2002, and his Ph.D. degree in pattern recognition and intelligent systems from the Institute of Automation, Chinese Academy of Sciences in 2007. He is currently an assistant professor at the Shenzhen Institute of Advanced Technology, Chinese Academy of Sciences. His research interests include computer vision, image processing, pattern recognition and artificial intelligence.

Hen Zhao received the B.S. degree in automatic control from Xi'an Jiaotong University in 1996, and the Ph.D. degree in circuit and system from Xidian University in 2005. From 1996 to 1999, he worked as an assistant researcher at Flight Automatic Control Research Institute in Xi'an, China. Currently, he is an associate professor at the Life Science Research Center in the School of Electronic Engineering, Xidian University. His research interests include data mining, pattern recognition, and image processing.

Xiaoli Zhou received the B.S. and M.S. degrees in electrical engineering from the Beijing University of Posts and Telecommunications, Beijing, China, in 1998 and 2001, the Ph.D. degree at the University of California, Riverside (UCR) in 2008. Her research interests were in machine learning, computer vision, pattern recognition, and image processing. At the Center for Research in Intelligent Systems, UCR, her research was mainly concerned with fusion of biometrics for human recognition at a distance in video. She is currently working in Microsoft Live Search, Microsoft Corporation, Redmond.

Index

A

ability 3, 12, 15, 24, 27
Artimetrics 399, 400, 401, 408, 409

B

behavioral biometric characteristics, forgeries
of 49
behavioral biometrics 57, 58, 61, 63, 64, 65,
66, 69, 70, 72, 76, 101, 449, 102, 103,
104, 109, 114, 117, 118, 121, 131, 150,
207, 208, 211, 223, 290, 291, 294, 308,
312, 314, 343, 313
behavioral biometrics, authorship-based 2, 10,
12, 14, 17, 34, 36, 40, 459, 461, 466,
468, 483
behavioral biometrics, human computer interaction (HCI) 2, 6, 12, 20, 26, 37, 471
behavioral biometrics, indirect HCI 2, 6, 27,
29, 42, 489
behavioral biometrics, motor-skills 3, 26
behavioral biometrics, pure 3, 25, 31
behavioral biometrics, pure, generalized algorithm for 25, 26
behavioral biometric systems 44, 49, 51, 52, 54
behavioral biometric systems, security evaluation of 44, 45, 47, 54, 55, 459, 464
behavioral features 291
behavioral signature 385
behaviour, environmental factors of 1, 4
bilinear models 169, 171, 172, 173, 174, 175,
176, 177, 178, 184
biofeedback 101, 103, 115
biometric application programming interface
(BioAPI) 57, 58, 59, 60, 70, 72, 73
biometric authentication 65, 72, 73, 455, 463,
464, 473
biometric helper 368
biometric identification 57, 58, 60, 61, 62, 64,
66, 69, 73
biometric-key 368, 369, 370
biometrics 207, 208, 209, 211, 221, 222, 223,
478
biometrics, behavioral 448
biometrics classifiers 151, 158
biometrics, fingerprints-based 138
biometrics, gaze-based 237, 238, 450, 239,
240, 241, 242, 243, 244, 245, 246, 247,
249, 251, 463, 253, 466, 256, 467, 257,
258, 469, 259, 260, 261, 262, 473, 263,
474, 477, 490
biometrics, handwriting 317, 318, 320, 327,
330, 335, 337, 339
biometrics, iris and retina based 121, 139, 140,
141, 143, 144, 145, 448, 452, 454, 457,
460
biometrics, keystroke-based 342, 343, 344,
346, 362, 363, 364, 365, 456, 486
biometrics, lip movement-based 135, 136, 137,
149
biometrics, mouse and keyboard dynamics-
based 137, 138, 143, 148, 448
biometrics, multimodal 61
biometrics, painting style-based 137
biometrics, physical 76
biometrics, physiological 121, 138, 207, 290,
291, 312
biometrics, signature-based 131, 132, 135, 145,
146, 147, 148, 150, 465, 469, 491
biometric standards 58